BRAVING THE WARTIME SEAS

BRAVING THE WARTIME SEAS

A Tribute to the Cadets and Graduates of
the U.S. Merchant Marine Academy and
Cadet Corps Who Died during World War II

1946 War Memorial

The American Maritime
History Project
George J. Ryan, Editor
Thomas F. McCaffery, Primary Researcher

Library of Congress Control Number: 2014906640
ISBN: Hardcover   978-1-4931-8614-3
                Softcover   978-1-4931-8615-0
                eBook   978-1-4931-8613-6

Rev. date: 06/16/2014

To order additional copies of this book, contact:
Xlibris LLC
1-888-795-4274
www.Xlibris.com
Orders@Xlibris.com
550565

Contents

Braving the Wartime Seas:
A Tribute to the Cadets and Graduates of the U.S. Merchant Marine Academy and Cadet Corps Who Died during World War II

Construction of Kings Point 1942   **Inspection at Pass Christian, Mississippi**

San Mateo, California, buildings

Editor:
George J. Ryan, Chairman, American Maritime History Project,
Class of 1957, Kings Point

Primary Researcher
Thomas F. McCaffery, Class of 1976, Kings Point
McCaffery & Associates, Inc., 107 S. West Street, #709, Alexandria, VA 22314

Research Contributors
Roy Corsa, Class of 1957, Kings Point
George J. Ryan, Class of 1957, Kings Point
Thomas Schroeder, Class of 1957, Kings Point

Editorial Assistance
Bob Aimone, Class of 1957, Kings Point
R. E. (Bob) McDermott, Class of 1973, Kings Point
Donald R. Yearwood, Class of 1961, Kings Point

Tribute by President Franklin D. Roosevelt On the Seventh Anniversary of the Merchant Marine Cadet Corps

WAR SHIPPING ADMINISTRATION, Washington
Thursday, March 15, 1945

"A tribute to the Cadet-Midshipmen of the United States Merchant Marine Academy at Kings Point, Long Island, N. Y., which is celebrating its seventh anniversary today, was conveyed in a letter from President Roosevelt to Vice Admiral Emory S. Land, USN, retired, War Shipping Administrator.

Since its founding in 1938, the Academy has graduated 6,000 young Americans as merchant ship officers. More than 140 have lost their lives in war service as the result of enemy action.

President Roosevelt's letter, read to the Cadet Corps at the ceremonies this afternoon at Kings Point by Captain Edward Macauley, USN, retired, Deputy War Shipping Administrator, follows:"

> "On the seventh anniversary of the founding of the United States Merchant Marine Cadet Corps, I extend my congratulations upon the service the Cadet Corps is rendering the Nation by adequately and efficiently training young men as officers of our Merchant Marine.
>
> I know that the young Cadet-Midshipmen of the Cadet Corps have gone to sea in the face of peril and that many have sacrificed their lives. They and the price they have paid toward maintaining freedom shall long endure in the memory of a grateful nation. I know of their love for the sea, their loyalty to their ships, and I am confident of their continued success in the ultimate peacetime commerce in which this country must surely engage.

To the United States Merchant Marine Cadet Corps and to the Training Organization of the War Shipping Administration, of which it is a part, I send my congratulations and best wishes."

From the condolence letter sent by the War Shipping Administration to the next of kin of merchant seamen killed during World War II. The letter was written by American playwright Eugene O'Neill, who drew upon his own experience as a merchant seaman.

With a deeper understanding than is given to most landsmen, a seafaring man whose life has been spent contesting the elements finds man-made tyranny and inequalities insufferable. Perhaps that is why men such as your son have shown themselves ready to give their lives in a Service where the rewards of heroism are few, and which demands of its men the grimmest form of courage. It takes an iron fortitude and indifference to danger to be a good merchant seaman in this war. Their duty is to face on every voyage the constant threat of death and to go on with their work, accepting this threat as a commonplace risk of each day's job. And when their luck runs out, their duty is to accept death, too, in the same spirit of unflinching loyalty to their Service and the task assigned them.

TEAMWORK WINS
You Build 'em
We'll Sail 'em
UNITED STATES MARITIME COMMISSION

Foreword

The American Maritime History Project proudly offers this book as a tribute to the men who died in World War II while serving as U.S. Maritime Commission Cadets, Cadet Officers, Cadet-Midshipmen, or as officers on merchant ships or in military service after finishing any of these training programs. Collectively they were known as Kings Pointers, although many never stepped foot on the Academy grounds at Kings Point, New York. Some were Maritime Commission Cadets before Kings Point was conceived, some were graduates of State Maritime Academies who enrolled in the Maritime Commission Cadet Officer program; others attended regional U.S. Merchant Marine officer preliminary training schools at Pass Christian, Mississippi, San Mateo, California, and Kings Point, New York. This latter group of men from the training schools was sent to sea as Cadets to complete six or more months of on board ship training, and they were expected to report to Kings Point for their advanced training; unfortunately, many made their final voyage to rest in a watery grave.

While this project specifically honors the Kings Pointers who died, we will never forget nor minimize the estimated 243,000 men and women who served in the merchant marine during WWII and the estimated 8,421 who were killed at sea, killed as prisoners of war, and those who died from wounds later ashore. According to *usmm.org*, there was a casualty rate of 3.9 percent. Kings Point records indicate that the youngest Cadet-Midshipman to die was 17 years and 11 months of age; the eldest was 24 years and 10 months, the average age of the deceased Cadet-Midshipmen was 20.5 years of age. The last two Cadet-Midshipmen to die in WWII were John Artist and Dante Polcari on April 9, 1945.

Because of their supreme sacrifice, the U.S. Merchant Marine Academy is privileged—among the nation's five federal academies—to be the only institution authorized to carry a Battle Standard flag as part of its color guard. The proud and colorful Battle Standard perpetuates the memory of 142 Kings Point Cadet-Midshipmen who died during World War II. Kings

Point is the only federal Academy that sends its students into "harms way" during their training.

The names of the Cadet-Midshipmen, Cadet Officers, and graduates who died are remembered on the 1946 War Memorial Monument at the Academy. Since wartime record-keeping is never exact, it was not an easy task to come up with the precise number and the names of the men who constitute the 142 Cadet-Midshipmen and the many Maritime Commission and Kings Point graduates who died. Thus, we believe there are a few inaccuracies on the Monument. In this tribute we include those men who died between January 1, 1941 and December 31, 1945.The authors believe there are three men whose names should not be on the Monument: Cadet Andrew Hoggatt who died in 1940, James W. McCarthy who died in 1946, and Semon Leroy Teague, who died in 1997. The authors believe there are five men whose names should be on the Monument: Cadets Carl Brandler, Kenneth McAuliffe, and Robert N. Simmons and Cadet Officer Coffey and Cadet-Midshipman Graduate Seperski. We have researched as many documents as possible to tell the story of each young man; in some cases the information is sparse, but that is all the information we uncovered.

Some Cadet-Midshipmen died in training accidents or from illnesses while in the United States; others died of accidents ashore or afloat while serving on their ship during the war. The authors found that some graduates also died of nonbattle related accidents ashore or afloat, and at least three died from a self-inflicted wound, not unlike the same tragedy that has occurred during the extreme stress of every war. Details may be found in Appendices A and B. There may be more Cadets who died of accidents or illnesses while in training during World War II whose names may not be included here because of poor wartime record-keeping. Others, as merchant marine Cadet-Midshipmen, became U.S. Navy Midshipmen and officers and never returned to the Academy; we do not know if any of them died in the war.

German and Japanese submarines and aircrafts and mines sunk, damaged, captured, or detained 1,768 ships during the war (*usmm.org*). Many sailors, including Cadet-Midshipmen, survived. The Kings Point survivors, over four hundred Cadet-Midshipmen, formed an exclusive club called the Tin Fish Club when they returned to the Academy to continue serving their country. The names of many of the Tin Fish Club members are found in Appendix C.

The end of the hostilities of World War II did not end the continued contributions of the U.S. Merchant Marine Academy graduates to their country. Many Kings Pointers continued to serve in all branches of the military services in peacetime, and in the wars that have followed—Korea, Vietnam, Iraq, and Afghanistan. Other graduates and Cadet-Midshipmen served on merchant ships in these war zones. Since 1947, eight Kings Point graduates serving in the Air Force, Marines, and Navy have died in aircraft accidents in training or while teaching others to fly. Eliot See, class of 1949, a member of the NASA space program, died in 1966 when his T-38 jet trainer crashed. He was scheduled to be the prime pilot on the Gemini 9 space capsule. Six graduates died as military officers in Vietnam, Iraq, and Afghanistan. Two graduates died while serving as merchant marine officers during the Vietnam War. Two graduates were killed when terrorists flew commercial jets into the World Trade Center in New York City on September 11, 2001. See Appendix F.

U.S. Merchant Marine Academy Cadet-Midshipmen and graduates continue to serve their country today just as they served in World War II, and their service is recognized and honored.

Acknowledgments

Braving the Wartime Seas is the final product of the vision of many Academy graduates, but in particular of Eliot Lumbard, class of 1945. Memories of his training period as a Cadet-Midshipman during World War II, serving on convoys to the Mediterranean remained embedded in his mind. The shock of the bombing raids on his convoy, and his personal observations of the total loss of several ships, and the cruel deaths of untold numbers of military personnel and merchant mariners were instrumental in his conception of this book to honor his comrades and other Cadet-Midshipmen and graduates.

Before Eliot Lumbard turned his attention to this tribute, he formed a Board of Directors and solicited contributions to support the publication of two book-length histories— *The Way of the Ship*, a history of the U.S. Merchant Marine from 1600 to 2000 and *In Peace and War*, a history of the U.S. Merchant Marine Academy. The board also approved the publication of other materials that are of importance to the mission of the Academy. Unfortunately, Eliot became ill and was unable to direct the project to its completion.

Cadet-Midshipman Eliot Lumbard,
Class of 1944

Lumbard engaged Jeff Cruikshank, coauthor of *In Peace and War*, to conduct groundwork research for *Braving the Wartime Seas*. We thank Jeff Cruikshank and Chloe G. Kline for the initial research they provided to Eliot.

When the publication appeared to languish without Eliot at the helm, George Ryan, class of 1957, was asked by Captain Warren G. Leback,

17

class of 1944, to assume the chairmanship of the project. A new Board and advisory committee were formed, and their names are listed below.

Tom Schroeder, class of 1957; and Jim Hoffman, class of 1944, provided valuable encouragement and research findings on the men who died and their families. Tony Romano, class of 1957, continued on as treasurer and filed the necessary documents to retain our not-for-profit tax status. Roy Corsa, class of 1957, became assistant treasurer and assisted with obtaining and identifying photographs of the Cadet-Midshipmen and graduates and became the project contact at the alumni foundation. Bob Aimone, class of 1957 and R. E. ("Bob") McDermott, class of 1973, aided with editing.

In some research we were assisted by Dr. George Billy, Chief Librarian at the Academy, and by Dr. Warren Mazek, retired Dean of USMMA, in matters too numerous to recount. Thanks are extended to Toni Horodysky, who is responsible for the website *usmm.org*, honoring all the merchant mariners who died in World War II.

Of major assistance in bringing the project to fruition is Thomas F. McCaffery, class of 1976, who offered to complete the research and to arrange the documents on the fatalities in a way that honors each individual Cadet-Midshipman or graduate with a separate page and photographs. Tom McCaffery and his staff of other Kings Pointers have worked at no charge because of their affection for the Academy and their belief that the men who sacrificed their lives should be honored.

We thank all of these persons for their encouragement and support. Last, but not least, on behalf of the Board of Directors, past and present, I extend heartfelt and profound thanks for the financial generosity of many contributors who made the past publications possible and to now complete *Braving the Wartime Seas.*

The American Maritime History Project rings up *Finished with Engines* as this book is published.

George J. Ryan, Chairman
Acta Non Verba

Directors, American Maritime History Project
Allen, Virgil R., class of 1973
Corsa, Roy, class of 1957
Cushing, Charles R., class of 1956
Hanley, Edward F., class of 1985
Herberger, Albert J., class of 1955
Mazek, Dr. Warren, former Academic Dean, USMMA
McCaffery, Thomas F., class of 1976
Romano, Anthony P., Jr., class of 1957, Treasurer
Ryan, George J., class of 1957, Chairman
Sherman, Fred S., class of 1955
Yearwood, Donald R., class of 1961
Yocum, James H., class of 1947

Advisory Committee
Renick, Charles M., class of 1947
Schroeder, Tom, class of 1957
Stewart, Vice Admiral Joseph D., ninth Superintendent, USMMA

The Battle Standard

The U.S. Merchant Marine Academy is privileged—among the nation's five federal academies—to be the only institution authorized to carry a Battle Standard as part of its color guard. The proud and colorful Battle Standard perpetuates the memory of the 142 Academy Cadet-Midshipmen who died during World War II.

The 142

The number 142 is enshrined at the U.S. Merchant Marine Academy. Every plebe learns within days of reporting to Kings Point that 142 Cadet-Midshipmen died during World War II. Their names, along with the names of graduates who died, are cast in bronze on the memorial facing Long Island Sound. Captain Kenneth R. Force, USMS, Director of Music composed a March to honor the 142.

Yet a review of the following pages will find that that hallowed number was hard to pin down in regard to the circumstances and other details of their death. Several of the 142 died while in training—by accident or illness in the United States, far from the enemy's torpedoes or bombs. Others, even while overseas in combat areas, died of disease, shipboard accidents, or in a traffic accident while ashore seeing the sights of exotic foreign lands. The same is also true for the Academy's alumni who died during the war.

There is some confusion about how the number 142 came about. A *New York Times* article on March 16, 1946, mentions, "War memorial services for the 132 Cadet-Midshipmen who lost their lives in training at sea with the Cadet Corps." Other accounts indicate that Vice Admiral Gordon McClintock, the Academy's longest serving Superintendent, simply decreed that 142 was the number and ordered his staff to make the number work.

Research into the Academy's historical documents, both at the Academy and in the National Archives, shows that the end of World War II was a chaotic period in many ways. One of the methods of determining which of the thousands of wartime U.S. Maritime Commission Cadets, Cadet Officers, Cadet-Midshipmen, and Academy's graduates had died was by sending letters to their last known address—on the assumption that the Post Office would forward the letters and the recipient would respond. This method worked very well, but not perfectly. Thus, the name of one alumnus who did not actually die until 1997 is on the War Memorial. Nothing is perfect, especially when dealing with human beings during wartime.

However, the importance of 142 to Kings Point and Kings Pointers is not whether the number is factually correct. The actual number is irrelevant; 142 is the symbol that defines Kings Point as a unique institution, the only federal Academy that routinely sends its students into combat. Only Kings Point has the honor of having a Regimental Battle Standard. The Academy would still have its Regimental Battle Standard if only fourteen Cadet-Midshipmen had died in World War II combat.

Should the War Memorial be "corrected" or 142 changed? No. The names of Kings Pointers on the memorial who didn't die in World War II represents all the thousands of Kings Pointers who volunteered to go into combat, came back, graduated, and moved on with their lives.

The names on the War Memorial include the 142, Maritime Commission Cadet Officers, and Kings Point graduates; every one of them, whoever they might be, represents the ultimate expression of the Academy's motto, "*Acta Non Verba*—Deeds not words."

Every Kings Pointer is a volunteer, just like the 142. No one can force a person to go to Kings Point, let alone graduate; just like no one could force the 142 to go where they would ultimately die. This is the real message of the 142 to the generations of Kings Pointers who made the Academy what it is today and for those that will shape its future.

PART ONE

The U.S. Merchant Marine Cadet Corps during World War II

It was, as President Franklin Delano Roosevelt solemnly intoned, a "date that would live in infamy." On December 7, 1941, Japanese planes attacked the United States naval base at Pearl Harbor, killing 2,403 Americans and injuring an additional 1,178, destroying or damaging eight Navy battleships, and abruptly plunging the United States into war.

Although the dawn attack was unexpected, a global conflagration was already underway. Pearl Harbor, and the subsequent declaration of war on the Axis powers, only accelerated a massive mobilization of the U.S. Armed Forces and private industry that was already in process. Less than a month later, President Roosevelt announced production goals for 1942 that included sixty thousand planes, forty-five thousand tanks, twenty thousand antiaircraft guns, and eighteen million deadweight tons of merchant shipping. These were staggering, almost unbelievable targets for a nation that had long indulged its isolationist streak.

Almost overnight, the rules had to be rewritten. Suddenly, scrap metal was no longer disposable. Idle talk was no longer harmless. For most Americans, the world had changed irrevocably.

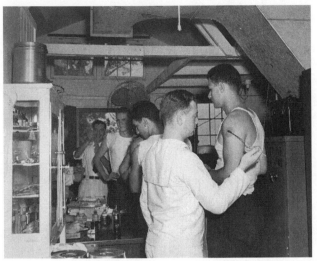

U.S. Navy physical exam and immunizations.

In cities across the country, the world had also changed for 395 young men who, only a day earlier on December 6, 1941, had taken the fifth national competitive exam to qualify as Cadets in the fledgling Merchant Marine Cadet Corps. The Corps, which had been founded two years earlier by the U.S. Maritime Commission to train officers for the U.S. merchant marine industry, had been selecting highly qualified young men from every state in the nation to become part of an elite training unit. However, in the new post—Pearl Harbor world of merchant shipping, every able-bodied young man was needed; thus, the December 6 exams were never graded. All applications to the corps were accepted, as long as the applicants met Naval Reserve physical fitness standards.

Over the next several months, many of those who had taken the exam would report to one of three Cadet Corps officer training schools to begin training for service in the U.S. merchant marine. In subsequent months and years, these men, and thousands of others like them, would find themselves serving as part of the fourth arm of national defense, the U.S. Flag Merchant Marine, and on the front lines of war.

Putting the Foundations in Place

Founded in 1939 under the auspices of the U.S. Maritime Commission, the Cadet Corps replaced an older system of Cadet maritime training on U.S. flag mail ships and the private Company Cadet program. Although storm clouds were already gathering in Europe, the immediate impetus for expanded merchant marine training in the United States was not the anticipation of war but a series of accidents involving passenger liners, including the infamous SS *Morro Castle* disaster. These disasters were made worse by the actions of incompetent ships' officers. In this era, before transoceanic air travel, ships were the only lifelines linking Europe and Asia with the Americas; disasters at sea had a profound resonance in the United States.

The Cadet Corps was initially a sea-based operation in which ninety-nine Cadets were placed on merchant ships for training under the ship's officers. In addition to shipboard work assigned by the officers, the Cadets also worked on correspondence lessons that they completed onboard the ship. The lessons were then mailed to supervisors at the ports of New York, San Francisco, and New Orleans for grading.

The Maritime Commission also had a Cadet Officer program whereby graduates with licenses from state maritime academies or school ships could be assigned as excess billet Cadet Officers onboard the ships owned by companies receiving government subsidies. These officers would be evaluated and promoted to licensed officer positions on the ships of those companies. The majority of these Cadet Officer appointments were made in the 1939-1940 time frames, when permanent jobs were difficult to obtain. All these Cadet Officers were a component of the Maritime Commission Cadet program, just as the Cadets at Kings Point were. Those Cadet Officers who died during the war were memorialized on the Academy Monument facing Long Island Sound, just as the Kings Point Cadet-Midshipmen and graduates were memorialized.

By 1941 the Cadet complement had grown to 425 Cadets. With growth came change in the sea-based component of the program. Regulations published by the Maritime Commission in October 1939 specified a four-year training course, of which three years would be spent at sea, working on merchant vessels and one year of shore training. Administrators in Washington set in motion plans to establish a shore-based officer training school on each of the three coasts. However, by the fall of 1941, only temporary facilities had been acquired for the New York, California, and Louisiana schools.

On the Gulf Coast, the Maritime Commission began training in Algiers, Louisiana. Cadets were assigned to live in the large, white naval base Commander's house. Jim Risk '42 reported there in January 1942. The quarters were dubbed the country club house by Cadet Paul Snider '44, who reported there in September 1941. Each room had four midshipmen, two double deck bunks, and a large study hall table with four chairs. Later they were moved to the M/V *North Star,* a large private yacht previously owned by Dr. Mayo of Rochester, Minnesota. It was large enough to serve as a berth for all the Cadets; they went from four in a room to two in a room, but they still ate at the officers' mess. The *North Star* was later moved to the Maritime Commission basic school at Old Spanish Fort, Bayou Saint John, New Orleans, where land was leased to berth the *North Star* and a 120-foot houseboat, according to John Woodrow '44. He said old Civilian Conservation Corps buildings were reassembled on the site.

On the West Coast, before San Mateo was opened, the Maritime Commission made arrangements with the California Maritime Academy to send the first four Cadets in 1939 to the T/S *California State*; but that ended when the training ship went on its annual training cruise in January 1940. Under a new arrangement with the U.S. Navy, Cadets for basic training were sent to Treasure Island, California, where they were berthed onboard the floating naval barracks *Delta King* and later to the sister ship, *Delta Queen.* William Figari '42 said naval personnel trained him at the adjacent base.

On the East Coast, the Maritime Commission made arrangements with the New York State Maritime Academy, Fort Schuyler, New York for federal Cadets to live there; the first Cadets were assigned in October 1939. Due to the need to make new arrangements when the T/S *Empire State* took all Cadets and staff on a training cruise, a brief arrangement was made with the Admiral Billard Academy in New London, Connecticut, to act as a receiving station for Cadets until the operation would return to Fort Schuyler, where it remained until the move to Kings Point.

Many graduates and Cadets got their start at Fort Schuyler. In October 1940, J. Richard Kelahan '42 was ordered to Fort Schuyler; he said that Maritime Commission Cadet Officers who graduated from California Maritime School were also there. Rear Admiral Tom King '42 reported to Fort Schuyler in January 1941; after some basic training, he was assigned to merchant ships for Cadet training. In November 1941, Tom King returned to Fort Schuyler for naval science training, a prerequisite for Midshipman commission. In June 1941, Joe Mahoney '43 was sent to Fort Schuyler for prelim training, and from there was assigned to his first ship.

The attack on Pearl Harbor immediately intensified the search for new quarters on each coast. Within months, permanent facilities were established in New York, California, and Mississippi. The New York school found a home on the late Walter P. Chrysler's former estate, which comprised twelve waterfront acres and several buildings in the village of Kings Point, on Long Island's northern shore. In January 1942, twenty acres of land on the rocky Coyote Point, outcropping of San Mateo Point, was acquired for the California school. In August 1942, the Louisiana school located a permanent home at a forty-acre former resort in Pass Christian, Mississippi.

Guard at entrance to old Chrysler estate

Within nine months of Pearl Harbor, the Maritime Commission could proudly point to three officer training schools ready to begin the deadly serious job of training wartime merchant ship officers and naval reserve officers.

Building the Schools

The Cadet program was structured to have three phases. The first phase, which was conducted at the New York, Mississippi, and California schools, provided new Cadets with sufficient skills and knowledge to make the most of their second phase, shipboard training. Upon completion of their shipboard training, unless directed elsewhere, all Cadet-Midshipmen reported to the New York school for the final phase. This school soon became known simply as Kings Point. During their advanced training, Cadet-Midshipmen were prepared to take and pass their U.S. Coast Guard license examinations. As the only school organized to provide both preliminary and final training, Kings Point quickly became the centerpiece of the program. As a result, the development of Kings Point was the most complex.

The Kings Point advance party, including engineering instructor Lauren McCready, arrived at the former Chrysler estate on the afternoon of January 24, 1942. Gerald Early '43, who lived in nearby Manhasset, was assigned to Kings Point on February 11, 1942. Men coming back from their sea assignment began to receive orders to Kings Point for the advanced training as berthing space opened up. Jim Risk '42 said he reported to Kings Point in July 1942, and the first few nights were spent in the mansion; later he was billeted at the just-acquired Schenck house. Over the next several months, the government purchased other adjoining properties, thus by October 1943 growing the campus to forty-six acres with fifty-three permanent buildings.

**1942 First Cadets occupy Chrysler mansion for berthing,
classes, and mess hall**

McCready had been a company Cadet and a Wiper before he received his license. Captain McNulty knew of him and appointed him Cadet Training Instructor in Washington, DC. He was highly recommended for the job ahead. The challenge facing McCready and the other staff was that they not only had to make an immediately useful school, but at the same time keep an eye toward the future, allowing for the longer-term evolution of the Cadet Corps. Making the necessary trade-offs was far from a simple exercise, especially because the officers responsible for overseeing the physical redevelopment process were also creating the new curriculum, more or less from scratch, at the same time.

Greenhouse was Engineering Dept. in 1942

One clever, interim solution involved the use of twelve forest-green wooden buildings left over from the New Deal's Civilian Conservation Corps (CCC) days. Disassembled and trucked down from New York's Adirondacks Park region and from New Jersey's Fort Dix, these structures would serve a variety of purposes until more permanent solutions could be devised. Delivered on February 18, 1942, they required fourteen weeks to be installed and equipped for their new purposes, using almost exclusively Cadet labor. Rear Admiral Carl Seiberlich '43 remembered being part of a team of Cadets that helped reassemble the CCC buildings on-site. "The first two weeks I was there," Seiberlich recalled, "that's all we did."

The CCC barracks Corsair, Defiance, and Eclipse

Meanwhile, the existing buildings also were pressed into service. One of the former Chrysler garages housed the seamanship course; other existing structures became classrooms and an armory. The estate's greenhouses morphed into washrooms, and most other buildings served as barracks. However, constructing temporary buildings and retrofitting existing mansions and their outbuildings represented only a partial solution. The fast-growing Academy also needed new buildings. Shortly after installation of the CCC structures was completed, contractors began pouring concrete for the foundations of Palmer Hall, the first in what was to be a cluster of six new barracks.

Temporary mess hall

Making up double deck bunks in the CCC Barracks

The building program caused headaches for Cadets trying to learn their trade in the midst of construction, mud, and temporary facilities. Milton Nottingham '44 recalls, "The conditions were rather primitive. We were quartered in old CCC barracks buildings that lined the oval in front of Wiley Hall . . . And each one of those buildings housed, I would think, about 125 or 150 Cadet-Midshipmen. We had double-decker bunks, and we were in sections of 25 young men each." Jack Weinberger '44 was a prelim in 1943 and lived in the Corsair barracks. It was cold in February; the only heat was a coal-fired potbelly stove. There was still not enough berthing space to accommodate all the basic Cadets from the East Coast in 1943; for example, Jim Baker '45 from Connecticut was sent to San Mateo.

Ens. Turner - one of that big draft of Navy Ensigns who came in July '42 - among them Gaudreaux, Thomas, Carlson, who later built long and fine records at the Academy.

The Academy classrooms were also primitive and inadequately supplied. Weather permitting; some classes took place outdoors with tree stumps occasionally standing in as pedestals for teaching equipment. The Academy's young instructors soon found that their own resourcefulness was an indispensable contributor to the rapid evolution of a campus. Lauren McCready, named head of the Engineering Department in 1942, recalls an opportunity that arose in the furnace room of the Chrysler residence:

> Luckily for us, they had a big industrial boiler, not an ordinary residential boiler. A big, cast iron monster, probably eight feet by seven feet. It had an oil burner, pressure gauges, try-cocks, water-gauge glasses, siphons, stop valves, safety valves, and so on. I was able to use that system to teach the Cadets everything they needed to know about boilers. Primitive perhaps, but that boiler probably saved the lives of many men.

The machine shop was even more primitive. For the first several weeks of the new Academy's existence, the shop consisted of a bucket of tools that went wherever it was needed.

In a process that might kindly be described as chaotic, McCready and his colleagues built an Academy from the ground up. They improvised, made do, went without, and scavenged spare parts from the nearby Brooklyn Navy Yard to respond to the day's most urgent need. Meanwhile, similar feats were being accomplished at both Pass Christian and San Mateo. Because these two schools offered only preliminary instruction, their equipment and infrastructure needs were less elaborate than those of their sister school in New York.

The distractions and turmoil of construction, however, were similar on all three coasts. When Charles Renick '47 arrived at Pass Christian for basic training in July of 1944, almost a year after work had begun on the campus, the Cadets still found themselves being conscripted into work parties between lessons. Although the Pass Christian Cadets sometimes felt frustrated that their merchant marine training included land-based construction projects, they also recognized the need to complete the facilities. At no time was this more evident than at taps; when, in the absence of completed dormitories, all three-hundred Cadet-Midshipmen had to bunk down on cots in the gymnasium. Renick recalls that the facilities were so inadequate for the number of students on the half-finished campus that Cadets would often wake themselves at 2:00 or 3:00 in the morning in order to use the heads without a half-hour queue.

On the West Coast, construction moved more quickly, in part because the buildings on the site were conceived as temporary structures. On June 25, 1942, Architect Gardiner Dailey's plans were approved, and grading and tree clearing began the next day. Cadet-Midshipmen and faculty moved into the facilities on August 15, 1942, with the formal dedication of the school taking place two weeks later.

Abandon ship drill in San Mateo, California

The Training Programs

The training programs were tailored to the needs of the war. At times, "special" Cadet-Midshipmen were sent to other locations to take and pass their U.S. Coast Guard license examinations. These men did not follow any preset curriculum. Marc Enright '50 described the specials in the fall 1991 *Kings Pointer*, "Generally, they were Cadets and Cadet-Midshipmen who experienced an inordinately long sea year. The classes of '42-'48 had them, the classes of '42, '43 and '44 were conspicuous by their presence . . . The demands of the war and the goals of the Academy forced endless changes to the programs for the Cadets . . . If they were too long at sea, it became more difficult to assimilate them into the existing programs upon their return . . . They had generally sailed in berths above that of Cadet and were more than qualified . . . To get these specials back into the mainstream of the war as quickly as possible, they were given condensed refresher courses, tutored for their license exam, and graduated."

Rear Admiral Tom King, USMS, '42 said that in early 1942, "We were 'special' Cadets. The people they were really interested in were the new fellows who were coming in without examination. They would present their credentials: a high school diploma and the proper courses, and they took them in as plebes. They were beginning to form the regiment then. We were specials; we thought we were quite salty, I'm sure, but we were kept separate from the others."

Roger Shaw '42 said that in early 1942, the Navy took over his ship, the *Delargentina*, and the Maritime Commission ordered him off his ship to report to the Navy station at Algiers to study for his license. He said it was all Navy there; in fact, all his training was onboard the ship as a Cadet and a little from the Maritime Commission office in New Orleans. Phil Krepps '42 was at Pennsylvania Nautical School when the school closed temporarily, and he was immediately shipped out as a Maritime Commission Cadet and was at sea as a Cadet for long periods, including six weeks in England. Upon return to New York City, he was ordered to sit for his license. His only experience at Kings Point was the twelve days he was there to study for his license.

William Figari '42 said his ship was turned over to the Navy for conversion to the USS *Elizabeth Stanton* (AP-69). Figari was asked by the Navy if he would accept appointment as an Ensign, but he declined. He was detached and sent to Kings Point as a special, and he took classes with other Cadets. Frank Varga '43, after having been at sea as a Cadet for sixteen months rather than six, was pulled off the ship and sent to Kings Point as a special. Varga underwent two months of closely-monitored self-study under the guidance of a nautical science professor who was transferred up from the *Seneca*. He said the prof made his life miserable following the tradition of the *Seneca* where instructors encouraged and, at times, participated in the "boot" hazing. Varga noted that after a week of living at the Academy while taking the exam, he passed and was given the Third Mate license, an Ensign commission, and was told he had graduated and to move out of quarters by 1700! So much for ceremony! About a year after the war, in 1946, he received his diploma in the mail.

Vice Admiral Bob Scarborough, USCG, class of '44, took his prelim training at Pass Christian; and when he had enough time to sit for his license, was ordered to Pass Christian as a special for license prep training. Bob never spent a night at Kings Point during training, but is a loyal Kings Pointer.

Harry S. ("Stick") Riley '44 had his basic training at Kings Point. He made the Murmansk run; when he had enough sea time to sit for his license, he was sent to special school at Pass Christian. John Woodrow '44 and Michael Slezak '44 also were sent to Pass Christian for a month as an advanced Cadet special to prepare for the license exam and to pass along their seagoing experiences to the Cadets in basic training. Woodrow said that at that time there were ten to twelve specials at the school.

Philip Torf '44, a member of the Tin Fish Club, lost his sea project when his ship went down, and when he returned to the West Coast, was given a test at San Mateo; he passed and was shipped out again. When he finished his Cadet time, the Maritime Commission said they needed officers, and he was directed to do his advanced training as a special onboard the ship to prepare for his license. Torf was not the only one sent back to sea to study; since at times there was no berthing space at Kings Point, a Cadet-Midshipman was given an advanced sea project to complete onboard the ship in order to prepare for a license exam.

Ed Kavanagh '44 was assigned to the MV *Artigus*, Panamanian flag; by the end of February 1944, he had his time at sea and was ordered to the Academy as a special. He was assigned to a group of specials in a section where he was appointed the adjutant. He believed they looked like a bunch of prisoners marching; at one point, Gunny Horton observed them responding to the command "eyes left" as they passed a young woman. The section was put on report, and they all had to work off demerits. He had to take two exams—one to get out of the Academy and one to pass the license. He did not spend the training time at the Academy to get any certificate of graduation.

1942 scene coaling the Emery Rice. She used to make little cruises up and down Long Island sound. "Bing" Crosby was her Chief.

Coaling the Emory Rice

The prewar training program of the Merchant Marine Cadet Corps had been conceived with lofty goals in mind. The Maritime Commission aimed to produce nothing less than officers of the merchant marine who would be equally comfortable at sea and in industry roles ashore. In addition to the shipboard necessities of navigation, seamanship, and cargo handling, Deck Cadets would be required to learn maritime law, economics, and commercial practices. Engine Cadets would be taught not only basic electrical theory and the use of the lathe and related tools, but also advanced mathematics, thermodynamics, and physics.

Our toolroom Sebastian lathe, as well as the rest of the greenhouse shop, is in view. It was an excellent shop, 30'x90'; warm and light; but in the autumn of '42 it had to be taken down. It was reassembled over the School pool

However, due to the limited amount of time available to meet wartime manpower demands, many of these high-minded goals had to be temporarily set aside. Under enormous pressure to get troops and supplies to fronts around the world, Cadet-Midshipmen would have to learn on the job. With the outbreak of war, the training program was reduced from four years to twenty-two months, and then eighteen months. By December 1942, the fourth classmen basic prelim instruction period at San Mateo, Pass Christian, and Kings Point was just twelve weeks long. This was followed by a minimum of six months as third classmen on merchant vessels. Finally, second and first class Cadet-Midshipmen were to spend thirty-six weeks of instruction at Kings Point. Groups of Deck and Engine Cadet-Midshipmen completed the program, graduated, and shipped out every two weeks with Coast Guard license and Ensign, USNR commission in hand, to start playing their critical role in the global war.

The severe time constraints meant that priorities had to be established for its war-bound Cadets. Deck Cadet-Midshipmen needed to master navigation and the handling of ships, cargo, and men. Engine Cadet-Midshipmen needed to become sound machinists and practical electricians, skilled in the operation and maintenance of shipboard power plants, and also experts in the handling of men. Thus, engineering, seamanship, and navigation became the Academy's top priorities in the early months of 1942. Naval science was added to the curriculum in August 1942, when all federal Cadets were officially named Midshipmen in the U.S. Naval Reserve. Visual signaling was another early priority for Deck Cadets.

The lack of suitable equipment for engineering classes posed a difficult challenge since little serviceable equipment could be spared for training. Until funds and authorizations to purchase equipment began to roll in during the late spring, the machine shop was entirely equipped with cast-offs scrounged by Lauren McCready and his instructors.

Much of the curriculum, too, was borrowed, reflecting both the relative inexperience of the instructors and the extremely limited time allotted for lesson planning. Teaching at this time was accomplished mainly through a lecture-demonstration method, with liberal use of visual aids (when they were available) and laboratory work. Instructors were given detailed lesson plans, prepared by officers in the Maritime Commission Educational Unit located in Washington, defining the precise content of each lesson. This assured the standardization of instruction across three widely scattered campuses, crucial in light of the high turnover of personnel dictated by the war.

Cadet-Midshipmen in advanced training also made numerous field trips in these early years to compensate for areas in which the Academy lacked expertise or equipment. For example, in August and September 1942, groups of Cadets visited Brooklyn's Sperry Gyroscope Plant, the Hayden Planetarium in the Museum of Natural History, and General Electric's service shop on West Thirteenth Street in Lower Manhattan.

Gunnery instruction, added in early 1943, underscored the dangerous circumstances that Cadet-Midshipmen were facing during their sea training. The outside of the gymnasium (O'Hara Hall) became the gunnery training school, complete with large gun-loading machines, the 20-millimeter Bofors AA gun, the .50-caliber Browning, and the .30-caliber Lewis machine gun. For additional live-fire instruction, Cadet-Midshipmen were bused to the Navy firing range at Long Beach, on Long Island's South Shore, where they shot 20-millimeter guns seaward at aircraft-towed targets.

Cadet-Midshipmen also received instruction in the deadly serious task of manning and navigating lifeboats—a task made all the more relevant to the younger Cadet-Midshipmen with the steady drumbeat of tales of ship sinkings being brought home from the war zones by upperclassmen. Lauren McCready recalls that these drills were both rigorous and frequent:

The training here was all centered on the war, and lifeboat work was absolutely preeminent. These fellows had to have survival skills taught thoroughly. Survivors would come back and lecture them: Never do this, and always that. Bring your compass and warm clothing. Don't do this; do that. And they had overnight lifeboat trips in the winter. These poor things would row out into the Sound any day of the year— on the 10th of February, in sleet, rain, anything. They'd go right down to Manhasset Bay freezing to death, huddled in the lifeboat all night and come back congealed the next morning.

Eliot Lumbard '45 recalls the exhausting work of lowering the Monomoy rowboats down to the water, then rowing them with their heavy eight-foot oak oars, and then sailing them around Long Island Sound to get a feel for boat handling. Then they had to haul them up out of the water. Cadet-Midshipmen were also instructed on the proper way to swim out from under a burning oil field, and how to jump into the water from a fifteen-foot tower. Again, Lauren McCready recalls the grim purposefulness of the training:

> We had a life-jumping tower at the pool . . . a big high tower at the edge of the pool, where these guys had to practice abandoning ship, with a lifejacket on. They had to learn to plunge correctly into the water, and they were told how to swim through burning oil. You go under. You surface and thrash wildly to drive the flames away. Then you gulp air, and go under again, and try to emerge from the slick of burning oil. So it was really very rigorous and purposeful training.

Cadet-Midshipmen were given a rubber "zoot suit" to wear while jumping from the tower. By the end of the session, the suit would often be so full of water that the hapless Cadet who was at the end of the line would sink like a stone, requiring rescue by his fellow Cadets.

In September 1942, another addition was made to the curriculum. Up until this time, study on ships was essentially a continuation of the prewar correspondence school approach. This method was replaced by the "sea project," which the Cadet newspaper *Polaris* described as "another step towards making this Academy the Annapolis of the Merchant Marine." The sea project was formulated along practical lines, with an emphasis on actual experience. The projects, each one a series of weekly exercises created by instructors on the Academy faculty, were specific to the deck and engine specialties. A typical exercise in the engine sea project involved preparing a diagrammatic sketch of the fuel cycle, from double bottoms to boilers. The deck sea projects included problems such as, "Explain by word and sketch how you would rig a bos'n chair. Indicate size, type, and length of rope used." These exercises, which were graded at Kings Point after the Cadet returned to shore, helped familiarize the Cadets with every key system on their ship.

Moving a critical piece of the learning experience offshore created new kinds of risks and difficulties. Cadet-Midshipmen on merchant ships faced the same dangers as officers and seamen. They were bombed, strafed, torpedoed, and sometimes sunk. The average eighteen-year-old, most likely only recently graduated from high school and on his first ocean voyage, found it hard to concentrate on a sea project after a terrifying air raid, or a life-and-death engagement with a U-boat. When a Cadet-Midshipman survived a sinking, his sea project generally did not. In most such cases, the Cadet simply got a new ship and started over.

The sea project also underscored the challenges of administering an educational program that sent its students directly into a global conflict. Simply keeping track of where all the Cadets were, at any given point in time, was a nearly impossible task. Many Cadet-Midshipmen changed vessels multiple times during their six months at sea. Even in the best of circumstances, the supervision of Cadets in foreign ports was hit or miss. As a result, some Cadets remained stuck at sea for many months, or even years, hoping to run into someone with the authority to send them back to the Academy. One San Mateo Cadet, Douglass C. North '43, a future Nobel Laureate in Economics, was twice promoted on his ship in the Pacific; and therefore never made it to the Academy for his advanced training.

Training at San Mateo and Pass Christian

Life at the sister academies bore many similarities to life at Kings Point, with one fundamental exception: the training was focused solely on preliminary instruction—that is, giving Cadets just enough shipboard knowledge to make them useful from their first hour aboard ship and enough gunnery training to keep them alive. Charlie Renick '47 recalls the focus of those early weeks of training:

DE-NO 178. Jan. 29 & - Pass Christian C-M during check-up week spend two days at
30, 1945.   U. S. Navy Firing Range, Shell Beach, La., before assign-
                 ment to sea duty. View of firing line from control tower
                 showing .50 cal., 20mm, 3" and 5"-.38 cal. guns.

They taught us basic seamanship and things so that when you got aboard ship you wouldn't embarrass the school. So you'd know the bow from the stern, and you'd know a little about the compass and basic things. I know they prepared us very well in those three months because I felt confident when I went aboard ship. And they sent us, while we were there, to a place called Pebble Beach, where there was a Navy antiaircraft school. And we all learned to shoot the twenty-millimeter machine guns and would have planes fly by and drag a sleeve that you would shoot at. Of course, there's always somebody that gets mixed up and shoots at the plane. That happened in our class.

Other firing ranges were at Shell Beach, Louisiana.

Since Pass Christian and San Mateo housed and trained only preliminary Cadets, Cadet-Midshipmen at these schools had limited exposure to the firsthand tales of war that infused the Kings Point community. Lieutenant Commander Ralph Sheaf, Commanding Officer in San Mateo, came up with a plan to close this gap, hosting mariners who had survived attacks at sea and were in a position to warn the Cadets about the dangers they soon would be facing. A description of one of these events was later published in *Polaris*:

"C. W. Boylston, Second Mate of a freighter, related two torpedoings he had experienced recently. The freighter he was on was sunk and he was rescued by a Dutch ship, which was also sent down by a torpedo. He later was picked up by a passing freighter."

Among suggestions made by Mr. Boylston were: attempt to keep yourself prepared for immediate abandonment of ship at all times; wear as many articles of clothing as possible; try to simulate conditions that most probably will exist in case of actual emergency.

Pass Christian Cadet-Midshipmen received their own version of this cautionary indoctrination. On one memorable occasion, Cadets heard a hair-raising lecture from Superintendent Stedman during one of his infrequent visits to the New Orleans area school. Stedman spent a full hour warning Cadets not to sleep on the hatches of their ship while at sea— and proceeded to provide horrific details about the fates of those who had failed to heed this elementary warning.

Of course, a visit from the Superintendent was the rare exception to the routines of training. Most of the time, Cadet-Midshipmen learned their lessons in makeshift classes and laboratories, with occasional instruction out on the water. Within months of the opening of Pass Christian, for example, Cadet-Midshipmen were enjoying weekly training cruises in the Mississippi Sound, offering a first glimpse of their future responsibilities at sea. Half-hour watches, leadsman, pilot, lookout, and emergency stations were assigned to the Deck Cadets. Shortly after leaving the pier, a fire drill was conducted with all hands participating.

As at Kings Point, the Pass Christian Cadet-Midshipmen were generally too busy to pursue recreational activities—which was just as well since the hastily converted campus offered little in the way of amenities. On the other hand, the rough-and-ready campus had few rules, at least at the outset. As James Hoffman '44 recalls,

**Cadet Section E-7, San Mateo,
California, August 25, 1943**

When I got there, just as the campus was opening, you could smoke anyplace on the grounds. Then, as things moved along, new rules were put into effect. The smoking lamp would be lit only in certain places, and at certain times. And in general, as things took shape, things went from being pretty informal to being much more organized.

The regimental system did not take root as forcefully at the satellite campuses as it did at Kings Point. The Cadet-Midshipmen faced drills, to be sure, but they encountered little in the way of precision marching or the other fine points of the regiment. At Pass Christian, for example, reveille sounded at 5:45 a.m., which rousted all the Cadets out onto the parade ground for calisthenics. But lacking a band and a drillmaster, Pass Christian never got to the point of full-dress regimental reviews.

Cadet Life

Much of the tenor of daily life at Kings Point, the Pass Christian and San Mateo schools was defined by the regiment, which was created under the charismatic second superintendent of Kings Point, Giles C. Stedman. Stedman and his first Cadet regimental Commander, George Agee, put in place many of the rules and traditions that came to define the Kings Point experience.

Agee is best remembered for his invention of a local version of West Point's demerit system, which many decades later, in a much-modified form, still sets limits on the regiment and imposes sanctions on wayward Cadet-Midshipmen. (Graduates from that era can still recite samples of Agee's terse prose: Word, failure to get . . . six demerits.) Although Cadets had participated in regular drills since the inception of the Academy, it was not until the interventions of Stedman and Agee that the regimental system became expanded and codified.

As the training program gathered momentum, Cadet-Midshipmen were accepted in sections of twenty students. The sections completed basic training together, were shipped out on merchant ships in small groups and, if possible, later reunited at the Academy for their advanced training. Though this system created major administrative headaches, as many subjects had to be taught continuously, it allowed Kings Point to graduate groups of Cadet-Midshipmen every two weeks; thereby providing a steady flow of new officers to the U.S. Merchant Marine and U.S. Navy.

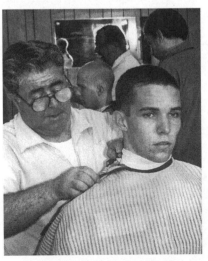

Regulation haircut for all!

46

The section quickly became the new Cadet's family. Sections ate together, attended classes together, got their vaccinations together, worked together, and came to grips with the hair-raising stories of wartime life at sea that were beginning to make their way back to the Academy. This bonding began on day one. The following account details the experience of the members of a typical section, in this case, section 074, as they arrived at Kings Point and were immersed in the life of a Cadet-Midshipman:

> *Friday and Saturday*: Ten men arrived by train or plane. Three find they have traveled 3,000 miles in the same airliner without knowing of their common destination. Others believe denim-clad Cadets to be laborers; all anxious to change into whites, demand, "When do we eat?"

> *Sunday*: The section receives two more members, both from California, gets church leave, attend Catholic or Episcopalian services. Later, baseball at Grace Estate; is served iced tea and cakes.
>
> *Monday*: Cadets become oriented to barracks discipline; some swim in Schenck pool; others spend day reading Sunday's funnies, investigating Academy's environs. All are given physical fitness tests by Mr. Cohen.
>
> *Tuesday*: Men begin week of work detail, break scrap iron until noon—reduce heterogeneity of dress by purchasing dungarees

and shirts at canteen—are moved from separate, scattered quarters to the "Bonita" barracks.

Wednesday, Thursday: New Cadets continue work detail—are given jobs for which they are best fitted—groan over aptitude tests and prospect of Kings Point duty for next week. Are measured for blues; told uniforms will be ready in two weeks.

Friday and Saturday: Last of preliminary sections, still incomplete, undergoes barracks inspection. Dust flies Friday night, and no white cotton gloves are dirtied Saturday morning as officers investigate high beams, shelf recesses, immaculate bunks, closets. Sprained ankle, injured shoulder, and stomach ache send three men to sick bay.

As the Cadet Corps grew, the rhythms of the first week solidified and became the core of what would later become a formal indoctrination ("indoc") period. Even before the end of the war, the first week of training exerted a profound impact that Cadets would later recall with some nostalgia. One Cadet's account of the experiences gives a strong sense of the new world into which these Cadet-Midshipmen were thrust into:

> Memories of our first week will remain with us forever. Some of the events are written indelibly on our souls—that short haircut, all those clothes to be stenciled, that huge armful of books, making the first bunk, folding so neatly the first blanket, learning how to brace, memorizing the Plebe Pledge, and falling in for our first muster.

Another ritual of the first week was the lecture given to incoming plebes by the executive officer of the Cadet Corps, Lieutenant Commander John F. ("Jackie") Wilson. The corps had no room for candidates who couldn't handle the pace, workload, or demands of war. Wilson's lecture gave the new recruits a clear picture of what would be required of them:

> [You] must spend every waking moment with the exception of recreation period in study. The instruction which you will receive in small-boat work must be taken seriously, and during your period of outdoor instruction you must refrain from any conversation whatever. Listen intently, bearing in mind that the instruction may aid you in saving your life or that of a shipmate. You must also remember that absolute silence must be maintained during group study . . . .

> When you return to the Academy, your advanced course of instruction will be stiff and you must prepare yourself well in advance of your

reporting here. You must choose your shipmates carefully; protect your personal property and the books and uniforms which have been entrusted to you. Your attention is called to the fact that should you resign, be requested to resign, or be dismissed, you will be required to turn in all government property which you have in your possession.

Wilson wasn't exaggerating; he was simply stating the facts. Many men did not make it through the first few weeks of their Kings Point experience, even though they were faced with the certainty of the draft if they left; and many of those who did had to struggle to survive. Cadets soon learned that the best way to make it through, indeed, the only way to make it through, was through teamwork. Upperclassmen refer to the fourth class program as an accelerated course—that is the acme of understatement. It is a super-accelerated maelstrom of physical and mental activities, and God help the bottom man on the totem pole.

The twenty-eight men in one section occupied one large room on the third deck of Furuseth Barracks. Here they lived the axiom that barracks life is the intro to military discipline. Limited quarters were a source of great confusion during the first few days, but the disorder gradually diminished and eventually disappeared. They learned almost immediately that intelligent cooperation was of paramount importance. Four months ago they were total strangers, and they became a veteran section, intimately associated and closely allied in thought, word, and deed; working and studying in harmony for the mutual benefit of all hands.

In spite of the busy schedule and cramped conditions, and the grim tidings of war that were beginning to filter back to the Academy, the Cadets managed to create a vibrant and optimistic community at each school. As the first two sections of Cadets who had begun their training at Kings Point graduated, the editors of *Polaris* took a moment to acknowledge the achievements of these trailblazers:

"18 Deck Cadets and 16 Engine Cadets have completed their prescribed course of training at the USMMA. They comprise the first group to have this distinction. They have had the honor of watching the Academy grow. Despite the many fond memories of comradeship and pleasant days of work and study, these Cadets are anxious to return to their careers at sea.

"They, the Cadets of 1-H-1, 1-H-2 realize their country is in greater need of their services now than at any period in her history. They, too, realize that they were instrumental in building the Academy to its present status.

This group formed the first class organization and held its first meeting June 2, 1942. Its aims were: 1) to build an organization with honorable traditions, 2) to provide the Upper-classmen with the necessary social functions, and 3) to indoctrinate the Lower-classmen.

"On July 18, 1942, the first dance sponsored by this class was held at the Academy. The plan to publish the Cadet Corps' own publication, *The Polaris*, was instituted by Cadets of this class . . . The tradition of tossing coins at Amphitrite's pool was born of this group. They carried out the suggestion that this money be placed in a fund to acquire a memorial for Cadets Lost at Sea."

The first classes of Cadets had laid an admirable foundation. Along with faculty, local administrators, and the Maritime Commission, they had helped put their Academy on a special course. Generations to come would benefit from their persistence, patience, and inventiveness.

Band Rehearsal

Who Were the Members of the Cadet Corps?

They were young men from all across the country, from all walks of life, who answered their country's call and enrolled in the Cadet Corps. Some came from seafaring traditions; others had never seen the ocean, but couldn't wait to escape the confines of the small towns in which they had grown up. Some chose the merchant marine because the path to officer rank was speedier than in the corresponding Army and Navy programs. Others were drawn by the romance of the sea.

Their backgrounds were as diverse as their motivations. One Cadet-Midshipman, writing in *Polaris*, described in detail the diverse origins of his section mates:

> Our section represents an excellent cross section of American youth . . . One lad is the son of a bank president who left Harvard to join the Cadet Corps. Another owned and operated a truck farm in Idaho; his locker is filled with seed catalogs. Another is a former Yale swimming star. One lad was an assistant buyer for Sears Roebuck. They hail from all walks of life and are truly a heterogeneous conglomeration. The clown of the section is a former bell-hop from a Chicago hotel . . . He has been on extra duty squad working off demerits ever since his second week.

Another *Polaris* article provided a tally of the prewar occupations of many Cadets, showcasing the variety of experiences (and the sometimes dry sense of humor) that students brought to their alma mater.

Cadet-Midshipman Allan Gibson: "Before entering the Cadet Corps, I was employed as a fire underwriter, which is one of the many branches of the insurance game." Cadet-Midshipman R. A. Perlatti: "I operated a surface grinder for the Eaton Manufacturing Co. in the aircraft division." Cadet-Midshipman Alva Andrus: "I got through Junior college by doing watch repair work, as well as being a clerk in a small jewelry firm in Salinas, CA. During the summer months, I was first trumpet with the Monterey County Symphony Orchestra."

All too often, war turns individuals into statistics, grim statistics. When reading accounts of the terrible trials of the merchant marine in World War II, it is worth remembering that the service was no more or less than a fleet of individual ships; and those ships were manned, in large part, by young people who had only begun to live their lives and pursue their dreams. They were from Iowa farms and small coastal cities in Massachusetts. They were clerks, trumpeters, machine-tool operators, and salesmen. As they embarked upon dangerous waters, they left behind anxious parents, fiancées, and friends. Many were sons of recent immigrants.

On balance, they were probably no braver than any other random assortment of young Americans, but they were soon called upon to be so.

Red-letter Days

The grinding routine of classes, examinations, and graduations at Kings Point was punctuated by a few standout dates during the war years. These were moments of reflection that prompted a contemplation of the important work already being done, and the enormous challenges still to be overcome.

Cadet Midshipman Frederick Zito receiving Distinguished Service Medal on September 30, 1943 during dedication of O'Hara Hall

One of these days was the formal dedication of the U.S. Merchant Marine Academy on September 30, 1943. Little more than a year and a half had passed since Cadets first set foot on its grounds, but Kings Point had undergone a complete transformation. The former Chrysler mansion, now the administration building, had been renamed in honor of Admiral Wiley, the first Maritime Commissioner in charge of training, who died in May 1943 at the age of seventy-three. Six new barracks, a mess hall, and several academic buildings had been erected; and the training facility was now nearly self-sufficient, with its own heating system (powered by two

Liberty ship boilers also used for engine instruction), fire department, and water supply.

The dedication ceremony was held in O'Hara Hall in front of the regiment of 2,500 Cadet-Midshipmen and 2,000 guests. A nationwide radio hookup allowed several million more listeners across the country to listen. The ceremony began with a letter from President Franklin Delano Roosevelt that was read to the assembled visitors by Sam Schell, executive officer of the War Shipping Administration. Roosevelt's words were complimentary and inspiring. One phrase in particular became both a touchstone and a point of affirmation for the young Academy,

> *"This Academy serves the Merchant Marine as West Point serves the Army and Annapolis serves the Navy."*

Maritime Commissioner Macauley followed Schell and used the occasion to present the Merchant Marine Distinguished Service Medal to Cadet-Midshipman Frederick Zito. Zito had risked his own life to save that of a ship's Fireman who, in the process of abandoning their torpedoed ship, had become entangled in the rope of a cargo net and was hanging upside down off the side of the ship. The young Cadet climbed up the boat falls from his lifeboat, extricated the Fireman, and both fell into the sea, from which they were rescued.

First Lady Eleanor Roosevelt toured the Academy grounds in the convertible owned by Engineering Professor Lauren McCready. She is escorted by Superintendent Giles C. Stedman and Chief of Staff P. C. Mahady

"For your quick thinking and coolness under action and your valor shown on this occasion," Macauley read to the assembled crowd, "you are hereby commended."

Commissioner Telfair Knight also spoke, paying tribute to Richard R. McNulty, the Supervisor of the Cadet Corps in Washington, and the man aptly called the guiding genius of the Academy. McNulty himself was not in attendance. Disliking ceremony of any sort, he had arranged to be in California at the time of the dedication.

Following Knight's speech, Macauley officially presented Captain James Harvey Tomb, USN, with the command of the Academy. This presentation was only a formality; the well-respected Tomb had been Superintendent of the Academy since April 11. Following the ceremony, the crowds moved to Kendrick Field (later renamed Tomb Field), where a formal review of the 2,500 Cadet-Midshipmen, divided into three battalions and eighteen companies, was held on the grounds. Captain Giles C. Stedman, Commandant of Cadets and soon-to-be-named the second Superintendent of the Academy, presented the regiment before approximately 8,900 guests. More than seventy-six busloads of people had been ferried in from the Great Neck train station, and some 1,200 cars were crammed into every corner of the Academy. It was a stirring occasion for those who had witnessed the birth of the school and who believed in its potential for the future.

Another red-letter day for the Academy was the May 5, 1944, visit of First Lady Eleanor Roosevelt. After a tour of the buildings and a review of the regiment, Roosevelt toured the grounds in the freshly washed convertible of Engineering Professor Lauren McCready, escorted by Superintendent Giles C. Stedman, and Chief of Staff P. C. Mahady. Her account of the visit was later reprinted in *Polaris*:

Regiment passes in Formal Review by First Lady Eleanor Roosevelt on Dedication Day September 30, 1943; it was rainy and windy!

"Saturday morning at 10 o'clock, Captain Giles G. Stedman, USNR, called for me and we went to visit the USMMA at Kings Point, NY. This is a very unique spot, beautifully landscaped and with permanent buildings. The old Chrysler house has been painted to conform with the newer buildings . . . The first thing I did on arrival was to be conducted to the Amphitrist [sic] pool, where just before exams the Cadet-Midshipmen toss in pennies. They brought a supply for my use, but when I delved into my pocketbook, I found two. Luckily, the second one landed in the correct spot, which I suppose indicated that I would pass my exam when I took it.

"Those pennies have an ultimate purpose, as well as an immediate one. Someday, they hope to erect a memorial to the group who have died at sea during the war. Already 124 have died, and some are missing, for the Merchant Marine is a dangerous service. There are some fine stories of heroism on which to begin building the traditions of the Cadet-Midshipmen of the Merchant Marine Academy.

Regimental salute in front of newly opened Delano Hall

"As they marched past us in review I was greatly impressed by them. The work must be extraordinarily heavy. 42 hours a week is a hard schedule, and they still find time to engage in extracurricular activities . . . I decided they never slept."

The memory of Cadet Elliott Earnest '44 was at variance with the official records of the dedication day with regard to the weather; he said that on September 30, 1943, there was bad weather, sufficient to cancel a regatta. Since there were more than eight thousand guests and the event was moved to O'Hara Hall, most Cadets were confined to the barracks. He said that when the regiment was assembled in front of Delano Hall for photographs, the wind blew so hard that many lost their hats, and Cadets and guests were wet from the rain!

A major milestone in Kings Point's social history occurred on July 18, 1942, when faculty and students gathered for the Academy's first dance, the midsummer hop, presented by the upperclassmen. With music furnished by Noble Sissle and his orchestra (brought in for the occasion from Billy Rose's Diamond Horseshoe nightclub in New York), four hundred officers, Cadet-Midshipmen, and young women "danced from 1600 to 2000 on the nautically decorated Quarter Deck and entire main floor of the Administration Building."

The event was a great success by all accounts. It was notable, in part, for its sheer normalcy. A group of young men and women got together on a Saturday night to flirt, brag, and boast; and otherwise enjoy each other's company. Surely, the uniformed men in attendance had earned the right to let their hair down and, if only briefly, put thoughts of war out of their minds.

Of course the biggest red-letter day for each Cadet-Midshipman was the day he was assigned to his first ship. He was prepared professionally and physically. Many were sent off after a meeting with the Chaplain, who gave them a straightforward talk about life at sea. In some cases, the Chaplain gave a prayer book, and for the Catholic men, a rosary and medals and he would send a letter to the family, advising them that their son was in his prayers.

Cadet Midshipman Howard P. Conway at Pass Christian; he died on board SS *Liberator* on March 19, 1942 when his ship was torpedoed. It was thought that he was the first Cadet to die since at that time it was unknown that Cadet-Midshipmen Lewis and See had actually been lost in a sinking of the SS *Azalea City* on February 20, 1942.

In the Line of Duty

World War II was fought, in part, on and around the merchant ships that served as the extended classrooms of the young Academy. In the two weeks following Pearl Harbor, Cadets Roger T. Wayland and Donald J. Stephenson watched in horror as Japanese planes made daily runs over Manila Harbor, dropping tons of high explosives on their ship and the other American vessels in the harbor. One of these ships was badly damaged, and the crew was captured. Among them was Cadet-Midshipman William V. Mitchell, whose completion of advanced education and graduation was postponed by more than three terrible years as a Japanese prisoner of war.

The Merchant Marine Cadet Corps sent its students out into active theaters of war. Administrators at Kings Point and in Washington understood full well the risks that their Cadet-Midshipmen were incurring. At first, there were attempts to keep Cadet-Midshipman out of the most dangerous areas. Very quickly though, the exigencies of war overwhelmed these efforts, and Cadets shipped out on any available U.S. merchant vessel and some foreign-flag ships.

In addition to the Four Chaplains who died on the SS Dorchester on January 19, 1943 Cadet-Midshipmen Edward G. Gavin and Samuel T. Tyler were among the 675 persons who perished

For a short time, Academy Cadet-Midshipmen escaped the ultimate sacrifice. Throughout the winter of 1941-42, Cadets and administrators held their breath, hoping somehow to avoid the inevitable. On March 20, 1942, the dreaded news finally arrived that Cadet-Midshipman Howard P. Conway Jr. had been lost when the SS *Liberator* was torpedoed. The Kings Point gymnasium was to be named after him, but upon knowing of the heroism of Cadet-Midshipman Edwin J. O'Hara, that gym was named O'Hara Hall. The gymnasium/naval science center at Pass Christian was named Conway Hall. When the war ended, German archives revealed that, in fact, Cadets Richard Lewis and Robert J. See were the first Cadets to die when their ship, the SS *Azalea City*, was torpedoed on February 20, 1942.

The United States Merchant Marine Academy is the only federal Academy to put its students in harm's way, but this distinction comes at a price paid in human life. Between 1942 and 1945, 142 Cadets died, primarily from submarine and aircraft attacks. Some others died from illness and accidents while on training ashore and afloat. Countless others survived sinkings and attacks from the icy waters off Murmansk, to the once-tranquil ports of Sicily, and from the Gulf of Mexico, to the ports of Indonesia. There is no exact count, but something like 650 ships sank with Cadets onboard.

Kings Point also lost members of its small, but rapidly burgeoning alumni. More than sixty graduates of the Academy and the U.S. Maritime Commission Cadet Officer Corps died during World War II, as members of the merchant marine and as naval officers. Kings Point and Merchant Marine Cadet Corps graduates served as mates and engineers on merchant ships as well as naval officers on destroyers, submarines, mine sweepers, and troopships. Like their not very much younger colleagues, they gave their lives in the line of duty.

At the beginning of the war, the U.S. Navy accepted many graduates into active duty because of the acute shortage of qualified officers, and at that time, the assembly lines for building merchant ships had not accelerated sufficiently to require those graduates on merchant ships. Toward the end of the war, the Navy had many officer training programs in place, such as the "90-day wonders" from colleges; and there was a vital need for merchant marine officers on the merchant ships. Thomas King '42 stated in *To Die Gallantly* that the Navy was desperate for manpower, particularly on the engineering side. In 1942, the Navy activated fifty-five Cadet-Midshipmen and assigned some of them to combat ships. It is believed that these men were the only U.S. Navy Midshipmen to serve aboard combatant ships in combat since the days of fighting sail.

According to Marc Enright '50, "A number of Cadets were activated into the Navy while serving their sea year." They served as assistant Engineering Officers and acting Engineering Officers on Navy ships while holding the rank of Midshipman. J. Richard Kelahan '42 never took a course at Kings Point. While he was a Cadet-Midshipman on a Navy-controlled ship, where he was serving in the capacity as Third Assistant Engineer, he was sent to Treasure Island to study for his third assistant license, which he passed. Elliott Earnest reported that graduation came on March 3, 1944, after passing the license exams. He had desired to go to the Navy upon graduation, but the Navy was encouraging merchant mariners to stay in the merchant marine since it took only ninety days to make an Ensign and eighteen months or more to make a merchant marine officer; and they were in short supply. Unfortunately, those decisions to serve where there was a greater need deprived graduates of the GI Bill, with its education and other monetary benefits; graduates who served on merchant ships found that they were not eligible for the GI Bill, unlike their classmates who served in the Navy. John Lively '44 said that on graduation he tried to join the Navy, but he was told there were too many Ensigns, and it would take six months before he could have his commission activated; he went back to the merchant marine. Captain Tom Saul '45 said he was one of the two in his section who went on active duty with the Navy, and thus, he was eligible for the GI Bill benefits that permitted him to attend college.

The Hot Spots

The Cadet-Midshipmen and graduates of Kings Point who died in the war succumbed to various causes. Some were taken ill onboard the ship, in the stifling heat of the Philippines, or the icy cold of Murmansk, or died of fever or infection onboard the ship. Others were victims of accidents, either onboard the ship or during brief visits ashore. Still, others were victims of storms and collisions at sea.

Most were killed as a result of a direct engagement with the enemy; they were killed by torpedoes launched from enemy submarine, and they were killed by bombs or torpedoes dropped from enemy aircraft. Whatever their ship or destination, every Cadet-Midshipman and graduate faced danger on every voyage. Throughout the war, the fate of the Academy's Cadets closely mirrored the fortunes of the U.S. Merchant Marine in general. As the theater of operations shifted, so did the hot spots in which Cadet-Midshipmen found themselves in the greatest danger. In roughly chronological order as the war progressed, these hot spots were the following: the U.S. East Coast, the Caribbean, the Murmansk run, the North Atlantic, the Mediterranean, the Indian Ocean, and finally, the South Pacific. (Details of the merchant ships sunk by German submarines may be found in www.uboat.net).

The first danger zone for merchant shipping emerged along the east coast of the United States—an area that became known as U-boat Lane or torpedo alley in the early months of 1942. In a campaign named Operation Paukenschlag (Drumbeat), five German submarines arrived off the east coast on January 11, 1942. During the next month, these subs sank twenty-two merchant ships. When they returned to Germany, they were replaced by another five submarines, which sank an additional nineteen ships. This was known to the German crews as the "happy time." Among the ships lost with Cadets onboard during this early phase of the war were the SS *Azalea City*, the SS *Liberator*, and the SS *Jonathan Sturges*.

Possible U.S. countermeasures to Operation Drumbeat were hampered by official denials of the severity of the situation. Fearing a general panic, the U.S. Navy claimed to be sinking German submarines and denied serious losses. Navy brass, including Admiral Ernest J. King, spurned elementary tactics, such as coastal blackouts and convoys that could have afforded at least some protection to the merchant ships.

As merchant ship losses mounted in the summer of 1942, the U.S. Navy started a coastal convoy system. Navy air and surface escorts forced the U-boats to make their way to the Caribbean where convoys had not yet been implemented. The Caribbean soon became known as The Bloody Sea. In a little more than a month, between mid-February and mid-March, six German submarines sank twenty-six merchant ships. The U-boats moved with impunity in the area, often trailing ships within sight of land. U-boats even launched surface gun attacks on ships to conserve their precious torpedoes. Many ships carrying Cadet-Midshipmen were lost in the Caribbean in 1942, including the SS *Nathaniel Hawthorne*, the SS *Alcoa Pilgrim*, the SS *Robert E. Lee*, the SS *Heredia*, the SS *Wichita*, the SS *Coamo*, the SS *Tela*, and the SS *West Chetac*.

Extension of the U.S. coastal convoys to the Caribbean, along with increasing numbers of escorts and aircraft, ended the happy time, forcing U-boats to look for prey in the North Atlantic. The Battle of the Atlantic was a prolonged war of attrition fought by the allied merchant marine and navies against coordinated groups of German submarines. The outcome of this struggle ultimately determined the course of the war in Europe. Initially, the North Atlantic suffered from the same lack of organization and effective antisubmarine ships and aircraft as the East Coast and Caribbean. However, unlike the East Coast and Caribbean, escorted convoys had been used by the British since 1940. The difference was the German "wolfpack," a group of U-boats who were able to find a convoy, and then coordinate their attacks on the convoy and overwhelm its escorts.

Few convoys arrived at their destination with all the ships they started out with, until the latter stages of the Battle of the Atlantic. A harsh reality of this struggle was the fate of ships damaged but not sunk in the initial attack. These ships could not keep up with the convoy and were left to their own devices. The fate of many of these "cripples" was unknown until after the war, when German records could be reviewed. Although certainly a godsend to mariners, convoys had their limitations. They required enormous coordination, and because so many ships arrived at the destination port at once, they often created huge congestion, which made an attractive target for air attacks, such as those at Bari, Italy.

Among the U.S. ships lost in the North Atlantic with Cadet-Midshipmen aboard were the SS *Stone Street*, the SS *James McKay*, the SS *Henry Mallory*, the SS *Jonathan Sturges*, and the SS *Meriwether Lewis*. The North Atlantic route saw the Academy's deadliest sinking during the entire war—that of the SS *Louise Lykes*; with five Cadets and two graduates onboard; in terms of Cadet losses, this was the single deadliest sinking in the Academy's history. Two Cadets were also killed in the tragic sinking of USAT SS *Dorchester*, in which 675 persons were lost, including four Army chaplains who chose to remain on deck, praying, as the ship went down after giving their life preservers to soldiers.

At sea, they were often subjected to ferocious battering by wind and waves. Monstrous rogue waves sometimes snapped ships in half. Ice buildups added weight and introduced other hazards. In his memoir of wartime experiences, Captain Richard Heinicke Jr. '44 spotlights another hazard of the North Atlantic, the extreme weather. Merchant ships were loaded to capacity and beyond.

> Weather in the North Atlantic in the winter of 1942-43 was horrendous. It was very cold throughout the crossings and extremely rough. Winds were at force 7-8 most of the time. Maintaining convoy

position was difficult for most of the slower ships, but the *Darien* [Heinicke's ship] was able to keep up. The main problem with our ship was that it was smaller than most and deeper in the water, requiring a constant battle to keep ice from building up on the standing rigging and upper decks. More time and effort was spent chopping ice than on vessel maintenance, which was difficult at best. Our lifeboats could not be swung out for fear of losing them in a heavy sea, so they remained up tight in their davits and chocks, partially frozen in place. Not a particularly pleasant thought.

The North Atlantic included one of the most dreaded of all shipping routes, the Murmansk run, one of three primary supply routes to Russia. Countless merchant sailors were lost and shipwrecked along this route. One Academy Cadet-Midshipman, Raymond Holubowicz, famously survived three sinkings along the Murmansk run and was later awarded the Russian Medal for Distinction in Action by the Russian government. On one trip to Murmansk (Convoy PQ-16), the naval Armed Guard Commander aboard the SS *Richard Henry Lee* reported running out of ammunition for the .50-caliber antiaircraft guns and breaking into the ship's cargo to keep the guns firing.

One of the most infamous convoys of the war, Convoy PQ-17, was a Murmansk convoy from Iceland. In the face of deteriorating weather and constant German air and submarine attacks, the convoy was ordered to scatter, and each ship proceeded to Murmansk or Archangel on its own. Of the thirty-three merchant ships that began the journey, twenty-three were sunk by bombs and torpedoes along the route after being abandoned to their fate by their British and American escort vessels. Among the vessels carrying Cadet-Midshipmen that were lost on the Murmansk run were the SS *Syros*, the SS *Pan Atlantic*, the SS *Richard Henry Lee*, the SS *William Clark*, and the SS *Richard Bland*.

**Cadet Henry Orndorff and survivors of the sinking of the James B. Stevens
with crew of British crash boat that found their lifeboat off Durban,
South Africa. Photo provided by Henry Orndorff**

David F. White, maritime author, notes that something like 36,200 Allied
sailors, airmen, and servicemen, and women died in the North Atlantic
between 1939 and 1945. Less heralded, but no less valiant, were the
merchant mariners who died with them:

> Alongside these, some 36,000 merchant ship sailors were lost, many
> dying terrible deaths, plunging to the bottom of the Atlantic in ships
> which disappeared from the surface with all hands in less than twenty
> seconds; many others were succumbing to isolation, exposure, or
> starvation in open lifeboats or on rafts.

Although the North Atlantic was the most treacherous region of the
Atlantic, epic sea battles were also waged in the South and Central
Atlantic. Given that ships in these regions were less likely to be protected
by convoys, except near the African and South American coasts, ships
frequently disappeared on these routes with all hands lost and no witnesses
to tell the stories of their destruction. In many cases, nothing was known
of the fate of these ships until years after the war.

The crews of some ships, like the SS *American Leader*, were treated
honorably by their German captors, only to be turned over to the Japanese.
A few, like the SS *Stephen Hopkins*, managed to fight back. The *Stephen
Hopkins* stumbled upon the German commerce raider *Stier* and the
supply ship *Tannenfels*. Unable to run away, the *Stephen Hopkins's* gun
crews inflicted grievous wounds on their attackers. Cadet-Midshipman

Edwin J. O'Hara fired the five shells left in the ready service locker for the four-inch gun and died along with most of the crew. The *Stier* was so severely damaged that she was scuttled by its crew shortly after the *Stephen Hopkins* sank.

In November 1942, the Mediterranean became the focal point in the war as Allied forces invaded North Africa at Oran and Algiers. These and other North African ports quickly became vital supply and staging areas. However, with German and Italian air bases well within range, the "narrow sea" became increasingly treacherous for any ship. submarines were more vulnerable in the confined seas and, thus, less of a threat to shipping; but the combination of air attacks and mines wreaked havoc on the Allied supply route.

In one particularly deadly attack, the vital Italian coastal port of Bari was attacked in early December 1943 by 105 German aircraft. Seventeen of the fifty ships moored in the harbor were sunk, including one with a cargo of poison gas. More than a thousand seamen and civilians, including six Academy Cadet-Midshipmen, died in the ensuing catastrophe and were subsequently buried in local cemeteries. Those who survived the initial attacks quickly succumbed to the deadly mustard gas that was released into the air by the explosions on the SS *John Harvey*. (The gas was to be secretly stockpiled at Bari by the Allied powers in the event that Germany resorted to chemical warfare.) Another Cadet, George Baist, onboard the SS *Lyman Abbott*, survived the attack but was hospitalized for shrapnel wounds and mustard gas exposure.

Other ships lost with Cadet-Midshipmen onboard, in the Mediterranean in the fall and winter of 1943-44, included the SS *Bushrod Washington*, the SS *John L. Motley*, the SS *Samuel J. Tilden*, the SS *Robert Erskine*, and the SS *Paul Hamilton*.

German, Italian, and Japanese submarines patrolled the shipping lanes along the east coast of Africa and Indian Ocean during the war. In the years 1939-45, there were 385 ships sunk—a total of 1,790,000 tons. These attacks were especially deadly during 1942 and 1943. In 1942, 242 Allied merchant ships were sunk in the Indian Ocean, with a loss of 715,000 tons of shipping. In April 1942, in a matter of days, Japanese subs and destroyers sank twenty-three Allied ships in the Bay of Bengal alone. Among the ships lost in the Indian Ocean with Cadets aboard were the *Bienville, Cornelia P. Spencer, Firethorn, LaSalle, Sawokla, John Drayton*,

William King, and the *Samuel Heintzelman*. Most notorious of these was the crew of the *Jean Nicolet*, most of who were tortured and murdered by the crew of a Japanese submarine.

The South Pacific began the war as a relatively safe part of the world for merchant ships, but that ended with the Allied invasion of the Philippines. American and Allied forces suffered significant losses with the invasions of the Philippines, Iwo Jima, and Okinawa—from Japanese suicide planes (kamikaze). In all, forty-four merchant ships—primarily Liberty ships— were sunk in the South Pacific, mostly by kamikaze planes. Among those lost with Cadet-Midshipmen onboard were the SS *John Burke*, the SS *Hobbs Victory*, and the SS *Saint Mihiel*.

Life at Sea

At all times, the specter of death at sea hung over each Cadet-Midshipman. Those who had not yet shipped out heard harrowing tales. Most, if not all, would have asked themselves, "How will I hold up under fire when the time comes?" Constant reminders of death at sea were the Kings Point upperclassmen wearing the ribbon of a new and distinctive club, which was known first as the Tin Fish Club.

This club was comprised of Academy Cadet-Midshipmen who had survived ship sinkings caused by enemy action. The club was suggested by Lieutenant William Slate, USMS, Public Relations Department, who noted that few, if any, students of other institutions had been subjected to hostile fire during their training. The concept was well received; within two months the club had 147 members. A Cadet-Midshipman whose ship had been lost through enemy action received a ribbon bar with a silver star by the War Shipping Administration. Each attack or sinking merited additional silver stars. By December 1943, some Cadets were sporting as many as six silver stars.

Stories of sinkings were also published regularly in *Polaris* by Kings Point Cadet-Midshipmen, with key identifying details obscured for security reasons. New Cadets, in May of 1944, might have read the harrowing tale of Cadet-Midshipman Roberts, whose six months at sea had stretched to fourteen and included icy North Atlantic crossings, trips threated by air attacks in the Mediterranean, two torpedoings, and three classmates lost. In addition to the stories of survivors, Cadets were constantly surrounded by visual reminders of those who had not made it back to the Academy. Pictures of the missing and confirmed dead were hung in their respective departments in Fulton and Bowditch Halls. *Polaris* regularly published the names of those Lost at Sea.

Of course, most Cadet-Midshipmen did not have a ship sunk out from under them. The vast majority went to sea, did their best to make a contribution to the ship's crew that was engaged in a strange, difficult, and sometimes dangerous mission, and eventually made their way home again.

In that spirit, *Polaris* offered tips not only on how to survive but also about how to be successful, both as a Cadet-Midshipman and as an officer. Cadets were urged, for example, to show humility, lend a hand whenever possible, and work without complaint.

"Foremost in the requisites of a successful Cadet is to have the proper respect for superiors—not the showy type of respect but rather a deeply ingrained appreciation of the fact that the men in command are in command because of their knowledge and experience. You will never find it necessary to salute on board most merchant ships today but if you lack the proper respect of which we speak you will have your 'oral hatch' battened down in short order. Have deference too for the veterans of the foc'sle. All this may leave the 'prelim' wondering who will pay homage to his nice new uniform. The answer is blunt. No one . . . .

"Generally you will take orders from no one but the mate or first. But be ready at all times to lend a hand where you can. Your working day may vary. Some Cadets stand the regular watches, four hours on and eight hours off. Others may be given 'day work,' which means working on deck or below for about six hours a day. Use your study time to best advantage. You are given an invaluable opportunity to check the theory with the practical. Don't hesitate to ask questions. You will find the average mariner helpful if he sees you are willing and eager to learn.

"Adjust yourself to doing menial tasks. Remember to leave your dignity with your baby pictures. Sweeping decks is part of the game. On shipboard you will find very few places barred to you. Be sure though to knock on anyone's door before entering. Deck Cadets should be most wary of how they behave on the bridge and in the chart room . . ."

At the end of the day though, it came down to the luck of the draw. Every voyage combined tedium and terror in its own particular mix. Cadet-Midshipmen might be called upon to perform heroics, but were always called upon to perform menial and, occasionally, ridiculous tasks until he knew better. Cadets were told to have their clothes, knife, lifebelt, and flashlight on them at all times. They were also cautioned to keep their cabin door open while at sea, never sleep on hatch covers, and to stay lucky. Cadets frequently kept their seaman's papers and sea project in one of the life boats wrapped in an oilskin packet. Cadet-Midshipman William "Boots" Lyman's letters sent home, in late 1942 and early 1943, suggested that he was one of the lucky ones; although there's reason to suspect that he downplayed the dangers he faced in an effort to reassure his worried family.

"This business of going to sea is all right. We had a pleasant trip so far with no mishaps. There's been a continual roll to the ship which seems quite natural, and though I did feel slightly nauseous when I was below decks, I did not get seasick. The other Cadets aboard are good eggs, the Captain and the Mates the same. Of course, we don't see the old man very much, but when we do he seems gruff, but good-natured.

"The other Deck Cadet and I stand 6-hour watches as that part of our working day. Two hours on the company and two hours on our own time complete the day, the four-hour period being study time. We stand our watches mostly on the bridge with the mates on watch. Though they are busy with keeping station in the convoy and all that, they manage to answer our questions, and make any necessary explanations. We will learn more as things become less rushed, and then the mates will let us help with the navigation and all that which will be still more interesting. Even now though, we have plenty to do and we are learning all the time.

"The slop chest is open once a week, and you can buy most anything you want there, from shirts to slippers, and back again. The thing that tickles me is buying a carton of cigarettes for $.60 or two for the price of one. We have playtime too aboard ship. In the evening when there's nothing to do, we often go topside and get out the semaphore flags to talk to neighboring ships. So far we've found plenty of Cadets, but I don't think any from my section are around."

"A pleasant trip. No mishaps. Playtime."

Six months after this letter was written; Lyman's luck ran out. His ship, the SS *Timothy Pickering*, was carrying a devil's brew of explosives and high-octane fuels and was anchored seven hundred yards off the coast of Avola, Sicily, when it was attacked by a lone Stuka raider. A bomb dropped into the open number four hatch, and Lyman's ship seemed to dissolve into thin air, in an explosion that was heard fifty miles out to sea. Lyman was one of three Cadets to perish at Avola that day.

Life at Sea after the War Ended

When the war ended, graduates and Cadet-Midshipmen were employed to provide food and material to rebuild war-torn Europe. Additionally, they manned the ships returning American troops to the United States, American POWs from Germany and Japan to the United States, war brides and children to the United States, German POWs to Germany, Japanese who were interred in Canada to Japan, and Allied foreign nationals held in captivity by the Japanese back to Europe.

While the threat of torpedoes and bombings had ended, the mined harbors were still extremely dangerous to navigate. Charles Hart '45 was onboard the SS *Cedar Mills*, American Petroleum Transport Co., when the ship hit a floating mine off Taranto, Italy, on November 19, 1945. He was in the boiler room when it exploded; and he was found on top of the engine room by Third Mate Fred Welford, who was awarded the mariners medal for the rescue. The explosion was so intense that it almost broke the vessel in two at the after end of the midship house; in fact, there were only two plates on the starboard side that held the *Cedar Mills* together. The vessel was beached and declared a total loss. The last ship to become a casualty of mine warfare was in 1947.

Many Cadet-Midshipmen who served during the war returned to Kings Point to finish their education and graduated in the classes of 1946 through 1948. Other men chose to leave the merchant marine and find other careers.

PART TWO

Bearing Witness

The following pages detail the individual stories of the Cadet-Midshipmen of Kings Point, San Mateo, and Pass Christian, and the graduates of Kings Point and the Maritime Commission Cadet Officer program, who braved the seas to carry the war to the enemy and, in the process, lost their lives.

Very few of these men came from seafaring families or backgrounds. They were farm boys and city boys, rich boys and poor boys. Some of them grew up in loving families with a mother and father, some didn't. Some were an only child, while others came from large families. Many were sons of immigrant families. Each man was a neighbor, a friend, a classmate to others. The lives of some are remembered in the names of buildings, ships, streets, ball fields, or on a piece of stone in a cemetery, while others have no such Monument to their lives. However, in a very real sense, the men whose short lives are chronicled in the book were more of a cross section of America then Kings Pointers are today.

The ages of the Cadets who died were generally between eighteen and twenty-four; J. W. Artist was seventeen-years-old. The hometown that is listed in the book is believed to be where they were living at the time they enrolled into the Cadet Corps. Many were born in other states, and some in other countries.

The Cadet-Midshipmen came from twenty-nine states and the District of Columbia. The majority of these young men (eighty) were from the eastern states of New York, Pennsylvania, New Jersey, Connecticut, and Massachusetts. The Midwest states of Ohio, Illinois, Michigan, and Minnesota each had four or more men who gave their lives to their country—twenty-one in total. Of the other states, five men were from

California; fewer in number came from Alabama, Arkansas, Florida, Georgia, Indiana, Kansas, Kentucky, Louisiana, Maine, Maryland, Missouri, North Carolina, Oklahoma, South Carolina, Texas, Utah, Vermont, Virginia, Washington, and Wisconsin.

Most of the men were victims of enemy action. Some succumbed to illness and others to violent storms. Some graduated from the Cadet Corps months or years before their deaths. Many of the men died on their first ship, others were still Cadet-Midshipmen at the Academy at the Academy. Some had witnesses to their passing. Others disappeared along with their ships, leaving their fates unknown for months or years afterward. All were volunteers who freely accepted the hazards of their chosen profession.

Some are still remembered by friends and family they left behind. All are remembered by the many graduates of Kings Point who followed in their footsteps. They should also be remembered by a grateful nation that is forever indebted to them for their sacrifice.

U.S. Merchant Marine Academy Cadet-Midshipmen Who Died during World War II

The men listed in this section were Cadets or Cadet-Midshipmen who died during World War II while members of the Cadet Corps. All but two of them have their names on the War Memorial Monument at Kings Point; Carl Brandler and Kenneth McAuliffe. McAuliffe was a United Fruit Company Cadet; not a U.S. Maritime Commission Cadet. He is included since he died following a torpedo attack on his ship; his form of Cadet training was one of the practices before the USMC Cadet training program was established. We have only family history to tell us that Brandler was in the Merchant Marine Cadet Corps. See Index A for a list of the Cadet-Midshipmen and the reference to pages where they are named.

As with other military organizations, not all deaths during the war were directly caused by enemy actions. Among those killed, there were 119 young men who were killed in direct action against the enemy; they died from aerial and submarine torpedoes, bombings, and kamikaze attacks, and German raider shelling. Nine Cadet-Midshipmen and graduates received the highest merchant marine award, the Distinguished Service Medal for their valor. (See Appendices D and E for details of the Medal citations and other medals and awards.)

The enemy was not the only peril faced by merchant mariners at war. The supply line had to be maintained at all costs; ships sailed in every weather condition and navigated perilously close to each other in tightly packed convoys day and night. Ships were prohibited from showing navigation lights and were compelled to zigzag, changing course as a group in the dark of night, often in heavy seas. Collisions were the inevitable result; six Cadet-Midshipmen died in collisions. Three died when their ships sank in violent storms. They all died serving in the line of duty, supplying war material to the Allied forces.

Unlike Navy ships, merchant ships carried no medical personnel, although some Pursers were trained as Pharmacist's Mates. Primary treatment was usually provided onboard with the aid of a first aid manual; and medical treatment was deferred until the next port, days or weeks away. Delayed treatment often exacerbated medical problems. Seven men died of illnesses contracted while on duty onboard ship or in training.

Ships are dangerous places for the uninitiated in the best of times, and in the rush to man the burgeoning fleet, training was accelerated to a breakneck pace. Much was left to the initiative of the Cadets; some mishaps were inevitable. Five men died in shore-based training or shipboard accidents.

Three men died ashore in foreign ports, in accidents not specifically related to a military action. They were serving honorably at the time of their deaths, and their names are inscribed on the Kings Point War Memorial.

Edward Joseph Ackerlind Jr.

Born:	May 9, 1920
Hometown:	Minneapolis, MN
Class:	1943
Service:	Merchant Marine
Position / Rank:	Engine Cadet
Date / Place of death:	December 31, 1942
	40-10 N, 72-02 W
Date / Place of burial:	December 31, 1942
	40-10 N, 72-02 W
	Lost at Sea
Age:	22

Edward J. Ackerlind signed on aboard his first ship, the SS *Maiden Creek*, at Mobile, Alabama, on July 7, 1942. His classmate Deck Cadet Warren B. Carriere had signed on a week earlier. The *Maiden Creek*, a World War I "Hog Islander" built in 1919, was owned by the Waterman Steamship Company.

SS *Maiden Creek*

On November 11, 1942, the *Maiden Creek* sailed from New York with a cargo of aviation gasoline in drums for the Army Air Corps airfield designated Bluie West Eight (later Sondrestrom AFB). On its return trip, after completing loading a cargo of ore concentrates, the *Maiden Creek* sailed from Botwood, Newfoundland, on December 15 to meet a convoy bound for New York. However, the old ship could not keep up with the convoy in the heavy seas it encountered. On December 19, the *Maiden Creek* diverted to Halifax, Nova Scotia. When the ship arrived on December 22, inspection of the ship found that the ship's chain locker, forepeak, and number 1 hold were flooded due to the heavy seas. Although the forepeak and chain locker were secured and pumped out, the water in number 1 hold could not be pumped out because of the characteristics of the cargo.

On December 27, despite having significantly reduced freeboard forward due to the flooded number 1 hold, the *Maiden Creek* sailed from Halifax on December 27 with eleven other ships and three escorts. The next day the ships joined Convoy ON-152 bound for New York. On December 30, as the convoy was nearing New York, the heavy weather resumed. By the afternoon of December 31, the hatch cover for number 1 hold was leaking again, and the hatch cover for number 2 hold had begun leaking. The water in the *Maiden Creek* holds eventually brought the propeller and rudder out of the water.

With the ship adrift in heavy seas about seventy miles south of Block Island, the Captain ordered the Radio Operator to send out an SOS. The Captain then called together the officers and informed them that they would have to abandon the ship. At about 1700, number 3 lifeboat was launched with eighteen crew members, including the two Cadet-Midshipmen and five Armed Guard sailors. A second lifeboat was launched at about thirty minutes later with all but two of the remaining crew and Armed Guard sailors aboard, a total of thirty-one men. Two men had to remain aboard because lowering a boat from the *Maiden Creek* antiquated lifeboat davits could only be done manually. The two Able Bodied seamen attempted to climb down the falls to the boat, but the rough seas carried the boat away before the men could get aboard. One man fell into the water and, despite attempts to pull him aboard, was lost. The other seaman climbed back on board the *Maiden Creek* and eventually went down with the vessel.

In heavy seas and growing darkness, the two lifeboats soon lost sight of each other. The lifeboat with thirty-one men aboard was spotted by the Army, Navy, and Coast Guard patrol planes in the ensuing days. However, it was not until January 3 that a patrol plane was able to transmit the position of the lifeboat to a ship close enough to affect a rescue. At about 1840 that day, the MS *Staghound* rescued the men in the *Maiden Creek*'s lifeboat. The men aboard the first lifeboat, including Cadet-Midshipmen Ackerlind and Carriere, were never seen again.

Cadet-Midshipman Edward J. Ackerlind was posthumously awarded the Atlantic War Zone Bar, the Victory Medal, and the Presidential Testimonial Letter.

Edward J. "Joseph" Ackerlind was the only son and youngest of Edward J. Ackerlind Sr. and Catherine Ackerlind's two children. Edward's sister Margaret was just three years older. According to the 1940 U.S. Census, Edward Sr. was a barber who owned his own shop. Edward Jr. worked as an assistant salesman at a bottling company, while his sister was a stenographer at the Land O'Lakes Creameries. Edward Sr. passed away on August 25, 1943, just a few months after the death of his son.

Joseph Peter Alexander

Born:	April 24, 1921
Hometown:	Attica, GA
Class:	1943
Service:	Merchant Marine
Position / Rank:	Deck Cadet
Date / Place of death:	October 18, 1942 / North Atlantic 49-39 N, 30-20 W
Date / Place of burial:	October 18, 1942 / North Atlantic 49-39 N, 30-20 W— Lost at Sea
Age:	21

Joseph P. Alexander signed on as Deck Cadet aboard the SS *Angelina* at Pensacola, Florida, on June 20, 1942. He was the ship's only Cadet until September 9 when Joseph Krusko signed on as the Engine Cadet. After a voyage to Liverpool, the *Angelina* was returning in ballast to New York in Convoy ON-137.

SS *Angelina*

On October 17, 1942, gale force winds caused the *Angelina* to straggle behind the convoy. However, a Canadian corvette had also been forced to fall behind the convoy and was keeping station off the *Angelina* as they coped with the heavy seas. Due to the heavy seas, neither ship was zigzagging.

At about 2345 (GCT), one torpedo fired by *U-618* struck the *Angelina* on its starboard side at number 4 hold. The *Angelina* listed to starboard after the impact, and the well deck flooded, preventing the gun crew from manning the four-inch gun on the stern. Fortunately, although the *Angelina*'s radio could not send a distress signal, the corvette did send an SOS. The general alarm sounded soon after the first torpedo struck, and all hands prepared to abandon ship in the vessel's port lifeboat and rafts. About twenty minutes after firing on the *Angelina*, *U-618* fired another torpedo, hitting the stern on the starboard side and detonated the ammunition magazine there. The *Angelina* sank at about 0030 (GCT), within minutes of the second torpedo hitting the ship.

Despite getting away from their sinking ship, the weather was not in the crew's favor. Many men were washed overboard and drowned in the heavy seas. The port (number 2) lifeboat, which was launched successfully, capsized in the waves, and only half of the occupants were able to seize hold of the overturned boat. The few who remained were gradually losing their hold, though the heroic efforts of the Carpenter kept five men clinging to the hull. Another six men managed to stay on a raft.

Fortunately, the convoy's rescue ship, the SS *Bury*, received the corvette's SOS and arrived on the scene at 0345 (GCT) and rescued the six men on the life raft. After searching for over two hours, the *Bury* found the capsized lifeboat, rescuing the three men still hanging on to it. The Armed Guard Commander, Ensign A. J. Gartland, USNR, cited the ship's Chief Mate, E. A. L. Koonig, and the Carpenter, Gus Alm, for heroism during the abandonment and boarding the *Bury*, respectively. Sadly, one of the men rescued by the *Bury*, Felix Posario, died before the *Bury* reached St. John's, Newfoundland, a week later. The other forty-six crew members of the *Angelina*, including Cadets Joseph Alexander and Joseph Krusko, were Lost at Sea.

Cadet-Midshipman Joseph Alexander was posthumously awarded the Mariner's Medal, the Combat Bar with star, the Atlantic War Zone Bar, the Victory Medal, and the Presidential Testimonial Letter.

Joseph P. "Peter" Alexander was the oldest of Read Alexander and Mary R. Alexander's four children, Joseph, Robert, Charles, and George. According to the 1940 U.S. Census, Read Alexander was a feed and fertilizer salesman to the local farmers.

Rachel Alexander McMahon was not born when her uncle Pete died, but she recalls the many stories of his life in Athens, Georgia, and how he was a great big brother to his little brothers. Rachael said that Pete's mother, her grandmother, kept his Cadet portrait in his dress whites and officer's hat on her bedroom wall; to her, he was forever twenty-one.

Norbert Amborski

Born:	September 6, 1920	
Hometown:	Buffalo, NY	
Class:	1943	
Service:	Merchant Marine	
Position / Rank:	Engine Cadet	
Date / Place of death:	September 13, 1942 /	
	North Atlantic	
48-18 N, 39-43 W		
Date / Place of burial:	September 13, 1942 /	
	North Atlantic	
	48-18 N, 39-43 W	
	Lost at Sea	
Age:	22	

Norbert Amborski signed on as Engine Cadet aboard the SS *Stone Street* on June 29, 1942, at the Port of New York. The *Stone Street* (ex-*Cara*), a twenty-year-old Italian freighter seized at Savannah, Georgia, in December 1941, was scheduled to sail for Belfast, Northern Ireland, on July 6, 1942. Built in 1922, the ex-*Cara*'s Italian boilers were difficult for its crew to operate and maintain. The *Stone Street*'s Armed Guard officer noted in his report that it was not unusual for the ship to throw a "tremendous shower of sparks from our funnel."

The SS *Stone Street* left Liverpool in ballast on September 5, 1942, in a two-column coastal convoy. On September 6, the two-column group joined up with Convoy ON-127 north of Ireland for the return voyage to New York. The convoy was accompanied by a Royal Canadian Navy Escort Group of two destroyers and four corvettes. For four days, the westward voyage, shielded by stormy weather, proceeded without loss or mishap. Around midday on September 10, the convoy was located and attacked by *U-96*, one of the twelve submarines of wolfpack "Vorwarts." This first attack began a five-day running battle between the convoy and the wolfpack.

On the evening of September 12, the *Stone Street* was ordered to leave the convoy because of its inability to keep up with the convoy and constant marking of the convoy's position with its smoke and sparks. The *Stone Street* took up a course parallel to the convoy about twelve miles off its starboard side. At 0130, September 13, the *Stone Street*'s lookouts observed a huge explosion in the direction of the convoy. The Captain ordered the *Stone Street* to pull another twelve miles away from the convoy. The maneuvering proved fruitless. At 1045, 575 miles east of Newfoundland, the *Stone Street* was found by *U-594*, one of the wolfpack submarines. The submarine fired three torpedoes at the straggling ship with one hitting amidships on the port side.

The ship immediately listed forty-five degrees to port, making it impossible to man the guns or lower the port side lifeboats. Although the Radio Operator tried to send an "SOS," the signal was not received since the radio antenna was knocked out by the torpedo explosion. The Captain gave the order to abandon ship, but the crew was only able to successfully launch one of its two un-damaged lifeboats. Fortunately, two of its life rafts were also launched. Accounts differ on how Cadet-Midshipman Norbert Amborski wound up in the water, but all agree that he died when he was pulled into the ships propeller while it was turning. One crew member, Messman John Watt, was killed trying to save Norbert Amborski. Several other crew members drowned while attempting to make it to the lifeboat.

Cadet-Midshipman Vetter and ten other volunteers were left on one of the life rafts, with Vetter in charge, while the Captain took the lifeboat and picked survivors out of the water. The Captain was still picking up survivors when *U-594* surfaced and approached the raft, asking for the Captain and chief engineer. Cadet Vetter directed them to the lifeboat. In the process, the *U-594* capsized the lifeboat, although the crew rescued the seventeen men who had been on it and placed them on two rafts with food and provisions. However, the *U-594* took Captain Harold Anderson prisoner. Two days later, the men in the rafts found the capsized lifeboat and were able to right it, finding nearly all of the provisions and supplies intact. On September 19, the neutral Irish ship, SS *Irish Larch,* found and rescued the twenty-nine survivors of the *Stone Street*'s crew and ten of the ship's Naval Armed Guard. Eleven of the *Stone Street*'s crew, including Engine Cadet Norbert Amborski and two Naval Armed Guard sailors, were lost.

Cadet-Midshipman Norbert Amborski was posthumously awarded the Combat Bar with star, the Mariner's Medal, the Atlantic War Zone Bar, the Victory Medal, and the Presidential Testimonial Letter.

Norbert Amborski was the oldest of the two sons and two daughters of Nicholas and Angeline Amborski of Buffalo, New York. Nicholas Amborski was a pressman for the local newspaper. Norbert was remembered by his brother, Dr. Leonard Amborski (author of *The Last Voyage*, a tribute to his brother and the others who died aboard the *Stone Street*), as a devout Catholic and a good student who finished high school with the highest grades in his class. After graduating from high school, Norbert and his brother Leonard both entered Canisius College in the class of 1943. However, after only one year, Norbert dropped out to accept an appointment to the U.S. Coast Guard Academy at New London, Connecticut. He later resigned from the Coast Guard Academy but was subsequently accepted for admission to Kings Point. He was the first student from his high school to give his life in World War II.

According to Leonard, he frequently told his mother that he would buy the family a house one day. In the end, he did, with the insurance money from his death.

John Walter Artist

Born:	April 22, 1927
Hometown:	Brooklyn, NY
Class:	1946
Service:	Merchant Marine
Position / Rank:	Engine Cadet
Date / Place of death:	April 9, 1945 / North Atlantic, 37-31 N, 64-26 W
Date / Place of burial:	April 9, 1945 / North Atlantic, 37-31 N, 64-26 W / Lost at Sea
Age:	17

Cadet-Midshipmen John W. Artist and Dante L. Polcari were the last two Academy Cadets to lose their lives in WW II. The two Cadets signed on aboard the T2-SE-A1 tanker, SS *Saint Mihiel*, on March 20, 1945, at Philadelphia, Pennsylvania. This was one day after the ship was delivered from its builder, Sun Shipbuilding, to the War Shipping Administration. The vessel sailed in ballast to Corpus Christi, Texas, where it picked up a full load of aviation gasoline bound for Cherbourg, France. After leaving Corpus Christi, the *Saint Mihiel* was ordered to New York where Convoy CU-65, a fast convoy of tankers and other high value ships, was forming. On April 8, the *Saint Mihiel* and the other ships of the convoy sailed from New York and began forming the convoy.

On the night of April 9 the *Saint Mihiel* and another tanker, SS *Nashbulk*, collided. Part of the *Saint Mihiel*'s cargo of gasoline immediately burst into flame, destroying the navigating bridge located amidships and killing most of the deck officers. The surviving crew abandoned ship as soon as possible and after about two hours in the water were picked up by the USS *Stewart* (DE 238). Of the fifty crew members and twenty-nine Naval Armed Guard members, only twenty-three of the crew and nineteen Navy sailors survived. Cadets John W. Artist and Dante L. Polcari were among those missing and presumed dead. Also among the dead was Third Assistant Engineer James Maloney, a 1944 USMMA graduate.

On the morning of April 10, the *Saint Mihiel* was still afloat, although some of the cargo was still burning. The ship's senior surviving deck officer, Second Mate Bruno Baretich, assembled some of the *Saint Mihiel*'s survivors to board the *Saint Mihiel* to see if it could be salvaged. Aided by crewmen from the *Stewart* and another escort, Baretich reboarded the ship, put out the fires, and got the ship under way for New York. Although the ship was ultimately a constructive total loss, over 80 percent of the gasoline cargo was saved. For his actions, Baretich, a former vaudeville performer and song arranger for Irving Berlin, received the Merchant Marine Distinguished Service Medal.

Cadet-Midshipman John W. Artist was posthumously awarded the Atlantic War Zone Bar, the Victory Medal, and the Presidential Testimonial Award.

John W. Artist was the son of John J. Artist and Frances Artist. When he died, John Artist was one month shy of his eighteenth birthday; possibly the youngest of the Academy Cadets to lose his life. A musical prodigy, John began taking piano lessons at age four and had accumulated several awards by the time he was nine. For high school, he attended the Professional Children's School in New York City, a special school for child actors and entertainers. Although he was an accomplished pianist and singer, John was also active in several sports and was popular with both his classmates and his teachers. He graduated from the Professional Children's School in 1944 and enrolled at the Academy soon after.

Alan Arlington Atchison Jr.

Born: November 6, 1922
Hometown: Saint Louis, MO
Class: 1944
Service: Merchant Marine
Position / Rank: Deck Cadet
Date / Place of death: September 20, 1943 /
                           North Atlantic
                           57-03 N; 28-08 W
Date / Place of burial: September 20, 1943 /
                           North Atlantic
                           57-03 N; 28-08 W /
                           Lost at Sea
Age: 20

Cadet-Midshipman Alan A. Atchison Jr. reported for training at the Pass Christian, Mississippi, Basic School, around April 15, 1943. After completing Basic School, he signed on as Deck Cadet aboard the SS *Theodore Dwight Weld* at Mobile, Alabama, on July 27, 1943. Engine Cadet Frank H. Cain was also on board. After sailing to England, the *Weld*, loaded with 1,200 tons of sand ballast, sailed from Liverpool, England, on September 15, 1943, en route to New York in Convoy ON-202. The ship had a crew of forty-two merchant mariners, including two Cadets and twenty-eight Naval Armed Guard Sailors.

This "fast" convoy was composed of thirty-eight ships, escorted by a Canadian Navy escort group composed of two destroyers (HMCS *Gatineau* and HMCS *Icarus*), a frigate HMS *Lagan,* and three corvettes, HMCS *Drumheller*, HMCS *Kamloops*, and HMS *Polyanthus*. A "slow" convoy of twenty-seven ships bound for Halifax, Nova Scotia, ONS-18, sailed on September 12 with seven escorts that followed an almost identical route as ON-202. On September 19, *U-270*, one of twenty-one submarines assigned to wolfpack Leuthen damaged HMS *Langan*. Aware that Convoy ON-202 was heading into a large wolfpack, the British Admiralty ordered Convoy ON-202 to join up with ONS-18 on September 21. In addition, another escort group with a destroyer, frigate, and three corvettes was ordered to reinforce the combined convoy. Thus began one of the major convoy engagements of the Battle of the Atlantic.

On the morning of September 20, the *Theodore Dwight Weld* was the first ship in the second column of Convoy ON-202. The convoy was making 9.5 knots in clear weather and choppy seas but was not taking any evasive action. The *Theodore Dwight Weld* had posted numerous lookouts. At 0736 (GMT), one of four torpedoes fired by *U-238* struck the SS *Frederick Douglas* in the next column over from the *Weld*. The *Weld*'s alarm bells immediately began ringing. One minute later, at 0737, when the ship was about five hundred miles southwest of Iceland, the ship was hit by at least one of the other three torpedoes fired by *U-238*.

Engine Cadet Frank H. Cain later reported that he was just beginning an inspection of the degaussing system that morning when he heard a series of short rings on the general alarm. Noting the urgency of the ringing, he rushed to his quarters on the bridge deck to don his life jacket. There he crossed paths with Alan Atchison, the Deck Cadet. Atchison had just put his own life jacket on and was proceeding to the lifeboats. Just after Atchison left the room, the torpedo hit the vessel on the port side, amidships, at number 3 hold. Observers noticed a large white flash but no smoke. About twenty seconds after the impact, the engine room blew up, breaking the ship in half, just forward of the accommodation house.

According to his report, Cain was blown into the air by the force of the explosion and nearly fell through a gaping hole in the deck. Fortunately, he was able to pull himself up and rushed to the starboard boat deck. The ship was listing heavily to starboard and beginning to break up. Cadet-Midshipman Alan Atchison along with the First Mate and several other crew members had lowered number 3 boat into the water. However, the sea was already breaking over the *Weld*'s main deck; and the lifeboat, the only one not damaged by the torpedo explosion, was destroyed before it could get away from the ship. Several crew members, including the Captain, were washed overboard by the breaking seas. Cain was washed overboard as he tried to help the Captain back aboard. In the process, Cain reported that he became entangled in the lifeboat falls as the ship sank.

After freeing himself from his entanglement, Cain swam to the surface. He said he could see the after gun mount of the ship going under and managed to cling to a fragment of one of the *Weld*'s lifeboats. After about two hours in what he nonchalantly termed "cold" water, Cain and the thirty-six survivors were picked up by the rescue ship SS *Rathlin*. Alan A. Atchison Jr. was among the nineteen crewmen and thirteen Armed Guard sailors that were missing and presumed lost.

Cadet-Midshipman Alan A. Atchison Jr. was posthumously awarded the Mariner's Medal, the Combat Bar, the Atlantic War Zone Bar, the Victory Medal, and the Presidential Testimonial Letter.

Alan A. Atchison was the only son and youngest of Alan A. and Cecelie Atchison's two children. Alan's sister was Alice, who was nine years older. Alan Sr. was the president of Lacquer Service Corporation and later the owner of the Atchison Celucoating Company.

Burton Gale Bergeson

Born:	June 3, 1922
Hometown:	Lake Park, MN
Class:	1943
Service:	Merchant Marine
Position / Rank:	Deck Cadet
Date / Place of death:	September 24, 1942 / North Atlantic, 56 N, 31 W
Date / Place of burial:	September 24, 1942 / North Atlantic, 56 N, 31 W / Lost at Sea
Age:	20

Burton G. Bergeson signed on as Deck Cadet aboard the SS *John Winthrop* on August 12, 1942, at Boston, Massachusetts, shortly after the ship was completed and delivered to the War Shipping Administration. He joined Cadet-Midshipman Jonathan F. Sturges, who signed on as Engine Cadet. After a voyage to the United Kingdom, the *John Winthrop* sailed from Glasgow, Scotland, to join sixty other merchant ships and seventeen escorts of Convoy ON-131 bound for New York.

On September 21, 1942, the *John Winthrop* straggled from the convoy. For three days the straggling *John Winthrop* managed to evade German U-boats prowling the area. However, according to records of the German Navy, on the evening of September 24, the straggler was found by *U-619*. The submarine fired five torpedoes, breaking the *John Winthrop* into two pieces, which remained afloat. *U-619* then surfaced and sunk the remaining portions of the ship with its deck gun. There were no survivors among the *John Winthrop*'s crew of thirty-nine Armed Guard complement of fifteen.

Of the sixty-one ships in Convoy ON-131, the *John Winthrop* was the only ship sunk.

Cadets Bergeson and Sturges received the Atlantic War Zone Bar, the Combat Bar, the Mariner's Medal, the Presidential Testimonial Letter, and the Victory Medal.

Burton G. Bergeson was the eldest of Reno Rino Selmer Bergeson and Anna Joanna Skei Bergeson's five children. He had two little brothers, Rudolph (three years younger) and Harold (six years younger). Burton's two sisters were Enid (one year younger) and Janice (two years younger). According to the 1940 U.S. Census, Reno Bergeson was an insurance salesman.

According to recollections of his sister Janice, Burton was considered a role model for his siblings. Janice recalls that Burton walked to school, was a good student, and attended church regularly. She also remembers a childhood filled with outdoor sports both summer and winter. Janice

Memorial in Lake Park Cemetery, Lake Park, MN

recalled that in one notable year, Burton "rolled up his sleeves" to help install indoor plumbing in the family home. During summer vacations in high school, Burton worked for the Northern Pacific Railroad. He graduated with highest honors from Lake Park High School, where he played both football and basketball. After graduation, he enrolled in Concordia College. However, the war broke out during his freshman year, and he applied for entrance into the U.S. Merchant Marine Academy—changing the course of his life.

Peter John Biemel

Born:	September 13, 1924
Hometown:	Cleveland, OH
Class:	1944
Service:	Merchant Marine
Position / Rank:	Engine Cadet
Date / Place of death:	November 1, 1943 / off Naples, Italy
Date / Place of burial:	November 3, 1943 / Grave 27, Row 8, Plot C, Sicily-Rome American Cemetery, Nettuno, Italy
Age:	19

Peter J. Biemel signed on the SS *Salmon P. Chase* as Engine Cadet at New York, New York, on July 19, 1943. By October 23, 1943, the *Salmon P. Chase*, which was carrying troops and cargo between Mediterranean ports, sailed from Algiers, Algeria bound for Naples, Italy, via Augusta, Sicily. Among the ship's cargo were troops and equipment of the 450th Antiaircraft Artillery Battalion, an all-black unit. The ship joined Convoy UGS-20 for the Algiers to Malta leg of its voyage, breaking off from the main convoy on October 26 in a smaller five-ship convoy to Augusta. After arrival at Augusta on the following day, the ship worked cargo until departing on October 30 for Naples. The ship arrived in Naples on the morning of November 1, 1943.

At 1845, while the *Salmon P. Chase* was at anchor in Naples Bay, thirty-eight Ju-88 bombers attacked the area. According to the report of Lt. (jg) William F. Saunders, USNR, the Armed Guard officer, the ship's general alarm sounded simultaneously with the air raid signal ashore. The Armed Guard sailors immediately manned their guns while the Army unit, under the command of Lieutenant Whiteside, USA, broke out two 40 mm guns and four .50-caliber machine guns and readied them for action.

Although the gunners aboard the *Salmon P. Chase* initially withheld their fire so as not to disclose their position; within five minutes of sounding the alarm, flares illuminated the *Salmon P. Chase,* and the order was given to fire on the attacking aircraft. At 1920, an aircraft attacked the ship's starboard bow and was taken under fire by the three-inch gun manned by Navy sailors spoiling its attack and shooting it down. Ten minutes later, another plane attacked the port bow. While the three-inch gun could not take it under fire, one of the Army 40 mm guns could and shot it down. Shortly thereafter, the smoke screen being laid by naval escorts shrouded the ship, concealing it from the attacking planes. The attack ended at 1950, with the sounding of the "all clear" signal. During the attack, sailors, soldiers, and merchant mariners aboard the *Salmon P. Chase* crewed and fired fifteen guns, expending 28 rounds of three-inch, 800 rounds of 40 mm, 1,595 rounds of 20 mm, and 1,000 rounds of .50 cal. ammunition.

Except for Peter J. Biemel, none of the ship's crew, Armed Guard sailors, or Army "passengers" was injured in the attack. Biemel, whose battle station was at the Carbon Dioxide Firefighting unit in the engine room, insisted on going on deck during the attack. According to Lieutenant Saunders's report, the crew attempted twice to restrain Biemel from going on deck to observe the action. However, on his third attempt, Biemel made it out onto the boat deck. Soon after, he staggered back inside, bleeding from the nose, mouth, and ears. Although he had no visible wounds other than that on the tip of his tongue and a front tooth was missing, the ship's first-aid party and Army medical personnel were unable to stop the bleeding. At 2030, a doctor from the British destroyer HMS *Lookout* (G32) came on board in response to the ship's request for medical help. However, Biemel died at 2100 while the doctor was working on him.

Cadet-Midshipman Peter J. Biemel's body was taken ashore the following morning and turned over to Army medical authorities for autopsy and burial. According to Lieutenant Saunders's report, Army medical personnel concluded after the autopsy that Peter J. Biemel's death was caused by a hemorrhage at the apex of his lung from piece of lead, possibly from a .50 cal. bullet, which entered through his right nostril and passed down his throat. Peter Biemel's body was interred in a temporary cemetery and permanently interred at the Sicily-Rome American Cemetery after the war.

Peter J. Biemel was posthumously awarded the Atlantic War Zone Bar, the Mediterranean-Middle East War Zone Bar, the Combat Bar, the Mariner's Medal, the Victory Medal, and the Presidential Testimonial Letter.

Peter John Biemel was the youngest of three children, and the only son of Peter and Anna Radler Biemel of Cleveland, Ohio. According to the 1930 U.S. Census, Mr. Biemel was a crane operator for an automotive business in Cleveland. Peter's older sister Marie describes him as a quiet and dignified young man who was very close to her and his mother during his youth. An above-average student and a hard worker, he graduated from West Technical High School's Machine Shop program in 1942. At West Technical, he was known as "Bruno" and was involved in student government. His sister Marie noted that Peter drew to himself a number of lasting friends. She also noted that the unsung hero of Peter's short life was his mother, who sacrificed not for herself but to shape and make a life for her son.

"My mother was the making of me."

Henry James Bogardus Jr.

Born: March 12, 1923
Hometown: Montclair, NJ
Class: 1944
Service: Merchant Marine
Position / Rank: Engine Cadet
Date / Place of death: June 6, 1943 / Indian
                               Ocean,
                               30-10 S, 34-10 E
Date / Place of burial: June 6, 1943 / Indian
                               Ocean,
                               30-10 S, 34-10 E, Lost
                               at Sea
Age: 20

Henry J. Bogardus signed aboard the SS *William King* as Engine Cadet on November 16, 1942, at Philadelphia, Pennsylvania. According to the report submitted by one of the ship's other Cadets, John H. Lueddecke, the ship sailed from Philadelphia loaded with Army trucks, ammunition, food, blankets, medical supplies, and railroad car axles bound for Bushehr, Iran. The *William King* sailed in convoy to the Panama Canal and then down the west coast of South America, around Cape Horn to Karachi, India, and its destination. After unloading its cargo in the Persian Gulf, the *William King* sailed from Basra, Iran, refueled in Saudi Arabia, and sailed for Cape Town, South Africa. On May 28, the ship received a message from the British Admiralty via the radio station at Mombasa, Kenya, to divert to Durban.

At about 1140 (GCT) on June 6, when the *William King* was about two hundred miles east of Durban, it was sighted and attacked by *U-198*. The submarine first torpedo hit the ship on the port side at number 3 hatch and the engine room. Both of the ship's two boilers exploded, stopping the ship immediately and starting a fire in the engine room. The crew members in the engine room, including Engine Cadet Henry J. Bogardus Jr., were believed to have been killed instantly.

Captain Owen Harvey Reed immediately ordered the crew to abandon ship, using the two starboard lifeboats and a life raft (the port lifeboats had been destroyed in the attack). The Captain, the Second Mate, and the Armed Guard remained on board for another forty minutes, attempting to fire on the submarine until a second torpedo missed the stern of the ship by about fifteen feet. Shortly after they abandoned ship in three life rafts, *U-198* fired one more torpedo, which hit on the starboard side amidships. A large explosion and shooting flames ensued, and the ship sank almost immediately.

After the entire crew had abandoned ship, the German submarine surfaced and questioned the survivors about their nationality and the name, tonnage, and destination of the ship. The U-boat crew also demanded to know where the Captain was and fired several rounds of submachine gun bullets into the water. Captain Reed gave himself up, said goodbye to his crew, and boarded the submarine. Three weeks later, he was turned over to *U-196*'s supply ship, the *Charlotte Schliemann*. In turn, the *Charlotte Schliemann* turned its prisoners over to a Japanese prisoner of war camp in Batavia, Java, in August 1943. Captain Reed, along with 2,300 other POW, was aboard the "hell ship" SS *Junyo Maru*, which perished when the ship was sunk by HMS *Tradewind* (P 329) on September 18, 1944.

The gun crews in the life rafts were rescued after thirty-six hours in the water by the antisubmarine trawler HMS *Northern Chief*. Twelve hours later, the *Northern Chief* found one of the lifeboats. The survivors in the other lifeboat (who had managed to sail within fourteen miles of land) were picked up on June 12 by the British destroyer HMS *Relentless* (H85). The fifty-nine survivors of the sinking of the SS *William King*, including Cadets Patrick F. Canavan, Joseph A. Gagliano, and John H. Lueddecke, were brought to Durban.

Cadet Midshipman Henry J. Bogardus posthumously received the Mariner's Medal, the Combat Bar, the Atlantic War Zone Bar, the Mediterranean-Middle East War Zone Bar, the Victory Medal, and the Presidential Testimonial Letter.

Henry J. Bogardus was the eldest son of Adelaide V. Bogardus. Henry was raised in Montclair, New Jersey, with his older sister, Dorothy, and younger sister, Beatrice, and brother, Robert. The family survived difficult times during the Great Depression. Bogardus was a talented musician and played tuba in his school marching band and bugle at Boy Scout camp in the summers. Despite suffering from asthma that kept him out of athletics, he was an Eagle Scout and an excellent student. After high school, Bogardus enrolled at Cooper Union College night school and worked at

Union Carbide Co. in New York City before attending the U.S. Merchant Marine Academy.

His brother Robert says,

> Henry lived by the fine motto of the Boy Scouts of America: Be prepared. It should be said that he paid the price by preparing for achievement!

Capt. Richard R. McNulty, supervisor of the Cadet Corps, received a letter from R. H. Farinholt, chief of the Merchant Marine Personnel Records and Welfare Section, on June 16, 1943, informing him of Bogardus's death. A handwritten note in McNulty's hand at the bottom of the page reads,

> This is 100th gone. Too damned many of these fine lads gone. Wish there was more we could do to minimize losses.

Robert J. Bole, III

Born:	July 7, 1920
Hometown:	Drexel Hill, PA
Class:	1943
Service:	Merchant Marine
Position / Rank:	Deck Cadet
Date / Place of death:	September 19, 1942 / 11-20 N, 58-50 W
Date / Place of burial:	September 19, 1942 / Lost at Sea 11-20 N, 58-50 W
Age:	22

Robert J. Bole signed on the freighter MS *Wichita* as Deck Cadet on May 21, 1942, at New Orleans, Louisiana. He joined Cadet-Midshipman Chester E. Klein, who had signed on a few days earlier as Engine Cadet. Ceslaus A. Maciorowski, who had received his license as Third Assistant Engineer just days before, signed on as Third Assistant Engineer on May 20. The *Wichita* was originally a World War I—era "Hog Islander" but was converted from steam turbine to diesel propulsion in 1929. The ship departed for Africa in late May. After calling at several ports, the final loading port was Takoradi, Ghana and they sailed for the United States loaded with general cargo on September 1, 1942, bound for St. Thomas, U.S. Virgin Islands without any escort.

MS *Wichita*

According to German Navy records, the *Wichita* was located and attacked by *U-516* on the morning of September 19, 1942, when the *Wichita* was about three hundred miles east of Barbados. The submarine's initial attack was unsuccessful. Despite the *Wichita* zigzagging at a speed of about 11 knots, the *U-516* repositioned itself and hit the *Wichita* with a torpedo between the foremast and the bridge. The *Wichita* sank in less than a minute with no survivors.

The *U-516*'s logbook states that the submarine surfaced and searched the sinking area but found neither survivors nor lifeboats. Cadet-Midshipmen Robert J. Bole III, Chester E. Klein, and Third Assistant Engineer Ceslau Maciorowski were all killed in the attack.

Cadet-Midshipman Robert J. Bole was posthumously awarded the Mariner's Medal, the Combat Bar, the Atlantic War Zone Bar, the Victory Medal, and the Presidential Testimonial Letter.

Bole was the oldest of six sons and three daughters of Robert J. Bole and Elizabeth Doris O'Rourke Bole. Known as "Bobby," he was adored by his younger siblings. He attended the Pennsylvania Nautical School for some period of time and applied to the U.S. Naval Academy. However, by December 1941, he was a freshman engineering student at Drexel University. He subsequently applied for and was accepted for the Maritime Commission's new Cadet program. One of his brothers says that the following quote from William Shakespeare describes Bobby Bole best,

> Heaven doeth with us, as we with torches do;
> Not light them for themselves; for if our virtues
> Did not go forth for us, 'twere all alike as if we had them not.

Robert Bole (rt) with brothers (l-r) Ted, Bill, Tom (in back), and Ken

Robert Bole (rt) aboard ship with crew member he rescued after he fell overboard

Randall Price Bourell

Born:	January 4, 1921
Hometown:	Olney, IL
Class:	1944
Service:	Merchant Marine
Position / Rank:	Deck Cadet
Date / Place of death:	March 2, 1943 / North Atlantic, 62-10 N, 28-25 W
Date / Place of burial:	March 2, 1943 / North Atlantic, 62-10 N, 28-25 W / Lost at Sea
Age:	22

Randall P. Bourell signed on aboard the SS *Meriwether Lewis* as Deck Cadet on October 15, 1942, at New York, New York. His classmate Alan Clark had signed on as Deck Cadet two days earlier. The ship's two Engine Cadets were Walter E. Johnson and Daniel J. Maher. Former USMCC Cadet Officer James J. Coffey was Second Mate. After an uneventful voyage to Casablanca, French Morocco, the ship returned to New York on January 10, 1943. Johnson was replaced by Francis McCann around January 25, 1943. On February 18, 1943, the *Meriwether Lewis,* with its four Kings Point Cadets, sailed from New York as part of Convoy HX-227 bound for the United Kingdom and then to Murmansk, Russia. The ship was loaded with a cargo of vehicle tires, ammunition, and, based upon some references, a deck cargo of PT boats.

According to German Navy records, the *Meriwether Lewis* was identified as a straggler from a convoy and unsuccessfully attacked by U-759 in the early morning of March 2. The submarine was unable to reattack the *Meriwether Lewis* due to problems with the sub's engines, but it was able to contact *U-634* and lead it to the straggler. The *U-634* fired four torpedoes at the *Meriwether Lewis*, hitting it with one of them. The damage was apparently sufficient to stop the ship, but did not sink it. The submarine hit the *Meriwether Lewis* with two more torpedoes, the last of which detonated the ship's ammunition cargo. Although there was plenty of time to abandon ship, the USCGC *Ingham* (WPG 35) found only a thirty-mile line of floating tires during its two-day-long search for the *Meriwether Lewis* and crew. Thus, the ship's entire crew of forty-four, including Second Mate James J. Coffey and the four Kings Point Cadets, and twenty-eight members of the Naval Armed Guard perished in the sinking.

Cadet-Midshipman Randall P. Bourell was posthumously awarded the Mariner's Medal, the Combat Bar, the Atlantic War Zone Bar, the Victory Medal, and the Presidential Testimonial Letter.

Randall P. "Bud" Bourell, described as five feet eleven inches tall and 180 pounds, was the youngest child and only son of Claude A. and Aileen L. Bourell. According to his niece, he loved the outdoors and spent his early summers fishing, swimming, and boating at the family cabin on a lake. During his teenage years, Bud was a lifeguard at the Olney community pool. He was a standout athlete who was voted the football team's most valuable player for two years in a row and captain of the team in his senior year. He graduated from Olney High School in 1939. He was also an accomplished woodworker and built a bedstead for his parents that they slept on for the rest of their lives. Randall's name was engraved on his parents' tombstone in the Haven Hill Cemetery, Olney, Illinois.

Carl A. Brandler

Born:	1918
Hometown:	Mabank, TX
Class:	1943
Service:	Merchant Marine
Position / Rank:	Engine Cadet
Date / Place of death:	May 4, 1942 / Gulf of Mexico, 25-17 N, 83-57 W
Date / Place of burial:	May 4, 1942 / Gulf of Mexico, 25-17 N, 83-57 W— Lost at Sea
Age:	24

No Photograph Available

According to his family history, Carl A. Brandler entered the Cadet Corps in March 1942. Given his Texas residence, he probably attended the Pass Christian Basic School and was then assigned to the tanker SS *Munger T. Ball*.

SS *Munger T. Ball*

On May 4, 1942, the *Munger T. Ball* was traveling from Smith's Bluff, Texas, to Wilmington, North Carolina, carrying a cargo of sixty-five thousand barrels of gasoline. At 1840 (EWT), when the *Munger T. Ball* was eighty miles northwest of Dry Tortugas Island, it was sighted and attacked by *U-507*. The ship was hit on the port side by two torpedoes, one amidships and one in the engine room in the ship's stern. The explosion of the first torpedo ignited the gasoline cargo, while the explosion of the second torpedo killed the engine room crew and many in the crew accommodations. The flames from the burning gasoline prevented the launching of ship's lifeboats and life rafts.

Four of the thirty-three-man crew survived the attack by leaping from the ship and swimming clear of the burning gasoline on the surface of the water. All of the other members of the crew, including Engine Cadet Carl A. Brandler, perished in the attack.

According to the survivors, within minutes of the second explosion, *U-507*, the attacking submarine surfaced on the port side of the vessel and fired a machine gun at the ship from stem to stern. The four survivors were picked up by the MV *Katy* at 2055 (EWT). The *Katy* had been about nine miles away from the *Munger T. Ball* when it was attacked.

At this point in the war, the Navy did not believe that German submarines were operating in the Gulf of Mexico, so ships traveling through the Gulf were neither escorted nor expected to zigzag. However, the German Navy had just sent the submarines of the Tenth U-boat Flotilla into the Gulf of Mexico to disrupt the flow of oil and other cargos from the Gulf of Mexico to the East Coast and Caribbean. The *Munger T. Ball* was one of fifty-six ships sunk by these German submarines during May 1942.

Carl A. Brandler was posthumously awarded the Mariner's Medal, the Combat Bar, and the Atlantic War Zone Bar. According to the 1930 census, Carl was the youngest son of Charles Hubert and Winnie Myrtle Bates Bandler's four children. Carl grew up on farms and small towns in Henderson and Kaufman Counties in Northeast Texas.

Philip George Branigan

Born:	July 6, 1922
Hometown:	Teaneck, NJ
Class:	1943
Service:	Merchant Marine
Position / Rank:	Deck Cadet
Date / Place of death:	December 7, 1942 / North Atlantic, 57-50 N, 23-10 W
Date / Place of burial:	December 7, 1942 / North Atlantic, 57-50 N, 23-10 W / Lost at Sea
Age:	20

Philip G. Branigan signed on the SS *James McKay* as Deck Cadet on November 11, 1942, at New York, New York. Three other Kings Point Cadet-Midshipmen, Leonard L. Ehrlich (engine), Walter C. Hetrick (engine), and John J. McKelvey (deck), were also aboard. In addition, the Third Assistant Engineer, Henry E. Harris, was a 1942 Kings Point graduate.

SS *James McKay*

The *James McKay* sailed from New York with Convoy HX-216 bound for Belfast, Northern Ireland, and Cardiff, Wales, on November 19. On November 25, the convoy encountered a northwest gale and reduced visibility that caused the convoy to partly scatter. The weather was sufficiently rough to cause the *James McKay*'s general cargo to shift, endangering its stability; the ship left the convoy and sailed into St. John's, Newfoundland, on November 29 to restow its cargo.

After restowing its cargo, the *James McKay* sailed from Newfoundland to join up with the next eastbound convoy, HX-217. However, there is no indication that the *James McKay* ever actually joined up with HX-217, possibly due to the convoy being scattered in a southwesterly gale from December 2 to 4.

Philip George Branigan

According to German Navy records, the *James McKay* was located and attacked by *U-600* on the night of December 7/8, 1943, about four hundred miles south of Iceland. Three torpedoes hit the *James McKay*, one amidships and the other two in the after portion of the ship. The ship stopped and sent out distress signals, and the crew abandoned ship in two lifeboats although the ship was still afloat. It required two more torpedoes from *U-600* to sink the *James McKay*. Neither the two lifeboats nor any of her crew were ever seen again.

Cadet-Midshipman Philip G. Branigan was posthumously awarded the Mariner's Medal, the Combat Bar with star, the Atlantic War Zone Bar, the Victory Medal, and the Presidential Testimonial Letter.

According to his niece, Maureen C. Bridger, Philip Branigan was very close to his sister Rose, Maureen's mother. Rose, who was just fifteen months older than Philip, shared a wide circle of friends, and went to dances, war bond rallies, and other social events together. When they were little, their grandfather took them out on his boat with him to go crabbing.

Maureen's mother told her that Uncle Phil was a talented singer and musician who played the bass fiddle. Phil was also an avid reader. At the beginning of the war, Phil tried to join the Navy but had been rejected because his eardrums had been damaged by ear infections as a child. He was determined to serve his country at sea and was accepted at Kings Point. In going to Kings Point, he became the first member of his family to enroll in a postsecondary educational institution. At the time of his death, Philip was engaged to a young woman named Evelyn.

Maureen remembers going on a shopping trip with her mother to New York when her mother thought she saw Philip in a crowd. After running to catch the person only to learn, of course, that it wasn't Phil.

Maureen said that her mother always thought it fitting that Phil died just as he had wanted—aboard a ship serving his country.

Phil's mother put a gold star in the window of her house after learning of his death. The gold star signified that someone on the house had died in action during World War II. Mrs. Branigan kept the gold star in her window even though neighborhood women criticized her for doing so because they felt that Philip wasn't a "real soldier or sailor."

John Paulson Brewster

Born:	March 9, 1919
Hometown:	Teaneck, NJ
Class:	1943
Service:	Merchant Marine
Position / Rank:	Engine Cadet
Date / Place of death:	May 26, 1942 / North Atlantic, 72-35 N, 5-30 E
Date / Place of burial:	May 26, 1942 / North Atlantic, 72-35 N, 5-30 E / Lost at Sea
Age:	23

John P. Brewster and his Kings Point classmate Raymond Holubowicz signed on aboard the SS *Syros* at Philadelphia, Pennsylvania, in early May 1942. The ship sailed loaded with general cargo and ammunition bound for Murmansk, Russia, via Reykjavik, Iceland. When the *Syros* sailed from Reykjavik on May 21, 1942, it joined Convoy PQ-16. The convoy was located by German "Condor" search planes on May 25 and remained under nearly constant air and submarine attack for the next four days due to the nearly constant daylight of the northern summer.

In the early morning hours of May 26, when the ship was about two hundred miles southwest of Bear Island, the *Syros* was sighted and attacked by *U-703*. Two of *U-703*'s torpedoes hit the *Syros* despite the sub being seen and fired on by other ships in the convoy. The first torpedo hit amidships at the engine room, while the second hit at the number 2 hatch, detonating the ship's ammunition cargo. The ship sank in thirty seconds, carrying Holubowicz down with it, but he was able to break free and reach the surface. According to Holubowicz' report, Engine Cadet John Brewster was among the men on watch in the engine room when the torpedo hit and was most likely killed instantly.

With no time to launch any of the lifeboats or life rafts, the survivors hung on to one life raft that broke loose from the ship and floating wreckage. Fortunately, one of the escorts, the minesweeper HMS *Hazard* (J02), was able to rescue thirty men from the icy waters. However, two of these men died on board the *Hazard* and were buried at sea. The twenty-eight survivors were taken to Murmansk and placed aboard ships bound for Iceland. Eleven of the *Syros*'s crew, including all of the engineers on duty in the engine room and the Captain, perished in the sinking.

John P. Brewster was posthumously awarded the Mariner's Medal, the Combat Bar, the Atlantic War Zone Bar, the Victory Medal, the Presidential Testimonial Letter, the Merchant Marine Service Emblem, and the Honorable Service Button.

John P. Brewster was the youngest of Charles F. Brewster Sr. and Amie Brewster's three children. John's sister was Marjorie, who was eight years older. His brother, Charles Jr., was five years older. John's mother, Amie, was born in the Virgin Islands and had immigrated to the United States from the Virgin Islands. The 1940 U.S. Census indicates that both Charles Sr. and Jr. were involved in sales in the "electric industry," while John was working as an office boy in a nearby manufacturing plant.

John P. Brewster is remembered by his shipmate Raymond Holubowicz as being a practical young man, made friends rapidly, was at home in any type of situation, and "fearless in pursuing his goal of superior service aboard ship."

SS *Syros*

After surviving the sinking of the *Syros*, Raymond Holubowicz's voyage home took longer than he anticipated. Once at Murmansk, Holubowicz signed on aboard the SS *Hybert* as Deck Cadet, only to be sunk again by "friendly" mines off the coast of Iceland. Rescued and taken to Reykjavik, Holubowicz was assigned to the Murmansk bound Liberty ship, SS *J. L. M. Curry,* which made it safely to Murmansk. The ship discharged its cargo while under constant enemy air attack and sailed for home. However, the *Curry* broke into three pieces during a gale. Rescued once more, this time by a British vessel, Holubowicz finally made it back to Kings Point a year after first shipping out. In 1985, Holubowicz, along with other veterans of the "Murmansk Run," received medals from the Russian government to honor their service and heroism.

Marvin William Brodie Jr.

Born:	February 15, 1922
Hometown:	Columbus, OH
Class:	1944
Service:	Merchant Marine
Position / Rank:	Engine Cadet
Date / Place of death:	December 2, 1943 / Bari, Italy
Date / Place of burial:	December 2, 1943 / Bari, Italy / Lost at Sea
Age:	21

Marvin W. Brodie signed on aboard the SS *John Harvey* as Engine Cadet on October 5, 1943, at Baltimore, Maryland. Three other Kings Point Cadets also signed on the *John Harvey:* James L. Cahill (deck), Richard B. Glauche (deck), and Alvin H. Justis (engine). According to a report filed by Cadet-Midshipman Cahill, the ship sailed to Norfolk, Virginia, to finish loading and joined a convoy that sailed for Oran, Algeria, on October 15. Unbeknownst to most of the crew, part of the ship's cargo was two thousand M47A1 mustard gas bombs. The bombs had been loaded at Baltimore between September 30 and October 8 under the supervision of a seven-man detail of chemical warfare specialists from the Army's Eastern Chemical Warfare Depot. The seven men remained aboard the *John Harvey* to monitor the condition of the bombs while at sea and supervise their discharge. The bombs were being sent to the Mediterranean as a precaution so that American forces could retaliate if the Germans resorted to chemical warfare.

The *John Harvey* arrived in Oran on November 2, discharged its cargo other than the mustard gas bombs, and then loaded a cargo of ammunition. A convoy of about forty ships, including the *John Harvey*, sailed from Oran for Augusta, Sicily, on November 19, arriving there on November 25. The *John Harvey* sailed the next day in a convoy of thirty ships bound for the ports of Taranto and Bari on the Italian mainland, with the Bari bound ships arriving there on November 28. The port facilities at Bari were unable to keep up with the number of ships in the port, resulting in days-long delays in discharging ships anchored in the port. Because of the high level of secrecy surrounding its cargo, the *John Harvey* was held in port for several days awaiting discharge, moored alongside other ships loaded with ammunition and gasoline, including the Victory Ship ships *John L. Motley*, the *John Bascom*, and the *Samuel J. Tilden*.

Because of its distance from German airfields, an air attack on Bari was not considered likely, so the port was not protected by the normal air defenses. As a result, a German attack force of more than one hundred Ju88s was able to completely surprise the few defenders of Bari on the evening of December 2, 1943. Due to the lights being left on, the bombers were able to accurately bomb the ships in the port and port facilities with only the loss of a single aircraft. They left behind twenty-eight ships sunk, twelve more damaged, over one thousand merchant mariners and military personnel killed, and a port so badly damaged that it took three weeks to resume discharging ships.

According to the few surviving eye witnesses, the *John L. Motley* and the *Samuel J. Tilden* were among the first ships to be hit by the bombers. However, after the second wave of aircraft finished their attack, the *John Harvey* was in flames from stem to stern. With the fires threatening the *John Harvey*'s cargo of ammunition, its crew fought desperately to save the ship, and their lives. However, the damaged *John L. Motley* had broken free from its mooring lines and, completely engulfed in flames, was drifting toward the *John Harvey*. Suddenly, the *John L. Motley* exploded, destroying the ship and detonating the *John Harvey*'s cargo. The *John Harvey* disintegrated, sending the contents of its cargo of mustard gas bombs into the air and water throughout the port.

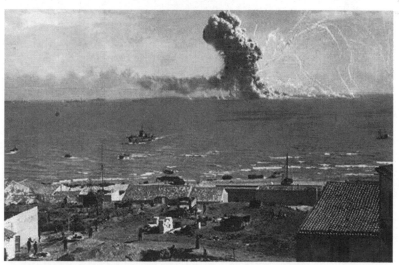

Explosion of either SS *John Harvey* or SS *John L. Motley* at Bari, Italy

Thirty-six of the ship's crew, all twenty-eight members of its Armed Guard and the Army chemical warfare specialists perished instantly, including Cadet-Midshipmen Marvin W. Brodie, Richard B. Glauche, and Alvin H. Justis. The only survivors from the *John Harvey* were Cadet-Midshipman James L. Cahill and one of the ship's able-bodied seaman who was ashore when the attack began. One of the major factors in the high number of casualties from the attack is that doctors and other medical personnel attending to the wounded did not diagnose their signs and symptoms as those of mustard gas poisoning, since no mustard gas was believed to be in the area.

Cadet-Midshipman Marvin W. Brodie was posthumously awarded the Mariner's Medal, the Combat Bar, the Atlantic War Zone Bar, the Mediterranean-Middle East War Zone Bar, the Victory Medal, and the Presidential Testimonial Letter.

Marvin W. Brodie was the only son and youngest child of Marvin W. Brodie Sr. Marvin's sister was Catherine. Marvin Sr. was employed by the post office. The 1930s were hard on the Brodie family. According to the 1930 U.S. Census; the Brodie children were lodging with the Cullison family. According to Columbus, Ohio, city directories, Marvin Sr. was living at the YMCA since 1926. The same records indicate that Marvin Sr. had secured a home for himself and the children by 1932. None of the available records indicate that Marvin Sr. was married from 1926 onward, so Marvin and Catherine lost their mother at a very young age. Marvin attended West High School in Columbus, where he was a member of the chorus. After graduating from high school, he attended Ohio State University before applying to Kings Point.

Glenn Ray Bruaw

Born:	November 19, 1921
Hometown:	York Haven, PA
Class:	1943
Service:	Merchant Marine
Position / Rank:	Deck Cadet
Date / Place of death:	May 19, 1942 / Gulf of Mexico, 28-53 N, 91-03 W
Date / Place of burial:	May 19, 1942 / Gulf of Mexico, 28-53 N, 91-03 W / Lost at Sea
Age:	20

Glenn R. Bruaw signed on aboard the passenger-cargo ship SS *Heredia* as Deck Cadet on April 23, 1942, at New Orleans, Louisiana. In addition to Glenn Bruaw, Engine Cadet Irwin S. Ebel was also part of the ship's crew. On May 19, 1942, the ship was returning to New Orleans from Puerto Barrios, Guatemala, loaded with forty thousand stems of bananas and five thousand bags of coffee. The ship was traveling without an escort and was not zigzagging, since the Navy did not believe that any German submarines were operating in the Gulf of Mexico. However, the German Navy had recently ordered the submarines of their Tenth U-boat Flotilla to begin operating in the Gulf of Mexico to interrupt the flow of petroleum products and supplies to the U.S. East Coast and Caribbean. During the month of May 1942, these submarines sank fifty-six ships, including the *Heredia*.

SS *Heredia*

At about 0200 (CWT), when the *Heredia* was about two miles south of the Ship Shoal Buoy off the Louisiana coast, the ship was sighted and attacked by *U-506*. Two torpedoes hit the *Heredia* on the port side at number 3 and number 4 holds. Survivors reported a third torpedo hit on the starboard side amidships, leading them to conclude that the ship was attacked by two submarines. However, German naval records do not identify a second submarine operating in the same area as *U-506*.

The torpedo explosions on the port side destroyed the lifeboats there. No distress signal was sent, and the passengers, crew, and Armed Guard abandoned ship in two life rafts. The survivors were rescued by several shrimp boats (*Papa Joe*, *Conquest*, *J. Edwin Treakle*, and *Shellwater*) and by a seaplane. Of the *Heredia*'s eight passengers, forty-eight crewmen, and six Armed Guard Sailors,

Bruaw family memorial, Pleasant Grove Cemetery, York Haven, PA

one passenger, five Armed Guard Sailors, and thirty crewmen, including Cadet-Midshipmen Glenn Bruaw and Irwin Ebel perished.

Cadet-Midshipman Glen R. Bruaw was posthumously awarded the Mariner's Medal, the Combat Bar with star, the Atlantic War Zone Bar, the Victory Medal, and the Presidential Testimonial Letter.

Glen R. Bruaw was the only child of Raymond Stephen Bruaw and Lottie M. Stoner Bruaw.

Atlee Hoover, a family friend, said the following about Glen:

> Cadet Glen Bruaw had an ideal American boyhood. Born on a small farm in the village of Cly in Newberry Township, York County, Pennsylvania, he attended a one-room school for eight years. His youthful days were spent playing baseball, hunting, and fishing the nearby Susquehanna River. Growing up in the historic Pennsylvania Dutch country no doubt contributed to the formation of his patriotic character. He graduated from New Cumberland High School.

Michael Buck Jr.

Born:	February 15, 1920
Hometown:	Mount Kisco, NY
Class:	1944
Service:	Merchant Marine
Position / Rank:	Engine Cadet
Date / Place of death:	March 10, 1943 / Caribbean Sea, 19-49 N, 74-38 W
Date / Place of burial:	March 10, 1943 / Caribbean Sea, 19-49 N, 74-38 W / Lost at Sea
Age:	23

Michael Buck signed on aboard the brand new Liberty ship SS *James Sprunt* as Engine Cadet on February 23, 1943, at Charleston, South Carolina. He was joined by his Academy classmates, Howard McGrath (engine), James Rowley (deck), and John Tucek (deck). The ship was loaded with general cargo and four thousand tons of high explosives at Charleston for a voyage to Karachi, India, via Texas and the Panama Canal.

SS *James Sprunt* shortly after completion

On the morning of March 10, 1943, the *James Sprunt* was traveling in Convoy KG-123 about three miles southeast of Guantanamo Bay, Cuba. Another ship in the convoy, the *Virginia Sinclair*, had been torpedoed at

0430 on the same morning. At 0809, *U-185* fired torpedoes at the convoy, hitting the *James Sprunt*.

The *James Sprunt*'s cargo of explosives blew up with extraordinary force, disintegrating the ship completely. The glare from the explosion was seen more than forty miles away, and witnesses on other ships recalled the violent tremors and debris that fell like hail on the other ships. There were no survivors among the forty-three crew members and twenty-eight Naval Armed Guard members, including all four of the ship's Cadets, Engine Cadet Michael Buck, Engine Cadet Howard McGrath, Deck Cadet James Rowley, and Deck Cadet John Tucek.

The thirty-day life of the SS *James Sprunt* may have been the shortest life span of any Liberty ship. The ship was delivered from North Carolina Shipbuilding to the War Shipping Administration on February 13, 1943, loaded cargo from the nineteenth to the twenty-ninth, and was destroyed on March 10, 1943.

Cadet-Midshipman Michael Buck was posthumously awarded the Mariner's Medal, the Combat Bar, the Atlantic War Zone Bar, the Victory Medal, and the Presidential Testimonial Letter.

Michael Buck Jr. was the fourth of Michael Buck Sr. and Veronica Buck's five sons (Alexander, John, Joseph, Michael, and Peter). The Bucks also had four daughters of which Anna and Mary were Michael's big sisters, while Veronica and Helen were his little sisters. Based on the 1930 and 1940 U.S. Census, it appears that Michael was known as Marion (Maryan) by the rest of his family.

Harry Moulton Burlison

Born:	December 11, 1921
Hometown:	Minneapolis, MN
Class:	1944
Service:	Merchant Marine
Position / Rank:	Deck Cadet
Date / Place of death:	February 23, 1943 / North Atlantic, 46-15 N, 38-11 W
Date / Place of burial:	February 23, 1943 / North Atlantic, 46-15 N, 38-11 W / Lost at Sea
Age:	21

Harry M. Burlison signed on as Deck Cadet aboard the SS *Jonathan Sturges* at the Port of New York on January 12, 1943. Also on board were Cadet-Midshipmen Ralph Kohlmeyer (engine), Grover Leitz (engine), and William Wilson (deck). The ship's Chief Mate was 1940 Cadet Officer David L. Edwards. After safely delivering its cargo to England, the *Jonathan Sturges* was returning to New York with Convoy ON-166 from Liverpool to New York City when it fell behind the convoy on the night of February 23/24, 1943. The ship, with a crew of forty-four merchant mariners and a Naval Armed Guard of thirty-one, was carrying 1,500 tons of sand ballast. In bad weather and poor visibility, the *Sturges* was making 6 knots, about half its full speed.

At about 1:00 a.m., the vessel was struck in the forward part of the ship by two torpedoes fired by *U-707*. The engines were secured, but the ship, which had apparently been broken in two, began to sink bow first. Survivors recalled that the explosions gave off a sweet odor and left a sweet taste in their mouths for hours after the incident.

Although the Radio Officer was able to send a distress signal, there was no time to await a reply, as the crew abandoned ship. Two lifeboats and four life rafts were successfully launched. According to the post sinking report of the survivors, nineteen men were able to get into one lifeboat while the Master, Chief Mate David Edwards, and fifteen others were in the other boat. The other twenty-four survivors were able to reach the four life rafts. The boats and rafts were soon separated.

On February 27, three days after the sinking, the boat with nineteen men aboard met up with a lifeboat carrying three survivors from the Dutch ship SS *Madoera* who had been in the same convoy. Eight of the *Sturges* survivors climbed into the *Madoera*'s boat. Although one of the *Jonathan Sturges* crew eventually died of exposure, the other eighteen (along with the three *Madoera*'s survivors) were rescued by the USS *Belknap* (DD 251) on March 12, 1943. The other lifeboat with its seventeen survivors was never seen again. Of the twenty-four men on the life rafts, only six survived. These men were rescued on April 5 by *U-336* and spent the rest of the war as prisoners of war. Cadet-Midshipman Harry M. Burlison, along with the three other Cadet-Midshipmen, died.

Cadet-Midshipman Harry M. Burlison was posthumously awarded the Mariner's Medal, the Combat Bar, the Atlantic War Zone Bar, the Victory Medal, and the Presidential Testimonial Letter.

Harry M. Burlison was the eldest of Harry Miles and Mertel Burlison's two sons and daughter. According to his brother Richard, a 1944 graduate of Kings Point, Harry attended the public schools in Minneapolis from kindergarten through high school. In 1942, he enrolled in the Northwestern Naval Preparatory School, in anticipation of acceptance at the U.S. Naval Academy. As a child, Harry was skilled at building rafts and boating activities. He was a skilled musician, following in the steps of his father, an accomplished pianist. Unfortunately, Harry's father passed away when he was only nine, leaving his mother to raise three children during the Depression.

Lee Thomas Byrd

Born:	April 29, 1922
Hometown:	Benson, NC
Class:	1944
Service:	Merchant Marine
Position / Rank:	Deck Cadet
Date / Place of death:	March 17, 1943 / North Atlantic, 50-38 N, 34-46 W
Date / Place of burial:	March 17, 1943 / North Atlantic, 50-38 N, 34-46 W Lost at Sea
Age:	25

Lee T. Byrd signed on aboard the SS *Harry Luckenbach* as Engine Cadet on March 2, 1943, at New York, New York. In addition to Byrd, the *Harry Luckenbach* had three other Kings Point Cadets aboard: Walter J. Meyer, Francis R. Miller, and William H. Parker. The Third Mate, LeRoy W. Kernan, was a 1942 graduate. The ship sailed from New York on March 8 as one of forty ships in Convoy HX-229, bound for Liverpool with a general cargo of war supplies. A second HX convoy, HX-229A, with more ships sailed about ten hours after the ships of HX-229. During their transit of the North Atlantic, the two convoys overtook a slower convoy, SC-122. The three convoys, with a total of 110 ships, but less than twenty escorts, would be the centerpiece of what has been described as the greatest convoy battle of World War II.

SS *Harry Luckenbach*

The ships of Convoy HX-229 had proceeded without incident or attack until March 16. For the next three days, the convoy was under attack by over forty U-boats. On the morning of March 17, when HX-229 was about four hundred miles east-southeast of Cape Farrell, *U-91* fired five torpedoes at the convoy, not aiming at any specific ship. The *Harry Luckenbach* in the starboard forward corner of the convoy was hit by two of the torpedoes at the engine room. The ship sank in minutes, but amazingly, three lifeboats were able to get away from the sinking vessel. One or more of the boats were later sighted by HMS *Beverley* (H-64), HMS *Pennywort* (K-111), HMS *Volunteer* (D-71), and possibly, HMS *Abelia* (K-184). However, none of these ships were able to pick up the survivors from the boats. None of the fifty-four crew members and twenty-six Naval Armed Guard of the *Harry Luckenbach* survived the sinking.

By March 20, the surviving ships of the three convoys arrived in the United Kingdom, having lost twenty-two ships and their crews, while sinking just one of the attacking U-boats. According to a Royal Navy report on the convoy battle,

> The Germans never came so near to disrupting communications between the New World and the Old as in the first twenty days of March 1943.

The fact that the Germans were unable to do so is a testament to the courage of merchant mariners like Lee T. Byrd, and the example that he set for the Kings Pointers that came after him.

Cadet-Midshipman Lee T. Byrd was posthumously awarded the Mariner's Medal, the Combat Bar with star, the Atlantic War Zone Bar, the Victory Medal, and the Presidential Testimonial Letter.

Lee T. Byrd was the eldest of Zebedee B. Byrd and Callie Geneva Byrd's two sons.Lee's younger brother was Zebedee. The family lived on their farm in Elevation Township, Johnston County, North Carolina. When Lee registered for the draft, he indicated that he was employed by Newport News Shipbuilding and Drydock Company, in Newport News, Virginia. According to Academy records, Lee reported to Kings Point for his initial training on January 3, 1943.

Thomas Bernard Carey Jr.

Born:	October 31, 1924
Hometown:	Hartford, CT
Class:	1944
Service:	Merchant Marine
Position / Rank:	Engine Cadet
Date / Place of death:	November 2, 1944 / U.S. Naval Hospital, St. Albans, NY
Date / Place of burial:	November 1944 / Mount Saint Benedict Cemetery, Bloomfield, CT
Age:	20

Cadet-Midshipman Thomas B. Carey signed on as Engine Cadet aboard the SS *Golden Eagle* on April 29, 1943, at San Francisco, California, after completing initial training at the San Mateo Basic School on April 5. The *Golden Eagle*, a refrigerated cargo ship, had just been delivered from its builder and was ready for its maiden voyage. On October 12, 1943, following the *Golden Eagle*'s arrival at New York, New York, from Cardiff, Wales, Thomas Carey left the ship to begin his final training at Kings Point.

Just a few months later, in January 1944, Thomas Carey contracted scarlet fever. In the following weeks, Carey appeared to improve, but complications set in. By early April, the complications had become so severe, including accumulation of fluid in his body tissues and renal failure, that he was admitted to the Academy's Patten Hospital. However, his condition continued to deteriorate. On May 23, 1944, after six weeks of treatment at Patten Hospital, Thomas Carey was transferred to the U.S. Naval Hospital at St. Albans, New York. Although he showed some brief periods of improvement, Carey's condition gradually deteriorated. He died at St. Albans at 1030 on November 2, 1944. The official cause of death is listed as acute nephritis, a serious inflammation of the kidneys. An autopsy was not performed at the request of Carey's parents.

For his time at sea, Cadet-Midshipman Thomas B. Carey earned the Pacific War Zone Bar, the Atlantic War Zone Bar, the Victory Medal, and the Presidential Testimonial Letter.

According to the 1930 U.S. Census, Thomas B. Carey was the only child of Thomas Bernard and Mary Carey. Thomas's father was a detective in the Hartford Police Department.

**Headstone for Cadet-Midshipman Thomas B. Carey Jr.,
Mount St. Benedict Cemetery, Bloomfield, CT**

Warren Benjamin Carriere

Born:	August 14, 1919
Hometown:	New Orleans, LA
Class:	1943
Service:	Merchant Marine
Position / Rank:	Deck Cadet
Date / Place of death:	December 31, 1942 / 40-10 N, 72-02 W
Date / Place of burial:	December 31, 1942 / Lost at Sea—40-10 N, 72-02 W
Age:	23

Warren B. Carriere signed on aboard his first ship, the SS *Maiden Creek*, as Deck Cadet at Mobile, Alabama, on June 29, 1942. A week later, he was joined by Cadet-Midshipman Edward J. Ackerlind, who signed as Engine Cadet. The *Maiden Creek*, a World War I "Hog Islander" built in 1919, was owned by the Waterman Steamship Company.

SS *Maiden Creek*

On November 11, 1942, the *Maiden Creek* sailed from New York with a cargo of aviation gasoline in drums for the Army Air Corps airfield designated Bluie West Eight (later Sondrestrom AFB). For its return trip, it was to load a cargo of ore concentrates. After completing loading of its return cargo, the *Maiden Creek* sailed from Botwood, Newfoundland, on December 15 to meet a convoy bound for New York. However, the old ship could not keep up with the convoy in the heavy seas it encountered. On December 19, the *Maiden Creek* diverted to Halifax, Nova Scotia. When the ship arrived on December 22, inspection of the ship found that the ship's chain locker, forepeak, and number 1 hold were flooded due to the heavy seas. Although the forepeak and chain locker were secured and pumped out, the water in number 1 hold could not be pumped out because of the characteristics of the cargo.

On December 27, despite having significantly reduced freeboard forward due to the flooded number 1 hold, the *Maiden Creek* sailed from Halifax on December 27 with eleven other ships and three escorts. The ship joined Convoy ON-152, bound for New York, the next day. On December 30, as the convoy was nearing New York, the heavy weather resumed. By the afternoon of December 31, the hatch cover for number 1 hold was leaking again, and the hatch cover for number 2 hold had begun leaking. The water in the *Maiden Creek*'s holds eventually brought the propeller and rudder out of the water. With the ship adrift in heavy seas about seventy miles south of Block Island, the Captain ordered the Radio Officer to send out an SOS. The Captain then called together the officers and informed them that they would have to abandon the ship.

At about 1700, number 3 lifeboat was launched with eighteen crew members, including the two Cadet-Midshipmen and five Armed Guard sailors. A second lifeboat was launched about thirty minutes later with all but two of the remaining crew and Armed Guard sailors aboard, a total of thirty-one men. Two men had to remain aboard because lowering a boat from the *Maiden Creek* antiquated lifeboat davits could only be done manually. The two able-bodied seamen attempted to climb down the falls to the boat, but the rough seas carried the boat away before the men could get aboard. One man fell into the water and was lost, despite attempts to pull him aboard. The other seaman climbed back on board the *Maiden Creek* and eventually went down with the vessel.

In heavy seas and growing darkness, the two lifeboats soon lost sight of each other. The lifeboat with thirty-one men aboard was spotted by Army, Navy, and Coast Guard patrol planes in the ensuing days. However, it was not until January 3 that a patrol plane was able to transmit the position of the lifeboat to a ship close enough to affect a rescue. At about 1840 that day, the MS *Staghound* rescued the men in the *Maiden Creek* lifeboat. The twenty-three men aboard the first lifeboat, including Cadet-Midshipmen Carriere and Ackerlind, were never seen again.

Warren B. Carriere

Cadet-Midshipman Warren B. Carriere was posthumously awarded the Atlantic War Zone Bar, the Victory Medal, and the Presidential Testimonial Letter.

Warren B. Carriere, known as "Benny" by his family, was the tenth of eleven children born to Charles Pierre Carriere and Lydia Marie Guibert Carriere. He is recalled by his niece, Sr. Mary Carriere Daniel, a Dominican nun whom he nicknamed "Tweedles," as the linchpin of his family. Sister Daniel also recalls that Benny's sister Lydia loved him dearly and spoke of him with great affection. Lydia recalled one of the last times she saw Benny. She had planned to make him a special breakfast but was delayed in getting home for some reason. When she got home, she found Benny making the eggs for breakfast but was substituting milk for some of the eggs. Sister Daniel describes Benny as being a thoughtful son with a droll sense of humor and a person who never met anyone he didn't like. During the war, Benny had four brothers in the service, all stationed in Europe.

John McCormick Carter

Born:	June 16, 1921	
Hometown:	Rockville, MD	
Class:	1944	
Service:	Merchant Marine	
Position / Rank:	Engine Cadet	
Date / Place of death:	June 10, 1943 / U.S. East Coast, 31-02 N, 79-17 W	
Date / Place of burial:	June 10, 1943 / U.S. East Coast, 31-02 N, 79-17 W	
	Lost at Sea	
Age:	21	

John M. Carter signed on aboard the SS *Esso Gettysburg* as Engine Cadet on May 27, 1943, at New York, New York. The ship was engaged in the coastal oil trade, running from the Gulf of Mexico to the East Coast. Also aboard the ship were Kings Point Cadet-Midshipmen Joseph Landron (engine), Alfonse Miller (deck), and Eugene Quidort (deck). The ship sailed on June 6 from Port Arthur, Texas, bound for Philadelphia, Pennsylvania, loaded with 120,000 barrels of west Texas crude oil for the Atlantic Refining Company's refinery there.

Esso Gettysburg

On the afternoon of June 10, the ship was under way about one hundred miles southeast of Savannah, Georgia, traveling without escort, apparently due to its ability to make more than 15 knots. However, the ship was steering evasive courses. Although the vessel had been warned after rounding Key West that submarines were in the area, none had been sighted by the lookouts.

At around 1400, local time, 1900 (GCT), the *Esso Gettysburg* was sighted and attacked by *U-66*. The submarine's two torpedoes hit the ship's port side, the first one aft of midships, while the second torpedo hit the engine room in the stern. The impacts ruptured twenty-five feet of deck and hull, and raised a one-hundred-foot geyser of oil and water. The crude oil exploded on impact, transforming the ship into an inferno. A thick cloud of black smoke rose almost a thousand feet in the air. The ship settled by the stern and began to list to port.

At the time of the attack, Alphonse Miller was painting the starboard side of the afterdeck with an AB. John Carter was on duty with the Second Assistant Engineer in the engine room. Joseph Landron, who was not on watch, was sleeping in his room. The fact that Eugene Quidort was off watch on the flying bridge near the compass probably saved his life. Carter, along with the rest of the engine crew on duty, was killed instantly. Miller was seen to run along the catwalk toward midships, where he was caught in the flames and killed. Landron made way for the lifeboats, but when these caught fire, he jumped into the water with the rest of the survivors. He was last seen by an Able Seaman fighting the flames in the water.

Eugene Quidort also jumped overboard after unsuccessfully attempting to help the Chief Mate lower one of the lifeboats into the sea. He was able to swim away from the burning oil, towing Ensign John S. Arnold, the Armed Guard officer for a while. Quidort eventually found a burned lifeboat to hang on to. Several hours later, he was rescued by the Chief Mate and Second Mate, who had managed to climb aboard a partially burned lifeboat and pulled aboard six crew members and seven Navy men—the only survivors among forty-five crew members and twenty-seven Naval Armed Guard sailors. The following day, the survivors were spotted by an Army B-25 patrol plane. They were picked up by the SS *George Washington* and taken to Charleston, South Carolina.

The Armed Guard, under the command of Ensign John S. Arnold, USNR, did manage to fire one shot in the direction of the submarine before being forced to abandon their post by the flames. Ensign Arnold survived the sinking and was awarded the Navy Cross for his actions.

Cadet-Midshipman John Carter was posthumously awarded the Mariner's Medal, the Combat Bar, the Atlantic War Zone Bar, the Victory Medal, and the Presidential Testimonial Letter.

John M. Carter was one of five sons of Guy L. and Mary H. Carter. Although the family lived on a dairy farm in Rockville, Maryland, John's father is identified in the 1930 census as being a clerk for the U.S. government. John's older brother Guy also served in the merchant marine and perished aboard the SS *John Harvey* at Bari, Italy, on December 2, 1943. Carter Field at Glenora Park in Rockville, Maryland, is dedicated to their memory. John's younger brother Hilton served as an Army officer during the war while his youngest brother, Robert, graduated from the U.S. Naval Academy after the war.

Ball field dedicated to the Carter brothers

Vincent Gordon Cathey

Born:	January 7, 1923
Hometown:	Andrews, NC
Class:	1943
Service:	Merchant Marine
Position / Rank:	Engine Cadet
Date / Place of death:	July 30, 1942 / Gulf of Mexico, 28-40 N, 88-30 W
Date / Place of burial:	July 30, 1942 / Gulf of Mexico, 28-40 N, 88-30 W / Lost at Sea
Age:	19

Cadet-Midshipman Vincent G. Cathey signed on aboard his first ship, the passenger ship SS *Robert E. Lee*, as Engine Cadet on July 2, 1942, at the port of New Orleans, Louisiana. Also aboard the ship were Cadet-Midshipmen Carl C. Gross (deck) and Howard A. Hanson (engine).

SS *Robert E. Lee*

In late July 1942, the *Robert E. Lee* sailed from Port of Spain, Trinidad, bound for Tampa, Florida, in Convoy TAW-7 with 270 passengers and forty-seven tons of general cargo. The latter was identified as being mostly the personal effects of the passengers. Many of the *Robert E. Lee's* passengers were survivors of ships that had previously been torpedoed, including the MV *Andrea Brovig* and SS *Stanvac Palembang*. Upon arrival at Key West, Florida, the convoy and its escorts dispersed to their assigned discharge ports. However, when the *Robert E. Lee*, escorted by USS *PC 566*, arrived off Tampa on July 29, no pilots were available to take the ship into port. After discussion with the Commanding Officer of *PC 566* by blinker light, the *Robert E. Lee's* Master decided to proceed to New Orleans. The *PC 566* was ordered to accompany the *Robert E. Lee* to New Orleans.

At 1630, Central War Time (CWT), the following day, the *Robert E. Lee* and *PC 566* were about thirty miles south of the mouth of the Mississippi River. Unfortunately, this was also where *U-166* was hunting for targets to sink. The submarine fired one torpedo, hitting the *Robert E. Lee* just aft of the engine room. The explosion destroyed the number 3 hold, its radio, and engines. At the time of the explosion, Engine Cadet Vincent Cathey and the First Assistant Engineer were working in the shaft alley. Both men are believed to have been killed instantly. Immediately following the torpedoing, *PC 566* detected *U-166* on its sonar and began dropping depth charges, sinking the submarine and its crew of fifty-six men. The wreck of *U-166* lies near its last victim, the *Robert E. Lee*.

Immediately after being hit by the torpedo, the Captain, William C. Heath, ordered the passengers and crew to abandon ship. Six lifeboats and sixteen life rafts were launched in the minutes following the attack. Thanks to a speedy evacuation, warm water, sufficient boats and rafts, and the nearby shore, only the First Assistant Engineer, Herman J. Coates, Engine Cadet Vincent G. Cathey, eight other crewmen, and fifteen passengers of the 407 people aboard the *Robert E. Lee* were lost in the incident. The survivors were picked up by *PC-566*, another patrol boat, USS *SC 519,* as well as the tug *Underwriter*, and were landed at Venice, Louisiana.

Cadet-Midshipman Vincent G. Cathey was posthumously awarded the Mariner's Medal, the Combat Bar, the Atlantic War Zone Bar, the Victory Medal, and the Presidential Testimonial Letter.

Vincent G. Cathey was, according to the 1930 census, the youngest of Andrew R. and Cora Greene Cathey's three children. Vincent, who went by Gordon, grew up on the family farm outside of Andrews, North Carolina.

Gordon was a 1942 graduate of Andrews High School, where he was remembered as a popular student. He was in the cast of the Junior class play and was selected to be the toastmaster for the annual Junior-senior banquet. The Catheys were members of the Andrews Lutheran Church, where Gordon was the president of the Luther League and active in the church's "Light Brigade." After Gordon's death, his family presented a pair of altar vases in his name, which are believed to still be in the church.

Arthur Richard Chamberlin Jr.

Born:	November 24, 1921
Hometown:	Piedmont, CA
Class:	1943
Service:	Merchant Marine
Position / Rank:	Deck Cadet
Date / Place of death:	September 27, 1942/ South Atlantic, 28-08 S, 11-59 W
Date / Place of burial:	September 27, 1942 / South Atlantic, 28-08 S, 11-59 W
	Lost at Sea
Age:	20

Arthur R. Chamberlin signed on aboard the newly delivered Liberty ship SS *Stephen Hopkins* as Deck Cadet on May 16, 1942, at San Francisco, California. Also signing on as Engine Cadet on the same day was Edwin J. O'Hara.

After sailing across the Pacific with war cargo, the *Stephen Hopkins* called at Durban and Cape Town, South Africa, before sailing across the South Atlantic, bound for Paramaribo, Suriname. On September 27, 1942, the visibility was reduced due to fog and haze. Despite having five lookouts, no one aboard the *Stephen Hopkins* sighted either the German Raider *Stier* (known as *Raider J*) or its supply ship, *Tannenfels,* until 1235 GCT when they appeared out of the mist. Ordered to stop by the *Stier*, the *Stephen Hopkins*'s Master, Captain Paul Buck, refused and turned the ship away from the Germans to bring his heaviest weapon to bear, a single four-inch gun.

The *Stier* was armed with six 150 mm guns, one 75 mm gun, a twin 37 mm antiaircraft gun, and four 20 mm antiaircraft guns with modern fire control and trained naval gunners. The ship also had two float planes and two torpedo tubes. The *Tannenfels* was only armed with antiaircraft machine guns. Against this armament, the *Stephen Hopkins* had one four-inch gun, two 37 mm, and several .50—and .30-caliber antiaircraft machine guns manned by a small detachment of Naval Armed Guard and the ship's crew.

At 1238, the *Stier* began firing on the *Stephen Hopkins* at close range. Shrapnel and machine gun bullets rained down on the *Stephen Hopkins*'s crew, wounding or killing several men, including the Armed Guard Commander, Lt. (jg) Kenneth M. Willett, USNR. Despite his wounds, Willett got the guns manned and began returning fire at a range of about one thousand yards. Willett steadfastly continued to direct fire from the *Stephen Hopkins* on the two German vessels, while Captain Buck maneuvered to keep the ships stern pointed at the German ships. In their exposed post, the Naval Armed Guard crew was decimated by shells and machine gun bullets, leaving only the wounded Willett to keep the four-inch gun firing at the *Stier*'s waterline, inflicting heavy damage. When the ammunition magazine for the four-inch gun magazine exploded, Willett was out of action. Cadet Edwin J. O'Hara, who was nearby, rushed forward to take his place, firing the five shells left in the ready service locker. O'Hara fired the five remaining shells on the *Tannenfels* before being mortally wounded by enemy fire.

After twenty minutes of intense shelling, with the ship on fire and sinking, Captain Buck gave the order to abandon ship. The Second Assistant Engineer and the Steward lowered the only undamaged lifeboat over the side, and several other crew members lowered rafts. When last seen, Lieutenant Willett was cutting loose life rafts. The lifeboat then made the rounds in the water, collecting those crew members on rafts that it could reach until the men in the lifeboat could no longer see in the fog and mist. One raft with five men, including possibly Captain Buck, could not be reached and was never seen again. The survivors were able to see the *Stephen Hopkins* sink stern first and shortly afterward heard the detonation of the *Stier*'s ammunition magazines, sinking that ship. Only nineteen of the sixty men aboard the *Stephen Hopkins* made it to the lifeboat, including five wounded men. Among those who did not survive the battle were Cadets Edwin J. O'Hara and Arthur R. Chamberlin.

On September 28, the survivors of the *Stephen Hopkins* set their course west for South America. After a voyage of thirty-one days and 2,200 miles, fifteen of the men arrived at Barra-do-Itabapoana, Brazil, on October 27. The survivors told the story of the *Stephen Hopkins*'s fight with the two German ships the next day to Timothy J. Mahoney, the American vice consul in Brazil. However, press reports of the *Stephen Hopkins* did not appear until December.

When the press was able to report the story of the *Stephen Hopkins,* the ship was hailed as a "Hero Ship" and cited the action as the first between a German surface raider and U.S. merchant ship, which resulted in sinking the raider. For the action of September 27, 1942, the *Stephen Hopkins* and its crew were awarded the U.S. Maritime Commission's Gallant Ship Unit Citation.

The men of the *Stephen Hopkins* were also honored by a grateful nation. Lt. (jg) Kenneth M. Willett, USNR, was posthumously awarded the Navy Cross for his actions. Of the crew, Paul Buck, (Master), George S. Cronk (Second Assistant Engineer), Joseph Earl Layman (Second Mate), Richard Moczkowski (Chief Mate), Edwin J. O'Hara (Engine Cadet) and Ford Stilson (Chief Steward) were awarded the Merchant Marine Distinguished Service Medal. The awards for Buck, Layman, Moczkowski, and O'Hara were made posthumously.

Five ships were named in honor of the crew of the *Stephen Hopkins* and of the ship itself.

SS *Paul Buck*   SS *Richard Moczkowski*
SS *Edwin Joseph O'Hara*   SS *Stephen Hopkins II*
USS *Kenneth M. Willett* (DE 354)

In addition to the Gallant Ship Unit Citation, Cadet Arthur R. Chamberlin was posthumously awarded the Mariner's Medal, the Combat Bar, the Atlantic War Zone Bar, the Pacific War Zone Bar, the Victory Medal, and the Presidential Testimonial Letter.

Arthur "Artie" Chamberlin was the oldest of Arthur R. and Sadie Chamberlin's three sons. According to the 1930 census, Arthur Sr. was an x-ray technician. Artie is remembered by his brothers, John and Bob, as a great sailor and a skillful "scrounger." John recalled that as a boy, Arthur caught a few pollywogs and traded them for a Boy Scout knife, which he traded for a flashlight, which he traded for a pair of roller skates, right up the line, ultimately ending with a Snipe sailboat that he kept at the Berkeley Yacht Harbor. During the Depression, Arthur always had spending money because he had two paper routes and also worked at the Sixth Street Market in Oakland. In his "spare time," Artie also sold Christmas trees during the holidays and magazines "door to door" throughout the year. Bob fondly remembered sailing trips with his oldest brother on Lake Merritt in Oakland and on San Francisco Bay. The latter included an adventurous overnight sail in San Francisco Bay that was very impressive to his eight-year-old brother.

Artie Chamberlin at home

In his book, *Unsung Sailors: The Naval Armed Guard in World War II*, Justin F. Gleichauf reports that Arthur Chamberlin formed a close friendship with Wallace Breck, one of the *Hopkins*'s Armed Guard gunners. According to Gleichauf, Chamberlin taught Breck seamanship and navigation. Breck survived the sinking of the *Hopkins* and visited Chamberlin's family to offer his sympathy and share the details of Chamberlin's death.

The Chamberlin brothers with their mother (l-r John, Bob, and Arthur)

John, Bob, and Artie in the tub

Denniston Charlton Jr.

Born: December 28, 1923
Hometown: Great Neck, NY
Class: 1944
Service: Merchant Marine
Position / Rank: Deck Cadet
Date / Place of death: January 1, 1943 /
                           Mediterranean Sea,
                           35-34 N, 00-4 W
Date / Place of burial: January 1, 1943 /
                           Mediterranean Sea,
                           35-34 N, 00-45 W /
                           Lost at Sea
Age: 19

Denniston Charlton signed on aboard the SS *Arthur Middleton* as Deck Cadet on November 21, 1942, at New York, New York. Also aboard was Engine Cadet Ben Gafford. At New York and Norfolk, Virginia, the *Arthur Middleton* loaded a cargo of ammunition, explosives, and mail with *LCT-21* stowed on deck. The ship sailed from Hampton Roads on December 12, 1942, for Oran, Algeria as part of a "slow" convoy, UGS-3 with forty-two crew, twenty-seven Armed Guard, and twelve passengers (eleven crew from *LCT-21* and one Army officer).

Upon arrival at Casablanca, Morocco, eleven ships bound for nearby Oran split off from the convoy and proceeded to their destination. When the eleven ships were about eight miles away from Oran, the convoy slowed, and the signal was given for single column for entry into the harbor. The SS *Rhode Island*, the Commodore's ship, was maneuvering at slow speed to line up for the harbor approach, while the other ships formed a line astern.

The *Arthur Middleton* was near the port quarter of the *Rhode Island* when it was struck near the bow by two torpedoes fired by *U-73* at 1411 (GCT). According to *U-73*'s Commanding Officer, the *Arthur Middleton* violently exploded less than twenty seconds after being hit by the torpedoes, sending flames and parts of the ship soaring one thousand feet into the air. The front half of the ship disintegrated from the number 5 hatch to the bow, but a small section of the stern remained afloat for about a minute. Of the eighty-one men on board, only three men, members of the Armed

Guard who had been stationed on the after section and were able to jump overboard, survived. These three were picked up twenty-five minutes after the attack by the HMS *Boreas* (H77) and transferred to the British Hospital Ship, HMHS *Oxfordshire*. Denniston Charlton Jr. and Ben P. Gafford were among those lost in the attack.

Cadet-Midshipman Denniston Charlton was posthumously awarded the Mariner's Medal, the Combat Bar, the Atlantic War Zone Bar, the Mediterranean-Middle East War Zone Bar, the Victory Medal, and the Presidential Testimonial Letter.

Denniston Charlton Jr. was the son of Denniston and Lois Wibberly Charlton. He had one older sister, Lois Elizabeth. According to passenger lists for ships arriving in the Port of New York, Denniston and his sister visited Havana, Cuba, with their mother in 1926 and 1928. The senior Charlton was a successful produce manager in a Connecticut supermarket. The family moved to Great Neck, Long Island, sometime before 1939, where Denniston Jr. finished high school.

Marion Michael Chrobak

Born:	September 8, 1921
Hometown:	Linden, NJ
Class:	1944
Service:	Merchant Marine
Position / Rank:	Engine Cadet
Date / Place of death:	January 9, 1943 / North Atlantic, 56-15 N, 22-00 W
Date / Place of burial:	January 9, 1943 / North Atlantic, 56-15 N, 22-00 W / Lost at Sea
Age:	21

Marion M. Chrobak signed on as Engine Cadet aboard the SS *Louise Lykes* on December 29, 1942, at the Port of New York. He joined four other Kings Point Cadet-Midshipmen: Charles Gassner (deck), Allen Miller (deck), Robert Vancure (engine), and Eugene Walters (deck), who had made the ship's previous voyage to the Mediterranean. In addition, the ship's Third Assistant Engineer, Frederick Baumann, and Third Mate, Harry Wolfe, were former U.S. Maritime Commission Cadet Officers.

The SS *Louise Lykes* sailed without escort from New York on January 2, 1943, carrying a cargo of ammunition and other war supplies bound for Belfast, Northern Ireland. The ship was hit by four torpedoes fired from the surfaced *U-384* at 2025 on the evening of January 9, 1943. According to German Navy records, the *Louise Lykes* cargo exploded with what was described as "a terrible blast," forcing *U-384* to dive to avoid being struck by pieces of the wreckage. There were no survivors among the fifty merchant crew, thirty-four Naval Armed Guard, and ten U.S. Army personnel aboard. This was the single deadliest sinking in the Academy's history in terms of Cadet losses.

Marion Michael Chrobak was posthumously awarded the Mariner's Medal, the Combat Bar, the Atlantic War Zone Bar, the Victory Medal, and the Presidential Testimonial Letter.

Marion M. Chrobak was the eldest son of Stanislaw and Frances Chrobak, Polish immigrants. According to the 1930 U.S. Census, Stanislaw Chrobak was employed as a pipe fitter at a factory in New Jersey, while Frances worked as a housekeeper for another family. Marion had an older sister, Sophie, and a younger brother, Chester.

SS *Louise Lykes*

Peter Nicholas Chunosoff

Born: November 10, 1922
Hometown: Brooklyn, NY
Class: 1943
Service: Merchant Marine
Position / Rank: Deck Cadet
Date / Place of death: May 28, 1942 /
                         Caribbean,
                         16-28 N, 67-37 W
Date / Place of burial: May 28, 1942 /
                         Caribbean,
                         16-28 N, 67-37 W /
                         Lost at Sea
Age: 19

Peter N. Chunosoff was assigned as Deck Cadet aboard the SS *Alcoa Pilgrim* from the New Orleans Basic School on March 4, 1942. Also aboard the *Alcoa Pilgrim* was Cadet-Midshipman Edward T. Ursin, the Engine Cadet.

SS *Alcoa Puritan* (yard sister ship of the SS *Alcoa Pilgrim*)

On the night of May 27/28, the *Alcoa Pilgrim* was en route from Port of Spain, Trinidad, to Mobile, Alabama, loaded with 9,500 tons of bauxite. According to the Navy report on the sinking, the *Alcoa Pilgrim* was unarmed and zigzagging on a westerly heading at 15.5 knots. Around 0100 (GCT), when the *Alcoa Pilgrim* was about 150 miles south of the Mona Passage, the ship was sighted by *U-502* in the bright moonlight. Shortly thereafter, *U-502* fired one torpedo, which struck the *Alcoa Pilgrim* on the starboard side at the engine room, just below the water line. The engine room was destroyed in the explosion, and the ship sank in the next ninety seconds without being able to send a distress signal.

No boats were successfully launched, though at least one was lowered as the ship began to sink. Deck Cadet Peter Chunosoff was lost overboard when this lifeboat capsized. Engine Cadet Edward T. Ursin was able to escape on one of the two life rafts that managed to get clear of the ship.

Shortly after the sinking, *U-502* approached one of the rafts. The submarine's Commander asked in fluent English for the name and nationality of the ship, the tonnage and cargo, and whether the life raft had a sail. The *U-502* then left the area at full speed. Only nine of the forty crew members survived the sinking. The survivors, including Cadet Ursin, were picked up from the two life rafts on June 2 by the SS *Thomas Nelson* and landed at Port of Spain on June 5, 1942.

Cadet-Midshipman Peter N. Chunosoff was posthumously awarded the Mariner's Medal, the Combat Bar, the Atlantic War Zone Bar, the Merchant Marine Defense Bar, the Victory Medal, and the Presidential Testimonial Letter.

Peter N. Chunosoff was the eldest child of Nicholas, a Russian immigrant, and Cecilia Chunosoff. According to the 1940 U.S. Census, Nicholas was employed as a shipping clerk in a department store. Peter had a sister, Laura, who was three years younger than he. Crew lists on file in Boston, New York, indicate that Peter signed on as Ordinary Seaman aboard the SS *Express* at New York, New York, on June 3, 1941, and was discharged there after a voyage to India in late September 1941. He was described as being six feet one inch tall and weighing 163 pounds. Given the dates, it appears that he applied for admission to the Merchant Marine Cadet Corps shortly after leaving the SS *Express* and began his training in early 1942.

Alan R. Clarke

Born:	February 8, 1922
Hometown:	Ridgewood, NJ
Class:	1944
Service:	Merchant Marine
Position / Rank:	Deck Cadet
Date / Place of death:	March 2, 1943 / North Atlantic, 62-10 N, 28-25 W
Date / Place of burial:	March 2, 1943 / North Atlantic, 62-10 N, 28-25 W / Lost at Sea
Age:	21

Alan R. Clarke signed on aboard the SS *Meriwether Lewis* as Deck Cadet on October 13, 1942, at New York, New York. His classmate Randall Bourell signed on as Deck Cadet two days later. The two Engine Cadets were Walter E. Johnson and Daniel J. Maher. Former USMCC Cadet Officer James J. Coffey was Second Mate. After an uneventful voyage to Casablanca, French Morocco, the ship returned to New York on January 10, 1943. Johnson was replaced by Francis McCann around January 25, 1943. On February 18, 1943, the *Meriwether Lewis* with its four Kings Point Cadets sailed from New York as part of Convoy HX-227 bound for the United Kingdom and then to Murmansk, Russia. The ship was loaded with a cargo of vehicle tires, ammunition, and based upon some references, a deck cargo of PT boats.

According to German Navy records, the *Meriwether Lewis* was identified as a straggler from a convoy and unsuccessfully attacked by *U-759* in the early morning of March 2. The submarine was unable to re-attack the *Meriwether Lewis* due to the sub's problems with its engines, but it was able to contact *U-634* and lead it to the straggler. The *U-634* fired four torpedoes at the *Meriwether Lewis*, hitting it with one of them. The damage was apparently sufficient to stop the ship, but did not sink it. The submarine hit the *Meriwether Lewis* with two more torpedoes, the last of which detonated the ship's ammunition cargo. Although there was plenty of time to abandon ship, the USCGC *Ingham* (WPG 35) found only a thirty-mile line of floating tires during its two-day-long search for the *Meriwether Lewis* and crew. Thus, the ship's entire crew of forty-four, including Second Mate James J. Coffey and the four Kings Point Cadets, and twenty-eight members of the Naval Armed Guard perished in the sinking.

Cadet-Midshipman Alan R. Clarke was posthumously awarded the Mariner's Medal, the Combat Bar, the Atlantic War Zone Bar, the Victory Medal, and the Presidential Testimonial Letter.

Alan R. Clarke was the only son of Robert Clarke and Ruth Clarke. According to his classmate, David Douglas (KP '44), Robert Clarke was a senior executive of the Seamen's Bank for Savings in New York. David Douglas said that he was told by his grandmother that both of the Clarkes died of grief not long after Alan's death.

Aubrey George Connors

Born: November 6, 1922
Hometown: Lincolnville, ME
Class: 1944
Service: Merchant Marine
Position / Rank: Deck Cadet
Date / Place of death: April 23, 1943/ 57-30N, 43-00W
Date / Place of burial: April 23, 1943/ Lost at Sea—57-30 N, 43-00 W
Age: 20

Aubrey G. Connors signed on the SS *Robert Gray* as Deck Cadet on April 3, 1943, at the port of Baltimore, New York. His classmate Stephen Siviglia signed on the same day as Engine Cadet. A week later, on April 12, 1943, the ship sailed from New York with a number of other ships in Convoy HX 234 bound for Liverpool, England, loaded with a cargo that included ammunition or explosives. For unknown reasons, the *Robert Gray* fell back from the convoy on the night of April 13/14. Although ordered to return to Halifax, the ship apparently attempted to follow or rejoin the convoy but was never heard from again.

After the war, German Navy records told the rest of the story. The ship was spotted by *U-108* at a little before 3:00 a.m. on April 19 while the submarine was running on the surface about 125 miles south of Cape Farrell, Greenland. The submarine fired four torpedoes and heard two explosions. However, the ship did not sink immediately, and its gun crews began firing at the surfaced submarine, forcing it to dive. While submerged, *U-108* fired two more torpedoes, with the final torpedo hitting the *Robert Gray* a little after 5:00 a.m., local time. This caused a fire and explosion in the ship's cargo, sinking the ship quickly by the stern. There were no survivors among the crew of thirty-nine and the twenty-three Naval Armed Guard sailors. On June 14, 1943, the Navy Department determined that since the *Robert Gray* had not been heard from since April 13/14, it must be presumed lost.

Cadet-Midshipman Aubrey G. Connors was posthumously awarded the Mariner's Medal, the Combat Bar with star, the Atlantic War Zone Bar, the Victory Medal, and the Presidential Testimonial Letter.

**1939 high school
graduation photo**

Aubrey G. Connors, the second of three children of Wilbur S. Connors and Ellen J. Connors, was born in Yarmouth, Nova Scotia. In 1927, the Connors family left their farm in Nova Scotia and moved to Brooklyn, New York, where Aubrey started grade school in 1928 at PS 132. The family moved again in 1934 to a farm near Lincolnville, Maine. Aubrey, his older brother, Ernest, and younger sister, Lucille, attended elementary school there through eighth grade. After eighth grade, he moved on to the high school in nearby Camden, where Aubrey graduated in 1939. In addition to being an avid sportsman, Aubrey was also a talented bass horn player in the Camden and Lincolnville bands.

In 1941, Aubrey accepted a job at Sperry Gyroscope Company and moved to Brooklyn. He was able to continue playing music with the Sperry Gyroscope Band. While he was employed at Sperry, Aubrey's older brother, Ernest, entered Kings Point and graduated in 1943. Aubrey followed his brother to Kings Point, entering in 1942. While the Connors boys were at Kings Point, their sister, Lucille, was attending Columbia University.

**From left to right: Aubrey (4), Lucy (2),
and Ernest (6 ½)**

Howard Payne Conway Jr.

Born:	January 9, 1919
Hometown:	Charlotte, NC
Class:	1943
Service:	Merchant Marine
Position / Rank:	Engine Cadet
Date / Place of death:	March 19, 1942 / U.S. East Coast, 35-05 N, 75-30 W
Date / Place of burial:	March 19, 1942 / U.S. East Coast, 35-05 N, 75-30 W / Lost at Sea
Age:	23

Howard P. Conway signed on the SS *Liberator* as Engine Cadet on March 4, 1942, at New Orleans, Louisiana. He had previously served aboard the SS *Howell Lykes*. Sometime thereafter, the ship loaded eleven thousand tons of sulfur at Galveston and was bound for the Port of New York without escort. On the morning of March 19, 1942, the ship was three miles west of the Diamond Shoals buoy when it was sighted by *U-332*. The fact that the *Liberator* was not steering an evasive course made the ship an easy target for the submarine, which fired one torpedo at the ship. At 1619 (GCT), the torpedo hit the *Liberator*'s port side, destroying the engine room and killing five men, including Engine Cadet Conway. The explosion destroyed one lifeboat and blew the hatch off of number 4 hold. However, during the twenty minutes or so the ship remained afloat; the thirty-one surviving crew members launched the rest of the lifeboats and got away from the ship. They were picked up later the same day by the Navy tug, USS *Umpqua* (AT-25), and transported to Morehead City, North Carolina.

Although Cadet-Midshipmen Lewis and See had actually been lost in a sinking almost a month before this, the news of Cadet Conway's fate was the first confirmation of a fatality to reach the U.S. Merchant Marine Cadet Corps schools at Kings Point and Pass Christian. At both schools, Conway was mourned as the first Cadet to die in the conflict. The mess hall at Pass Christian was later named in his honor.

Cadet-Midshipman Howard P. Conway was posthumously awarded the Mariners Medal, Combat Bar with star, Atlantic War Zone Bar, the Victory Medal and the Presidential Testimonial Letter.

Howard P. Conway Jr. was the only child of Howard Payne and Miriam Parker Conway. The elder Conway was the southern district manager for Grinnell Company and also for the General Fire Extinguisher Company, based in Charlotte, North Carolina. Father and son often took saltwater fishing trips. Howard Jr. attended Woodberry Forest Preparatory School in Virginia, where he was elected senior prefect in recognition of his personal integrity. After graduating from Woodberry Forest, Howard attended and graduated from Williams College.

James Sinclair Cordua

Born:	January 14, 1922	
Hometown:	Lost Creek, WV	
Class:	1944	
Service:	Merchant Marine	
Position / Rank:	Deck Cadet	
Date / Place of death:	March 10, 1943 / North Atlantic, 51-35 N, 28-30 W	
Date / Place of burial:	March 10, 1943 / North Atlantic, 51-35 N, 28-3 W / Lost at Sea	
Age:	21	

James S. Cordua signed on the SS *William C. Gorgas* as Deck Cadet in Mobile, Alabama, on January 27, 1943, shortly after the ship was delivered to the War Shipping Administration from its builder. Joining Cadet-Midshipman Cordua were three of his classmates, Edwin Hanzik, James Moon, and Edwin Wiggin. Already aboard was the ship's Third Mate, 1942 Cadet Corps alumnus Rafael R. Rivera. Six weeks later, on March 10, 1943, the *Gorgas* was traveling in Convoy HX-228 en route from New York to Liverpool loaded with general cargo, including nine hundred tons of explosives and a deck cargo of an LCT and two PT boats. The ship carried a crew of forty-one merchant mariners and twenty-six Naval Armed Guard sailors.

At around 2030 on March 10, another ship in the convoy was torpedoed, and the general alarm was sounded. The crew remained on alert, with the Naval Armed Guard manning the battle stations. The weather was hazy, with moderate to heavy swells and ten to fifteen knot winds in bright moonlight. At 2330, the *Gorgas* was hit on the starboard side amidships by a torpedo fired by *U-757*. The explosion destroyed the engine room, instantly killing the three engineers on watch. The Master ordered the crew to abandon ship. By 2350, when 51 survivors in lifeboats and rafts had left the ship, snow had begun falling in higher winds. The *U-757* located one of the boats and questioned the survivors. Shortly thereafter the submarine found the ship still afloat and fired another torpedo to sink it. Immediately after the ship settled under the waves its ammunition cargo exploded, damaging *U-757* so much that it was unable to dive. The submarine was escorted on the surface back to France by another submarine.

The *Gorgas*'s fifty-one survivors were picked up at about 0700 on March 11 by the destroyer HMS *Harvester* (H 19). Shortly after rescuing the *Gorgas*'s survivors, the *Harvester* sighted *U-444* on the surface. Although the submarine dove to escape the *Harvester*'s gunfire, a depth charge attack brought the submarine to the surface. It is unclear why the *Harvester*'s Commander made his decision, but *U-444* was rammed at full speed by the *Harvester*, severely damaging both ships.

Although *U-444* was able to break free of the *Harvester*, it was rammed again and sunk by the Free French corvette *Aconit* (K 58). The almost motionless *Harvester* was easy prey for *U-432,* which fired two torpedoes, quickly sinking the destroyer with nearly all of its crew and thirty-nine of the *Gorgas*'s survivors. The *Aconit* was immediately on scene attacking the *U-432* with depth charges and forcing it to the surface. The *Aconit* fired at the surfaced submarine and then rammed it, sending the *U-432* and all but twenty of its crew to the bottom. With this vital task accomplished, the *Aconit* rescued twelve *Gorgas*'s survivors, forty-eight survivors of HMS *Harvester*, and twenty-four German sailors from *U-444* and *U-432*.

Launching of SS *William C. Gorgas*

After the *Harvester* sank, the Master of the *Gorgas*, James Calvin Ellis Jr., was seen by some of the survivors floating in a life ring in the cold seas. When he was offered a place on a life raft by one of the seamen, he declined, telling the man to keep his place. Soon after, he lost his grip on the life ring and was lost in the icy waters.

James Cordua, his three U.S. Merchant Marine Academy classmates, and 1942 graduate Rafael R. Rivera were among those lost. It is believed that all five survived the initial attack but were lost in the subsequent sinking of HMS *Harvester*.

Cadet-Midshipman James S. Cordua was posthumously awarded the Mariner's Medal, the Combat Bar with star, the Atlantic War Zone Bar, the Victory Medal, and the Presidential Testimonial Letter.

James S. Cordua listed his sister, Marcella K. Cordua Grazzini, who was living in Washington DC, as his next of kin. No other information about his background could be located.

Vincent Jerome Corrigan

Born: July 19, 1922
Hometown: Glendale, NY
Class: 1944
Service: Merchant Marine
Position / Rank: Engine Cadet
Date / Place of death: January 27, 1943 /
                           Atlantic, 36-37 N,
                           30-55 W
Date / Place of burial: January 27, 1943 /
                           Atlantic, 36-37 N,
                           30-55 W / Lost at Sea
Age: 22

Vincent J. Corrigan signed on the SS *Charles C. Pinckney* as Engine Cadet on January 1, 1943, at the Port of New York. Joining him on the ship was his classmate, Deck Cadet Robert Lamac. On the same day, Theodore Scharpf, a former Merchant Marine Cadet Corps Cadet Officer, signed on as First Assistant Engineer.

The *Pinckney* sailed with Convoy UGS-4 from Hampton Roads, Virginia, on January 13, 1943, loaded with ammunition, a general cargo of war supplies, and mechanized equipment bound for Casablanca. On the night of January 21, 1943, the *Charles Pinckney*, the SS *City of Flint*, and the SS *Julia Ward Howe* straggled from the convoy. All three, no longer protected by the convoy escort of six U.S. Navy destroyers, were sunk by U-boats within a week.

On January 27 the *Pinckney* was about two hundred miles south-southwest of Fayal Island, Azores. During the morning, the watch sighted a submarine far off on the horizon, traveling parallel to the *Pinckney*, apparently at great speed. The gun crew fired a few shots at the submarine, but even at maximum elevation, these did not come close to their target. The *Pinckney* then increased to its maximum speed of 11 knots.

Late in the afternoon, the *Pinckney* changed its course to proceed directly away from the submarine, but the crew was unable to tell whether or not the submarine followed. At about 2145, local time, the Chief Mate observed a torpedo, fired by *U-514,* heading directly for the ship, and ordered a hard-right rudder. The order came too late, and the torpedo struck just behind the ship's bow, detonating part of the cargo. The explosion blew off the bow, killing two men in the forward gun crew. On the Captain's order, the crew abandoned ship immediately, with all but one of the boats lowered successfully. The gun crew remained on the ship at great peril to their own lives, given the cargo of munitions on board. When the German submarine, which had fired the torpedo, later surfaced near the port beam, the gun crew fired on the sub. Although the gun crew claimed they sunk the submarine, it had actually made an emergency dive.

Since the ship did not immediately sink, the crew reboarded the ship to see if it could be repaired. After inspecting the ship's engines, the Chief Engineer reported that it would not be possible to raise steam and continue sailing the ship. However, the crew was able to collect additional supplies and send a distress signal. Around midnight, *U-514* fired two more torpedoes; the second torpedo hit the *Pinckney,* and the crew abandoned ship again. Soon thereafter, *U-514* approached the boats and questioned the survivors.

The four lifeboats began making way for the Azores but were unable to stay together in heavy seas during the second night. One lifeboat, carrying six crew members, including the second officer, and eight Naval Armed Guard sailors, was picked up on February 8 by the Swiss ship *Caritas I* and later landed at Horta, Faial Island, Azores. The other three lifeboats were never seen again. Of the seventy-three persons aboard the *Pinckney* (forty-two crew, twenty-nine Naval Armed Guard, and two U.S. Army security officers), only the above mentioned fourteen were rescued. Cadet-Midshipmen Vincent Corrigan and Robert Louis Lamac, along with First Assistant Engineer Theodore Scharpf, were among those lost.

Cadet-Midshipman Vincent J. Corrigan was posthumously awarded the Mariner's Medal, the Combat Bar with star, the Atlantic War Zone Bar, the Victory Medal, and the Presidential Testimonial Letter.

Vincent J. Corrigan was the only son of Alice Corrigan. According to U.S. Census records Vincent and his mother lived with his grandparents, Michael and Marry Corrigan, and their three adult children in Queens, New York. Vincent started his Basic School training at Kings Point in October 1942.

Robert John Derick

Born:	April 2, 1923
Hometown:	East Hartford, CT
Class:	1944
Service:	Merchant Marine
Position / Rank:	Engine Cadet
Date / Place of death:	August 19, 1943 / North Atlantic, 36-37 N, 30-55 W
Date / Place of burial:	September 3, 1943 / Sydney, Nova Scotia; 1949 / Jefferson Barracks National Cemetery, St. Louis, MO, Section 82 Site 7-10
Age:	20

Robert J. Derick signed on as Engine Cadet aboard the SS *J. Pinckney Henderson* on July 23, 1943, with his classmate, Deck Cadet Roscoe J. Prickett Jr. By August 14, 1943, the *J. Pinckney Henderson* had been loaded with a cargo of magnesium, glycerin, resin, oil, and wax and sailed for Liverpool as part of Convoy HX-252.

The weather from August 14 onward was bad, with both high seas and fog. On the evening of August 19, the *Henderson* collided with the Panamanian flag tanker *J. H. Senior*. The *J. H. Senior* was carrying aviation gasoline, which exploded, showering both ships with burning high-octane gasoline. Within moments, both ships were transformed into infernos. Three crew members on the *Henderson* and six others on the *J. H. Senior* were able to leap into the sea and save themselves. The remaining crew members of both ships, including Cadet-Midshipmen John R. Derick and Roscoe J. Prickett, were killed in the fire.

The *J. Pinckney Henderson* was initially thought to be salvageable and was towed to Sydney, Nova Scotia, while still in flames. However, she continued to burn for another month and was eventually declared a total loss. The hulk was later towed to Philadelphia and scrapped. On September 3, 1943, the charred remains of thirty-four unidentifiable bodies were buried with naval honors in a mass grave at Sydney. A Monument was also erected there in their honor. Sometime around 1949, the remains were exhumed and reinterred in a mass grave at the Jefferson Barracks National Cemetery. At the same time, the Monument to the crew of the *J. P. Henderson* was moved to Kings Point.

The Monument to the men of the *J.P. Henderson* languished in relative anonymity until 2004 when it was installed in a place of honor at the entrance of the American Merchant Marine Museum adjacent to the U.S. Merchant Marine Academy.

**Headstone for the mass grave of the deceased of the
SS *J. Pinckney Henderson*, Jefferson Barracks National Cemetery,
St. Louis, Missouri**

Cadet-Midshipman Robert J. Derick was posthumously awarded the Mariner's Medal, the Atlantic War Zone Bar, the Victory Medal, and the Presidential Testimonial Letter.

Robert J. Derick was the son of Sarah M. Derick of East Hartford, Connecticut. No other information on his background could be located.

Joseph Carlo DiCicco

Born:	September 10, 1922
Hometown:	Brooklyn, NY
Class:	1943
Service:	Merchant Marine
Position / Rank:	Engine Cadet
Date / Place of death:	September 10, 1942 / South Atlantic
Date / Place of burial:	September 10, 1942 / South Atlantic—Buried at Sea
Age:	21

Joseph C. DiCicco signed on as Engine Cadet aboard the MS *American Leader* on April 13, 1942, at the Port of New York. According to the account of Captain George Duffy, then the Third Mate; the ship was carrying a general cargo of war supplies, including boots, barbed wire, and vehicles, along with a deck cargo of nine twin-engine bombers from New York to the Persian Gulf for Russia. The ship was also carrying several thousand tons of steel ingots for India. The *American Leader* was armed with what a survivor characterized as an "ancient four-inch cannon on our stern plus four machine guns—two of which never fired one round without jamming."

MS *American Leader*

The ship arrived safely in the Persian Gulf and loaded a cargo of rugs and chemicals before sailing for Colombo, Ceylon (Sri Lanka), to load a cargo of rubber and latex. The *American Leader* headed alone down the coast of Africa to Cape Town, South Africa. Upon arrival at Cape Town on September 7, 1942, the ship was ordered to continue westward, without escort, toward the Straits of Magellan and the Pacific Ocean. At about 1930, on September 10, the *American Leader* ran afoul of the German Navy commerce raider, *Michel*, a converted merchant ship that had been operating in the South Atlantic.

The *Michel*, disguised as a neutral merchant ship, fired on the *American Leader* with deck guns and then launched two torpedoes. The *Michel*'s crew managed to destroy two of the lifeboats as the crew attempted to launch them, forcing the crew to abandon in life rafts. The *American Leader* sank in about twenty-five minutes, and ten crew members, including Cadet-Midshipmen Joseph C. DiCicco and Gordon Tyne, were killed in the attack. The thirty-nine crew members and nine Naval Armed Guard sailors who survived the sinking were taken prisoner by the *Michel*.

In addition to the survivors, the crew of the *Michel* recovered one body, which could not be recognized. After interviewing George Duffy, the *Michel*'s doctor determined that the body was that of DiCicco. Cadet-Midshipman Joseph C. DiCicco was buried at sea on the evening of September 10, 1942, with full military honors, including an American flag to cover him. The *Michel*'s Commanding Officer, Helmuth von Ruckteschell, invited the *American Leader*'s Captain, Chief Officer, and First Assistant Engineer to the service. During the service, von Ruckteschell reportedly said, "If all the people of the world held each other in the same respect as their seamen do, we would not be in this terrible situation on board here tonight." Joseph DiCicco is believed to be the only U.S. Merchant Marine Academy Cadet-Midshipman to have been given a formal funeral by the enemy.

The survivors, now prisoners of war, including the *American Leader*'s Second Mate, 1940 Cadet Officer Walter Hay Lee, were handed over to the Japanese in Batavia, Java (present-day Djakarta, Indonesia), in November 1942. In September 1944, Lee and several other *American Leader* survivors were killed in the sinking of the prisoner transport *Junyo Maru* when it was torpedoed by HMS *Tradewind* (P 329). Other *American Leader*'s survivors were killed in the sinking of the Japanese prisoner transport *Tomahaku Maru*. Of the fifty-eight merchant seamen and Naval

Armed Guard on the *American Leader*, only twenty-eight (including Captain Duffy) eventually made it home. All of these had survived more than two years as prisoners of war.

Joseph C. DiCicco at left in Color Guard at KP in 1942

Cadet-Midshipman Joseph C. DiCicco was posthumously awarded the Mariner's Medal, the Combat Bar, the Atlantic War Zone Bar, the Mediterranean-Middle East War Zone Bar, the Victory Medal, and the Presidential Testimonial Letter.

Joseph C. DiCicco was the oldest child and only son of Joseph and Elizabeth DiCicco. According to the 1930 U.S. Census, the elder DiCicco was a Carpenter and they had a daughter Dorothy who was two years old.

Joseph Leonard Driscoll

Born:	August 20, 1923
Hometown:	Brooklyn, NY
Class:	1945
Service:	Merchant Marine
Position / Rank:	Deck Cadet
Date / Place of death:	January 6, 1944 / Mediterranean, 37-22 N, 9-55 E
Date / Place of burial:	January 8 1944 / 2nd Corps U.S. Army Cemetery, Mateur, Tunisia, Plot E, Row 5, Grave 23
Age:	22

Joseph L. Driscoll signed on as Deck Cadet aboard the SS *Robert Erskine* on July 17, 1943, at the Port of New York. In the coming months, the *Robert Erskine* made two voyages across the Atlantic to ports in the United Kingdom and returned to New York. On September 29, 1943, Joseph Driscoll was joined by Cadet-Midshipman Robert W. Hempel, Engine Cadet. The *Robert Erskine* sailed from Norfolk, Virginia, on its third voyage on December 14, 1943, as part of Convoy UGS-27 bound for Naples, Italy. The ship's cargo was five-hundred-pound aircraft bombs, detonators, aircraft engines, and Army trucks.

SS *Robert Erskine*

On January 2, 1944, the convoy passed through the Straits of Gibraltar and began to split into groups headed to different ports. The *Robert Erskine*, with about seventy-five other vessels, proceeded to the port of Bizerte, Tunisia, to await a convoy to Naples, Italy. The vessel dropped anchor just inside the submarine nets at the harbor entrance a little after 2230, local time, January 5, 1944, in a heavy storm. However, by 0200, local time, on January 6, 1944, the ship's anchor chain began jumping off of the wildcat on the anchor windlass due to the heavy seas. The Captain decided to pull up the anchor and cruise just outside the harbor until daylight.

The ship returned to Bizerte Harbor and dropped anchor again at about 0500 on January 6. However, the anchors began dragging in the heavy seas. By 0520, the *Robert Erskine* was hard aground inside Bizerte Harbor and was unable to work itself off. At 0730, the ship broke in two just forward of the engine room. The crew was ordered to collect their personal effects and be ready to be taken off by an Army tugboat. However, after waiting for an hour, the *Erskine* was informed that the tug was unable to come alongside due to the heavy seas. At this point, the Captain ordered the crew to abandon ship. Despite the heavy seas and interference from the drifting forward portion of the ship, the ship's motor lifeboat and a life raft were launched. Both of the craft were overturned before reaching shore, throwing their occupants into the sea. Fortunately, the occupants were able to swim to the safety of the nearby beach.

The Captain next ordered Cadets Driscoll and Hempel, along with an Ordinary Seaman and the ship's Carpenter, to try to make shore in a small "doughnut" raft. Just as with the larger craft, the raft and its four occupants overturned in heavy seas. No sooner did the men clamber back onto the raft than it overturned again. Cadet Hempel, noticing that the raft was snagged in a rope, took out his knife and cut the rope. Hempel, Driscoll, and the Carpenter managed to climb on once again, but the Ordinary Seaman could not reach the raft and eventually made it to shore. The raft then began to drift back toward the ship. The cold and exhausted men decided to swim back to the ship. Hempel and the Carpenter made it back to the ship, but Hempel discovered that Driscoll had remained on the raft. It is unclear from the available reports whether Cadet-Midshipman Driscoll actually returned aboard the *Robert Erskine* on January 6, 1945. His body was found on the beach and identified by Hempel on January 8, 1945. He was buried in the Second Corps Army Cemetery at Mateur, Tunisia, with full military honors. At some point after the war, his remains were exhumed and returned to the United States for final burial.

Cadet-Midshipman Hempel and the rest of the crew were rescued from the remains of the wreck on the morning of January 7, when the seas had calmed sufficiently to permit a rescue by boat. The salvage of the *Robert Erskine*'s cargo lasted until February. Several members of the engine crew, including Engine Cadet Hempel, remained to provide steam to the cargo winches. They, along with most of the crew of the *Robert Erskine,* were transferred to the bomb-damaged Liberty ship SS *James W. Marshall,* which was being repaired for return to the United States. Cadet-Midshipman Hempel sailed on the *James Marshall* as acting Third Assistant Engineer until its arrival in England in March. Hempel and other members of the *Robert Erskine*'s crew boarded the SS *Emma Willard* to return to the United States and the Academy for further training.

Cadet-Midshipman Joseph L. Driscoll was posthumously awarded the Mariner's Medal, the Atlantic War Zone Bar, the Mediterranean-Middle East War Zone Bar, the Victory Medal, and the Presidential Testimonial Letter.

On the *Robert Erskine*'s crew lists, Joseph L. Driscoll is described as being five feet six inches tall and weighing 130 pounds. He was the son of Dorothy E. Wells of Brooklyn, New York. Norman S. Wells, a sibling, lives in Arlington, VA.

Roy Joseph DuChene Jr.

Born: February 1, 1926
Hometown: Detroit, MI
Class: 1945
Service: Merchant Marine
Position / Rank: Deck Cadet
Date / Place of death: January 30, 1945 /
                         Detroit, MI
Date / Place of burial: Unknown / Detroit, MI
Age: 18

Roy J. DuChene signed on as Deck Cadet aboard the SS *Examiner* on September 7, 1944, at the Port of New York. He signed off on or about January 15, 1945, after voyages to ports in the United Kingdom. He apparently traveled to his home in Detroit, Michigan, and became ill. He died on January 30, 1945, at a hospital in Detroit, Michigan. The cause of death was listed as viral pneumonia, congestive heart failure, and nephritis.

Based on his merchant marine service aboard the SS *Examiner*, Cadet-Midshipman Roy J. Duchene Jr. would have been posthumously awarded the Atlantic War Zone Bar, the Victory Medal, and the Presidential Testimonial Letter.

Roy was the younger of Roy J. and Isabel DuChene's two sons. Roy Sr. was a purchasing agent for a factory in Detroit. By 1940, Roy's older brother James was working as a salesman at an electrical supply house. The crew lists for the SS *Examiner* described Roy as being five feet six inches tall and weighing 145 pounds.

Irwin Stutz Ebel

Born: March 13, 1923
Hometown: Brooklyn, NY
Class: 1943
Service: Merchant Marine
Position / Rank: Engine Cadet
Date / Place of death: May 19, 1942 / 28-53 N, 91-03 W
Date / Place of burial: May 19, 1942 / Lost at Sea— 28-53 N, 91-03 W
Age: 19

Cadet-Midshipman Irwin S. Ebel signed on aboard the passenger cargo ship SS *Heredia* as Engine Cadet on April 23, 1942, at New Orleans, Louisiana. In addition to Ebel, Cadet-Midshipman Glenn Bruaw, Deck Cadet was also aboard.

SS *Heredia*

On May 19, 1942, the ship was returning to New Orleans from Puerto Barrios, Guatemala, loaded with forty thousand stems of bananas and five thousand bags of coffee. The ship was traveling without an escort and was not zigzagging, since the Navy did not believe that any German submarines were operating in the Gulf of Mexico. However, the German Navy had recently ordered the submarines of their Tenth U-boat Flotilla to begin operating in the Gulf of Mexico to interrupt the flow of petroleum products and supplies to the U.S. East Coast and Caribbean. During the month of May 1942, these submarines sank fifty-six ships, including the SS *Heredia*.

At about 0200 (CWT), when the SS *Heredia* was about two miles south of the Ship Shoal Buoy off the Louisiana coast, the ship was sighted and attacked by *U-506*. Two torpedoes hit the *Heredia* on the port side at number 3 and number 4 holds. Survivors reported a third torpedo hit on the starboard side amidships, leading them to conclude that the ship was attacked by two submarines. However, German naval records do not identify a second submarine operating in the same area as *U-506*.

The torpedo explosions on the port side destroyed the lifeboats there. No distress signal was sent, and the passengers, crew, and Armed Guard abandoned ship in two life rafts. The survivors were rescued by several shrimp boats (*Papa Joe, Conquest, J. Edwin Treakle,* and *Shellwater*) and by a seaplane.

Of the *Heredia*'s eight passengers, forty-eight crewmen, and six Armed Guard sailors, one passenger, five Armed Guard sailors, and thirty crewmen, including Cadet-Midshipmen Irwin Ebel and Glenn Bruaw, perished.

Cadet-Midshipman Irwin S. Ebel was posthumously awarded the Mariner's Medal, the Combat Bar with star, the Atlantic War Zone Bar, the Victory Medal, and the Presidential Testimonial Letter.

Irwin was the youngest of Frank Ebel and Rose Ebel's three children. Frank Ebel, an Austrian immigrant, owned and operated an automotive repair business. Irwin's older siblings were named Maxine and Lester. The 1941 college year book for the University of North Carolina, Chapel Hill, identifies Irwin as a sophomore attending the school.

Meyer Egenthal

Born:	March 17, 1922
Hometown:	Brooklyn, NY
Class:	1943
Service:	Merchant Marine
Position / Rank:	Engine Cadet
Date / Place of death:	November 29, 1942 / 28 S, 54 E
Date / Place of burial:	November 29, 1942 / Lost at Sea 28 S, 54 E
Age:	20

Meyer Egenthal signed on as Engine Cadet aboard the MS *Sawokla* at the Port of New York on June 16, 1942. Also aboard with him was his classmate William O'Hara, Deck Cadet. The ship sailed two days later loaded with general war cargo bound for the Soviet Union via Abadan, Iran. After arriving in Abadan via Port of Spain, Trinidad, and Cape Town, South Africa, the *Sawokla* delivered its cargo. The ship sailed in ballast for Colombo and then to Calcutta, India, where it loaded a cargo of gunny sacks in bales. The *Sawokla* returned to Colombo for sailing directions and to pick up some homebound passengers.

On November 21, 1942, the *Sawokla* sailed from Colombo with a crew of forty-one, a Navy Armed Guard contingent of thirteen, and five passengers. Eight days out of port and about four hundred miles south of Madagascar, the *Sawokla* was sighted and attacked by the German surface raider *Michel*. Junior Third Mate Stanley Willner, a Merchant Marine Cadet Corps Cadet Officer on his first voyage as a ship's officer, was standing watch on the bridge on the eight-to-twelve watch. After the war, Willner reported that about 2035, he saw the outlines of a ship take shape in the darkness and immediately called the Captain to the bridge. However, just as the Captain was opening his cabin at door at 2037, the *Michel* opened fire on *Sawokla*, targeting the bridge and radio shack with its main battery of six 150 mm guns.

The Captain was killed immediately, as were most of the bridge watch and forecastle lookout. The *Michel* also launched a motor torpedo boat, which circled the *Sawokla*, spraying the decks with machine gun fire and preventing the crew from launching any of the lifeboats. Willner reported that eight minutes after the attack began; the *Sawokla* was on fire from stem to stern and sank. The crew, Armed Guard, and passengers who survived the initial attack were forced to jump overboard into the rough seas. Cadet-Midshipmen Meyer Egenthal and William V. O'Hara were among those seen jumping overboard by other crew members.

According to Willner, the *Michel*, including its two aircraft, spent two days searching for *Sawokla*'s survivors. Willner and thirty-eight other men were rescued by the *Michel* and its crew. *Sawokla*'s wounded survivors, including Willner, were treated by the *Michel*'s medical staff. However, neither Meyer Egenthal nor his classmate William O'Hara were among those rescued by the *Michel* and are presumed to have drowned.

For those that had survived the initial attack, the ordeal had just begun. On February 19, 1943, the *Michel* arrived in Singapore, where its prisoners were handed over to the Japanese by the *Michel* crew, which was their normal procedure. The prisoners were taken to the prisoner of war camp at the former Changi Prison. According to Willner, when the *Sawokla*'s survivors arrived at Changi, they were "fairly fit." However, after a few months, about half of the survivors were taken from the camp, while most of the remaining men were taken to work on the Thailand-Burma Railway, sometimes known as the "Death Railway" and immortalized in the film *The Bridge over the River Kwai*. Willner and the men of his group returned to Singapore in December 1943 and remained there until the camp was liberated September 7, 1945.

Willner, along with his shipmate Dennis Roland, worked for decades to earn official veteran's status for merchant seamen in World War II, serving as a named plaintiff in litigation that finally bore fruit in 1988, more than four decades after Willner's ordeal.

Cadet-Midshipman Meyer Egenthal was posthumously awarded the Mariner's Medal, the Combat Bar with star, the Atlantic War Zone Bar, the Mediterranean-Middle East War Zone Bar, the Victory Medal, and the Presidential Testimonial Letter.

Meyer Egenthal was the only son of Abraham Egenthal, a Polish immigrant, and Pauline Egenthal a Romanian immigrant. Meyer was the middle child of a family that included his older sister, Fay, and his younger sister, Freida. By 1940, Fanny was employed as a sales clerk in a department store, while Meyer attended the Manual Training High School in Brooklyn. In high school, he was active in athletics and received a varsity letter in track. Abraham owned a grocery store in Brooklyn where Meyer worked part time. His outgoing nature and cheerful service made him popular with the customers. According to his family, Meyer was ambitious and had a strong desire to make himself valuable to the family business. His family also said that Meyer had learned that the priceless value of a good nature costs nothing and benefits the individual and those around him. Meyer's "magnetic" personality resulted from his unusual mental, social, and emotional characteristics.

Abraham, Meyer, and Pauline Egenthal

Leonard Laurence Ehrlich

Born:	June 28, 1923
Hometown:	Brooklyn, NY
Class:	1943
Service:	Merchant Marine
Position / Rank:	Engine Cadet
Date / Place of death:	December 7, 1942 / North Atlantic, 57-50 N, 23-10 W
Date / Place of burial:	December 7, 1942 / North Atlantic, 57-50 N, 23-10 W/ Lost at Sea
Age:	19

Leonard L. Ehrlich signed on as Engine Cadet aboard the SS *John Penn* at Boston, Massachusetts, on June 11, 1942. During his assignment to the *John Penn*, it sailed to Murmansk, Russia, in Convoy PQ-18. On September 19, 1942, the *John Penn* was attacked and sunk by German aircraft. Fortunately, Ehrlich survived the sinking of the *John Penn* and returned to Boston, Massachusetts, aboard the SS *Queen Mary* on October 15, 1942, as a member of the "Tin Fish Club." After spending almost a month to visit his family and replace the clothing and personnel effects lost on the *John Penn*, he was ordered to report to a new ship to complete his at-sea training.

Leonard L. Ehrlich signed on the SS *James McKay* as Engine Cadet on November 11, 1942, at New York, New York. Three other Kings Point Cadet-Midshipmen, Philip G. Branigan (deck), Walter C. Hetrick (engine), and John J. McKelvey (deck) were also aboard. In addition to the four Cadets, the ship's Third Assistant Engineer, Henry E. Harris, was a 1942 Cadet Corps alumnus.

SS *James McKay*

The *James McKay* sailed from New York with Convoy HX-216 bound for Belfast, Northern Ireland, and Cardiff, Wales, on November 19. On November 25, the convoy encountered a northwest gale and reduced visibility that caused the convoy to partly scatter. The weather was sufficiently rough to cause the *James McKay*'s general cargo to shift, endangering its stability. As a result, the ship left the convoy and sailed into St. John's, Newfoundland, on November 29 to restow its cargo.

After restowing its cargo, the *James McKay* sailed from Newfoundland to join up with the next eastbound convoy, HX-217. However, there is no indication that the *James McKay* ever actually joined up with HX-217, possibly due to the convoy being scattered in a southwesterly gale from December 2 to 4.

According to German Navy records, the *James McKay* was located and attacked by *U-600* on the night of December 7/8, 1943, when the ship was about four hundred miles south of Iceland. Three of *U-600*'s torpedoes hit the *James McKay*, one amidships and the other two in the after portion of the ship. The ship stopped and sent out distress signals, and the crew abandoned ship in two lifeboats, although the ship was still afloat. It required two more torpedoes from *U-600* to sink the *James McKay*. Neither the two lifeboats nor any of the people aboard the *James McKay* were ever seen again.

Cadet-Midshipman Leonard L. Ehrlich was posthumously awarded the Mariner's Medal, the Combat Bar with two stars, the Atlantic War Zone Bar, the Victory Medal, and the Presidential Testimonial Letter.

Leonard L. Ehrlich was the only son of William and Rebecca Ehrlich. According to U.S. Census records, William Ehrlich worked as a clerk for a tobacco distributor. By 1940, Leonard's older sister, Shirley, was also working in a similar position, possibly with her father. Leonard arrived at Kings Point in February 1942 and completed his initial training while the school was still under construction.

Robert Ray Everhart

Born:	March 30, 1922
Hometown:	Bala Cynwyd, PA
Class:	1943
Service:	Merchant Marine
Position / Rank:	Deck Cadet
Date / Place of death:	November 4, 1942 / Norwegian Sea, 71-05 N, 13-20 W
Date / Place of burial:	November 4, 1942 / Norwegian Sea, 71-05 N, 13-20 W—Lost at Sea
Age:	20

Robert R. Everhart reported aboard the SS *William Clark* in New York harbor on August 17, 1942. Joining the ship on the same day were Cadet-Midshipmen Herman Garritsen, Richard Holland, and Peter Smith. They joined a crew of thirty-eight merchant ship officers and seamen, along with thirty officers and men of the Navy's Armed Guard.

SS *William Clark*

The ship sailed on August 22, 1942, carrying a cargo of general military supplies in its holds and a deck cargo of aircraft and tanks to Murmansk, Russia. The *William Clark* traveled with convoys via Boston (BX-35) and Halifax, Nova Scotia (SC-99), to Reykjavik, Iceland, where the ship would normally have joined a Murmansk-bound convoy. However, due to the high losses of the previous two Murmansk Convoys, PQ-17 and PQ-18, and the demand for warships to support the landings in North Africa, the Murmansk convoys were suspended. In the interim, supplies still had to flow to Russia. One Russian, seven British, and five U.S. merchant ships that would have been in the next Murmansk convoy were ordered to sail independently from Reykjavik in twelve-hour intervals between October 29 and November 2, 1942, in what was called Operation FB. Of the thirteen ships, three turned back to Reykjavik, five arrived safely, and five ships, including the *William Clark*, were lost.

At 1135 on November 4, 1942, near Jan Mayen Island, Norway, the *William Clark* was hit on the port side, amidships, by one of three torpedoes fired by *U-354*. The explosion completely destroyed the engine room, killing all five of the engineers on duty, including Engine Cadet Peter J. Smith. The remaining crew abandoned ship into two lifeboats and a motorboat. Although the motorboat was able to keep the survivors together by towing the lifeboats, the towline was eventually broken, and the boats became separated. One boat with twenty-six survivors was rescued after three days afloat by HMS *Elstan* (FY 240). The second boat with fourteen survivors was rescued by HMS *Cape Passiser* (FY 256) after over a week at sea. Robert Everhart apparently was in the motorboat that, with twenty other crew members, was under the command of the Captain. This boat was never heard from again.

Cadet-Midshipman Robert R. Everhart was posthumously awarded the Mariner's Medal, the Combat Bar with star, the Atlantic War Zone Bar, the Victory Medal, and the Presidential Testimonial Letter.

Robert R. Everhart was the youngest son of William T. and Helen Louisa Van Reed Everhart. His older brothers were Jack and William. Bob attended Lower Merion High School in Ardmore, Pennsylvania. He is described by his family as an excellent tennis player who was respected by his teammates and the student body in general. According to his niece, Bob was deeply loved by his family.

And when the stream
Which overflowed the soul has passed away, A consciousness
remained that it had left Deposited upon the silent shore
Of memory images and precious thoughts That shall not die,
and cannot be destroyed

William Wordsworth

Richard Paul Farrell

Born:	July 27, 1920
Hometown:	Los Angeles, CA
Class:	1943
Service:	Merchant Marine
Position / Rank:	Deck Cadet
Date / Place of death:	November 7, 1942 / Caribbean 11-34 N, 63-26 W
Date / Place of burial:	November 7, 1942 / Caribbean 11-34 N, 63-26 W / Lost at Sea
Age:	22

Richard P. Farrell signed on aboard the SS *Nathaniel Hawthorne* as Deck Cadet on May 10, 1942, at Portland, Oregon, just a week after the ship was delivered to the War Shipping Administration by its builder, Oregon Shipbuilding. Joining him on the ship was his West Coast Basic School classmate, William Weis. By November 1942, the ship was en route from Georgetown, British Guiana, to New York via Trinidad loaded with a cargo of 7,576 tons of bauxite. The vessel was traveling in Convoy TAG-19 and carried a complement of forty crew members, ten Naval Armed Guard, and two passengers.

At 0340 on November 7, while the convoy was traveling about forty miles northeast of Isla de Margarita, Venezuela, the *Nathaniel Hawthorne* was struck on the port side at number 1 hold by a torpedo fired by *U-508*. Seconds later, another torpedo struck the port side near the engine room. The engines stopped after the second hit, and the entire midsection of the ship was blown to pieces. The ship listed to port and, after a third explosion (most likely involving the acetylene supply on board), sank quickly.

Of the fifty-two men on board, only ten crew members, three Naval Armed Guard sailors, and one passenger survived. Cadet-Midshipmen Richard P. Farrell and William R. Weis Jr. were lost in the attack. Those who survived had managed to jump overboard and swim to one of three rafts that floated free of the ship after it sank. Thirty-nine hours later, they were rescued by the crew of the USS *Biddle* (DD 151). The *Nathaniel Hawthorne*'s

Armed Guard officer, Ensign Kenneth H. Muir, USNR, was awarded the Navy Cross for directing his men to safety as the ship sank, despite being severely wounded.

Launching of SS *Nathaniel Hawthorne*

Cadet-Midshipman Richard P. Farrell was posthumously awarded the Mariner's Medal, the Combat Bar, the Atlantic War Zone Bar, the Pacific War Zone Bar, the Victory Medal, and the Presidential Testimonial Letter.

Richard P. Farrell was the younger of David A. and Virginia B. Farrell's two sons. Richard's older brother, David Jr., was about seven years older. The 1930 U.S. Census indicates that the Farrell family owned a business selling electric furnaces in which both parents worked.

According to information assembled by James Hoffman, Richard Farrell sailed as an unlicensed deck seaman aboard the SS *Pacific Sun* in December 1941. Shortly thereafter, he reported for his basic training at the West Coast Basic School's temporary home, the Navy's Training Base at Treasure Island in the middle of San Francisco Bay. He was one of the earliest Cadet-Midshipmen to begin training on the West Coast.

Calvert Sumner Foote

Born:	April 22, 1922
Hometown:	Scranton, PA
Class:	1943
Service:	Merchant Marine
Position / Rank:	Deck Cadet
Date / Place of death:	July 6, 1942 / 71 N 45 E
Date / Place of burial:	July 6, 1942 / 71 N 45 E / Lost at Sea
Age:	20

Calvert Foote signed on aboard the SS *Pan Atlantic* as Deck Cadet on April 6, 1942, at Philadelphia, Pennsylvania. He was joined by his classmate, Cadet-Midshipman Carl E. Anderson. The *Pan Atlantic*, built in 1919, sailed from Philadelphia on April 22 for Russia via Halifax, Nova Scotia, Scotland, and Reykjavik, Iceland, with a cargo of tanks, steel, nickel, aluminum, food, petroleum equipment, and explosives.

SS *Pan Atlantic*

At Reykjavik, the *Pan Atlantic* joined with thirty-three other merchant ships, plus an Oiler and three rescue ships, to form Convoy PQ-17 to Murmansk. The convoy sailed from Reykjavik (Hvalfjord) on June 27, 1942, bound for the Russian port of Archangel via an evasive route north of Bear Island into the Barents Sea. The convoy was escorted by three groups of British and American warships, including covering forces of cruisers and battleships.

All went well for the first few days, although three ships had to return to Iceland. The convoy itself was not spotted by the Germans until July 1. Between July 1 and July 4, the convoy and its escorts beat back attacks by German torpedo bombers, losing two of the remaining ships.

On July 4, the British Admiralty became convinced that the battleship *Tirpitz* and its escorts were sailing to attack the convoy and its escorts. Shortly after 2100, unwilling to risk the limited numbers of heavy warships in waters controlled by German aircraft, heavy surface ships, and submarines, the Admiralty ordered the convoy's covering cruiser force to sail west, out of harm's way, at high speed. A few minutes later, the Convoy Commodore was ordered to disperse the convoy to proceed to Archangel independently. The result was as catastrophic as it was predictable. Shorn of their escorts, the merchant ships bravely tried their best to deliver the goods in the face of overwhelming odds. For many of the ships and their crews, their best was not good enough.

Among the ships lost was the *Pan Atlantic*. By pluck and luck, the ship survived all day July 5 and most of July 6. At about 1610 (GMT), when the ship was about 270 miles north of Cape Kanine, Russia, a German dive bomber found the *Pan Atlantic*. The *Pan Atlantic*'s Armed Guard sailors and its crew manned all of the guns and fiercely defended the ship. About five minutes later, the aircraft dove on the ship, pulling out just out of the machine gun's range and dropping two bombs. The bombs hit forward of the bridge, setting off an explosion in the cargo that broke the ship in half. Three minutes later, the ship sank.

One boat was successfully launched from the *Pan Atlantic* by the Chief Mate, two crewmen, and two Armed Guard sailors. This boat pulled eighteen other men from the water or life rafts, including the Captain and Cadet-Midshipman Anderson. Cadet-Midshipman Calvert Foote was one of the twenty-five men killed during the attack. The men in the lifeboat spent three days in the frigid weather before being rescued by the corvette HMS *Lotus (K 130)* on July 9. However, their ordeal was not over. The crew of the HMS *Lotus* and the survivors aboard had to endure another seven and a half to eight hours of German air attacks before they arrived in Archangel on July 11. Many of the survivors had to stay in Russia for weeks before they could get aboard a ship and make their way back to the United States. Even then, the return trip was as hazardous as the first trip. Many survivors, like Cadet-Midshipman Anderson, had to survive a second sinking before reaching home.

Cadet-Midshipman Calvert Foote was posthumously awarded the Mariner's Medal, the Combat Bar, the Atlantic War Zone Bar, the Victory Medal, and the Presidential Testimonial Letter.

Calvert S. "Jack" Foote was the only son of the Reverend Adrian B. and Irene L. Foote. The Foote family traveled extensively as Reverend Foote moved from church to church. Jack and his sister Marjorie were born in South Dakota, but by the time Jack was seven and Marjorie was six, they were living in Whitney Point, New York. Five years later, in 1935, the family had moved to Pennsylvania, where Calvert attended the Methodist School in Wyoming Valley, Pennsylvania. Marjorie graduated from Johns Hopkins Medical School in Baltimore, Maryland. She practiced medicine in Massachusetts until her death in 1976.

David Hogan Frohn

Born:	July 30, 1921
Hometown:	Los Angeles, CA
Class:	1943
Service:	Merchant Marine
Position / Rank:	Deck Cadet
Date / Place of death:	November 7, 1942 / Champerico, Guatemala
Date / Place of burial:	November 9, 1942 / Champerico, Guatemala (initial) June 8, 1943 / Holy Cross Cemetery, Los Angeles, CA (final)
Age:	21

David H. Frohn signed on as Deck Cadet aboard the SS *Francis Drake* on September 3, 1942, at Los Angeles, California. This was his first ship after completing the curriculum at the San Mateo, California, Basic School. He joined Cadet-Midshipman Victor Hugo, Engine Cadet for the voyage to South and Central America.

On November 7, 1942, the *Francis Drake* was anchored about a mile off of Champerico, Guatemala. As was customary in that port, transportation to and from ships anchored offshore were provided by a harbor launch towing a small lighter. At 1900 hours on November 7, 1942, David Frohn and seven other crew members, including Second Mate Carey, and Armed Guard Commander, Lieutenant Brady, boarded the lighter for the short trip ashore. Unfortunately, the short trip ended in tragedy.

According to the report made by the ship's Master, S. Chapman, to the American Consul in Guatemala City, at about 1915, as the launch and its lighter made its turn to come alongside the pier, a swell capsized the launch. The Second Mate and Lieutenant Brady realized that the lighter would likely collide with the capsized launch. They shouted to the rest of the men to jump in the water and swim for the beach. However, only the two officers jumped into the water. They successfully made their way to the beach.

When the lighter collided with the capsized launch, the Radio Officer, a Steward, and possibly David Frohn were thrown into the water. Due to the darkness and their efforts to keep the lighter from sinking, the men aboard the lighter lost track of the men in the water. Only after everyone else had made it ashore did anyone realize that Frohn was missing. A search for him was organized immediately and continued for several hours after the accident without success. David Frohn's body was recovered the following day, November 8, when it washed up on the beach about a mile from the accident.

Burial services for Cadet-Midshipman David Frohn began at November 9 at 1400 when pall bearers, four of the ship's officers and crew and four of the ship's Armed Guard sailors, bore the flag-draped casket and body to Champerico's Catholic Chapel, where a requiem High Mass was celebrated by Fr. August F. Herrera. From the chapel, the body was taken to the local Catholic cemetery, where David Frohn was buried with his rosary and prayer book.

David Frohn's belongings and wages were turned over to the U.S. Shipping Commissioner in Los Angeles when the ship arrived there a few weeks later. Although Guatemalan authorities normally required the deceased's body to remain in a Guatemalan cemetery for at least four years, David Frohn's remains were exhumed in April 1943. His remains were brought back to his parents in Los Angeles for a final service at St. Gregory's Catholic Church and burial at Holy Cross Cemetery on June 8, 1943.

Cadet-Midshipman David H. Frohn was posthumously awarded the Pacific War Zone Bar, the Victory Medal, and the Presidential Testimonial Letter.

David H. Frohn was the only son of David Watson Frohn and Helen Frohn. The elder Frohn, who went by his middle name, was a linotypist for the *Los Angeles Times*. David was born in Clarksdale, Massachusetts.

Benjamin Prentice Gafford

Born:	March 21, 1922
Hometown:	Sherman, TX
Class:	1943
Service:	Merchant Marine
Position / Rank:	Engine Cadet
Date / Place of death:	January 1, 1943 / Mediterranean, 35-45 N, 00-45 W
Date / Place of burial:	January 1, 1943 / Mediterranean, 35-45 N, 00-45 W / Lost at Sea
Age:	22

Benjamin P. Gafford signed on the SS *Arthur Middleton* as Engine Cadet on November 21, 1942, at New York, New York. Also aboard was Deck Cadet Denniston Charlton. At New York and Norfolk, Virginia, the *Arthur Middleton* loaded a cargo of ammunition, explosives, and mail, with *LCT-21* stowed on deck. The ship sailed from Hampton Roads on December 12, 1942, for Oran as part of a "slow" convoy, UGS-3, with forty-two crew, twenty-seven Armed Guard, and twelve passengers (eleven crew from *LCT-21* and one Army officer).

Upon arrival at Casablanca, eleven ships bound for nearby Oran, Algeria, split off from the convoy and proceeded to their destination. When the eleven ships were about eight miles away from Oran, the convoy slowed, and the signal was given for single column for entry into the harbor. The SS *Rhode Island*, the Commodore's ship, was maneuvering at slow speed to line up for the harbor approach, while the other ships formed a line astern.

The *Arthur Middleton* was near the port quarter of the *Rhode Island* when it was struck near the bow by two torpedoes fired by *U-73* at 1411 (GCT). According to *U-73*'s Commanding Officer, the *Arthur Middleton* violently exploded less than twenty seconds after being hit by the torpedoes, sending flames and parts of the ship soaring one thousand feet into the air. The ship disintegrated from number 5 hatch to the bow, but a small section of the stern remained afloat for about a minute. Of the eighty-one men on board, only three men survived; they were members of the Armed Guard who had been stationed on the after section and were able to jump overboard. These three were picked up twenty-five minutes after the attack by the HMS *Boreas* (H77) and transferred to the British Hospital Ship, HMHS *Oxfordshire*. Cadet-Midshipmen Benjamin P. Gafford and Denniston Charlton Jr. were among those lost in the attack.

Cadet-Midshipman Benjamin P. Gafford was posthumously awarded the Mariner's Medal, the Combat Bar, the Atlantic War Zone Bar, the Mediterranean-Middle East War Zone Bar, the Victory Medal, and the Presidential Testimonial Letter.

Ben Prentice Gafford

Before joining the SS *Arthur Middleton*, Ben Gafford had sailed aboard the SS *Nishmaha* from January to March 1942. For unknown reasons, perhaps illness, passenger lists on file in New York, New York, list Ben Gafford as a passenger, along with two other U.S. merchant seamen, aboard the MS *Kota Gede*, a Dutch passenger cargo ship. The ship arrived at New York on June 28, 1942, after a month long voyage from Durban, South Africa.

Ben Gafford was the only son of George Prentice and Allie Belle Gafford. George P. Gafford, better known as "Prentice," was identified in the 1930 U.S. Census as clerk of the district court in Sherman, Texas.

According to the notation for Ben Prentice Gafford in the Austin College memorial for its World War II Dead,

> He entered Austin College in the fall of 1940. At the end of his freshman year, Ben Prentice declined a nomination to Annapolis as second alternate and entered the merchant marine.
>
> After passing a competitive examination, he reported to New Orleans for 8 weeks of shore training. In his twenty months of

service he completed voyages to South America, South Africa, and the West Indies. At the time of his death he would have received his commission on completion of the voyage.

A memorial to Ben Prentice Gafford was added to his family's grave markers in the West Hill Cemetery, Sherman, Texas.

Herman Gerard Garritsen

Born:	February 23, 1922
Hometown:	Ridgewood, NJ
Class:	1943
Service:	Merchant Marine
Position / Rank:	Engine Cadet
Date / Place of death:	November 4, 1942 / North Atlantic 71-02 N, 13-05 W
Date / Place of burial:	November 4, 1942 / North Atlantic 71-02 N, 13-05 W / Lost at Sea
Age:	20

Herman G. Garritsen signed on as Engine Cadet aboard the SS *William Clark* in New York harbor on August 17, 1942. Also joining the ship on the same day were Engine Cadets Richard Holland and Peter Smith and Deck Cadet Robert Everhart. They joined a crew of thirty-eight merchant ship officers and seamen, along with thirty officers and men of the Navy's Armed Guard.

SS *William Clark*

The ship sailed on August 22, 1942, carrying a cargo of general military supplies in its holds and a deck cargo of aircraft and tanks to Murmansk, Russia. The *William Clark* traveled with convoys via Boston (BX-35) and Halifax, Nova Scotia (SC-99), to Reykjavik, Iceland, where the ship would normally have joined a Murmansk bound convoy. However, due to the high losses of the previous two Murmansk Convoys, PQ-17 and PQ-18, and the demand for warships to support the landings in North Africa, the Murmansk convoys were suspended. In the interim, supplies still had to flow to Russia. The one Russian, seven British, and five U.S. merchant ships that would have been in the next Murmansk convoy were ordered to sail independently from Reykjavik in twelve-hour intervals between October 29 and November 2, 1942, in what was called Operation FB. Of the thirteen ships, three turned back to Reykjavik, five arrived safely, and five, including the SS *William Clark*, were lost.

At 1135 on November 4, 1942, near Jan Mayen Island, Norway, the *William Clark* was hit on the port side, amidships, by one of three torpedoes fired by *U-354*. The explosion completely destroyed the engine room, killing all five of the engineers on duty, including Engine Cadet Peter J. Smith. The remaining crew abandoned ship into two lifeboats and a motorboat. Although the motorboat was able to keep the survivors together by towing the lifeboats, the towline was eventually broken, and the boats became separated. One boat with twenty-six survivors was rescued after three days afloat by HMS *Elstan* (FY 240). The second boat with fourteen survivors was rescued by HMS *Cape Passiser* (FY 256) after over a week at sea. Herman Garritsen apparently was in the motorboat that, with twenty other crew members, was under the command of the Captain. This boat was never heard from again.

Cadet-Midshipman Herman G. Garritsen was posthumously awarded the Mariner's Medal, the Combat Bar with star, the Atlantic War Zone Bar, the Victory Medal, and the Presidential Testimonial Letter.

Herman Garritsen was the only son and youngest child of Herman H. and Bernadine Peters Garritsen. According to the 1930 U.S. Census, the elder Garritsen was a house painter. Herman Jr. started his seagoing career early, sailing across the Atlantic in 1925, when he was three years old, to visit relatives with his mother. His nephew, Frank Ludica, said that he was known as a precocious youngster with a lively interest in music, sports, photography, science, and journalism. He was an accomplished pianist who wrote and arranged his own music.

Frank said,

> I remember him as an outstanding basketball player on his high school team. He went on to study at Columbia University before entering the Academy. As my uncle, he was a role model and a loss I feel very deeply!

Charles Conrad Gassner

Born:	November 17, 1921
Hometown:	Pittsburgh, PA
Class:	1943
Service:	Merchant Marine
Position / Rank:	Deck Cadet
Date / Place of death:	January 9, 1943 / 56-15 N, 22 W
Date / Place of burial:	January 9, 1943 / Lost at Sea—56-15 N, 22 W
Age:	21

Charles Gassner signed on aboard the SS *Louise Lykes* as Deck Cadet on October 18, 1942, at New York, New York. He was joined by three other Kings Point Cadet-Midshipmen, Allen Miller (deck), Robert Vancure (engine), and Eugene Walters (deck). In addition, the Third Assistant Engineer, Frederick Baumann, and Third Mate, Harry Wolfe, were former U.S. Maritime Commission Cadet Officers. The *Louise Lykes* made one voyage to the Mediterranean and returned to New York on December 12, 1942. A fifth Cadet-Midshipman, Marion Chrobak (engine), joined the ship for its next voyage. The ship sailed on January 2, 1943, loaded with general cargo and ammunition bound for Belfast, Northern Ireland. For unknown reasons, the ship did not sail in a convoy and was not escorted. On January 9, 1943, the ship was in mid-Atlantic several hundred miles south of Iceland.

SS *Louise Lykes*

On the evening of January 9, 1943, *U-384* located the solitary ship and fired four torpedoes while surfaced. According to German Navy records, two torpedoes hit the ship, disintegrating her in a massive explosion. The Captain of the *U-384* reported that he had to submerge the submarine to prevent damage from falling debris. When the submarine resurfaced five minutes later, there was no sign of the ship or its crew. There were no other witnesses to the disaster, and there were no survivors among the fifty merchant crew, thirty-four Naval Armed Guard sailors, and ten U.S. Army personnel aboard, including the five Cadet-Midshipmen and two former Cadet Officers. This was the single deadliest sinking in the Academy's history.

Cadet-Midshipman Charles Gassner was posthumously awarded the Mariner's Medal, the Combat Bar, the Atlantic War Zone Bar, the Victory Medal, and the Presidential Testimonial Letter.

Charles C. Gassner was the youngest son of Charles C. Gassner, a stationary engineer at a meat-packing plant in Pittsburgh, Pennsylvania. Charles lived with his father, Grandfather Conrad, Grandmother Elizabeth, and his brothers Elmer C. and Robert J. on Prospect Street in Pittsburgh. Charles Sr. and his parents were immigrants from the Alsace-Lorraine area of the French/ German border. According to the 1940 U.S. Census, Charles Sr. was no longer living at the same address as his parents and children. Since Charles Gassner's next of kin is listed as his grandfather, Conrad, it is possible that Charles Sr. died, leaving the boys to be raised by their grandparents.

Edward James Gavin

Born:	April 23, 1923
Hometown:	West Orange, NJ
Class:	1944
Service:	Merchant Marine
Position / Rank:	Engine Cadet
Date / Place of death:	February 3, 1943 / North Atlantic 59-22 N, 48-42 W
Date / Place of burial:	February 3, 1943 / North Atlantic 59-22 N, 48-42 W/ Lost at Sea
Age:	19

Edward J. Gavin signed on aboard the U.S. Army troop transport SS *Dorchester* on January 19, 1943, in the Port of New York, New York, as Engine Cadet. He was joined by Samuel T. Tyler, Deck Cadet. On February 3, 1943, the *Dorchester* was about 150 miles west of Cape Farrell, Greenland, in a small convoy with two other ships (Convoy SG-19). The ship carried a complement of 130 crew members, 23 Naval Armed Guard sailors, and 751 passengers (made up of U.S. Army personnel, civilian workers, Danish citizens, and U.S. Coast Guard personnel). The vessel, which was traveling between St. John's, Newfoundland, and Narsarssuak, Greenland, was also laden with 1,069 tons of general cargo and lumber, and sixty bags of mail and parcel post.

Just before 5:00 a.m., one of five torpedoes fired by *U-223* struck the *Dorchester* on the starboard side near the engine room. There were no submarine sightings before or after the attack, and those on watch did not notice any wake indicating a torpedo attack. Survivors recalled little noise but a considerable concussion. A gaping hole in the starboard side of the ship caused extremely rapid flooding, and the engines were completely destroyed. Two of the lifeboats were also destroyed by the impact of the torpedo.

Only three minutes after the vessel was hit, the Captain gave the order to abandon ship. However, only two boats were successfully launched. Whether because of shock, confusion, or limited space, hundreds of passengers and crew remained on board and went down with the ship when it sank about thirty minutes after being hit. Some were apparently unaware of the seriousness of the situation. Two of the convoy's U.S. Coast Guard escorts, USCGC *Escanaba* (WPG 77) and USCGC *Comanche* (WPG 76), remained at the site of the disaster, picking up survivors throughout the night and into the following day. In all, only 229 of the *Dorchester*'s 904 passengers and crew survived the sinking. Cadet-Midshipmen Edward G. Gavin and Samuel T. Tyler were among those missing and presumed lost.

USAT *Dorchester*

In a renowned act of bravery, four U.S. Army chaplains on board the ship gave their life jackets to nearby soldiers who had none. The four men held hands and prayed as the ship went down. Each was posthumously awarded the Purple Heart and the Distinguished Service Cross. A stamp honoring the four men was issued by the post office in 1948.

Cadet-Midshipman Edward J. Gavin was posthumously awarded the Mariner's Medal, the Combat Bar, the Atlantic War Zone Bar, the Victory Medal, and the Presidential Testimonial Letter.

Edward J. Gavin was the only son of James and Linda Gavin. According to the 1940 U.S. Census, the elder Gavin was a salesman for a printer. Edward's sister, Alyce, who was fifteen years older, is identified in the same document as being a clerk in a department store. Edward, known as "Eddie" by friends and family, was remembered as a reserved and unselfish young man with an innate mechanical ability. After graduating from West Orange High School, he worked briefly for Western Electric Company before attending Kings Point.

Charles Frederick Gerstacker

Born:	July 4, 1920
Hometown:	Cleveland, OH
Class:	1944
Service:	Merchant Marine
Position / Rank:	Engine Cadet
Date / Place of death:	October 4, 1944 / U.S. Merchant Marine Cadet Basic School, San Mateo, CA
Date / Place of burial:	October 1944 / Cleveland, Ohio
Age:	24

Charles F. Gerstacker drowned during swimming training in the pool at the San Mateo Basic School at 1130 on October 4, 1944. Gerstacker apparently became incapacitated while in the water, but his distress went unnoticed. His death was not discovered until the other forty-six men of his section mustered on the pool deck upon completion of the class. He was removed from the pool, and a doctor placed the time of death at 1130. After the investigation of his death, his remains were returned to Cleveland, Ohio, for burial.

Cadet-Midshipman Gerstacker had been at San Mateo just three months. Based on the amount of time he had been at San Mateo, it appears that Charles Gerstacker reported to the San Mateo Basic School on or around his twenty-fourth birthday. Charles Gerstacker is described on his U.S. Coast Guard records as being five feet seven inches tall, blond hair, gray eyes, fair complexion, and weighing 145 pounds.

Charles was the younger of Oliver John and Mary Nelson Gerstacker's two sons. William, Charles brother, was seven years older than Charles. The 1930 U.S. Census indicates that Oliver Gerstacker was a draftsman for an oil exploration company. Charles's mother, Mary, died in December 1936 when he was sixteen. In the 1940 U.S. Census, Charles's occupation is identified as draftsman for a Cleveland manufacturing company, while his father is identified as Chief Engineer for another firm.

William Bernard Ginnelly

Born: October 8, 1922
Hometown: Philadelphia, PA
Class: 1943
Service: Merchant Marine
Position / Rank: Engine Cadet
Date / Place of death: November 14, 1942 /
South Atlantic 12 N, 30 W
Date / Place of burial: November 14, 1942 /
South Atlantic 12 N, 30
W /Lost at Sea
Age: 19

William Ginnelly reported to Kings Point for Basic School on April 6, 1942. He signed on as Engine Cadet aboard the SS *Scapa Flow* on August 1, 1942, at Lynnhaven Road, Virginia. Deck Cadet Robert E. Benson signed on the same day. The *Scapa Flow* was built in 1914 at a German shipyard. In December 1941, less than three weeks after attack on Pearl Harbor, the Finnish flagged ship was requisitioned by the War Shipping Administration. Renamed, registered in Panama, and crewed with a combination of U.S. and non-U.S. sailors, the ship began serving the U.S. war effort.

SS *Scapa Flow*

The ship sailed shortly after the new Cadets signed on bound for Trinidad and Takoradi, West Africa. At Takoradi, the ship picked up an Armed

Guard sailor who had been left behind in the hospital there and loaded a cargo of manganese. The ship proceeded on its scheduled calls to ports on the west coast of Africa, including Marshall, Liberia, where it loaded additional cargo of latex in drums and bales of rubber. At Freetown, Liberia, the ship picked up another Armed Guard sailor, a survivor from the sinking of the Liberty ship SS *John Carter Rose* a month before. The *Scapa Flow* also loaded the metal lifeboat from the *John Carter Rose* to replace one of its own boats. On November 7, 1942, the *Scapa Flow* sailed unescorted from Freetown bound for Trinidad and the U.S. East Coast with a crew of forty-seven and a thirteen-man Armed Guard contingent.

Seven days later, approximately 700 miles northwest of Freetown, and 350 miles southeast of the Cape Verde Islands, the *Scapa Flow* was located by *U-134*. Due to a boiler casualty, the ship was making a little more than 6 knots and was not steering evasive courses. According to German naval records, the *U-134* had to request permission from German Naval Headquarters to attack the *Scapa Flow*. After receiving permission to attack the *Scapa Flow, U-134* positioned itself and fired. The *Scapa Flow* was hit almost simultaneously at about 1430 by two torpedoes on the port side at number 2 hatch and amidships, just below the bridge. The damage caused the ship to sink within forty-five seconds of the impact.

In the words of Cadet-Midshipman Robert Benson, the torpedoes simply "ripped the ship apart." Another survivor reported that the "bottom seemed to fall out of the ship." Of all the ship's lifeboats and rafts, only the lifeboat from the SS *John Carter Rose* could be launched, although a hole in its hull had to be plugged with life jackets to keep the boat afloat. In the hours after the sinking, this boat was able to pick up twenty-one members of the crew and seven Armed Guard sailors. The survivors did not include Cadet-Midshipman William B. Ginnelly.

According to survivor's accounts, sometime within an hour or so of the sinking, *U-134* surfaced. After questioning the survivors, the submarine's Commander and its crew offered the survivors bandages for the badly injured and gave them their position. Although the Cape Verde Islands were closer, adverse wind and current conditions prevented the lifeboat making the course. Sailing with the wind, they set sail for Freetown instead.

The survivors spent seventeen days on board the lifeboat under the command of the ship's Fourth Officer, Mr. Keel. On December 1, 1942, the boat was spotted and rescued by HMS *Armeria* (K 187), a convoy escort bound for Freetown.

Cadet-Midshipman William B. Ginnelly was posthumously awarded the Mariner's Medal, the Combat Bar with star, the Atlantic War Zone Bar, the Victory Medal, and the Presidential Testimonial Letter.

William B. Ginnelly was the youngest of John Ginnelly and Nora Ginnelly's two sons and daughter. William's siblings were Catherine (twelve years older) and John Jr. (seven years older). William's father and sister worked at an electric storage battery manufacturer where John was a molder and Catherine an inspector. Documents from Kings Point show that William Ginnelly reported to Kings Point for Basic School on the afternoon of April 6, 1942.

Joseph Giovinco

Born:	April 2, 1924
Hometown:	Brooklyn, NY
Class:	1943
Service:	Merchant Marine
Position / Rank:	Deck Cadet
Date / Place of death:	December 2, 1942 / North Atlantic 48-45 N, 23-30 W
Date / Place of burial:	December 2, 1942 / North Atlantic 48-45 N, 23-30 W / Lost at Sea
Age:	18

Joseph Giovinco signed on the SS *Coamo* at New York, New York, as Deck Cadet on October 2, 1942. He was joined by Cadet-Midshipman Henry Levett, Deck Cadet. The *Coamo* was built in 1925 for the East Coast to Puerto Rico passenger trade. When World War II began, the ship was chartered by the Army Transport Service for use as a troop ship.

After a voyage to Algiers, the *Coamo* sailed with sixteen other merchant ships in Convoy MKF-3 on November 23, 1942, bound for the west coast of Scotland. On December 1, 1942, as the convoy was nearing the British Isles, the *Coamo* was ordered by the British admiralty to proceed independently to New York without escort.

On the evening of the following day, the *Coamo* was sighted by *U-604* in a rising gale. According to German Navy records, *U-604* closed to within eight hundred yards of its target and fired one torpedo. At 1818 (GCT), the torpedo struck the *Coamo* underneath its bridge. The *Coamo* sank within five minutes of the attack without launching a single lifeboat. Although the submarine's crew reported seeing some survivors leave the ship on rafts, none of the 133 crew, 37 Armed Guard sailors, and 16 passengers, including Cadet-Midshipmen Joseph Giovinco and Henry Levett, were seen again. It is believed that any survivors who left the *Coamo* died in the gale that swept the area for three days. The sinking of the *Coamo* was the largest loss of merchant crew on any U.S. Flag merchant vessel during the Second World War. It is interesting to note that all of the other ships in Convoy MKF-3 arrived safely at their destinations.

Cadet-Midshipman Joseph Giovinco was posthumously awarded the Mariner's Medal, the Combat Bar, the Atlantic War Zone Bar, the Mediterranean-Middle East War Zone Bar, the Victory Medal, and the Presidential Testimonial Letter.

Joseph Giovinco was the eldest of Italian immigrants Saverio and Mary Giovinco's four children (Joseph, Frank, Anthony, and Frances). The 1940 U.S. Census identifies Saverio's occupation as shoemaker and Mary's as a seamstress in a clothing factory. Joseph's brother Anthony remembers that Joe was very intelligent and was always exempt from final exams at Grover Cleveland High School because of his high grades. By the time Joe was five, he spoke fluent Italian, which he learned from his parents. However, after being laughed at in kindergarten because he spoke Italian, his parents spoke only English at the home. Anthony says that Joe was an excellent swimmer and played football for the Ridgewood Crusaders. Joe was also a good dancer. In fact, he was so good that while dancing at an event at 1939-40 World's Fair, actress Joan Crawford noticed Joseph dancing and asked him to dance with her.

According to Anthony,

> Joe had many friends, and as his younger brother, I was an admirer of his!

Richard Burton Glauche

Born:	April 7, 1924
Hometown:	Chicago, IL
Class:	1944
Service:	Merchant Marine
Position / Rank:	Deck Cadet
Date / Place of death:	December 2, 1943 / Bari, Italy
Date / Place of burial:	December 2, 1943 / Bari, Italy
	Lost at Sea
Age:	19

Richard B. Glauche signed on aboard the SS *John Harvey* as Deck Cadet on October 5, 1943, at Baltimore, Maryland. Three other Kings Point Cadets also signed on the *John Harvey*: Marvin W. Brodie (engine), James L. Cahill (deck), and Alvin H. Justis (engine). According to a report filed by Cadet-Midshipman Cahill, the ship sailed to Norfolk, Virginia, to finish loading and joined a convoy that sailed for Oran, Algeria, on October 15. Unbeknownst to most of the crew, part of the ship's cargo were two thousand M47A1 mustard gas bombs. The bombs had been loaded at Baltimore between September 30 and October 8 under the supervision of a seven-man detail of chemical warfare specialists from the Army's eastern chemical warfare depot. The seven men remained aboard the *John Harvey* to monitor the condition of the bombs while at sea and supervise their discharge. The bombs were being sent to the Mediterranean as a precaution so that American forces could retaliate if the Germans resorted to chemical warfare.

The *John Harvey* arrived in Oran on November 2, discharged its cargo other than the mustard gas bombs, and then loaded a cargo of ammunition. A convoy of about forty ships, including the *John Harvey*, sailed from Oran for Augusta, Sicily, on November 19, arriving there on November 25. The *John Harvey* sailed the next day in a convoy of thirty ships bound for the ports of Taranto and Bari on the Italian mainland with the Bari-bound ships arriving there on November 28. The port facilities at Bari were unable to keep up with the number of ships in the port, resulting in days-long delays in discharging ships anchored in the port. Because of the high level of secrecy surrounding its cargo, the *John Harvey* was held in port for several days awaiting discharge, moored alongside other ships loaded with ammunition and gasoline, including the Liberty ships *John L. Motley*, the *John Bascom*, and the *Samuel J. Tilden*.

Because of its distance from German airfields, an air attack on Bari was not considered likely, so the port was not protected by the normal air defenses. As a result, a German attack force of more than one hundred Ju88s was able to completely surprise the few defenders of Bari on the evening of December 2, 1943. Due to the lights being left on, the bombers were able to accurately bomb the ships in the port and port facilities with only the loss of a single aircraft. They left behind twenty-eight ships sunk, twelve more damaged, over one thousand merchant mariners and military personnel killed, and a port so badly damaged that it took three weeks to resume discharging ships.

According to the few surviving eye witnesses, the *John L. Motley* and the *Samuel J. Tilden* were among the first ships to be hit by the bombers. However, after the second wave of aircraft finished their attack, the *John Harvey* was in flames from stem to stern. With the fires threatening the *John Harvey*'s cargo of ammunition, its crew fought desperately to save the ship and their lives. However, the damaged *John L. Motley* had broken free from its mooring lines and, completely engulfed in flames, was drifting toward the *John Harvey*. Suddenly, the *John Motley* exploded, destroying the ship and detonating the *John Harvey*'s cargo. The *John Harvey* disintegrated, sending the contents of its cargo of mustard gas bombs into the air and water throughout the port area.

Explosion of either SS *John Harvey* or SS *John L. Motley* at Bari, Italy

Thirty-six of the ship's crew, all twenty-eight members of its Armed Guard, and the Army Chemical Warfare specialists perished instantly, including Cadet-Midshipmen Richard B. Glauche, Marvin H. Brodie, and Alvin H. Justis. The only survivors from the *John Harvey* were Cadet-Midshipman James L. Cahill and one of the ship's able-bodied seamen who were ashore when the attack began. One of the major factors in the high number of casualties from the attack is that doctors and other medical personnel attending to the wounded did not diagnose their signs and symptoms as those of mustard gas poisoning, since no mustard gas was believed to be in the area.

Cadet-Midshipman Richard B. Glauche was posthumously awarded the Mariner's Medal, the Combat Bar, the Atlantic War Zone Bar, the Mediterranean-Middle East War Zone Bar, the Victory Medal, and the Presidential Testimonial Letter. According to the *Chicago Daily Tribune*, Richard Glauche continued firing his antiaircraft gun until the *John Harvey* exploded.

Richard Glauche was the only son of Fred R. and Edna Snyder Glauche. According to the 1930 and 1940 census, Fred Glauche was a postal clerk. Richard graduated from William J. Onahan School and went on to attend Schurz High School and to graduate from William H. Taft High School. He was attending Maine Township Junior College when he was accepted for Kings Point on his nineteenth birthday.

Known as "Dick" to his friends, Richard was remembered by his Kings Point classmate Juel Hansen as a quiet, conservative young man with a subtle sense of humor. He was extremely neat in his clothing and personal habits, and was a disciplined student, and was a member of the swim team. Juel Hansen recalled that Dick never lost his temper or engaged in heated arguments. He always considered Dick to be a well-mannered, gentle, and intelligent friend.

A memorial service for Richard Glauche was held on what would have been his twenty-first birthday at the Onahan School. The centerpiece of the memorial was the creation of the Richard B. Glauche Memorial in the school's library. The money for the memorial was raised by William V. Jackson, a boyhood friend of Richard. The initial memorial consisted of sixty books and a fifteen-drawer card catalog with subsequent additions by Jackson and others who knew Richard Glauche and were dedicated to keeping his memory alive.

John Robert Gordon Jr.

Born: January 6, 1920
Hometown: Brooklyn, NY
Class: 1944
Service: Merchant Marine
Position / Rank: Engine Cadet
Date / Place of death: February 24, 1943 /
Mediterranean 36-04 N,
0-02.5 W
Date / Place of burial: February 24, 1943 /
Mediterranean 36-04 N,
0-02.5 W / Lost at Sea
Age: 23

John R. Gordon Jr. signed on the SS *Nathaniel Greene* as Engine Cadet in March 1942, shortly after it was delivered from North Carolina Shipbuilding. He was joined by his classmate Deck Cadet John A. Harley.

Gallant Ship SS *Nathaniel Greene*

According to Harley's report, the *Nathaniel Greene* sailed from New York for Russia via ports in the United Kingdom. On September 2, 1942, the *Nathaniel Greene* sailed from Loch Ewe, Scotland, with Convoy PQ-18 for Russia. After the near disaster of the previous Russia convoy, PQ-17, the convoy was accompanied by an escort aircraft carrier, HMS *Avenger* (D 14), and a heavy escort of cruisers, destroyers, corvettes, minesweepers, and submarines.

Despite losing thirteen of its forty-one ships to enemy action, Convoy PQ-18 was considered to be a success. The *Nathaniel Greene* and its gun crews were commended for her courageous action during this trip, which included the destruction of five enemy planes. On September 15, the Commodore of the convoy signaled to the ship, "Reverences to your gunners, you are at the top of the class." Despite being hit by bombs and shrapnel that damaged bulkheads and destroyed the ship's compass, the *Nathaniel Greene* arrived in Russia, where it discharged its cargo and made repairs.

The return trip with Convoy QP-15 sailed from Russia on November 17, 1942, and almost immediately ran into a severe gale, which scattered the convoy for ten days. However, the Germans were unable to take advantage of the situation due to lack of daylight and the bad weather. The *Nathaniel Greene* arrived safely at Loch Ewe and discharged its cargo in Glasgow and then loaded cargo and sailed for North Africa on January 21, 1943.

The *Nathaniel Greene* arrived safely at Mostaganem, Algeria, on February 5 and discharged all but about eight hundred tons of food there. On February 24, the ship sailed at noon (GCT) to meet up with Convoy MKS-8 for protection as it sailed for other Algerian ports to deliver its cargo. Escorted by the HMS *Brixham* (J 105), a minesweeper, the *Nathaniel Greene*'s crew could see the convoy on the horizon. However, *U-565* was patrolling off of the port and sighted the *Nathaniel Greene*. The submarine's Captain maneuvered into position and fired three torpedoes. At 1351 (GCT), one torpedo struck the ship on the starboard side at the number 2 hold, while another hit amidships at the engine room. As the *Nathaniel Greene* began to settle by the head, German dive and torpedo bombers began attacking the convoy.

The antiaircraft cruiser HMS *Scylla* (98) promptly commenced firing on the attacking aircraft. Along with the efforts of two Hurricane fighters, the attack was broken up. However, the attacking aircraft spotted the crippled *Nathaniel Greene* and turned their attention to safer prey. Although the *Nathaniel Greene*'s gun crews were able to shoot one attacker down, the ship was hit by three other torpedoes in the forward part of the ship. Cadet-Midshipman John Harley described the scene that ensued:

> Shrapnel was raining from the sky . . . The midship section was engulfed in smoke and could not be seen. The deck cargo was littered with debris. In the excitement the two forward life rafts had been cast adrift, their painters parted and they drifted astern.

HMS *Brixton* came alongside the crippled *Nathaniel Greene* to take off its wounded and survivors. Other survivors who able to escape in numbers 2 and 4 lifeboats were also picked up by the *Brixham*. The *Brixham* then began towing the sinking vessel back to shore to beach it so that its cargo could be salvaged. The vessel was beached late the next day, at Salamanda, Algeria, four miles west of Mostaganem. Only four of the forty-four crew and seventeen Armed Guard sailors died in the attack on the *Nathaniel Greene*, but the four included Cadet-Midshipman John R. Gordon, who was last seen at his assigned station in the engine room, working the grease extractors. For its actions in the Russian convoys and at Algeria, the *Nathaniel Greene* was awarded the Gallant Ship Unit Citation.

Mr. and Mrs. John R. Gordon at the christening of SS *John R. Gordon*

Cadet-Midshipman John R. Gordon was posthumously awarded the Gallant Ship Citation Bar, the Mariner's Medal, the Combat Bar, the Atlantic War Zone Bar, the Mediterranean-Middle East War Zone Bar, the Victory Medal, and the Presidential Testimonial Letter. The Liberty ship SS *John Robert Gordon*, named in his honor, was launched on May 22, 1945, at South Portland, Maine, and began service in June 1945.

John was the only son of John R. and Kathleen Gordon. According to the 1940 census, the senior Gordon owned a hardware store.

Mrs. John R. Gordon christens Liberty ship named after her son, John Robert Gordon Jr.

Arthur Jack Gradus

Born:	June 17, 1923	
Hometown:	Long Island City, NY	
Class:	1944	
Service:	Merchant Marine	
Position / Rank:	Deck Cadet	
Date / Place of death:	March 10, 1943 / North Atlantic 66-53 N, 14-10 W	
Date / Place of burial:	March 10, 1943 / North Atlantic 66-53 N, 14-10 W / Lost at Sea	
Age:	19	

Arthur J. Gradus signed on aboard the SS *Richard Bland* as Deck Cadet on April 17, 1942, at Philadelphia, Pennsylvania. He was joined by his Academy classmate Charles W. Tamplin, who also signed on as Deck Cadet. Although the *Richard Bland* was originally assigned to the infamous Convoy PQ-17 to Murmansk, Russia, the ship apparently ran aground shortly after leaving port and was towed back for repairs. After completing the necessary repairs, the ship subsequently sailed to deliver its cargo to Murmansk with Convoy JW-51A, which arrived in Kola Inlet, Russia, without the loss of a single ship on December 25, 1942.

SS *Richard Bland*

After discharging its cargo, the *Richard Bland*, loaded with four thousand tons of lumber, general cargo, and deck cargo, sailed from Kola Inlet on March 1, 1943, with the other ships of Convoy RA-53, bound for Loch Ewe, Scotland. At about 0930, local time, March 5, 1943, *U-255* fired three torpedoes at the convoy. Two torpedoes hit the SS *Executive* and exploded, sinking the ship. The third torpedo fired by *U-255* hit the *Richard Bland* on the starboard side at number 1 hold and out the other side of the ship, causing the deck to crack and other structural damage. While the ship did not sink, the impact of the torpedo partially disabled the ship, leaving her unable to keep up with the convoy for several hours. Although the *Bland* was able to rejoin the convoy, by the afternoon, heavy weather that night found the ship falling behind again.

At about 1530, local time, on March 10, *U-255* found the *Richard Bland* again, about thirty-five miles off the coast of Langanes, Iceland. The *Bland* was hit by one torpedo on the port side at the number 4 hatch, but the *Bland* remained afloat. Although the boats were lowered to their embarkation stations, the ship was not abandoned. A distress signal was sent and acknowledged by a shore station, and the ship's confidential papers were thrown overboard. An attempt to lower the windward boats and bring them into the lee of the ship failed, leaving two boats and eight men adrift. At about 1835, local time, the ship was hit amidships by another torpedo from *U-255*. The explosion caused the ship to break in half, just forward of the bridge. The forward half broke free and remained afloat, while the after portion sank.

As the ship began to break up, the Captain ordered the two remaining lifeboats lowered and life rafts launched. There were heavy seas at the time of the attack, as well as intermittent snow, and several life rafts were lost as the crew attempted to launch them. The nearly sixty remaining crew and Armed Guard sailors quickly abandoned ship into lifeboats, designed to hold twenty persons each. One survivor, Lt. (jg) William A. Carter, USNR, reported that his boat was so overloaded that they had only a few inches of freeboard; they were shipping water over the sides and had to bail the water out to keep afloat.

After a long night in a cramped lifeboat in high seas, twenty-seven survivors in the boat commanded by the Third Mate were picked up by the HMS *Impulsive* (D11) at about 0730 the following morning. The *Impulsive* also rescued one of the windward boats and its crew of four, while another destroyer rescued the other boat and its crew of four. The last lifeboat, under the command of the Master, was never seen again. Fifteen Armed Guard sailors and nineteen merchant crew members were aboard this boat, including Cadet-Midshipmen Arthur Gradus and Charles Tamplin.

Louis Chirillo and Arthur Gradus (right) Outside Wiley Hall 1942

Arthur J. Gradus was posthumously awarded the Mariner's Medal, the Combat Bar with star, the Atlantic War Zone Bar, the Victory Medal, and the Presidential Testimonial Letter.

Arthur was the only son of Jacob and Martha Gradus. According to the 1930 and 1940 U.S. Census, Jacob Gradus was a foreman and clerk for post office.

William Henry Green Jr.

Born:	November 6, 1922
Hometown:	Louisiana, MO
Class:	1944
Service:	Merchant Marine
Position / Rank:	Engine Cadet
Date / Place of death:	July 9, 1943 / Indian Ocean 9-00 S, 81-00 E
Date / Place of burial:	July 9, 1943 / Indian Ocean 9-00 S, 81-00 E / Lost at Sea
Age:	20

William H. Green signed on as Engine Cadet aboard the SS *Samuel Heintzelman* at Charleston, South Carolina, on May 11, 1943. He was joined by his Pass Christian classmate Deck Cadet John N. Stewart. The ship sailed the same day for Fremantle, Australia, via the Panama Canal.

After safely crossing the Pacific, the *Samuel Heintzelman* sailed from Fremantle, Australia, on July 1, en route to Calcutta by way of Colombo and Karachi with a cargo of ammunition and general cargo. The *Heintzelman* was due to arrive in Colombo on July 14, but she never arrived; and for months, her disappearance was a mystery. Then on September 29, a plank marked with the ship's name, along with several boxes of ammunition and boxes of glass vials with an unidentified powder, washed up on the beach of Minni-Minni, a village on Diego Garcia, in the Chagos Archipelago. Villagers had also noticed two unoccupied ship's boats the previous day, but these were never recovered.

After the war, German records showed that the ship had been torpedoed on July 9, 1943, by *U-511*. The submarine submerged after shooting its torpedoes, but the crew heard underwater explosions. When *U-511* surfaced, there was no sign of the ship or any survivors, only debris floating on the surface of the ocean. All of the seventy-five people aboard the *Samuel Heintzelman* (forty-two crew, twenty-seven Armed Guard sailors, and six passengers) were lost.

Cadet-Midshipman William H. Green was posthumously awarded the Mariner's Medal, the Combat Bar, the Atlantic War Zone Bar, the Pacific War Zone Bar, the Victory Medal, and the Presidential Testimonial Letter.

William H. "Billy" Green was the only son and oldest child of William H. "Willie" and Lucy Protzman Green. According to the 1930 U.S. Census, Willie Green was a printer who worked for a nursery. Billy's younger sister, Margaret Lucile, known as "Peggy," was four years younger. According to information on his "family tree," Billy attended the Missouri School of Mines at Rolla, Missouri, before he was accepted into the U.S. Merchant Marine Cadet Corps.

Billy Green, age 11

Billy was remembered by neighbors and friends as a standout student who studied trigonometry in a special advanced class his senior year in high school. He was described as a handsome and well-mannered young man who was welcome in every circle in the community located about eighty miles north of St. Louis. Friends recall that he was a fine singer and often performed in Louisiana with his girlfriend Honey, who was an accomplished pianist. Billy was appointed to the U.S. Merchant Marine Academy on December 17, 1942, and entered the Pass Christian Basic School in January. Because of his short stature, Billy needed, and received, a waiver of the minimum height requirement for his appointment in the Merchant Marine Reserve.

Proud mother says goodbye to son

One of the chaplains at Pass Christian wrote to William Green's parents several times before his death. In one letter, he spoke highly of William's personality and his faith:

> As you know, by this time your son has left the Cadet Basic School to continue his studies at sea. During the time that he was here it was my privilege to be associated with him and all of our contacts were very pleasant. During the last few days he was here I talked with him and his spirits were high and his belief in God was as great as ever.

Billy and his girlfriend "Honey"   **Last day at home**

Family with Billy at train station before joining his ship

George Edgar Guilford

Born: July 22, 1921
Hometown: Centralia, KS
Class: 1943
Service: Merchant Marine
Position / Rank: Engine Cadet
Date / Place of death: November 7, 1942 /
Indian Ocean
40-00 S, 21-30 E
Date / Place of burial November 7, 1942 / Lost
at Sea / Indian Ocean
40-00 S, 21-30 E
Age: 21

George E. Guilford attended Basic School at Pass Christian, Mississippi. According to Academy records, he signed on aboard the SS *La Salle* as Engine Cadet at Balboa, in the Panama Canal Zone, on September 26, 1942. Also aboard the ship were the Deck Cadet, his Pass Christian classmate Fred Pennington, and 1942 alumnus James D. Herndon, Third Assistant Engineer. Shortly after signing on, the *La Salle* sailed for Cape Town, South Africa, loaded with a cargo of trucks, steel, and ammunition. However, the *La Salle* never arrived at Cape Town, and the fate of the *La Salle* remained a mystery until after the war. The vessel was officially marked as "presumed lost" on December 2, 1942.

SS *Wynah*, a shipyard sister to the SS *La Salle*

After the war, German Navy records solved the mystery. On November 7, 1942, when the *La Salle* was nearing the end of its voyage, the unescorted freighter was sighted by *U-159* about 350 miles southeast of the Cape of Good Hope. The submarine chased *La Salle* for over five hours, missing with one torpedo, until it managed to achieve a better target solution and fired another torpedo. The explosion of that torpedo detonated *La Salle* ammunition cargo, instantly destroying the ship. The crew of *U-159* reported that the explosion sent pillars of flame hundreds of feet into the air. Three of the submarine's crew were wounded by the debris that rained down on the submarine for several minutes after the explosion. It was later claimed that the explosion could be heard three hundred miles away, at South Africa's Cape Point Lighthouse.

Everyone aboard the *La Salle* was killed instantly, including Cadet-Midshipmen George E. Guilford and Fred Pennington and Third Assistant Engineer James D. Herndon. Also among the dead was the ship's Armed Guard officer, the former Mayor of Milwaukee, Wisconsin, Lt. Carl F. Zeidler, USNR. After resigning as Mayor so that he could be commissioned, Zeidler is said to have asked for the most dangerous job in the Navy. He was then assigned to command a merchant ship Armed Guard detachment.

George E. Guilford was posthumously awarded the Mariner's Medal, the Combat Bar, the Atlantic War Zone Bar, the Pacific War Zone Bar, the Victory Medal, and the Presidential Testimonial Letter.

George Edgar (Edward according to his family) Guilford was the older of Harvey Dickerson Guilford and Hazel Zeola Condit Guilford's two sons; they grew up on a farm outside of Centralia, Kansas. George's younger brother, William E. Guilford, was killed at Aachen, Germany, in 1944 while serving in the U.S. Army.

Jay Arthur Hammershoy

Born: March 14, 1922
Hometown: Glenbrook, CT
Class: 1944
Service: Merchant Marine
Position / Rank: Engine Cadet
Date / Place of death: February 7, 1943
                    North Atlantic 55-18 N,
                    26-29 W
Date / Place of burial: February 7, 1943
                    North Atlantic 55-18 N,
                    26-29 W / Lost at Sea
Age: 20

According to crew lists on file in Boston, Massachusetts, James A. Hammershoy signed on aboard the U.S. Army Transport SS *Henry R. Mallory* as Engine Cadet on November 7, 1942, at New York, New York. Also aboard the ship were Cadet-Midshipmen Joseph E. Best (deck) and Phillip G. O'Reilly. After completing one voyage, O'Reilly signed off, and four new Cadet-Midshipmen signed on: Robert Helling, Richard E. Holland, George R. Race, and Frank C. Roberts. The *Henry R. Mallory* sailed on January 24, 1943, as part of slow convoy SC-118 bound for Liverpool via Nova Scotia. However, the *Henry R. Mallory* and several other ships were to split off from the convoy on February 9 and to proceed to Iceland. Loaded with 383 Army, Navy, Marine Corps, and civilian passengers, the ship was also carrying a mixed cargo of clothing, food, trucks, tanks, cigarettes, liquor, and 610 sacks of mail.

U.S. Army Transport SS *Henry R. Mallory* (ca. 1918)

On February 4, 1943, German submarines sighted the convoy and began attacking it. The attacks continued until the afternoon of February 7. At 0538 (GCT) on February 7, despite the rising sea and snow falling, a torpedo fired by *U-402* struck the starboard side of the *Henry R. Mallory* at hold number 3, damaging the engines and blowing the hatch covers off of number 4 hold. At the time of the explosion, the *Henry R. Mallory* was traveling at about 7 knots and was not steering an evasive course. According to some survivors, the ship began sinking immediately, while others, apparently including the Captain, believed that the ship would remain afloat. As a result, neither distress messages nor flares were launched. In addition, after the sinking, survivors reported that the general alarm was not rung and no order was given to abandon ship. In the confusion of the greater attack on the convoy, none of the other ships in the convoy knew that the *Henry R. Mallory* had been hit.

However, the *Henry R. Mallory*'s engines were badly damaged and quickly shut down. Two of the aft lifeboats had been damaged in the explosion, while others were damaged by the heavy seas, but the remainder seemed secure. When the ship suddenly began sinking faster by the stern, the abrupt change caused panic among passengers and crew. Men rushed on deck amid frigid temperatures without proper protective clothing. In the chaos, only three boats were lowered successfully, and each of these was dangerously overloaded either during launching or after picking up survivors from the water. Several other boats capsized as crew and passengers tried to launch them. Many of the life rafts could not be launched either because they were tied or frozen in place. Others were insufficiently trained in how to use their rafts and did not properly deploy key parts of the raft to prevent capsizing in the heavy seas. Hundreds of the men aboard jumped overboard.

Meanwhile, the situation on the overloaded lifeboats was perilous. According to Cadet-Midshipman Joseph Best, his lifeboat was intended for fifty men but held eighty. With so much weight, the boat's gunwales were just inches above the water, and the high seas threatened to either capsize or simply sink the boat. Many of the men frantically bailed with anything they could lay their hands on to keep the boat afloat, while others jettisoned anything that did not appear to be necessary to survive their imminent sinking. However, Cadet-Midshipman Best took custody of the distress rockets and flares because he thought ". . . they might become useful."

With daylight, the men in Best's boat sighted the U.S. Coast Guard Cutter *Bibb* (WPG 31). The rockets hoarded by Best were fired into the air, while Cadet-Midshipman Frank C. Roberts waved a yellow flag to attract the *Bibb*'s attention. The *Bibb* saved 205 freezing survivors of the *Mallory*, including those in the lifeboat with Cadet-Midshipmen Best and Roberts. The *Bibb*'s sister ship, USCGC *Ingham* (WPG 35), also picked up some survivors. According to the official U.S. Coast Guard history of the USCGC *Bibb*,

> Lookouts aboard the *Bibb* sighted one of the *Mallory*'s lifeboats at 1000, and, disobeying an order to return to the convoy, *Bibb*'s Commanding Officer, CDR Roy Raney, ordered his cutter to begin rescuing survivors.

Many of *Bibb*'s crewmen leapt into the water to assist the nearly frozen survivors, and the cutter *Ingham* assisted. One of *Ingham*'s crew described the scene, a dreadfully common one along the North Atlantic that year:

> I never saw anything like it, wood all over the place and bodies in life jackets . . . never saw so many dead fellows in my whole life. Saw lots of mail bags, boxes, wood, wood splinters, empty life jackets, oars, upturned boats, empty life rafts, bodies, parts of bodies, clothes, cork, and a million other things that ships have in them. I hope I never see another drowned man as long as I live.

Among the 272 men who died in the frigid water were Jay A. Hammershoy, George R. Race, and Richard E. Holland. In a sad twist of fate, Richard Holland had survived the sinking of the SS *William Clark* three months earlier.

Cadet-Midshipman Jay A. Hammershoy was posthumously awarded the Mariner's Medal, the Combat Bar with star, the Atlantic War Zone Bar, the Victory Medal, and the Presidential Testimonial Letter.

According to Academy records, Jay Hammershoy was sworn in as Cadet-Midshipman, USNR, on October 14, 1942. He was the oldest child and only son of Joseph and Mary Hammershoy. Jay's father was born in Denmark and worked in 1930 as a railroad foreman.

Edwin Hanzik

Born:	February 11, 1922
Hometown:	Huntington Station, NY
Class:	1944
Service:	Merchant Marine
Position / Rank:	Deck Cadet
Date / Place of death:	March 11, 1943, North Atlantic 51-35 N, 28-30 W
Date / Place of burial:	March 11, 1943, North Atlantic 51-35 N, 28-30 W / Lost at Sea
Age:	21

Edwin Hanzik signed on aboard the SS *William C. Gorgas* as Deck Cadet in Mobile, Alabama, on January 27, 1943, shortly after the ship was delivered to the War Shipping Administration from its builder. Joining Cadet-Midshipman Hanzik were three of his classmates, James Cordua, James Moon, and Edwin Wiggin. Already aboard was Third Mate Rafael R. Rivera, 1942 Cadet Corps alumnus. Six weeks later, on March 10, 1943, the *Gorgas* was traveling in Convoy IIX-228 en route from New York to Liverpool loaded with general cargo, including nine hundred tons of explosives and a deck cargo of an LCT and two PT boats. The ship carried a crew of forty-one merchant mariners and twenty-six Naval Armed Guard sailors.

At around 2030 on March 10, another ship in the convoy was torpedoed, and the general alarm was sounded. The crew remained on alert, with the Naval Armed Guard manning the battle stations. The weather was hazy, with moderate to heavy swells and ten to fifteen knot winds in bright moonlight. At 2330, the *Gorgas* was hit on the starboard side amidships by a torpedo fired by *U-757*. The explosion destroyed the engine room, instantly killing the three engineers on watch. The Master ordered the crew to abandon ship. By 2350, when 51 survivors in lifeboats and rafts had left the ship, snow had begun falling in higher winds. The *U-757* located one of the boats and questioned the survivors. Shortly thereafter the submarine found the ship still afloat and fired another torpedo to sink it. Immediately after the ship settled under the waves its ammunition cargo exploded, damaging *U-757* so much that it was unable to dive. The submarine was escorted on the surface back to France by another submarine.

The *Gorgas*'s fifty-one survivors were picked up at about 0700 on March 11 by the destroyer HMS *Harvester* (H 19). Shortly after rescuing the *Gorgas*'s survivors, the *Harvester* sighted *U-444* on the surface. Although the submarine dove to escape the *Harvester*'s gunfire, a depth charge attack brought the submarine to the surface. It is unclear why the *Harvester*'s Commander made his decision, but *U-444* was rammed at full speed by the *Harvester*, severely damaging both ships.

Although *U-444* was able to break free of the *Harvester*, it was rammed again and sunk by the Free French corvette *Aconit* (K 58). However, the almost-motionless *Harvester* was easy prey for *U-432,* which fired two torpedoes, quickly sinking the destroyer with nearly all of its crew and thirty-nine of the *Gorgas*'s survivors. The *Aconit* was immediately on scene attacking the *U-432* with depth charges and forcing it to the surface. The *Aconit* fired at the surfaced submarine and then rammed it, sending the *U-432* and all but twenty of its crew to the bottom. With this vital task accomplished, the *Aconit* rescued twelve *Gorgas*'s survivors, forty-eight survivors of the *Harvester*, and twenty-four German sailors from *U-444* and *U-432*.

Launching of SS *William C. Gorgas*

After the *Harvester* sank, the Master of the *Gorgas*, James Calvin Ellis Jr., was seen by some of the survivors floating in a life ring in the cold seas. When he was offered a place on a life raft by one of the seamen, he declined, telling the man to keep his place. Soon after, he lost his grip on the life ring and was lost in the icy waters.

Edwin Hanzik, his three U.S. Merchant Marine Academy classmates, and 1942 graduate Rafael R. Rivera were among those lost. It is believed that all five survived the initial attack but were lost in the subsequent sinking of the *Harvester*.

Cadet-Midshipman Edwin Hanzik was posthumously awarded the Mariner's Medal, the Combat Bar with star, the Atlantic War Zone Bar, the Victory Medal, and the Presidential Testimonial Medal.

He was the youngest of Joseph and Anna Hanzik's four children. Joseph Hanzik was a baker. Edwin's sisters and brother were all much older (fourteen to nineteen years) than he.

Alexander Walker Harris

Born:	November 9, 1925
Hometown:	Greenville, SC
Class:	1946
Service:	Merchant Marine
Position / Rank:	Deck Cadet
Date / Place of death:	April 6, 1945, Kerama Retto, off Okinawa, 26-05 N, 127-14 E
Date / Place of burial:	April 6, 1945, Kerama Retto, off Okinawa, 26-05 N, 127-14 E, Lost at Sea
Age:	19

Alexander W. Harris signed on aboard the new SS *Hobbs Victory* as Deck Cadet on February 14, 1945, at San Francisco, California. He was joined by Cadet-Midshipman John L. Danner, Engine Cadet. The ship sailed independently for the South Pacific on February 25, 1945, loaded with a cargo of U.S. Army ammunition bound for Okinawa. On its way to Okinawa, the *Hobbs Victory* called at Eniwetok and the U.S. Navy fleet base at Ulithi Atoll. From Ulithi, the *Hobbs Victory* sailed for Okinawa in convoy with six other ships.

The *Hobbs Victory* arrived at the harbor of Kerama Retto, the fleet anchorage and logistics base near Okinawa, on the morning of April 6, 1945. That afternoon, the *Hobbs Victory*, along with the other ships in the explosives anchorage, the SS *Pierre Victory* and the SS *Logan Victory* were subjected to three separate attacks by Japanese kamikaze aircraft. During these attacks, the SS *Logan Victory* and USS *LST 447* were hit and eventually sank. In order to stay clear of the burning *Logan Victory*, the *Hobbs Victory* got under way until early evening when it anchored again.

However, within minutes of anchoring, two more Japanese aircraft flew parallel to the *Hobbs Victory* from about three thousand feet away. The *Hobbs Victory*'s Armed Guard managed to shoot down one of the planes, but the second aircraft changed course and headed directly toward the vessel. The gun crews damaged the aircraft but could not prevent it from hitting the ship. At 1845, the kamikaze smashed into the *Hobbs Victory* just forward of number 4 lifeboat at boat deck level, causing a terrific explosion, killing all hands in the engine room, and destroying the port side lifeboats.

According to accounts of the survivors, the entire port side of the house and boat deck was blown out by the explosion. Within minutes, the port side of the midship house was engulfed in flames, which spread to number 4 hold. After thirty minutes of trying to fight the fire, the Captain ordered the surviving crew to abandon ship. The survivors were picked up by the minesweeper USS *Success* (AM 310) and subsequently transferred to the USS *Gosper* (APA 170) for medical evaluation and treatment. Fourteen of the ninety-eight men aboard the SS *Hobbs Victory*, including Cadet-Midshipman Alexander Harris, died in the attack or of their wounds. Both Cadet-Midshipman Danner and the Master reported that Alexander Harris had just finished blacking out the vessel and believed that he was in or near his room in the midship house when the kamikaze hit the ship. Despite the best efforts of a Navy fireboat, the fires aboard the *Hobbs Victory* could not be controlled, and the ship sank early the next morning.

Cadet-Midshipman Alexander W. Harris was posthumously awarded the Mariner's Medal, the Combat Bar, the Pacific War Zone Bar, the Victory Medal, and the Presidential Testimonial Letter.

Alexander W. Harris was the younger of Donald Ryan Harris and Frances Weldon Walker Harris's two sons. He reported to the Basic School at Pass Christian, Mississippi, and was appointed a Midshipman, Merchant Marine Reserve, USNR, on July 1, 1944. While Alexander was growing up, the family lived in North Carolina and Pennsylvania before settling in Mobile, Alabama. Donald Harris was involved in the automobile business. In 1941, Alexander entered Christ School in Asheville, North Carolina, a boarding school where his grandfather, Rev. Reuben R. Harris, had been the headmaster. At Christ School, Alexander was president of his Junior and senior classes and the Gamma Lambda Sigma Fraternity. As a senior, he was named one of the school's prefects and elected president of the student council. Alexander was a natural athlete and was elected team Captain for both the football and basketball teams. In his senior year, Alexander became the first Christ School student to win the school's highest athletic ward, the Athletic Trophy, and its highest overall honor, the Headmaster's Cup.

In a letter to his parents, the Master of the *Hobbs Victory* wrote,

> His willingness to do anything at all times to help out and learn was a pleasure to see. He was exceptionally well liked by all the crew. There were many clean jokes played on him in fun and he took them all in good spirit. One thing he was continually kidded about was his enormous appetite. It seemed as though he was always hungry and could never get enough to eat. He was therefore often found between meals fixing up a little snack for himself. His breakfast each morning was a wonder in itself. It consisted of eight large pancakes, an order of bacon or ham, and eggs and few other small items. It was a sight to watch him get away with it and never stagger under the load. Now and then the Cooks would add a few extra cakes to the stack and watch to see if he could eat them all. He took and relished all that came.
>
> Your son was a fine clean and strong young man and it was a pleasure having him sail with me. In closing, I extend my deepest sympathies.

Walter Charles Hetrick Jr.

Born:	August 14, 1920
Hometown:	Lawrence, NY
Class:	1943
Service:	Merchant Marine
Position / Rank:	Deck Cadet
Date / Place of death:	December 7, 1942 / North Atlantic 57-50 N, 23-10 W
Date / Place of burial:	December 7, 1942 / North Atlantic 57-50 N, 23-10 W / Lost at Sea
Age:	20

Walter C. Hetrick signed on the SS *James McKay* as Deck Cadet on November 11, 1942, at New York, New York. Three other Kings Point Cadet-Midshipmen, Philip G. Branigan (deck), Leonard L. Ehrlich (engine), and John J. McKelvey (deck), were also aboard. In addition to the four Cadets, Third Assistant Engineer, Henry E. Harris, was a Cadet Corps alumnus. According to crew lists on file in New York, New York, Walter Hetrick had previously sailed as Engine Cadet aboard the SS *Aquarius*, signing off just a few days before signing on aboard the *James McKay*.

SS *James McKay*

The *James McKay* sailed from New York with Convoy HX-216 bound for Belfast, Northern Ireland, and Cardiff, Wales, on November 19. On November 25, the convoy encountered a northwest gale and reduced visibility that caused the convoy to partly scatter. The weather was sufficiently rough to cause the *James McKay*'s general cargo to shift, endangering its stability; the ship left the convoy and sailed into St. John's, Newfoundland, on November 29 to restow its cargo.

After restowing its cargo, the *James McKay* sailed from Newfoundland to join up with the next east-bound convoy, HX-217. However, there is no indication that the *James McKay* ever actually joined up with HX-217, possibly due to the convoy being scattered in a southwesterly gale from December 2 to 4.

According to German Navy records, the *James McKay* was located and attacked by *U-600* on the night of December 7/8, 1943, when the ship was about four hundred miles south of Iceland. Three of *U-600*'s torpedoes hit the *James McKay*, one amidships and the other two in the after portion of the ship. The ship stopped and sent out distress signals, and the crew abandoned ship in two lifeboats, although the ship was still afloat. It required two more torpedoes from *U-600* to sink the *James McKay*. Neither the two lifeboats nor any of the people aboard the *James McKay* were ever seen again.

Cadet-Midshipman Walter C. Hetrick was posthumously awarded the Mariner's Medal, the Combat Bar with star, the Atlantic War Zone Bar, the Victory Medal, and the Presidential Testimonial Letter.

Walter Jr. was the oldest of three sons of Walter Sr. and May V. Hetrick. Walter's next younger brother, William Hetrick, also graduated from Kings Point and became a Master with Farrell Lines. According to Albert D. Wood, class of 1947, Walter Sr. was a successful Cedarhurst, Long Island, businessman. He said that even though May never got over the loss of her eldest son, she became like a mother to a generation of Kings Pointers from her apartment over Jack's Bar in Cedarhurst. Many of her "boys" went on to successful careers with Farrell Lines.

According to his youngest brother, Robert, Walter graduated from Cedarhurst High School on Long Island. He was interested in sports, loved the outdoors, and became an accomplished horseman. Robert said,

> Friends flocked to him. He developed the finer qualities and abilities
> of manhood and earned the admiration of the community.

Robert felt that the following from Shakespeare sums up Walter's life:

> Heaven doth with us, as we with torches do;
> Not light them for ourselves; for if our virtues
> Did not go forth of us, 'twere all alike as if we had them not.

Richard Homer Holbrook

Born:	January 9, 1922
Hometown:	Wayland, NY
Class:	1943
Service:	Merchant Marine
Position / Rank:	Engine Cadet
Date / Place of death:	April 11, 1942 / Berhampur, India
Date / Place of burial:	April 12, 1942 / Catholic Cemetery, Berhampur, India
Age:	20

Richard H. Holbrook signed on as Engine Cadet aboard the SS *Bienville* at the Port of New York on December 12, 1941, less than a week after the United States officially entered World War II. He was joined by his Academy classmate Deck Cadet Robert W. Corliss. According to Corliss's report, the *Bienville* sailed from New York on December 15, 1941, bound for Suez and other ports in the Middle East as directed. After discharging their cargo, the *Bienville* was ordered to Calcutta, India, to load a cargo of manganese ore, jute, burlap, and general cargo. The ship sailed from Calcutta on April 3, bound for Colombo, Ceylon. Unfortunately, the ship was also bound for a collision with six Japanese aircraft carriers, escorted by cruisers and destroyers on a raid into the Bay of Bengal known by the Japanese Navy as "Operation C."

During the morning four-to-eight watch on April 6, 1942, Cadet-Midshipman Robert Corliss was a lookout on the bridge when he heard gunfire ahead. In light of the situation, he was ordered to wake all hands. At 0718, the *Bienville* was attacked by Japanese aircraft and was hit at number 2 hatch, starting a fire. While the crew was fighting the fire, two more Japanese aircraft attacked the *Bienville*, but without hitting the ship. At this early point in the war, the *Bienville* had no defensive armament.

In the growing light, the crew of the *Bienville* could see a Japanese aircraft carrier, later identified as the IJNS *Ryujo*, and its escorting cruisers and destroyers. The Captain ordered *Bienville* to put its stern toward the Japanese ships and make full speed while the Chief Engineer attempted to lay a smoke screen. However, the efforts to hide the old ship were in vain.

At about 0740, a Japanese cruiser, identified after the war as the heavy cruiser IJNS *Chokai*, opened fire from less than two miles away, hitting the ship at least five times and severely wounding Richard Holbrook.

As the firing began, the Captain ordered the crew to abandon ship. However, by this time, three of the ship's four lifeboats had been destroyed. Most of the crew had to jump into the ocean and swim for life rafts. Cadet-Midshipman Corliss joined a group of men at the number 4 hatch who were trying to launch a life raft there. However, due to their wounds, the men could not get the raft launched. The men cut the raft loose in hopes that it would float clear of the *Bienville* as it sank. Incredibly, the raft did just that.

The one lifeboat that had survived the sinking picked up twenty-four men, including Cadet-Midshipmen Corliss and Holbrook. After a little more than a day at sea, the lifeboat reached land. The wounded, including Richard Holbrook, were taken to the government headquarters hospital in Berhampur, India, for treatment. After several days of treatment, Richard Holbrook died at 0835 on April 11, 1942, of a fractured skull and penetrating wounds of the abdomen. He was buried in the Catholic Cemetery in Berhampur. Four other survivors also died of their wounds.

Cadet-Midshipman Corliss's return to the United States was a lengthy adventure in which he found himself at sea in a lifeboat again after his second ship was torpedoed. He was subsequently assigned to a ship so short of crew that he was rated Ordinary Seaman at the Captain's request to fill out the crew. Corliss arrived at Philadelphia, Pennsylvania, on August 20, 1942, nine months after he left New York aboard the *Bienville*.

In a historical note, in 1944, the Japanese cruiser *Chokai* that sank the *Bienville* was sunk with all hands by U.S. Navy ships and aircraft at the Battle off Samar.

Cadet-Midshipman Richard H. Holbrook was posthumously awarded the Mariner's Medal, the Combat Bar with star, the Atlantic, the Mediterranean-Middle East, and Pacific War Zone Bars, the Victory Medal, and the Presidential Testimonial Letter.

Richard H. Holbrook was the older of Pearl W. Holbrook and Myrtle R. Holbrook's two sons. He had an older sister, Flora, a younger brother, William, and two younger sisters, Kathryn and Sharon. The Holbrook family lived in the village of Wayland, New York, in West Central New

York. In 1940, Richard was working part time as a waiter in a restaurant, while his father worked as a weaver in a silk mill. Richard's sister Sharon said that while Richard had some health problems as a young boy, hockey was his favorite sport at school. He was consistently outgoing and became popular with his classmates. Sharon and the rest of the Holbrook family remember Richard as patriotic and a consistent worker at the United Brethren Church in Wayland. She believed that the following quote from W. Drummond best summarizes her recollections of Richard:

> There are some men and women in whose company we are always at our best. All the best stops in our nature are drawn out, and we find music in our souls never felt before.

Richard Edmund Holland

Born:	May 13, 1922
Hometown:	Scranton, PA
Class:	1944
Service:	Merchant Marine
Position / Rank:	Deck Cadet
Date / Place of death:	February 7, 1943, North Atlantic / 55-18 N, 26-29 W
Date / Place of Burial:	February 7, 1943, North Atlantic/ 55-18N, 26-29 W / Lost at Sea
Age:	20

Richard E. Holland signed on as Deck Cadet aboard the U.S. Army Transport SS *Henry R. Mallory* on January 24, 1943, at Boston, Massachusetts. He had recently returned to the United States from Reykjavik, Iceland, aboard the Army Transport SS *Chateau Thierry*. His first ship, the SS *William Clark*, was sunk on November 4, 1942, en route to Murmansk, Russia. Signing on at about the same time were Cadet-Midshipmen Robert Helling, George R. Race, and Frank C. Roberts. The men joined Cadet-Midshipmen James A. Hammershoy (Engine) and Joseph E. Best (Deck), who had sailed aboard the *Henry R. Mallory* on its previous voyage.

U.S. Army Transport SS *Henry R. Mallory* (ca. 1918)

The *Henry R. Mallory* sailed on January 24, 1943, as part of slow convoy SC-118 bound for Liverpool via Nova Scotia. However, the *Henry R. Mallory* and several other ships were to split off from the convoy on February 9 and to proceed to Iceland. Loaded with 383 Army, Navy, Marine Corps, and civilian passengers, the ship was also carrying a mixed cargo of clothing, food, trucks, tanks, cigarettes, liquor, and 610 sacks of mail.

On February 4, 1943, German submarines sighted the convoy and began attacking it. The attacks continued until the afternoon of February 7. At 0538 (GCT) on February 7, despite the rising sea and snow, a torpedo fired by *U-402* struck the starboard side of the *Henry R. Mallory* at hold number 3, damaging the engines and blowing the hatch covers off of number 4 hold. Although two of the aft lifeboats had been damaged in the explosion and others were damaged by the heavy seas, the rest of the boats seemed secure.

According to some survivors, the ship began sinking immediately, while others, apparently including the Captain, believed that the ship would remain afloat. As a result, distress messages were not sent, and flares were not fired to alert other ships to the *Henry R. Mallory*'s distress. Survivors also reported that the general alarm was not rung, and no order was given to abandon ship. Thus, between the failure to communicate its distress and the confusion of the greater attack on the convoy, none of the other ships in the convoy knew that the *Henry R. Mallory* was sinking.

Unfortunately, after a period of perceived stability, the ship suddenly began sinking faster by the stern. The abrupt change caused panic among passengers and crew. Men rushed on deck amid frigid temperatures without proper protective clothing. In the chaos, only three boats were lowered successfully. However, each of these was dangerously overloaded either during launching or after picking up survivors from the water. Several other boats capsized as crew and passengers tried to launch them in the heavy seas. According to Cadet-Midshipman Joseph Best, his lifeboat was intended for fifty men but held eighty. With so much weight, the boat's gunwales were just inches above the water, and the high seas threatened to either capsize or simply sink the boat. Many of the men frantically bailed with anything they could lay their hands on to keep the boat afloat, while others jettisoned anything that did not appear to be necessary to survive their imminent sinking. Fortunately, Best took custody of the distress rockets and flares because he thought ". . . they might become useful."

Although the ship was also equipped with life rafts, several of these could not be launched because they were either tied or frozen in place. Further, the men on the life rafts that could be launched were insufficiently trained in how to use their rafts. As a result, they did not properly deploy key parts of the raft to prevent capsizing in the heavy seas. Hundreds of the men aboard jumped overboard.

With daylight, the men in Best's boat sighted the U.S. Coast Guard Cutter *Bibb* (WPG 31). The rockets hoarded by Best were fired into the air, while Cadet-Midshipman Frank C. Roberts waved a yellow flag to attract the *Bibb*'s attention. The *Bibb* saved 205 freezing survivors of the *Mallory*, including those in the lifeboat with Cadet-Midshipmen Best and Roberts. The *Bibb*'s sister ship, USCGC *Ingham* (WPG 35), also picked up some survivors. According to the official U.S. Coast Guard history of the USCGC *Bibb*,

> Lookouts aboard the *Bibb* sighted one of the *Mallory*'s lifeboats at 1000 and, disobeying an order to return to the convoy, *Bibb*'s Commanding Officer, CDR Roy Raney, ordered his cutter to begin rescuing survivors.

Many of *Bibb*'s crewmen leapt into the water to assist the nearly frozen survivors, and the cutter *Ingham* assisted. One of *Ingham*'s crew described the scene, a dreadfully common one along the North Atlantic that year:

> I never saw anything like it, wood all over the place and bodies in life jackets . . . never saw so many dead fellows in my whole life. Saw lots of mail bags, boxes, wood, wood splinters, empty life jackets, oars, upturned boats, empty life rafts, bodies, parts of bodies, clothes, cork, and a million other things that ships have in them. I hope I never see another drowned man as long as I live.

Among the 272 men who died in the frigid water were Cadet-Midshipmen Richard E. Holland, Jay A. Hammershoy, and George R. Race.

Cadet-Midshipman Richard E. Holland was posthumously awarded the Mariner's Medal, the Combat Bar with two stars, the Atlantic War Zone Bar, the Victory Medal, and the Presidential Testimonial Letter.

Richard Holland was one of seven children of James C. Holland and Helen Bender Holland. The 1930 U.S. Census finds the Holland family living in Scranton, Pennsylvania, where Richard's father worked in an electric generating plant and his mother managed a grocery store. Richard's father died in April 1933, and the family of six boys and one girl were raised by their mother. Richard joined the Civilian Conservation Corps and was assigned to a camp in New Mexico. When he returned from New Mexico, he applied for entrance to Kings Point and was accepted.

Maxwell Hollander

Born:	September 23, 1918
Hometown:	Atlantic Beach, NY
Class:	1944
Service:	Merchant Marine
Position / Rank:	Deck Cadet
Date / Place of death:	February 21, 1943 / North Atlantic 50-30 N, 24-38 W
Date / Place of burial:	February 21, 1943 / North Atlantic 50-30 N, 24-38 W / Lost at Sea
Age:	24

Maxwell Hollander signed on as Deck Cadet aboard the SS *Rosario*, a World War I—era freighter, on September 27, 1943, at the Port of New York. He joined Cadet-Midshipman Edward F. Welch, Deck Cadet. The ship sailed a few days later for England, discharged its cargo, and sailed for New York in ballast from Avonmouth, England, on February 9, joining Convoy ON 167, which sailed from Liverpool on February 14.

SS *Rosario*

On the evening of February 21, when the convoy was approximately 550 miles west of Fastnet, Ireland, it was located by *U-664*. After making its approach on a dark calm night, at 2035 (GMT), the *U-664* fired four torpedoes at the convoy. Two of the torpedoes struck the *Rosario*'s starboard side at number 2 and number 5 holds, blowing their hatch covers off and throwing their sand and slag ballast into the air.

Cadet-Midshipman Edward Welch, who was on watch on the bridge at the time, saw no signs of the torpedoes before the impact. Within three minutes of the explosions, the ship was listing over forty-five degrees to starboard. The ship sank so quickly that the crew was unable to launch the lifeboats, leaving the survivors no choice but to jump into the frigid water clinging to what wreckage they could find. Fortunately, two of the ship's life rafts had floated free. One Armed Guard sailor, Seaman First Class Clarence J. Bennett, USNR, distinguished himself by climbing aboard a raft and pulling ten men from the water onto the raft who might otherwise have perished. When that raft was full, he then swam to the other raft and rescued several other men.

After almost two hours in the water, the survivors were picked up by lifeboats from the other ship torpedoed by *U-644*, the tanker *H. H. Rogers*, and by the convoy's rescue ship, SS *Rathlin*. The *Rathlin* landed its human cargo at Halifax, Nova Scotia, on March 6, 1943. Of the sixty-three men aboard the *Rosario*, thirty of its crew, including Cadet-Midshipman Maxwell Hollander and all but one of the officers, and three Armed Guard sailors, perished.

Cadet-Midshipman Maxwell Hollander was posthumously awarded the Combat Bar with star, the Mariner's Medal, the Victory Medal, and the Presidential Testimonial Letter.

Maxwell Hollander was the youngest son of Harry Hollander and Hazel Hollander. Maxwell's father Harry was an oral surgeon on Long Island. His older brother, James, survived World War II and retired as a Captain in the U.S. Naval Reserve. Maxwell had an older sister, Augusta, and a younger sister, Gloria.

James Arthur Hope

Born:	April 15, 1921
Hometown:	Avalon, PA
Class:	1944
Service:	Merchant Marine
Position / Rank:	Deck Cadet
Date / Place of death:	April 11, 1943 / North Atlantic 50 N, 39 W
Date / Place of burial:	April 11, 1943 / North Atlantic 50 N, 39 W / Lost at Sea
Age:	22

James A. Hope signed on as Deck Cadet aboard the new Liberty ship SS *Edward B. Dudley* at Savannah, Georgia, on March 1, 1943, just days after its delivery from North Carolina Shipbuilding. James Hope was joined aboard the *Edward B. Dudley* by his classmate Deck Cadet James J. Magee.

After loading a cargo of cotton in Savannah, the *Edward B. Dudley* sailed on its maiden voyage for New York. At New York, the ship loaded more cargo, including either ammunition or explosives. The *Edward B. Dudley* sailed from New York with Convoy HX 232 on April 1, 1943, bound for Liverpool via Halifax, Nova Scotia.

At some point after the convoy sailed from Halifax, the *Edward B. Dudley* straggled behind the convoy due to, according to some sources, a bent propeller blade. German naval records indicate that the *Edward B. Dudley* was located by *U-615* on April 10. The submerged submarine fired a four-torpedo spread at the ship. Only one of the four torpedoes was seen by *U-615* to hit the ship, and it failed to explode.

Alerted to the danger, the *Edward B. Dudley* began zigzagging, but it was unable to shake off the pursuit by *U-615*. The pursuit lasted all night, with *U-615* finally getting ahead of the *Edward B. Dudley* and setting up its approach on the surface. When the *Edward B. Dudley* was in *U-615*'s sights, it fired two torpedoes at the ship, hitting it amidships and stopping the ship. However, the *Edward B. Dudley* would not sink. Twenty minutes after the first torpedoes hit the *Edward B. Dudley;* the *U-615* closed to within a half mile of the ship and fired another torpedo, which hit the stern. The explosion of this torpedo detonated the ammunition for the five-inch gun there, but the *Edward B. Dudley* still remained afloat. At this point, the crew of the *U-615* witnessed the crew abandoning ship in the lifeboats.

The *U-615* then moved even closer to the crippled ship and fired a fourth torpedo, which hit under the bridge, detonating the ship's cargo and totally destroying her. Falling debris from the explosion wounded the *U-615*'s Captain and slightly damaged its conning tower, forcing the submarine to abort its patrol and return to base. The *U-615* itself was sunk by Allied aircraft in the Caribbean on its next patrol.

Although the *U-615*'s Captain and other crew members had seen boats being lowered, no survivors of the *Edward B. Dudley*, including Cadet-Midshipmen James A. Hope and Joseph J. Magee, were ever heard from. Given the extent of the explosion of the *Edward B. Dudley*'s cargo, any survivors who were in the lifeboats perished in the explosion.

Cadet-Midshipman James A. Hope was posthumously awarded the Combat Bar with star, the Mariner's Medal, the Atlantic War Zone Bar, the Victory Medal, and the Presidential Testimonial Letter.

James A. Hope was the middle of three boys, Keith (George Keith), James, and Dean, born to George Cowan Thompson Hope and Margaretta Agatha Barnhart Hope. The boys were born in Hamilton, Canada, but the family moved to America in 1923. George Hope, a civil engineer and World War I veteran, died in 1924. They were raised from 1925 to 1940 by their aunt and uncle, George and Helen Hess. However, by the 1940 U.S. Census, all three boys were living with their mother. George K. was identified as working in a steel mill, while their mother took in boarders. According to Dean, James and he caddied at a local country club during high school. James was also the quarterback on his high school football team. After graduating from high school, James worked briefly at American Bridge Company before going to Kings Point.

Edwin David Howard

Born:	May 28, 1924
Hometown:	Sylvania, OH
Class:	1944
Service:	Merchant Marine
Position / Rank:	Deck Cadet
Date / Place of death:	December 2, 1943 / Bari, Italy
Date / Place of burial:	December 2, 1943 / Bari, Italy / Lost at Sea
Age:	19

Edwin D. Howard signed on as Deck Cadet aboard the SS *John L. Motley* at Philadelphia, Pennsylvania, on October 16, 1943. He was joined by his classmate Engine Cadet Jay F. Litton. Already aboard from the ship's maiden voyage was an Academy alumnus, Second Mate Fulton E. Yewell. After loading a cargo of ammunition, the *John L. Motley* sailed on its second voyage, bound for the Mediterranean. The ship reached the crowded harbor of Bari, Italy, on November 28, 1943.

On December 2, 1943, the *John L. Motley* was moored alongside the jetty at Bari, Italy, discharging its cargo when a massive German air attack on the port took defenders by surprise. The attack and ensuing explosions sank seventeen ships and put the harbor out of use for three weeks. This attack became known as "Little Pearl Harbor."

A Naval Armed Guard member on the SS *John Bascom*, moored next to the *John L. Motley,* reported that the vessel sustained three bomb hits, one in number 5 hold, one in number 3 hold, and one down the vessel's stack. The crew was able to control the fires caused by the first strike, but after the second hit, the fires on board raged out of control, burning through the vessel's mooring lines and setting her adrift. The subsequent explosion of the *Motley*'s cargo killed everyone on board, including Kings Point graduate Second Mate Fulton Edison Yewell Jr., along with the two Cadets, Edwin D. Howard and Jay F. Litton.

However, the damage caused by German bombs to the *John L. Motley* did not end there. When the *Motley* blew up, the ship was only fifty feet or so distant from the SS *John Bascom.* The *Motley*'s explosion destroyed the port side of the *Bascom*, sinking the ship within minutes. The explosion on the *John L. Motley* also set off a chain reaction on the nearby Liberty ship SS *John Harvey*, which was carrying a secret cargo of mustard gas munitions. The *John Harvey*, which had already been hit and was on fire, disintegrated when the *John L. Motley exploded*, releasing deadly mustard gas into the air and water around the vessel.

Explosion of either *John L. Motley* or SS *John Harvey* at Bari, Italy

The death toll in Bari was more than one thousand civilians and Allied seamen. Six Kings Point Cadets were lost on three different vessels. Thousands more seamen and civilians sustained serious injuries caused by the exposure to mustard gas. The effect of these injuries was exacerbated by the fact that doctors in the area didn't realize they were treating mustard gas victims.

Cadet-Midshipman Edwin D. Howard was posthumously awarded the Mariner's Medal, the Combat Bar, the Atlantic War Zone Bar, the Mediterranean-Middle East War Zone Bar, the Victory Medal, and the Presidential Testimonial Letter.

Edwin Howard was the oldest of Edwin C. Howard and Mary A. Howard's two sons and the middle of their three children. He is remembered by his sister as a trickster, and enormously popular among both classmates and teachers. The 1940 U.S. Census indicates that Edwin C. Howard was the vice president and manager of a gas and oil company. Though slow to grow, Edwin surprised everyone by suddenly growing twelve inches during his senior year in high school. Edwin was engaged to a young woman from his high school and asked his sister to accompany him to buy the engagement ring. Although Edwin had his pilot's license, he was unable to enter the Army Air Force due to an allergy. His sister recalled a letter Edwin sent home from the Mediterranean shortly before his death, in which he told his family, "Don't worry about me—I am invincible."

The Liberty ship SS *Edwin D. Howard*, built by J. A. Jones Construction Company, Panama City, Florida, in March 1945, was named in honor of Cadet-Midshipman Howard. The ship was later acquired by the Navy and converted to the Radar Picket Ship USS *Scanner* (AGR 5).

Alvin Harris Justis Jr.

Born: August 23, 1924
Hometown: Lynchburg, VA
Class: 1944
Service: Merchant Marine
Position / Rank: Engine Cadet
Date / Place of death: December 2, 1943 /
Bari, Italy
Date / Place of burial: December 2, 1943 /
Lost at Sea—Bari, Italy
Age: 19

Alvin H. Justis signed on aboard the SS *John Harvey* as Engine Cadet on October 5, 1943, at Baltimore, Maryland. Three other Cadet-Midshipmen also signed on aboard the *John Harvey* were Marvin W. Brodie (engine), James L. Cahill (deck), and Richard B. Glauche (deck). According to a report filed by Cadet-Midshipman Cahill, the ship sailed to Norfolk, Virginia, to finish loading and joined a convoy that sailed for Oran, Algeria, on October 15. Unbeknownst to most of the crew, part of the ship's cargo were two thousand M47A1 mustard gas bombs. The bombs were being sent to the Mediterranean so that American forces could retaliate if the Germans resorted to chemical warfare.

The *John Harvey* arrived in Oran on November 2, discharged its cargo other than the mustard gas bombs, and then loaded a cargo of ammunition. A convoy of about forty ships, including the *John Harvey*, sailed from Oran for Augusta, Sicily, on November 19, arriving there on November 25. The *John Harvey* sailed the next day in a convoy of thirty ships bound for the ports of Taranto and Bari on the Italian mainland, with the Bari-bound ships arriving there on November 28. The port facilities at Bari were unable to keep up with the number of ships in the port, resulting in days-long delays in discharging ships anchored in the port. Because of the high level of secrecy surrounding its cargo, the *John Harvey* was held in port for several days awaiting discharge, moored alongside other ships loaded with ammunition and gasoline, including the SS *John L. Motley*, the SS *John Bascom*, and the SS *Samuel J. Tilden*.

Because of its distance from German airfields, an air attack on Bari was not considered likely, so the port was not protected by the normal air defenses. As a result, a German attack force of more than one hundred

Ju88s was able to completely surprise the few defenders of Bari on the evening of December 2, 1943. Due to the lights being left on, the bombers were able to accurately bomb the ships in the port and port facilities with only the loss of a single aircraft. They left behind twenty-eight ships sunk, twelve more damaged, over one thousand merchant mariners and military personnel killed, and a port so badly damaged that it took three weeks to resume discharging ships.

Explosion of either SS *John Harvey* or SS *John L. Motley* at Bari, Italy

According to the few surviving eye witnesses, the *John L. Motley* and the *Samuel J. Tilden* were among the first ships to be hit by the bombers. However, after the second wave of aircraft finished their attack, the *John Harvey* was in flames from stem to stern. With the fires threatening the *John Harvey* cargo of ammunition, its crew fought desperately to save the ship, and their lives. However, the damaged *John L. Motley* had broken free from its mooring lines and, completely engulfed in flames, was drifting toward the *John Harvey*. Suddenly, the *John L. Motley* exploded, destroying the ship and detonating the *John Harvey* cargo. The *John Harvey* disintegrated, sending the contents of its cargo of mustard gas bombs into the air and water throughout the port.

Everyone aboard the *John Harvey*, including Cadet-Midshipmen Alvin H. Justis, Marvin H. Brodie, and Richard B. Glauche, perished instantly. The only survivors from the *John Harvey* were Cadet-Midshipman James L. Cahill and one of the ship's able-bodied seamen who were ashore when the attack began. One of the major factors in the high number of casualties from the attack is that doctors and other medical personnel attending to the wounded did not diagnose their signs and symptoms as those of mustard gas poisoning, since no mustard gas was believed to be in the area.

Cadet-Midshipman Alvin H. Justis Jr. was posthumously awarded the Mariner's Medal, the Combat Bar, the Atlantic War Zone Bar, the Mediterranean-Middle East War Zone Bar, the Victory Medal, and the Presidential Testimonial Letter.

Alvin H. Justis was the only son and oldest child of Alvin Harris Justis and Lavie Clyde Grissett Justis. Alvin's sister, Marie, was two years younger. According to the 1940 U.S. Census, the Justis family was hard working, with only Marie identified as not having some type of employment. Alvin Sr. worked as a clerk for the Norfolk and Western Railroad in Lynchburg; Lavie worked part time as a "fancy stitcher" in a shoe factory; and at age fifteen, Alvin worked about nine hours per week driving a truck for a local grocery store. A graduate of E. C. Glass High School in Lynchburg, Alvin Justis was a member of the football and baseball teams. Nicknamed "Shorty" because of his short stature, Alvin stood tall when it counted.

Donald James Kannitzer

Born:	October 14, 1925
Hometown:	Seattle, WA
Class:	1945
Service:	Merchant Marine
Position / Rank:	Deck Cadet
Date / Place of death:	December 28, 1944 / between Leyte and Mindoro Islands
Date / Place of burial:	December 28, 1944 / Lost At Sea between Leyte and Mindoro Islands
Age:	19

Cadet-Midshipman Donald J. Kannitzer, a graduate of the San Mateo, California, Basic School, signed on aboard the SS *John Burke* as Deck Cadet on October 5, 1944, at Honolulu, Hawaii. The ship sailed on October 10, loaded with ammunition bound for the Philippines. It is unknown how Donald Kannitzer came to be in Honolulu, as this was not a normal port for taking new crew.

SS *John Burke* hit by kamikaze

By December 28, 1944, the *John Burke* and its crew were part of a convoy of merchant ships and landing craft en route from Leyte to Mindoro loaded with ammunition for the new air bases to be built there. According to to the deck logbook of the USS *Bush* (DD 529), one of the convoy's escorts, the convoy came under a Japanese kamikaze attack at about 1012 (local time). At 1020, Val (Aichi D3A) dive bombers crashed into the SS *John Burke* and SS *William Sharon*. The after action report of the Commander, LST Group 43, who was in charge of all of the LSTs in the convoy, stated,

> Within two minutes after the *John Burke* had been hit she exploded and left no evidence. Debris from this ship killed 3 Army personnel and 1 Navy, wounded 23 Army and Navy on ships in the vicinity. LST 750 suffered heavily with several serious casualties and some ship damage.

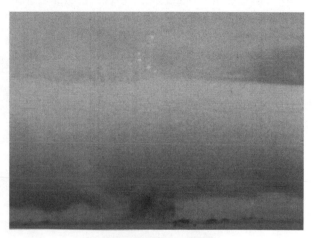

SS *John Burke* exploding

When the attack began, the medical officer of the USS *Bush,* Lt. George Johnson, MC, USNR, began filming the attack with his 16 mm movie camera. This film captured the last moments of the SS *John Burke*. The SS *John Burke* was one of two ships with Kings Pointers aboard that were lost with all hands in the Mindoro invasion. The other was the SS *Lewis L. Dyche*, whose Third Assistant Engineer was Kings Point graduate Peter Chung Ying Chue.

Cadet-Midshipman Donald J. Kannitzer was posthumously awarded the Mariner's Medal, the Combat Bar with star, the Philippine Liberation Ribbon, the Pacific War Zone Bar, the Victory Medal, and the Presidential Testimonial Letter.

SS *John Burke* explosion

Donald J. Kannitzer was the youngest of Julius S. and Marie L. Kannitzer's three sons. His twin older brothers, Lyle and Clyde, were four years older than Donald. Donald's father was a baker at the Ballard Baking Company.

According to his uncle, Ernest Frey, Donald was an excellent student who was well known for his good citizenship qualities. He applied himself with determination in the pursuit of high marks in his scholastic studies. Donald's favorite form of relaxation was to go fishing. He was sought out by his classmates because of his character and flawless conduct record. He was a source of pride to his family. Ernest Frey offered the following about his nephew:

> The aim of every man should be to secure the highest and most harmonious development of his powers to a complete and consistent whole.

Thomas Kellegrew

Born:	October 22, 1921
Hometown:	Brooklyn, New York
Class:	1944
Service:	Merchant Marine
Position / Rank:	Engine Cadet
Date / Place of death:	May 19, 1943 /At Sea
Date / Place of burial:	(Initial) May 22, 1943 Stellawood Cemetery Durban, South Africa (Final) Date Unknown / North Africa American Cemetery, Carthage, Tunisia, Plot H, Row 18, Grave 5
Age:	21

Thomas Kellegrew signed on as Engine Cadet aboard the SS *John Drayton* by September 17, 1942, at Wilmington, North Carolina, where the ship had been built. His Academy classmate Herman E. Rosen (deck) also signed on at Wilmington, North Carolina, before the ship sailed to load cargo in New York for its maiden voyage. In New York, Cadet-Midshipmen Morton Deitz (deck) and Jack Stadstad (engine) joined the ship.

The *John Drayton* sailed on October 12 from New York bound for Abadan, Iran, loaded with a general cargo of military supplies, including canned goods, ammunition, tanks, and aircraft. From January 31 to April 1, 1943, the *John Drayton* discharged and loaded cargo at several ports in Iran. On April 4, the ship sailed from Bandar Abbas for Cape Town. With the exception of the first two days, the *John Drayton* was not escorted.

On the evening of April 21, 1943, the *John Drayton* was approximately 275 miles east of Durban, South Africa, when its luck ran out. According to the Navy report on the sinking, the ship came under attack at 1700 (GCT) when the crew reported seeing torpedoes miss the ship. The ship maintained its speed but was zigzagging around its original course. Later that evening, the ship turned to evade what appeared to be a surfaced submarine. Upon returning to course, another torpedo, later determined to have been fired by the Italian submarine *Leonardo Da Vinci*, struck the

John Drayton on the starboard side at the number 3 lifeboat, destroying the engines and killing the men on watch, including Cadet-Midshipman Stadstad. Cadet-Midshipman Morton Deitz stated in his report,

> A large gaping hole was blown in the hull, demolishing the #3 boat, and since the torpedo hit about at the generator platform in the engine room, all lights were blown out. Immediately after the explosion of the torpedo, the abandon ship signal was given from the bridge and all hands proceeded to their respective boat stations. The crew of the #3 boat was ordered to distribute themselves among the remaining boats.

Cadet-Midshipman Rosen was actually assigned to boat number 4, but because he left his station to collect clothing and a blanket from his cabin, he was accidentally left aboard. His only option was to jump into the water and swim for number 2 boat, which already had Cadet-Midshipmen Deitz, Kellegrew, and twenty-one other survivors on board. The men in number 1 and number 4 boats were all rescued within a week of the sinking.

However, the voyage of the *John Drayton* number 2 boat started out poorly and never recovered. The two deck officers aboard, the Chief Mate and Third Mate, were unable to effectively command the boat due to illness and their injuries. Gale force winds prevented the survivors from raising its sail until the next morning when they attempted to set course for Durban. After six days of stormy weather, the boat capsized, resulting in the loss of everything aboard, including the survivor's food, water, and clothing. By what Rosen described as a "miracle of seamanship," the boat was righted and bailed out by the twenty-four men. For the next three weeks, they were, in Rosen's words, "wet and frozen by night and baked and thirsty by day."

After the capsizing, the survivors, including the two deck officers, began dying, mainly due to drinking seawater. Eventually, command of the boat fell upon Cadet-Midshipman Rosen, although he ". . . felt immature and unequal to the task." Unknown to Rosen and the other survivors, the search for the John Drayton's lifeboat had been called off on May 8. Cadet-Midshipman Thomas Kellegrew died in Herman Rosen's arms just hours before they were rescued on May 20 by the Greek freighter SS *Mount Rhodope*. At that point, the boat was just twenty miles from land but contained only eight survivors of which three later died in the hospital.

Cadet-Midshipman Thomas Kellegrew was posthumously awarded the Mariner's Medal, the Combat Bar with star, the Atlantic War Zone Bar, the Pacific War Zone Bar, the Mediterranean-Middle East War Zone Bar, the Victory Medal, and the Presidential Testimonial Letter. Although he was initially buried in Durban on May 22, 1943, Thomas Kellegrew's final resting place is in the North Africa American Cemetery in Carthage, Tunisia. Two other Kings Pointers, Otto E. Kern Jr. and Niles Stevens, are buried in the same cemetery. The name of another Kings Pointer, Frederick Whitehead, is inscribed on the cemetery's list of those Lost at Sea.

Thomas Kellegrew was the only son of Alexander R. Kellegrew, an attorney, and Adelaide Kellegrew. His sister, Joyce, who was four years younger, traveled to Europe in 1938 with her parents, while Thomas, apparently, had to stay in school.

Herman Rosen wrote a moving account of the loss of the SS *John Drayton* in his book, *Gallant Ship, Brave Men*. In October 2004, he said,

> Tom Kellegrew, Engine Cadet aboard S.S. John Drayton was popular aboard our ship. He was always pleasant and eager to do more than his share. He stood extra watches in the Engine Room when the Third Assistant Engineer was ill. He was often praised by the Chief Engineer for his dedication. Tom hoped to make a career of the sea. In our Lifeboat he rowed until his hands blistered. He was constantly cheerful, expecting rescue day after day. He boosted morale! He was my buddy and died in the lifeboat on the 30th day, only hours before our rescue.
>
> Tom's mother visited me while I was hospitalized at Staten Island, NY. She insisted on giving me his pocket watch engraved "TK" which I have and treasure to this day!

Donald Anderson Kennedy

Born: May 20, 1924
Hometown: Brooklyn, New York
Class: 1944
Service: Merchant Marine
Position / Rank: Engine Cadet
Date / Place of death: June 30, 1943
Date / Place of burial: July 5, 1943 / Calvary
                               Cemetery, Brooklyn,
                               NY
Age: 19

Donald A. Kennedy signed on as Engine Cadet aboard the new Liberty ship SS *Lee Overman* on June 30, 1943, at Norfolk, Virginia. The next morning, his body was found at the bottom of the ship's number 4 hold. He was pronounced dead at 0935 on July 1, 1943. The cause of death is an accidental fall. According to his death certificate, his remains were shipped to Brooklyn, New York, for burial at the Calvary Cemetery.

Cadet-Midshipman Donald A. Kennedy was posthumously awarded the Merchant Marine Service Medal.

Donald Kennedy was the younger of the two sons of Raymond J. S. Kennedy and Estelle Kennedy. He graduated from Midwood High School in Brooklyn, New York. His brother, Everett, was four years older. According to the 1930 U.S. Census, Raymond Kennedy was a railroad engineer. However, various crew lists indicate that Raymond J. S. Kennedy sailed as Chief Engineer on various ships during World War II.

Otto Edward Kern Jr.

Born:	February 17, 1921
Hometown:	Detroit, MI
Class:	1943
Service:	Merchant Marine
Position / Rank:	Deck Cadet
Date / Place of death:	November 18, 1942 / Oran, Algeria
Date / Place of burial:	November 19, 1942 / U.S. Army Cemetery, Oran, Algeria, (Final) Date Unknown / North Africa American Cemetery, Carthage, Tunisia; Plot A Row 15 Grave 13
Age:	21

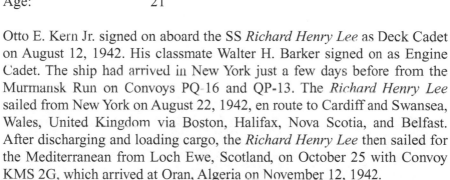

Otto E. Kern Jr. signed on aboard the SS *Richard Henry Lee* as Deck Cadet on August 12, 1942. His classmate Walter H. Barker signed on as Engine Cadet. The ship had arrived in New York just a few days before from the Murmansk Run on Convoys PQ-16 and QP-13. The *Richard Henry Lee* sailed from New York on August 22, 1942, en route to Cardiff and Swansea, Wales, United Kingdom via Boston, Halifax, Nova Scotia, and Belfast. After discharging and loading cargo, the *Richard Henry Lee* then sailed for the Mediterranean from Loch Ewe, Scotland, on October 25 with Convoy KMS 2G, which arrived at Oran, Algeria on November 12, 1942.

On November 17, 1942, the *Richard Henry Lee* was at the French naval base at Mers-el-Kebir, now a suburb of the city of Oran. That evening, Cadet-Midshipman Otto E. Kern, along with Oiler Edward Blechel and Able Seamen Jose N. Roberts and Clarence Bovay, went into Oran. At about 0015, local time, the men asked for rides back to their ship from an Army military police jeep patrol that was headed toward Mers-el-Kebir. Sgt. Harold L. O'Brien, who was in charge of the patrol, agreed to take the men as far as he could; the four merchant seamen and an Army corporal crowded into the back of the jeep, which was driven by Private Alfred L. Dyer.

Near Fort St. Andre in Oran, the jeep passed a convoy of Army trucks heading in the opposite direction. One of the trucks hit the jeep on the left side, throwing it into the curb on the right with enough force to break the stock on Private Dyer's "tommy gun." None of trucks in the convoy stopped or even slowed down for the accident. When Private Dyer was able to bring the jeep to a stop, two of the men sitting in the rear of the jeep, Cadet-Midshipman Otto Kern and Able Seaman Jose N. Roberts, were lying in the center of the road about twenty-five feet away. Private Dyer radioed for an ambulance, while Sergeant O'Brien and Edward Blechl drove in the jeep to a nearby dispensary to bring medical help for Cadet-Midshipman Kern. However, the French doctor they brought to the scene declared that both Kern and Roberts were dead when he arrived. Two Army officers arrived shortly thereafter to take charge of the investigation and remove the bodies. Army authorities informed the Master of the *Richard Henry Lee* of the accident and deaths soon after.

Cadet-Midshipman Otto E. Kern Jr. was buried the following day at the U.S. Army cemetery in Oran. After the war, Kern's remains were moved to the North Africa American Cemetery in Carthage, Tunisia. He is buried near two other Kings Pointers, Niles Stevens and Thomas Kellegrew. The name of another Kings Pointer, Frederick Whitehead, is inscribed on the cemetery's list of those Lost at Sea.

Otto E. Kern Jr. was posthumously awarded the Atlantic War Zone Bar, the Mediterranean-Middle East War Zone Bar, the Victory Medal, and the Presidential Testimonial Letter.

Kern's Department Store, Detroit, MI, 1942

Otto Kern was the youngest of Otto Kern and Katherine Helen H. Kern's four children. His older siblings were Ernst, Richard, and Mary Louise. The senior Kern was an executive of Kern's, one of Detroit's "Big Three" department stores, which had been started by his father. The land where the main store was located is now the site of the Compuware Corporation Headquarters. The family sold the company in 1957, and the stores closed in 1959.

The Otto Kern family lived in Bloomfield Heights, Michigan, one of Detroit's northern suburbs, where they were prominent members of the Catholic Church. Otto Jr. was a Boy Scout and a member of the Cranbrook High School wrestling and track teams. He was remembered by his high school classmates as being a man with a "fun" personality who was popular with the girls. His family and friends found that he developed a power of self-reliance that was apparent to all. One of Otto's brothers believed that the following statement by Abraham Lincoln best summarized his brother.

> And having chosen our course, let us renew our trust in God and go forward without fear and with manly hearts.

Chester Edward Klein

Born:	June 5, 1920
Hometown:	Elmhurst, NY
Class:	1943
Service:	Merchant Marine
Position / Rank:	Engine Cadet
Date / Place of death:	September 19, 1942 / 11-20 N, 58-50 W
Date / Place of burial:	September 19, 1942 / Lost at Sea—11-20 N, 58-50 W
Age:	22

Chester E. Klein signed on as Engine Cadet aboard the MS *Wichita* on May 1 at New Orleans, Louisiana. He had been assigned to the MS *Blenheim* from the Cadet school in New Orleans but was abruptly transferred to the *Wichita* on April 30. He was joined on May 20 by recent graduate Third Assistant Engineer Ceslaus (Chester) Maciorowski. The next day, Cadet-Midshipman Robert J. Bole signed on as Deck Cadet. The MS *Wichita* was a World War I era "Hog Islander" converted from steam turbine to diesel propulsion in 1929. The ship departed for Africa in late May. After calling at several ports, the final loading port was Takoradi, Ghana and they sailed for the United States loaded with general cargo on September 1, 1942, bound for St. Thomas, U.S. Virgin Islands without any escort.

MS *Wichita*

According to German Navy records, the *Wichita* was located and attacked by *U-516* on the morning of September 19, 1942, when the *Wichita* was about three hundred miles east of Barbados. The submarine's initial attack was unsuccessful. Despite the *Wichita* zigzagging at a speed of about 11 knots, the *U-516* repositioned itself and hit the *Wichita* with a torpedo between the foremast and the bridge. The *Wichita* sank in less than a minute with no survivors.

The *U-516*'s logbook states that the submarine surfaced and searched the area but found neither survivors nor lifeboats. Cadet-Midshipmen Chester E. Klein, Robert J. Bole III, and Third Assistant Engineer Ceslau Maciorowski all died in the attack.

Cadet-Midshipman Chester E. Klein was posthumously awarded the Mariner's Medal, the Combat Bar with star, the Atlantic War Zone Bar, the Victory Medal, and the Presidential Testimonial Letter.

Chester E. Klein

Chester (Chet) Edward Klein was the oldest of Dr. Henry Klein and Lucy Ermold Klein's two children, and their only son. His sister, Lucy, also known as "Sis," was one year younger. When Chet and Sis were young teenagers, the Klein family moved to Beacon, New York, to be closer to the families of Lucy's father, George, and Uncle Edward Ermold, owners of successful manufacturing businesses. Chet, Sis, and John Ermold, a favorite cousin, spent a great deal of time together on Edward Ermold's yacht. Chet and Sis attended Newtown High School in Elmhurst, New York.

Chet attended Middlebury College for one year after graduating from high school. However, according to his family, the next year, Chet entered Pratt Institute of Technology to prepare him for his responsibilities running the Ermold family manufacturing businesses.

However, after entering Pratt, Chet applied for and was accepted to the U.S. Merchant Marine Cadet Corps and reported for training at the

Lucy and Chester

Cadet School at New Orleans, Louisiana. Letters to his family reveal that he enjoyed his merchant marine training and life. In his last letters, Chet said he was looking forward to a short trip of three months and then to return for shore school for ten months after which he would seek active duty in the Navy.

According to Lucy's son, Mark Lofgren, in her last days, his mother frequently asked for "Chet" and that being told she would meet him soon eased her last days.

Ralph Jacob Kohlmeyer

Born: October 28, 1919
Hometown: Rego Park, NY
Class: 1944
Service: Merchant Marine
Position / Rank: Engine Cadet
Date / Place of death: February 23, 1943 /
North Atlantic,
46-15 N, 38-11 W
Date / Place of burial: February 23, 1943 /
Lost At Sea, North
Atlantic
46-15 N, 38-11 W
Age: 23

Ralph J. Kohlmeyer signed on as Engine Cadet aboard the SS *Jonathan Sturges* at the Port of New York on January 12, 1943. He was sworn in as a Midshipman, USNR, on September 18, 1942. Also on board were Cadet-Midshipmen Harry Burlison (deck), Grover Lietz (engine), and William Wilson (deck). David L. Edwards, Chief Mate was a 1940 Cadet Officer. After safely delivering its cargo to England, the *Jonathan Sturges* was returning to New York with Convoy ON-166 from Liverpool when it fell behind the convoy on the night of February 23/24, 1943. The ship, with a crew of forty-four merchant mariners and a Naval Armed Guard of thirty-one, was carrying 1,500 tons of sand ballast. In bad weather and poor visibility, the *Sturges* was making 6 knots, about half its full speed.

At about 1:00 a.m., the vessel was struck in the forward part of the ship by two torpedoes fired by *U-707*. The engines were secured, but the ship, which had apparently been broken in two, began to sink bow first. Survivors recalled that the explosions gave off a sweet odor and left a sweet taste in their mouths for hours after the incident.

Although the Radio Officer was able to send a distress signal, there was no time to await a reply, as the crew abandoned ship. Two lifeboats and four life rafts were successfully launched. According to the post sinking report of the survivors, nineteen men were able to get into one lifeboat, while the Master, Chief Mate David Edwards, and fifteen others were in a second boat. The other twenty-four survivors were able to reach the four life rafts. However, the boats and rafts were soon separated.

On February 27, three days after the sinking, the boat with nineteen men aboard met up with a lifeboat carrying three survivors from the Dutch ship SS *Madoera* which had been in the same convoy. Eight of the *Sturges* survivors climbed into the *Madoera*'s boat. Although one of the *Jonathan Sturges* crew eventually died of exposure, the other eighteen (along with the three *Madoera*'s survivors) were rescued by the USS *Belknap* (DD 251) on March 12, 1943. However, the other lifeboat with its seventeen survivors was never seen again. Of the twenty-four men on the life rafts, only six survived. These men were rescued on April 5 by *U-336* and spent the rest of the war as prisoners of war.

Cadet-Midshipman Ralph J. Kohlmeyer, along with the three other Cadets, was killed in the incident. He was posthumously awarded the Mariner's Medal, the Combat Bar, the Atlantic War Zone Bar, the Victory Medal, and the Presidential Testimonial Letter.

Ralph Kohlmeyer was the youngest, by thirteen years, of Jacob Kohlmeyer and Matilda Kohlmeyer's two sons. According to Ralph's niece, Joan Cabble, Ralph loved dancing and was a frequent listener to the *Make Believe Ballroom* radio show. While he was attending Richmond Hill High School, he worked as a lifeguard. The yearbook for his senior year (1939) lists his accomplishments as receiving the "Scholarship Pin," being a "Junior Arista," and being involved with the Commercial Honor Society, Who's Who Committee, and basketball intramurals. According to the 1940 census, after graduating from high school, Ralph was employed as a clerk in a brokerage house.

Joseph William Krusko

Born:	March 19, 1920
Hometown:	Yonkers, New York
Class:	1944
Service:	Merchant Marine
Position / Rank:	Deck Cadet
Date / Place of death:	October 17, 1942 / North Atlantic 49-39 N, 30-20 W
Date / Place of burial:	October 17, 1942 / Lost At Sea, North Atlantic 49-39 N, 30-20 W
Age:	23

Joseph W. Krusko signed on as Deck Cadet aboard the SS *Angelina* on September 9, 1942, at the Port of New York. He joined Cadet-Midshipman Joseph P. Alexander who had signed on as Deck Cadet three months earlier. After a voyage to Liverpool, the *Angelina* was returning to New York in ballast with Convoy ON-137.

SS *Angelina*

On October 17, 1942, gale force winds had resulted in the *Angelina* straggling behind the convoy. However, a Canadian corvette had also been forced to fall behind the convoy and was keeping station off the *Angelina* as they coped with the heavy seas. Due to the heavy seas, neither ship was zigzagging.

At about 2345 (GCT), one torpedo fired by *U-618* struck the *Angelina* on its starboard side at number 4 hold. The *Angelina* listed to starboard after the impact, and the well deck flooded, preventing the gun crew from manning the four-inch gun on the stern. Fortunately, although the *Angelina*'s radio could not send a distress signal, the corvette did send an SOS. The general alarm sounded soon after the first torpedo struck, and all hands prepared to abandon ship in the port lifeboat and rafts. About twenty minutes after firing on the *Angelina*, *U-618* fired another torpedo, hitting the stern on the starboard side and detonating the ammunition magazine there. The *Angelina* sank at about 0030 (GCT), within minutes of the second torpedo hitting the ship.

However, despite getting away from their sinking ship, the weather was not in the crew's favor. Many men were washed overboard and drowned in the heavy seas. The port (number 2) lifeboat, which was launched successfully, capsized in the waves, and only half of the occupants were able to seize hold of the overturned boat. The few who remained were gradually losing their hold, through the heroic efforts of the Carpenter five men kept clinging to the hull. Another six men managed to stay on a raft.

Fortunately, the convoy's rescue ship, the SS *Bury*, received the corvette's SOS and arrived on the scene at 0345 (GCT) and rescued the six men on the life raft. After searching for over two hours, the *Bury* found the capsized lifeboat, rescuing the three men still hanging on to it. The Armed Guard Commander, Ensign A. J. Gartland, USNR, cited the ship's Chief Mate, E. A. L. Koonig, and the Carpenter, Gus Alm, for heroism during the abandonment and boarding the *Bury*, respectively. One of the men rescued by the *Bury*, Felix Posario, died before the *Bury* reached St. John's, Newfoundland, a week later. The other forty-six crew members of the *Angelina*, including Cadets Joseph Alexander and Joseph Krusko, were Lost at Sea.

Cadet-Midshipman Joseph W. Krusko was posthumously awarded the Mariner's Medal, the Combat Bar with star, the Atlantic War Zone Bar, the Victory Medal, and the Presidential Testimonial Letter.

Joseph W. Krusko was the youngest son and fifth of the six children of Slovakian immigrants William and Susan Krusko of Bayonne, New Jersey. Based on U.S. Census data, it appears that Joseph, his brothers, and his sisters lost their parents at some time in the 1930s. The 1940 U.S. Census shows that John Krusko, the oldest child, was "head of the household."

Ginny Sidorik, Joseph's niece, recalled his "sparkling personality" and his "widespread popularity" in the schools he attended in Yonkers. Joseph

Krusko graduated from Saunders Trade and Technical High School, and was later employed by Ward Leonard Electric Company in Mount Vernon, New York, before attending the Academy. The 1940 U.S. Census shows that he was employed as a radio mechanic.

Robert Louis Lamac

Born:	September 14, 1921
Hometown:	Bronx, NY
Class:	1944
Service:	Merchant Marine
Position / Rank:	Deck Cadet
Date / Place of death:	January 27, 1943 / Atlantic, 36-37 N, 30-55 W
Date / Place of burial:	January 27, 1943 / Lost At Sea, Atlantic, 36-37 N, 30-55 W
Age:	21

Robert L. Lamac signed on aboard the SS *Charles C. Pinckney* as Deck Cadet on January 1, 1943, at the Port of New York. Joining him on the ship was his classmate, Engine Cadet Vincent Corrigan. On the same day, First Assistant Engineer Theodore Scharpf, a former Cadet Officer, also signed on.

The *Pinckney* sailed with Convoy UGS-4 from Hampton Roads, Virginia, on January 13, 1943, loaded with ammunition, a general cargo of war supplies, and mechanized equipment bound for Casablanca. On the night of January 21, 1943, the *Charles Pinckney*, the SS *City of Flint*, and the SS *Julia Ward Howe* straggled from the convoy. All three, no longer protected by the convoy escort of six U.S. Navy destroyers, were sunk by U-boats within a week.

On January 27, the *Pinckney* was about two hundred miles south-southwest of Fayal Island, Azores. During the morning, the watch sighted a submarine far off on the horizon, traveling parallel to the *Pinckney*, apparently at great speed. The gun crew fired a few shots at the submarine, but even at maximum elevation, these did not come close to their target. The *Pinckney* then increased to its maximum speed of 11 knots.

Late in the afternoon, the *Pinckney* changed course to proceed directly away from the submarine, but the crew was unable to tell whether or not the submarine followed. At about 2145, local time, the Chief Mate observed a torpedo, fired by *U-514*, heading directly for the ship and ordered a hard-right rudder. The order came too late, and the torpedo struck just behind the ship's bow, detonating part of the cargo. The explosion blew off the bow, killing two men in the forward gun crew. On the Captain's order, the crew abandoned ship immediately, with all but one of the boats lowered successfully. The gun crew remained on the ship at great peril to their own lives, given the cargo of munitions on board. When the German submarine surfaced near the port beam, the gun crew engaged, forcing the sub into an emergency dive, and leading the gun crew to believe they'd sunk the sub.

Since the ship did not immediately sink, the crew reboarded the ship to see if it could be repaired. After inspecting the ship's engines, the Chief Engineer reported that it would not be possible to raise steam and continue sailing the ship. However, the crew was able to collect additional supplies and send a distress signal. Around midnight, *U-514* fired two more torpedoes; the second torpedo hit the *Pinckney,* and the crew abandoned ship again. Soon thereafter, *U-514* approached the boats and questioned the survivors.

The four lifeboats began making way for the Azores but were unable to stay together in heavy seas during the second night. One lifeboat, carrying six crew members, including the Second Officer, and eight Naval Armed Guard sailors, was picked up on February 8 by the Swiss ship *Caritas I* and later landed at Horta, Fayal Island, Azores. The other three lifeboats were never seen again. Of the seventy-three persons aboard the *Pinckney* (forty-two crew, twenty-nine Naval Armed Guard sailors, and two U.S. Army security officers), only these fourteen were rescued. Cadet-Midshipmen Robert L. Lamac and Vincent Corrigan, along with First Assistant Engineer Theodore Scharpf, were among those lost.

Cadet-Midshipman Robert L. Lamac was posthumously awarded the Mariner's Medal, the Combat Bar with star, the Atlantic War Zone Bar, the Victory Medal, and the Presidential Testimonial Letter.

Robert L. Lamac was the older of Emil and Mary Lamac's two sons. According to the 1930 U.S. Census, Emil was a machinist at an instrument manufacturing company.

John Robert Lambert

Born:	May 22, 1924
Hometown:	Del Rio, TX
Class:	1944
Service:	Merchant Marine
Position / Rank:	Deck Cadet
Date / Place of death:	March 16, 1943 / North Atlantic, 50-38 N, 34-46 W
Date / Place of burial:	March 16, 1943 / Lost at Sea
50-38 N, 34-46 W	
Age:	18

John R. Lambert signed on as Deck Cadet aboard the new Liberty ship SS *James Oglethorpe* on February 22, 1943, at Savannah, Georgia, just a few days after it was completed. He joined three other Cadet-Midshipmen who were already aboard: Wayne D. Fajans (engine), William H. Ford (deck), and Richard Record (engine). The *James Oglethorpe* completed the installation of its armament, final fitting out, and adjustments, and the ship sailed for its first loading port. The ship joined Convoy HX-229 in New York on March 9, 1943, for a journey to Liverpool, England. The *James Oglethorpe* was loaded with a cargo of steel, cotton, and food in the holds, and a deck cargo of aircraft, tractors, and trucks. It had a crew of forty-four merchant sailors, twenty-six Naval Armed Guard sailors, and four Navy passengers.

Cadet-Midshipmen Fajans later reported that

> the weather was the usual kind experienced during this time of year in the North Atlantic, i.e., dirty and heavy seas.

In his report of the sinking, Cadet-Midshipman Ford stated,

> The day before our vessel was lost number 2 boat was carried away by heavy seas and numbers 1 and 3 extensively damaged. As a result of this damage, our available life savings equipment was materially reduced.

Early on the evening of March 16, Fajan was at his gun station when he spotted the conning tower of a submarine on the starboard side of the ship and notified the gunnery officer. However, no action was taken by the ship's gun crews. Analysis of German Navy records found that the submarine reported to have been seen by Fajans was not one of the submarines that later attacked the *James Oglethorpe*.

At 2120 (GCT) on March 16, 1943, *U-758* fired a "spread" of four torpedoes at Convoy HX-229, hitting and sinking the M/V *Zaanland* with one torpedo and the *James Oglethorpe* with another. The *U-758*'s other two torpedoes missed. The *James Oglethorpe* was hit in either number 1 or number 2 hold (survivor reports differ). The torpedo's impact started a fire in the cargo, which was quickly extinguished. According to the accounts of survivors, although the ship settled about three feet lower in the water, it did not appear to be in danger of sinking. However, the Captain did give permission, or at least some crew members believed that he had given the crew permission, to abandon ship despite the ship being in a hard-left turn with its engines still running. Of the remaining lifeboats (numbers 4, 5, and 6) only number 6 boat was safely launched. Cadet-Midshipman Fajans, who was in number 5 boat, fell into the sea when the boat's forward fall broke. Seeing the chaos occurring with lowering the boats, the Chief Mate and Cadet-Midshipman William Ford jumped into the sea, joining the men from numbers 4 and 5 boats in the water. The crew of number 6 lifeboat was able to pick up some of the men in the water. The nine men in this boat were rescued by the corvette HMS *Pennywort* (K 111). The destroyer HMS *Beverly* (H 64, ex-USS *Branch* [DD 197]) rescued twenty-one other men from the water. These men were landed in Scotland (HMS *Pennywort*) and Northern Ireland (HMS *Beverly*). Some of the men, including Cadet-Midshipman Ford, returned to the United States aboard the SS *Queen Mary*.

About thirty members of the crew stayed on board to help the Captain sail the ship to St. John's, Newfoundland, the nearest harbor. The *James Oglethorpe* was last seen by those in the lifeboat and in the water at about 0200 (GCT), still afloat and under way. The ship, and its remaining crew, was never seen again. Although some accounts credit *U-91* with sinking the crippled *James Oglethorpe* on March 17, German Navy records only credit *U-91* with sinking the SS *Irenee Du Pont* and SS *Nariva*. It is likely that the *James Oglethorpe* foundered due to the torpedo damage and high seas.

From the accounts of the thirty survivors, it is unknown whether Cadet-Midshipmen John Lambert and Richard Record were among the seventeen men who perished abandoning the ship on March 16 or were among the thirty men lost when the *James Oglethorpe* sank.

Cadet-Midshipman John R. Lambert was posthumously awarded the Mariner's Medal, the Combat Bar with star, the Atlantic War Zone Bar, the Victory Medal, and the Presidential Testimonial Letter.

John R. Lambert was the only son of Gladys Lambert, a registered nurse. At some point between 1935 and 1940, the Lamberts moved from Ypsilanti, Michigan, to Del Rio, Texas.

Joseph J. Landron Jr.

Born:	October 5, 1922
Hometown:	Brooklyn, NY
Class:	1944
Service:	Merchant Marine
Position / Rank:	Engine Cadet
Date / Place of death:	June 10, 1943 / U.S. East Coast, 31-02 N, 79-17 W
Date / Place of burial:	June 10, 1943 / Lost at Sea—U.S. East Coast, 31-02 N, 79-17 W
Age:	20

Joseph J. Landron signed on aboard the SS *Esso Gettysburg* as Engine Cadet on May 27, 1943, at New York, New York. The ship was engaged in the coastal oil trade, running from the Gulf of Mexico to the East Coast. Also aboard the ship were Kings Point Cadet-Midshipmen John M. Carter (engine), Alfonse Miller (deck), and Eugene Quidort (deck). The ship sailed on June 6 from Port Arthur, Texas, bound for Philadelphia, Pennsylvania, loaded with 120,000 barrels of west Texas crude oil for the Atlantic Refining Company's refinery there.

Esso Gettysburg

On the afternoon of June 10, the ship was under way about one hundred miles southeast of Savannah, Georgia, traveling without escort, apparently due to its ability to make more than 15 knots. However, the ship was steering evasive courses. Although the vessel had been warned after rounding Key West that submarines were in the area, none had been sighted by the lookouts.

At around 1400, local time, 1900 (GCT), the *Esso Gettysburg* was sighted and attacked by *U-66*. The submarine's two torpedoes hit the ship's port side, the first one aft of midships, while the second torpedo hit the engine room in the stern. The impacts ruptured twenty-five feet of deck and hull, and raised a one-hundred-foot geyser of oil and water. The crude oil exploded on impact, transforming the ship into an inferno. A thick cloud of black smoke rose almost a thousand feet in the air. The ship settled by the stern and began to list to port.

At the time of the attack, Alphonse Miller was painting the starboard side of the afterdeck with an AB. John Carter was on duty with the Second Assistant Engineer in the engine room. Joseph Landron, who was not on watch, was sleeping in his room. The fact that Eugene Quidort was off watch on the flying bridge near the compass probably saved his life. Carter, along with the rest of the engine crew on duty, was killed instantly. Miller was seen to run along the catwalk toward midships, where he was caught in the flames and killed. Landron made way for the lifeboats, but when these caught fire, he jumped into the water with the rest of the survivors. He was last seen by another crew member fighting the flames in the water.

Cadet-Midshipman Eugene Quidort also jumped overboard after unsuccessfully attempting to help the Chief Mate lower one of the lifeboats into the sea. He was able to swim away from the burning oil, towing for a while Ensign John S. Arnold, the Armed Guard officer. Quidort eventually found a burned lifeboat to hang on to. Several hours later, he was rescued by the Chief Mate and Second Mate, who had managed to climb aboard another partially burned lifeboat, and pulled aboard six crew members and seven Navy men—the only survivors among forty-five crew members and twenty-seven Naval Armed Guard sailors. The following day, the survivors were spotted by an Army B-25 patrol plane. They were picked up by the SS *George Washington* and taken to Charleston, South Carolina.

The Armed Guard, under the command of Ensign John S. Arnold, USNR, did manage to fire one shot in the direction of the submarine before being forced to abandon their post by the flames. Ensign Arnold survived the sinking and was awarded the Navy Cross for his actions.

Cadet-Midshipman Joseph J. Landron Jr. was posthumously awarded the Mariner's Medal, the Combat Bar with star, the Atlantic War Zone Bar, the Victory Medal, and the Presidential Testimonial Letter.

Joseph Landron was the older of Joseph and Carmen Landron's two sons. The family moved to Brooklyn, New York, by 1925 when Joseph Jr. was a small boy. According to the 1930 and 1940 U.S. Census, Joseph Sr. was a compositor for a printer.

Leroy Pinneo Lawrence

Born:	July 10, 1921
Hometown:	Hartford, CT
Class:	1945
Service:	Merchant Marine
Position / Rank:	Deck Cadet
Date / Place of death:	August 30, 1944 / North Atlantic, 55-30 N, 7-30 W
Date / Place of burial:	August 30, 1944 / North Atlantic, 55-30 N, 7-30 W—Lost at Sea
Age:	23

Leroy P. Lawrence signed on aboard his second ship, the tanker SS *Jacksonville*, as Deck Cadet on August 18, 1944, at the Port of New York. He had previously served as Deck Cadet aboard the SS *Henry S. Sanford*. Another Kings Pointer, Third Assistant Engineer Robie K. Wentworth, who had just graduated, also signed on. The ship sailed shortly afterward loaded with a cargo of aviation gasoline.

SS *Jacksonville*

On August 30, about fifty miles north of Londonderry, Northern Ireland, the *Jacksonville* was nearing the end of its voyage when tragedy struck. The vessel was one of five ships in Convoy CU-36 destined for Loch Ewe, Scotland, which were separating from the main convoy. The *Jacksonville* had just completed an eighty-six-degree turn to take its place at the end of a single column on the port side of the convoy when it was struck by a torpedo from *U-482*.

The *Jacksonville*'s gasoline cargo quickly ignited. Within minutes, the entire ship was enveloped in flames, and ammunition in the stern ready boxes could be heard exploding. Although the ship was on fire, it was not sinking. The Captain of *U-482* fired another torpedo, which broke the ship in two. Even then, the tough tanker didn't sink. Convoy escorts had to sink the after portion with gunfire and depth charges to remove the hazard to navigation. The forward section continued burning and sank the following day.

The ship's crew had no time to launch any lifeboats or rafts, and nearly all succumbed rapidly to the raging fire. The only two survivors, a Fireman and a member of the Naval Armed Guard, jumped over the side of the ship into the flaming water and swam away from the doomed vessel. The attacking sub was never sighted, and witnesses initially thought that the ship had hit a mine. Cadet-Midshipman Leroy Lawrence and Third Assistant Engineer Robie Knowles Wentworth were among those lost in the sinking.

Cadet-Midshipman Leroy P. Lawrence was posthumously awarded the Mariner's Medal, the Combat Bar, the Atlantic War Zone Bar, the Victory Medal, and the Presidential Testimonial Letter.

Leroy P. Lawrence was the third of Edward S. and Pauline Lawrence's four children and their second son. Leroy had an older brother, Edward, an older sister, Edith, and a younger brother, Donald. According to the 1930 and 1940 U.S. Census, Edward Lawrence owned a battery service company.

Leroy graduated from Hartford High School, where he was active in the student government and a member of the National Honor Society. In 1940, Leroy entered Wesleyan University with the class of 1943. During his college years, he was a member of the John Wesley Club, president of both the Debating Society and the International Relations Club. Socially, he was a member of the university's Phi Nu Theta "Eclectic Society" or Fraternity.

Henry Alexander Levett

Born:	January 21, 1923
Hometown:	Summit, NJ
Class:	1943
Service:	Merchant Marine
Position / Rank:	Deck Cadet
Date / Place of death:	December 2, 1942 / North Atlantic, 48-45 N, 23-30 W
Date / Place of burial:	December 2, 1942 / Lost at Sea—North Atlantic, 48-45 N, 23-30 W
Age:	19

Henry A. Levett signed on as Deck Cadet aboard the SS *Coamo* on October 2, 1942, at New York, New York. He was joined by Cadet-Midshipman Joseph Giovinco, Deck Cadet. The *Coamo* was built in 1925 for the East Coast to Puerto Rico passenger trade. When World War II began, the ship was chartered by the Army Transport Service for use as a troop ship.

SS *Coamo*

After a voyage to Algiers, the *Coamo* sailed with sixteen other merchant ships in Convoy MKF-3 on November 23, 1942, bound for the west coast of Scotland. On December 1, 1942, as the convoy was nearing the British Isles, the *Coamo* was ordered by British Admiralty to proceed independently to New York without escort.

On the evening of the following day, the *Coamo* was sighted by *U-604* in a rising gale. According to German Navy records, *U-604* closed to within eight hundred yards of its target and fired one torpedo. At 1818 (GCT), the torpedo struck the *Coamo* underneath its bridge. The *Coamo* sank within five minutes of the attack without launching a single lifeboat. Although the submarine's crew reported seeing some survivors leave the ship on rafts, none of the 133 crew, 37 Armed Guard sailors, and 16 passengers, including Cadet-Midshipmen Henry Levett and Joseph Giovinco was seen again. It is believed that any survivors who left the *Coamo* died in the gale that swept the area for three days. The sinking of the *Coamo* was the largest loss of merchant crew on any U.S. Flag merchant vessel during the Second World War. It is interesting to note that all of the other ships in Convoy MKF-3 arrived safely at their destinations.

Cadet-Midshipman Henry A. Levett was posthumously awarded the Mariner's Medal, the Combat Bar, the Atlantic War Zone Bar, the Mediterranean-Middle East War Zone Bar, the Victory Medal, and the Presidential Testimonial Letter.

Henry Levett was the younger of Charles Martin Everett and Laura M. Levett's two sons. According to the 1940 U.S. Census, Charles Everett was a bond salesman in a brokerage. Henry's older brother, Charles Jr., was working as a clerk in a life insurance office. Laura Levett was a puppeteer.

Richard Erwin Lewis

Born:	April 5, 1923
Hometown:	Oswego, New York
Class:	1943
Service:	Merchant Marine
Position / Rank:	Deck Cadet
Date / Place of death:	February 20, 1942 / 38-00 N, 78-00 W
Date / Place of burial:	February 20, 1942 / Lost at Sea—38-00 N, 78-00 W
Age:	18

Richard E. Lewis signed on as Deck Cadet aboard the SS *Azalea City* at New York, New York, on the day the United States began combat in World War II, December 7, 1941. Also joining him was his classmate, Cadet-Midshipman Robert See, Engine Cadet. Two months later, on February 12, 1942, the freighter *Azalea City* left the island of Trinidad, en route from Bahia Blanca, Argentina, to Philadelphia, Pennsylvania, with a cargo of flaxseed. The vessel, with a crew of thirty-eight, was traveling alone and not zigzagging. When the *Azalea City* failed to arrive in Philadelphia after several months, the ship was presumed lost, though its exact fate remained a mystery.

SS *Azalea City*

The details of the loss were discovered after World War II in the records of the German Navy. On February 20, 1942, *U-432* sited the *Azalea City* about 125 miles east-southeast from Ocean City, Maryland. Over several hours, *U-432* fired three torpedoes at the *Azalea City;* two of which struck the ship. For some reason, the ship was unable to send a distress signal after the first torpedo struck the ship and the crew did not abandon ship. Apparently, the ship capsized immediately after the second torpedo hit, taking all hands with it, including Cadet-Midshipmen Robert See and Richard Lewis. These men were the first two Academy Cadets killed through enemy action. However, due to the nature of the disaster, their fate remained unknown for months, and Cadet-Midshipman Howard P. Conway was mourned at the Academy as the first Cadet to give his life in service of his country.

Cadet-Midshipman Richard E. Lewis was posthumously awarded the Mariner's Medal, the Combat Bar, the Atlantic War Zone Bar, the Victory Medal, and the Presidential Testimonial Letter.

Richard E. Lewis was the only child of Henry M. Lewis and Edith M. Lewis. Although the 1930 U.S. Census identifies Henry Lewis as a real estate and insurance salesman by the 1940 census, his occupation was listed as a gatekeeper for a construction company.

Grover Paul Lietz

Born:	March 21, 1921
Hometown:	Okawville, IL
Class:	1944
Service:	Merchant Marine
Position / Rank:	Engine Cadet
Date / Place of death:	February 23, 1943 / 46-15 N, 38-11 W
Date / Place of burial:	February 23, 1943 / Lost at Sea—46-15 N, 38-11 W
Age:	21

Grover P. Lietz signed on as Engine Cadet aboard the SS *Jonathan Sturges* at the Port of New York on January 12, 1943. Also on board were Cadet-Midshipmen Harry Burlison (deck), Ralph Kohlmeyer (engine), and William Wilson (deck). Chief Mate David L. Edwards was a 1940 Cadet Officer. After safely delivering its cargo to England, the *Jonathan Sturges* was returning to New York with Convoy ON-166 from Liverpool when it fell behind the convoy on the night of February 23/24, 1943. The ship, with a crew of forty-four merchant mariners and a Naval Armed Guard of thirty-one, was carrying 1,500 tons of sand ballast. In bad weather and poor visibility, the *Sturges* was making 6 knots, about half its full speed.

At about 1:00 a.m., the vessel was struck in the forward part of the ship by two torpedoes fired by *U-707*. The engines were secured, but the ship broke in two and began to sink by the bow. Survivors recalled that the explosions gave off a sweet odor and left a sweet taste in their mouths for hours after the incident.

Although the Radio Officer was able to send a distress signal, there was no time to await a reply, as the crew abandoned ship. Two lifeboats and four life rafts were successfully launched. According to the post sinking report of the survivors, nineteen men were able to get into one lifeboat, while the Master, Chief Mate David Edwards, and fifteen others were in the other boat. The other twenty-four survivors were able to reach the four life rafts. However, the boats and rafts were soon separated.

On February 27, three days after the sinking, the boat with nineteen men aboard met up with a lifeboat carrying three survivors from the Dutch ship SS *Madoera* which had been in the same convoy. Eight of the *Sturges* survivors climbed into the *Madoera*'s boat. Although one of the *Jonathan Sturges* crew eventually died of exposure, the other eighteen (along with the three *Madoera* survivors) were rescued by the USS *Belknap* (DD 251) on March 12, 1943. However, the other lifeboat with its seventeen survivors was never seen again. Of the twenty-four men on the life rafts, only six survived. These men were rescued on April 5 by *U-336* and spent the rest of the war as prisoners of war.

Cadet-Midshipman Grover P. Lietz, along with the three other Cadets, was killed in the incident. He was posthumously awarded the Mariner's Medal, the Combat Bar with star, the Atlantic War Zone Bar, the Victory Medal, and the Presidential Testimonial Letter.

Grover Lietz was the son of Edwin Lietz and Susie Lietz. He grew up on a farm in rural Washington County, Illinois, with his four brothers (Elmo, Lavern, Darrell, and Enos) and three sisters (Vergal, Dolores, and Juanita). However, by the 1940 U.S. Census, Grover was living with Vergal and her husband, Earl McGuire, in St. Louis, Missouri. The records show that Grover was a messenger for a railroad.

According to his brother Enos, Grover was popular with his classmates at Okawville High School, where he was Captain of the basketball team. Grover is credited by teammate Warren D. Stricker as being his inspiration for attending and graduating from Kings Point in 1945.

1936-37 Okawville High School basketball team. Team Captain Grover Lietz (center), Warren D. Stricker (USMMA '45) on left wearing number 1

Albert Milton Limehouse

Born:	November 16, 1921
Hometown:	Birmingham, AL
Class:	1944
Service:	Merchant Marine
Position / Rank:	Basic School Cadet
Date / Place of death:	January 5, 1943 / New Orleans, LA
Date / Place of burial:	January 9, 1943 / Elmwood Cemetery, Birmingham, Alabama
Age:	21

Cadet-Midshipman Albert Limehouse was taking part in a training cruise aboard the TV *Robert Waterman* from the Pass Christian Basic School in December 1942. On December 19, 1942, he was admitted to the U.S. Public Health Service's Marine Hospital in New Orleans. On January 1, 1943, he suffered a loss of blood supply to his lungs and kidneys; he died on the evening of January 5, just a few weeks after his twenty-first birthday. According to his death certificate, Albert was suffering from pulmonary and renal infarction, brought on by nephrosis, a disease of the kidneys. On January 6, his remains were returned to his parents in Birmingham, Alabama.

Albert Limehouse was the second of Benjamin P. Limehouse and Virginia Stott Limehouse's three sons. According to a 1942 Birmingham city directory, Benjamin Sr. owned a grocery store in which his wife and youngest son, Donald, worked as clerks. The same directory indicates that Albert Limehouse was employed as a payroll clerk by the Tennessee Coal, Iron and Railroad Company, a major employer in the Birmingham area. According to U.S. Navy records, Albert Limehouse enlisted in the U.S. Naval Reserve on January 30, 1939. He served on active duty twice for two weeks each in 1939 and 1940 aboard the World War I -era destroyers USS *Dickerson* (DD 157) and USS *Swasey* (DD 273). He attained the rate of seaman second class before being discharged on June 13, 1941.

Albert's older brother, Benjamin Jr., was a naval aviator. He was declared missing in action in the Pacific, likely near Okinawa, on March 1, 1945. At that time, he had already been awarded the Distinguished Flying Cross and the Air Medal.

William Rutherford Linde

Born:	October 10, 1921
Hometown:	Hartford, CT
Class:	1944
Service:	Merchant Marine
Position / Rank:	Engine Cadet
Date / Place of death:	February 2, 1943 / 54-50 N, 28-55 W
Date / Place of burial:	February 2, 1943 / Lost at Sea—54-50 N, 28-55 W
Age:	21

William R. Linde signed on as Engine Cadet aboard the SS *Jeremiah Van Rennselaer* on January 1, 1943. Joining the ship on the same day was Cadet-Midshipman William G. Holby, Deck Cadet. Upon completion of loading a cargo of general Army supplies, plus a deck cargo that included a railroad tank car, five trucks, telephone poles, and oil in barrels, the ship sailed from New York on January 22, 1943, in Convoy HX-224, bound for the United Kingdom. In his report on the sinking, William Holby recalled that the trip was very rough, stating,

> Heavy seas caused part of the ship's deck cargo consisting of oil in barrels to be washed overboard.

The Armed Guard Commander, Lt. (jg) Marshall T. Ismond, USNR, reported that the ship had lost the convoy on at least four occasions after sailing from New York and managed to keep its proper station in the convoy only one night in seven. He reported that the ship's deck officers felt that there was greater danger of collision from other ships in the convoy than from submarines. During the afternoon of February 1, the *Jeremiah Van Rennselaer* was ordered to change its position in the convoy from the front to the rear of the convoy. During the maneuver, the ship lost sight of the convoy and was unable to rejoin it.

On the early morning of February 2, the straggling *Jeremiah Van Rennselaer* was located by *U-456*. At 0320 (GCT), one of *U-456*'s torpedoes hit the ship at number 1 hold on the port side, blowing a large hole in the hull. A second torpedo hit about three minutes later in about the same place. According to survivors, five minutes later, another torpedo struck the ship at number 4 hold.

The explosions from the torpedoes started fires in the deck cargo, which may have caused the crew to assume that the ship was sinking. Without actually receiving orders from the Master to abandon ship, the crew hastily took to the boats. According to his report, Cadet-Midshipman William Holby reported for duty in the wheelhouse but found it deserted, except for the Captain on the starboard bridge wing. In a letter to the Linde family in 2008, William Holby said that when the first torpedo hit,

> I was sitting on my bunk reading and quickly started getting dressed. Bill jumped out of his bunk and ran out on deck. Most of the crew was out on the boat deck getting life boats over the side. With the ship rolling as it was this became a very difficult operation.

In a letter to William Linde's parents written in July 1943, another crewman, William K. McLean, confirms that the inexperienced crew lost their heads and mishandled what he called the most important job: abandoning ship. According to McLean's letter, both he and Cadet-Midshipman Linde were able to get into number 1 lifeboat, which, he says, was lowered safely to the water. However, more men than the boat could safely hold climbed into the boat, which quickly filled with water and sank. Cadet-Midshipman Linde spotted a nearby raft and jumped from the sinking lifeboat to the raft. The raft was eventually covered three deep with men desperately holding on to keep themselves from being washed overboard in the heavy seas.

Among the frozen men aboard the raft, McLean said that William Linde was one of the few who could move. He said that despite the cold, William put a light on the end of an oar and stood up on the pitching life raft for two hours, hoping that someone would see the light. McLean said that William tried to keep all of the men on the raft awake, knowing that going to sleep in those conditions would be fatal. However, in the letter, McLean said,

> It seems to me that we were about 2 hours or so out when Bill said something like this, "I am sorry, boys, but I am frozen," and passed on. His body was washed overboard a short time later.

> As I said before, I am sure you will be proud of the way your son passed on. I am and I know others who lived thought and feel the same way.

Ironically, despite the hasty abandonment of the *Jeremiah Van Rennselaer*, the ship remained afloat while many of its crew drowned or froze to death. The convoy's rescue ship, SS *Accrington*, was able to locate and rescue the men in number 4 lifeboat and several others who were able to get aboard, and stay aboard, some of the life rafts. According to the account of the SS *Accrington*'s chief officer,

> The torpedoed ship was later boarded by a third officer, the wireless engineer and 2nd Engineer where they found one man alive on the burning ship. The engines were discovered to be in order but the fuel had not been shut off and the boilers were found to be red hot. Thus she could not be salvaged under her own steam.

To prevent the ship from becoming a hazard to navigation, the *Jeremiah Van Rennselaer* was sunk by one of the convoy's escorts. Of the *Rennselaer*'s seventy men (forty-two crew and twenty-eight Armed Guard sailors), only seven crew members and seventeen Navy gunners survived. Based on reports of the survivors, many of those who died might have lived.

Cadet-Midshipman William R. Linde was posthumously awarded the Mariner's Medal, the Combat Bar with star, the Atlantic War Zone Bar, the Victory Medal, and the Presidential Testimonial Letter.

William R. Linde was the oldest son of Carl H. Linde and Elizabeth McDougal Pollock Linde's four children. According to the 1930 and 1940 U.S. Census, Carl Linde was employed by the post office. The family

William at home on leave

lived in Hartford, Connecticut, at 190 Hawthorn Street, described by local residents as one of the most attractive streets in the city.

William attended West Middle School and Hartford High School. As the oldest brother, he established a paper route that was passed on from brother to brother. He established a reputation for his brothers to live up to when he delivered the newspaper by boat in a flood. Another job "pioneered" by William for his younger brothers was working at Highland Dairy. He was later employed by Aetna Life Insurance Company while attending Hillyer College to study accounting.

The boys all lived in one room in the house where William posted the following:

> Think big and your deeds will grow
> Think small and you'll fall behind
> Think that you can and you will.
> It's all in the state of mind.

**William R. Linde,
age sixteen**

William was a member of Boy Scout Troop 22, which he said was a very important part of his life, along with the First Presbyterian Church. William's sister, Marion, believes that he was a person of strong Christian faith. To this day, in thinking about the circumstances of William's untimely death, Marion takes some comfort in the thought that the hope of his faith could have sustained and strengthened him at the end.

To honor his older brother, William's youngest brother, Capt. David Joy Linde, USCG, awarded the diplomas to the Kings Point graduating class of 1981.

Jay Francis Litton

Born:	August 11, 1924
Hometown:	Detroit, MI
Class:	1944
Service:	Merchant Marine
Position / Rank:	Engine Cadet
Date / Place of death:	December 2, 1943 / Bari, Italy
Date / Place of burial:	December 2, 1943 / Lost at Sea
Age:	19

Jay F. Litton signed on as Engine Cadet aboard the SS *John L. Motley* at Philadelphia, Pennsylvania, on June 4, 1943, shortly after it was delivered from its builders, Bethlehem-Fairfield Shipbuilding, to the War Shipping Administration. He joined his classmate Edward D. Howard, Deck Cadet, and Academy alumnus Second Mate Fulton E. Yewell. The *John L. Motley* made one voyage to the Mediterranean and returned to New York from Oran in mid-September 1943. After loading a cargo of ammunition, the *John L. Motley* sailed on its second voyage to the Mediterranean, reaching the crowded harbor of Bari, Italy, on November 28, 1943.

On December 2, 1943, the *John L. Motley* was moored alongside the jetty at Bari, Italy, discharging its cargo when a massive German air attack on the port took defenders by surprise. The attack and ensuing explosions sank seventeen ships and put the harbor out of use for three weeks. This attack became known as "Little Pearl Harbor."

A Naval Armed Guard member on the SS *John Bascom*, moored next to the *John L. Motley*, reported that the vessel sustained three bomb hits, one in the number 5 hold, one in the number 3 hold, and one down the vessel's stack. The crew was able to control the fires caused by the first strike, but after the second hit, the fires on board raged out of control, burning through the vessel's mooring lines and setting her adrift. The subsequent explosion of the *Motley*'s cargo killed everyone on board, including Second Mate Fulton Edison Yewell Jr., along with the two Cadets, Edward D. Howard and Jay F. Litton.

However, the damage caused by German bombs to the *John L. Motley* did not end there. When the *Motley* blew up, the ship was only fifty feet or so distant from the SS *John Bascom*. The *Motley*'s explosion destroyed the port side of the *Bascom*, sinking the ship within minutes. The explosion on the *John Motley* also set off a chain reaction on the nearby Liberty ship SS *John Harvey*, which was carrying a secret cargo of mustard gas munitions. The *John Harvey*, which had already been hit and was on fire, disintegrated when the *Motley* exploded, releasing deadly mustard gas into the air and water around the vessel.

Explosion of either *John L. Motley* or SS *John Harvey* at Bari, Italy

The death toll in Bari was more than one thousand civilians and Allied seamen. Six Kings Point Cadets were lost on three different vessels. Thousands more seamen and civilians sustained serious injuries caused by the exposure to mustard gas. The effect of these injuries was exacerbated by the fact that doctors in the area didn't realize they were treating mustard gas victims.

Cadet-Midshipman Jay F. Litton was posthumously awarded the Mariner's Medal, the Combat Bar, the Atlantic War Zone Bar, the Mediterranean-Middle East War Zone Bar, the Victory Medal, and the Presidential Testimonial Letter.

Jay Litton was the older of John Litton and Grace Litton's two sons. He attended Southeastern High School, where his younger brother, Jack, remembered him as a leader in all his activities. He was president of his high-school class and was selected to be a senator at Michigan Boys State. He is also remembered as being a leader in his church group and among his friends. Jay was an avid athlete who concentrated his efforts on baseball, but also played varsity tennis. He also enjoyed stamp collecting, and at the time of his death, he was "going steady" with a girl from his high-school class.

William Lowry Lyman Jr.

Born:	March 25, 1923
Hometown:	Upper Montclair, NJ
Class:	1944
Service:	Merchant Marine
Position / Rank:	Deck Cadet
Date / Place of death:	July 14, 1943 / Avola, Sicily
Date / Place of burial:	July 14, 1943 / Lost at Sea—Avola, Sicily
Age:	20

William L. Lyman signed on aboard the SS *Timothy Pickering* as Deck Cadet on December 11, 1942, at the Port of New York. He was joined by Christopher C. Brennan (deck), Warren P. Marks (engine), and Lawrence D. McLaughlin (engine). Second Mate George Alther, a former Cadet Officer, also signed on.

The Allied Invasion of Sicily, "Operation Husky," involved amphibious assaults near Gela, Sicily, by U.S. Forces and Avola, Sicily, by British Forces on the morning of July 10, 1943. Shortly thereafter, the *Timothy Pickering* arrived off Avola after sailing in convoy from Alexandria, Egypt, on July 6 with 130 British soldiers and a cargo of munitions, TNT, high-octane gasoline, artillery pieces, and trucks. On the morning of July 13, the vessel was anchored in the harbor, about half a mile from shore, with the bow in and the starboard side closest to the shore. The crew had begun unloading the vessel's cargo.

At 1040 (GCT), the Allied shipping off Avola was attacked by German dive bombers. One of them dropped a single five-hundred-pound bomb on the *Timothy Pickering* at its number 4 hold. The bomb detonated in the ship's engine room, causing a massive explosion of the ship's cargo with resulting fire. The explosion left a gaping hole in the starboard side of the ship, causing it to quickly begin sinking.

With no time to either launch lifeboats or be given an order to abandon ship, the crew began to leave the ship immediately, leaping over the side into the oily waters or sliding down ropes and the anchor chain. In May 1944, the Academy's newspaper, *Polaris*, printed a report on the loss of

the *Timothy Pickering,* which expanded on the report of the sinking by Cadet-Midshipman Brennan, one of only twenty-nine survivors.

> The ticklish cargo of explosives and high-test octane was being gently worked over the side to waiting supply barges when one such raider appeared and began to attack. The plane's bomb landed squarely into the open number four hatch of Brennan's ship. The explosion was instantaneous. Sheets of yellow flame and billowing clouds of smoke rose hundreds of feet in the air. Two adjacent ships were set afire; others were bombarded with huge chunks of metal. Cadet-Midshipmen on other vessels heard the explosion some 50 miles out at sea. To stunned observers nearby, the doomed ship seemed to dissolve into thin air.

The *Timothy Pickering's* other Cadet-Midshipmen were not as lucky as Brennan. According to Brennan's report, William Lyman was in his quarters when the ship was hit by the bomb and was not seen afterward. Warren Marks was in the engine room at the time of the explosion and was killed instantly. Brennan states that Lawrence McLaughlin was seen jumping over the side of the ship but drifted into the burning oil that surrounded the blazing ship. Along with the three Cadet-Midshipmen, nineteen other crew members, eight Naval Armed Guard sailors, and one hundred British soldiers died in the attack. Also among the dead was Second Mate George W. Alther Jr., whose heroic actions during the disaster were recognized by the award of the Merchant Marine Distinguished Service Medal.

Cadet-Midshipman William L. Lyman was posthumously awarded the Mariner's Medal, the Combat Bar, the Atlantic War Zone Bar, the Mediterranean-Middle East War Zone Bar, the Presidential Testimonial Letter, and the Victory Medal.

William L. Lyman was the eldest of William Sr. and Edith Lyman's three sons. William's family nickname was"Boots," although none of his brothers remember how he came by it. His younger brother Peter recalled that Boots was a leader for the rest of the family, especially after their mother, Edith, died in 1935, when William was only twelve. The 1930 U.S. Census lists William Sr.'s occupation as treasurer and manager of a manufacturing firm. By the 1940 U.S. Census, William Sr. had remarried a widow, Maple Adams, whose son, David, was the same age as William.

During summer vacations on Cape Cod, Boots led Peter and his youngest brother, David, on expeditions on the beach or crabbing in nearby rivers. Boots enjoyed hunting small game. According to Peter, William would occasionally bring home a squirrel or bird, which he would keep in the refrigerator until he could try his hand at taxidermy. The boys knew when their stepmom had found William's latest taxidermy by her ear-splitting shriek. At Montclair High School, Boots was a pole-vaulter on the track and field team and also played six-man football. In the fall of 1941, he enrolled at Colby College. After finishing the academic year, however, he left Colby to attend the U.S. Merchant Marine Academy.

A memorial to William L. Lyman Jr. was placed at Mount Hebron Cemetery in Montclair, New Jersey, by his family.

James Joseph Magee

Born: September 26, 1923
Hometown: Philadelphia, PA
Class: unknown   1944
Service: Merchant Marine
Position / Rank: Deck Cadet
Date / Place of death: April 11, 1943 / 53-00
                           N, 39-00 W
Date / Place of burial: April 11, 1943 / Lost at
                           Sea—53-00 N, 39-00 W
Age: 19

James J. Magee signed on as Deck Cadet aboard the new SS *Edward B. Dudley* at Savannah, Georgia, on March 1, 1943, just days after its delivery from North Carolina Shipbuilding. Magee was joined aboard the *Edward B. Dudley* by Cadet-Midshipman James Hope, also sailing as Deck Cadet.

After loading a cargo of cotton in Savannah, the *Edward B. Dudley* sailed on its maiden voyage for New York. At New York, the ship loaded more cargo, including either ammunition or explosives. The *Edward B. Dudley* sailed from New York with Convoy HX 232 on April 1, 1943, bound for Liverpool via Halifax, Nova Scotia.

At some point after the convoy sailed from Halifax, the *Edward B. Dudley* straggled behind the convoy due to, according to some sources, a bent propeller blade. According to German naval records, the *Edward B. Dudley* was located by *U-615* on April 10. The submerged submarine fired a four-torpedo spread at the ship. Only one of the four torpedoes was seen by *U-615* to hit the ship, and it failed to explode.

Alerted to the danger, the *Edward B. Dudley* began zigzagging, but it was unable to shake off the pursuit by *U-615*. The pursuit lasted all night, with *U-615* finally getting ahead of the *Edward B. Dudley* and setting up its approach on the surface. When the *Edward B. Dudley* was in *U-615*'s sights, it fired two torpedoes at the ship, hitting it amidships and stopping the ship. However, the *Edward B. Dudley* would not sink. Twenty minutes after the first torpedoes hit the *Edward B. Dudley;* the *U-615* closed to within half mile of the ship and fired another torpedo, which hit the stern.

The explosion of this torpedo detonated the ammunition for the five-inch gun there, but the *Edward B. Dudley* still remained afloat. At this point, the crew of the *U-615* witnessed the crew abandoning ship in the lifeboats.

The *U-615* then moved even closer to the crippled ship and fired a fourth torpedo, which hit under the bridge, detonating the ship's cargo and totally destroying her. Falling debris from the explosion wounded the *U-615*'s Captain and slightly damaged its conning tower, forcing the submarine to abort its patrol and return to base. The *U-615* itself was sunk by Allied aircraft in the Caribbean on its next patrol.

Although the *U-615*'s Captain and other crew members had seen boats being lowered, no survivors of the *Edward B. Dudley*, including Cadet-Midshipmen Joseph J. Magee and James A. Hope, were ever heard from. Given the extent of the explosion of the *Edward B. Dudley*'s cargo, any survivors who were in the lifeboats perished in the explosion.

Ironically, Magee was supposed to do his at-sea training aboard another Liberty ship, the SS *Daniel Heister,* and signed on aboard the ship as Deck Cadet on January 28, 1943. However, a few days later, he came down with a case of what the ship's Master noted as "grippe" (today known as influenza). He was sent ashore to a hospital in New York for treatment and was left behind when the ship sailed. The *Daniel Heister* survived the war without incident.

Cadet-Midshipman James J. Magee was posthumously awarded the Mariner's Medal, the Combat Bar, the Atlantic War Zone Bar, the Victory Medal, and the Presidential Testimonial Letter.

James J. Magee was the middle son of John Charles Magee Sr. and Anna C. McShea Magee of Philadelphia. Anna Magee died on November 5, 1930, leaving her husband to raise three young boys with the help of her mother, Annie Margaret McShea. Following Anna's death the brothers took care of the family with the help of their grandmother. Neighbors in Philadelphia thought highly of James, who was always willing to cut a lawn or shovel some snow. Many thought he might later become a priest. Robert Magee, the youngest son in the family, remembers his brother Jim as an excellent student at West Catholic High School, and a member of the crew team, the student government, and the senior prom committee. He also recalled that his brother could be tough on the youngest son in the family! James Magee attended Drexel University for one year before enrolling at Kings Point. Robert P. Magee Jr., the son of James's brother

Robert, graduated from Kings Point in the class of 1969. According to Robert Magee, when his sister Diane asked their father about whether he thought about his brother often, he said,

No, but I never forget him.

Daniel Joseph Maher

Born:	July 17, 1923
Hometown:	East Boston, MA
Class:	1944
Service:	Merchant Marine
Position / Rank:	Engine Cadet
Date / Place of death:	March 2, 1943 / 62-10 N, 28-25 W
Date / Place of burial:	March 2, 1943 / Lost at Sea—62-10 N, 28-25 W
Age:	19

Daniel J. Maher signed on aboard the SS *Meriwether Lewis* as Engine Cadet on October 15, 1942, at New York, New York. Cadet-Midshipman Walter E. Johnson, Engine Cadet, had signed on a few days earlier. The ship's two Deck Cadets were Randall Bourell and Alan Clarke. Former Cadet Officer James J. Coffey was Second Mate. After an uneventful voyage to Casablanca, French Morocco, the ship returned to New York on January 10, 1943. Johnson was replaced by Francis McCann around January 25, 1943. On February 18, 1943, the *Meriwether Lewis,* with its four Kings Point Cadets, sailed from New York as part of Convoy HX-227 bound for the United Kingdom and then to Murmansk, Russia. The ship was loaded with a cargo of vehicle tires, ammunition, and based upon some references, a deck cargo of PT boats.

According to German Navy records, the *Meriwether Lewis* was identified as a straggler from a convoy and unsuccessfully attacked by *U-759* in the early morning of March 2. The submarine was unable to reattack the *Meriwether Lewis* due to problems with the sub's engines, but it was able to contact *U-634* and lead it to the straggler. The *U-634* fired four torpedoes at the *Meriwether Lewis*, hitting it with one of them. The damage was sufficient to stop the ship, but did not sink it. The submarine hit the *Meriwether Lewis* with two more torpedoes; the last of which detonated the ship's ammunition cargo. Although there was plenty of time to abandon ship, the USCGC *Ingham* (WPG 35) found only a thirty-mile line of floating tires during its two-day-long search for the *Meriwether Lewis* and crew. Thus, the ship's entire crew of forty-four, including Second Mate James J. Coffey and the four Kings Point Cadets, and twenty-eight members of the Naval Armed Guard sailors perished in the sinking.

Cadet-Midshipman Daniel J. Maher was posthumously awarded the Mariner's Medal, the Combat Bar with star, the Atlantic War Zone Bar, the Victory Medal, and the Presidential Testimonial Letter. He had previously earned the Pacific War Zone Bar for service aboard the SS *Charles Kurz* and SS *Argentina*. Crew lists on file in New York indicate that he had signed on aboard the SS *Argentina* as a Fireman at San Francisco on April 15, 1942.

CALLING UP HOME FROM 200 MILES OUT
Danny Maher, aged eight, calls up his mother in East Boston from Capt. Maher's cabin. This was Danny's first sea voyage.

Danny Maher (age 8) and father call home on his first voyage to sea

Daniel J. Maher, known to his family as "Dannie," was the youngest of Capt. Daniel J. and Annie M. J. Maher's three children. The oldest was his sister, Rita, who, according to the 1940 U.S. Census, worked in a hospital. The middle child was Dannie's brother, William, who was working in a fish processing and cold storage plant in 1940. Dannie's father was Captain of the trawler MV *Foam*. On May 17, 1942, while off the coast of Nova Scotia, the *Foam* was the first American fishing trawler sunk by a German submarine in World War II. Dannie graduated from Tilton Parochial School and East Boston High School in 1941. He was an active member of the Sea Scouts and was remembered by his sister, Rita, for his excellent character and his love of life and for the sea.

Warren Prime Marks

Born:	September 20, 1923
Hometown:	Nutley, NJ
Class:	1944
Service:	Merchant Marine
Position / Rank:	Engine Cadet
Date / Place of death:	July 14, 1943 / Avola, Sicily
Date / Place of burial:	July 14, 1943 / Lost at Sea—
	Avola, Sicily
Age:	19

Warren P. Marks signed on aboard the SS *Timothy Pickering* as Engine Cadet on December 11, 1942, at the Port of New York. He was joined by Christopher C. Brennan (deck), William L. Lyman (deck), and Lawrence D. McLaughlin (engine). Second Mate George Alther was a former Cadet Officer.

The Allied Invasion of Sicily, "Operation Husky," involved amphibious assaults near Gela (U.S. Forces) and Avola (British Forces), Sicily, on the morning of July 10, 1943. Shortly thereafter, the *Timothy Pickering* arrived off Avola after sailing in convoy from Alexandria, Egypt, on July 6 with 130 British soldiers and a cargo of munitions, TNT, high-octane gasoline, artillery pieces, and trucks. On the morning of July 13, the vessel was anchored in the harbor, about half a mile from shore, with the bow in and the starboard side closest to the shore. The crew had begun unloading the vessel's cargo.

At 1040 (GCT), the Allied shipping off Avola was attacked by German dive bombers. One of them dropped a single five-hundred-pound bomb on the *Timothy Pickering* at its number 4 hold. The bomb detonated in the ship's engine room, causing a massive explosion of the ship's cargo with resulting fire. The explosion left a gaping hole in the starboard side of the ship, causing it to quickly begin sinking.

With no time to either launch lifeboats or be given an order to abandon ship, the crew began to leave the ship immediately, leaping over the side into the oily waters or sliding down ropes and the anchor chain. In May 1944, the Academy's newspaper, *Polaris*, printed a report on the loss of

the *Timothy Pickering,* which expanded on the report of the sinking by Cadet-Midshipman Brennan, one of only twenty-nine survivors.

> The ticklish cargo of explosives and high-test octane was being gently worked over the side to waiting supply barges when one such raider appeared and began to attack. The plane's bomb landed squarely into the open number four hatch of Brennan's ship. The explosion was instantaneous. Sheets of yellow flame and billowing clouds of smoke rose hundreds of feet in the air. Two adjacent ships were set afire; others were bombarded with huge chunks of metal. Cadet-Midshipmen on other vessels heard the explosion some 50 miles out at sea. To stunned observers nearby, the doomed ship seemed to dissolve into thin air.

The *Timothy Pickering*'s other Cadet-Midshipmen were not as lucky as Brennan. According to Brennan's report, Warren Marks was in the engine room at the time of the explosion and was killed instantly. William Lyman was in his quarters when the ship was hit by the bomb and was not seen afterward. Brennan states that Lawrence McLaughlin was seen jumping over the side of the ship but drifted into the burning oil that surrounded the blazing ship. Along with the three Cadet-Midshipmen, nineteen other crew members, eight Naval Armed Guard sailors, and one hundred British soldiers died in the attack. Also among the dead was Second Mate George W. Alther Jr., whose heroic actions during the disaster were recognized by the award of the Merchant Marine Distinguished Service Medal.

Marks family portrait, 1931

Cadet-Midshipman Warren P. Marks was posthumously awarded the Mariner's Medal, the Combat Bar, the Atlantic War Zone Bar, the Mediterranean-Middle East War Zone Bar, the Presidential Testimonial Letter, and the Victory Medal.

Warren P. "Moose" Marks was the oldest of Sylvester Wade Marks and Arabella "Belle" Florence Prime Marks's three children. He had one sister, Annis Jean, and a brother, Roger. The 1940 U.S. Census lists Sylvester Marks's occupation as assistant manager of a five and ten-cent store. Warren attended public schools in Nutley, New Jersey, graduating from Nutley High School in January 1941. At school, Warren was a member of the dramatic club. He was also a member of the Vincent Methodist Church.

A Liberty ship, SS *Warren P. Marks,* was named after Warren. This ship later became the USS *Protector* (AGR 11), a radar picket or early warning ship that operated as part of the nation's early warning radar network from 1956 to 1965.

Kenneth McAuliffe

Born:	1924
Hometown:	Metairie, LA
Class:	United Fruit Company Cadet
Service:	Merchant Marine
Position / Rank:	United Fruit Company Cadet
Date / Place of death:	June 8, 1942/18-15 N, 85-20 W
Date / Place of burial:	June 8, 1942 / Lost at Sea—18-15 N, 85-20 W
Age:	18

Kenneth McAuliffe, on May 31, 1942, at New Orleans, Louisiana, signed on as Cadet (no deck/engine designation on the shipping articles) aboard the SS *Tela*, a "banana boat" "owned" by Empress Honduran Vapores and operated by United Fruit Company. He was the son of a United Fruit Company executive. The ship had already been armed by March 7, 1942; however, the Navy did not provide any Armed Guard personnel, as the ship was still foreign flagged. The *Tela* was scheduled to sail from New Orleans on June 2, bound for Port Limon, Costa Rica. He had sailed as Cadet on another United Fruit Company ship, the SS *Musa*, the previous summer.

SS *Tela*

On the night of June 8, the *Tela*, which was traveling at 15 knots on a zigzag course under clear skies, was sighted by *U-504*. The submarine fired two torpedoes at the *Tela*. Both torpedoes hit the *Tela* on its port side, one at the engine room and the other at the number 3 hatch. The first torpedo destroyed the engine room, while the second caused the ship to burst into flames, illuminating the entire ship.

The forty-three survivors of the attack were able to launch two lifeboats and two rafts before the ship sank stern first, just five minutes after being hit. The *Tela* went to the bottom with eleven of its crew, including Kenneth McAuliffe. Eventually, all of the men on the rafts were taken aboard the two lifeboats. After about twelve hours in the lifeboats, the *Tela*'s survivors were picked up by the MV *Port Montreal*. Two of the *Tela*'s survivors died from their injuries while aboard the *Port Montreal*.

On June 10, 1942, the *Port Montreal* was sighted by *U-68*. Although the *U-68* was poorly positioned for an attack, its Captain fired what he later described as a "desperation" shot that he described as a "very lucky" shot. The torpedo exploded in the ship's stern, causing it to sink quickly. However, the forty-one remaining survivors of the *Tela*'s sinking were all able to take to the boats again. After three days afloat the *Port Montreal* lifeboats were located by the Colombian schooner *Hilda* and the survivors were landed at Cristobal, Panama Canal Zone, on June 16, 1942.

Kenneth McAuliffe was posthumously awarded the Mariner's Medal, the Combat Bar with star, the Atlantic War Zone Bar, the Victory Medal, and the Presidential Testimonial Letter.

Kenneth "Ken" McAuliffe was the middle son of Daniel J. McAuliffe and Catherine McAuliffe's three sons (Ernest, Kenneth, and Edwin). Daniel McAuliffe was a senior executive of the United Fruit Company. Edwin McAuliffe clearly remembers that in high school, his brother played football at St. Stanislaus College, in Bay St. Louis, Mississippi. That team was famously led to an undefeated season in 1941 by "Doc" Blanchard, who later was the first college Junior to win the Heisman Trophy in 1945. According to Edwin, because there were a lot of native Spanish-speaking students at St. Stanislaus, Ken wanted to improve his mastery of Spanish. So for the summer of 1941, Ken's father had him assigned to work in the engine room of the SS *Musa,* which had an all-Spanish-speaking crew. By the end of the summer, Ken was nearly fluent in Spanish. He had also picked up a love of going to sea and marine engineering.

Upon graduation from St. Stanislaus, Ken decided to go back to sea in the merchant marine rather than enlist in the Army. Daniel McAuliffe, wanting to be sure that his son was in good hands, arranged for his son to sign on aboard a ship, the SS *Tela*, commanded by a Captain he knew personally. According to Edwin, one of Daniel McAuliffe's jobs at United Fruit Company was to interview survivors of company ships that had been sunk. Edwin recalls that one of the *Tela*'s survivors told his father that he was about to relieve Ken just as the torpedo hit the engine room, killing Ken, the chief engineer, and seven other men instantly. Shortly after this interview, Daniel McAuliffe left United Fruit to start his own business. According to Edwin, the death of his son Kenneth was a contributing factor to his decision to leave United Fruit.

George Duncan McCall

Born:	March 13, 1922
Hometown:	Hartselle, AL
Class:	1944
Service:	Merchant Marine
Position / Rank:	Deck Cadet
Date / Place of death:	July 14, 1943 / 15-25 S, 41-13 E
Date / Place of burial:	July 14, 1943 / Lost at Sea—15-25 S, 41-13E
Age:	21

George D. McCall signed on as Deck Cadet aboard the newly completed Liberty ship SS *Robert Bacon* on March 3, 1943, at New Orleans, Louisiana. He was joined by three other Cadet-Midshipmen from the Pass Christian Basic School: Francis T. Joos (deck), Edward S. O'Connell (engine), and Charles C. Wendt (engine). The ship sailed from New Orleans on March 19 loaded with general cargo and explosives bound for Durban, South Africa, via Guantanamo Bay, Cuba, the Panama Canal, and Cape Town. After discharging cargo in Cape Town and Durban, the ship was routed to Aden, Port Tewfik, on the Suez Canal. At Port Tewfik, the ship loaded the personnel effects of approximately 250 deceased Army officers, along with some mail, and sailed for Cape Town via Mombasa, Kenya. The *Robert Bacon* sailed from Mombasa on July 12 via the Mozambique Channel.

Late in the evening or early morning of July 13/14, the *Robert Bacon* was sighted by *U-178*. At 0235, local time, on July 14, 1943 (2335 [GMT], July 13, 1943), the *Robert Bacon* was hit by a torpedo forward on the port side at the number 2 hold. The shock of the explosion was reported by the survivors to have caused extensive damage on the main deck and filling the number 1 and number 2 lifeboats with water and fuel oil. In the engine room, all of the main and auxiliary steam lines were reported to have parted while the fuel pumps were blown off of their foundations. Although the ship was slowly flooding by 2350, the crew had abandoned ship in numbers 3, 4 and 6 lifeboats and the ship's life rafts.

According to the report of Cadet-Midshipman Edward O'Connell, number 5 lifeboat was launched but was swamped by the heavy seas, rendering it useless. Cadet-Midshipman George McCall, who had been helping to launch number 5 lifeboat, began climbing down the embarkation net to see if the boat could be bailed out. However, he became entangled in the net and was trapped between the lifeboat and the side of the ship. For whatever reason, he was unable to climb back up the net to safety. Edward O'Connell noted that throughout the abandon ship process, George McCall could be heard calling for help. Unfortunately, due to where he was, the weather, and darkness, none of the other boats could get near him. Edward O'Connell reported that he and two other crewmen attempted to rescue George McCall by pulling number 3 life raft up to where he was trapped. However, the men accidentally released the raft from the ship, which prevented them from reaching him.

About five minutes after the *Robert Bacon*'s crew had gotten away from their sinking ship; *U-178* fired a second torpedo, which hit the ship under the stack, close to where McCall was clinging to the net. Edward O'Connell believed that his classmate, George McCall, perished in the explosion of the torpedo. The ship was still not sinking fast enough for the *U-178*. Half an hour later, a third torpedo was fired, which sent the ship plunging down into the sea by the bow, carrying the remains of George McCall with it. The submarine later surfaced and approached the lifeboats, asking for the Captain. The crew claimed they didn't know where the Captain was, and the sub Commander then left, pointing them toward land and wishing them luck. Eventually, all but six of the *Robert Bacon*'s seventy-one crew and Armed Guard sailors were rescued and arrived safe ashore.

**George D. McCall (front row, sixth from left) with his Preliminary
Section at the Pass Christian Basic School**

Cadet-Midshipman George D. McCall was posthumously awarded the Mariner's Medal, the Combat Bar with star, the Atlantic War Zone Bar, the Mediterranean-Middle East War Zone Bar, the Victory Medal, and the Presidential Testimonial Letter.

George D. McCall was the only son and oldest child of Nora A. McCall. His sister Mary Frances was two years younger. Another sister, Aileen, was identified in an unpublished photograph with George and Mary Frances, but there is no mention of her in either the 1930 or 1940 U.S. Census. According to the 1930 U.S. Census, Nora McCall was the head of the household, indicating that George and Mary Frances lost their father at an early age. The 1940 U.S. Census indicates that George was working as a clerk in the Citizen's Bank in Hartselle, Alabama. During his school years, George McCall was president of the Morgan County High School student body, where he was also on the football and tennis teams. Described as a self-assured and determined young man, George taught Sunday school and was a soloist at the family church. After graduating from high school, George volunteered to help coach the Morgan County High School football team until he broke his leg during a practice scrimmage. While working at the bank, George evaluated several careers and decided to enter the merchant marine. According to his sister, Mary Frances,

> There is nothing more beautiful than the dedicated love of a son for his Mother and sisters. This was George Duncan McCall!

Francis Thomas McCann

Born:	March 8, 1924	
Hometown:	Johnson City, NY	
Class:	1944	
Service:	Merchant Marine	
Position / Rank:	Engine Cadet	
Date / Place of death:	March 2, 1943 / 62-10 N, 28-25 W	
Date / Place of burial:	March 2, 1943 / Lost at Sea—62-10 N, 28-25 W	
Age:	18	

Francis T. McCann signed on aboard the SS *Meriwether Lewis* as Engine Cadet on January 25, 1943, at New York, New York, replacing Walter E. Johnson. He joined Randall Bourell (deck), Alan Clarke (deck), and Daniel Maher (engine), who had made the previous voyage to Casablanca, French Morocco. Former USMCC Cadet Officer James J. Coffey was Second Mate. On February 18, 1943, the *Meriwether Lewis,* with its four Kings Point Cadets, sailed from New York as part of Convoy HX-227 bound for the United Kingdom and then to Murmansk, Russia. The ship was loaded with a cargo of vehicle tires, ammunition, and perhaps a deck cargo of PT boats.

According to German Navy records, the *Meriwether Lewis* was identified as a straggler from a convoy and unsuccessfully attacked by *U-759* in the early morning of March 2. The submarine was unable to re-attack the *Meriwether Lewis* due to problems with the sub's engines, but it was able to contact *U-634* and lead it to the straggler. The *U-634* fired four torpedoes at the *Meriwether Lewis*, hitting it with one of them. The damage was apparently sufficient to stop the ship, but did not sink it. The submarine hit the *Meriwether Lewis* with two more torpedoes; the last of which detonated the ship's ammunition cargo. Although there was plenty of time to abandon ship, the USCGC *Ingham* (WPG 35) found only a thirty-mile line of floating tires during its two-day-long search for the SS *Meriwether Lewis* and crew. Thus, the ship's entire crew of forty-four, including Second Mate James J. Coffey and the four Kings Point Cadets, and twenty-eight members of the Naval Armed Guard perished in the sinking.

Cadet-Midshipman Francis T. McCann was posthumously awarded the Mariner's Medal, the Combat Bar with star, the Atlantic War Zone Bar, the Victory Medal, and the Presidential Testimonial Letter.

The McCann siblings (l to r) Francis, Joseph, Mary Lou

Francis T. McCann was the oldest of Thomas V. McCann and Helen G. McCann's two sons and daughter. Although he had been a coal miner when Francis was born, by 1930, the family had moved from Pennsylvania to Johnson City, New York. There Thomas McCann worked in a shoe factory, while Helen was a registered nurse. Francis's sister, Mary Lou, was just two years younger, while his brother, Joseph, was much younger. Although called Francis by his parents, he was known as "Nippy" to others, owing to his resemblance to a comic strip character whose hair was similarly parted in the middle. As a boy, McCann was a fan of the 1930s St. Louis Cardinals (the "Gas House Gang") and the Fighting Irish of Notre Dame. When he was home for Christmas 1942, just before joining the *Meriwether Lewis*, Francis became engaged to his childhood sweetheart.

Joseph McCann, Francis's brother, said,

> I do remember, like it was yesterday when he came to my room to say goodbye. He had my Mother give him a pair of baby shoes to take for good luck.

William Edward McCann

Born: September 12, 1920
Hometown: Detroit, MI
Class: 1944
Service: Merchant Marine
Position / Rank: Engine Cadet
Date / Place of death: August 4, 1943 / SS *Thomas Paine*
Date / Place of burial: August 6, 1943 / Saint Patrick's Cemetery, Madras, India, Grave number 24
Age: 22

William E. McCann signed on as Engine Cadet aboard the SS *Thomas Paine* on April 12, 1943, at Baltimore, Maryland. By July, the ship was discharging cargo in India. On July 28, 1943, the ship left Calcutta bound for New York with planned stops in several Indian ports for cargo before sailing via Ceylon, Australia, the Panama Canal, and Key West. During the vessel's trip down the eastern coast of India, the crew suffered greatly from malaria. Lieutenant (jg) J. N. Heroy, USNR, Commanding Officer of the ship's Naval Armed Guard, estimated that 83 percent of the gun crew was ill during one three-week period.

The *Thomas Paine* arrived in Vizagapatam (Visakhapatnam), India, a port in the Madras section of India, on August 1. Several crew members, including William McCann, were so ill that the Master asked the ship's local agent to have an Indian doctor to come aboard the ship and examine them. According to Lieutenant (jg) Heroy's voyage report, the doctor believed that McCann would make it to Colombo, Ceylon, a major British naval base, where more adequate medical assistance was available. However, shortly after sailing for Madras, the ship's next port of call before Colombo, McCann's condition worsened. According to his report of the death of an American citizen, Cadet-Midshipman William E. McCann died at 4:00 a.m., local time, aboard the *Thomas Paine* in Madras Harbor. He was buried in Saint Patrick's Cemetery, Madras, India, on August 6; the day after the *Thomas Paine* sailed for Colombo.

In his voyage report, Lieutenant (jg) Heroy stated that the Indian doctors obtained by the ship's agent in these ports were ". . . superficial, disinterested and professionally incompetent." He mentions that one of his sailors was examined three times by Indian doctors who were unable to diagnose his condition, while a British Navy doctor in Colombo instantly diagnosed the man as having malaria. He noted that in each port, there were large numbers of British Army troops and concluded that they would have their own doctors. Based on this conclusion, he recommended to Naval Armed Guard Commanders that Allied military medical personnel be called to provide medical attention for merchant ship crews and Armed Guard sailors in these ports rather than relying on local medical personnel. He concluded,

> I believe that Cadet McCann could have been saved had competent medical assistance been available.

Cadet-Midshipman William E. McCann was posthumously awarded the Atlantic War Zone Bar, the Mediterranean-Middle East War Zone Bar, the Victory Medal, and the Presidential Testimonial Letter.

William E. McCann was born in Ontario, Canada, and the youngest of John J. and Mary McCann's three sons; his brothers were Francis and Joseph. According to the 1930 U.S. Census, John McCann worked in one of Detroit's automobile factories. William attended Holy Redeemer High School, where he was active on the football and basketball teams. He was noted as being able to draw out the best in his teammates. In addition, he also served as an altar boy in his parish church. William's sister-in-law, Kathleen, recalled that he had an innate mechanical ability and a natural inclination for engineering training. Though he initially gravitated toward aviation, he ended up applying to the Merchant Marine Academy soon after graduating from high school in 1939. Kathleen said the following about her brother-in-law:

> Religious strength was a sustaining force in his life reflecting the wisdom that he concentrated on things that would outlast his mortality."

Howard Timothy McGrath

Born:	June 10, 1923
Hometown:	New York City, NY
Class:	1944
Service:	Merchant Marine
Position / Rank:	Engine Cadet
Date / Place of death:	March 10, 1943 / 19-49 N, 74-38 W
Date / Place of burial:	March 10, 1943 / Lost at Sea
19-49 N, 74-38 W	
Age:	19

Howard T. McGrath signed on aboard the brand-new SS *James Sprunt* as Engine Cadet on February 23, 1943, at Charleston, South Carolina. He was joined by his Academy classmates Michael Buck (engine), James Rowley (deck), and John Tucek (deck). The ship was loaded with general cargo and four thousand tons of high explosives at Charleston for a voyage to Karachi, India, via Texas and the Panama Canal.

SS *James Sprunt* shortly after completion

On the morning of March 10, 1943, the *James Sprunt* was traveling in Convoy KG-123 about three miles southeast of Guantanamo Bay, Cuba. Another ship in the convoy, the *Virginia Sinclair*, had been torpedoed at 0430 on the same morning. At 0809, *U-185* fired torpedoes at the convoy, hitting the *James Sprunt*.

The *James Sprunt*'s cargo of explosives blew up with extraordinary force, completely disintegrating the ship. The glare from the explosion was seen more than forty miles away. Witnesses on other ships recalled the violent tremors and debris that fell like hail on the other ships. There were no survivors among the forty-three crew members. Twenty-eight Naval Armed Guard members, including all four Kings Point Cadet-Midshipmen: Michael Buck, Howard McGrath, James Rowley, and John Tucek were lost.

The thirty-day life of the *James Sprunt* may have been the shortest life span of any Liberty ship. The ship was delivered from North Carolina Shipbuilding to the War Shipping Administration on February 13, 1943, loaded cargo from the nineteenth to the twenty-ninth and destroyed on March 10, 1943.

Cadet-Midshipman Howard T. McGrath was posthumously awarded the Mariner's Medal, the Combat Bar, the Atlantic War Zone Bar, the Victory Medal, and the Presidential Testimonial Letter.

Howard McGrath was the oldest son and second child of Timothy and Winifred McGrath. His sister, Helen, was five years older, while Howard was nine years older than Robert. The family lived at 322 Holly Avenue, in the Throgs Neck neighborhood of the Bronx in New York City. Just across Long Island Sound from Throgs Neck is Kings Point, the home of the U.S. Merchant Marine Academy. According to the 1940 U.S. Census, Timothy McGrath was an inspector for the Interborough Rapid Transit Railroad, part of New York City's subway system. He had previously worked for them as an electrician.

Howard's brother Robert said that Howard loved to be fishing on Long Island Sound. According to Robert, their father built Howard a number of rowboats from which he would come home with buckets of flounder. The fish fed the family, friends, and neighbors, while the remains were used to fertilize their father's prize roses. Robert said that Howard wrote to his mother every day and enjoyed his short career.

John James McKelvey

Born:	October 13, 1920
Hometown:	Patterson, NJ
Class:	1943
Service:	Merchant Marine
Position / Rank:	Deck Cadet
Date / Place of death:	December 7, 1942/ 57-50 N, 23-10 W
Date / Place of burial:	December 7, 1942 / Lost at Sea—57-50 N, 23-10 W
Age:	22

James J. McKelvey signed on the SS *James McKay* as Deck Cadet on November 11, 1942, at New York, New York. Three other Kings Point Cadet-Midshipmen, Philip Branigan (deck), Leonard L. Ehrlich (engine), and Walter C. Hetrick (engine), joined him. Third Assistant Engineer Henry E. Harris was a Cadet Corps alumnus.

SS *James McKay*

The *James McKay* sailed from New York with Convoy HX-216 bound for Belfast, Northern Ireland, and Cardiff, Wales, on November 19. On November 25, the convoy encountered a northwest gale and reduced visibility that caused the convoy to partly scatter. The weather was sufficiently rough to cause the *James McKay*'s general cargo to shift, endangering its stability; the ship left the convoy and sailed into St. John's, Newfoundland, on November 29 to restow its cargo.

After restowing its cargo, the *James McKay* sailed from Newfoundland to join up with the next east-bound convoy, HX-217. However, there is no indication that the *James McKay* ever actually joined up with HX-217, possibly due to the convoy being scattered in a southwesterly gale from December 2 to 4.

According to German Navy records, the *James McKay* was located and attacked by *U-600* on the night of December 7/8, 1943, when the ship was about four hundred miles south of Iceland. Three of *U-600*'s torpedoes hit the *James McKay*, one amidships and the other two in the after portion of the ship. The ship stopped and sent out distress signals, and the crew abandoned ship in two lifeboats, although the ship was still afloat. It required two more torpedoes from *U-600* to sink the *James McKay*. Neither the two lifeboats nor any of the people aboard the *James McKay* was ever seen again.

Cadet-Midshipman John McKelvey was already a member of the Academy's "Tin Fish Club" for surviving the sinking of the SS *Oliver Ellsworth* in October of 1942 on the "Murmansk Run." He was posthumously awarded the Mariner's Medal, the Combat Bar with two stars, the Atlantic War Zone Bar, the Victory Medal, and the Presidential Testimonial Letter.

John McKelvey was the oldest child and only son of John and Irene McKelvey. He had a younger sister Carolyn (Carol) who was seven years younger. According to Academy records, John reported to Kings Point on the afternoon of April 6, 1942, to begin his training.

John's sister Carol recalls that, despite the real danger surrounding John every day at sea, he continued to send cheerful letters home to his family. She recalls that although he was granted a longer leave after surviving the sinking of the *Oliver Ellsworth*, John insisted on going right back to sea. When he left home for the *James McKay*, he took all of his uniforms with him, as he had no idea where the ship was going or where it would go from there. Carol said that John's letters, despite being cut up by the military censors, assured his family and reminded them to make sure to set a place for him at Christmas dinner. In his letters, John specifically asked his father to listen to the Army-Navy football game for him. According to Carol,

> The love he sent from sea to shore was a treasured gift. We could ask for no more. His qualities of honesty, sincerity, gratitude and patriotism made our family proud of this young man.

Lawrence Daniel McLaughlin

Born:	August 31, 1923
Hometown:	Woodbridge, NJ
Class:	1944
Service:	Merchant Marine
Position / Rank:	Engine Cadet
Date/Place of death:	July 14, 1943/Avola, Sicily
Date/Place of burial:	July 14, 1943/Avola, Sicily
Age:	19

Lawrence D. McLaughlin signed on aboard the SS *Timothy Pickering* as Engine Cadet on December 4, 1942, at the Port of New York. Over the next few days, he was joined by Christopher C. Brennan (deck), William L. Lyman (deck), and Warren P. Marks (engine). Second Mate George Alther was a former Cadet Officer.

The Allied Invasion of Sicily, "Operation Husky," involved amphibious assaults near Gela (U.S. Forces) and Avola (British Forces), Sicily, on the morning of July 10, 1943. Shortly thereafter, the *Timothy Pickering* arrived off Avola after sailing in convoy from Alexandria, Egypt, on July 6 with 130 British soldiers and a cargo of munitions, TNT, high-octane gasoline, artillery pieces, and trucks. On the morning of July 13, the vessel was anchored in the harbor, about half a mile from shore, with the bow in and the starboard side closest to the shore. The crew had begun unloading the vessel's cargo.

At 1040 (GCT), the Allied shipping off Avola was attacked by German dive bombers. One of them dropped a single five-hundred-pound bomb on the *Timothy Pickering* in its number 4 hold. The bomb detonated in the ship's engine room, causing a massive explosion of the ship's cargo with resulting fire. The explosion left a gaping hole in the starboard side of the ship, causing it to quickly begin sinking.

With no time to either launch lifeboats or be given an order to abandon ship, the crew began to leave the ship immediately, leaping over the side into the oily waters or sliding down ropes and the anchor chain. In May 1944, the Academy's newspaper, *Polaris*, printed a report on the loss of

the *Timothy Pickering,* which expanded on the report of the sinking by Cadet-Midshipman Brennan, one of only twenty-nine survivors.

> The ticklish cargo of explosives and high-test octane was being gently worked over the side to waiting supply barges when one such raider appeared and began to attack. The plane's bomb landed squarely into the open number four hatch of Brennan's ship. The explosion was instantaneous. Sheets of yellow flame and billowing clouds of smoke rose hundreds of feet in the air. Two adjacent ships were set afire; others were bombarded with huge chunks of metal. Cadet-Midshipmen on other vessels heard the explosion some 50 miles out at sea. To stunned observers nearby, the doomed ship seemed to dissolve into thin air.

The *Timothy Pickering*'s other Cadet-Midshipmen were not as lucky as Brennan. According to Brennan's report, Warren Marks was in the engine room at the time of the explosion and was killed instantly. William Lyman was in his quarters when the ship was hit by the bomb and was not seen afterward. Brennan states that Lawrence McLaughlin was seen jumping over the side of the ship but drifted into the burning oil that surrounded the blazing ship. Along with the three Cadet-Midshipmen, nineteen other crew members, eight Naval Armed Guard sailors, and one hundred British soldiers died in the attack. Also among the dead was Second Mate George W. Alther Jr., whose heroic actions during the disaster were recognized by the award of the Merchant Marine Distinguished Service Medal.

Cadet-Midshipman Lawrence D. McLaughlin was posthumously awarded the Mariner's Medal, the Combat Bar, the Atlantic War Zone Bar, the Mediterranean-Middle East War Zone Bar, the Presidential Testimonial Letter, and the Victory Medal.

Lawrence McLaughlin was the youngest son, and third child of Joseph F. McLaughlin and Marguerite Dolan McLaughlin. His older brother was Joseph, and his younger sister was Alice. According to the 1930 and 1940 U.S. Census, Lawrence's father worked as a clerk for the railroad. Lawrence's name is inscribed on his family's memorial in the Saint James Cemetery and Mausoleum, Woodbridge, New Jersey. The same memorial indicates that his father died in 1940.

Walter John Meyer

Born:	February 12, 1922
Hometown:	New York, NY
Class:	1944
Service:	Merchant Marine
Position / Rank:	Engine Cadet
Date / Place of death:	March 17, 1943 / 50-38 N, 34-46 W
Date / Place of burial:	March 17, 1943 / 50-38 N, 34-46 W—Lost at Sea
Age:	21

Walter J. Meyer signed on aboard the SS *Harry Luckenbach* as Engine Cadet on March 2, 1943, at New York, New York. In addition to Meyer, the *Harry Luckenbach* had three other Kings Point Cadets aboard: Lee T. Byrd (deck), Francis R. Miller (engine), and William H. Parker (deck). Third Mate Leroy W. Kernan was a 1942 graduate. The ship sailed from New York on March 8 as one of forty ships in Convoy HX-229 bound for Liverpool with a general cargo of war supplies. A second HX convoy, HX-229A, with more ships, sailed about ten hours after the ships of HX-229. During their transit of the North Atlantic, the two convoys overtook a slower convoy, SC-122. The three convoys, with a total of 110 ships, but less than twenty escorts, would be the centerpiece of what has been described as the greatest convoy battle of World War II.

SS *Harry Luckenbach*

The ships of Convoy HX-229 had proceeded without incident or attack until March 16. For the next three days, the convoy was under attack by over forty U-boats. On the morning of March 17, when HX-229 was about four hundred miles east-southeast of Cape Farrell, *U-91* fired five torpedoes at the convoy, not aiming at any specific ship. The *Harry Luckenbach* in the starboard forward corner of the convoy was hit by two of the torpedoes at the engine room. The ship sank in minutes, but amazingly, three lifeboats were able to get away from the sinking vessel. One or more of the boats were later sighted by HMS *Beverley* (H-64), HMS *Pennywort* (K-111), HMS *Volunteer* (D-71) and, possibly, HMS *Abelia* (K-184). However, none of these ships were able to pick up the survivors from the boats. None of the fifty-four crew members and twenty-six Naval Armed Guard sailors of the *Harry Luckenbach* survived the sinking.

By March 20, the surviving ships of the three convoys arrived in the United Kingdom, having lost twenty-two ships and their crews while sinking just one of the attacking U-boats. According to a Royal Navy report on the convoy battle,

> The Germans never came so near to disrupting communications between the New World and the Old as in the first twenty days of March 1943.

The fact that the Germans were unable to do so is a testament to the courage of merchant mariners like Walter J. Meyer, and the example that he set for the Kings Pointers that came after him.

Cadet-Midshipman Walter J. Meyer was posthumously awarded the Mariner's Medal, the Combat with star, the Atlantic War Zone Bar, the Victory Medal, and the Presidential Testimonial Letter.

Walter J. Meyer was the only son and eldest child of Walter H. Meyer and Agnes Meyer. Lois, nine years younger, was Walter's little sister. Walter reported to Kings Point on February 15, 1942.

Allen George Miller Jr.

Born:	September 25, 1923
Hometown:	Philadelphia, PA
Class:	1944
Service:	Merchant Marine
Position / Rank:	Deck Cadet
Date / Place of death:	January 9, 1943/ 56-15 N, 22 W
Date / Place of burial:	January 9, 1943 / Lost at Sea—56-15 N, 22 W
Age:	19

Allen Miller signed on aboard the SS *Louise Lykes* as Deck Cadet on October 18, 1942, at New York, New York. He was joined by three other Kings Point Cadet-Midshipmen, Charles Gassner (deck), Robert Vancure (engine), and Eugene Walters (deck). Third Assistant Engineer, Frederick Baumann, and Third Mate Harry Wolfe were former Cadet Officers. The *Louise Lykes* made one voyage to the Mediterranean and returned to New York on December 12, 1942. A fifth Cadet-Midshipman, Marion Chrobak (engine), joined the ship for its next voyage. The ship sailed on January 2, 1943, loaded with general cargo and ammunition bound for Belfast, Northern Ireland. For unknown reasons, the ship did not sail in a convoy and was not escorted. On January 9, 1943, the ship was in mid-Atlantic several hundred miles south of Iceland.

SS *Louise Lykes*

On the evening of January 9, 1943, *U-384* located the solitary ship and fired four torpedoes while surfaced. Two torpedoes hit the ship, which, according to German Navy records, disintegrated in a massive explosion.

The Captain of the *U-384* reported that he had to submerge the submarine to prevent damage from falling debris. When the submarine resurfaced five minutes later, there was no sign of the ship or its crew. There were no other witnesses to the disaster, and there were no survivors among the fifty merchant crew, thirty-four Naval Armed Guard sailors, and ten U.S. Army personnel aboard, including the five Cadet-Midshipmen and two Cadet Officers. This was the single deadliest sinking in the Academy's history.

Cadet-Midshipmen Allen Miller was posthumously awarded the Mariner's Medal, the Combat Bar, the Atlantic War Zone Bar, the Victory Medal, and the Presidential Testimonial Letter.

Allen G. Miller was the youngest child and third of three sons of Allen G. Miller Sr. and Bessie H. Miller. The oldest child was Allen's sister, Elizabeth. His brothers were James and William. According to the 1940 U.S. Census, Allen Sr. was a bookkeeper in a Philadelphia sugar factory.

Alphonse Ignatius Miller

Born:	July 10, 1923
Hometown:	Toledo, OH
Class:	1944
Service:	Merchant Marine
Position / Rank:	Deck Cadet
Date / Place of death:	June 10, 1943 / 31-02 N, 79-17 W
Date / Place of burial:	June 10, 1943 / Lost at Sea—31-02 N, 79-17 W
Age:	19

Alphonse I. Miller signed on aboard the SS *Esso Gettysburg* as Deck Cadet on May 27, 1943, at New York, New York. The ship was engaged in the coastal oil trade, running from the Gulf of Mexico to the East Coast. Also aboard the ship were Kings Point Cadet-Midshipmen John M. Carter (engine), Joseph J. Landron (engine), and Eugene Quidort (deck). The ship sailed on June 6 from Port Arthur, Texas, bound for Philadelphia, Pennsylvania, loaded with 120,000 barrels of west Texas crude oil for the Atlantic Refining Company's refinery there.

SS *Esso Gettysburg*

On the afternoon of June 10, the ship was under way about one hundred miles southeast of Savannah, Georgia, traveling without escort, apparently due to its ability to make more than 15 knots. However, the ship was steering evasive courses. Although the vessel had been warned after rounding Key West that submarines were in the area, none had been sighted by the lookouts.

At around 1400, local time, 1900 (GCT), the *Esso Gettysburg* was sighted and attacked by *U-66*. The submarine's two torpedoes hit the ship's port side, the first one aft of midships while the second torpedo hit the engine room in the stern. The impacts ruptured twenty-five feet of deck and hull, and raised a one-hundred-foot geyser of oil and water. The crude oil exploded on impact, transforming the ship into an inferno. A thick cloud of black smoke rose almost a thousand feet in the air. The ship settled by the stern and began to list to port.

At the time of the attack, Alphonse Miller was painting the starboard side of the afterdeck with an AB. John Carter was on duty with the Second Assistant Engineer in the engine room. Joseph Landron, who was not on watch, was sleeping in his room. The fact that Eugene Quidort was off watch on the flying bridge near the compass probably saved his life. Carter, along with the rest of the engine crew on duty, was killed instantly. Miller was seen to run along the catwalk toward midships, where he was caught in the flames and killed. Landron made way for the lifeboats, but when these caught fire, he jumped into the water with the rest of the survivors. He was last seen by an Able Seaman fighting the flames in the water.

Cadet-Midshipman Eugene Quidort also jumped overboard after unsuccessfully attempting to help the Chief Mate lower one of the lifeboats into the sea. He was able to swim away from the burning oil, towing for a while Ensign John S. Arnold, the Armed Guard officer. Quidort eventually found a burned lifeboat to hang on to. Several hours later, he was rescued by the Chief Mate and Second Mate, who had managed to climb aboard another partially burned lifeboat and pulled aboard six crew members and seven Navy men—the only survivors among forty-five crew members and twenty-seven Naval Armed Guard sailors. The following day, the survivors were spotted by an Army B-25 patrol plane. They were picked up by the SS *George Washington* and taken to Charleston, South Carolina.

The Armed Guard, under the command of Ensign John S. Arnold, USNR, did manage to fire one shot in the direction of the submarine before being forced to abandon their post by the flames. Ensign Arnold survived the sinking and was awarded the Navy Cross for his actions.

Cadet-Midshipman Alphonse I. Miller was posthumously awarded the Mariner's Medal, the Combat Bar with star, the Atlantic War Zone Bar, the Victory Medal, and the Presidential Testimonial Letter.

Alphonse I. Miller was the youngest of Alphonse A. Miller and Theresa Miller's two sons and the fourth of five children. Alphonse' siblings were

Norbert, Germaine, Rosemary, and Dolores. According the 1930 U.S. Census, the elder Alphonse, a German immigrant, was the proprietor of a confectionary store. As a sophomore at Toledo's Central Catholic High School in 1939, Alphonse was a member of the student council and the St. John Berchmans Society. In his Junior year, he was a member of the "4 A List" and the "Al-Geo-Trig Club," and participated in the school's drama club. Following his graduation from Central Catholic High School in 1941, Alphonse Miller attended the University of Toledo before being accepted at Kings Point.

Francis Robert Miller

Born:	November 11, 1924
Hometown:	Chestertown, MD
Class:	1944
Service:	Merchant Marine
Position / Rank:	Engine Cadet
Date / Place of death:	March 17, 1943 / 50-38 N, 34-46 W
Date / Place of burial:	March 17, 1943 / Lost at Sea—50-38 N, 34-46 W
Age:	21

Francis R. Miller signed on aboard the SS *Harry Luckenbach* as Deck Cadet on March 2, 1943, at New York, New York. In addition to Meyer, the *Harry Luckenbach* had three other Kings Point Cadets aboard: Lee T. Byrd (deck), Walter J. Meyer (engine), and William H. Parker (deck). Third Mate Leroy W. Kernan was a 1942 graduate. The ship sailed from New York on March 8 as one of forty ships in Convoy HX-229, bound for Liverpool with a general cargo of war supplies. A second HX convoy, HX-229A, with more ships, sailed about ten hours after the ships of HX-229. During their transit of the North Atlantic, the two convoys overtook a slower convoy, SC-122. The three convoys, with a total of 110 ships, but less than twenty escorts, would be the centerpiece of what has been described as the greatest convoy battle of World War II.

SS Harry Luckenbach

The ships of Convoy HX-229 had proceeded without incident or attack until March 16. For the next three days, the convoy was under attack by over forty U-boats. On the morning of March 17, when HX-229 was about four hundred miles east-southeast of Cape Farrell, *U-91* fired five torpedoes at the convoy, not aiming at any specific ship. The *Harry Luckenbach* in the starboard forward corner of the convoy was hit by two of the torpedoes at the engine room. The ship sank in minutes, but amazingly, three lifeboats were able to get away from the sinking vessel. One or more of the boats were later sighted by HMS *Beverley* (H-64), HMS *Pennywort* (K-111), HMS *Volunteer* (D-71), and, possibly, HMS *Abelia* (K-184). However, none of these ships were able to pick up the survivors from the boats. None of the fifty-four crew members and twenty-six Naval Armed Guard sailors of the *Harry Luckenbach* survived the sinking.

By March 20, the surviving ships of the three convoys arrived in the United Kingdom, having lost twenty-two ships and their crews while sinking just one of the attacking U-boats. According to a Royal Navy report on the convoy battle,

> The Germans never came so near to disrupting communications between the New World and the Old as in the first twenty days of March 1943.

The fact that the Germans were unable to do so is a testament to the courage of merchant mariners like Francis R. Miller, and the example that he set for the Kings Pointers that came after him.

Cadet-Midshipman Francis R. Miller was posthumously awarded the Mariner's Medal, the Combat with star, the Atlantic War Zone Bar, the Victory Medal, and the Presidential Testimonial Letter.

Francis "Bob" Miller was the second of six sons of William T. Miller Sr. and Elisabeth C. Miller of Chestertown, Maryland. The 1930 U.S. Census indicates the Bob's father was an assistant manager for an insurance company.

"Bob" Miller with his mother, 1943

George Carter Miller Jr.

Born:	April 18, 1923
Hometown:	Jacksonville, FL
Class:	1943
Service:	Merchant Marine
Position / Rank:	Deck Cadet
Date / Place of death:	February 28, 1943 / 59-49 N, 34-43 W
Date / Place of burial:	February 28, 1943 / Lost at Sea—59-49 N, 34-43 W
Age:	19

George C. Miller signed on as Deck Cadet aboard the SS *Wade Hampton* on December 1, 1942, at New Orleans, Louisiana, upon its delivery from Delta Shipbuilding Company. He was joined by three Pass Christian classmates, Leland B. Anderson (engine), James Hoffman (engine), and Paul L. Milligan (deck). According to the Chief Mate John W. Clark, 1940 Cadet Corps alumnus, the ship sailed from New Orleans with cargo for the Navy base at Guantanamo Bay, Cuba. After discharging its Navy cargo, the ship was ordered to sail in ballast for Santiago, Cuba, where it loaded a cargo of sugar destined for Baltimore, Maryland. The Chief Mate later recalled that Cadet-Midshipman Miller helped him take soundings of Santiago harbor. After discharging the sugar at Baltimore, the *Wade Hampton* sailed for New York via Chesapeake Bay and the C & D Canal. Clark recalls that Miller was of great assistance in helping him deal with navigating in the thick fog surrounding the entrance to the C & D Canal.

The *Wade Hampton* arrived in New York on January 28, 1943. Upon arrival, it began loading eight thousand tons of general cargo bound for Russia. The cargo stowed in the holds included explosives. As was typical of the time, the *Wade Hampton* was also loaded with a deck cargo of two PT boats, automobile parts, and acid in carboys. When the ship sailed on February 18 to join Convoy HX-227, it had a crew of thirty-seven and fourteen Naval Armed Guard sailors aboard.

Convoy HX-227 was bound from New York for Liverpool. As the convoy approached the United Kingdom, the *Wade Hampton* was to leave the convoy with other ships carrying cargo bound for Russia and sail to Loch Ewe, Scotland, where their convoy to Murmansk would assemble. The convoy, which consisted of about seventy merchant ships, was escorted by eighteen American and British naval vessels.

According to the accounts of several survivors, including John Clark, on the morning of February 28, Chief Mate John Clark believed that the *Wade Hampton*'s deck cargo was in jeopardy of shifting due to the heavy weather the ship was encountering. Despite messages about submarines being sighted in the convoy's vicinity, Clark convinced the Master to drop behind the convoy so that the ship's deck crew could safely inspect and resecure the deck cargo. At the same time, the ship's lifeboats could also be swung in and better secured so they would not be lost, depriving the ship's crew of a means to abandon ship.

By the time the deck cargo had been inspected and, where necessary, resecured, the *Wade Hampton* had fallen behind the convoy and its escorts. The Master then ordered the engineers to bring the ship to full speed so that it could catch back up to the convoy. By evening, the ship had gained approximately ten miles on the convoy but was still about five miles behind.

At around 2030, two torpedoes, launched by *U-405*, hit the ship almost simultaneously on the port side at number 5 hold. Four members of the gun crew, whose bunks were near the impact site, were killed instantly in the explosion. The propeller, steering gear, and the entire stern of the ship broke loose and were carried away. There was no sign of the submarine, and no counter attack could be made. The order was given to abandon ship, and all hands reported to lifeboat stations.

At the time of the explosion, Cadet-Midshipmen Miller and Milligan were in their cabin. Somehow, Paul Milligan slept through the explosion, but roused by his cabin mate; he quickly dressed and headed with George Miller for their abandon ship station, number 3 lifeboat. On the starboard side, the ship's officers were dividing the men between the number 2 and number 4 lifeboats, as these were in the lee of the wind and seas. Cadet-Midshipmen Miller and Milligan climbed into the number 3 lifeboat and prepared to launch this boat from the ship's windward side. At the same time, Cadet-Midshipman James Hoffman was helping to launch the number 1 lifeboat just ahead of the number 3 boat.

The ship's Boatswain and several sailors began lowering number 3 boat in conditions that Milligan reported made it almost impossible to see. According to Milligan's account, while the sailors were lowering the boat away, the forward fall came off the cleat, allowing the fall to run away.

This almost instantaneously left the boat hanging by its after fall with its bow pointed down toward the sea. All six men aboard the boat, including Cadet-Midshipmen Miller and Milligan, were thrown into the water. Cadet-Midshipman Milligan was able to keep afloat in the icy water until the forward fall could be recovered to bring the bow back into position. When the boat was properly launched, Milligan was picked up. However, Miller never resurfaced. In his report on the sinking of the *Wade Hampton*, Cadet-Midshipman James Hoffman, who saw the incident, believed that George Miller may have hit the side of the boat or the ship during his fall, causing him to lose consciousness and drown.

In any event, all four of the *Wade Hampton*'s lifeboats were eventually launched without further incident and pulled away with nearly all of the crew aboard. The survivors on board these lifeboats were rescued later that day by the rescue vessel HMS *Vervain* (K190) and the SS *Bayano*. The Master and Chief Engineer elected to stay on the portion of the ship that remained afloat. They were rescued the following day by the *Vervain*. In all, only four crew members and five Navy gunners died, including the Naval Armed Guard officer, Ensign K. H. Cram, USNR, who refused to leave the ship without being sure that all of his men were accounted for.

Cadet-Midshipman George C. Miller was posthumously awarded the Mariner's Medal, the Combat Bar with star, the Atlantic War Zone Bar, the Victory Medal, and the Presidential Testimonial Letter.

George C. Miller was the oldest son and middle child of Captain George C. Miller, USN, and Frances H. Miller. George's siblings were Jane and Francis.

George Miller's shipmate, James Hoffman, survived the rest of his sea year, graduated in 1944, and survived the rest of the war. He was profoundly affected by the loss of George Miller and the other 141 Kings Pointers lost during World War II. Jim later spent many years tracking down the families of the lost Cadets in order to see that they received the appropriate military awards for their service in the war. (See the epilogue for James Hoffman.)

James Oscar Moon

Born:	June 14, 1923	
Hometown:	Stone Mountain, GA	
Class:	1943	
Service:	Merchant Marine	
Position / Rank:	Engine Cadet	
Date / Place of death:	March 11, 1943 / 51-35 N, 28-30 W	
Date / Place of burial:	March 11, 1943 / Lost at Sea—51-35 N, 28-30 W	
Age:	19	

James O. Moon signed on aboard the SS *William C. Gorgas* as Engine Cadet in Mobile, Alabama, on January 27, 1943, shortly after the ship was delivered to the War Shipping Administration from its builder. Joining Cadet-Midshipman Moon were three of his classmates, James Cordua, Edwin Hanzik, and Edwin Wiggin. Third Mate Rafael R. Rivera, 1942 Cadet Corps alumnus, was already aboard. Six weeks later, on March 10, 1943, the *Gorgas* was traveling in Convoy HX-228 en route from New York to Liverpool loaded with general cargo, including nine hundred tons of explosives and a deck cargo of an LCT and two PT boats. The ship carried a crew of forty-one merchant mariners and twenty-six Naval Armed Guard sailors.

At around 2030 on March 10, another ship in the convoy was torpedoed, and the general alarm was sounded. The crew remained on alert, with the Naval Armed Guard manning the battle stations. The weather was hazy, with moderate to heavy swells and ten to fifteen knot winds in bright moonlight. At 2330, the *Gorgas* was hit on the starboard side amidships by a torpedo fired by *U-757*. The explosion destroyed the engine room, instantly killing the three engineers on watch. The Master ordered the crew to abandon ship. By 2350, when 51 survivors in lifeboats and rafts had left the ship, snow had begun falling in higher winds. The *U-757* located one of the boats and questioned the survivors. Shortly thereafter the submarine found the ship still afloat and fired another torpedo to sink it. Immediately after the ship settled under the waves its ammunition cargo exploded, damaging *U-757* so much that it was unable to dive. The submarine was escorted on the surface back to France by another submarine.

The *Gorgas*'s fifty-one survivors were picked up at about 0700 on March 11 by the destroyer HMS *Harvester* (H 19). Shortly after rescuing the *Gorgas*'s survivors, the *Harvester* sighted *U-444* on the surface. Although the submarine dove to escape the *Harvester*'s gunfire, a depth charge attack brought the submarine to the surface. It is unclear why the *Harvester*'s Commander made his decision, but *U-444* was rammed at full speed by the *Harvester*, severely damaging both ships.

Although *U-444* was able to break free of the *Harvester*, it was rammed again and sunk by the Free French corvette *Aconit* (K 58). However, the almost-motionless *Harvester* was easy prey for *U-432,* which fired two torpedoes, quickly sinking the destroyer with nearly all of its crew and thirty-nine of the *Gorgas*'s survivors. The *Aconit* was immediately on scene attacking the *U-432* with depth charges and forcing it to the surface. The *Aconit* fired at the surfaced submarine and then rammed it, sending the *U-432* and all but twenty of its crew to the bottom. With this vital task accomplished, the *Aconit* rescued twelve *Gorgas*'s survivors, forty-eight survivors of the *Harvester*, and twenty-four German Sailors from *U-444* and *U-432*.

Launching of SS *William S. Gorgas*

After the *Harvester* sank, the Master of the *Gorgas*, James Calvin Ellis Jr., was seen by some of the survivors floating in a life ring in the cold seas. When he was offered a place on a life raft by one of the seamen, he declined, telling the man to keep his place. Soon after, he lost his grip on the life ring and was lost in the icy waters.

James Moon, his three U.S. Merchant Marine Academy classmates, and 1942 graduate Rafael R. Rivera were among those lost. It is believed that all five survived the initial attack but were lost in the subsequent sinking of the *Harvester*.

Cadet-Midshipman James O. Moon was posthumously awarded the Mariner's Medal, the Combat Bar with two stars, the Atlantic War Zone Bar, the Victory Medal, and the Presidential Testimonial Letter.

James O. Moon was the youngest son of Charles Emory Moon and Mary Elizabeth "Molly" Odom Moon. He was one of seven children, although, according to his family genealogy, one of his brothers died in infancy before James was born. According to the 1930 and 1940 U.S. Census, the Moon family were farmers in rural Georgia. By 1940, James was working at the local school as a school aide and groundskeeper while attending high school. According to some Academy records, James Moon had served aboard the SS *Jeremiah Wadsworth* on its maiden voyage when it was torpedoed off South Africa. As the survivor of a torpedoing, his name should have been listed as a member of the Academy's "Tin Fish Club."

Robert Shepard Nauman

Born:	September 2, 1921
Hometown:	Chicago, IL
Class:	1943
Service:	Merchant Marine
Position / Rank:	Deck Cadet
Date / Place of death:	October 7, 1942 / 34-00 S, 17-05 E
Date / Place of burial:	October 7, 1942 / Lost at Sea 34-00 S, 17-05 E; Memorial at Highland Cemetery, Lawton, OK
Age:	21

Robert S. Nauman signed on as Deck Cadet aboard the MS *Firethorn* on September 6, 1942, at the Port of New York. The *Firethorn* was originally a Danish vessel, the *Norden*, which had been requisitioned by presidential executive order on July 12, 1941. Now owned by the War Shipping Administration, it was registered in Panama and bareboat chartered to United States Lines. On February 26, 1942, the ship began operation by U.S. Lines under a general agency agreement.

Cadet-Midshipman Nauman was joined by Cadet-Midshipman Louis J. Rovella, Engine Cadet. The ship was crewed with forty foreign merchant mariners and twenty-one Armed Guard sailors. Cadet-Midshipmen Louis Rovella and Robert Nauman were the only American merchant mariners in the ship's crew. When the ship sailed, it was loaded with a cargo of general war supplies and a deck cargo of tanks.

SS *Firethorn* (ex-*Norden*)

On October 7, the *Firethorn* was passing about sixty miles northwest of Cape Town, en route from New York to Suez, Egypt. Traveling at about 12 knots, she was zigzagging under overcast skies. At approximately 0830, two torpedoes launched by the German submarine *U-172* struck the vessel in quick succession. The first torpedo hit the ship on the port side at the number 3 hatch, tearing open the hull and exploding on contact. The second struck the engine room on the port side, penetrating the hull before exploding. The ship sank in less than ninety seconds.

The crew had no time to launch the lifeboats, but the rafts and one boat floated free as the vessel went down, undoubtedly saving those crew members who had survived the initial explosions. Of the sixty-one men aboard the *Firethorn*, the Captain, eight merchant seamen, two Armed Guard sailors, and Cadet-Midshipmen Robert Nauman and Louis Rovella were lost. Survivors collected on four rafts and in one boat that had floated free of the sinking ship. The rafts were lashed together and remained in the vicinity of the sinking, while six men manned the boat and made for the coast of South Africa. The survivors on the boat were picked up by the HMS *Rockrose* (K 51) on October 8. The following day, the *Rockrose* picked up the survivors on the rafts. All were taken to Cape Town.

Cadet-Midshipman Robert S. Nauman was posthumously awarded the Mariner's Medal, the Combat Bar with star, the Atlantic War Zone Bar, the Victory Medal, and the Presidential Testimonial Letter.

Robert Nauman was the older of the two sons of Robert M. Nauman and Margaret H. Nauman. Robert's brother, seven years younger, was Jacob.

According to U.S. Census data, the family had moved around quite a bit when Robert was younger, and Robert Sr. managed restaurants in Des Moines, Iowa, and St. Paul, Minnesota. A memorial to Robert is located on the grave of his mother and brother at Highland Cemetery, Lawton, Oklahoma.

Robert S. Nauman Memorial, Lawton, OK

Roland Edward Netcott Jr.

Born:	1920
Hometown:	Independence, IA
Class:	1944
Service:	Merchant Marine
Position / Rank:	Engine Cadet
Date / Place of death:	September 26, 1943
Date / Place of burial:	Oakwood Cemetery, Independence, IA
Age:	23

Roland E. Netcott entered the U.S. Merchant Marine Cadet Corps on September 18, 1942, at Kings Point. He received his appointment as Cadet-Midshipman, USNR, on October 2, 1942. He was assigned to the SS *Tabitha Brown* on October 22, 1942. Crew lists on file in New York indicate that he signed on as Engine Cadet in Portland, Oregon, on October 26. He signed off the ship upon its arrival in New York from Trinidad on March 20, 1943.

Cadet-Midshipman Roland E. Netcott was discharged from the U.S. Naval Reserve and presumably the U.S. Merchant Marine Cadet Corps on July 16, 1943. Since Academy records indicate that he died on September 26, 1943, just two months after his discharge, the reason for his discharge may have been either injury or illness.

Roland Netcott Memorial, Independence, IA

For his merchant marine service, Cadet-Midshipman Roland E. Netcott earned the Atlantic and Pacific War Zone Bars, the Victory Medal, and the Presidential Testimonial Letter.

Roland E. Netcott was the only son and youngest of Ronald E. Netcott Sr. and Irene Netcott's two children. Roland's sister was Avenel, two years older then he. The Netcott family was well established in Independence,

Iowa, where Roland's father and Uncle Harry were architects practicing together in the firm of Netcott and Netcott. Growing up, Roland was a Boy Scout. In April 1934, when he was thirteen years old, he was awarded a medal and gold watch for preventing a fast freight train from derailing near Independence.

Ronald Earl Nolan

Born:	November 30, 1924
Hometown:	Algiers, Louisiana
Class:	1945
Service:	Merchant Marine
Position / Rank:	Deck Cadet
Date / Place of death:	January 10, 1944 / 16-20 N, 73-53 W
Date / Place of burial:	January 10, 1944 / At Sea—16-20 N, 73-53 W
Age:	19

Ronald E. Nolan signed on as Deck Cadet aboard the SS *Wildwood,* a World War I vintage "Hog Islander," on December 30, 1943, at New Orleans, Louisiana. Shortly after sailing, Cadet-Midshipman Nolan became ill and subsequently developed pneumonia. On January 19, 1944, the *Wildwood*'s Master reported to the American consul at Port of Spain, Trinidad that Ronald E. Nolan died of pneumonia just after midnight on January 10, 1944. He was buried at sea on the same day at around 1400 hours.

In his voyage report, Ensign Verne Stewart, USNR, Commander of *Wildwood*'s Naval Armed Guard, noted that the forward crew quarters on the *Wildwood* were "unlivable," with temperatures sometimes rising above 130 degrees Fahrenheit. He added that

> there has been much sickness on the ship and I am certain that this improvement (to the ship's ventilation) would decrease same.

Cadet-Midshipman Ronald E. Nolan was posthumously awarded the Atlantic War Zone Bar, the Victory Medal, and the Presidential Testimonial Letter.

Ronald Nolan was the oldest of William E. Nolan and Elvera B. Nolan's four sons. Ronald's younger siblings were the twins Emile and John, who were three years younger, and little brother, William, who was thirteen years younger. According to the 1930 and 1940 census, William Nolan was a machinist.

Edwin Joseph O'Hara

Born:	November 27, 1923
Hometown:	Lindsay, CA
Class:	1943
Service:	Merchant Marine
Position / Rank:	Engine Cadet
Date / Place of death:	September 27, 1942 / 28-08 S, 11-59 W
Date / Place of burial:	September 27, 1942 / Lost at Sea—28-08 S, 11-59 W
Age:	18

Before he sailed into history, Edwin J. O'Hara was just another Cadet from the Maritime Commission's West Coast Basic School. Although he was initially appointed as a Deck Cadet, Edwin O'Hara signed on aboard the SS *Mariposa* as Engine Cadet on March 14, 1942. In a unique twist of fate, Edwin O'Hara signed off the *Mariposa* after it arrived in San Francisco on May 3, 1942, due to an infection in his knee. On May 16, 1942, with the infection cleared up and ready for duty, he and Cadet-Midshipman Arthur R. Chamberlin (deck) signed on aboard the newly delivered SS *Stephen Hopkins* at San Francisco, California.

After sailing across the Pacific with war cargo, the *Stephen Hopkins* called at Durban and Cape Town, South Africa, before sailing across the South Atlantic, bound for Paramaribo, Suriname. On September 27, 1942, the visibility was reduced due to fog and haze. Despite having five lookouts, no one aboard the *Stephen Hopkins* sighted either the German Raider *Stier* (known as Raider J) or its supply ship *Tannenfels* until 1235 (GCT), when they appeared out of the mist. Ordered to stop by the *Stier*, the *Stephen Hopkins*'s Master, Captain Paul Buck, refused and turned the ship away from the Germans to bring his heaviest weapon to bear, a single four-inch gun.

The *Stier* was armed with six 150 mm guns, one 75 mm gun, a twin 37 mm antiaircraft gun, and four 20 mm antiaircraft guns with modern fire control and trained naval gunners. The ship also had two float planes and two torpedo tubes. The *Tannenfels* was only armed with antiaircraft machine guns. Against this armament, the *Stephen Hopkins* had one four-inch gun, two 37 mm, and several .50—and .30-caliber antiaircraft machine guns manned by a small detachment of Naval Armed Guard and the ship's crew.

At 1238, the *Stier* began firing on the *Stephen Hopkins* at close range. Shrapnel and machine gun bullets wounded several men, including the Armed Guard Commander, Lt. (jg) Kenneth M. Willett, USNR, while killing others. Despite his wounds, Willett got the guns manned and began returning fire at a range of about one thousand yards. Lieutenant Willett steadfastly continued to direct gunfire from the *Stephen Hopkins* at the two German vessels, while the Captain maneuvered to keep the stern pointed at the German ships. In their exposed post, the Naval Armed Guard crew was decimated by shells and machine gun bullets, leaving only the wounded Willett to keep the four-inch gun firing at the *Stier*'s waterline, inflicting heavy damage. When the ammunition magazine for the four-inch gun magazine exploded, Willett was knocked out. However, Cadet-Midshipman Edwin J. O'Hara, who was nearby, rushed forward to take Willett's place. Before being mortally wounded by enemy fire, O'Hara fired the five shells remaining in the gun mount's ready service locker at the *Tannenfels*.

After twenty minutes of uneven combat, the *Stephen Hopkins* was on fire and sinking. With no other recourse, Captain Buck gave the order to abandon ship. The Second Assistant Engineer and the Steward lowered the only undamaged lifeboat over the side, while other crew members, including the now-conscious Lieutenant Willett, lowered or cut rafts loose. The lifeboat then collected crew members that were in the water or on rafts until the men in the lifeboat could no longer see in the fog and mist. One raft with five men, including possibly Captain Buck, was lost in the fog and was never seen again. The survivors were able to see the *Stephen Hopkins* sink stern first. Shortly afterward, they were rewarded by the sound of the *Stier*'s ammunition magazines exploding, sinking their attacker. Only nineteen of the sixty men aboard the *Stephen Hopkins* made it to the lifeboat, including five wounded men. Among those who did not survive the battle were Cadet-Midshipmen Edwin J. O'Hara and Arthur R. Chamberlin.

On September 28, the survivors of the *Stephen Hopkins* set their course west for South America. After a voyage of thirty-one days and 2,200 miles, fifteen of the men arrived at Barra-do-Itabapoana, Brazil, on October 27. The next day, the survivors told the story of the *Stephen Hopkins*'s fight with the two German ships to Timothy J. Mahoney, the American vice consul in Brazil. However, press reports of the *Stephen Hopkins* did not appear until December.

When the press was able to report the story of the *Stephen Hopkins,* the ship was hailed as a "hero ship." The accounts cited the action as the first between a German surface raider and U.S. merchant ship, which resulted in sinking the raider. For the action of September 27, 1942, the SS *Stephen Hopkins* and its crew were awarded the U.S. Maritime Commission's Gallant Ship Unit Citation.

The men of the *Stephen Hopkins* were also honored by a grateful nation. Lt. (jg) Kenneth M. Willett, USNR, was posthumously awarded the Navy Cross.

Of the crew, Paul Buck (Master), George S. Cronk (Second Assistant Engineer), Joseph Earl Layman (Second Mate), Richard Moczkowski (Chief Mate), and Ford Stilson (Chief Steward) were awarded the Merchant Marine Distinguished Service Medal. The awards for Buck, Layman, and Moczkowski were made posthumously.

For his brave sacrifice of his own life in manning the *Stephen Hopkins*'s four-inch gun and firing the last five shots into the *Tannenfels*, O'Hara was also posthumously awarded the Distinguished Service Medal.

Five ships were named in honor of the crew of the *Stephen Hopkins* and of the ship itself.

SS *Paul Buck*
SS *Edwin Joseph O'Hara*
USS *Kenneth M. Willett* (DE 354)

SS *Richard Moczkowski*
SS *Stephen Hopkins II*

**Artist's depiction of *Edwin J. O'Hara* firing
SS *Stephen Hopkins*'s last five shells**

Cadet Edwin Joseph O'Hara is one of six Cadet-Midshipmen to be awarded the Distinguished Service Medal. He is the only Cadet to receive the award posthumously. O'Hara Hall, the Academy's athletic center, is named in his honor. In addition to the Distinguished Service Medal and Gallant Ship Unit Citation, Cadet-Midshipman Edwin J. O'Hara was posthumously awarded the Mariner's Medal, the Combat Bar with star, the Atlantic War Zone Bar, the Pacific War Zone Bar, the Victory Medal, and the Presidential Testimonial Letter.

Edwin J. O'Hara was the youngest son of Joseph C. O'Hara and Elma Fugle O'Hara. He grew up on the family farm near Lindsay, California, where his father grew oranges and wheat. According to his younger sister Dorothy O. Norris, Edwin, a member of the Future Farmers of America, disliked sitting at a desk and needed to be "doing things." In his off time, he worked on three old cars and dreamt of seeing the world. As graduation from Lindsay High School approached, he started looking for ways to turn his dreams into reality. Although the Navy's submarine service interested him, he was also interested in the Maritime Commission's Cadet Program, which had a Basic School at nearby Treasure Island in San Francisco Bay. However, with the war still distant, Edwin's parents persuaded him to attend a local Junior college in the spring of 1941. When the Japanese attacked Pearl Harbor on December 7,

Edwin Joseph O'Hara
Lindsay High School
Graduation, 1941

1941, Edwin O'Hara applied for the Cadet program and was quickly accepted. Dorothy recalls that on his only weekend leave home from the Basic School, his family and friends found a new and happier man than they had known previously. However, all too soon, his leave was over, and he was away to sea, never to return except to the pages of history as a symbol to all Kings Pointers of the motto, *Acta Non Verba*.

William Vaughan O'Hara

Born:	August 15, 1921
Hometown:	Cambridge, MA
Class:	1943
Service:	Merchant Marine
Position / Rank:	Deck Cadet
Date / Place of death:	November 29, 1942 / 28-00 S, 54-00 E
Date / Place of burial:	November 29, 1942 / Lost at Sea—28-00 S, 54-00 E
Age:	21

William V. O'Hara signed on as Deck Cadet aboard the MS *Sawokla* at the Port of New York on June 16, 1942. Also aboard was his classmate Meyer Egenthal, Engine Cadet. The ship sailed two days later loaded with general war cargo bound for the Soviet Union via Abadan, Iran. After arriving in Abadan via Port of Spain, Trinidad, and Cape Town, South Africa, the *Sawokla* delivered its cargo. The ship then sailed in ballast for Colombo and then to Calcutta, India, where it loaded a cargo of gunny sacks in bales. The *Sawokla* returned to Colombo for sailing directions and to pick up some homebound passengers.

MS *Sawokla*

On November 21, 1942, the *Sawokla* sailed from Colombo with a crew of forty-one, a Navy Armed Guard contingent of thirteen, and five passengers. Eight days out of port and about four hundred miles south of Madagascar, the *Sawokla* was sighted and attacked by the German surface raider *Michel*. Junior Third Mate Stanley Willner, a Merchant Marine Cadet Corps Cadet Officer on his first voyage as a ship's officer, was standing watch on the bridge on the eight-to-twelve watch the night of November 19, 1942. According to Willner, at about 2035, he saw the outlines of a ship take shape in the darkness and immediately called the Captain to the bridge. However, just as the Captain was opening his cabin door, the *Michel* opened fire on *Sawokla,* hitting the bridge and radio shack with its main battery.

The Captain was killed immediately, as were most of the bridge watch and forecastle lookout. During the attack, all of the ship's lifeboats had been so badly damaged by the gunfire that they were no longer seaworthy. The crew, Armed Guard sailors, and passengers who survived the initial attack were forced to jump overboard into the rough seas. Willner and thirty-eight other men were rescued by the *Michel* and its crew, who remained in the area for two days searching for survivors. In the very precise and detailed report written by Stanley Willner after the war, he stated that according to his questioning of the other crew members, Cadet-Midshipmen William V. O'Hara and Meyer Egenthal were seen jumping overboard after the attack but were not seen again.

For those that had survived the initial attack, the ordeal had just begun. On February 19, 1943, the *Michel* arrived in Singapore, where its prisoners were taken to the Japanese prisoner of war camp at the former Changi Prison. According to Willner, on May 17, 1943, he, five other officers from the *Sawokla,* and one of the *Sawokla* passengers were among eight thousand officer POWs taken from Changi to work as slave labor on the Thailand-Burma Railway. This railroad is sometimes known as the "Death Railway" and immortalized in the book and film *The Bridge over the River Kwai*. Willner was one of approximately three thousand survivors of his group. When Changi Prison was liberated on September 7, 1945, Willner weighed seventy-five pounds, almost half of his normal 135 pounds.

Willner, along with the *Sawokla* Second Mate, Dennis Roland, worked for decades to earn official veteran's status for merchant seamen in World War II. As part of this effort, Stanley Willner served as a named plaintiff in litigation that finally bore fruit in 1988, more than four decades after Willner's ordeal.

Cadet-Midshipman William V. O'Hara was posthumously awarded the Mariner's Medal, the Combat Bar with star, the Atlantic War Zone Bar, the Mediterranean-Middle East War Zone Bar, the Victory Medal, and the Presidential Testimonial Letter.

William V. O'Hara was the youngest son and second of Thomas E. O'Hara and Bernice J. O'Hara's four children. William's older brother was Thomas, while his younger sisters were (Bernice) Jane and Ruth. According to the 1930 U.S. Census, Thomas O'Hara was a dentist in Cambridge, Massachusetts. Following his graduation from high school, William entered Northeastern University, where he was a member of their class of 1945. However, based on the dates of his service, William V. O'Hara left Northeastern in early 1942, shortly after America officially entered World War II.

Robert Valentine Palmer

Born:	October 22, 1922
Hometown:	Richmond Hill, NY
Class:	1943
Service:	Merchant Marine
Position / Rank:	Engine Cadet
Date / Place of death:	September 24, 1942 / 8-05 N, 58-08 W
Date / Place of burial:	September 24, 1942 / Lost at Sea—8-05 N, 58-08 W
Age:	19

Robert V. Palmer signed on as Engine Cadet aboard the SS *West Chetac* in June 1942 at the Port of New York. He was joined by Cadet-Midshipman Arthur Z. Brown, Deck Cadet. The ship sailed from New York on June 22, 1942, stopping at Philadelphia and Norfolk to load additional cargo bound for the Persian Gulf. After sailing from Norfolk in Convoy TAW-14, the ship called at Key West, Florida, Aruba, and Trinidad, where the convoy disbanded on September 23.

SS *West Chetac*

On September 24, the *West Chetac* was about one hundred miles north of Georgetown, British Guyana, and proceeding on an easterly course at 7 knots without zigzagging when it was located by *U-175*. According to German naval records, the submarine fired a spread of three torpedoes at the *West Chetac* earlier that morning, which missed. The submarine also reported that the ship had been escorted by an aircraft for some time.

Some of the survivors reported that the ship had been circled by a twin-engine patrol plane, which they believed gave the ship's position away, not knowing that they were already being stalked by a submarine.

At 0715, the ship made a complete circle to avoid what was believed to be the wake of a submarine's conning tower. Fifteen minutes later, when the ship had steadied up on its course, a torpedo fired by *U-175* hit the port side of number 2 hold, destroying the hatch covers and causing the vessel to sink by the bow in less than two minutes. Between the rush to get the boats launched and the high sea running, all four lifeboats capsized, throwing their occupants into the water. In his report of the sinking, Cadet-Midshipman Arthur Brown stated,

> I had been standing near the after part of the amidships house talking to a crew member and had just left, on my way to my quarters, when the ship was hit. I immediately got my lifebelt and went to my station on the boat deck. The order to lower away was given by the Chief Officer. I released the pelican hook to the bridle, and then proceeded into the boat to secure the plug. Since another man was doing this I started to unlash and clear the gear in the boat. At the time water was coming over the Number Three hatch, the vessel was settling fast. There was a heavy swell which caused the lifeboat to turn over, toward the outboard side. Falling out of the boat I swam for a hatch cover. I then sighted a raft and proceeded to swim for it. Aboard the raft was a messman. He and I assisted others in getting aboard the raft. No boats had been able to get away.

After the *West Chetac* sank, *U-175* surfaced, interrogated some of the survivors, and the sub departed on the surface. Cadet-Midshipman Brown reported that he had been told that his shipmate Robert V. Palmer reached the boat deck but was not one of the survivors. Of the fifty men aboard the *West Chetac,* only seventeen crew members and two Naval Armed Guard sailors survived the sinking. The nineteen men were able to get aboard three rafts and keep them together until they were picked up by the USS *Roe* (DD 418) on October 1, eight days later. The survivors were taken to Port of Spain, Trinidad.

Cadet-Midshipman Palmer was posthumously awarded the Mariner's Medal, the Combat Bar with star, the Atlantic War Zone Bar, the Victory Medal, and the Presidential Testimonial Letter. According to the 1930 Census, Charles D. and Florence Palmer had five children; Charles, Adeline, Florence, Edith, and Robert who was the youngest.

George Edward Pancratz

Born:	April 13, 1923
Hometown:	Little Falls, MN
Class:	1944
Service:	Merchant Marine
Position / Rank:	Deck Cadet
Date / Place of death:	September 18, 1943 / Tunisia
Date / Place of burial:	September 19, 1943 / U.S. Military Cemetery, Mateur, Tunisia; April 2, 1949 / Calvary Cemetery, Little Falls, MN
Age:	20

George E. Pancratz signed on as Deck Cadet aboard the SS *Bushrod Washington* on May 7, 1943, at New York, New York, just two weeks after the ship had been completed. He was joined the same day by his classmate William S. Sempell, Engine Cadet. Shortly thereafter, the *Bushrod Washington* sailed for the Mediterranean, where it remained for the rest of its short life.

On September 3, 1943, the *Bushrod Washington* sailed from Oran with a convoy bound for the landing beaches at Salerno, Italy, with a cargo of ammunition, high-octane aviation gasoline in drums, bombs, C rations, Army trucks, and landing craft. The vessel arrived at Salerno on September 11 and anchored about three-quarters of a mile off Salerno Beach, in a northeast-southwest direction, stern to shore. The *Bushrod Washington* was carrying a crew of forty-two merchant seamen and thirty-three Naval Armed Guard sailors. The Master was Jonathan Wainwright V, son of Gen. Jonathan Wainwright, the American Commander at Corregidor and Bataan in the Philippines.

On September 14, at 1322, the vessel was attacked by either German dive bombers or a glide bomb. Much of the cargo had been unloaded over the previous days, but the gasoline and explosives were still on board. The plane dropped two bombs on the *Washington*, one of which missed the ship by about 150 feet. The other struck the vessel in the midship house between lifeboats number 2 and number 4, penetrating through the crew mess room and exploding below the main deck. Reports differ on whether the bomb hit the engine room directly or landed in the ice machine room nearby. In either case, the ship's engines were moved to starboard by the force of the explosion, and the port boiler exploded. The engine crew on duty, which included the First Assistant Engineer and Engine Cadet William Sempell, never made it out of the engine room.

The explosion also ignited the gasoline in number 4 hold, and within minutes, the entire ship was a raging inferno. At 1352, the Captain ordered the crew to abandon ship. Many crew members made it into # 1 and 3 lifeboats. Others jumped overboard and were rescued by small boats that came alongside the ship. Captain Wainwright and four other crew members later reboarded the ship in an attempt to extinguish the fire, but this proved impossible, and the ship was finally abandoned. Six members of the *Bushrod Washington*'s crew, including Cadet-Midshipman William Sempell, and one of the Naval Armed Guard sailors were lost in the bombing.

The injured crew members, including badly burned Cadet-Midshipman George Pancratz, were placed aboard the Royal Navy hospital ship HMHS *Amarapoora* for care and transportation to hospitals in North Africa. George Pancratz died of his wounds four days later and was buried in the U.S. Military Cemetery at Mateur, Tunisia.

Cadet-Midshipman George E. Pancratz was posthumously awarded the Combat Bar with two stars, the Mariner's Medal, the Atlantic War Zone Bar, the Mediterranean-Middle East War Zone Bar, the Victory Medal, and the Presidential Testimonial Letter. Although Academy records indicate that Cadet-Midshipman Pancratz was a member of the "Tin Fish Club," the name of the ship he served aboard before the *Bushrod Washington* could not be determined.

George Pancratz was the oldest son and the second of four children of Lambert Pancratz and Irene Tanner Pancratz. George had an older sister named Gertrude and younger siblings named Thomas and Barbara. Lambert Pancratz owned a sheet metal shop specializing in fabrication and repair of roofs and heating/ventilation systems. Although George's body was initially buried in an American military cemetery in Tunisia, his body was returned to his parents in 1949. On April 2, 1949, his body was reinterred at the Calvary Cemetery in Little Falls, Minnesota.

William Henry Parker

Born:	May 1, 1923
Hometown:	Newport News, VA
Class:	1944
Service:	Merchant Marine
Position / Rank:	Deck Cadet
Date / Place of death:	March 17, 1943 / 50-38 N, 34-46 W
Date / Place of burial:	March 17, 1943 / Lost at Sea—50-38 N, 34-46 W
Age:	19

William H. Parker signed on aboard the SS *Harry Luckenbach* as Deck Cadet on March 2, 1943, at New York, New York. In addition to Parker, the *Harry Luckenbach* had three other Kings Point Cadets aboard: Lee T. Byrd (deck), Walter J. Meyer (engine), and Francis R. Miller (engine). Third Mate Leroy W. Kernan was a 1942 graduate. The ship sailed from New York on March 8 as one of forty ships in Convoy HX-229, bound for Liverpool with a general cargo of war supplies. A second HX convoy, HX-229A, with more ships, sailed about ten hours after the ships of HX-229. During their transit of the North Atlantic, the two convoys overtook a slower convoy, SC-122. The three convoys, with a total of 110 ships, but less than twenty escorts, would be the centerpiece of what has been described as the greatest convoy battle of World War II.

SS *Harry Luckenbach*

The ships of Convoy HX-229 had proceeded without incident or attack until March 16. For the next three days, the convoy was under attack by over forty U-boats. On the morning of March 17, when HX-229 was about four hundred miles east-southeast of Cape Farrell, *U-91* fired five torpedoes at the convoy, not aiming at any specific ship. However, the *Harry Luckenbach* in the starboard forward corner of the convoy was hit by two of the torpedoes at the engine room. The ship sank in minutes, but amazingly, three lifeboats were able to get away from the sinking vessel. One or more of the boats were later sighted by HMS *Beverley* (H-64), HMS *Pennywort* (K-111), HMS *Volunteer* (D-71) and, possibly, HMS *Abelia* (K-184). However, none of these ships were able to pick up the survivors from the boats. None of the fifty-four crew members and twenty-six Naval Armed Guard sailors of the *Harry Luckenbach* survived the sinking.

By March 20, the surviving ships of the three convoys arrived in the United Kingdom, having lost twenty-two ships and their crews, while sinking just one of the attacking U-boats. According to a Royal Navy report on the convoy battle,

> The Germans never came so near to disrupting communications between the New World and the Old as in the first twenty days of March 1943.

The fact that the Germans were unable to do so is a testament to the courage of merchant mariners like William H. Parker, and the example that he set for the Kings Pointers that came after him.

Cadet-Midshipman William H. Parker was posthumously awarded the Mariner's Medal, the Combat Bar with star, the Atlantic War Zone Bar, the Victory Medal, and the Presidential Testimonial Letter.

William H. Parker was the younger of Arthur B. Parker and Irma Parker's two sons. William's big brother was Arthur Jr., who was several years older. According to the 1940 U.S. Census, Arthur Sr. was a manager for a life insurance company.

Fred Pennington

Born:	October 17, 1921
Hometown:	Newville, AL
Class:	1943
Service:	Merchant Marine
Position / Rank:	Deck Cadet
Date / Place of death:	November 7, 1942 / 40 S, 21-30 E
Date / Place of burial:	November 7, 1942 / Lost at Sea—40 S, 21-30 E
Age:	21

Fred Pennington attended Basic School at Pass Christian, Mississippi. According to Academy records, he signed on aboard the SS *La Salle* as Deck Cadet at Balboa, in the Panama Canal Zone, on September 26, 1942. Also aboard the ship was his Pass Christian classmate Engine Cadet George E. Guilford and 1942 alumnus Third Assistant Engineer James D. Herndon. Shortly after signing on, the *La Salle* sailed for Cape Town, South Africa, loaded with a cargo of trucks, steel, and ammunition. However, the *La Salle* never arrived at Cape Town, and the ship's remained a mystery until after the war. The vessel was officially marked as "presumed lost" on December 2, 1942.

SS *Wynah*, a shipyard sister to the SS *La Salle*

After the war, German Navy records solved the mystery. On November 7, 1942, when the *La Salle* was nearing the end of its voyage, the unescorted freighter was sighted by *U-159* about 350 miles southeast of the Cape of Good Hope. The submarine chased the *La Salle* for over five hours, missing with one torpedo, until it managed to achieve a better target solution and fired another torpedo. The explosion of that torpedo detonated the *La Salle* ammunition cargo, instantly destroying the ship and killing every member of its crew of thirty-nine and thirteen Armed Guard sailors.

The crew of *U-159* reported that the explosion sent pillars of flame hundreds of feet into the air. Three of the submarine's crew were wounded by the debris that rained down on the submarine for several minutes after the explosion. It was later claimed that the explosion could be heard at South Africa's Cape Point Lighthouse, three hundred miles away. All of the fifty-two men aboard the ship (thirty-nine ship's crew plus thirteen Naval Armed Guard sailors) died in the explosion, including Cadet-Midshipmen Fred Pennington and George E. Guilford and Third Assistant Engineer James D. Herndon. Also among the dead was the ship's Armed Guard officer, the former Mayor of Milwaukee, Wisconsin, Lt. Carl F. Zeidler, USNR. Carl Zeidler had resigned as Mayor to accept a commission in the Navy. When asked what assignment he wanted, he is said to have asked for the most dangerous job in the Navy. He was then assigned to command a merchant ship Armed Guard detachment.

Cadet-Midshipman Fred Pennington was posthumously awarded the Mariner's Medal, the Combat Bar, the Atlantic War Zone Bar, the Pacific War Zone Bar, the Victory Medal, and the Presidential Testimonial Letter.

Fred Pennington was the youngest of three sons and one daughter of Charles Pennington and Mary Pennington. The Pennington children were Edna, Charles Jr., Ted, and Fred. According to the 1930 U.S. Census, Charles Sr. was a brick mason.

David Harold Pitzely

Born:	July 31, 1924
Hometown:	Bronx, NY
Class:	1944
Service:	Merchant Marine
Position / Rank:	Deck Cadet
Date / Place of death:	February 5, 1943 / 52 N, 33 W
Date / Place of burial:	February 5, 1943 / Lost at Sea—52 N, 33 W
Age:	18

Two months before his seventeenth birthday, David Pitzely's parents gave him permission to begin sailing in the merchant marine. He initially signed on aboard the passenger ship SS *Talamanca* in May 23, 1941, as part of the Stewards Department. However, he subsequently sailed as Ordinary Seaman aboard the SS *Hibueras,* the SS *Mormacyork,* and the SS *Santa Monica* between June 26, 1941, and September 9, 1942. The Deck Cadets aboard each of these ships may have been David's inspiration for applying to Kings Point, as he entered Kings Point days after signing off of the SS *Santa Monica*.

David H. Pitzely signed on as Deck Cadet aboard the SS *West Portal* on December 24, 1942, at New York, New York. He joined his Academy classmate Cadet-Midshipman James Province, Engine Cadet who had signed on a few days earlier. The World War I -era "Hog Islander" sailed on January 24, 1943, for Liverpool via Nova Scotia in Convoy SC-118. Aboard the ship on sailing from Nova Scotia were eight officers, the two Cadets, thirty crewmen, twenty-five Navy Armed Guard, and twelve passengers.

SS *West Portal* (ex-*Emergency Aid*)

The slow ships of Convoy SC-118 were sailing right behind a convoy of higher-speed ships, HX 224. A survivor from one of the four ships sunk in this convoy was rescued by *U-632*. He told his rescuers that a large convoy of slow speed ships was behind his convoy. The German Navy's high command alerted every available U-boat upon receiving the news from *U-632*. U-boats were sent to locations along Convoy SC-118's most likely route from Nova Scotia to the United Kingdom. On February 4, the convoy's location was revealed to searching U-boats by the inadvertent firing of a signal rocket.

For whatever reason, the SS *West Portal* straggled behind the convoy on the evening of February 4. According to German naval records that became available only after the end of World War II, the SS *West Portal* was sighted by *U-143* on the afternoon of February 5. The *U-143* initially fired a spread of four torpedoes at the zigzagging *West Portal* from almost two miles away. Only the third torpedo hit the *West Portal*. The submarine closed the range for a final shot but reported that it missed. A sixth and final torpedo was reported to have hit the ship near the stern, which finally sunk the ship.

The *U-143*'s Captain reported seeing some of the ship's crew and passengers abandoning ship in the lifeboats. One of the convoy escorts, HMS *Vanessa (D 29),* received the *West Portal*'s distress message and was ordered to leave the convoy to search for survivors. However, the radio message did not provide a location, so the search proved fruitless. Neither the *West Portal*'s lifeboats nor any of the men aboard the *West Portal* were ever seen again.

Benjamin, David, and Minnie Pitzely

The battle to get Convoy SC-118's remaining ships to port was one of the largest during the Battle of the Atlantic. Seven other merchant ships were sunk, while the convoy's escorts sank three U-boats and damaged two more.

Cadet-Midshipman David H. Pitzely was posthumously awarded the Mariner's Medal, the Combat Bar with star, the Atlantic War Zone Bar, the Merchant Marine Defense Bar, the Victory Medal, and the Presidential Testimonial Letter.

David Pitzely was the older of Benjamin Pitzely and Minnie Silverstein Pitzely's two sons. David's brother, Lewis, was four years younger. According to the 1930 U.S. Census, Benjamin Pitzely was employed as a chauffeur. David's cousin Arthur Silverstein recalled David as a young man with a deep love of ships and the sea. As a youth, he had belonged to one of New York's many Junior naval organizations before starting his life at sea.

Dante Ludivico Polcari

Born:	April 20, 1921
Hometown:	Medford, MA
Class:	1946
Service:	Merchant Marine
Position / Rank:	Deck Cadet
Date / Place of death:	April 9, 1945 / 37-31 N, 64-26 W
Date / Place of burial:	April 9, 1945 / Lost at Sea—37-31 N, 64-26 W
Age:	23

Dante L. Polcari signed on as Deck Cadet aboard the T2-SE-A1 tanker, SS *Saint Mihiel*, on March 20, 1945, at Philadelphia, Pennsylvania. This was one day after the ship was delivered from its builder, Sun Shipbuilding, to the War Shipping Administration. He was joined by his classmate Engine Cadet John W. Artist. The vessel sailed in ballast to Corpus Christi, Texas, where it picked up a full load of aviation gasoline bound for Cherbourg, France. After leaving Corpus Christi, the *Saint Mihiel* was ordered to New York, where Convoy CU-65, a fast convoy of tankers and other high-value ships, was forming. On April 8, the *Saint Mihiel* and the other ships of the convoy sailed from New York and began forming the convoy.

On the night of April 9 the *Saint Mihiel* and another tanker, SS *Nashbulk*, collided. Part of the *Saint Mihiel*'s cargo of gasoline immediately burst into flame, destroying the navigating bridge located amidships and killing most of the deck officers. The surviving crew abandoned ship as soon as possible and were picked up by the USS *Stewart* (DE 238) after about two hours in the water. Of the fifty crew members and twenty-nine Naval Armed Guard members, only twenty-three of the crew and nineteen Navy sailors survived. Cadets John W. Artist and Dante L. Polcari were among those missing and presumed dead. Also among the dead was Third Assistant Engineer James LeRoy Maloney, a 1944 USMMA graduate.

On the morning of April 10, the *Saint Mihiel* was still afloat, although some of the cargo was still burning. The ship's senior surviving deck officer, Second Mate Bruno Baretich, assembled some of the *Saint Mihiel*'s survivors to board the *Saint Mihiel* to see if it could be salvaged. Aided by crewmen from the *Stewart* and another escort, Baretich reboarded the ship, put out the fires, and got the ship under way for New

York. Although the ship was ultimately a constructive total loss, over 80 percent of the gasoline cargo was saved. For his actions, Baretich, a former vaudeville performer and song arranger for Irving Berlin, received the Merchant Marine Distinguished Service Medal. Cadet-Midshipmen John W. Artist and Dante L. Polcari were the last two Academy Cadets to lose their lives in WWII.

Cadet-Midshipman Dante L. Polcari was posthumously awarded the Atlantic War Zone Bar, the Victory Medal, and the Presidential Testimonial Letter.

Dante L. Polcari was the oldest of Raffaele (Ralph) Polcari and Rosalia D'Antonio Polcari's four children. Dante's younger siblings were the twins John and Tony, two years younger, and his sister, Nancy. Ralph, an immigrant from Italy, owned a barbershop in Medford, Massachusetts.

Roscoe Joseph Prickett Jr.

Born:	December 16, 1924
Hometown:	Little Rock, Arkansas
Class:	1944
Service:	Merchant Marine
Position / Rank:	Deck Cadet
Date / Place of death:	August 19, 1943 / 36-37 N, 30-55 W
Date / Place of burial:	September 3, 1943 / Sydney, Nova Scotia
Age:	18

Roscoe J. Prickett Jr. signed on as Deck Cadet aboard the SS *J. Pinckney Henderson* on July 24, 1943. His classmate Engine Cadet Robert J. Derick had signed on the day before. By August 14, 1943, the *J. Pinckney Henderson* had been loaded with a cargo of magnesium, glycerin, resin, oil, and wax and sailed for Liverpool as part of Convoy HX-252. The weather from August 14 onward was bad, with both high seas and fog. On the evening of August 19, the *Henderson* collided with the Panamanian flag tanker *J. H. Senior*. The *J. H. Senior* was carrying aviation gasoline, which exploded, showering both ships with burning high-octane gasoline. Within moments, both ships were transformed into infernos. Three crew members on the *Henderson* and six others on the *J. H. Senior* were able to leap into the sea and save themselves. The remaining crew members of both ships, including Cadet-Midshipmen Roscoe J. Prickett and John R. Derick, were killed in the fire.

The *J. Pinckney Henderson* was initially thought to be salvageable and was towed to Sydney, Nova Scotia, still in flames. However, she continued to burn for another month and was eventually declared a total loss. The hulk was later towed to Philadelphia and scrapped. On September 3, 1943, the charred remains of thirty-four unidentifiable bodies were buried with naval honors in a mass grave at Sydney. A Monument was also erected there in their honor. Sometime around 1949, the remains were exhumed and reinterred in a mass grave at the Jefferson Barracks National Cemetery. However, the name of Roscoe J. Prickett, along those of several other men who died aboard the SS *J. P. Henderson*, was not among the fifty-six names inscribed on the memorial placed there. It can only be assumed that the identity of his remains was determined during the exhumation process and returned to his family for burial.

When the remains of the deceased were removed for reburial, the Monument to the crew of the *J. P. Henderson* erected by the citizens of Sydney, Nova Scotia, was moved to Kings Point. The Monument languished in relative anonymity until 2004, when it was installed in a place of honor at the entrance of the American Merchant Marine Museum adjacent to the U.S. Merchant Marine Academy.

Cadet-Midshipman Roscoe J. Prickett Jr. was posthumously awarded the Atlantic War Zone Bar, the Victory Medal, and the Presidential Testimonial Letter.

Roscoe J. Prickett Jr. was the only child of Roscoe J. Prickett and Maude Christen Prickett. According to the 1930 U.S. Census, Roscoe Sr. was employed as a truck driver, while Maude worked as a stenographer in a law firm. Roscoe Sr. died in 1940, leaving Maude to finish raising Roscoe Jr.

James Henry Province

Born:	October 10, 1920
Hometown:	Detroit, MI
Class:	1944
Service:	Merchant Marine
Position / Rank:	Engine Cadet
Date / Place of death:	February 5, 1943 / 52 N, 33 W
Date / Place of burial:	February 5, 1943 / Lost at Sea—52 N, 33 W
Age:	22

James H. Province signed on as Engine Cadet aboard the SS *West Portal* on December 21, 1942, at New York, New York. He was joined a few days later by his Academy classmate Cadet-Midshipman David H. Pitzely, Deck Cadet. The World War I -era "Hog Islander" sailed on January 24, 1943, for Liverpool via Nova Scotia in Convoy SC-118. Aboard the ship on sailing from Nova Scotia were eight officers, the two Cadets, thirty crewmen, twenty-five Navy Armed Guard sailors, and twelve passengers.

SS *West Portal* (ex-*Emergency Aid*)

The slow ships of Convoy SC-118 were sailing right behind a convoy of higher speed ships, HX 224. A survivor from one of the four ships sunk in this convoy was rescued by U-632. He told his rescuers that a large convoy of slow-speed ships was behind his convoy. The German Navy's high command alerted every available U-boat upon receiving the news from *U-632*. U-boats were sent to locations along Convoy SC-118 most likely route from Nova Scotia to the United Kingdom. On February 4, the convoy's location was revealed to searching U-boats by the inadvertent firing of a signal rocket.

For whatever reason, the SS *West Portal* straggled behind the convoy on the evening of February 4. According to German naval records that became available only after the end of World War II, the SS *West Portal* was sighted by *U-143* on the afternoon of February 5. The *U-143* initially fired a spread of four torpedoes at the zigzagging *West Portal* from almost two miles away. Only the third torpedo hit the *West Portal*. The submarine closed the range for a final shot but reported that it missed. A sixth and final torpedo was reported to have hit the ship near the stern, which finally sunk the ship.

The *U-143*'s Captain reported seeing some of the ship's crew and passengers abandoning ship in the lifeboats. One of the convoy escorts, HMS *Vanessa (D 29)*, received the *West Portal*'s distress message and was ordered to leave the convoy to search for survivors. However, the radio message did not provide a location, so the search proved fruitless. Neither the *West Portal*'s lifeboats nor any of the men aboard the *West Portal* were ever seen again.

The battle to get Convoy SC-118's remaining ships to port was one of the largest during the Battle of the Atlantic. Seven other merchant ships were sunk, while the convoy's escorts sank three U-boats and damaged two more.

Cadet-Midshipman James H. Province was posthumously awarded the Mariner's Medal, the Combat Bar with star, the Atlantic War Zone Bar, the Victory Medal, and the Presidential Testimonial Letter.

James Province was the oldest of James Province and Vivian Lee Page Province's five children (James, Dorothy, Terry, Beth, and Billy). Based on the 1930 U.S. Census, the elder James Province died in 1929 when James was eight years old. With the death of her husband, Vivian Province moved in with her parents. By the 1940 U.S. Census, James and Billy are identified as the "foster sons" of Terry A. Page and his wife Ruth of Russellville, Kentucky. This indicates that Vivian died before 1940, and the Province children had been sent to live with other members of the Page family. Before his final voyage, James had designated his uncle, Claude J. Page of Detroit, Michigan, as his next of kin.

According to the Province family, to help make ends meet, James held part-time jobs as a movie projectionist and "soda jerk" at the local drugstore. He is remembered as an intelligent man with a quiet demeanor who was kind and gentle to everyone.

Harry Quayle Jr.

Born:	May 2, 1922
Hometown:	Garfield, UT
Class:	1944
Service:	Merchant Marine
Position / Rank:	Deck Cadet
Date / Place of death:	February 13, 1943 / Castel Benito Airfield, Libya
Date / Place of burial:	February 17, 1943 / Catholic Military Cemetery, Tripoli, Libya; Re-interred June 8, 1948 / Salt Lake City Cemetery, Salt Lake City, UT
Age:	20

Harry Quayle Jr. signed on as Deck Cadet aboard the SS *Daniel H. Lownsdale* on August 18, 1942, at Portland, Oregon, after completing Basic School at the San Mateo campus. After the ship completed loading, the *Daniel H. Lownsdale* sailed for Wellington, New Zealand, via San Francisco, California. From Wellington, the *Daniel H. Lownsdale* sailed for duty in the Mediterranean via Aden and the Suez Canal, arriving at Port Said, Egypt, on November 18, 1942. The ship operated between various ports in the Mediterranean carrying cargo for British Army and Navy units. On February 10, 1943, the *Daniel H. Lownsdale* arrived in Tripoli, Libya, to load more cargo.

On Saturday, February 13, 1943, Cadet-Midshipman Harry Quayle accompanied the *Daniel H. Lownsdale*'s Armed Guard officer ashore to the former Italian air force base at Castel Benito, perhaps to inspect some of the abandoned Italian aircraft there. During the visit, Harry Quayle picked up, or otherwise disturbed, what was described in a Navy dispatch as a "hand grenade." The device exploded, fatally injuring him. He was buried on February 17, at the Catholic Military Cemetery in Tripoli. Armed Guard sailors from the *Daniel H. Lownsdale* rendered military honors to Midshipman Harry Quayle, USNR, at his burial. In 1949, his remains were returned to his parents and reinterred at Salt Lake City Cemetery, Salt Lake City, Utah.

Cadet-Midshipman Harry Quayle Jr. was posthumously awarded the Mariner's Medal, the Combat Bar, the Atlantic War Zone Bar, the Mediterranean-Middle East War Zone Bar, the Pacific War Zone Bar, the Victory Medal, and the Presidential Testimonial Letter.

Harry Quayle was the oldest of Harry Quayle and Thelma Walker Quayle's four children. Harry had two younger brothers, Paul and Vernon, and a sister, Donna. According to the 1940 U.S. Census, Harry Sr. worked as a stenographer at a copper mine, while Harry Jr. was working in the foundry of a copper mill. Harry initially attended the public schools in Salt Lake City. The family later moved to nearby Garfield. In 1939, Harry graduated from Cyprus High School in nearby Magna, Utah. Harry was a member of the Cyprus High School football team. He was also a skilled photographer and operated his own darkroom.

Cemetery Marker for Harry Quayle, Jr.

George Robert Race

Born:	April 18, 1919
Hometown:	Schenectady, NY
Service:	Merchant Marine
Position / Rank:	Engine Cadet
Class:	1944
Date / Place of death:	February 7, 1943 / 55-18 N, 26-29 W
Date / Place of burial:	February 7, 1943 / Lost at Sea—55-18 N, 26-29 W
Age:	24

George R. Race signed on aboard the U.S. Army Transport SS *Henry R. Mallory* as Engine Cadet on January 15, 1943, at Boston, Massachusetts. Joining him were Cadet-Midshipmen Robert Helling, Richard E. Holland (deck), and Frank C. Roberts (deck). Two Cadet-Midshipmen were already aboard from the ship's previous voyage: Joseph E. Best (deck) and James A. Hammershoy (engine).

U.S. Army Transport SS *Henry R. Mallory* (ca. 1918)

The *Henry R. Mallory* sailed on January 24, 1943, as part of slow convoy SC-118 bound for Liverpool via Nova Scotia. However, the *Henry R. Mallory* and several other ships were to split off from the convoy on February 9 to proceed to Iceland. Loaded with 383 Army, Navy, Marine

Corps, and civilian passengers, the ship was also carrying a mixed cargo of clothing, food, trucks, tanks, cigarettes, liquor, and 610 sacks of mail.

On February 4, 1943, German submarines sighted the convoy and began attacking it. The attacks continued until the afternoon of February 7. At 0538 (GCT), on February 7, despite the rising sea and snow falling, a torpedo fired by *U-402* struck the starboard side of the *Henry R. Mallory* at hold number 3, damaging the engines and blowing the hatch covers off of hold number 4. At the time of the explosion, the *Henry R. Mallory* was traveling at about 7 knots and was not steering an evasive course. According to some survivors, the ship began sinking immediately, while others, apparently including the Captain, believed that the ship would remain afloat. As a result, neither distress messages nor flares were launched. In addition, after the sinking, survivors reported that the general alarm was not rung, and no order was given to abandon ship. In the confusion of the greater attack on the convoy, none of the other ships in the convoy knew that the *Henry R. Mallory* had been hit.

However, the *Henry R. Mallory*'s engines were badly damaged and quickly shut down. Two of the aft lifeboats had been damaged in the explosion, while others were damaged by the heavy seas, but the remainder seemed secure. When the ship suddenly began sinking faster by the stern, the abrupt change caused panic among passengers and crew. Men rushed on deck amid frigid temperatures without proper protective clothing. In the chaos, only three boats were lowered successfully, and each of these was dangerously overloaded either during launching or after picking up survivors from the water. Several other boats capsized as crew and passengers tried to launch them. Many of the life rafts could not be launched either because they were tied or frozen in place. Others were insufficiently trained in how to use their rafts and did not properly deploy key parts of the raft to prevent capsizing in the heavy seas. Hundreds of the men aboard jumped overboard.

Meanwhile, the situation on the overloaded lifeboats was perilous. According to Cadet-Midshipman Joseph Best, his lifeboat was intended for fifty men but held eighty. With so much weight, the boat's gunwales were just inches above the water, and the high seas threatened to either capsize or simply sink the boat. Many of the men frantically bailed with anything they could lay their hands on to keep the boat afloat, while others jettisoned anything that did not appear to be necessary to survive their imminent sinking. However, Cadet-Midshipman Best took custody of the distress rockets and flares because he thought ". . . they might become useful."

With daylight, the men in Best's boat sighted the USCGC *Bibb* *(WPG 31)*. The rockets hoarded by Best were fired into the air, while Cadet-Midshipman Frank C. Roberts waved a yellow flag to attract the *Bibb*'s attention. The *Bibb* saved 205 freezing survivors of the *Mallory*, including those in the lifeboat with Cadet-Midshipmen Best and Roberts. The *Bibb*'s sister ship, USCGC *Ingham (WPG 35),* also picked up some survivors. According to the official U.S. Coast Guard history of the USCGC *Bibb*,

> lookouts aboard the *Bibb* sighted one of the *Mallory*'s lifeboats at 1000, and disobeying an order to return to the convoy, *Bibb*'s Commanding Officer, CDR Roy Raney, ordered his cutter to begin rescuing survivors.

Many of *Bibb*'s crewmen leapt into the water to assist the nearly frozen survivors, and the cutter Ingham assisted. One of Ingham's crew described the scene, a dreadfully common one along the North Atlantic that year:

> I never saw anything like it, wood all over the place and bodies in life jackets . . . never saw so many dead fellows in my whole life. Saw lots of mail bags, boxes, wood, wood splinters, empty life jackets, oars, upturned boats, empty life rafts, bodies, parts of bodies, clothes, cork, and a million other things that ships have in them. I hope I never see another drowned man as long as I live.

Among the 272 men who died in the frigid water were Cadet-Midshipmen George R. Race, Jay A. Hammershoy, and Richard E. Holland. In a sad twist of fate, Richard Holland had survived the sinking of the SS *William Clark* three months earlier.

Cadet-Midshipman George R. Race was posthumously awarded the Mariner's Medal, the Combat Bar with star, the Atlantic War Zone Bar, the Victory Medal, and the Presidential Testimonial Letter.

George R. Race was the second son of Nicholas Racz and Magdalena Helen Racz, who had immigrated to the United States before World War I. According to the 1940 U.S. Census, George's family name was spelled Racz, although it became "Americanized" within the following two years.

In 1940, George was working as an apprentice electrician, while his father worked in a bakery. George reported to Kings Point in October 1942. George's older brother, Victor, sailed aboard U.S. Army Transports in the Atlantic and Pacific during World War II.

Richard Marion Record

Born: June 1, 1924
Hometown: Oklahoma City, OK
Service: Merchant Marine
Position / Rank: Engine Cadet
Class: 1944
Date / Place of death: March 16, 1943 / 50-38 N, 34-46 W
Date / Place of burial: March 16, 1943 / Lost at Sea—50-38 N, 34-46 W
Age: 18

According to Academy records, Richard M. Record signed on as Engine Cadet aboard the SS *James Oglethorpe* in February 1943 at Savannah, Georgia, just a few days after it was completed. Around the same time, two other Cadet-Midshipmen also signed on: Wayne D. Fajans (engine) and William H. Ford (deck). Cadet-Midshipman John Lambert signed on as the second Deck Cadet a few days later. After the SS *James Oglethorpe* completed the installation of its armament and final fitting out and adjustments; the ship sailed for its first loading port. The ship joined Convoy HX-229 in New York on March 9, 1943, for a journey to Liverpool, England. The *James Oglethorpe* was loaded with a cargo of steel, cotton, and food in the holds, and a deck cargo of aircraft, tractors, and trucks. It had a crew of forty-four merchant sailors, twenty-six Naval Armed Guard sailors, and four Navy passengers.

Cadet-Midshipmen Fajans later reported that

> the weather was the usual kind experienced during this time of year in the North Atlantic, i.e., dirty and heavy seas.

In his report of the sinking, Cadet-Midshipman Ford stated,

> The day before our vessel was lost Number 2 boat was carried away by heavy seas and Nos. 1 and 3 extensively damaged. As a result of this damage, our available life savings equipment was materially reduced.

Early in the evening of March 16, Cadet-Midshipman Wayne D. Fajans reported that he had seen the conning tower of a submarine on the starboard side of the ship while at his gun station and reported this fact to the gunnery officer. However, no action was taken by the ship's gun crews. Analysis of German Navy records found that the submarine reported to have been seen by Cadet-Midshipman Fajans was not one of the submarines that later attacked the *James Oglethorpe*.

At 2120 (GCT) on March 16, 1943, *U-758* fired a "spread" of four torpedoes at Convoy HX-229, hitting and sinking the M/V *Zaaland* with one torpedo and the *James Oglethorpe* with another. The *U-758*'s other two torpedoes missed. The *James Oglethorpe* was hit in either hold number 1 or number 2 (survivor reports differ). The torpedo's impact started a fire in the cargo, which was quickly extinguished, very likely by the water flooding into the hold. According to the accounts of survivors, although the ship settled about three feet lower in the water, it did not appear to be in danger of sinking. However, the Captain did give permission, or at least some crew members believed that he had given the crew permission, to abandon ship despite the ship being in a hard-left turn with its engines still running. Of the remaining lifeboats (numbers 4, 5, and 6), only number 6 boat was safely launched. Cadet-Midshipman Fajans, who was in number 5 boat, fell into the sea when the boat's forward fall broke. Seeing the chaos occurring with lowering the boats, the Chief Mate and Cadet-Midshipman William Ford jumped into the sea, joining the men from numbers 4 and 5 boats in the water. The crew of number 6 lifeboat was able to pick up some of the men in the water. The nine men in this boat were rescued by the corvette HMS *Pennywort* (*K 111*). The destroyer HMS *Beverly* (*H 64*, ex-USS *Branch* [*DD 197*)) rescued twenty-one other men from the water. These men were landed in Scotland (HMS *Pennywort*) and Northern Ireland (HMS *Beverly*). Some of the men, including Cadet-Midshipman Ford, returned to the United States aboard the SS *Queen Mary*.

About thirty members of the crew stayed on board to help the Captain sail the ship to St. John's, Newfoundland, the nearest harbor. The *James Oglethorpe* was last seen by those in the lifeboat and in the water at about 0200 (GCT) still afloat and under way. The ship, and its remaining crew, was never seen again. Although some accounts credit *U-91* with sinking the crippled SS *James Oglethorpe* on March 17, German Navy records only credit *U-91* with sinking the SS *Irenee Du Pont* and SS *Nariva*. It is likely that the SS *James Oglethorpe* foundered due to the torpedo damage and high seas. From the accounts of the thirty survivors, it is unknown whether Cadet-Midshipmen Richard Record and John Lambert were among the seventeen men who perished, abandoning the ship on March 16, or were among the thirty men lost when the *James Oglethorpe* sank.

Cadet-Midshipman Richard M. Record was posthumously awarded the Mariner's Medal, the Combat Bar with star, the Atlantic War Zone Bar, the Victory Medal, and the Presidential Testimonial Letter.

Richard M. Record was the older of Marion Record and Louise G. Record's two sons. Richard's brother, Jack, was four years younger. According to the 1940 U.S. Census, Marion Record was an electrician.

Jay Richard Rosenbloom

Born: June 19, 1926
Hometown: Kansas City, MO
Class: 1945
Service: Merchant Marine
Position / Rank: Deck Cadet
Date / Place of death: April 9, 1945 / Bari, Italy
Date / Place of burial: Bari, Italy
Age: 18

Jay R. Rosenbloom signed on as Deck Cadet aboard the SS *Charles Henderson* on February 24, 1945, at New York. He was the only Cadet signed on aboard the ship. The ship sailed the next day for Norfolk, Virginia, where it loaded 6,675 tons of aircraft bombs in its holds. Loading was completed, and the ship sailed for Bari, Italy, on March 9. However, the *Charles Henderson* returned to Norfolk the same day to repair its condenser's main induction valve. The ship waited five days for the next convoy bound for the Mediterranean, UGS-80. Upon the convoy's arrival at Gibraltar, the *Charles Henderson* proceeded independently to Bari via Augusta, Sicily, arriving on April 5.

According to *The Liberty Ships*, by L. A. Sawyer and W. H. Mitchell, by April 9, the *Charles Henderson*, berthed in the center of the Bari dock complex, had discharged over one-half of its cargo. Gangs of Italian longshoremen were working in each of the ship's five holds under the supervision of British Army engineers. Just before noon, observers ashore saw a sheet of flame, followed by an explosion from the after part of the ship, which still held one thousand tons of bombs. The after portion of the ship disintegrated, while a column of smoke rose a thousand feet into the air. The forward part of the ship containing the remaining bombs slammed into Berth 14 and burst into fire. The detonation of these bombs demolished the facilities at Berth 14. A piece of the *Charles Henderson*'s deckhouse weighing sixty tons landed on a nearby pier, where it set buildings afire. When another Kings Point Cadet arrived in Bari a month later, the wreck of the *Henderson*'s deckhouse was still resting on the pier. Five other vessels in the harbor caught fire from the explosion, although none was damaged beyond repair. Although heavily damaged, the port of Bari was back in action one month later just as the war in Europe ended. However, the wreck of the *Charles Henderson* remained in Bari until

1948 when it was sold for scrap. The cause of the explosion was never determined, but a 1992 review of the record by the Department of Defense Explosives Safety Board indicates that rough handling of the bombs by the longshoremen may have been the cause. Jay Rosenbloom, along with everyone else on board the *Charles Henderson*, died in the explosion. The only survivor among the crew was the chief engineer, who was ashore at the time.

Cadet-Midshipman Jay R. Rosenbloom was awarded the Atlantic War Zone Bar, the Mediterranean-Middle East War Zone Bar, the Victory Medal, and the Presidential Testimonial Letter. Because his death was not due to enemy action, neither he nor any other member of the ship's crew or Armed Guard was eligible to receive awards for death in combat.

Jay R. Rosenbloom was the younger of Joe W. Rosenbloom and Eva Rosenbloom's two sons. Joe Rosenbloom owned a company that manufactured and sold store fixtures. Jay attended Southwest High School in Kansas City, where he was a member of the National Honor Society.

Louis Joseph Rovella

Born: June 5, 1923
Hometown: Philadelphia, PA
Class: 1943
Service: Merchant Marine
Position / Rank: Engine Cadet
Date / Place of death: October 7, 1942 / 34 S, 17-05 E
Date / Place of burial: October 7, 1942 / Lost at Sea
                             34 S, 17-0 E
Age: 19

Louis Rovella signed on as Engine Cadet aboard the MS *Firethorn* on September 6, 1942, at the Port of New York. He was joined by Cadet-Midshipman Robert Nauman, Deck Cadet. The ship was crewed with forty foreign merchant mariners and twenty-one Armed Guard sailors. Cadet-Midshipmen Louis Rovella and Robert Nauman were the only American merchant mariners in the ship's crew. When the ship sailed, it was loaded with a cargo of general war supplies and a deck cargo of tanks.

SS *Firethorn* (ex-*Norden*)

The MS *Firethorn* was originally a Danish vessel, the *Norden,* which had been requisitioned by presidential executive order on July 12, 1941. Now owned by the War Shipping Administration, it was registered in Panama and bareboat chartered to United States Lines. On February 26, 1942, the ship began operation by U.S. Lines under a general agency agreement.

On October 7, the *Firethorn* was passing about sixty miles northwest of Cape Town, en route from New York to Suez, Egypt. Traveling at about 12 knots, she was zigzagging under overcast skies. At approximately 0830, two torpedoes launched by *U-172* struck the vessel in quick succession. The first torpedo hit the ship on the port side at number 3 hatch, tearing open the hull and exploding on contact. The second struck the engine room on the port side, penetrating the hull before exploding. The ship sank in less than ninety seconds.

The crew had no time to launch the lifeboats, but the rafts floated free as the vessel went down, undoubtedly saving those crew members who had survived the initial explosions. Of the sixty-one men aboard the *Firethorn,* the Captain, eight merchant seamen, two Armed Guard sailors, and Cadet-Midshipmen Rovella and Nauman were lost.

Survivors collected on four rafts and in one boat that had floated free of the sinking ship. The rafts were lashed together and remained in the vicinity of the sinking, while six men manned the boat and made for the coast of South Africa. The survivors on the boat were picked up by the HMS *Rockrose (K 51)* on October 8. The following day, the *Rockrose* picked up the survivors on the rafts. All were taken to Cape Town.

Sadly, many of the survivors of the *Firethorn* were later placed on the MS *Zaandam* for repatriation to the United States. This vessel was sunk on November 2, 1942, about four hundred miles north of the coast of Brazil. Six Navy gunners and two of the merchant crew who had survived the sinking of the *Firethorn* were lost in the sinking of the *Zaandam.*

Cadet-Midshipman Louis J. Rovella was posthumously awarded the Mariner's Medal, the Combat Bar with star, the Atlantic War Zone Bar, the Victory Medal, and the Presidential Testimonial Letter.

Louis J. Rovella was the only son and youngest child of Santo Rovella and Maria Curcio Rovella. His older sister was Mary. According to the 1940 U.S. Census, Santo Rovella was a mechanic for the Philadelphia Street Car (Traction) Company. Merchant Marine Academy records show that Louis Rovella reported to Kings Point on the evening of April 23, 1942. However, Louis Rovella was no stranger to the sea as the Rovella family traveled from the United States to Naples, Italy, and back in 1930 aboard the SS *Vulcania.*

James Volney Rowley

Born:	March 30, 1922
Hometown:	Little Neck, NY
Class:	1944
Service:	Merchant Marine
Position / Rank:	Deck Cadet
Date / Place of death:	March 10, 1943 / 19-49 N, 74-38 W
Date / Place of burial:	March 10, 1943 / Lost at Sea—19-49 N, 74-38 W
Age:	20

James Rowley signed on aboard the brand-new SS *James Sprunt* as Deck Cadet on February 23, 1943, at Charleston, South Carolina. He was joined by his Academy classmates Cadet-Midshipmen Michael Buck (engine), Howard McGrath (engine), and John Tucek (deck). The ship was loaded with general cargo and four thousand tons of high explosives at Charleston for a voyage to Karachi, India, via Texas and the Panama Canal.

SS *James Sprunt* shortly after completion

On the morning of March 10, 1943, the *James Sprunt* was traveling in Convoy KG-123 about three miles southeast of Guantanamo Bay, Cuba. Another ship in the convoy, the *Virginia Sinclair*, had been torpedoed at 0430 on the same morning. At 0809, *U-185* fired torpedoes at the convoy, hitting the *James Sprunt*.

The *James Sprunt*'s cargo of explosives blew up with extraordinary force, completely disintegrating the ship. The glare from the explosion was seen more than forty miles away, and witnesses on other ships recalled the violent tremors and debris that fell like hail on the other ships. There were no survivors among the forty-three crew members and twenty-eight Naval Armed Guard members, including all four Kings Point Cadet-Midshipmen, Michael Buck, Howard McGrath, James Rowley, and John Tucek.

The thirty-day life of the SS *James Sprunt* may have been the shortest life span of any Liberty ship. The ship was delivered from North Carolina Shipbuilding to the War Shipping Administration on February 13, 1943, loaded cargo from the nineteenth to the twenty-ninth and was destroyed on March 10, 1943.

Cadet-Midshipman James R. Rowley was posthumously awarded the Mariner's Medal, the Combat Bar, the Atlantic War Zone Bar, the Victory Medal, and the Presidential Testimonial Letter.

James V. Rowley was the only son and youngest child of James L. Rowley and Abbie Chase Rowley. James's sister, Kathryn, was two years older. According to the 1930 and 1940 U.S. Census, the Rowley family lived in the Chicago, Illinois, area where James's father was an office equipment salesman. However, on his U.S. Coast Guard records, James listed his mother as his next of kin living in Little Neck, New York, which is close to Kings Point.

Samuel Schuster

Born:	February 19, 1923
Hometown:	Philadelphia, PA
Class:	1943
Service:	Merchant Marine
Position / Rank:	Deck Cadet
Date / Place of death:	October 9, 1942 / 34-52 S, 18-30 E
Date / Place of burial:	October 9, 1942 / Lost at Sea—34-52 S, 18-30 E
Age:	19

Samuel Schuster signed on as Deck Cadet aboard the freighter SS *Examelia*, a World War I "Hog Islander" at New York, New York, on May 22, 1942. He was joined by Cadet-Midshipman Bernard W. Spillman, Engine Cadet. Also on board was Walter P. Seperski, a recent USMMCC graduate who signed on as an AB Seaman. On October 9, 1942, the ship was traveling unescorted and not zigzagging, about fifty miles south of the Cape of Good Hope bound from Colombo, Ceylon, to Cape Town, South Africa, loaded with a cargo of chrome ore, jute, and hemp. According to a report submitted by the Commanding Officer of the ship's Naval Armed Guard, at 0148, local time, on October 9, 1942, the ship was hit by a torpedo on the starboard side at the bulkhead between the fire room and engine room. Postwar reports identify the submarine that fired the torpedo as *U-68*. The torpedo explosion immediately disabled the engines, and the ship sank in minutes.

SS *Examelia*

Of the fifty-one merchant crew and Naval Armed Guard, forty-three succeeded in getting into two of the lifeboats. Three men died either during the launching or immediately afterward. Cadet-Midshipman Samuel Schuster was one of the eleven men that did not get safely away from the *Examelia*.

Although the forty survivors were rescued by the SS *John Lykes* about twelve hours later, this was not the end of their misfortunes. On October 21, 1942, the *Examelia*'s survivors sailed aboard the Dutch passenger ship *Zaandam* for return to the United States. However, the *Zaandam* was torpedoed on November 2, 1942, killing twenty-one of the *Examelia*'s survivors. Of the nineteen men who survived the second sinking, three more died before they could be rescued. Among the dead from the sinking of the *Zaandam* were Cadet-Midshipman Bernard W. Spillman and AB Walter Seperski.

Cadet-Midshipman Samuel Schuster was posthumously awarded the Mariner's Medal, the Combat Bar with star, the Atlantic War Zone Bar, the Mediterranean-Middle East War Zone Bar, the Victory Medal, and the Presidential Testimonial Letter.

Samuel Schuster was the son of Morris Schuster and Pauline Schuster. According to the 1920 Census, Samuel had 3 older sibling, brothers George and Herman and a sister Francis.

Although Samuel Schuster was a Kings Pointer, he had previously attended the Pennsylvania Nautical School. It is interesting to note the relationship between Kings Point and the Pennsylvania Nautical School (PNS). Administration of the Pennsylvania Nautical School was transferred to the U.S. Maritime Commission in 1940 and renamed the Pennsylvania Maritime Academy. In March 1942, the Maritime Commission ended its administration of the Pennsylvania Maritime Academy, closing the school. The school ship *Seneca*, a former Coast Guard cutter, was assigned to other duties. All of the Cadets and their instructors were sent to Kings Point to complete their training. However, in September 1942, the Pennsylvania Maritime Academy reopened under state control. The *Seneca* was returned to the Pennsylvania Maritime Academy and renamed *Keystone State*. At Kings Point, the former Pennsylvania Maritime Academy instructors and Cadets that desired to return to Pennsylvania Maritime Academy were allowed to do so, while some remained at Kings Point. Although the official name of the institution from 1940 onward was Pennsylvania Maritime Academy, the institution was commonly referred to as the Pennsylvania Nautical School.

Robert James See

Born:	February 3, 1919
Hometown:	Brooklyn, NY
Class:	1943
Service:	Merchant Marine
Position / Rank:	Engine Cadet
Date / Place of death:	February 20, 1942 / 38 N, 78 W
Date / Place of burial:	February 20, 1942 / Lost at Sea—38 N, 78 W
Age:	23

Robert J. See signed on as Engine Cadet aboard the SS *Azalea City* at New York, New York, on November 29, 1941. This was just days before the United States officially entered in World War II. Also joining him was his classmate Cadet-Midshipman Richard E. Lewis, Deck Cadet. Two months later, on February 12, 1942, the SS *Azalea City* left the island of Trinidad, en route from Bahia Blanca, Argentina, to Philadelphia, Pennsylvania, with a cargo of flaxseed. The vessel, with a crew of thirty-eight, was traveling alone and not zigzagging. When the *Azalea City* failed to arrive in Philadelphia after several months, the ship was presumed lost, though its exact fate remained a mystery.

SS *Azalea City*

The details of the loss were discovered after World War II in the records of the German Navy. On February 20, 1942, *U-432* sighted the *Azalea City* about 125 miles east-southeast from Ocean City, Maryland. Over several hours, *U-432* fired three torpedoes at the *Azalea City;* two of which struck the ship. For some reason, the ship was unable to send a distress signal after the first torpedo struck the ship, and the crew did not abandon ship. Apparently, the ship capsized immediately after the second torpedo hit, taking all hands with it, including Cadet-Midshipmen Robert See and Richard Lewis.

These men were the first two Academy Cadets killed through enemy action. However, due to the nature of the disaster, their fate remained unknown for months, and Cadet-Midshipman Howard P. Conway was mourned at the Academy as the first Cadet to give his life in service of his country.

Cadet-Midshipman Robert J. See was posthumously awarded the Mariner's Medal, the Combat Bar with star, the Atlantic War Zone Bar, the Victory Medal, and the Presidential Testimonial Letter.

Robert J. See was the oldest of Ella H. See's two sons; both were born in Panama. According to the 1930 U.S. Census, Robert J. See, along with his younger brother Kenneth, was living with their aunts, Mary Kilbride and Margaret Kilbride, at 25 Prospect Place, Brooklyn, New York. Passenger lists on file in New York indicate that Ella See and her two sons spent part of each year in New York and the other part of the year in Central America until Robert was about four years old. Their address was 25 Prospect Place, Brooklyn, New York. In 1931, Robert, then eleven years old, visited Bermuda with his aunt, Mary Kilbride. Robert enlisted in the New York National Guard on September 29, 1937, and served in Battery A, 245th Coast Artillery. He reenlisted in September 1940 but was discharged on September 28, 1941, apparently so that he could attend Kings Point.

William Stewart Sempell

Born:	January 23, 1924
Hometown:	Brooklyn, NY
Class:	1944
Service:	Merchant Marine
Position / Rank:	Engine Cadet
Date / Place of death:	September 14, 1943 / Gulf of Salerno
Date / Place of burial:	September 14, 1943 / Gulf of Salerno—Lost at Sea
Age:	19

William S. Sempell signed on as Engine Cadet aboard the SS *Bushrod Washington* on May 7, 1943, at New York, New York, just two weeks after the ship had been completed. He was joined the same day by his classmate Cadet-Midshipman George E. Pancratz, Deck Cadet. Shortly thereafter, the *Bushrod Washington* sailed for the Mediterranean, where it remained for the rest of its short life.

On September 3, 1943, the *Bushrod Washington* sailed from Oran with a convoy bound for the landing beaches at Salerno, Italy, with a cargo of ammunition, high-octane aviation gasoline in drums, bombs, C rations, Army trucks, and landing craft. The vessel arrived at Salerno on September 11 and anchored about three-quarters of a mile off Salerno Beach, in a northeast-southwest direction, stern to shore. The *Bushrod Washington* was carrying a crew of forty-two merchant seamen and thirty-three Naval Armed Guard sailors. The Master was Captain Jonathan Wainwright V, son of General Jonathan Wainwright, the American Commander at Corregidor and Bataan in the Philippines.

On September 14, at 1322, the vessel was attacked by either German dive bombers or glide bombs. Much of the cargo had been unloaded over the previous days, but the gasoline and explosives were still on board. One bomb missed the ship by about 150 feet, while another struck the vessel in the midship house between lifeboats number 2 and number 4. This bomb went through the crew mess room and exploded below the main deck. Reports differ on whether the bomb hit the engine room directly or landed in the ice machine room nearby. In either case, the ship's engines were moved to starboard by the force of the explosion, and the port boiler exploded. The engine crew on duty, which included the First Assistant Engineer and Cadet-Midshipman William Sempell, never made it out of the engine room.

The explosion also ignited the gasoline in the number 4 hold, and within minutes, the entire ship was a raging inferno. At 1352, the Captain ordered the crew to abandon ship. Many crew members made it into the number 1 and number 3 lifeboats. Others jumped overboard and were rescued by small boats that came alongside the ship. The injured crew members were placed on a hospital ship. The Captain and four other crew members later reboarded the ship in an attempt to extinguish the fire, but this proved impossible, and the ship was finally abandoned. Six members of the *Bushrod Washington*'s crew and one of the Naval Armed Guard sailors were lost in the bombing.

Cadet-Midshipman William S. Sempell was posthumously awarded the Mariner's Medal, the Combat Bar with star, the Atlantic War Zone Bar, the Mediterranean-Middle East War Zone Bar, the Victory Medal, and the Presidential Testimonial Letter.

William "Bill" Sempell was the oldest son and second of Otto William Sempell and Helen Sempell's three children. Bill's sister was Carol, while his brother was Warren. The family lived in the Flatbush section of Brooklyn, where Otto was employed as a plumber. According to the Sempell family, William was baptized by his great-grandfather, a minister in Ocean Grove, New Jersey, where the family had a summer home.

Bill's sister Carol recalled that he sold magazines on the street as a child and later ushered in local movie theaters. Bill was a Boy Scout, was active in his church, and often took advantage of the cultural events in nearby New York City. Carol recalled that he spent many days at the New York World's Fair in 1939 and also visited Radio City Music Hall soon after its opening. After Bill graduated from Erasmus High School, he applied to the U.S. Merchant Marine Academy. Helen Sempell, who lived to be 106, always kept a framed picture of Bill near her. Otto Sempell always led the Memorial Day activities in Pocantico Hills, New York, where the family moved in 1945. Warren, Bill's younger brother, followed Bill to Kings Point. He began his Sea Year on January 1, 1945, as a Deck Cadet aboard the SS *Alden Besse*, less than two years after his brother's death.

Bernard Shultz

Born:	October 6, 1922
Hometown:	Brooklyn, NY
Class:	1945
Service:	Merchant Marine
Position / Rank:	Deck Cadet
Date / Place of death:	July 18, 1944 / Milne Bay, New Guinea
Date / Place of burial:	July 1944 / Grave number 265, U.S. Army Air Force Cemetery number 2, Milne Bay, New Guinea; February 7, 1949 / Mount Carmel Cemetery, Queens, NY
Age:	21

Bernard Shultz signed on as Deck Cadet aboard the MV *Cape Ugat* at San Francisco, California, on February 4, 1944. He joined Cadet-Midshipman William N. Johnson, who signed on as Deck Cadet on February 2. The ship made one voyage to the Pacific and returned to Los Angeles to load cargo.

According to the ship's official logbook, at 0800 June 6, 1944, two days after sailing from Los Angeles, Bernard Shultz "reported something in his throat" to the Master. He was relieved of duty and placed in the sick bay, where he was given a course of the antibiotic sulfadiazine, hot packs, and a modified diet. Almost three weeks later, the *Cape Ugat* arrived at Milne Bay, New Guinea. At 2030, on June 26, 1944, a few hours after the ship arrived, Cadet-Midshipman Shultz was taken ashore to U.S. Army Station Hospital number 174. After several blood transfusions and operations, Bernard Shultz died on July 18 of acute Ludwig's angina. This is an infection of the lower mouth usually caused by dental treatment such as the removal of a tooth.

Cadet-Midshipman Bernard Shultz was posthumously awarded the Pacific War Zone Bar, the Victory Medal, and the Presidential Testimonial Letter.

Bernard Shultz was the oldest son of Sam Shultz and Minnie Glick Shultz. Before being accepted to Kings Point, Bernard Shultz enlisted in the Naval Reserve on September 11, 1942, and was called to active duty as an aviation Cadet on April 14, 1943. However, he was discharged on September 2, 1943, so that he could report to Kings Point. He was appointed a Midshipman, MMR, USNR, on October 25, 1943.

According to Bernard Shultz' uncle, at the time of Bernard's death, his father, brother, and another uncle were all in the area aboard U.S. Navy ships but did not know he was in the area. One of Bernard Shultz's cousins provided the following poem written by Bernard while he was at Kings Point:

I am a Jew. Most of the boys here are Catholics or Protestants.
They are my friends so I went with them to the Christmas party at the base.

The choir sang a hymn. I don't know the name, but I can recognize the tune.
It has the word, "Peace on earth, Good will to men."

I heard several boys sniffle. There were tears in the eyes of several boys near me. My eyes were moist. I felt sorry for these boys, most of whom were away for the first Christmas. They were here instead, though they didn't know why.

They knew this country was at war. I knew too. They knew we had to fight this war. I knew too.

They knew we had to win this war. They knew it, so did I. But they did not know why we had to fight.

G_D, one man had a sword, and one man had a shield. So a larger sword was made, and for every defense invented, a greater weapon was invented, a greater weapon was created.

G_D, why must we fight? Why can't man live with man?

Why must we be always destroying each other?
G_D, I am not speaking to you in the name of Abraham or Jesus:

I'm asking you in the names of all the men who have suffered because of war.

I'm asking in the name of every woman who gave up her man!

Stephen Neuman Siviglia

Born:	May 28, 1924
Hometown:	Brooklyn, NY
Class:	1944
Service:	Merchant Marine
Position / Rank:	Engine Cadet
Date / Place of death:	April 23, 1943 / North Atlantic, 57-30 N, 43-00 W
Date / Place of burial:	April 23, 1943 / North Atlantic, 57-30 N, 43-00 W—Lost at Sea
Age:	19

On April 3, 1943, Engine Cadet Stephen Siviglia and Deck Cadet Aubrey Connors reported aboard the SS *Robert Gray* at Baltimore, Maryland. A week later, on April 12, 1943, the ship sailed from New York with a number of other ships in Convoy HX 234 bound for Liverpool, England, loaded with a cargo that included ammunition or explosives. For unknown reasons, the *Robert Gray* fell back from the convoy on the night of April 13/14. Although ordered to return to Halifax, the ship apparently attempted to follow or rejoin the convoy but was never heard from again.

After the war, German Navy records told the rest of the story. The ship was spotted by *U-108* at a little before 3:00 a.m. on April 19 while the submarine was running on the surface about 125 miles south of Cape Farrell, Greenland. The submarine fired four torpedoes and heard two explosions. However, the ship did not sink immediately, and its gun crews began firing at the surfaced submarine, forcing it to dive. While submerged, *U-108* fired two more torpedoes, with the final torpedo hitting the *Robert Gray* a little after 5:00 a.m., local time. This caused a fire and explosion in the ship's cargo, sinking the ship quickly by the stern. There were no survivors among the crew of thirty-nine and the twenty-three Naval Armed Guard sailors. On June 14, 1943, the Navy Department determined that since the *Robert Gray* had not been heard from since April 13/14, it must be presumed lost.

Cadet-Midshipman Stephen N. Siviglia was posthumously awarded the Mariner's Medal, the Combat Bar, the Atlantic War Zone Bar, the Victory Medal, and the Presidential Testimonial Letter.

According to the 1940 U.S. Census, Stephen Siviglia was living with his mother, Rose Siviglia Zagorski, stepfather, Stanley Zagorski, and their young son, Victor Zagorski. The census noted that the family had been living at the same address in Brooklyn, New York, since 1935. Stanley Zagorski worked as a rigger at the New York Naval Shipyard.

Peter Joseph Smith

Born:	July 9, 1921
Hometown:	Norwood, MA
Class:	1943
Service:	Merchant Marine
Position / Rank:	Engine Cadet
Date / Place of death:	November 4, 1942 / 71-05 N, 13-20 W
Date / Place of burial:	November 4, 1942 / Lost at Sea—71-05 N, 13-20 W
Age:	21

Peter J. Smith reported aboard the SS *William Clark* in New York harbor on August 17, 1942. Also joining the ship on the same day were Cadet-Midshipmen Robert Everhart (deck), Herman Garritsen (engine), and Richard Holland (engine). They joined a crew of thirty-eight merchant ship officers and seamen, along with thirty officers and men of the Navy's Armed Guard. The ship sailed on August 22, 1942, carrying a cargo of general military supplies in its holds and a deck cargo of aircraft and tanks bound for Murmansk, Russia.

SS *William Clark*

The *William Clark* traveled with convoys via Boston (BX-35) and Halifax, Nova Scotia (SC-99), to Reykjavik, Iceland, where the ship would normally have joined a Murmansk-bound convoy. However, due to the high losses of the previous two Murmansk convoys, PQ-17 and PQ-18, and the demand for warships to support the landings in North Africa, the Murmansk convoys were suspended. In the interim, supplies still had to flow to Russia. So the thirteen ships (seven British, five United States, and one Russian) that would have been in the next Murmansk convoy were ordered to sail independently from Reykjavik. The ships left port at twelve-hour intervals between October 29 and November 2, 1942, in what was called Operation FB. Of the thirteen ships, three turned back to Reykjavik, five arrived safely, and five, including the SS *William Clark*, were lost.

At 1135, on November 4, 1942, near Jan Mayen Island, Norway, the SS *William Clark* was hit on the port side, amidships, by one of three torpedoes fired by *U-354*. The explosion completely destroyed the engine room, killing all five of the engineers on duty, including Engine Cadet Peter Joseph Smith. The remaining crew abandoned ship into two lifeboats and a motorboat. Although the motorboat was able to keep the survivors together by towing the lifeboats, the towline eventually broke, causing the boats to drift apart. One boat with twenty-six survivors was found after three days afloat by HMS *Elstan (FY 240)*. The second boat with fourteen survivors was found by HMS *Cape Passiser (FY 256)* after over a week at sea. The Master and other survivors in the motor boat were never seen again.

Cadet-Midshipman Peter J. Smith was posthumously awarded the Mariner's Medal, the Combat Bar with star, the Atlantic War Zone Bar, the Victory Medal, and the Presidential Testimonial Letter.

**Peter J. Smith's
high school graduation**

Peter J. Smith was born in East Walpole, Massachusetts, one of seven children (four brothers and two sisters) of Mrs. Annie Smith. The close-knit family was active in St. George's Catholic Church in Norwood, Massachusetts. Nicknamed "Sarge" at Norwood High School, Peter is remembered by members of the Norwood community as being popular with his classmates and as a young man of fine character who was welcome in all social circles. He was active in school activities, including track, drama, and the senior prom.

Bernard Washington Spilman

Born:	December 20, 1920	
Hometown:	Arlington, VA	
Class:	1943	
Service:	Merchant Marine	
Position / Rank:	Engine Cadet	
Date / Place of death:	November 2, 1942 / 01-25 N, 36-22 W	
Date / Place of burial:	November 2, 1942 / Lost at Sea 01-25 N, 36-22 W; Memorial at Greenwood Cemetery, Greenville, NC	
Age:	21	

Bernard W. Spilman signed on as Engine Cadet aboard the freighter SS *Examelia*, a World War I "Hog Islander," at New York, New York, on May 22, 1942. This was just two months after he reported to Kings Point to begin Basic School on March 24, 1942. He was joined by Cadet-Midshipman Samuel Schuster, who signed on as Deck Cadet. Also on board was Walter P. Seperski, a recent USMMCC graduate who signed on as an AB Seaman. On October 9, 1942, the ship was traveling unescorted and not zigzagging, about fifty miles south of the Cape of Good Hope bound from Colombo, Ceylon, to Cape Town, South Africa, loaded with a cargo of chrome ore, jute, and hemp. According to a report submitted by the Commanding Officer of the Naval Armed Guard, at 0148, local time, on October 9, 1942, the ship was hit by a torpedo on the starboard side at the bulkhead between the fire room and engine room. Postwar reports identify the submarine that fired the torpedo as *U-68*. The torpedo explosion immediately disabled the engines, and the ship sank in minutes.

Cadet-Midshipman Spilman and Walter Seperski survived the sinking of the SS *Examelia*, although Samuel Schuster perished. After their rescue, Spilman and the other survivors in his boat were landed at Port Elizabeth, South Africa. They were then taken by train to Cape Town, where they could catch a ship bound for the United States. At Cape Town, the *Examelia*'s survivors were assigned to the Dutch cargo passenger ship *MV Zaandam* for return to the United States. In addition to the *Examelia*'s survivors, the *Zaandam*'s 169 passengers were mostly merchant seamen from other ships, which had met the same fate as the *Examelia*.

At 1627, on November 2, 1942, when the *Zaandam* was about four hundred miles north of Recife, Brazil, it was torpedoed by *U-174*. The torpedo struck the vessel at the port engine room, destroying the main engines and the decks above the engine room. The crew prepared to abandon ship, but the Captain, who believed that it was only a minor engine room explosion, ordered them to remain on board. Ten minutes later, another torpedo struck the *Zaandam*, between number 2 and number 3 hold on the port side. At this point, the Zaandam began to sink rapidly. The crew was able to launch three of the lifeboats and several rafts. Number 2 lifeboat capsized, but the crew managed to right the boat. Sharks attracted to the scene by blood in the water caused many casualties.

Three lifeboats with survivors were picked up within days of the sinking. Three survivors spent eighty-three days in a life raft before being rescued by the USS *PC 576*. In total, 165 of the 299 individuals on the *Zaandam* survived the sinking. However, 74 of the 169 passengers, including Cadet-Midshipman Bernard W. Spilman and Walter Seperski, perished.

Cadet-Midshipman Bernard W. Spilman was posthumously awarded the Mariner's Medal, the Combat Bar with two stars, the Atlantic War Zone Bar, the Mediterranean-Middle East War Zone Bar, the Victory Medal, and the Presidential Testimonial Letter.

Bernard W. Spilman was the youngest of John Barham Spilman and Johnetta Webb Spilman's three children. His brother was John Jr., and his older sister was Frances. Bernard's father died in 1935, leaving his mother to finish raising the family. The 1940 U.S. Census indicates that the family was still living in the same home as they had in 1935. At the time, John Jr.'s occupation is identified as foreman in a tobacco factory. When Bernard registered for the draft in 1940, he was employed by the Reconstruction Finance Corporation in Washington DC and was living in Arlington, Virginia. On his U.S. Coast Guard documents, he listed his mother as next of kin at his Arlington, Virginia, address.

Bernard W. Spilman's memorial, Greenville, NC

Bernard is remembered by his brother, John B. Spilman Jr., as being an individual of steel nerves and stoic manner who had an outstanding sense of humor and a large circle of friends. After graduating from Greenville High School, he attended Wake Forest University for one year before enrolling at the U.S. Merchant Marine Academy. According to his brother, Bernard enjoyed being in top physical condition and was a long-distance hiker.

Jack Norman Stadstad

Born:	November 29, 1921
Hometown:	Garden City, NY
Class:	1944
Service:	Merchant Marine
Position / Rank:	Engine Cadet
Date / Place of death:	April 21, 1943 / Indian Ocean/Red Sea, 32-10 S, 34-50 E
Date / Place of burial:	April 21, 1943 / Indian Ocean/Red Sea, 32-10 S, 34-50 E—Lost at Sea
Age:	21

Jack N. Stadstad signed on as Engine Cadet aboard the SS *John Drayton* on October 7, 1942, at the Port of New York. Already on board were Cadet-Midshipmen Thomas Kellegrew (deck) and Herman E. Rosen (deck). Cadet-Midshipman Morton Deitz, Deck Cadet, signed on two days later. The *John Drayton* sailed on October 12 from New York bound for Abadan, Iran, via Cuba, the Panama Canal, Cape Horn, and Durban, South Africa, loaded with a general cargo of military supplies, including canned goods, ammunition, tanks, and aircraft. Upon arrival at Abadan on January 31, 1943, the *John Drayton* spent the next several months discharging its cargo there and at Khorramshahr. The ship sailed from Khorramshahr on April 1 bound for Cape Town, South Africa. The ship, along with other ships bound from the Persian Gulf to Cape Town was part of Convoy PB 34, which sailed from Bandar Abbas, Iran, on April 4. On April 6, the Cape Town bound ships broke off from the convoy and sailed independently.

By the moonless evening of April 21, 1943, the *John Drayton* was approximately 275 miles east of Durban, South Africa. The Navy report on the sinking, based on the statements of the survivors, indicates that the crew reported a near miss by a torpedo across the bow at about 1700 (GCT). Shortly thereafter, the crew spotted what appeared to be two vessels on the horizon. The Master ordered the ship to turn away from the ships and to increase speed to emergency full ahead. However, the Master and Chief Mate determined after discussion that due to the ship's nearness to Durban that the ships were probably patrol vessels. The ship returned to its course and normal speed. Forty-five minutes after the crew reported the first miss by a torpedo, another torpedo was seen to miss the ship; but nothing was seen, and the crew dismissed from general quarters.

Roughly two hours after the first torpedo was sighted, the ship turned to evade what appeared to be a surfaced submarine. Upon returning to course, another torpedo, later determined to have been fired by the Italian submarine *Leonardo Da Vinci*, struck the *John Drayton* on the starboard side at number 3 lifeboat. Cadet-Midshipman Rosen, who was on watch at the time, went with the Master to ascertain the extent of the damage. The abandon ship order was given almost immediately. Afterward, according to Rosen's report,

> The writer started down to the engine room to help Engine Cadet-Midshipman Jack Stadstad who was on watch, the Third Assistant Engineer or the Oiler or Fireman, but the smoke and steam prevented the writer from going down the ladder. Suddenly the Fireman appeared on deck, covered from head to foot with oil and burns. The writer questioned him about the others and was told there was no hope for them.

According to the accounts of Rosen, Dietz, and other survivors, the abandonment of the *John Drayton* in boats numbers 1, 2, and 4 was orderly. Although the *John Drayton's* engines were destroyed, the ship was still afloat and apparently not sinking when the *Leonardo Da Vinci* surfaced and began firing on the *John Drayton* with its deck gun. Although none of the survivors witnessed the ship sink, they all concluded the ship was sunk by gunfire.

The men in the number 1 and number 4 boats were all rescued within a week of sinking. One boat with eleven survivors was rescued by the Swedish freighter SS *Oscar Gorthon* on April 23. The other boat, with the Master and thirteen other survivors, was rescued on April 27 by HMS *Relentless* (H85). Unfortunately, the men aboard the *John Drayton's* number 2 boat, including Cadet-Midshipmen Dietz, Kellegrew, and Rosen, were not so lucky. By the time they were rescued on May 20, only eight out of twenty-four original survivors were still alive. Among the dead was Cadet-Midshipman Thomas Kellegrew. In all, twenty-six men out of the ship's crew of fifty-six (forty-one merchant and fifteen Armed Guard sailors) perished in either the sinking or its aftermath.

Cadet-Midshipman Jack N. Stadstad was posthumously awarded the Mariner's Medal, the Combat Bar, the Atlantic War Zone Bar, the Pacific War Zone Bar, the Mediterranean-Middle East War Zone Bar, the Victory Medal, and the Presidential Testimonial Letter.

Jack N. Stadstad was the only son and youngest child of Ole Stadstad and Jessie Cavanah Stadstad. His sister was Vesle. Although Jack was born in Long Beach, California, by 1930, the two Stadstad children were living in Manhattan with the Loeser family, one of their mother's relatives. After spending Jack's earliest days in Manhattan, the Loeser and Stadstad families moved to Garden City, Long Island. The 1940 U.S. Census identifies Jessie Stadstad as a telephone operator.

Jack is recalled by his niece, Ann Festermaker Olson, as a tall young man with a dry sense of humor, who was quick to make friends. His friends and classmates remember him as a natural athlete and an outstanding swimmer. According to Ann Olson, Jack Stadstad left a family that is uniformly proud of everything that Jack stood for in his character and actions.

John Norton Stewart Jr.

Born:	February 26, 1924
Hometown:	Pass Christian, MS
Class:	1944
Service:	Merchant Marine
Position / Rank:	Deck Cadet
Date / Place of death:	July 9, 1943 / Indian Ocean, 9-00 S, 81-00 E
Date / Place of burial:	July 9, 1943 / Indian Ocean, 9-00 S, 81-00 E—Lost at Sea
Age:	19

Deck Cadet John N. Stewart reported aboard the SS *Samuel Heintzelman* at Charleston, South Carolina. The ship sailed on July 1, 1943, from Freemantle, Australia, bound for Calcutta via Columba, and Karachi, India, with a cargo of ammunition and general cargo. The *Heintzelman* was due to arrive in Colombo on July 14, but never arrived after being last seen on July 4. For months, her disappearance was a mystery. Then on September 29, a plank marked with the ship's name, along with several boxes of ammunition and boxes of glass vials filled with an unidentified powder, washed up on the beach of Minni-Minni village, in the Maldives. Villagers had also noticed two unoccupied ship's boats the previous day, but these were never recovered.

After the war, German records showed that the ship had been torpedoed on July 9 by *U-511*. The submarine submerged after firing on the vessel, but the crew heard underwater explosions. When the submarine resurfaced, there was no sign of the *Heintzelman* or any survivors. All of the forty-two crew members and nineteen Naval Armed Guard sailors perished.

John N. Stewart, a graduate of the Basic School at Pass Christian, received the Atlantic War Zone Bar, the Mediterranean-Middle East War Zone Bar, the Pacific War Zone Bar, the Combat Bar, the Mariner's Medal, the Victory Medal, and the Presidential Testimonial Letter.

John N. Stewart listed his mother, Beth L. Stewart, of Pass Christian, Mississippi, as his next of kin. He had a sister, Nancy.

Jonathan Ford Sturges

Born:	June 19, 1919
Hometown:	Fairfield, CT
Class:	1943
Service:	Merchant Marine
Position / Rank:	Engine Cadet
Date / Place of death:	September 24, 1942 / 56 N, 31W
Date / Place of burial:	September 24, 1942 / Lost at Sea—56 N, 31W
Age:	23

Jonathan F. Sturges signed on as Engine Cadet aboard the SS *John Winthrop* on August 3, 1942, at Boston, shortly after the ship was completed and delivered to the War Shipping Administration. After a voyage to the United Kingdom, the *John Winthrop*, with its crew of thirty-nine and fifteen Naval Armed Guard sailors aboard, sailed for Liverpool to join Convoy ON-131. On September 18, 1942, the sixty-one ships of the convoy and seventeen escorts sailed into the stormy North Atlantic bound for New York.

By September 21, 1942, the *John Winthrop* was unable to keep up with the convoy and became a straggler, the favorite prey of U-boats. For three days, the *John Winthrop* managed to evade detection. However, on the evening of September 24, the *John Winthrop*'s luck ran out. The ship was detected, stalked, and attacked by *U-619,* which hit the ship with five torpedoes. According to German naval records, the *John Winthrop* broke into two pieces, which remained afloat. In order to finish the job, *U-619* surfaced and sunk the remnants of the SS *John Winthrop* with its deck gun. The SS *Jonathan Winthrop* was the only ship of the more than sixty ships in Convoy ON-131 that sunk.

Cadet-Midshipman Jonathan Sturges was posthumously awarded the Mariner's Medal, the Combat Bar with star, the Atlantic War Zone Bar, the Victory Medal, and the Presidential Testimonial Letter. In addition, the Liberty ship *Jonathan Sturges* was named in his honor.

Jonathan F. Sturges was the only son and oldest child of Harold M. Sturges and Laura Ford Sturges. Jonathan had two sisters, Nancy and Priscilla. According to the 1930 and 1940 U.S. Census, Harold Sturges was an insurance salesman. At Roger Ludlowe High School, Jonathan was an officer of the Boys Home Economics Club and a member of the Public Health Club.

According to his sister Priscilla,

> As a youth growing up in New England, he developed a love for the sea and all maritime subjects. He impressed acquaintances and teachers with his outstanding intelligence and dedication to personal achievement. His mother, Laura Sturges, encouraged his hard work in school. The horizon for Jonathan soon included Sea Scouts and the opportunity to demonstrate his sea related talents. He was an eager student for the subjects offered in the Sea Scout program. He seemed destined to pursue a marine career of professional achievement. He found it easy to master the rules of seamanship safety. Jonathan was active in the Congregational Church. As the son of a well-recognized New England family, he was admired and welcomed by all community groups. With his interest in the sea, Jonathan had found his "true self" that was the mainspring within him. Progress *was* the mark of Jonathan.

John Odell Talbott Jr.

Born: October 13, 1923
Hometown: Bellefonte, PA
Class: 1944
Service: Merchant Marine
Position / Rank: Deck Cadet
Date / Place of death: June 1, 1943 / 36-53 N, 76 W
Date / Place of burial: June 1, 1943 / Lost at Sea—36-53 N, 76 W
Age: 19

John O. Talbott signed on as Deck Cadet aboard the SS *John Morgan* on May 19, 1943, at Philadelphia, Pennsylvania, a few days after the ship was delivered from its builder, Bethlehem-Fairfield Shipyard in Baltimore, Maryland. He was joined by Cadet-Midshipman Benjamin H. Wilkinson, Engine Cadet. After loading a cargo of five thousand tons of high explosives bound for the Persian Gulf, the ship, with a crew of forty-one plus twenty-eight Armed Guard sailors, sailed for Hampton Roads to join its convoy.

At about 0400, on June 1, 1943, the *John Morgan* was about twenty miles off Cape Henry, maneuvering with other ships to form up into their assigned positions in the convoy. As part of the maneuvering, the tanker SS *Montana* was crossing the *John Morgan*'s bow from starboard to port, apparently intending to pass port to port. According to survivors, during the maneuver, the *John Morgan* veered to the left, hitting the *Montana* on the port bow. The *Montana*'s petroleum cargo burst into flames and quickly spread to the *John Morgan*. Within minutes, the fire detonated the SS *John Morgan*'s cargo of explosives, disintegrating the ship and killing all but three of the men aboard, including Cadet-Midshipmen John Talbott and Benjamin Wilkinson.

Cadet-Midshipman John O. Talbott was posthumously awarded the Atlantic War Zone Bar, the Victory Medal, and the Presidential Testimonial Letter.

John O. "Jack" Talbott was the only son and youngest child of John O. Talbott Sr. and Margaret C. Talbott. Jack's sister Virginia was ten years older. According to the 1930 census, John Sr. was an accountant for a railroad. In 1933, the family moved to Bellefonte, Pennsylvania, when John Sr. was offered a position with the Bellefonte Central Railway, which ran between Bellefonte and State College, Pennsylvania. Jack attended high school in Bellefonte and apparently planned to attend nearby Pennsylvania State College before the outbreak of World War II changed his direction to Kings Point.

Charles Wallace Tamplin

Born:	August 8, 1923
Hometown:	Troy, OH
Class:	1944
Service:	Merchant Marine
Position / Rank:	Deck Cadet
Date / Place of death:	March 10, 1943 / 66-53 N, 14-10 W
Date / Place of burial:	March 10, 1943 / Lost at Sea—66-53 N, 14-10 W; Memorial at Riverside Cemetery, Troy, OH
Age:	19

Charles W. Tamplin signed on aboard the SS *Richard Bland* as Deck Cadet on April 17, 1942, at Philadelphia, Pennsylvania. He was joined by his classmate Cadet-Midshipman Arthur J. Gradus, who also signed on as Deck Cadet. Although the *Richard Bland* was originally assigned to the infamous Convoy PQ-17 bound for Murmansk, Russia, the ship apparently ran aground shortly after leaving port and was towed back for repairs. After completing the necessary repairs, the ship subsequently sailed to deliver its cargo to Murmansk with Convoy JW-51A, which arrived in Kola Inlet, Russia, without the loss of a single ship, on December 25, 1942.

SS *Richard Bland*

After discharging its cargo, the *Richard Bland*, loaded with four thousand tons of lumber, general cargo, and deck cargo, sailed from Kola Inlet on March 1, 1943, with the other ships of Convoy RA-53, bound for Loch

Ewe, Scotland. At about 0930, local time, March 5, 1943, *U-255* fired three torpedoes at the convoy. Two torpedoes hit the SS *Executive*, sinking the ship. The third torpedo fired by *U-255* hit the *Richard Bland* on the starboard side at the number 1 hold, passed through the hold, and out the other side of the ship. This caused the deck to crack and other structural damage. Although the ship did not sink, the impact of the torpedo partially disabled the ship, leaving her unable to keep up with the convoy for several hours. The *Richard Bland* was only able to briefly rejoin the convoy before heavy weather, combined with difficulties with its steering gear, caused the ship to become a straggler again.

At about 1530, local time, on March 10, *U-255* found the *Richard Bland* again, about thirty-five miles off the coast of Langanes, Iceland. The *Bland* was hit by one torpedo on the port side at the number 4 hatch, but remained afloat. Although the boats were lowered to their embarkation stations, the ship was not abandoned. A distress signal was sent and acknowledged by a shore station, and the ship's confidential papers were thrown overboard. The Captain decided to lower the windward boats to see if they could be brought around to the leeward side of the ship should they be needed. However, the four men in each boat were unable to bring them alongside in the heavy seas. The Armed Guard remained at their stations, but after an initial periscope sighting astern, nothing more was seen of the submarine. The Master requested the gun crews to stand down, hoping the submarine would leave them alone. This tactic was fruitless, as at about 1835, local time, the *Richard Bland* was hit amidships by another torpedo from *U-255*. The explosion broke the ship in half, just forward of the bridge.

As the ship began to break up, the Captain ordered the two remaining lifeboats lowered and life rafts launched. There were heavy seas at the time of the attack, as well as intermittent snow, and several life rafts were lost as the crew attempted to launch them. The nearly sixty remaining crew and Armed Guard quickly abandoned ship into lifeboats designed to hold twenty persons each. One survivor, Lt. (jg) William A. Carter, USNR, reported that his boat was so overloaded that they had only a few inches of freeboard.

After a long night in a cramped lifeboat in high seas, twenty-seven survivors in the boat commanded by the Third Mate were picked up by the HMS *Impulsive (D11)* at about 0730 the following morning. The *Impulsive* also rescued one of the windward boats and its crew of four, while another destroyer rescued the other boat and its crew of four. The last lifeboat, under the command of the Master, was never seen again. Of a total crew of sixty-nine, thirty-five survived. Fifteen Armed Guard sailors and nineteen merchant crew members were killed, including Cadet-Midshipmen Charles Tamplin and Arthur Gradus.

Cadet-Midshipman Charles W. Tamplin was posthumously awarded the Mariner's Medal, the Combat Bar with star, the Atlantic War Zone Bar, the Victory Medal, and the Presidential Testimonial Letter.

Charles Tamplin was the youngest child of Harry Halfield Tamplin and Erma Parke Tamplin. Charles's brother, Parke, was three years older. The boy's sister, Caroline, was eleven years older than Charles. Tragically, Erma died on August 8, 1923, while giving birth to Charles. According to the 1930 U.S. Census, Harry Tamplin remarried about a year after Erma's death. The two boys were raised by their step-mother, Gladys H. Tamplin, no doubt with the help of their sister Caroline. Harry Tamplin's occupation is listed in the 1930 and 1940 U.S. Census as being a real estate and insurance broker. Charles Tamplin's nephew, also named Charles, provided the following biography of him based on Charles Tamplin's letters home in 1942 and 1943.

> Charles placed family relations high on his priority list. He was popular with the opposite sex and managed to find a girl in each of his locations. During his initial basic training at Kings Point he was a sought after guest for Long Island dinner parties and dances. Charles attended the Methodist Church and found his contact with religion to be a support for the activities of his life.
>
> He applied himself to his studies and was always making extra effort. He was a favorite of the instructors who saw him as a willing student. He enjoyed music and looked forward to quality concerts that time and circumstances allowed him to attend.
>
> Charles maintained a close connection with his family members and was always responsive to their wishes! His correspondence to his family

was frequent and voluminous. He found time to construct his letters so that they were interesting to the reader. Perhaps we could say that he was willing to behave toward others as if receiving a great guest.

Charles W. Tamplin Memorial Riverside Cemetery, Troy, OH

Francis Bernard Tone

Born:	July 4, 1923
Hometown:	Easton, PA
Class:	1944
Service:	Merchant Marine
Position / Rank:	Engine Cadet
Date / Place of death:	December 2, 1943 / Bari, Italy
Date / Place of burial:	December 2, 1943 / Lost at Sea—Bari, Italy
Age:	20

Francis B. Tone signed on as Engine Cadet aboard the SS *Samuel J. Tilden* on July 14, 1943, at New York, New York, shortly before the ship sailed for Palermo, Sicily, in Convoy UGS-15. After arrival in Sicily, the ship was assigned to "shuttle" service between Allied ports in North Africa and Italy. The vessel generally traveled in a convoy of seventy to one hundred ships. On the vessel's last run, however, she traveled between Augusta, Sicily, and Bari, Italy, in a convoy of only three ships and a single armed British trawler. After stopping at Taranto, Italy, to pick up about three hundred military passengers and a cargo of gasoline, ammunition, and hospital units, the *Samuel J. Tilden* sailed for Bari, Italy, arriving on the evening of December 2, 1943.

Upon its arrival at Bari on the evening of December 2, 1943, the *Samuel J. Tilden* was anchored just outside of the port, waiting for a pilot to board the ship and enter the harbor. At the time, a shore searchlight operated by British port control authorities was playing on the vessel to guide the pilot boat to the ship. Under the fierce glare of the searchlight (which was not extinguished until seven minutes after the air raid began), the vessel was easy prey for the large force of German bombers that surprised the defenses of Bari. The catastrophic results of this attack became known as "Little Pearl Harbor."

Cadet-Midshipman Robert Donnelly, who survived the attack, later described the events of that evening in his a report on the loss of the SS *Samuel J. Tilden*.

> Approximately five minutes after the first flares were dropped; a bomb was dropped through the fiddley hatch, just aft of the stack.

This bomb completely demolished the engine room where the writer was on duty. The concussion blew the writer up to the next deck where he lay for fifteen minutes. The rest of the men on duty in the engine room, including the First Assistant Engineer, Second Assistant, Third Assistant, two Oilers and two firemen, are all believed to be lost. As the writer lay on the upper deck unconscious, another bomb hit on the starboard side amidships and the vessel began burning fiercely.

It is not known precisely how or where Cadet-Midshipman Francis Tone was when he died, but according to Donnelly's report,

the writer did not see Cadet-Midshipman Francis B. Tone, but it is believed that he was killed in the engine room when it was struck by the first bomb. He is classed as missing in action.

The ship's number 3 lifeboat was destroyed in the explosion of the first bomb and subsequent strafing of the ship by German bombers. The second bomb reported by Donnelly set the ship on fire, first forward and then aft, which caused the ammunition magazine in the stern to explode. The crew and passengers of the *Samuel J. Tilden* began abandoning ship after the attack was over in the remaining life rafts and lifeboats. Two boats were able to reach shore, while others were towed by harbor launches. Casualties included ten of the forty-one man crew of the *Samuel J. Tilden*, including Cadet-Midshipman Francis Tone, and fourteen passengers.

Cadet-Midshipman Francis B. Tone was posthumously awarded the Mariner's Medal, the Combat Bar with star, the Atlantic War Zone Bar, the Mediterranean-Middle East War Zone Bar, the Victory Medal, and the Presidential Testimonial Letter.

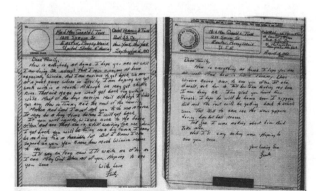

Letters home written by Francis B. Tone

Francis B. "Frank" Tone was the second of Gerald L. Tone and Florence Young Tone who had five sons and two daughters.

Frank's older brother, Gerald, graduated from Kings Point in 1944. Frank's younger siblings were his sisters, Mary Jane and Cynthia, and brothers William, Donald, and Philip.

According to the 1930 U.S. Census, Gerald L. Tone was employed as an electrician.

Known as "Fritz" to his friends, Francis Tone attended Easton High School, graduating in the class of 1942. He was an excellent basketball player, a leader among his friends, and an outgoing and well-respected young man.

John Paul Tucek Jr.

Born:	August 8, 1922
Hometown:	Rutherford, NJ
Class:	1944
Service:	Merchant Marine
Position / Rank:	Deck Cadet
Date / Place of death:	March 10, 1943 / Caribbean, 19-49 N, 74-38 W
Date / Place of burial:	March 10, 1943 / Caribbean, 19-49 N, 74-38 W— Lost at Sea
Age:	20

John P. Tucek signed on the brand-new Liberty ship SS *James Sprunt* on February 23, 1943 at Charleston, South Carolina. Also on board were his Academy classmates Cadet-Midshipmen Michael Buck (engine), Howard McGrath (engine), and James Rowley (deck). The ship was loaded with general cargo and four thousand tons of high explosives at Charleston for a voyage to Karachi, India, via Texas and the Panama Canal.

SS *James Sprunt* shortly after completion

On the morning of March 10, 1943, the *James Sprunt* was traveling in Convoy KG-123 about three miles southeast of Guantanamo Bay, Cuba. Another ship in the convoy, the *Virginia Sinclair*, had been torpedoed at 0430 on the same morning. At 0809, *U-185* fired torpedoes at the convoy, hitting the *James Sprunt*. At 0810, the *James Sprunt*'s cargo of explosives blew up with extraordinary force, disintegrating the ship completely. The glare from the explosion was seen more than forty miles away, and witnesses on other ships recalled the violent tremors and debris that fell like hail on the other ships. There were no survivors among the forty-three crew members and twenty-eight Naval Armed Guard members, including all four of the ship's Cadets, Engine Cadet Michael Buck, Engine Cadet Howard McGrath, Deck Cadet James Rowley, and Deck Cadet John Tucek.

The thirty-day life of the *James Sprunt* may have been the shortest life span of any Liberty ship. The ship was delivered from North Carolina Shipbuilding to the War Shipping Administration on February 13, 1943, loaded cargo from the nineteenth to the twenty-ninth and was destroyed on March 10, 1943.

Cadet-Midshipman John P. Tucek, the son of John Paul and Rose June Tucek, was posthumously awarded the Atlantic War Zone Bar, the Combat Bar, the Mariner's Medal, and the Merchant Marine Service Emblem.

John Tucek Jr. graduated from high school in Rutherford, New Jersey, in 1941, where he was the Captain and star of his high-school football team during his senior year. A passenger list on file in New York indicates that John and his mother took a trip to Curacao in 1934 aboard SS *Astrea*, so he was no stranger to the sea. John attended Washington and Lee University after graduation. After one year there, he decided to apply for admission to Kings Point in June 1942 and reported for his initial training in October 1942.

Samuel Thomas Tyler Jr.

Born:	February 12, 1924
Hometown:	Wilmington, NC
Class:	1943
Service:	Merchant Marine
Position / Rank:	Deck Cadet
Date / Place of death:	February 3, 1943 / North Atlantic, 59-22 N, 48-42 W
Date / Place of burial:	February 3, 1943 / North Atlantic, 59-22 N, 48-42 W Lost at Sea
Age:	18

Samuel T. Tyler, Deck Cadet, signed on aboard the U.S. Army troop transport SS *Dorchester* on January 19, 1943, in the Port of New York, New York. He was joined by Engine Cadet Edward J. Gavin. On February 3, 1943, the *Dorchester* was about 150 miles west of Cape Farrell, Greenland, in a small convoy with two other ships (Convoy SG-19). The ship carried a complement of 130 crew members, 23 Naval Armed Guard, and 751 passengers (made up of U.S. Army personnel, civilian workers, Danish citizens, and U.S. Coast Guard personnel). The vessel, which was traveling between St. John's, Newfoundland, and Narsarssuak, Greenland, was also laden with 1,069 tons of general cargo and lumber, and sixty bags of mail and parcel post.

Just before 5:00 a.m. on February 3, 1943, one of five torpedoes fired by *U-223* struck the *Dorchester* on the starboard side near the engine room. There were no submarine sightings before or after the attack, and those on watch did not notice any wake indicating a torpedo attack. Survivors recalled little noise, but a considerable concussion. A gaping hole in the starboard side of the ship caused extremely rapid flooding, and the engines were completely destroyed. Two of the lifeboats were also destroyed by the impact of the torpedo.

Only three minutes after the vessel was hit, the Captain gave the order to abandon ship. However, only two boats were successfully launched. Whether because of shock, confusion, or limited space, hundreds of passengers and crew remained on board and went down with the ship when it sank about thirty minutes after being hit. Some were apparently unaware of the seriousness of the situation. Two of the convoy's U.S. Coast Guard escorts, USCGC *Escanaba* (WPG 77) and USCGC *Comanche* (WPG 76), remained at the site of the disaster, picking up survivors throughout the night and into the following day. In all, 675 died; only 229 of the *Dorchester*'s 904 passengers and crew survived the sinking. Cadet-Midshipmen Samuel T. Tyler and Edward J. Gavin were among those missing and presumed lost.

USAT *Dorchester*

In a renowned act of bravery, four U.S. Army chaplains on board the ship gave their life jackets to nearby soldiers who had none. The four men held hands and prayed as the ship went down. Each was posthumously awarded the Purple Heart and the Distinguished Service Cross. A stamp honoring the four men was issued by the post office in 1948.

Cadet-Midshipman Samuel T. Tyler, who perished just days before his nineteenth birthday, was posthumously awarded the Mariner's Medal, the Combat Bar, the Atlantic War Zone Bar, the Victory Medal, and the Presidential Testimonial Letter.

Samuel T. Tyler was the youngest son of Samuel T. Tyler and Mary Dell Brown Tyler. He had an older brother, Horace. However, by the time he entered Kings Point, his mother was using the name Mary D. Thomas.

Gordon Ambrose Tyne

Born:	October 6, 1922
Hometown:	Gloucester, MA
Class:	1943
Service:	Merchant Marine
Position / Rank:	Deck Cadet
Date / Place of death:	September 10, 1942 / South Atlantic
Date / Place of burial:	September 10, 1942 / Lost at Sea—South Atlantic
Age:	19

Gordon A. Tyne signed on aboard the MS *American Leader*, a C-1 freighter, on April 13, 1942, at the Port of New York. Joining him on the same day was Cadet-Midshipman Joseph DiCicco, Engine Cadet. Already aboard was Second Mate Walter Hay Lee, a 1940 Cadet Corps graduate. According to the account of Captain George Duffy, then the ship's Third Mate, the ship was carrying a general cargo of war supplies, including boots, barbed wire, and vehicles, along with a deck cargo of nine twin-engine bombers, from New York to the Persian Gulf for Russia. The ship was also loaded with several thousand tons of steel ingots for India. The *American Leader* was armed with what a survivor characterized as an "ancient four-inch cannon on our stern plus four machine guns—two of which never fired one round without jamming."

MV *American Leader*

The ship arrived safely in the Persian Gulf and loaded a partial cargo of rugs and chemicals here before sailing for Colombo, Ceylon (Sri Lanka), to load a cargo of rubber and latex. The *American Leader* headed alone down the coast of Africa to Cape Town, South Africa. Upon arrival at Cape Town on September 7, 1942, the ship was ordered to continue westward, without escort, toward the Straits of Magellan and the Pacific Ocean.

At about 1930 on September 10, the *American Leader* ran afoul of the German Navy commerce raider, *Michel*, a converted merchant ship that had been operating in the South Atlantic. The *Michel*, disguised as a neutral merchant ship, fired on the *American Leader* with deck guns and then launched two torpedoes. The *Michel*'s crew managed to destroy two of the lifeboats as the *American Leader* crew attempted to launch them, forcing the crew to abandon in life rafts. The *American Leader* sank in about twenty-five minutes, and ten crew members, including Cadet-Midshipmen Gordon Tyne and Joseph C. DiCicco, were killed in the attack. The thirty-nine crew members and nine Naval Armed Guard sailors who survived the sinking were taken prisoner by the *Michel*.

The survivors, now prisoners of war, including the *American Leader* Second Mate Walter Lee, were handed over to the Japanese in Batavia, Java (present-day Djakarta, Indonesia), in November 1942. In September 1944, Lee and several other *American Leader* survivors were killed in the sinking of the prisoner transport *Junyo Maru* when it was torpedoed by HMS *Tradewind*. Other *American Leader* survivors were killed in the sinking of the Japanese prisoner transport *Tomahuku Maru*. Of the fifty-eight merchant seamen and Naval Armed Guard sailors on the *American Leader*, only twenty-eight (including Captain Duffy) eventually made it home. All of these had survived more than two years as prisoners of war.

Cadet-Midshipman Gordon A. Tyne was posthumously awarded the Mariner's Medal, the Combat Bar, the Atlantic War Zone Bar, the Mediterranean-Middle East War Zone Bar, the Victory Medal, and the Presidential Testimonial Letter.

**Gordon Tyne's memorial,
Gloucester, MA**

Gordon A. Tyne was the youngest son of Everett E. and Mary Ambrose Tyne two sons. According to the 1940 U.S. Census, Gordon's father and older brother, both named Everett, worked as printers. Gordon's name is inscribed on the family grave marker in the Wesleyan Cemetery, Gloucester, Massachusetts.

Robert Charles Vancure

Born:	October 27, 1919
Hometown:	Youngstown, OH
Class:	1944
Service:	Merchant Marine
Position / Rank:	Engine Cadet
Date / Place of death:	January 9, 1943 /56-15 N, 22-00 W
Date / Place of burial:	January 9, 1943 / Lost at Sea—56-15 N, 22-00 W
Age:	23

Robert Vancure signed on aboard the SS *Louise Lykes* as Engine Cadet on October 18, 1942, at New York, New York. He was joined by three other Kings Point Cadet-Midshipmen, Charles Gassner (deck), Allen Miller (deck), and Eugene Walters (deck). Also on board were Third Assistant Engineer, Frederick Baumann and Third Mate Harry Wolfe, former Cadet Officers. The *Louise Lykes* made one voyage to the Mediterranean and returned to New York on December 12, 1942. A fifth Cadet-Midshipman, Marion Chrobak (engine), joined the ship for its next voyage. The ship sailed on January 2, 1943, loaded with general cargo and ammunition bound for Belfast, Northern Ireland. For unknown reasons, the ship did not sail in a convoy and was not escorted. On January 9, 1943, the ship was in mid-Atlantic several hundred miles south of Iceland.

SS *Louise Lykes*

On the evening of January 9, 1943, *U-384* located the solitary ship and fired four torpedoes while surfaced. Two torpedoes hit the ship, which, according to German Navy records, disintegrated in a massive explosion. The Captain of the *U-384* reported that he had to submerge the submarine to prevent damage from falling debris. When the submarine resurfaced five minutes later, there was no sign of the ship or its crew. There were no other witnesses to the disaster, and there were no survivors among the fifty merchant crew, thirty-four Naval Armed Guard sailors, and ten U.S. Army personnel aboard, including the five Cadet-Midshipmen and two Cadet Officers. This was the single deadliest sinking in the Academy's history.

Cadet-Midshipman Robert Vancure was posthumously awarded the Atlantic War Zone Bar, the Combat Bar, the Mariner's Medal, the Victory Medal, and the Presidential Testimonial Letter.

Robert C. "Bob" Vancure was the eldest of Charles E. Vancure and Henrietta Bingham Vancure's five children. Bob had three brothers, John, William, and Thomas. His sister, Dorothy, remembered Bob as being very protective of her and his two younger brothers. Dorothy remembers that Bob always had some kind of part-time job to help out with the family finances and to maintain his Model T Ford. According to the 1940 U.S. Census, Bob was working as a machinist in a local steel mill. His sister said that he was training to follow in his father's footsteps as a tool and die maker. However, when the war came, his interest in ships and the sea led him to his training as an engineer at the Merchant Marine Academy. Dorothy specifically recalls,

> He was always cheerful, upbeat, and positive. He had a sense of humor that infected the lives of all who were a part of his short life.

George John Viridakis

Born:	May 1, 1924
Hometown:	New Haven, CT
Class:	1944
Service:	Merchant Marine
Position / Rank:	Cadet/Midshipman
Date / Place of death:	December 12, 1942 / New Haven, CT
Date / Place of burial:	December 14, 1942 / Beaverdale Cemetery, New Haven, CT
Age:	18

George Viridakis reported to the Academy in 1942 and was recommended for appointment as a Cadet, Merchant Marine Reserve, U.S. Naval Reserve, on June 30, 1942. Six months later, on November 27, 1942, he was admitted to the Laurel Heights Sanitarium in Fairfield, Connecticut, while he was home on sick leave from Kings Point. George Viridakis died on December 12, 1942, of miliary tuberculosis, a systemic disease. An honor guard of six Midshipmen and a bugler from Kings Point traveled to New Haven on December 14, 1942, for his funeral at Saint Barbara Greek Orthodox Church. He was buried at Beaverdale Cemetery, New Haven.

George Viridakis was the only son of John Viridakis and Anna K. Strigos Viridakis' three children. George's sisters were Rita (five years older) and Mary (two years younger).

According to the 1940 U.S. Census, both of George's parents, who were immigrants from Greece, worked to support the family. John was a watchmaker while Anna was a dress maker.

Eugene Weaver Walters

Born:	July 20, 1920
Hometown:	Brownsville, PA
Class:	1944
Service:	Merchant Marine
Position / Rank:	Deck Cadet
Date / Place of death:	January 9, 1943 / 56-15 N, 22 W
Date / Place of burial:	January 9, 1943 / Lost at Sea 56-15 N, 22 W
Age:	25

Eugene Walters signed on aboard the SS *Louise Lykes* as Deck Cadet on October 18, 1942, at New York, New York. He was joined by three other Kings Point Cadet-Midshipmen, Charles Gassner (deck), Allen Miller (deck), and Robert Vancure (engine). Also on board were Third Assistant Engineer Frederick Baumann, and Third Mate Harry Wolfe, former Cadet Officers. The *Louise Lykes* made one voyage to the Mediterranean and returned to New York on December 12, 1942. A fifth Cadet-Midshipman, Marion Chrobak (engine), joined the ship for its next voyage. The ship sailed on January 2, 1943, loaded with general cargo and ammunition bound for Belfast, Northern Ireland. For unknown reasons, the ship did not sail in a convoy and was not escorted. On January 9, 1943, the ship was in mid-Atlantic several hundred miles south of Iceland.

SS *Louise Lykes*

On the evening of January 9, 1943, *U-384* located the solitary ship and fired four torpedoes while surfaced. Two torpedoes hit the ship, which, according to German Navy records, disintegrated in a massive explosion.

The Captain of the *U-384* reported that he had to submerge the submarine to prevent damage from falling debris. When the submarine resurfaced five minutes later, there was no sign of the ship or its crew. There were no other witnesses to the disaster, and there were no survivors among the fifty merchant crew, thirty-four Naval Armed Guard sailors, and ten U.S. Army personnel aboard, including the five Cadet-Midshipmen and two Cadet Officers. This was the single deadliest sinking in the Academy's history.

Cadet-Midshipman Eugene Walters was posthumously awarded the Mariner's Medal, the Combat Bar with star, the Atlantic War Zone Bar, the Victory Medal, and the Presidential Testimonial Letter.

Eugene with Nancy and Dan

Eugene Walters was the eldest of Theophilus D. Walters and Hazel W. Walters's three children. The younger Walters were Dan (seven years younger) and Nancy (twelve years younger). His father, who went by "TD," was the manager of an A&P grocery store in Brownsville, where Eugene also worked as a clerk. A good student, Eugene enjoyed relaxing after school with his dog, Rex. After graduating from Brownsville High School, Eugene attended Washington & Jefferson

Nancy, Dan, TD, and Eugene

College in Washington, Pennsylvania, for two years. He then accepted a position with the Federal Bureau of Investigation in Washington DC. In Washington, Walters continued his education with evening classes at George Washington University before enrolling at the Merchant Marine Academy. Eugene's sister Nancy said of Eugene that "patriotic service of this country was always foremost in his mind!"

High School Graduation

John Henry Watson, III

Born:	August 15, 1921
Hometown:	Madison, NJ
Class:	1944
Service:	Merchant Marine
Position / Rank:	Deck Cadet
Date / Place of death:	July 8, 1943 / Bermuda Naval Base
Date / Place of burial:	July 9, 1943 / Catholic Cemetery, Prospect, Bermuda
	1947 / St. Vincent Cemetery, Madison, NJ
Age:	21

John H. Watson signed on aboard the SS *Peter Minuit* as a Deck Cadet at Baltimore Maryland on May 7, 1943. The ship sailed for New York, where it finished loading, and then for Casablanca, French Morocco, on May 14, 1943. The *Peter Minuit* arrived safely in Casablanca, discharged its cargo, and sailed for the return voyage to Baltimore, Maryland, on June 23, 1943, as one of the ships in Convoy GUS-8A.

At 1000, on July 5, Deck Cadet John Watson was on deck helping Chief Mate Jerome V. Cherry stream a fog buoy from the stern of the vessel. During this procedure, Watson's right leg got caught between the towing wire and the starboard chock, cutting his leg off below the knee. The ship's crew did their best to treat the injury, but the trauma was beyond their skill. An hour later, the doctor from one of the escort vessels, the USS *Stockton* (DD 646), boarded the vessel by small boat to treat Watson. After seeing the extent of the wounds, he decided to transfer Watson to the destroyer for treatment. At 1356, Watson arrived on board the *Stockton;* and later that day, the doctor amputated Watson's leg at the thigh. Shortly thereafter, the *Stockton* began a high-speed run to Bermuda to bring Watson to the medical facilities there.

When the *Stockton* arrived in Bermuda on the morning of July 7, 1943, Watson was transferred to the Naval Air Station Dispensary. He was given several blood transfusions throughout the day. However, at 0810 the following morning, Watson died from shock and loss of blood. At his request, last rites of the Roman Catholic Church were performed, and he was buried the following morning at the Catholic Cemetery in Prospect, Bermuda. A funeral mass was conducted by the Reverend A. G. Burman of St. Theresa's Roman Catholic Church. The American consul general of Bermuda, William H. Beck, attended the service, and six enlisted Navy men acted as pallbearers for Watson. In a letter to Watson's mother, Beck noted that a small silk American flag was found in Watson's wallet. According to Watson's sister, a Catholic nun, Watson's body was returned to the United States in 1947 against the wishes of his mother. He was reinterred with full military honors in the Watson family plot in St. Vincent's Cemetery, Madison, New Jersey.

USS *Stockton* (DD 646)

Cadet-Midshipman John H. Watson III was posthumously awarded the Atlantic War Zone Bar, the Mediterranean-Middle East War Zone Bar, the Victory Medal, and the Presidential Testimonial Letter.

John H. Watson was the youngest of Frederick G. Watson and Evangeline Shapter Watson's six children. Growing up, John had three older sisters (Evangeline, Margaret, and Frances) and two older brothers (Frederick Jr. and Harold). According to the 1930 U.S. Census, Frederick Watson was working as an attorney, while Frederick Jr. was employed as clerk in a law office, perhaps his father's. John's sister recalled that John wanted to become a banker. She said that after graduating from Madison High School, he went to night school where he was taking courses in banking. However, at some point, he wanted to join the merchant marine. A friend of the family who was a state senator helped to expedite John's admission to the U.S. Merchant Marine Academy at the request of his mother.

William Raymond Weis Jr.

Born:	March 19, 1921
Hometown:	Oakland, CA
Class:	1943
Service:	Merchant Marine
Position / Rank:	Deck Cadet
Date / Place of death:	November 7, 1942 /11-34 N, 63-26 W
Date / Place of burial:	November 7, 1942 / Lost at Sea—11-34 N, 63-26 W
Age:	22

Launching of SS Nathaniel Hawthorne

William R. Weis signed on aboard the SS *Nathaniel Hawthorne* as Deck Cadet on May 10, 1942, at Portland, Oregon, just a week after the ship was delivered to the War Shipping Administration by its builder, Oregon Shipbuilding.

Joining him on the ship was his Basic School classmate, Richard Farrell. By November 1942, the ship was en route from Georgetown, British Guiana, to New York, via Trinidad, loaded with a cargo of 7,576 tons of bauxite. The vessel was traveling in Convoy TAG-19 and carried a complement of forty crew members, ten Naval Armed Guard sailors, and two passengers.

At 0340 on November 7, while the convoy was traveling about forty miles northeast of Isla de Margarita, Venezuela, the *Nathaniel Hawthorne* was struck on the port side at number 1 hold by a torpedo fired from *U-508*. Seconds later, another torpedo struck the port side near the engine room. The engines stopped after the second hit, and the entire midsection of the ship was blown to pieces. As the ship listed to port and began sinking, a third explosion, believed to have been bottles of acetylene gas, sealed the ship's fate.

Of the fifty-two men on board, only ten crew members, three Naval Armed Guard sailors, and one passenger survived. Cadet-Midshipmen William R. Weis Jr. and Richard P. Farrell were lost in the attack. Those who survived had managed to jump overboard and swim to one of three rafts that floated free of the ship after it sank. Thirty-nine hours later, they were rescued by the crew of the USS *Biddle (DD 151)*. The *Nathaniel Hawthorne*'s Armed Guard officer, Ensign Kenneth H. Muir, USNR, was awarded the Navy Cross for directing his men to safety as the ship sank, despite being severely wounded.

Cadet-Midshipman William R. Weis was posthumously awarded the Mariner's Medal, the Combat Bar with star, the Atlantic War Zone Bar, the Pacific War Zone Bar, the Victory Medal, and the Presidential Testimonial Letter.

William R. Weis was the older of William Raymond Weis and Louella Haselton Weiss's two children. William's brother, Robert, was three years younger. According to the 1930 U.S. National Census, William R. Weis Sr. was employed as a meat inspector by the city of Oakland. By the 1940 U.S. Census, William was working as a switchboard operator at Saint Rose Hospital in Hayward, California. According to information assembled by James Hoffman, William Weis reported for his basic training at the West Coast Basic School's temporary home, the Navy's training base at Treasure Island in the middle of San Francisco Bay. He was one of the earliest Cadet-Midshipmen to begin training on the West Coast.

Edwin Parslow Wiggin

Born:	July 9, 1924	
Hometown:	Quicksand, KY	
Class:	1944	
Service:	Merchant Marine	
Position / Rank:	Deck Cadet	
Date / Place of death:	March 11, 1943 / North Atlantic, 51-35 N, 28-30 W	
Date / Place of burial:	March 11, 1943 / North Atlantic, 51-35 N, 28-30 W—Lost at Sea	
Age:	18	

Edwin P. Wiggin signed on aboard the SS *William C. Gorgas* as Deck Cadet in Mobile, Alabama, on January 27, 1943, shortly after the ship was delivered to the War Shipping Administration from its builder. Joining Cadet-Midshipman Wiggin were three of his classmates, James Cordua, Edwin Hanzik, and James Moon. Already aboard was Third Mate Rafael R. Rivera, 1942 Cadet Corps alumnus. Six weeks later, the *Gorgas* was traveling in Convoy HX-228 on March 10, 1943, en route from New York to Liverpool loaded with general cargo, including nine hundred tons of explosives and a deck cargo of an LCT and two PT boats. The ship carried a crew of forty-one merchant mariners and twenty-six Naval Armed Guard sailors.

At around 2030 on March 10, another ship in the convoy was torpedoed, and the general alarm was sounded. The crew remained on alert, with the Naval Armed Guard manning the battle stations. The weather was hazy, with moderate to heavy swells and ten to fifteen knot winds in bright moonlight. At 2330, the *Gorgas* was hit on the starboard side amidships by a torpedo fired by *U-757*. The explosion destroyed the engine room, instantly killing the three engineers on watch. The Master ordered the crew to abandon ship. By 2350, when 51 survivors in lifeboats and rafts had left the ship, snow had begun falling in higher winds. The *U-757* located one of the boats and questioned the survivors. Shortly thereafter the submarine found the ship still afloat and fired another torpedo to sink it. Immediately after the ship settled under the waves its ammunition cargo exploded, damaging *U-757* so much that it was unable to dive. The submarine was escorted on the surface back to France by another submarine.

The *Gorgas's* fifty-one survivors were picked up at about 0700 on March 11, by the destroyer HMS *Harvester* (H 19). Shortly after rescuing the *Gorgas's* survivors, the *Harvester* sighted *U-444* on the surface. Although the submarine dove to escape the *Harvester's* gunfire, a depth charge attack brought the submarine to the surface. It is unclear why the *Harvester's* Captain made his decision, but *U-444* was rammed at full speed by the *Harvester*, severely damaging both ships.

Although *U-444* was able to break free of the *Harvester*, it was rammed again and sunk by the Free French corvette *Aconit* (K 58). However, the almost-motionless *Harvester* was easy prey for *U-432,* which fired two torpedoes, quickly sinking the destroyer with nearly all of its crew and thirty-nine of the *Gorgas's* survivors. The *Aconit* was immediately on scene attacking the *U-432* with depth charges and forcing it to the surface. The *Aconit* fired at the surfaced submarine and then rammed it, sending the *U-432* and all but twenty of its crew to the bottom. With this vital task accomplished, the *Aconit* rescued twelve *Gorgas's* survivors, forty-eight survivors of *Harvester*, and twenty-four German sailors from *U-444* and *U-432*.

Launching of SS *William C. Gorgas*

After the *Harvester* sank, the Master of the *Gorgas*, James Calvin Ellis Jr., was seen by some of the survivors floating in a life ring in the cold seas. When he was offered a place on a life raft by one of the seamen, he declined, telling the man to keep his place. Soon after, he lost his grip on the life ring and was lost in the icy waters.

Cadet-Midshipman Edwin Wiggin, his three U.S. Merchant Marine Academy classmates, and 1942 graduate Rafael R. Ramirez were among those lost. It is believed that all five survived the initial attack but were lost in the subsequent sinking of HMS *Harvester*. He was posthumously awarded the Mariner's Medal, the Combat Bar with star, the Atlantic War Zone Bar, the Victory Medal, and the Presidential Testimonial Letter.

Edwin P. Wiggin was the son of Gilbert Henry "Bertie" Wiggin and Mabel Helen O'Dell Wiggin. At some point before attending Kings Point, he attended the University of Kentucky, where he is listed on their roll of World War II dead.

Benjamin Harris Wilkinson

Born:	July 24, 1918
Hometown:	Wilkinsburg, PA
Class:	1944
Service:	Merchant Marine
Position / Rank:	Deck Cadet
Date / Place of death:	June 1, 1943 / U.S. East Coast, 36-53 N, 76-00 W
Date / Place of burial:	June 1, 1943 / U.S. East Coast, 36-53 N, 76-00 W—Lost at Sea
Age:	24

Benjamin H. Wilkinson signed on as Engine Cadet aboard the SS *John Morgan* on May 19, 1943, at Philadelphia, Pennsylvania, a few days after the ship was delivered from its builder, Bethlehem-Fairfield Shipyard in Baltimore, Maryland. He was joined by Cadet-Midshipman John O. Talbott, Deck Cadet. After loading a cargo of five thousand tons of high explosives bound for the Persian Gulf, the ship with a crew of forty-one plus twenty-eight Armed Guard sailors sailed for Hampton Roads to join its convoy.

At about 0400, on June 1, 1943, the *John Morgan* was about twenty miles off Cape Henry, maneuvering with other ships to form up into their assigned positions in the convoy. As part of the maneuvering, the tanker SS *Montana* was crossing the *John Morgan*'s bow from starboard to port, apparently intending to pass port to port. According to survivors, during the maneuver, the *John Morgan* veered to the left, hitting the *Montana* on the port bow. The *Montana*'s petroleum cargo burst into flames and quickly spread to the *John Morgan*. Within minutes, the fire detonated the *Morgan*'s cargo of explosives, disintegrating the ship and killing all but three of the men aboard, including Cadet-Midshipmen Benjamin Wilkinson and John Talbott.

Cadet-Midshipman Benjamin H. Wilkinson was posthumously awarded the Atlantic War Zone Bar, the Victory Medal, and the Presidential Testimonial Letter.

Benjamin H. Wilkinson was the oldest of Benjamin H. Wilkinson Sr. and Virginia "Vergie" Ball Wilkinson's three sons. Benjamin's brothers were the twins Henry and Jack. According to U.S. Census data, Benjamin Sr. died in the 1920s, at which time Virginia moved in with her parents. In 1930, Virginia Wilkinson was working as a waitress in a restaurant. However, by 1940, Benjamin was working as a clerk in a steel mill, while Henry worked as a truck driver, and Jack was a pin setter in a bowling alley.

William Crocker Wilson

Born:	January 26, 1924
Hometown:	Loudonville, NY
Class:	1944
Service:	Merchant Marine
Position / Rank:	Deck Cadet
Date / Place of death:	February 23, 1943 / North Atlantic, 46-15 N, 38-11 W
Date / Place of burial:	February 23, 1943 / North Atlantic, 46-15 N, 38-11 W—Lost at Sea
Age:	19

William C. Wilson signed on as Deck Cadet aboard the SS *Jonathan Sturges* at the Port of New York on January 12, 1943. Also on board were Cadet-Midshipmen Harry Burlison (deck), Ralph Kohlmeyer (engine), and Grover Leitz (engine). Chief Mate David L. Edwards was a 1940 Cadet Officer. After safely delivering its cargo to England, the *Jonathan Sturges* was returning to New York with Convoy ON-166 from Liverpool to New York City when it fell behind the convoy on the night of February 23/24, 1943. The ship, with a crew of forty-four merchant mariners and a Naval Armed Guard of thirty-one, was carrying 1,500 tons of sand ballast. In bad weather and poor visibility, the *Sturges* was making 6 knots, about half its full speed.

At about 1:00 a.m., the vessel was struck in the forward part of the ship by two torpedoes fired by *U-707*. The engines were secured, but the ship, which had apparently been broken in two, began to sink bow first. Survivors recalled that the explosions gave off a sweet odor and left a sweet taste in their mouths for hours after the incident.

Although the Radio Officer was able to send a distress signal, there was no time to await a reply, as the crew abandoned ship. Two lifeboats and four life rafts were successfully launched. According to the post sinking report of the survivors, nineteen men were able to get into one lifeboat, while the Master, Chief Mate David Edwards, and fifteen others were in the other boat. The other twenty-four survivors were able to reach the four life rafts. However, the boats and rafts were soon separated.

On February 27, three days after the sinking, the boat with nineteen men aboard met up with a lifeboat carrying three survivors from the Dutch ship SS *Madoera* which had been in the same convoy. Eight of the *Sturges* survivors climbed into the *Madoera*'s boat. Although one of the *Jonathan Sturges* crew eventually died of exposure, the other eighteen (along with the three *Madoera*'s survivors) were rescued by the USS *Belknap (DD 251)* on March 12, 1943. However, the other lifeboat with its seventeen survivors was never seen again. Of the twenty-four men on the life rafts, only six survived. These men were rescued on April 5 by *U-336* and spent the rest of the war as prisoners of war. All four Cadet-Midshipmen plus David Edwards perished.

Cadet-Midshipman William Wilson was posthumously awarded the Mariner's Medal, the Combat Bar with star, the Atlantic War Zone Bar, the Victory Medal, and the Presidential Testimonial Letter.

William C. "Billy" Wilson was the younger of James Wilson and Emma Crocker Wilson's two sons. Billy's brother James was two years older. According to the 1930 U.S. Census, James Wilson and his wife's brother, William Crocker, both worked at a local gas station.

According to Ann Crocker Lawton, the daughter of William Crocker and Billy's first cousin, the Crockers and Wilsons lived in separate houses on the family farm. Although she was only six years old at the time of William's death, Ann remembers that he treated her like a "little sister." Her fondest memories of Billy are being taking for bareback rides on his horse, rides in the farm's buckboard, tobogganing, and ice skating with her on the pond in winter. She recalls that Billy had his own "combo," The Trubadors, in high school. He also played a "mean barroom piano," although his mother preferred him to play classical music.

Donald Samuels Wright

Born:	March 28, 1924	
Hometown:	Moline, IL	
Class:	1944	
Service:	Merchant Marine	
Position / Rank:	Deck Cadet	
Date / Place of death:	September 21, 1943 / 2-08 N, 50-10 E	
Date / Place of burial:	September 21, 1943 / Lost at Sea—2-08 N, 50-10 E	
Age:	19	

Donald S. Wright signed on aboard the SS *Cornelia P. Spencer* at Wilmington, North Carolina, on April 30, 1943, shortly after it was delivered by its builder, North Carolina Shipbuilding, to the War Shipping Administration. He was joined by Cadet-Midshipman Frederick Steingress (engine). By September 1943, the ship was in the British Crown Colony of Aden at the southern end of the Red Sea to refuel. The ship sailed from Aden on September 16 bound for Durban, South Africa, carrying a load of steel rails, steel plates, concrete reinforcing rods, and three hundred tons of gum Arabic. She was sailing alone in clear weather against a stiff current and was not zigzagging.

In the early morning of September 21, when the ship was about three hundred miles off the coast of Somalia, the *Cornelia P. Spencer* was located by *U-188*. At 0803, *U-188* fired one torpedo at the *Cornelia Spencer*, which hit the ship on the port side at number 5 hold. The explosion blew of the hatch cover and broke the propeller shaft, which made it impossible for the ship to maneuver. However, although the ship was damaged and adrift, it was not sinking. Alerted by the explosion, the crew, including Cadet-Midshipmen Wright and Steingress, made their way to their stations. Both Wright and Steingress helped the Armed Guard man the guns.

Seeing that the *Cornelia Spencer* was not sinking, the *U-188* attempted to surface, apparently to finish off the *Cornelia Spencer* with its deck gun. However, when *the U-188*'s conning tower appeared about one hundred yards off the *Cornelia Spencer*'s port quarter, the gun crews took the submarine under fire, forcing it to submerge. *U-188* fired another torpedo at the stubborn Liberty ship's port side, hitting near the stern. The explosion detonated the ammunition remaining in the magazine, destroying the after gun mount. Cadet-Midshipman Donald Wright and Able-Bodied Seaman Melvin H. Franklin were killed in the explosion, the only fatalities in the attack.

The lifeboats had been lowered to their embarkation stations after the first torpedo strike. Following the second hit, the crew made their way to the boats in order to abandon ship. One lifeboat, under the Third Mate, had to return to the ship, fighting the stiff current, in order to rescue remaining crew members, including Cadet-Midshipman Steingress, who along with several other crewmen and Armed Guard, had been wounded by the magazine explosion. The Armed Guard crew abandoned on rafts and were later picked up by the lifeboats. Most of the survivors were picked up either by the SS *Sandown Castle* or HMS *Relentless (H-85)* and taken to Aden. However, sixteen men in one lifeboat spent fifteen days before reaching land.

Cadet-Midshipman Donald S. Wright was posthumously awarded the Mariner's Medal, the Combat Bar with star, the Atlantic War Zone Bar, the Mediterranean-Middle East Bar, the Victory Medal, and the Presidential Testimonial Letter.

Donald Wright was the only son of Donald Wright Sr. and Florence Wright. According to the 1930 and 1940 U.S. Census, the Wrights were divorced when Donald was a small boy. He grew up in his grandparents' home in Moline, Illinois, with his mother. His grandfather was a mechanical engineer employed by Deere & Company, the well-known agricultural and tractor manufacturer. At this time, Donald's mother and grandmother taught people how to play contract bridge. By 1940, the family finances had improved, and Florence Wright was now working in a local law office.

In 1942, Donald graduated from Moline High School and joined the other young men of his class in making their contribution to the war effort. A friend of Donald's says that Donald had been involved in boating on the Mississippi River, and that may have influenced his decision to apply to the U.S. Merchant Marine Academy. The same friend said the following about him:

As he matured he was able to grasp the real value of life. Neighborly friendliness produced enjoyment as he grew up. He realized that life is a brief sojourn and he should enjoy each day as it was presented to him. Donald indeed, went forward with a cheerful, optimistic attitude. He carried his own "sunshine" with him. Friends gravitated to him. The devotion of his friends was not affected in the least by good fortune or the lack of it. His enduring friendships were based on what he was—rather than what he had.

Edward Steve Zapletal

Born:	January 27, 1923
Hometown:	Milwaukee, WI
Class:	1945
Service:	Merchant Marine
Position / Rank:	Deck Cadet
Date / Place of death:	April 20, 1944 / 37-02 N, 3-41 E
Date / Place of burial:	April 20, 1944 / Lost at Sea—37-02 N, 3-41 E
Age:	21

Edward S. Zapletal, a first-generation American of Croatian descent, signed on as Deck Cadet aboard the SS *Paul Hamilton* at Norfolk, Virginia, on March 26, 1944. Less than one month later, on April 20, 1944, the *Paul Hamilton* was traveling in Convoy UGS-38 off the Algerian coast, en route to Bizerte, Tunisia. The vessel, which had a crew of forty-seven merchant mariners, twenty-nine sailors of the Naval Armed Guard, and 504 U.S. Army passengers, was also carrying a cargo of high explosives. One of the officers aboard a convoy escort, USS *Lansdale (DD 426)*, Ensign Frederick C. Whitehead, USNR, was a recent Academy graduate.

SS *Paul Hamilton*

Destruction of SS *Paul Hamilton*

At 2055, the convoy was attacked by German Junkers 88 twin-engine torpedo bombers. One aircraft launched a torpedo that struck the *Paul Hamilton*. The resulting explosion completely disintegrated the ship in what the *Washington Post* described as a "great flare of fire and smoke, lighting the black heavens and rocking the ships around her." There were no survivors, and only one body was recovered.

Ironically, the exploding *Paul Hamilton* silhouetted the USS *Lansdale*, making it a better target for the German torpedo planes.

Kings Point graduate Frederick C. Whitehead was killed when a German torpedo exploded in the *Lansdale*'s forward fire room, where he was on duty.

Cadet-Midshipman Edward S. Zapletal was posthumously awarded the Mariner's Medal, the Combat Bar with star, the Atlantic War Zone Bar, the Mediterranean-Middle East War Zone Bar, the Victory Medal, and the Presidential Testimonial Letter.

Edward S. Zapletal was the older of Stefan (Steven) Zapletal and Anna Zapletal's two sons. The Zapletal's had immigrated to the United States from Croatia in the early 1900s. Edward's brother, Raymond, was just two years younger. According to the 1940 U.S. Census, in 1940, the two boys were living with their father, who was divorced from their mother by that time. Stefan's occupation is listed as being a buffer in a tannery.

Raymond Zapletal said the following about his brother:

> Edward was always an excellent student, an avid reader and inspiration to me. We often played sand lot baseball, football and in the summer we swam in Lake Michigan. After grade school Edward chose to attend Boys Technical High School, where in addition to his

academic studies he had to choose a trade. He chose print shop. He excelled at sports, especially track, swimming and weight lifting. In his leisure time he enjoyed chess and dating pretty girls!

He registered for the draft in December of 1941, and learning of an accelerated program to train ship's officers at Kings Point he applied and was accepted. January 27, 1944, his birthday was the date of the last letter he wrote me. Normally his letters were not nostalgic or sentimental; this one was different. He was reminiscing about our lives together.

U.S. Merchant Marine Academy Graduates Who Died during World War II

Among the forty-five graduates from Kings Point who died during WWII, there were twenty-eight men who were killed in direct enemy action from aerial and submarine torpedo attacks, bombings, and kamikaze raids; eleven others died supporting military operations in convoy or in port collisions, storms, cargo operations, travel to assignments, or from lack of adequate medical treatment. Eight graduates died in noncombat events. See Index B for a list of the Graduates and the reference to pages where they are named.

The supply line was maintained at all costs, and ships departed port in every weather and navigated perilously close to each other in tightly packed convoys day and night. Collisions were the inevitable result; two graduates died in collisions. Heavy weather was the cause of the death of a graduate serving as a naval officer in the North Pacific when his destroyer was sunk in a typhoon.

Four graduates died of shipboard accidents while serving the war effort. A Third Mate was crushed in cargo operations in New Guinea. An Engineer was one of over three hundred people who died in Port Chicago, California, when explosions destroyed his ship and the port. Another Third Mate was crushed in cargo operations in Iran. An Ensign died with 350 other crew in New Guinea when the ammunition ship on which he served exploded. Each of these men served and died in the line of duty. Two other graduates died in aircraft accidents; one in the crash of an Army Air Corps transport which crashed on takeoff from New Guinea en route to the United States; and the other when his aircraft went down in North Africa while attempting to rejoin his ship after surgery.

A graduate, a member of the Tin Fish Club, while serving as a Maritime Commission deck instructor, died in a sailing accident in Louisiana. Two graduates apparently commandeered a taxi in Norfolk, Virginia, and drove the taxi into a body of water and drowned. They had served honorably on previous ships in war operations and were facing another voyage on an ammunition ship at the time of their deaths.

Another graduate who survived his service in war zones, died in California on November 1945 of an accidental gunshot wound. Another man, a presumed graduate, died in the United States of an illness contracted while on duty aboard ship.

Three graduates while serving as Navy Officers took their own lives. Two of them were awarded medals and honors for their military service. Post-traumatic stress disorder (PTSD) led to many suicides during WWII, even among high ranking Navy Officers. In recent times, in the wars in Afghanistan and Iraq, suicides among combat troops exceeded deaths during combat.

The names of the above men are inscribed on the Kings Point War Memorial except for one man whose fate we learned of recently. The names of two graduates, Semon Teague, '43 and James McCarthy, '44 are on the War Memorial; we do not include them in the book as Teague died in 1997 and McCarthy died in 1946. The inaccuracy of names on the War Memorial may have been a result of poor communications after the war when the Academy was attempting to finalize the list of graduates who died during the war.

Drew Allen

Born: January 13, 1922
Hometown: Chappaqua, NY
Class: 1942
Service: Merchant Marine
Position / Rank: Engine Cadet
Date / Place of death: September 19, 1943 /
                             New York, NY
Date / Place of burial: Unknown
Age: 21

Drew Allen started his Cadet training at Fort Schuyler and completed it at Kings Point. According to Academy records, he was a member of Section 1-H-2 at the Academy; the section, that along with 1-H-1, formed the first Kings Point class organization, began publishing the Academy newspaper *Polaris*, and started the tradition of tossing coins at the feet of Amphitrite, the "Goddess of Passing Grades." Drew was nicknamed "Oilcan" while at the Academy due to his habit of carrying oil can "whenever possible."

Engine Cadet Drew served aboard the tanker SS *Beta*, from September 15, 1941, to May 1, 1942. The *Beta* was operating along the U.S. East Coast and into the Caribbean (West Indies) during this time. While he was aboard the SS *Beta,* he became ill with myasthenia gravis, a chronic autoimmune neuromuscular disorder.

Allen was first admitted to the U. S. Public Health Service Marine Hospital, Staten Island, New York, but this hospital did not have adequate facilities to treat Allen's disease, so he was transferred to Bellevue Hospital in New York. Drew Allen died on September 19, 1943, at Bellevue Hospital in New York from his disease.

Although listed as a graduate, his U.S. Coast Guard record contains no indication that he ever received his Third Assistant Engineer's license. Therefore, he may have graduated with his class in 1942 but may have been unable to meet the physical requirements to receive his license.

For his merchant marine service, Drew Allen earned the Merchant Marine Defense Bar, the Atlantic War Zone Bar, the Victory Medal, and the Presidential Testimonial Letter.

Drew Allen was the oldest son and third of Herbert D. Allen and Evelyn H. Allen's four children. Drew's older sisters were Sally and Deborah. According to the 1930 U.S. Census, Herbert Allen was an executive at a tea and coffee company.

Herbert Evald Anderson

Born:	1923
Hometown:	Worcester, MA
Class:	1943
Service:	Merchant Marine
Position / Rank:	Second Assistant Engineer
Date / Place of death:	April 18, 1945 / North Atlantic, 47-47 N, 6-26 W
Date / Place of burial:	April 18, 1945 / North Atlantic, 47-47 N, 6-26 W / Lost at Sea
Age:	22

Herbert E. Anderson sailed as Engine Cadet aboard the SS *Samuel Johnston* from July to December 1942 before returning to Kings Point to complete his training. After graduation in 1943, he sailed as Third Assistant Engineer aboard the SS *Hall J. Kelley*. On January 25, 1945, Herbert Anderson signed on as Second Assistant Engineer of the SS *Cyrus H. McCormick* at New York, New York. Four months later, the ship was part of Convoy HX-348 bound from New York to England loaded with 8,400 tons of Army engineer equipment, locomotives, cranes, and trucks.

On the morning of April 18, 1945, the ship was nearing the English Channel in clear weather with smooth seas. However, *U-1107* was on patrol in the area, unseen and undetected by the seventy-nine-ship convoy's escorts. At approximately 1008 (GCT), the tanker SS *Empire Gold*, just astern of the *Cyrus H. McCormick*, was hit by a torpedo fired by *U-1107*. The general quarters alarm was sounded on the *Cyrus H. McCormick*, and all hands were on the way to battle stations when a second torpedo hit the *Empire Gold*. Two minutes later, at 1010 (GCT), the *Cyrus H. McCormick* itself was struck between number 1 and number 2 holds on the port side by another of *U-1107*'s torpedoes. Almost immediately, the Captain ordered the engines to be secured and to abandon ship. Within three minutes of the torpedo hitting the ship, it sank.

All lifeboats were manned, but only boats 1 and 3 were lowered to the water and they capsized almost immediately, leaving the survivors to, as the Armed Guard Commander put it, "shift for themselves." However, within thirty minutes of hitting the water, the first survivors were being picked up by the convoy's designated "rescue ship," SS *Gothland*. By 1115, all of the survivors were aboard the *Gothland,* which, with the survivors of the *Empire Gold*, were landed at Gourock, Scotland. Of the total complement of fifty-four, four merchant crew, including Second Assistant Engineer Herbert E. Anderson, and two Armed Guard sailors were missing and presumed drowned in the incident.

Cadet-Midshipman Herbert E. Anderson

Based on the above, Herbert E. Anderson would have posthumously been awarded the Mariner's Medal, the Combat Bar, the Atlantic War Zone Bar, and the Presidential Testimonial Letter.

Herbert E. Anderson was the youngest of John Anderson and Anna M. Anderson's five children. His older brothers were Johann (twelve years older), Otto (nine years older), and Bertella (two years older). His sister Elin was five years older. According to the 1930 U.S. Census, John Anderson was employed as a factory watchman. However, at some point between 1930 and 1940, John Anderson died, leaving Anna Anderson a widow. In 1940, every member of the household was working, including Herbert, who was a newspaper boy while still attending high school.

SS *Cyrus H. McCormick*

Richard Pershing Anderson

Born: September 23, 1918
Hometown: Chicago, IL
Class: 1943
Service: USNR
Position / Rank: Chief Engineer/ Lt. (jg)
Date / Place of death: April 6, 1945 / Okinawa
Date / Place of burial: April 6, 1945 / Okinawa /
                               Tablets of the Missing,
                               Honolulu Memorial,
                               Honolulu, Hawaii
Age: 26

Richard P. Anderson was a member of Section 1-H-2 at the Academy, the section that along with 1-H-1, formed the first Kings Point class organization, began publishing the Academy newspaper *Polaris*, and started the tradition of tossing coins into the Amphitrite pool. These sections started their education at Fort Schuyler and completed their education at Kings Point when they returned from their at-sea training. Crew lists on file in New York indicate that Richard Anderson signed on as Engine Cadet aboard the SS *Shawnee* on November 28, 1941. According to Academy records, he was appointed a Cadet, Merchant Marine Reserve, on July 28, 1942.

After graduating from Kings Point in January 1943, Richard P. Anderson accepted his commission as an Ensign, U.S. Naval Reserve. The logbook of the USS *Bush* (DD-529) shows that he reported aboard the ship upon its commissioning on May 10, 1943. Normal Navy practice is for officers and most of the crew to report to the shipyard where the ship is being built several months in advance of commissioning. By April 1, 1944, he had been promoted to Lieutenant (Junior grade) and assigned to duty as the ship's Chief Engineer.

On April 1, 1945, the *Bush* was assigned to Radar Picket Station number 1, fifty-one miles north of Okinawa. The *Bush*'s mission was to give early warning of air attacks to the transports, auxiliaries, and cargo ships lying off of the landing beaches. On April 2 and 3, the *Bush* refueled from a tanker at Kerama Retto and returned to Radar Picket Station number 1.

For the next three days, the USS *Bush* fought off several kamikaze attacks every day. By the afternoon of April 6, the ship had already fought off seven separate attacks. However, at about 1513, a single Japanese plane, later identified as a "Jill" torpedo bomber, was sighted dead ahead, low on the water. Although the ship maneuvered violently so that all of the ship's guns could fire at the plane, the Japanese pilot flew through all of the exploding shells until it hit the ship between the ship's two stacks at 1515. The bomb carried by the plane exploded in the forward engine room, Lieutenant Anderson's station. Everyone on duty there, including Richard P. Anderson, was killed instantly. Although the *Bush* remained afloat after this attack, two more kamikaze hits sank the ship later in the day, carrying six other officers and eighty enlisted men out of a crew of 307 to their final resting place.

USS *Bush* (DD-529)

Lt. (jg) Richard P. Anderson, USNR, was posthumously awarded the Purple Heart and the Asiatic-Pacific Campaign Medal. For his merchant marine service, Anderson also earned the Merchant Marine Defense Bar, the Victory Medal, and the Presidential Testimonial Letter.

Richard P. Anderson was the younger of Harry Anderson and Ora Anderson's two children. Richard's brother, Harry Jr., was just two years older. According to the 1930 and 1940 U.S. Census, Ora Anderson died at some time between 1930 and 1940, leaving Harry Anderson to raise his two sons. Harry Sr. was a painter with an eighth-grade education, but by 1940, his older son had graduated from high school and was employed in a stock brokerage firm, with his youngest son well on his way in life.

A caption in his Academy yearbook credited Richard Anderson with frequently telling his classmates to "take it or leave it."

Alfredo Ignatius Anido

Born:	April 27, 1921
Hometown:	San Francisco, CA
Class:	1944
Service:	USN
Position / Rank:	Asst. Engineering Officer / Ensign
Date / Place of death:	December 18, 1944 / 14-57 N, 127-58 E
Date / Place of burial:	December 18, 1944 / Lost at Sea—14-57 N, 127-58 E; Tablets of the Missing, Manila American Cemetery, Manila, Philippines
Age:	23

Although Academy records list his name as Alfredo I. Anido, Navy and other records identify him as Alfred Anido. Crew lists on file at the Port of New York indicate that Cadet-Midshipman Alfred Anido signed on aboard the SS *Frederick Remington* as Engine Cadet in December 1942 shortly after the ship was delivered from its builder. Following his graduation from Kings Point in 1944, Alfred Anido was commissioned an Ensign, USNR, and reported for active duty aboard the USS *Hull* (DD 350) on May 9, 1944, where he was assigned as Assistant Engineering Officer. In December 1944, the ship was assigned to the Third Fleet, commanded by Vice Admiral William F. "Bill" or "Bull" Halsey, USN.

USS *Hull* (DD 350)

The *Hull* had been operating as one of three ships screening four fleet Oilers (Task Unit 30.8.3) servicing Task Force 38. On December 17, while the Oilers refueled the Task Force's six heavy carriers, seven light carriers, eight battleships, fifteen cruisers, and fifty destroyers, the *Hull* in addition to other duties scurried from ship to ship delivering mail. Late in the afternoon of December 17, the increasingly heavy seas heralded the arrival of Typhoon Cobra, which caused the task force Commander to suspend all refueling and resupply operations until calmer weather. Two destroyers and the escort aircraft carrier USS *Cape Esperance* (CVE 88) were ordered to join the *Hull*'s replenishment group.

The group steamed throughout the night in the heavy rain and mountainous seas of Typhoon Cobra, sometimes known as "Halsey's Typhoon." The following morning, at around 1100, the group changed course to 140 degrees. Sparks were jumping back and forth between electrical and electronic equipment in the Combat Information Center due to leaky seams in the hull plating. Shortly before noon, the power of the wind and sea overwhelmed the power of the Hull's engines and rudder, preventing the ship from steering the ordered course, which would have placed the wind and seas on the Hull's port quarter. Instead, the Hull's course yawed between eighty and one hundred degrees, putting the wind and seas square on the Hull's port side. The Hull began rolling so heavily that solid water was forced into the intakes for the boiler forced draft blowers in the forward fire room, putting the forward boilers out of commission. The crew in the engine room did what they could, but communications with the bridge were spotty. Ensign Anido was on the ship's bridge, manning the sound-powered telephones to the engine room, but had great difficulty in hearing because of the tremendous noise of the storm.

Lt. Cdr. James A. Marks, the *Hull*'s Commanding Officer, stated in his after action report that

> At a time I estimate roughly about 1130 the seas were mountainous and the wind increased to hurricane proportions . . . considerable damage was occurring as the storm became worse . . . at this point no man could have possibly existed in an exposed position topside_. . . . The bridge structure itself was under such great strain that I was greatly concerned that the structure itself or a portion thereof might be torn off the ship . . . the performance of duty by officers and crew was at all times high creditable previous to and subsequent to the loss of the ship. Orders were promptly and quietly carried out and there was no confusion.

Shortly after noon, the wind velocity increased to an estimated 110 knots, and the ship was laid steadily over on her starboard side at an angle of eighty degrees. Water flooded the upper structures, and the ship began to sink. The Captain remained on the port wing of the bridge until the water flooded up to him and then stepped off the bridge into the seas. The Captain was among only five officers and thirty-six enlisted men who survived the sinking and were later picked up by the USS *Tabberer* (DE-418). Among the 202 men missing and declared dead was Ensign Alfred Anido, USNR.

Ensign Alfred I. Anido, USNR, was posthumously awarded the Asiatic-Pacific Campaign Medal. For his merchant marine service, he earned the Atlantic War Zone Bar, the Pacific War Zone Bar, the Victory Medal, and the Presidential Testimonial Letter.

Alfred Anido was the youngest of Mrs. Remidios Perez Anido's three sons. According to the 1930 U.S. Census, Alfred's mother, Remidios, who was born in Spain, worked as a housekeeper while raising her three boys, Frank, Henry, and Alfred. The boy's father was not living in the home in 1930. The 1940 census identifies Remidios Anido as a widow. Although Alfred's oldest brother, Frank, was no longer living at home, both Henry and Alfred were working to help support their mother.

Howard Spencer Bartlett Jr.

Born:	January 5, 1923
Hometown:	Fresno, CA
Class:	1944
Service:	USNR
Position / Rank:	Jr. Division Officer/ Ensign
Date / Place of death:	May 11, 1945 / Okinawa
Date / Place of burial:	May 12, 1945 / Buried at sea. Tablets of the Missing, Honolulu Memorial, Honolulu, HI.
Age:	22

Howard S. Bartlett was appointed Cadet, Merchant Marine Reserve, on June 3, 1942. Crew lists on file in New York, New York, indicate that he signed on as Deck Cadet aboard the SS *George B. McClellan* at San Francisco, California, on June 30, 1942, and signed off articles at New York, New York, on April 3, 1943, after a voyage from Oran. Following his graduation from Kings Point in 1944, Howard Bartlett was commissioned an Ensign, USNR, and reported for active duty. He reported aboard the USS *Bunker Hill* (CV 17), on December 7, 1944, at Puget Sound Naval Shipyard. According to the *Bunker Hill*'s logbook, Ensign Bartlett was assigned as a Junior Division Officer, although which department and division he was assigned to is not indicated.

USS *Bunker Hill*—April 1945

The USS *Bunker Hill* sailed from Puget Sound Naval Shipyard on January 24, 1945, and was on duty with the Fifth Fleet's Carrier Task Force by mid-February when it launched air strikes on the Japanese home islands of Honshu and Nansei Shoto. These strikes were followed by supporting attacks for the invasion of Okinawa. On April 7, 1945, aircraft from the *Bunker Hill* and other Fifth Fleet aircraft carriers ended the last sea battle of the war by sinking the Japanese battleship *Yamato*. In the following weeks, the *Bunker Hill*'s aircraft defended the surrounding fleet from attacks by Japanese kamikaze suicide planes and supported ground troops in action on Okinawa.

On the morning of Friday, May 11, 1945, the *Bunker Hill* was the flagship of Vice Admiral Marc Mitscher's Fifth Fleet and was maneuvering as part of Task Group 58.3 with the USS *Essex* (CV 9) and other ships. By 0930 that morning, after fifty-eight straight days in action, the ship's crew had already gone to general quarters three times since 2:00 a.m. At about 0510, around dawn, the *Bunker Hill* began launching aircraft. By 0940, most of the aircraft launched earlier in the morning by the *Bunker Hill* had returned on board and were being serviced on the flight deck or on the hangar deck.

USS *Bunker Hill*—May 11, 1945

Twenty-five minutes later, apparently without warning, since the ship was not at general quarters, the USS *Bunker Hill* was hit by a Japanese Zero fighter that slipped through low cloud cover, dropped its bomb, and then crashed just aft of number 3 elevator. A minute later, a second Zero suicide plane and its bomb hit at the number 2 elevator. The bombs and gasoline aboard the kamikazes set off additional explosions and fires in the aircraft parked on the flight deck and in the hangar deck below.

For the next two hours, the crew fought to control and extinguish the fires and keep the ship afloat. At one point the flames were so intense that anti-aircraft gunners manning guns along the flight deck were unable to find safety aboard the ship. Fortunately they were rescued by escorting destroyers that came alongside the Bunker Hill to help fight the fires. The fire and explosions eventually caused the abandonment of fire rooms number 1 and number 2 and the forward engine room. By 1630, the fires were out; and the USS *Bunker Hill* was capable of moving under its own power. However, the badly damaged ship was no longer capable of functioning as a combat vessel. As a result, Vice Admiral Mitscher and the survivors of his staff were transferred to the USS *Enterprise*.

On Saturday, May 12, 1945, the USS *Bunker Hill* began counting its dead while continuing to treat the wounded and working to keep their ship afloat. Between 1:00 p.m. and 7:00 p.m., the ship held three burial-at-sea services for its 351 honored dead, including Ensign Howard S. Bartlett, USNR.

Ensign Howard S. Bartlett, USNR, was posthumously awarded the Purple Heart and the Asiatic-Pacific Campaign Medal. For its actions prior to and during Ensign Bartlett's service aboard, the USS *Bunker Hill* was awarded the Presidential Unit Citation. Cadet-Midshipman Howard Bartlett earned the Atlantic War Zone, the Pacific War Zone and Mediterranean-Middle East War Zone Bars, the Victory Medal, and the Presidential Testimonial Letter for his merchant marine service.

Howard S. Bartlett was the older of Howard S. Bartlett Sr. and Stella May Pheley Bartlett's two sons. Howard's brother, Robert, was six years younger. According to the 1940 U.S. Census, both of Howard's parents worked outside the home. Howard Sr. worked for the local power company as a repairman, while Stella worked as an assistant instructor for the local schools.

Floyd Kenneth Callesen

Born:	July 28, 1920
Hometown:	Elma, WA
Class:	1942
Service:	USNR
Position / Rank:	Chief Engineer/ Lt. (jg)
Date / Place of death:	June 12, 1944 / Pacific, Mios Woendi Lagoon
Date / Place of burial:	June 12, 1944 / Lost at Sea Mios Woendi Lagoon; Memorial Tablets at Manila National Cemetery
Age:	23

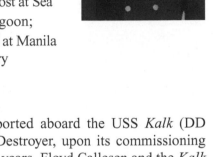

Ensign Floyd K. Callesen, USNR, reported aboard the USS *Kalk* (DD 611), a USS *Benson* (DD 421) Class Destroyer, upon its commissioning on October 17, 1942. Over the next two years, Floyd Callesen and the *Kalk* served in Alaskan and North Atlantic waters escorting convoys. In early 1944, the *Kalk* was transferred to the Pacific fleet. By June 1944, Floyd Callesen had been promoted to Lieutenant (jg) and assigned to duty as the *Kalk*'s Engineering Officer.

USS *Kalk* (DD 611)

On June 12, 1944, the *Kalk* was patrolling the Mios Woendi lagoon, providing support for several beached LSTs. At 1032, Japanese aircraft were reported in the area; and at 1036, an enemy plane was sighted diving into the ship from the starboard quarter. The *Kalk* began firing on the plane, but a bomb hit on the *Kalk*'s starboard side between the stacks before the *Kalk*'s gunners could shoot it down. The midships repair party, headed by Lieutenant Callesen, was stationed exactly where the bomb hit.

Almost every member of the midships repair party, including Lieutenant (jg) Callesen, was declared "missing in action."

Memorial aboard USS *Kalk* to those killed or missing in action, June 12, 1944

The *Kalk* was able to proceed on its port engine to Hollandia, New Guinea, for emergency repairs. The ship returned to San Francisco, where it was repaired and returned to action by the end of November. A memorial plaque to the ship's dead and missing was placed on the *Kalk* during its repairs by Bethlehem Steel Shipyard, San Francisco, the shipyard that built the ship. The USS *Kalk* was decommissioned after World War II, never served again, and was sunk as a target in 1969.

U.S. Navy and Merchant Marine Cadet Corps records indicate that Floyd K. Callesen began his "sea year" on May 1, 1941, serving as Engine Cadet aboard the USAT *St. Mihiel* and SS *President Coolidge*. He was appointed a Midshipman, USNR, on June 13, 1941. On November 3, 1941, he was placed on active duty in the U.S. Navy and assigned to the Transport USS *Henderson* (AP 1).

U.S. Merchant Marine Cadet Corps records show that Cadet-Midshipman Callesen was considered to be eligible to sit for his Third Assistant Engineers' license on or before November 30, 1942, after accumulating 505 days of sea time. However, since he reported aboard the USS *Kalk* as an Ensign, USNR, six weeks earlier, one must conclude that he never took his Third Assistant Engineer's license. The actual date of his graduation from Kings Point cannot be determined.

Lt. (jg) Floyd K. Callesen, USNR, was posthumously awarded the Purple Heart and the Asiatic-Pacific Campaign Medal. Based on his merchant marine service, he also earned the Merchant Marine Defense Bar. Callesen belongs to a very small group of about fifty Kings Point Cadet-Midshipmen that served on active duty in the Navy as midshipmen during World War II. It is believed that these men were the only U.S. Navy Midshipmen to serve aboard combatant ships in combat since the days of fighting sail.

Floyd (center) with his mother and sister Helen

Floyd's father, James P. Callesen

According to the 1930 U.S. Census, Floyd Callesen was one of four children of James Peter Callesen and Margaret Thomsen Callesen. Floyd had an older sister, Helen, and two brothers, Walter and Irving. The Callesens were Danish immigrants who had worked their way across the west from Minnesota, through Iowa, Nebraska, North Dakota, and finally settling in Elma, Washington. James Callesen was the town barber. At the time of his death, Floyd Callesen was married to Charlotte Elaine Hughes Callesen. Their daughter, Judith Elaine Callesen, was born May 11, 1943. According to the family genealogist, Sue Ellen Stetler, Judith has four sons (Kenneth, Stewart, Timothy, and Donald).

Peter Chung Ying Chue

Born:	August 15, 1920
Hometown:	Berkeley, CA
Class:	1944
Service:	Merchant Marine
Position / Rank:	Third Assistant Engineer
Date / Place of death:	January 4, 1945 / Mindoro, Philippines
Date / Place of burial:	January 4, 1945 / Lost at Sea Mindoro, Philippines; February 23, 1947, Memorial Service held at True Sunshine Episcopal Mission, Oakland, CA,
Age:	24

Peter C. Y. Chue graduated from the University of California, Berkeley, with a bachelor of science degree in plant pathology in May 1941. In November 1942, he began his Cadet training at the San Mateo Basic School. On January 23, 1943, he signed on as Engine Cadet aboard the SS *Egbert Benson* and returned to San Francisco from Australia on April 4. After making another voyage on the *Egbert Benson*, Chue was transferred to the brand-new Liberty ship SS *John Ross*, where he signed on as Engine Cadet on August 4, 1943; Chue had already been sailing for seven months. The *John Ross* returned to San Francisco from Milne Bay, New Guinea, on July 7, 1944 and Chue went to the Academy for advanced training. After graduating, Chue applied for active duty in the Navy but was rejected on the basis that he did not meet the physical requirements.

Shortly after graduation from Kings Point, Peter C. Y. Chue signed on aboard the SS *Lewis L. Dyche* as Third Assistant Engineer. On the morning of January 4, 1945, *the Lewis L. Dyche*, loaded with a cargo of ammunition and explosives, was anchored in Mindoro Harbor. Other ships, including the USS *Monadnock* (CM 9), the USS *Pecos* (AO 6), and the USS *Susquehanna* (AOG 5), were anchored nearby. At 0755 (GCT), an air raid warning was sent to the ships by Army authorities ashore, bringing the ship's crews to battle stations. Twenty-five minutes later, Japanese aircraft were sighted bombing the adjacent seaplane anchorage. Shortly thereafter, a Japanese "Val" dive bomber was seen diving on the SS *Lewis L. Dyche*. The attacking aircraft leveled off about twenty feet above the sea and headed straight for the *Dyche*, hitting it amidships.

According to the USS *Monadnock*'s after action report,

> The resultant explosion completely disintegrated the *Dyche* and showered this ship with debris which caused one death, twelve casualties and minor damage.

Peter C. Y. Chue was posthumously awarded the Mariner's Medal, the Combat Bar, the Pacific War Zone Bar, the Philippine Liberation Bar, the Victory Medal, and the Presidential Testimonial Letter.

Peter Chue was the only son of Bak Yuen (also known as Min Yin Shea) Chue's four children. The 1940 U.S. Census identifies Bak Yuen Chue as widow. Peter's sisters were Ruth (three years older), Alice (one year younger), and Helen (two years younger). The 1940 census identifies Bak Yuen Chue as a language instructor, while Ruth and Alice worked in a department store. The same document shows that Peter was working as a laboratory technician in a public health laboratory.

Peter's last letter to his family, dated December 26, 1944, tells of a Christmas morning trip ashore in the Philippines:

> We went ashore Christmas morning bright and early, and attended mass at a native Catholic church. The church is an old stone structure whose walls showed its age by the presence of moss and vines. It was a quiet and beautiful ceremony . . . We felt like bums walking into the service, the Filipinos wore neat white suits . . . and the womenfolk were well decked out. And here we came, tromping in our khakis and mud up to our knees!

Peter was remembered as being active in the Phi Epsilon Chi and Pi Alpha Pi fraternities and the UC Chinese Students Club in college. He taught English to Chinese boys at the Oakland True Sunshine Mission and helped with the church's Sunday school. The program for his memorial service included the following:

To Peter

Your life, too brief here among us,
Shines on within our hearts;
It lifts our thoughts from sorrow—
New hope and faith imparts.

Your brave devotion to duty
Will be a guiding light
To others who are seeking The
way to Peace with Right.

Your valiant spirit is with us,
Dispelling doubt and fear; It
bids us face the future
With Courage and Good Cheer!

Alfredo John Dell'Aquila

Born:	March 29, 1921
Hometown:	Bayside, NY
Class:	1944
Service:	USNR
Position / Rank:	Ensign
Date / Place of death:	May 5, 1945 / Four Miles West of Sorido Airstrip, Biak, Indonesia
Date / Place of burial:	March 23, 1952 / Jefferson Barracks National Cemetery, Section 85 Site 70
Age:	24

Alfredo J. Dell'Aquila was sworn in as a midshipman, USNR, on September 18, 1942. On November 2, 1942, he signed on as Engine Cadet aboard the SS *Examiner*. After at least two voyages aboard that ship, he signed off in early March 1943 and returned to Kings Point to complete his education. On September 24, 1943, he was recognized for academic achievement. Alfredo J. Dell'Aquila graduated from the Academy on January 8, 1944, a member of section A142. After graduation, Alfredo Dell'Aquila requested assignment to active duty with the Navy. On March 20, 1944, he reported aboard the USS *Jamestown* (AGP 3), a PT boat tender, and was assigned as Assistant Engineering Officer.

Memorial to victims of air crash at Sorido Air Strip, Biak, Indonesia, on May 5, 1945, Jefferson Barracks National Cemetery

Ensign Alfredo J. Dell'Aquila, USNR, was transferred to the Naval Base at Woendi, New Guinea, on May 1, 1945, for further transport to the United States. He died four days later, on May 5, 1945, in the crash of an Army Air Corps C-54 Transport (44-9043) on takeoff from the Sorido Air Strip, Biak, en route to Manus Island. The remains of the crash victims were initially buried in a common grave at Biak. In 1952, the remains were exhumed and reinterred in a mass grave at Jefferson Barracks National Cemetery, St. Louis, Missouri.

Ensign Alfredo J. Dell'Aquila, USNR, was posthumously awarded the Asiatic-Pacific Campaign Medal. For his merchant marine service, he earned the Combat Bar, the Atlantic War Zone Bar, the Mediterranean-Middle East War Zone Bar, the Victory Medal, and the Presidential Testimonial Letter.

At the time of his death, he was married to the former Marie C. Field of Bayside, Queens, New York. No further information on his background could be located.

Clarence Bert Dengler Jr.

Born: June 15, 1923
Hometown: Pottsville, PA
Class: 1944
Service: Merchant Marine
Position / Rank: Third Mate
Date / Place of death: February 5, 1945 / New York Harbor
Date / Place of burial: February 5, 1945 / Lost at Sea—New York Harbor; Memorial at Charles Barber Cemetery, Pottsville, PA
Age: 25

Clarence B. Dengler signed on as Third Mate of the T-2 tanker SS *Spring Hill* on February 1, 1945, just a few weeks after graduating from Kings Point in Section B-389. On February 5, 1945, the *Spring Hill* was anchored in Anchorage 27 off Pier 18, Staten Island, New York, loaded with 140,000 barrels of high-test gasoline. At around 0845, she was rammed on the port bow by the foreign flag merchant ship M/V *Clio*. The *Spring Hill*'s forward cargo tanks immediately exploded and burst into flames, ultimately consuming about one-third of the ship's cargo. Crew members who survived the explosion jumped overboard into the ice-choked water of New York harbor. Many men tried to make their way to the aft of the ship, where the flames were less intense, but most were unable to do so. In attempting to swim to other ships in the vicinity, several men were caught in burning gasoline floating on the surface of the water. Nine crew members, including Clarence Dengler, and eleven Armed Guard members died in the disaster. The remains of Clarence Dengler and four other members of the SS *Spring Hill*'s crew were never recovered. They were declared "presumptively dead" on February 20, 1945.

As the ship's least-experienced Third Mate, it is likely that he was on watch at the time of the collision. The report by the *Spring Hill*'s Armed Guard officer states, "The General Alarm was sounded by the mate on duty." Thus, Dengler's action may have saved several of the ship's crew by alerting them to the approaching danger.

Clarence "Curly" Dengler attended Basic School at Pass Christian and signed on as Deck Cadet aboard the SS *Curaca* on May 19, 1943, at New Orleans, Louisiana. One month later, he was hospitalized in Valparaiso, Chile, and left ashore when the SS *Curaca* sailed. A few weeks later, he was apparently fit for duty and signed on as Deck Cadet aboard the SS *Elias Howe,* which sailed from Valparaiso to Suez, loaded with nitrates. On September 24, 1943, the *Elias Howe* was torpedoed by the Japanese submarine *I-10* in the Gulf of Aden. The crew, including Cadet-Midshipman Clarence Dengler, was able to abandon ship before the cargo of nitrates exploded.

Clarence returned to the United States as a passenger aboard the British passenger ship SS *Stirling Castle* on November 7, 1943. Three weeks later, on November 30, 1943, Clarence Dengler signed on as Deck Cadet aboard the SS *Santa Cruz* at New York, New York. He was discharged at San Francisco, California, on March 18, 1944, completing his sea year. Upon his arrival at Kings Point for advanced training, he was welcomed into the Tin Fish Club and joined the Propeller Club. He graduated on December 22, 1944.

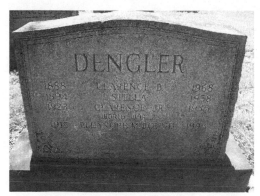

Dengler family memorial, Pottsville, PA

Based on his service as a Cadet-Midshipman, Clarence B. Dengler was posthumously awarded the Combat Bar with star, the Atlantic War Zone Bar, the Mediterranean-Middle East War Zone Bar, the Pacific War Zone Bar, the Victory Letter, and the Presidential Testimonial Letter.

Clarence was the only son and youngest of Clarence B. Dengler Sr. and Stella E. Covely Dengler's three children. According to U.S. Census and other records, Mr. Dengler was a shoemaker. Clarence's older sisters were named Eleanore and Anita.

Clarence B. Dengler died before the Academy's yearbook *Midships* could be published for his graduating section. The following was printed on his section's page:

It is with utmost regret that Kings Point announces the loss of her son, Ensign Clarence B. Dengler.

Ensign Dengler, while at the Academy, by his demeanor, personified in an exemplary manner, the finest qualities of an officer and a gentleman. His beaming smile and congenial personality warmed the hearts of those associated with him here.

We will ever cherish his friendship as a privilege that few of us will be so fortunate to share again.

Arthur Churchill Forsyth

Born: September 20, 1922
Hometown: Hempstead, Long Island, NY
Class: 1943
Service: Merchant Marine
Position / Rank: Third Mate
Date / Place of death: January 15, 1945 / Norfolk, VA
Date / Place of burial: Unknown
Age: 22

Arthur C. Forsyth signed on as Third Mate aboard the SS *Zebulon Pike* on December 28, 1944, at the Port of New York. He was joined by his Academy classmate Edward S. Sherman, who signed on as Second Mate the same day. The ship sailed from New York to Norfolk, Virginia, on January 1, to load cargo. On January 15, 1945, at 1900, Arthur Forsyth and Edward Sherman left their vessel. According to the *Zebulon Pike*'s official logbook, at 0245 on January 16, the Master was informed by Norfolk Police that the two men apparently commandeered a taxi, drove the taxi into a body of water, and drowned. Before the ship sailed on January 18, the personal effects and wages of Arthur Forsyth and Edward Sherman were left at the U.S. Shipping Commissioner's office for return to their families.

Forsyth and Sherman had served aboard the same ship at least twice. Both men signed on as Deck Cadets aboard the Liberty ship SS *Caleb Strong* on November 5, 1942. The men signed on as third and Second Mate, respectively, aboard the Liberty ship *Robert F. Stockton* at New York, New York, on January 20, 1944, and signed off on May 2, 1944, at the same port. At the time they signed aboard the *Stockton*, Forsyth is shown as having six months' sea time, while Sherman had seven months' time.

Arthur C. Forsyth was born in Hants, Nova Scotia, to John Stewart Grant Forsyth and Francis Churchill Forsyth. The family moved to the United States in 1924. Arthur's mother died in 1942 and his older brother Alfred was killed in Italy in 1944. His younger sister was Mary Elizabeth. John S. Forsyth is identified as a telephone engineer in the 1930 and 1940 U.S. Census. The Forsyth family lived on Staten Island in 1930 but moved to Hempstead, Long Island, by the 1940 U.S. Census. Crew lists identify Arthur Forsyth as being six feet tall and weighing 145 pounds.

Harry Grant

Born:	April 15, 1922
Hometown:	Winnetka, IL
Class:	1944
Service:	Merchant Marine
Position / Rank:	Third Mate
Date / Place of death:	October 31, 1944 / Port of Hollandia, New Guinea
Date / Place of burial:	November 1, 1944 / USAAF Cemetery, Hollandia, New Guinea, Grave number 123
Age:	22

Harry Grant signed on as Third Mate aboard the SS *Francis G. Newlands* at San Francisco, California, on August 14, 1944, two days after being issued his Coast Guard license. The ship sailed the same day to the South Pacific bound for Finschhafen, New Guinea, with a cargo described by the ship's Armed Guard officer as "heavy lifts and subsistence." Upon arrival in Finschhafen, the *Francis G. Newlands* awaited further routing orders until September 12, when it was ordered to sail to Hollandia, New Guinea. Hollandia was the headquarters for General MacArthur and the main staging base for the invasion of the Philippine Islands. From September 14 through November 14, 1944, the *Francis G. Newlands* was moored at Hollandia, delayed in the discharge of its cargo by the tremendous ship traffic (both merchant and Navy) in preparation for the invasion of the Philippines. On the afternoon of October 31, Harry Grant was supervising cargo operations at the after end of number 4 hatch. At 1620, local time, he was crushed between the ship's number 4 heavy boom and the pipe guard around the number 4 starboard winch. The *Francis G. Newlands*'s Third Mate was pronounced dead twenty-eight minutes later by Lt. Hugh Crawford, USNR, the medical officer assigned to the USS *Isherwood* (DD 520). The *Francis G. Newlands* sailed from Hollandia bound for Port Moresby, New Guinea, on November 14. The Captain had been unable to find a replacement for Grant, so the ship sailed without a Third Mate.

Harry Grant entered the San Mateo Basic School on November 11, 1942, roughly six weeks after his family name was changed from Goldstein to Grant. He signed on aboard the Liberty ship SS *Simon Bolivar* as Deck

Cadet on April 28, 1943. Fourteen months later, the *Simon Bolivar* arrived at San Francisco from Australia. Harry Grant signed off on June 13, 1944, and reported to Kings Point to complete his education. This culminated in his graduation later that summer and issuance of his Third Mate's license on August 12, 1944.

Based on his merchant marine service, Harry Grant was posthumously awarded the Pacific War Zone Bar, the Victory Medal, and the Presidential Testimonial Letter. Further it is likely that he was also entitled to the Combat Bar.

Harry (Goldstein) Grant was the only son and youngest child of Harry Goldstein and Lorraine Beilman Goldstein. His older sisters were Lois and Marian. According to the 1930 and 1940 U.S. Census, Harry Sr. was the manager/owner of a clothing factory in 1930 but was listed as a salesman for a clothing factory in 1940. After his death, Harry's sister Lois wrote to the Coast Guard for more details on her brother's death, but no further details were available. Most of the men buried overseas during World War II were either reinterred at permanent military cemeteries overseas or returned home for reburial by their family. There is no record of Harry Grant being buried in an overseas military cemetery, so his remains must have been returned to his parents for burial after the war.

Antonio Vito Graziano

Born:	February 5, 1922
Hometown:	Brooklyn, NY
Class:	1944
Service:	USNR
Position / Rank:	Boiler Officer / Ensign
Date / Place of death:	February 1, 1945 / Pacific Ocean, SE of Hawaii
Date / Place of burial:	St. John's Cemetery, Middle Village, Long Island, NY, Section 36, Range M, Plot 27, Graves 1 and 2
Age:	22

Anthony V. Graziano was sworn in as a midshipman, Merchant Marine Reserve, U.S. Naval Reserve, on December 24, 1942, four days before he completed his ten weeks of training at the Pass Christian Basic School. According to crew lists on file in New York, he signed on aboard the SS *David G. Farragut* as Engine Cadet on January 9, 1943. He signed off articles on September 14, 1943, after making voyages across the Atlantic and into the Mediterranean.

Upon reporting to Kings Point, he was assigned to Section B-116 and joined the Academy's boxing team. On May 19, 1944, he applied for an active duty commission in the Navy. He graduated on July 12, 1944, and was commissioned Ensign, USNR, on July 15, 1944. After reporting for duty on August 11, he was assigned to initial training at Newport, Rhode Island. Upon completion of his initial training, he was assigned to the pre-commissioning crew of the USS *Queens* (APA 103), then being constructed and converted into an attack troop transport at Bethlehem Steel Company's Sparrows Point, Maryland, shipyard.

The USS *Queens* was commissioned on December 16, 1944. Ensign Graziano was assigned to duty as the ship's Boiler's Officer. The ship and its crew trained in Chesapeake Bay. When the ship was ready for duty, it was assigned for duty to the Pacific Fleet and sailed from Norfolk, Virginia, for Pearl Harbor via the Panama Canal.

The afternoon deck logbook entries for the USS *Queens* for February 1, 1945, state, in part,

> 1330 Ensign Antonio V. Graziano, EM, USNR number 181430 sustained injuries to the head. 1509 Ensign Antonio V. Graziano died from gunshot wound, circumstances being investigated.

A board of investigation, headed by Commander M. H. Hegarty, USNR, the ship's Engineering Officer, convened a little more than an hour after Ensign Graziano's death. After several meetings, the board concluded that Ensign Graziano died of a self-inflicted gunshot wound to head. The board stated,

> At the time of the act, the deceased was temporarily insane caused by acts of duty as shown by changes in behavior and personality in the past six weeks as stated in the statements of witnesses. It is concluded that his death occurred in the line of duty and not the result of his own misconduct.

The Queens arrived at Pearl Harbor on February 7, 1945; two days after what would have been Antonio V. Graziano's twenty-third birthday. Ensign Graziano's body was transferred to U.S. Naval Hospital number 8, Aiea, Hawaii. He was buried in the Halawa Naval Cemetery in Pearl Harbor. After World War II, parents or next of kin of deceased military personnel buried outside the continental U.S. were given the option of either leaving the remains buried where they were or having the remains disinterred and returned to them for burial in their hometown. On November 21, 1947, a headstone for Ensign Graziano was ordered from the government. It was shipped on April 2, 1948, to St. John's Cemetery in Middle Village, Long Island, which is Antonio V. Graziano's final resting place.

According to U.S. Navy records, Graziano was awarded the Combat Bar, the Atlantic War Zone Bar, and the Mediterranean-Middle East War Zone Bar. During his service as a Cadet-Midshipman, he received a letter of commendation from the *David G. Farragut*'s Armed Guard officer for his participation in repelling aircraft attacks on the ship.

Antonio V. Graziano was the youngest of Michele (Michael) and Mary Graziano's two sons and third of their four children. His older brother was Daniel, and his two sisters were Angelina (older) and Elizabeth. According to the 1930 U.S. Census, Michele Graziano was a "boot black," or shoe shiner. The family lived at 1166 Forty-Third Street in Brooklyn, New

York. Antonio graduated from New Utrecht High School and took evening classes at Brooklyn College before his appointment to Kings Point. During the days before Kings Point, he worked as a clerk in a stationery and printing company, and as a diamond cutter's apprentice.

In a historical note, the USS *Queens* was decommissioned on June 10, 1946. The ship was converted into a trans-Atlantic passenger ship and renamed SS *Excambion*. As one of American Export Lines "Four Aces," the ship operated from the East Coast of the United States to Mediterranean ports until 1958. In 1965, the ship was assigned as the first training ship of the Texas Maritime Academy in Galveston, Texas. After many years of service, training new merchant mariners, the ship was retired. In 2007, the ship was sunk as a reef approximately seventeen nautical miles northeast of South Padre Island, Texas. Today, the ship is a popular scuba diving attraction.

George Pershing Grieshaber

Born:	October 19, 1918	
Hometown:	Union, NJ	
Class:	1943	
Service:	USNR	
Position / Rank:	Chief Engineer/ Lt. (jg)	
Date / Place of death:	April 11, 1945 / 90 miles East of Okinawa	
Date / Place of burial:	April 12, 1945 / Buried At Sea—23-25N, 131-58E; Tablets of the Missing, Honolulu Memorial, Honolulu, HI	
Age:	26	

George P. Grieshaber was appointed as Cadet, Merchant Marine Reserve, on November 22, 1941, upon completion of Basic School. According to crew lists on file in New York, New York, he signed on aboard the SS *Argentina* as Engine Cadet between November 22 and 24 of November, 1941. After the war began, the SS *Argentina* was taken over by the Army as a troop transport. He signed off on June 20, 1942. Upon reporting to the Academy to complete his training, he was assigned to Section A204.

USS *Kidd* (DD 661)

Upon his graduation from Kings Point, George Grieshaber was commissioned an Ensign, U.S. Naval Reserve, and called to active duty. He was subsequently assigned to the pre-commissioning unit for a new USS *Fletcher* (DD 445) Class Destroyer, USS *Kidd* (DD 661), then completing construction at Federal Shipbuilding and Drydock Company, Kearny, New Jersey. The USS *Kidd*, named after Rear Admiral Isaac C. Kidd Sr., who was killed aboard his flagship, USS *Arizona* (BB 39), on December 7, 1941, was commissioned on April 23, 1943.

The USS *Kidd*'s crew adopted the pirate "Captain Kidd" as their mascot as they began training for combat duty with the Pacific Fleet. From September 1943 to December 1944, the *Kidd* was in combat operations with the Pacific Fleet. During the ship's first overhaul, Lieutenant (Junior grade) Grieshaber was assigned as the ship's Engineering Officer. He was also one of very few of the ship's original officers remaining aboard.

The USS *Kidd* and its crew returned to combat in February 1945, escorting the aircraft carrier strike group Task Force 58. On April 11, 1945, the *Kidd* and three of its shipyard sisters were part of the escort group for three aircraft carriers. At 0343, the USS *Kidd* and its three sister ships of Destroyer Division 96 were assigned to radar picket duty twenty-five miles north of the task group. About ten hours later, the radar pickets were attacked by Japanese suicide planes.

According to the USS *Kidd*'s deck log, the ship's guns opened fire on the attacking aircraft at 1353. A few minutes later, the *Kidd* accelerated to its full speed of 35 knots and began maneuvering radically to avoid the attacking aircraft. However, twenty minutes later, the *Kidd*'s luck

Aircraft that hit USS *Kidd* seconds before impact (USS *Black* in background)

ran out. A kamikaze aircraft flew over the USS *Black*, and then dropped, skimming over the wave tops to crash into the *Kidd*'s starboard side. The *Kidd*'s 40 mm and 20 mm gunners scored several direct hits on the plane but could not destroy it before it struck the *Kidd* at the waterline at the forward fire room where Lt. (jg) George P. Grieshaber was checking a leaky gauge. He was killed instantly, along with all of the other crewmen in the space. In addition, the ship's Commanding Officer, doctor, and other officers and men were put out of action from multiple wounds.

At 1411, the badly wounded Executive Officer took command of the USS *Kidd,* which was on fire and dead in the water with holes in its hull on both sides of the forward fire room. However, within minutes, the *Kidd*'s Engineering Department had the ship back up to 5 knots and reported it was ready to make 25 knots. By 1427, a little more than fifteen minutes after being hit, fires were out on the Kidd, and it was ready to return to the protection of Task Group 58.3 escorted by its sister ships. That evening, the USS *Kidd*, escorted by the USS *McNair* (DD 679), was ordered to sail to the fleet base at Ulithi Atoll for repairs.

From 1030 to 1100, local time, on April 12, 1945, the crew of the USS *Kidd* buried their dead at sea, including Lt. (jg) George P. Grieshaber, USNR. The Commander, Destroyer Division Ninety-Six, said the following about the actions of the *Kidd*'s Engineering Department in his after action report for April 11-15, 1945:

> The quick recovery of the ship from personnel and material damage of such magnitude is considered to be remarkable and conclusive proof of the high standard of training existing on the KIDD.

As one of the ship's original engineers, and its Engineering Officer, much of this credit must lie with George P. Grieshaber. He was posthumously awarded the Purple Heart and the Asiatic-Pacific Campaign Medal in addition to his merchant marine awards. For his service aboard the SS *Argentina,* Cadet-Midshipman George P. Grieshaber was awarded the Atlantic War Zone Bar and the Pacific War Zone Bar.

George P. Grieshaber was the only child of George T. Grieshaber and Estelle P. Grieshaber. The senior Grieshaber's occupation is listed in the U.S. Census as draftsman and architect. A graduation note in the Academy newspaper *Polaris* reports that Grieshaber attended Union Junior College and Mississippi State College before enrolling at the Merchant Marine Academy. According to the note, George planned to obtain a degree in mechanical engineering after the war. At the time of his death, George P. Grieshaber was married to Grace Adelaid Grieshaber, whose residence was listed in the roster of the *Kidd*'s officers as 115-19 199th Street, St. Albans, Long Island, New York. On a trip to Bermuda in 1946, her occupation is listed as receptionist, living at the same address. No further information could be found about Mrs. Grieshaber.

In 1975, the decommissioned USS *Kidd* was selected to be preserved as a memorial and museum in Baton Rouge, Louisiana, where it has been returned to its World War II configuration. A proud fixture of the ship's quarterdeck is the plaque cast by the crew of the Destroyer Tender USS *Hamul* (AD 20) at Ulithi Atoll in 1945 to honor the dead of April 11, 1945.

Henry Edward Harris Jr.

Born:	November 27, 1921
Hometown:	Shamokin, PA
Class:	1942
Service:	Merchant Marine
Position / Rank:	Third Assistant Engineer
Date / Place of death:	December 7, 1942, North Atlantic 57-50 N, 23-10 W
Date / Place of burial:	December 7, 1942, North Atlantic 57-50 N, 23-10 W / Lost at Sea
Age:	21

Henry E. Harris graduated from Kings Point in October 1942. According to U.S. Coast Guard records, he was issued his license as Third Assistant Engineer (steam) on October 9 and his license as Third Assistant Engineer (diesel) on October 14, 1942. He signed on the SS *James McKay* as Third Assistant Engineer a few days later in the Port of New York upon the ship's arrival from Cape Town, South Africa. Four Kings Point Cadet-Midshipmen, Philip G. Branigan (deck), Leonard L. Ehrlich (engine), Walter C. Hetrick (engine), and John J. McKelvey (deck), were also aboard.

SS *James McKay*

According to U.S. Coast Guard and Academy records, Henry E. Harris had previously served as Engine Cadet aboard the SS *Almeria Lykes* from May 23, 1942, until it was torpedoed by German E-boats on August 13, 1942. He had also sailed as Engine Cadet aboard the SS *Margaret Lykes* in 1941.

The *James McKay* sailed from New York with Convoy HX-216 bound for Belfast, Northern Ireland, and Cardiff, Wales, on November 19. On November 25, the convoy encountered a northwest gale and reduced visibility that caused the convoy to partly scatter. The weather was sufficiently rough to cause the *James McKay*'s general cargo to shift, endangering the ship's stability; the ship left the convoy and sailed into St. John's, Newfoundland, on November 29 to restow its cargo.

After restowing its cargo, the *James McKay* sailed from Newfoundland to join up with the next east-bound convoy, HX-217. However, there is no indication that the *James McKay* ever actually joined up with HX-217, possibly due to the convoy being scattered in a southwesterly gale from December 2 to 4.

According to German Navy records, the *James McKay* was located and attacked by *U-600* on the night of December 7/8, 1943, about four hundred miles south of Iceland. Three torpedoes hit the *James McKay*, one amidships and the other two in the after portion of the ship. The ship stopped and sent out distress signals, and the crew abandoned ship in two lifeboats although the ship was still afloat. It required two more torpedoes from *U-600* to sink the *James McKay*. Neither the two lifeboats nor any of her crew were ever seen again.

Henry E. Harris was posthumously awarded the Mariner's Medal, the Combat Bar with two stars, the Atlantic War Zone Bar, the Mediterranean-Middle East War Zone Bar, the Victory Medal, and the Presidential Testimonial Letter.

He was the oldest of Henry Edward Harris Sr. and Helen Elizabeth Pflugner Harris's five children. Henry Sr. was on optometrist in Shamokin, a small town located in east central Pennsylvania.

James Dale Herndon

Born:	February 16, 1922
Hometown:	San Benito, TX
Class:	1942
Service:	Merchant Marine
Position / Rank:	Third Asst. Engineer
Date / Place of death:	November 7, 1942 / Indian Ocean 40-00 S, 21-30 E
Date / Place of burial	November 7, 1942 / Lost at Sea / Indian Ocean 40-00 S, 21-30 E
Age:	21

James D. Herndon was appointed as Cadet, U.S. Merchant Marine Cadet Corps, on June 27, 1940, and assigned to the Cadet school, Algiers, Louisiana. U.S. Coast Guard records indicate that James was originally designated as a Deck Cadet. However, according to Academy records and crew lists on file in Honolulu, Hawaii, he sailed as Engine Cadet aboard the SS *Pan Crescent* from August 1940 to November 1941. According to Academy records, he was joined aboard the SS *La Salle* on September 26, 1942, by Cadet-Midshipmen George E. Guilford (Engine Cadet) and Fred Pennington (Deck Cadet) from the Pass Christian, Mississippi, Basic School. The *La Salle* sailed the same day for Cape Town, South Africa, loaded with a cargo of trucks, steel, and ammunition. However, the *La Salle* never arrived at Cape Town, and the fate of the *La Salle* remained a mystery until after the war. The vessel was officially marked as "presumed lost" on December 2, 1942.

SS *Wynah*, a shipyard sister to the SS *La Salle*

After the war, German Navy records solved the mystery. On November 7, 1942, when the *La Salle* was nearing the end of its voyage, the unescorted freighter was sighted *by U-159* about 350 miles southeast of the Cape of Good Hope. The submarine chased the *La Salle* for over five hours, missing with one torpedo, until it managed to achieve a better target solution and fired another torpedo. The explosion of that torpedo detonated the *La Salle*'s ammunition cargo, instantly destroying the ship. The crew of *U-159* reported that the explosion sent pillars of flame hundreds of feet into the air. Three of the submarine's crew were wounded by the debris that rained down on the submarine for several minutes after the explosion. It was later claimed that the explosion could be heard three hundred miles away, at South Africa's Cape Point Lighthouse.

Everyone aboard the SS *La Salle* was killed instantly, including Third Assistant Engineer James D. Herndon and Cadet-Midshipmen George E. Guilford and Fred Pennington. Also among the dead was the ship's Armed Guard officer, the former Mayor of Milwaukee, Wisconsin, Lt. Carl F. Zeidler, USNR. After resigning as Mayor so that he could be commissioned, Zeidler is said to have asked for the most dangerous job in the Navy. He was then assigned to command a merchant ship Armed Guard detachment.

James D. Herndon was posthumously awarded the Mariner's Medal, the Combat Bar, the Atlantic War Zone Bar, the Pacific War Zone Bar, the Merchant Marine Defense Medal, the Victory Medal, and the Presidential Testimonial Letter.

James was the younger of Amos Allen Herndon and Ethel Mae Turvey Herndon's two adult sons. He grew up on a farm outside of San Benito, Texas, where all of the family worked either on the farm or at neighboring farms or businesses. In the 1940 U.S. Census, James was identified as a farm laborer, his brother Clarence as a truck driver, and his mother as a fruit picker.

Gordon Alan Herstam

Born:	May 7, 1923
Hometown:	Cleveland Heights, OH
Class:	1943
Service:	USNR
Position / Rank:	Asst. Beachmaster / Ensign
Date / Place of death:	April 2, 1945, USS Goodhue (APA 107) off Okinawa
Date / Place of burial	(Initial) April 3, 1945 / Army and Navy Cemetery Zamami-Shima, Kerama Retto, Okinawa (Final) March 25, 1949 / Arlington National Cemetery, Plot 34, Grave 4369
Age:	22

Gordon A. Herstam reported to the U.S. Merchant Marine Cadet Basic School at New Orleans, Louisiana, on May 6, 1942. According to crew lists on file in New Orleans, Louisiana, Cadet-Midshipman Herstam signed on aboard the United Fruit Company's SS *Atlantida* as Deck Cadet in early July 1942. Upon reporting to Kings Point, he was assigned to Section A221 for his final training. Crew lists on file in New York, New York, show that he signed on aboard the tanker SS *Little Big Horn* in January 1944, after his graduation from the Academy, apparently while waiting for his Navy commission to be activated.

Ensign Gordon A. Herstam, USNR, was a "plank owner" aboard the amphibious troop transport USS *Goodhue* (APA 107) when it was commissioned on November 11, 1944. According to the ship's logbook, Ensign Herstam was assigned to duty as one of the ship's Assistant Beachmasters. After shakedown training off of the U.S. West Coast, the new troop transport sailed on January 4, 1945, from San Diego, California, bound for the South Pacific. From January through late March 1945, the USS *Goodhue* carried cargo and troops in the South Pacific before loading for the assault on Okinawa.

The USS *Goodhue* (APA 107) sailed from Leyte Gulf on March 21, 1945, in a convoy bound for Kerama Retto, a group of islands designated as the fleet base for the ships assaulting Okinawa. On March 26, the *Goodhue*'s troops, along with troops from other ships in the formation, secured the islands of Kerama Retto and began building the base. For about a week, the *Goodhue* remained at Kerama Retto, unloading cargo during the day and withdrawing offshore overnight with the other transports. Even in the night retirement area, things were not peaceful. On Monday, April 2, 1945, the *Goodhue*'s deck log records the crew going to general quarters three times between midnight and 0742 when the ship anchored again off Kerama Retto. That afternoon, while getting under way to execute the fleet's night retirement plan, the troop transports came under a prolonged air attack by Japanese kamikazes. The *Goodhue*'s gunners started firing at 1837. Within minutes, the transports USS *Henrico* (APA 45) and USS *Telfair* (APA 210) had been hit or grazed by kamikazes.

The crew of the *Goodhue* fought back, desperately firing at the approaching planes, bringing one of them down on her starboard side. Meanwhile, a second kamikaze was stalking the *Goodhue* from about three thousand yards to starboard. As the plane turned toward the *Goodhue,* the ship's forward five-inch gun fired one shot, damaging the plane, before suffering a breakdown. The ship's 20 mm gunners continued firing on the aircraft, finally managing to set the plane on fire, but the kamikaze crashed into the *Goodhue*'s mainmast at the crosstrees. Part of the plane continued aft, exploding over the fantail; while another part of the plane, with at least one bomb, swung over the port side and exploded at deck level. The explosions immediately killed seventeen of the ship's crew, including Ensign Gordon A. Herstam, who was at his station and

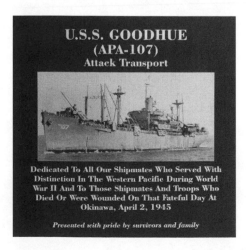

U.S.S. GOODHUE
(APA-107)
Attack Transport

Dedicated To All Our Shipmates Who Served With Distinction In The Western Pacific During World War II And To Those Shipmates And Troops Who Died Or Were Wounded On That Fateful Day At Okinawa, April 2, 1945

Presented with pride by survivors and family

suffered shrapnel wounds to his abdomen. Five more Army soldiers were killed, and many others subsequently died of their wounds in the following hours and days.

The *Goodhue* did not suffer structural damage and was able to continue on to Kerama Retto for repairs and further service. The *Goodhue*'s dead were buried at the Army and Navy cemetery at Zamami-Shima, on Kerama

Retto, the following day with full military honors. After World War II, the men buried in temporary cemeteries like those interred at Zamami-Shima were either reinterred at permanent military cemeteries or returned to the United States. Ensign Gordon A. Herstam's body was reinterred at Arlington National Cemetery on March 25, 1949. His grave is near that of another Kings Pointer, astronaut Elliot M. See, class of 1949.

Ensign Gordon A. Herstam, USNR, was posthumously awarded the Purple Heart and the Asiatic-Pacific Campaign Medal. As a Cadet-Midshipman, he earned the Atlantic War Zone Bar, the Victory Medal, and the Presidential Testimonial Letter.

Gordon A. Herstam was the only son of Nathan Herstam and Lilian Gordon Herstam. According to U.S. Census records, Nathan Herstam was a lawyer with a private practice. Gordon's sister Ruth was four years younger.

Charles Wayman Hogue

Born:	1923
Hometown:	Memphis, TN
Class:	1944
Service:	USNR
Position / Rank:	Asst. Engineering Officer / Ensign
Date / Place of death:	December 10, 1944 / Aboard USS Mercy (AH 8)
Date / Place of burial:	December 11, 1944 / USS Mercy (AH 8); Tablets of the Missing at Manila American Cemetery, Manila, Philippines
Age:	21

According to U.S. Navy records, Charles W. Hogue was appointed Midshipman, USNR, on August 15, 1942, although he was appointed a Cadet, U.S. Merchant Marine Cadet Corps, some months before. He signed on as Engine Cadet aboard the new SS *Peter Silvester* on June 24, 1942, at San Francisco, California. The ship returned to San Francisco, California, nearly a year later, on May 23, 1943, from Noumea, New Caledonia. From there, he reported to Kings Point to complete his education and receive his license as Third Assistant Engineer and his commission as Ensign, USNR.

USS *Lamson* (DD 367) off Vallejo, CA, 1944

Ensign Hogue reported aboard the USS *Lamson (DD 367)* as assistant Engineering Officer on April 26, 1944, at Mare Island Naval Shipyard. By July, the ship had completed its overhaul and was ready for action.

The USS *Lamson* reported for duty with the Fifth Fleet at Eniwetok on August 8. After two months of convoy escort duty, the *Lamson* was transferred to the Seventh Fleet for the amphibious assault on Leyte in the Philippine Islands. On the morning of December 7, 1944, three years after the war began; the *Lamson* was firing its guns on Japanese targets on Leyte in support of Army troops ashore. Later that morning, following air attacks that badly damaged the *Lamson*'s sister ship, the USS *Mahan (DD 364)*, the *Lamson* was ordered to take the *Mahan*'s place as the formation's fighter director ship.

At about 1400, the Japanese renewed their attack on the fleet, with *Lamson* guiding fighters to groups of enemy planes while shooting down one attacker. However, another plane flew around a nearby island and was able to approach to one thousand yards before being fired on by the *Lamson*'s guns. Despite the *Lamson*'s violent turn away from the plane, it struck the after stack with its right wing and spun around into the port side of the ship. The aircraft wreckage immediately enveloped the ship in flame from amidships to the bow. The impact of the crash on number 2 stack collapsed it, causing a flare back in the after fire room, burning the crew on duty there. The hatches to the forward fire room were jammed by the damage, trapping the men there.

USS *Lamson* (DD 367) with USS *ATR 31* alongside, December 7, 1944, Ormoc Bay, Philippines

With the fire threatening the forward ammunition magazines, and no water pressure in the fire mains, USS *ATR 31* came alongside to help fight the fire and remove the wounded.

The fires were soon under control, and *ATR 31* began towing the ship out of danger.

Despite continuous air attacks, the *Lamson*'s crew managed to keep their ship afloat and bring their over fifty wounded shipmates to medical treatment.

Among the injured was Ensign Charles W. Hogue. Due to the severity of his wounds, he was transferred to the hospital ship USS *Mercy (AH 8)* for transfer to a hospital in Hollandia, New Guinea.

Unfortunately, at 0130, on December 10, 1944, Ensign Charles Hogue died of his wounds. He was buried at sea the following day.

Ensign Charles W. Hogue, USNR, was posthumously awarded the Purple Heart and the Asiatic-Pacific Campaign Medal. For his merchant marine service, he earned the Pacific War Zone Bar, the Victory Medal and Presidential Testimonial Letter.

At the time of his death, Charles W. Hogue was married to Barbara Rosina Hogue. Charles was the youngest child of Abner E. Hogue and Florence Hogue of Memphis, Tennessee. In 1930, Charles, his parents, and older sister, Maxine, were living with his grandfather in Memphis, Tennessee.

Thomas George Jones

Born:	1921
Hometown:	North Bergen, NJ
Class:	1944
Service:	Merchant Marine
Position / Rank:	Third Assistant Engineer
Date / Place of death:	May 24, 1945, Nakagusuku Bay, Okinawa
Date / Place of burial:	May 24, 1945, Nakagusuku Bay, Okinawa / Lost at Sea
Age:	21

Thomas G. Jones signed on as Third Assistant Engineer aboard the SS *William B. Allison* in late January, 1945 at the Port of New York. This was probably his first job as a licensed officer after his graduation from Kings Point in 1944. He had previously sailed as Engine Cadet aboard the SS *David G. Farragut* on at least one voyage to the Mediterranean.

The *William B. Allison* sailed from New York on February 21, 1945, bound for the Panama Canal with Navy cargo for its bases on Espiritu Santo in the New Hebrides. Arriving at Espiritu Santo on March 26, the ship sailed on April 1 to deliver cargo to bases in the Russell and Solomon Islands, Eniwetok, and Ulithi Atoll. In the Russell Islands, the ship loaded Navy Construction Battalion equipment, which was accompanied by thirty-four "Seabees." The *William B. Allison* sailed from Ulithi on May 15, 1945, in a convoy with seventeen other ships bound for Okinawa. The ship was loaded with lumber, structural steel, vehicles, diesel fuel in drums, and its Seabee passengers.

On May 21, the *William B. Allison* anchored in Nakagusuku Wan (Bay) at Okinawa, where it began discharging its cargo under the watchful eyes of its passengers. On the early morning of May 25, 1945 (local time), the ship was at anchor, "blacked out" with no lights showing, and surrounded by a smoke screen. However, the anchorage was illuminated by a full moon. At 0305, a Japanese torpedo plane silently glided out of the smoke screen about three hundred yards from the bow, dropped a torpedo, and zoomed away. There was no time to alert the crew to the danger until after the torpedo hit the ship on the port side at the engine room. The after action report stated that the explosion blew a hole eighteen feet long and thirty feet high, extending some 4' to 5' above the water line to within 18" of the keel; it completely destroyed the engine room. Two of the men on watch in the engine room, Thomas G. Jones and an unlicensed engineer, were killed instantly along with one of the Navy Seabees. Four more members of the *William B. Allison* crew died of their injuries the following day.

Former SS *William B. Allison* aground off Okinawa, 1945

Although its engine room was completely wrecked, neither its cargo holds nor the cargo they contained was damaged as the ship settled a little lower in the water. With the help of steam from its shipyard sister, the USS *Mintaka* (AK 97) (ex-SS *Ansell Briggs*), which tied up alongside, all of the *William B. Allison* cargo was safely discharged. That job done, the *William B. Allison* was towed to the fleet repair base at Kerama Retto. There, although the *William B. Allison* was considered to be a constructive total loss, the hole in the engine room was plated over. After these basic repairs, the hulk was turned over to the Navy for use as a floating storage facility. The former *William B. Allison* continued to serve the fleet in this capacity until it ran aground after dragging its anchor during a typhoon in October 1945. At this point, the Navy considered that further repairs to the former *William B. Allison* were unwarranted and returned the ship to the War Shipping Administration for disposal. The hulk was finally sold for scrapping in 1948.

Based on his sailing career as a Cadet-Midshipman and licensed officer, Thomas George Jones was eligible for posthumous award of the Mariner's Medal, the Combat Bar, the Atlantic War Zone Bar, the Mediterranean-Middle East War Zone Bar, the Pacific War Zone Bar, the Victory Medal, and the Presidential Testimonial Letter.

Walter Frederick Kannberg Jr.

Born:	August 12, 1921
Hometown:	Chicago, IL
Class:	1944
Service:	Merchant Marine
Position / Rank:	Third Assistant Engineer
Date / Place of death:	July 17, 1944 / Port Chicago, California
Date / Place of burial:	July 17, 1944 / Lost at Sea—Port Chicago, California
Age:	22

Walter F. Kannberg joined the U.S. Merchant Marine Cadet Corps in 1942 and most likely attended the Pass Christian Basic School. He was issued his U.S. Coast Guard documents on October 13, 1942, at Chicago, Illinois. He signed on aboard the SS *Simon Willard* as Engine Cadet on January 1, 1943, at Mobile, Alabama. After a voyage to Cape Town, South Africa, and back via the Caribbean and South America, he signed off in New York in early May 1943.

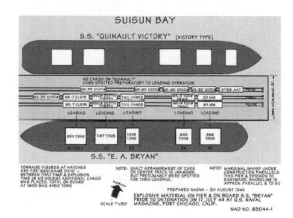

On July 11, 1944, Walter F. Kannberg signed on as Third Assistant Engineer of the SS *Quinault Victory* at Portland, Oregon. He had graduated from Kings Point just a few months earlier with Section A393. On July 17, 1944, the *Quinault Victory* was alongside the pier at the Naval Magazine, Port Chicago, California, preparing to load a cargo of ammunition for its maiden voyage.

Across the pier, the SS *E. A. Bryan* had loaded a little more than 4,600 tons of explosives and ammunition.

Over four hundred tons of ammunition and explosives were on the pier waiting to be loaded. At 2200, Pacific war time, ammunition loading was proceeding normally with the exception of some "new ship" faults aboard the *Quinault Victory*, which were being corrected so that loading could start by 2400.

Hulk of SS *Quinault Victory*, July 18, 1944

However, between 2218 and 2219, Pacific war time, the ammunition either aboard the *E. A. Bryan* or on the pier adjoining it exploded with a bright flash, leaving huge vertical column of smoke and fire. For a few seconds, smaller explosions were observed on the pier followed by a final major explosion, probably the cargo of the *E. A. Bryan*. The two explosions completely destroyed both ships, the pier, and everyone there at the time.

The explosions were felt across fourteen counties and left a death toll of 320, including 202 African American men assigned the dangerous task of loading and unloading munitions. Another 390 were wounded in the blasts.

For his merchant marine service, Walter F. Kannberg was posthumously awarded the Atlantic War Zone Bar, the Victory Medal, and the Presidential Testimonial Letter.

At the time of his death, Walter F. Kannberg was married to Anita Brooke Weaver. The two were married on April 16, 1944, with Walter's brother, Robert, present as a witness and, presumably, best man. Walter was the oldest son and middle of three children of Walter F. Kannberg Sr. and Martha Kamradt Kannberg. Walter's sister (one year older) was Ruth Georgiana. According to U.S. Census information, Walter Sr. was a painting contractor. In 1940, Ruth was working as a file clerk for a motor club; and Walter, who was nineteen in 1940, was working as a draftsman for an electrical manufacturing firm.

Interestingly, although Robert is not an alumnus of Kings Point, he also became a licensed marine engineer, sailing as third assistant on the SS *Maryville Victory* in 1945 and aboard the *Coe Victory* in 1950.

The tragedy could have been even worse for the Merchant Marine Academy as two Cadet-Midshipmen from San Mateo, Lynn Osborn and Rex Boone, were ordered to report to the ship on the afternoon of June 17. However, according to their classmate Jack M. Beggs, Osborn convinced Boone to stay ashore at a relative's home that night. When they woke up the next morning, the relative asked, "Did you hear the big explosion at Port Chicago last night?" Thus, because of the desire to stay ashore one more night, the "142" did not become the "144."

LeRoy William Kernan

Born: October 5, 1917

Hometown: Elgin, IL

Class: 1942

Service: Merchant Marine

Position / Rank: Third Mate

Date / Place of death: March 17, 1943 / North
                             Atlantic 50-38 N, 34-46 E

Date / Place of burial: March 17, 1943 / North
                             Atlantic 50-38 N, 34-46
                             E / Lost at Sea

Age: 25

Leroy W. Kernan was appointed a Cadet in the U.S. Merchant Marine Cadet Corps in February 1941, although he had received his Coast Guard papers as Deck Cadet on April 30, 1940, at New Orleans. He attended the Maritime Commission Cadet School at Algiers, Louisiana, and had begun sailing as Deck Cadet aboard the SS *Arizpa* on May 1, 1940. Following receipt of his unlimited Third Mate license on August 15, 1942, LeRoy Kernan signed on as Third Mate aboard the SS *Hawaiian Shipper* at New York on November 19, 1942, for a voyage to Casablanca and return.

SS *Harry Luckenbach*

On March 2, 1943, LeRoy Kernan signed on aboard the SS *Harry Luckenbach* as Third Mate at New York, New York. The *Harry Luckenbach* also had four Kings Point Cadet-Midshipmen aboard: Lee T. Byrd (deck), Walter J. Meyer (engine), Francis R. Miller (engine), and William H. Parker (deck). The ship sailed from New York on March 8 as one of forty ships in Convoy HX-229, bound for Liverpool with a general cargo of war supplies. A second HX convoy, HX-229A, with more ships, sailed about ten hours after the ships of HX-229. During their transit of the North Atlantic, the two convoys overtook a slower convoy, SC-122. The three convoys, with a total of 110 ships, but less than twenty escorts, would be the centerpiece of what has been described as the greatest convoy battle of World War II.

The ships of Convoy HX-229 had proceeded without incident or attack until March 16. For the next three days, the convoy was under attack by over forty U-boats. On the morning of March 17, when HX-229 was about four hundred miles east-southeast of Cape Farrell, *U-91* fired five torpedoes at the convoy, not aiming at any specific ship. However, the *Harry Luckenbach*, sailing in the starboard forward corner of the convoy, was hit by two of the torpedoes at the engine room. The ship sank in minutes, but amazingly, three lifeboats were able to get away from the sinking vessel. One or more of the boats were later sighted by HMS *Beverley* (H-64), HMS *Pennywort* (K-111), HMS *Volunteer* (D-71), and, possibly, the HMS *Abelia* (K-184). However, none of these ships were able to pick up the survivors from the boats. None of the fifty-four crew members and twenty-six Naval Armed Guard sailors of the *Harry Luckenbach* survived the sinking.

By March 20, the surviving ships of the three convoys arrived in the United Kingdom, having lost twenty-two ships and their crews, while sinking just one of the attacking U-boats. According to a Royal Navy report on the convoy battle,

> The Germans never came so near to disrupting communications between the New World and the Old as in the first twenty days of March 1943.

The fact that the Germans were unable to do so is a testament to the courage of merchant mariners like LeRoy W. Kernan, and the example that he set for the Kings Pointers that came after him.

Based on his sailing record, LeRoy W. Kernan was posthumously awarded the Mariner's Medal, the Combat Bar with star, the Atlantic War Zone Bar, the Mediterranean-Middle East War Zone Bar, the Pacific War Zone Bar, the Victory Medal, and the Presidential Testimonial Letter.

Leroy was the oldest of three children and only son of William W. Kernan and Cresentia Kernan. LeRoy's two sisters were named Lois and Lenore. According to the 1940 census, William Kernan was a Carpenter, while

LeRoy's occupation was listed as being a finisher in a pottery factory. However, Leroy had attended Illinois State Normal University at Normal, Illinois, in 1938, where he studied music after graduating from Elgin High School in Elgin, Illinois. In high school, he played violin in the school orchestra.

Michael Frank Kostal Jr.

Born:	September 12, 1922
Hometown:	Coraopolis, PA
Class:	1942
Service:	U.S. Navy
Position / Rank:	Lieutenant (Junior grade)
Date / Place of death:	June 1, 1944 / North Pacific, Near Matsuwa Island
Date / Place of burial:	June 1, 1944 / Lost at Sea, North Pacific near Matsuwa Island; Tablets of the Missing at Honolulu Memorial Honolulu, Hawaii
Age:	21

Michael F. Kostal Jr. entered the U.S. Merchant Marine Cadet Corps in the spring of 1941 and received his basic training at Fort Schuyler. After sailing as Engine Cadet aboard the SS *Mormacrey* and SS *Argentina*, he returned to Kings Point for his advanced training. While at the Academy, he earned the affectionate moniker "the Moving Man" because he was "always on the go." He was one of eleven members of the thirty-four young men in his graduating class to volunteer for active duty in the Navy.

After he received his commission on February 1, 1943, Michael Kostal was initially assigned to the USS *Stevens* (DD 479) as the Assistant Engineering Officer. In October, he was transferred to the USS *Pollack* (SS 180), where he served as the submarine's Assistant First Lieutenant until April 26, 1944. From April 28 to May 3, 1944, he was assigned to Submarine Division Forty-Three, where he served in relief crews aboard submarines undergoing overhaul between patrols.

USS *Herring* (SS 233)

At some point in early May, Michael Kostal reported aboard another submarine, the USS *Herring* (SS 233). On May 16, the *Herring* departed Pearl Harbor on its eighth war patrol. A week later, the *Herring* stopped at Midway Island to top off its fuel supply. From there, the submarine headed to a patrol area off the Kuril Islands. On May 31, the submarine had a rendezvous with the USS *Barb (*SS *220)*.

Later that day, the crew of the *Barb* heard depth charges and assumed the *Herring* was launching an attack. The *Barb* later picked up a prisoner who confirmed that the *Herring* had sunk an escort vessel for an enemy convoy.

Japanese records later revealed that the *Herring* had also sunk a merchantman in the convoy. The following day, the *Herring* attacked and sank another two merchant ships. However, in the attack, the submarine itself was sunk by a shore battery, which scored direct hits on the conning tower. Since there were no Allied witnesses to the attack, the fate of the *Herring* remained unknown for the duration of the war. When the submarine was not heard from by the middle of July, she was listed as missing and presumed lost.

Lt. (jg) Michael F. Kostal Jr., USNR, was posthumously awarded the Purple Heart, the Asiatic Pacific Campaign Medal, and the World War II Victory Medal. His name is engraved on the Tablets of the Missing at the Honolulu Memorial. For his merchant marine service, he earned the Atlantic War Zone Bar and the Presidential Testimonial Letter.

Michael F. Kostal Jr. was the only son and oldest child of Michael F. Kostal and Mary Kostal. His younger sister was Marie. The 1930 U.S. Census indicates that the senior Kostal was a "boat engineer" at a steel mill. Ten years later, Mr. Kostal's occupation was identified as "machinist" at a foundry.

Joseph Richard Lawrence Jr.

Born: March 19, 1919
Hometown: Allentown, PA
Class: 1942
Service: U. S. Navy
Position / Rank: Lieutenant (Junior grade)
Date / Place of Death: December 12, 1944 / aboard USS *Castle Rock* (AVP 35) in San Diego, CA
Date / Place of burial: Undetermined
Age: 25

Joseph R. Lawrence Jr. was appointed a Midshipman, USNR, on August 20, 1942 and was officially sworn in on September 22, 1942. During his sea year, Cadet-Midshipman Lawrence sailed as Deck Cadet aboard the SS *George Washington*, the SS *City of Flint,* and the SS *Topa Topa*. The latter ship was torpedoed and sunk on August 29, 1942. Joseph Lawrence was one of the thirty-five survivors and thus was one of the founders of the Tin Fish Club. The survivors were rescued the next day by the British SS *Clan McInnis* and repatriated to the United States aboard the Navy stores ship USS *Tarazed* (AF 13). After graduation from the Cadet Corps program in November 1942, Joseph Lawrence signed on aboard the SS *Pan Crescent* as Third Mate at the Port of New York in early December 1942.

On March 15, 1943, Joseph Lawrence was sworn in as an Ensign, USNR, with a date of rank from February 19, 1943. After a brief assignment in New York, Ensign Lawrence was assigned to the pre-commissioning crew of the USS *Schuylkill* (AO 76), a T2-SE-A1 tanker being converted into a Navy fleet Oiler. Ensign Lawrence officially joined the crew of the *Schuylkill* upon its commissioning on April 9, 1943. After more than a year of service aboard the *Schuylkill*, Joseph Lawrence was promoted to Lieutenant (Junior grade) on May 1, 1944. Three weeks later, he was detached to Naval Air Station, Dallas, for temporary duty involving flight instruction. However, on July 11, shortly after he reported for flight training, he was transferred to Lake Washington Shipyards in Houghton, Washington. When he arrived there, he was assigned to the pre-commissioning crew of the USS *Castle Rock* (AVP 35). Upon the commissioning of the *Castle Rock* on October 8, 1944, he was assigned to duty as the first division officer. For the next few months, the *Castle Rock* conducted the training necessary to prepare the ship for combat duty with the Pacific Fleet.

On December 12, 1944, just six days before the ship sailed for duty with the Pacific Fleet, the *Castle Rock* was moored at San Diego, California. At 2210 that evening, Lieutenant Lawrence returned from shore leave. Five minutes later, an enlisted man from another department aboard ship warned the Officer of the Deck that Lieutenant Lawrence might try to shoot himself. The Officer of the Deck proceeded to Lieutenant Lawrence's quarters, where he found Lawrence unconscious on his bunk, a gun in his right hand, and blood coming from his mouth.

The Officer of the Deck immediately summoned the ship's duty Pharmacist's Mate to provide medical treatment. Upon examination, the Pharmacist's Mate discovered a gunshot wound on the right side of Lieutenant Lawrence's chest. The Officer of the Deck then summoned an ambulance and a doctor. The doctor arrived within minutes. However, at 2224, fourteen minutes after he returned aboard the ship, Joseph R. Lawrence was pronounced dead.

On December 14, two days after Lawrence's death, a court of inquiry assembled on the ship to inquire into the circumstances of the death of Lt. (jg) Joseph R. Lawrence. The court called witnesses and deliberated from 0930 to 1150 when it "adjourned to await orders from the convening authority." The findings of the court inquiry could not be located.

Lt. (jg) Joseph R. Lawrence Jr. was posthumously awarded the World War II Victory Medal and the Asiatic Pacific Campaign Medal for his U.S. Navy service. For his merchant marine service, Cadet-Midshipman Joseph R. Lawrence earned the Combat Bar with star and the Atlantic and Pacific War Zone Bars.

Joseph R. Lawrence was the son of Joseph R. and Louise Lawrence of Allentown, Pennsylvania.

Edward Addis Lemerise

Born:	August 11, 1923
Hometown:	Fall River, MA
Class:	1943
Service:	USNR
Position / Rank:	Ensign / Assistant Engineering Officer
Date / Place of death:	October 10, 1944 / Portland, OR
Date / Place of burial:	October 1944 / St. Patrick's Cemetery, Fall River, MA
Age:	21

Ensign Edward Lemerise graduated from the U.S. Merchant Marine Academy on May 22, 1943. As a Cadet-Midshipman, he sailed as Engine Cadet aboard the SS *Exanthia*. He was sworn into the U.S. Naval Reserve as an Ensign on June 5, 1943. After initial training, Ensign Lemerise reported to the pre-commissioning detail for the USS *Rutland* (APA 192) at Astoria, Oregon. Upon the *Rutland* commissioning on September 29, 1944, Ensign Lemerise was assigned to duty as the ship's auxiliary machinery or "A" Division Officer and Assistant Engineering Officer.

On October 9, 1944, the *Rutland* was moored at U.S. Naval Station Astoria, Oregon, taking on supplies for her shakedown cruise off the West Coast. Ensign Lemerise left the ship but was due back aboard the ship by 1645 that afternoon. However, he did not return and was listed as absent without leave at the 0710 crew muster on October 10. Less than an hour later, the ship sailed from Astoria for Bremerton, Washington. Two days later, at 1036, on October 12, 1944, the *Rutland* received a message from the officer in charge of the receiving barracks in Portland saying that they had positively identified a deceased person as Ensign Lemerise.

Edward Lemerise's death certificate indicates that he may not have intended to return from liberty when he left the *Rutland* on October 9. His body was found on October 10 in Mount Calvary Cemetery in Portland, dead of a self-inflicted gunshot wound to his right temple. The death certificate indicates that he used a .45-caliber pistol, possibly his service pistol or one he borrowed from the ship before he left.

Ensign Lemerise's remains were returned to his wife, Elizabeth L. Lemerise, in Fall River, Massachusetts, where he is buried at St. Patrick's Cemetery. Edward A. Lemerise was the oldest of Edward Lemerise and Elizabeth C. Lemerise's three children. According to the 1940 U.S. Census, the elder Lemerise worked as a mechanic in a garage.

Gordon Wallace Lyons

Born:	December 4, 1917
Hometown:	Dallas, TX
Class:	1942
Service:	Merchant Marine
Position / Rank:	Chief Mate
Date / Place of death:	August 28, 1944 / 15-10 N, 55-18 E
Date / Place of burial:	August 28, 1944 / Lost at Sea—15-10 N, 55-18 E
Age:	26

According to Academy records, Gordon W. Lyons was one of forty-seven men who took the competitive examination to join the U.S. Merchant Marine Cadet Corps on November 16, 1940. He passed the examination and signed on as Deck Cadet aboard the SS *Zoella Lykes* at New Orleans on April 8, 1941. Crew lists show that he made at least two voyages to the Far East aboard the *Zoella Lykes*. Academy records also show that by December 1941, he had returned to the Maritime Commission Cadet School at Algiers, Louisiana, where he received twenty-five demerits for returning late from leave. The same record also shows that he had been sworn in as a midshipman, USNR, by that time. He was detached on December 30, 1941, and assigned as Deck Cadet to the SS *Nishmaha*. By January 7, 1943, Gordon signed on as Junior Third Mate aboard the SS *Frederick Lykes* at the Port of New York for a voyage to the Middle East. He signed off on March 11, 1943.

By July 1944, Gordon W. Lyons had raised his license to Chief Mate and was sailing in this position aboard the SS *John Barry* when it sailed from Philadelphia, Pennsylvania, on July 19, 1944, bound for Dhahran, Saudi Arabia. The ship was carrying a cargo of oil drilling equipment, pipe, vehicles, and other war material. In addition to the ship's normal cargo, it was also carrying hundreds of thousands of dollars' worth of silver Saudi riyals, newly struck at the Philadelphia Mint, to pay oil field workers in Saudi Arabia. After sailing in convoy to Port Said, Egypt, the *John Barry* passed through the Suez Canal, sailing unescorted en route to the Persian Gulf.

On the evening of August 28, 1944, the *John Barry* was off of the coast of Oman sailing in moderately rough seas under bright moonlight. The zigzagging freighter was spotted by *U-859,* which fired at least one torpedo at, or shortly after, 1800 (GCT). One torpedo hit the *John Barry*'s starboard side between number 2 and number 3 holds, destroying number 1 lifeboat.

The other lifeboats were reported to have been launched and in the water within fifteen minutes of the torpedo explosion. However, number 2 lifeboat, with Chief Mate Gordon Lyons aboard, was swamped and its crew thrown into the water during the launching. The boat was eventually righted, bailed out, and put back into use, picking up men in the water and on life rafts. Unfortunately, neither Gordon Lyons nor another crew member from number 2 lifeboat could be found once the lifeboat was righted. These two men, who are presumed to have drowned when the boat swamped, were the only fatalities in the sinking of the SS *John Barry*. The other sixty-six men were rescued the next day by the SS *Sunetta*, a Dutch tanker, and the SS *Benjamin Bourn*.

Forty-five minutes after the first torpedo hit the *John Barry;* *U-859* fired a second torpedo, which hit amidships, breaking the ship in two and sinking it in 8,500 feet of water. In 1989, a converted drill ship recovered a little less than half of the silver riyals stowed in the *John Barry*'s number 2 hold.

Gordon Lyons's photograph indicates that he had already been awarded the Atlantic War Zone, the Pacific War Zone, and the Mediterranean and Middle-East War Zone Bars before he signed on aboard the SS *John Barry*. For his service aboard the SS *John Barry,* he was posthumously awarded the Mariner's Medal and the Combat Bar with star.

According to U.S. Census information, Gordon W. Lyons was the oldest of Percy Lyons and Essie Lyons's three sons and three daughters. These records indicate that all of the Lyons children were born in Illinois, but in 1930, the Lyons family was living in Dallas, Texas, where Percy Lyons worked as a railroad engineer. In 1940, Gordon had graduated from high school and was living in New Orleans, where he was employed as a clerk in a warehouse.

Ceslaus Adam Maciorowski

Born:	November 27, 1917
Hometown:	Chicago, Illinois
Class:	1942
Service:	Merchant Marine
Position / Rank:	Third Assistant Engineer
Date / Place of death:	September 19, 1942 / 11-20 N, 58-50 W
Date / Place of burial:	September 19, 1942 / Lost at Sea—11-20 N, 58-50 W
Age:	24

Ceslaus "Chester" Maciorowski sailed as Engine Cadet aboard the passenger ship SS *Santa Rosa*. According to Merchant Marine Cadet Corps records, he signed off in June 1941 with eleven and a half months of experience aboard steamships. He spent the next few months in academic studies at Fort Schuyler before returning to sea to acquire additional sea time on diesel-powered ships. On November 18, 1941, Chester signed on as Engine Cadet aboard the MS *Wichita* at the Port of New York for a voyage to Australia. He signed off upon the ship's arrival in New Orleans in early April 1942. This gave him just enough time to sit for his license examinations in New Orleans on May 5 and 7, and return to the ship as its new Junior Third Assistant Engineer on May 20, 1942. Already aboard the ship was Cadet-Midshipman Chester E. Klein, who had signed on a few days earlier as Engine Cadet. Cadet-Midshipman Robert Bole signed on as Deck Cadet the next day. The MS *Wichita* was originally a World War I—era "Hog Islander" but was converted from steam turbine to diesel propulsion in 1929. The ship departed for Africa in late May. After calling at several ports, the final loading port was Takoradi, Ghana and they sailed for the United States loaded with general cargo on September 1, 1942, bound for St. Thomas, U.S. Virgin Islands without any escort.

MS *Wichita*

According to German Navy records, the *Wichita* was located and attacked by *U-516* on the morning of September 19, 1942, when the *Wichita* was about three hundred miles east of Barbados. The submarine's initial attack was unsuccessful. Despite the *Wichita* zigzagging at a speed of about 11 knots, the *U-516* repositioned itself and hit the *Wichita* with a torpedo between the foremast and the bridge. The *Wichita* sank in less than a minute with no survivors.

The *U-516*'s logbook states that the submarine surfaced and searched the sinking area but found neither survivors nor lifeboats. Ceslaus (Chester) Maciorowski, Cadet-Midshipmen Robert J. Bole III, and Chester E. Klein were among the dead.

Based on his sailing experience as an Engine Cadet, Ceslaus A. Maciorowski had already earned the Pacific, Atlantic, and American Defense Bars when he signed on aboard the MS *Wichita* for its final voyage. From his final voyage aboard the MS *Wichita,* he was posthumously awarded the Mariner's Medal, the Combat Bar with star, the Victory Medal, and the Presidential Testimonial Letter.

Chester Maciorowski was the middle of Adam Maciorowski and Camilla Maciorowski's three children and the older of their two sons. Chester's sister, Mary, was the oldest by three years; while John, the youngest, was three years younger. According to the 1940 U.S. Census, Adam Maciorowski was employed as a molder, while Chester was working full time as a machinist.

James LeRoy Maloney

Born:	November 20, 1924
Hometown:	Brooklyn, NY
Class:	1944
Service:	Merchant Marine
Position / Rank:	Third Assistant Engineer
Date / Place of death:	April 9, 1945 / 37-31 N, 64-26 W
Date / Place of burial:	April 9, 1945 / 37-31N, 64-26 W / Lost at Sea
Age:	21

Based on U.S. Coast Guard records, James Maloney applied for his Certificate as Lifeboatman on April 29, 1942, but his Merchant Marine Document as Engine Cadet was not issued until February 3, 1943. Crew lists on file in New York indicate that he signed on as Engine Cadet aboard the SS *Kemp P. Battle* on September 23, 1943, at Baltimore, Maryland. The ship arrived in New York from Algiers on February 5, 1944.

After graduation from Kings Point, James L. Maloney signed articles on March 19, 1945 as Third Assistant Engineer aboard the brand new T2-SE-A1 tanker, SS *Saint Mihiel*, at Sun Shipbuilding in Philadelphia, PA. The *Saint Mihiel* was James Maloney's first ship as a licensed officer. A few days later the *Saint Mihiel* sailed in ballast to Corpus Christi, TX where it picked up a full load of aviation gasoline bound for Cherbourg, France. After leaving Corpus Christi the *Saint Mihiel* was ordered to New York where convoy CU-65, a fast convoy of tankers and other high value ships, was forming. On April 8 the *Saint Mihiel* and the other ships of the convoy sailed from New York and began forming the convoy.

On the night of April 9 the *Saint Mihiel* and another tanker, SS *Nashbulk*, collided. Part of the *Saint Mihiel* cargo of gasoline immediately burst into flame, destroying the navigating bridge located amidships and killing most of the deck officers. The surviving crew abandoned ship as soon as possible and were picked up by the USS *Stewart* (DE 238) after about two hours in the water. Of the fifty crew members and twenty-nine Naval Armed Guard members, only twenty-three of the crew and nineteen Navy sailors survived. Among those missing and presumed dead were Third Assistant Engineer James LeRoy Maloney and Cadet-Midshipmen John

W. Artist and Dante L. Polcari. The two Cadet-Midshipmen were the last Cadet-Midshipmen to die in World War II.

On the morning of April 10, the *Saint Mihiel* was still afloat, although some of the cargo was burning. The ship's senior surviving deck officer, Second Mate Bruno Baretich, assembled some of the *Saint Mihiel*'s survivors to board the *Saint Mihiel* to see if it could be salvaged. Aided by crewmen from the *Stewart* and another escort, Baretich reboarded the ship, put out the fires, and got the ship under way for New York. Although the ship was ultimately a constructive total loss, over 80 percent of the gasoline cargo was saved. For his actions, Baretich, a former vaudeville performer and song arranger for Irving Berlin, received the Merchant Marine Distinguished Service Medal.

Based on the above, James L. Maloney was awarded the Atlantic and Mediterranean-Middle East Bars. For his service aboard the *Saint Mihiel*, he was posthumously awarded the Victory Medal and the Presidential Testimonial Letter.

No information was located regarding his next of kin.

Ralph Henry Nemitz

Born:	February 25, 1922
Hometown:	Chicago, IL
Class:	1943
Service:	U.S. Maritime Service
Position / Rank:	Lieutenant (Junior grade)
Date / Place of death:	June 10, 1945 / Lake Pontchartrain, LA
Date / Place of burial:	June 10, 1945 / Lost at Sea Lake Pontchartrain, LA
Age:	23

Ralph H. Nemitz entered Kings Point in May 1942 for Basic School and received his Cadet documents from the U.S. Coast Guard on June 14, 1942. He received his appointment as Cadet-Midshipman, USNR, on June 11, 1942. Ralph Nemitz began his sea year by signing on aboard the SS *John Carter Rose* as Deck Cadet on August 14, 1942, at Baltimore, Maryland, for the ship's maiden voyage. The ship was loaded with twenty-six thousand drums of gasoline along with other war material. On October 6, the ship was located by *U-201* and *U-202*. Through evasive maneuvering and gunfire from the *John Carter Rose* Armed Guard, the submarines were unable to launch a successful attack on the ship. Eventually, after a thirty-two-hour-long chase over a distance of about 290 miles and being missed by seven torpedoes, the ship was struck aft between number 2 and number 3 holds by one torpedo fired by *U-201*. The resulting explosion ignited the ship's gasoline cargo but did not immediately sink the ship. Because of the burning gasoline, the ship's crew had difficulty launching the lifeboats. Cadet-Midshipman Nemitz took charge of one of the lifeboats, successfully launched it, and was able to successfully maneuver the boat and its occupants to safety.

Surviving the sinking earned Nemitz membership in the Academy's Tin Fish Club, an organization he joined upon his safe return to the United States. Cadet-Midshipman Nemitz then was assigned to the SS *Monmouth* to complete his sea year. After signing off the *Monmouth* on March 3, 1943, he returned to Kings Point to complete his education and prepare for the U.S. Coast Guard examination for his Third Mate's license.

Nemitz graduated from Kings Point on December 3, 1943, with Section A-243. He was commissioned an Ensign, USNR, on December 15, 1943, but did not receive this Third Mate's license until December 28, 1943. With his new license in hand, Ralph Nemitz signed on aboard the SS *John F. Steffen* on January 18, 1944, and served aboard in that capacity until March 24. On April 1, 1944, he was promoted to acting Second Mate and served in that capacity until he signed off on September 4, 1944, a period including the *John F. Steffen's* participation in the Normandy Invasion. Ralph Nemitz received his Second Mate's license October 4, 1944.

On November 17, 1944 Ralph Nemitz wrote to the Chief of Naval Personnel informing him that he had been recalled to Active Duty with the U.S. Maritime Service and assigned to duty as Junior Instructor, U.S. Merchant Marine Cadet Corps at the office of the Officer-in-Charge of Cadet-Midshipmen, Baltimore, MD. In the same letter he requested that his next of kin be designated as his wife, Joan R. Nemitz at their home in Baltimore, MD.

This office apparently closed in January 1945 and Ralph Nemitz was transferred that month to the New Orleans office with similar duties. He was accidentally drowned on June 10, 1945, while sailing on Lake Pontchartrain, Louisiana. His body was not recovered. According to the Navy's Report of Casualty, his wife Joan R. Nemitz was living on Staten Island, NY at the time of his death.

Based on his U.S. Merchant Marine career to the time of his death, Lt. (j.g.) Ralph H. Nemitz, USMS had earned the Combat Bar with star, Atlantic War Zone Bar, the Victory Medal and Presidential Testimonial Letter.

Ralph Nemitz was the only son of Henry F. Nemitz and Frances Nemitz. Ralph's sister Edna was four years younger. According to U.S. Census data, Henry Nemitz was a life insurance salesman. Ralph Nemitz graduated from Chicago's Jones Commercial High School in 1940.

William John O'Neill Jr.

Born:	1922
Hometown:	Woodside, NY
Class:	1944
Service:	USNR
Position / Rank:	Asst. Engineering Officer / Ensign
Date / Place of death:	November 1, 1944 / 10-48N 125-22E
Date/ Place of burial:	November 1, 1944 / Lost at Sea—10-48 N 125-22 E; Tablets of the Missing at Manila American Cemetery
Age:	22

William John O'Neill Jr. graduated from the U.S. Merchant Marine Academy on February 28, 1944. During his sea year, Cadet-Midshipman O'Neill sailed as Engine Cadet aboard the Standard Oil company tanker SS *Dean Emery* from December 9, 1942, until May 28, 1943. During this time, the ship made voyages to the United Kingdom and Caribbean. Ensign O'Neill reported aboard the USS *Abner Read* (DD-526) on June 12, 1944 to become an Assistant Engineering Officer.

USS *Abner Read* (DD 536)

Beginning on October 29, the USS *Abner Read* was employed as a patrol and screen ship in Task Group 77, in Leyte Gulf. On November 1, the *Abner Read* was screening the USS *Mississippi* (BB-41) along with several other battleships and cruisers. These ships were part of the Seventh Fleet, which had destroyed a major Japanese fleet in the Battle of Surigao Strait.

At 0930, the formation was attacked by Japanese kamikaze aircraft, which damaged the USS *Claxton* (DD-571), the USS *Ammen* (DD-527), and the USS *Killen* (DD-593). The *Abner Read* was directed to leave the screen and stand by the *Claxton*, which was alternately lying to and going ahead slowly on one engine. After the *Abner Read* sent a boat with a medical officer, repair personnel, and oxygen over to the *Claxton,* the crippled ship was able to proceed toward the transport area at about 10 knots. The *Abner Read* escorted the vessel, traveling about 1,500 yards ahead of the *Claxton*.

At 1340, a Japanese aircraft crashed into the starboard side of the *Abner Read*, even after a wing had been shot off the aircraft during its attack. The impact caused a raging fire in the entire after portion of the ship, including the after fire room and engine room. There were no communications with the forward part of the ship, and much of the ship's firefighting capability had been disabled. About ten minutes later, one of the ammunition magazines in the after section of the ship exploded. With the ship on fire, listing ten degrees to port, and the rest of the after ammunition magazines ready to explode, the Commanding Officer ordered the crew to abandon ship. The *Abner Read* sank stern first at 1417, after the surviving crew had escaped. Ensign O'Neill was on duty in the after engine room when the ship was attacked. He remained in the after engine room until all his men had been evacuated and then directed the evacuation of wounded men off the stern of the ship. Ensign O'Neill's body was not recovered.

Ensign William J. O'Neill, USNR, was posthumously awarded the Silver Star and the Purple Heart. He is believed to be the first Kings Pointer to be awarded the Silver Star, the nation's third highest military decoration for valor. The recommendation for the award of the Silver Star to Ensign O'Neill states,

> As the officer in charge of the after engine room of a destroyer attacked by a suicidal Japanese dive bomber, he remained steadfastly at his post despite the immediate danger of nearby fire and explosion until all personnel under his authority were evacuated. Making his way to the main deck, he directed, with utter disregard for his own safety, the evacuation of wounded men trapped on the stern by flames, and was thereby instrumental in the major portion of these men reaching safety.

For his merchant marine service, Cadet-Midshipman O'Neill earned the Atlantic War Zone Bar, the Victory Medal, and the Presidential Testimonial Letter. At the time of his death, William J. O'Neill was married to Catherine Ann O'Neill, who was living in Woodside, Queens, New York.

Rafael Ramirez Rivera

Born:	1922
Hometown:	Mayaguez, Puerto Rico
Class:	1942
Service:	Merchant Marine
Position / Rank:	Third Mate
Date / Place of death:	March 11, 1943 / 51-35 N, 28-30 W
Date / Place of burial:	March 11, 1943 / Lost at Sea—51-35 N, 28-30 W
Age:	21

Merchant Marine Academy records indicate that Rafael R. Rivera joined the U.S. Merchant Marine Cadet Corps on November 28, 1940. However, Rafael Rivera was not appointed a Midshipman, USNR, because he did not meet the Navy's minimum standards for height, weight, and number of teeth. Despite not meeting Navy physical standards, he was assigned to the SS *Shawnee*, the SS *Mexico*, the SS *Oriente,* and the SS *Agwiprince* as Deck Cadet. He returned to Kings Point on February 27, 1942, to complete his education and prepare for the U.S. Coast Guard examination for Third Mate. He received his license as Third Mate, ocean, on June 4, 1942.

Rafael R. Rivera signed on aboard the SS *William C. Gorgas* as Third Mate in Mobile, Alabama, on January 27, 1943, shortly after the ship was delivered to the War Shipping Administration from its builder. Joining Rafael Rivera were four U.S. Merchant Marine Academy Cadet-Midshipmen, James Cordua, Edwin Hanzik, James Moon, and Edwin Wiggin. Six weeks later, on March 10, 1943, the *Gorgas* was traveling in Convoy HX-228 en route from New York to Liverpool loaded with general cargo, including nine hundred tons of explosives and a deck cargo of an LCT and two PT boats. The ship carried a crew of forty-one merchant mariners and twenty-six Naval Armed Guard sailors.

At around 2030 on March 10, another ship in the convoy was torpedoed, and the general alarm was sounded. The crew remained on alert, with the Naval Armed Guard manning the battle stations. The weather was hazy, with moderate to heavy swells and ten to fifteen knot winds in bright moonlight. At 2330, the *Gorgas* was hit on the starboard side amidships by a torpedo fired by *U-757*. The explosion destroyed the engine room, instantly killing the three engineers on watch. The Master ordered the crew to abandon ship. By 2350, when 51 survivors in lifeboats and rafts had left the ship, snow had begun falling in higher winds. The *U-757* located one of the boats and questioned the survivors. Shortly thereafter the submarine found the ship still afloat and fired another torpedo to sink it. Immediately after the ship settled under the waves its ammunition cargo exploded, damaging *U-757* so much that it was unable to dive. The submarine was escorted on the surface back to France by another submarine.

The *Gorgas*'s fifty-one survivors were picked up at about 0700 on March 11 by the destroyer HMS *Harvester (H 19)*. Shortly after rescuing the *Gorgas*'s survivors, the *Harvester* sighted *U-444* on the surface. Although the submarine dove to escape the *Harvester*'s gunfire, a depth charge attack brought the submarine to the surface. It is unclear why the *Harvester*'s Commander made his decision, but *U-444* was rammed at full speed by the *Harvester*, severely damaging both ships.

Although *U-444* was able to break free of the *Harvester*, it was rammed again and sunk by the Free French corvette *Aconit (K 58)*. However, the almost motionless *Harvester* was easy prey for *U-432,* which fired two torpedoes, quickly sinking the destroyer with nearly all of its crew and thirty-nine of the *Gorgas*'s survivors. The *Aconit* was immediately on scene attacking the *U-432* with depth charges and forcing it to the surface. The *Aconit* fired at the surfaced submarine and then rammed it, sending

the *U-432*, and all but twenty of its crew, to the bottom. With this vital task accomplished, the *Aconit* rescued twelve *Gorgas*'s survivors, forty-eight survivors of HMS *Harvester*, and twenty-four German sailors from *U-444* and U-432.

After the *Harvester* sank, the Master of the *Gorgas*, Captain James Calvin Ellis Jr., was seen by some of the survivors floating in a life ring in the cold seas. When he was offered a place on a life raft by one of the seamen, he declined, telling the man to keep his place. Soon after, he lost his grip on the life ring and was lost in the icy waters.

Launching of SS William C. Gorgas

Rafael R. Rivera and all four U.S. Merchant Marine Academy Cadet-Midshipmen were among those lost. It is believed that all five survived the initial attack but were lost in the subsequent sinking of HMS *Harvester*.

Rafael R. Rivera was posthumously awarded the Mariner's Medal, the Combat Bar with star, the Defense Bar, the Atlantic War Zone Bar, the Victory Medal, and the Presidential Testimonial Letter. In January 1945, a Liberty ship, built at J. A. Jones Construction Company, Panama City, FL, the SS *Rafael R. Rivera* was named after him.

Floyd Walter Roach

Born: September 18, 1921
Hometown: Park City, UT
Class: 1944
Service: Merchant Marine
Position / Rank: Second Assistant Engineer
Date / Place of death: July 2, 1944 / 3-28S, 74-30 E
Date / Place of burial: July 2, 1944 / Lost at Sea—3-28 S, 74-30 E
Age: 22

Floyd Walter Roach graduated from Kings Point on January 12, 1944. He had previously sailed as Engine Cadet aboard the SS *James Duncan* for its maiden voyage from Portland, Oregon. This single "voyage" lasted from September 18, 1942 to September 5, 1943, when the ship finally arrived in New York from Malta. After graduation, Floyd Roach signed on the SS *Jean Nicolet* on April 28, 1944, at San Francisco, California. Also signing on for the voyage as Third Mate was another Kings Pointer, George M. Rutan.

The *Jean Nicolet* sailed on May 12, 1944, from San Pedro, California, en route to Colombo, Ceylon, with a cargo of heavy machinery, trucks, steel plates, and other general cargo. As usual with wartime practice, the ship also had a deck cargo of steel mooring pontoons, disassembled barges, and more steel plates.

On July 2, 1944, the SS *Jean Nicolet* was traveling unescorted in the Indian Ocean. At 1907, local time, and shortly after securing from evening general quarters, she was attacked by the Japanese submarine I-8. Two torpedoes struck the *Jean Nicolet's* starboard side, thus beginning a chilling tale of death and atrocity.

After the impact, the ship began to list dangerously to port, and the engines were secured in preparation for abandoning ship. The Captain feared the ship would capsize and ordered the crew to abandon around 1920. Four lifeboats and two rafts were successfully lowered, and the entire complement, forty-one crew members, twenty-eight Naval Armed Guard sailors, twenty-six passengers, and one U.S. Army medic, abandoned ship. After the boats were lowered, the submarine began shelling the ship, and fires were seen on the main deck. The Radio Operator managed to send a distress signal before leaving the *Jean Nicolet*, an action that may have saved the lives of the twenty-three men who survived the Japanese atrocities to follow.

The Submarine Commander, Tetsunosuke Ariizumi, ordered the survivors to approach the sub, and all complied, except for five men who managed to pull away on a small raft, apparently unseen. Floyd Roach and the other survivors aboard the submarine were then subjected to brutal and violent treatment by their captors. After their hands were bound behind them with wire, many of the survivors were bayoneted and thrown into the water. Others were made to run through a gauntlet of Japanese crew members armed with steel stanchions, bayonets, and rifles. Many of the men died on the deck of the submarine; while the rest either drowned after being thrown into the water or were finished off by hungry sharks attracted to the scene by the blood in the water.

Only when an approaching plane was heard, several hours after the torpedoing, did the submarine submerge. Many of those left on deck drowned, their hands still bound. A few survivors managed to stay afloat until another plane, flying over at 0630 the next morning, dropped bread, water, and life jackets. A total of twenty-three men were eventually rescued by HMS *Hoxa (T-16)*. However, crewmen, Armed Guard sailors, and passengers, including Floyd Roach, either died at the hands of the Japanese or drowned. The Captain, the Radio Operator, and Francis J. O'Gara, a representative of the War Shipping Administration, were taken on board the submarine as prisoners. Of the three, only Mr. O'Gara survived to be liberated from a Japanese prisoner of war camp in 1945. Presuming that Mr. O'Gara died, the U.S. Maritime Commission named a Liberty ship after him, the only Liberty ship named after a living person.

The *I-8* was sunk later in the war by U.S. Navy destroyers, killing most of the crew, perpetrators of the atrocities not only on the survivors of the *Jean Nicolet*'s but also of those of the Dutch freighter SS *Tjisalak*. Upon learning of the Japanese surrender, Tetsunosuke Ariizumi committed suicide, evading a trail to determine responsibility for his actions. Two surviving crew members were convicted of their crimes by postwar tribunals and sentenced to prison terms.

Based on his service both as a Cadet-Midshipman and licensed officer, Roach was posthumously awarded the Mariner's Medal, the Combat Bar with star, the Atlantic War Zone Bar, the Mediterranean-Middle East

War Zone Bar, the Pacific War Zone Bar, the Victory Medal, and the Presidential Testimonial Letter.

Floyd W. Roach was the second of Earl Soren Roach and Amanda Burgess Roach's three sons. His older brother was Delbert and his younger brother was Dean. Floyd also had four younger sisters, Lona Beth, Vera, Melva, and Julia. According to the 1940 U.S. Census, the family was living in Park City, Utah, where Earl was the bookkeeper at a silver mine. The 1940 census lists both Floyd and Delbert as silver miners.

George Morris Rutan

Born: August 14, 1920
Hometown: Albany, CA
Class: 1944
Service: Merchant Marine
Position / Rank: Third Mate
Date / Place of death: July 2, 1944 / Indian
                          Ocean, 3-28 S, 74-30 E
Date / Place of burial: July 2, 1944 / Indian
                          Ocean, 3-28 S, 74-30
                          E—Lost at Sea
Age: 23

George M. Rutan graduated from the Merchant Marine Academy on January 12, 1944, and was issued a U.S. Coast Guard license as Third Mate at San Francisco, California, on April 12, 1944. He most likely signed shipping articles for what would turn out to be the last voyage of the Liberty ship SS *Jean Nicolet* on April 28, 1944, at San Francisco, California, with his Kings Point classmate Second Assistant Engineer Floyd Roach

The ship sailed on May 12, 1944, from San Pedro, California, en route to Colombo, Ceylon, with a cargo of heavy machinery, trucks, steel plates, and other general cargo. As usual with wartime practice, the ship also had a deck cargo of steel mooring pontoons, disassembled barges, and more steel plates.

On July 2, 1944, the SS *Jean Nicolet* was traveling unescorted in the Indian Ocean. At 1907, local time, and shortly after securing from evening general quarters, she was attacked by the Japanese Submarine I-8. Two torpedoes struck the *Jean Nicolet's* starboard side, thus beginning a chilling tale of death and atrocity.

After the impact, the ship began to list dangerously to port, and the engines were secured in preparation for abandoning ship. The Captain feared the ship would capsize and ordered the crew to abandon around 1920. Four lifeboats and two rafts were successfully lowered, and the entire complement, forty-one crew members, twenty-eight Naval Armed Guard sailors, twenty-six passengers, and one U.S. Army medic, abandoned ship. After the boats were lowered, the submarine began shelling the ship, and fires were seen on the main deck. The Radio

Operator managed to send a distress signal before leaving the *Jean Nicolet*, an action that may have saved the lives of the twenty-three men who survived the Japanese atrocities to follow.

The Submarine Commander, Tetsunosuke Ariizumi, ordered the survivors to approach the sub, and all complied, except for five men who managed to pull away on a small raft, apparently unseen. George Rutan and the other survivors aboard the submarine were then subjected to brutal and violent treatment by their captors. After their hands were bound behind them with wire, many of the survivors were bayoneted and thrown into the water. Others were made to run through a gauntlet of Japanese crew members armed with steel stanchions, bayonets, and rifles. Many of the men died on the deck of the submarine; while the rest either drowned after being thrown into the water or were finished off by hungry sharks attracted to the scene by the blood in the water.

Only when an approaching plane was heard, several hours after the torpedoing, did the submarine submerge. Many of those left on deck drowned, their hands still bound. A few survivors managed to stay afloat until another plane, flying over at 0630 the next morning, dropped bread, water, and life jackets. A total of twenty-three men were eventually rescued by HMS *Hoxa (T-16)*. However, crewmen, Armed Guard sailors, and passengers, including George Rutan, either died at the hands of the Japanese or drowned. The Captain, the Radio Operator, and Francis J. O'Gara, a representative of the War Shipping Administration, were taken on board the submarine as prisoners. Of the three, only Mr. O'Gara survived to be liberated from a Japanese prisoner of war camp in 1945. Presuming that Mr. O'Gara died, the U.S. Maritime Commission named a Liberty ship after him, the only Liberty ship named after a living person.

The *I-8* was sunk later in the war by U.S. Navy destroyers, killing most of the crew, which perpetrated the atrocities on the *Jean Nicolet*'s survivors and those of the Dutch freighter SS *Tjisalak*. Upon learning of the Japanese surrender, Tetsunosuke Ariizumi committed suicide, evading a trail to determine responsibility for his actions. Two surviving crew members were convicted of their crimes by postwar tribunals and sentenced to prison terms.

Based on his service both as a Cadet-Midshipman and licensed officer, Rutan was posthumously awarded the Mariner's Medal, the Combat Bar with star, the Atlantic War Zone Bar, the Mediterranean-Middle East

War Zone Bar, the Pacific War Zone Bar, the Victory Medal, and the Presidential Testimonial Letter.

George M. Rutan was the only son of George C. Rutan and Estelle M. (Mae) Rutan. The senior Rutan's occupation is listed as "driller" in the 1940 U.S. Census, while George M. Rutan is shown as being employed as a professional photographer while attending college.

Isidore Schaffer

Born:	November 14, 1921
Hometown:	Brooklyn, NY
Class:	1943
Service:	Merchant Marine
Position / Rank:	Second Assistant Engineer
Date / Place of death:	March 20, 1945 / 68-26 N, 33-40 E
Date / Place of burial:	March 20, 1945 / Lost at Sea—68-26 N, 33-40 E; Memorial at Baron Hirsch Cemetery, Staten Island, NY
Age:	23

Isidore Schaffer entered Kings Point in late 1941. On February 27, 1942, he signed on aboard the SS *Expositor* as Engine Cadet to begin his sea year. After surviving a convoy to Murmansk, Russia (PQ-15), he was reassigned to the SS *Exiria* to complete his sea year. He returned to the Academy in August 1942 to complete his studies and receive his license as Third Assistant Engineer. Following his graduation, he signed on as Third Assistant Engineer aboard the SS *John L. Motley*. He subsequently served aboard the SS *Exchange* before sailing as Second Assistant Engineer aboard the SS *Exminster* in 1944. After working aboard the SS *Exminster,* he served aboard the SS *William D. Burnham* until that vessel failed to rendezvous with its convoy and was sunk by torpedo fire from *U-978* on November 23, 1944. Eighteen crew members died in the attack, but Schaffer survived, earning him membership in the Tin Fish Club. He returned to New York aboard the British passenger/troopship SS *Aquitania*, arriving on January 12, 1945; he was ready to go to sea again.

After signing on aboard the SS *Thomas Donaldson* in February 1945, the ship sailed for Murmansk, Russia, via Gourock, Scotland, with a cargo of six thousand tons of explosives and general cargo including a deck cargo of railroad locomotives. On March 12, 1945, the twenty-six-ship convoy JW-65 sailed from Gourock escorted by two aircraft carriers, a cruiser, and eighteen smaller escorts. At 1220 (local) March 20, when the ship was about twenty miles from Kola Inlet, the approach to Murmansk, the ship was struck amidships by a torpedo fired by *U-968*. The impact destroyed the engine room, killing everyone on watch at the time, including Second Assistant Engineer Isidore Schaffer. Despite the damage and rapid flooding, the chief engineer, First Assistant Engineer, and Third Mate attempted to rescue the three men on watch in the engine room. However, by the time they got to the engine room, it was already completely flooded. Due to the ship's cargo of explosives, the Captain ordered the crew to abandon ship shortly after the torpedo struck. The Armed Guard was ordered to abandon ship at 1230. The survivors were rescued by HMS *Bamborough Castle* (K 412), one of the convoy's escorts. One of the survivors, the deck maintenance man, died aboard the *Bamborough Castle*.

However, since the ship did not immediately sink, the Master and several crewmen remained aboard to assist with towing and possible salvage of the ship and its cargo. There was no fire on board the ship, but a crack was observed in the hull, amidships on the port side. The *Thomas Donaldson* was taken in tow by HMS *Honeysuckle* (K 27). At about 1630, tow was passed to a Russian tugboat, but the ship sank shortly thereafter. Of the total complement of sixty-nine men (merchant crew plus Naval Armed Guard) the only fatalities were the three men in the engine room and a deck maintenance man wounded during the attack.

For his service aboard the SS *Thomas Donaldson* and his previous merchant marine service, Isidore Schaffer was posthumously awarded the Mariner's Medal, the Combat Bar with two stars, the Atlantic War Zone Bar, the Mediterranean-Middle East War Zone Bar, the Victory Medal, and the Presidential Testimonial Letter. He would also have been eligible for award of the Soviet Commemorative Medal awarded in 1995 by the then Soviet Union to U.S. Merchant Mariners who sailed in the Murmansk convoys.

Isidore Schaffer, known as "Izzy" during his time at the Academy, was the third of Joseph Schaffer and Rose Schaffer's six sons. His older brothers were Meyer and Herman, while his younger brothers were Roy, James, and Harold. He also had an older sister, Florence. By 1940, Joseph Schaffer had died, leaving Rose Schaffer a widow. Her four oldest children, including Isidore, all worked to support the family. Isidore's occupation is shown as being a helper in a metal trades company while attending his final year of high school.

The April 1943 edition of *Polaris* described Isidore Schaffer upon his graduation:

Isidore Schaffer hails from Brooklyn—'nuff sed. Izzy is good natured and easy going. Loves music and plays the phonograph in his spare time. Remembers the time he aspired to become a taffy puller. Loves Academy life . . .

On September 20, 2010, a wreath was laid over the site of the SS *Thomas Donaldson*'s sinking by Russian sailors and crew members from the USS *Taylor* (FFG 50) to honor Isidore Schaffer and his two shipmates. The visit by the USS *Taylor* was part of ceremonies commemorating the sixty-fifth anniversary of the end of World War II. The USS *Taylor* was the first U.S. warship to visit Murmansk since 1945.

William John Secunda

Born:	1924
Hometown:	Butler, PA
Class:	1943
Service:	Merchant Marine
Position / Rank:	Third Assistant Engineer
Date / Place of death:	April 19, 1944 / 54-15 N, 163-30 W
Date / Place of burial:	April 19, 1944 / Lost at Sea—54-15 N, 163-30 W
Age:	20

William J. Secunda reported to Kings Point in early 1942. On June 26, 1942, he signed on aboard the SS *William Johnson* as Engine Cadet to begin his sea year. Following his graduation, he signed on as Third Assistant Engineer aboard the SS *John Straub*, which had been delivered in December 1943.

On the night of April 18/19, 1944, the SS *John Straub* was sailing off the coast of Sanak Island, Alaska, en route from Seattle, Washington, to Attu Island in the Aleutians, with a cargo of diesel oil and high-octane gasoline. At about midnight, local time, the ship was destroyed by a series of violent explosions. The ship broke in half just aft of the deckhouse and engine room. The forward section of the ship sank within three minutes, while the stern remained afloat for fourteen hours. Because of the speed with which the forward section sank, no order was given to abandon ship.

Initially, the loss of the ship was attributed to either brittle fracture of the steel in the hull in the Arctic cold or some other internal source. However, postwar investigations proved that the ship was sunk by a torpedo fired by the Japanese Submarine *I-180*. Ironically, the Navy had declared the area "submarine-free" before the sinking.

The only survivors of the *Straub* were thirteen Naval Armed Guard members, the Third Mate, and an Able Seaman, all of whom were on the stern section of the ship at the time of the explosion. The survivors were picked up about nine hours after the stern section sank.

For his service aboard the SS *Joseph Straub* and his sea year, William J. Secunda was posthumously awarded the Mariner's Medal, the Combat Bar with star, the Atlantic War Zone Bar, the Pacific War Zone Bar, the Victory Medal, and the Presidential Testimonial Letter.

William Secunda was the oldest son and third of Joseph Secunda and Mary Secunda's six children. His older sisters were Mary and Elizabeth. John, Helen, and Paul were his younger siblings. According to the 1940 U.S. Census, Joseph Secunda was a blacksmith. Mary and Elizabeth are also identified working outside the home.

Walter Paul Seperski

Born:	1918
Hometown:	Pepperell, MA
Class:	1942
Service:	Merchant Marine
Position / Rank:	A. B. Seaman
Date / Place of death:	November 2, 1942 / 01-25 N, 36-22 W
Date / Place of burial:	November 2, 1942 / Lost at Sea—01-25 N, 36-22 W;
Age:	24

No Photograph Available

Walter P. Seperski was a Cadet-Midshipman graduate from the U.S. Merchant Marine Cadet Corps in 1942. As a Deck Cadet he sailed aboard the SS *George Washington* and SS *Manhattan* in 1940. In 1941 he sailed aboard the SS *Alcoa Ranger* and SS *West Honaker* from which he signed off in March 1942.

It is unknown why he signed on as A. B. Seaman aboard the freighter SS *Examelia*, a World War I "Hog Islander" at New York, NY on May 22, 1942. Perhaps even six months after the start of World War II shipping jobs were still scarce. In any event, two Kings Point Cadet-Midshipmen, Bernard Spillman and Schuster also joined the ship on the same day.

On October 9, 1942 the ship was traveling unescorted and not zig-zagging, about 50 miles south of the Cape of Good Hope bound from Colombo, Ceylon to Cape Town, South Africa loaded with a cargo of chrome ore, jute and hemp. According to a report submitted by the Commanding Officer of the ship's Naval Armed Guard, at 0148 local time on October 9, 1942 the ship was hit by a torpedo on the starboard side at the bulkhead between the Fire Room and Engine Room. Post-war reports identify the submarine that fired the torpedo as *U-68*. The torpedo explosion immediately disabled the engines and the ship sank in minutes.

Walter Seperski and Cadet-Midshipman Spilman survived the sinking of the SS *Examelia*, although Cadet-Midshipman Samuel Schuster perished. After their rescue, Seperski, Spilman and the other survivors were landed at Port Elizabeth, South Africa. They were then taken by train to Cape Town where they could catch a ship bound for the United

States. At Cape Town the *Examilia's* survivors were assigned to the Dutch cargo-passenger ship MV *Zaandam* for return to the United States. In addition to the *Examelia's* survivors, the *Zaandam's* 169 passengers were mostly merchant seamen from other ships which had met the same fate as the *Examelia*.

At 1627 on November 2, 1942, when the *Zaandam* was about 400 miles north of Receife, Brazil, it was torpedoed by *U-174*. The torpedo struck the vessel at the port engine room, destroying the main engines and the decks above the engine room. The crew prepared to abandon ship, but the Captain, who believed that it was only a minor engine room explosion, ordered them to remain on board. Ten minutes later, another torpedo struck the *Zaandam*, between Number 2 and 3 hold on the port side. At this point, the *Zaandam* began to sink rapidly. The crew was able to launch three of the lifeboats and several rafts. The #2 lifeboat capsized, but the crew managed to right the boat. Sharks, attracted to the scene by blood in the water, caused many casualties.
Three lifeboats with survivors were picked up within days of the sinking. However, three survivors spent 83 days in life raft, before being rescued by the USS *PC 576*. In total, 165 of the 299 individuals on the *Zaandam* survived the sinking. However, 74 of the 169 passengers, including Walter P. Seperski and Cadet-Midshipman Bernard W. Spilman perished.

Based on his service as Deck Cadet and as A. B. Seaman aboard the *SS Examelia* Walter P. Seperski was posthumously awarded the Mariners Medal, Combat Bar with two stars, the Atlantic War Zone Bar, Pacific War Zone Bar, the Victory Medal, and the Presidential Testimonial Letter.

Walter was the second of William Seperski and Stella Seperski's four sons. The Seperski's were Polish immigrants. Walter's only sister, Edna, was two years older. Stanley, Walter's older brother was three years older, while his two younger brothers, Louis and Edward, were three years and twelve years younger, respectively. In 1930 William Seperski was employed at a paper mill, but the 1940 U.S. Census does not list an occupation for him. However, the same census indicates that Stanley and Louis were working in forestry. The two censuses indicate that the family had lived in New Hampshire and Pennsylvania before settling in Massachusetts in the 1920's.

Edward Stanley Sherman

Born: Unknown
Hometown: Port Jefferson, NY
Class: 1943
Service: Merchant Marine
Position / Rank: Second Mate
Date / Place of death: January 15, 1945 /
                           Norfolk Harbor, Virginia
Date / Place of burial: Unknown
Age: Unknown

Edward Sherman signed on as Second Mate aboard the SS *Zebulon Pike* on December 28, 1944, at the Port of New York. He was joined by his Academy classmate Arthur C. Forsyth, who signed on as Third Mate the same day. The ship sailed from New York to Norfolk, Virginia, on January 1 to load cargo. On January 15, 1945, at 1900, Arthur Forsyth and Edward Sherman left their vessel. The ship, the SS *Zebulon Pike*, was moored in Norfolk Harbor at the U.S. Army base. According to the *Zebulon Pike* official logbook, at 0245, on January 16, the Master was informed by Norfolk Police that the two men apparently commandeered a taxi, drove the taxi into a body of water, and drowned. Before the ship sailed on January 18, the personal effects and wages of Arthur Forsyth and Edward Sherman were left at the U.S. Shipping Commissioner's office for return to their families.

Forsyth and Sherman had served aboard the same ship at least twice. Both men signed on as Deck Cadets aboard the Liberty ship SS *Caleb Strong* on November 5, 1942. The men signed on as third and Second Mate, respectively, aboard the Liberty ship *Robert F. Stockton* at New York, New York, on January 20, 1944, and signed off on May 2, 1944, at the same port. At the time they signed aboard the *Stockton*, Forsyth is shown as having six months sea time, while Sherman had seven months' time.

Edwin Ray Stauffacher Jr.

Born:	January 22, 1920
Hometown:	Glendale, CA
Class:	1944
Service:	Merchant Marine
Position / Rank:	Third Mate
Date / Place of death:	On or about January 2, 1945 / Mindoro Island, Philippines
Date / Place of burial:	Unknown
Age:	24

After completing Basic School at San Mateo, Edwin Stauffacher sailed as Deck Cadet aboard the SS *William B. Allison* and SS *Kit Carson*. It is likely that when Edwin Stauffacher signed on aboard the SS *John M. Clayton,* it was his first licensed position aboard ship.

The *John M. Clayton* was one of several merchant ships that carried troops and supplies to support the amphibious landings at Mindoro, in the Philippine Islands. On January 2, 1945, the ship was anchored off of White Beach, Mangarin Bay, after having unloaded all of her 401 Army troops and most of her cargo, which included Army vehicles.

At 1540, the ship was attacked by a Japanese aircraft with its motor silenced. The plane strafed the ship, riddling the lifeboats with bullets and destroying one of them. The plane dropped one bomb, which struck the port side of number 3 hold, exploding upon impact. The explosion blew off the hatch covers and started a fire in number 3 hold. The fire was put out in ten minutes and the ship was beached the next morning to prevent its sinking. Two members of the crew were killed, along with four of the twenty-nine Naval Armed Guard sailors. Among those lost was Third Mate Edwin R. Stauffacher, who was badly burned in the attack.

Two Academy Cadets were on board the *John Clayton* at the time of the attack. Cadet-Midshipman Lewis Little recalls the attack, the injuries sustained by his classmate, Cadet-Midshipman Paul White, and the efforts of the crew to save the ship:

> On the night of 1/1/45 while our vessel lay at anchor in Mindoro Gulf, Philippine Islands, an alert was sounded at 2030. Japanese planes

were spotted and immediately attacked us. The night was dark and the weather extremely calm. At the time of our attack, there were four other cargo vessels in the Gulf.

At 2340 [ship's time] while I was at my assigned post in the engine room, a torpedo dropped from the enemy aircraft hit in Number 3 hold causing fire which gutted the forward part of the deckhouse. Six men were burned alive and many other crew members received severe burns. We immediately fought the fire with water drawn from the engine room and after a difficult struggle were able to put the fire out although the vessel had been slowly sinking. Not many hands became excited during the attack and those few that did were immediately calmed down. The vast majority of the crew members conducted themselves with extreme calmness and coolness.

When the Captain gave the order to abandon ship, we went over the port side and were immediately placed into Army LCMs which were standing by. We were taken ashore where we remained for 11 days.

Cadet-Midshipman Paul V. White rec'd second degree burns on his hands and face. He was doing well at Mindoro in an Army hospital. The last time I saw him was when he was placed aboard a hospital plane and flown out of Mindoro.

Based on his service aboard the SS *John M. Clayton* and his previous merchant marine service, Edwin Stauffacher was posthumously awarded the Mariner's Medal, the Combat Bar with star, the Pacific War Zone Bar, the Philippine Liberation Bar, the Victory Medal, and the Presidential Testimonial Letter.

Edwin Stauffacher was the only child of Edwin R. Stauffacher Sr. and May Elizabeth McCann Stauffacher. According to the 1940 U.S. Census, Edwin Sr. was employed as an electrical engineer for the local power company. After graduating from high school, Edwin attended Glendale Junior College before applying to the Merchant Marine Academy.

Niles Kendall Stevens

Born:	November 4, 1921
Hometown:	Linesville, PA
Class:	1944
Service:	Merchant Marine
Position / Rank:	Second Mate
Date / Place of death:	February 23, 1945 / North of Wadi Seidna Airport, Khartoum, Sudan
Date / Place of burial:	March 1, 1945 / New Christian Cemetery, Khartoum, Sudan; Date Unknown / North Africa American Cemetery, Carthage, Tunisia, Plot D, Row 11, Grave 12
Age:	23

Niles K. Stevens enrolled in the U.S. Maritime Service on December 26, 1941. He received his initial training aboard the training ship SS *American Sailor,* which was located at the Coast Guard/U.S. Maritime Commission Training Station at Port Hueneme, California. However, although Niles Stevens received his Coast Guard papers as Ordinary Seaman/Wiper on April 9, 1942, he signed on aboard the SS *Santa Ana* as Deck Cadet on July 3, 1942, at San Francisco. Thus, he may well have been transferred from the *American Sailor* to the Basic School at San Mateo. Following his sea year aboard the *Santa Ana* in the South Pacific, Niles Kendall returned to Kings Point to complete his education and sit for his Coast Guard license as Third Mate. He signed on as Third Mate aboard the tanker SS *Red Canyon* on February 26, 1944. Niles Stevens made several voyages to the United Kingdom aboard the SS *Red Canyon* and was promoted to Second Mate in late July 1944.

On October 12, 1944, Niles Stevens signed on aboard the SS *George H. Williams* as Second Mate. He was signed off shipping articles on February 17, 1945, at Aden, Yemen, for an appendectomy. Within days, he was apparently sufficiently recovered to rejoin the SS *George H. Williams* for the return voyage to New York. By February 22, 1945, he had managed to make his way from Aden to Khartoum, Sudan. On the morning of February 23, 1945, Niles Kendall was one of the passengers aboard an Army Transportation Corps C-46A (number 42-96541) bound for Cairo, Egypt. The aircraft took off from Wadi Seidna Airport, a Royal air force base about twenty miles north of Khartoum, Sudan, around sunrise (0354 [GMT]).

Curtiss C-46A "Commando"

According to the log of radio traffic in the aircraft accident report, the takeoff was about one hour late for unknown reasons. After clearing airfield, the plane reported at 0402 (GMT) that it was climbing to eight thousand feet and would check in by radio at 0550. When the plane failed to check in at this time and no contact could be made for six minutes, the plane was declared overdue. When the limits of its known fuel load were past, the aircraft was declared missing. American, British, and Sudanese search efforts located the aircraft on February 27, 1945, about 116 miles north of Wadi Seidna Airport. A search and rescue party arrived at the crash site the following day.

Interviews with three witnesses and analysis of the crash site found that a fire started in the aircraft's left engine and spread into the structure of the left wing, which then fell away from the aircraft. The rest of the aircraft burned when it crashed into the earth, instantly killing all of the crew and passengers. Witnesses said that at the time the left wing collapsed, the plane was headed south, in the direction of Wadi Seidna. It was presumed that the pilot was attempting to return to Wadi Seidna due to the engine fire.

Niles Stevens's remains were initially interred in the New Christian Cemetery, Khartoum, after a Protestant service. However, after World War II, the remains of all those interred in temporary cemeteries were either returned to their next of kin or interred in a cemetery administered by the American Battle Monuments Commission.

Today, Niles K. Stevens's remains rest in Carthage, Tunisia at the North Africa American Cemetery, plot D, row 11, grave 12. The remains of two other Kings Pointers, Thomas Kellegrew and Otto Kern, are also buried there.

Based on his service both as a Cadet and licensed officer, Niles K. Stevens was posthumously awarded the Atlantic War Zone, the Mediterranean-Middle East War Zone and Pacific War Zone Bars, the Victory Medal, and the Presidential Testimonial Letter.

Niles K. Stevens was the youngest son of Myrl Levi Stevens and Pansie Kendall Stevens. According to the 1940 U.S. Census, Myrl Stevens was employed as a trackman for the Pennsylvania Railroad. At the time, Gordon, Niles's slightly older brother, was working as a clerk in an Atlantic & Pacific Tea Company grocery store.

In December 2011, Niles's brother, Gordon L. Stevens, of Lake City, Pennsylvania, wrote the following about him:

> My brother was born in 1921 in Linesville, PA. During high school he played varsity basketball. He graduated in 1939.
>
> Niles was always noted for his fascination with words. He was extremely articulate and he used his incredible vocabulary to challenge his teachers and parents. He used his skills to acquire two jobs simultaneously during the Great Depression while most individuals felt fortunate to have one.
>
> Although Niles was raised in a small town, he had dreams of becoming a cartoonist and traveling to see the world. Shortly after graduation from high school he and a school friend drove to Florida to work in the tourist business. Soon after he and his friend purchased a new car and drove to California where he worked in the ship buildering industry. He soon became foreman.
>
> While attending the Merchant Marine Academy my parents and I went by train to visit him at Kings Point.

Although Niles had a short life, I believe he had a full one and some of his dreams were realized. He was able to travel to places most of us only read about. I can only imagine what he would have achieved if his life had not ended so soon.

**Stevens family marker,
Linesville Cemetery, Linesville, PA**

Lloyd Stanley Strom

Born:	November 4, 1921
Hometown:	San Francisco, CA
Class:	1944
Service:	USNR
Position / Rank:	Asst. Engineering Officer / Ensign
Date / Place of death:	November 10, 1944 / Seeadler Harbor, Admiralty Islands, New Guinea
Date / Place of burial:	November 10, 1944 / Lost at Sea—Seeadler Harbor, Admiralty Islands, New Guinea; Tablets of the Missing at Manila American Cemetery Manila, Philippines
Age:	23

Lloyd S. Strom was appointed a Midshipman, USNR, on October 9, 1942, but was hospitalized for a hernia the following day. By November 20, he shipped out as Engine Cadet aboard the SS *Phillipa*. He graduated with Section A-156 on January 28, 1944, and was commissioned an Ensign, U.S. Naval Reserve.

USS *Mount Hood* (AE 11)

After training at Newport, Rhode Island, Ensign Strom reported to the pre-commissioning detail for the USS *Mount Hood (AE 11)*, a U.S. Maritime Commission C2-S-AJ1 cargo ship being converted into an ammunition ship.

Ensign Lloyd Strom officially reported aboard the USS *Mount Hood* upon its commissioning on July 1, 1944, as one of three Assistant Engineering Officers.

After a brief shakedown cruise, the ship reported for duty on August 5, 1944, loaded ammunition for Pacific Fleet ships, and sailed for Manus, Admiralty Islands, on August 21, 1944. On September 22, 1944, the *Hood* arrived at Manus and anchored in Seeadler Harbor, a major repair and logistical support site for ships participating in the Philippine invasion. The *Hood* was a primary provider of ammunition for all ships attached to the Third Fleet, and she was kept busy over the next weeks supplying ammunition to other ships in the harbor. Though the harbor had certain designated berths for ammunition ships, the USS *Hood* ended up taking a berth closer to the center of the harbor in order to more easily transfer ammunition to other ships.

The USS *Mount Hood* had an estimated 3,800 tons of ammunition aboard on the morning of November 10, 1944. Just before 0900, the ship was observed to have a landing craft alongside with aerial depth charges aboard while five hundred pound bombs were being loaded into the Number Three Hold from another landing craft. Meanwhile, .50-caliber machine gun ammunition in boxes were sitting on the deck of a nearby pontoon lighter, waiting to be loaded onto the *Hood*. Several other landing craft were also in the area, carrying unknown cargo. All five of the ship's cargo holds were open and being worked by, what the Board of Inquiry called, ". . . a relatively inexperienced crew."

USS *Mount Hood* (AE-11), Seeadler Harbor, Manus, Admiralty Islands, November 10, 1944

At around 0855, the ship's cargo detonated, completely disintegrating the ship as well as the nearby landing craft.

Everyone on board, including Ensign Lloyd Strom, was killed in the explosion. The Board of Inquiry concluded that there were several irregularities with the cargo and its handling that could have contributed to the disaster.

Ensign Lloyd Strom, USNR, was posthumously awarded the American Area Campaign Medal, the Asiatic-Pacific Campaign Medal, and the World War II Victory Medal for his U.S. Navy Service. For his merchant marine service, he had already earned the Pacific War Zone Bar, the Victory Medal, and the Presidential Testimonial Letter.

Lloyd S. Strom was the only son and oldest child of Louis Strom and Emily Strom. The 1930 U.S. Census identifies Louis Strom as a seaman working aboard a freighter. However, a 1941 San Francisco city directory indicates that Louis was employed as a stationary engineer. At the time of his death, Lloyd Strom was married to Rosemary Strom, who was living in San Francisco.

Keith William Treseder

Born:	January 20, 1921
Hometown:	Magna, UT
Class:	1944
Service:	Merchant Marine
Position / Rank:	Third Mate
Date / Place of death:	April 6, 1945 / Kerama Retto, Okinawa
Date / Place of burial:	April 6, 1945 / Lost at Sea—Kerama Retto, Okinawa
Age:	24

Keith W. Treseder, a 1944 graduate of Kings Point, signed on as Third Mate aboard the SS *Logan Victory* before it sailed from San Francisco, California, on February 18, 1945. Also on board were Cadet-Midshipmen William W. Lau (engine) and John R. Hawken (deck). Treseder had previously sailed as Junior Third Mate aboard the SS *Guatemala Victory* on a voyage to the South Pacific from September to December 1944. Cadet-Midshipman Treseder began his sea year aboard the SS *President Tyler* in February 1943. He subsequently served aboard the SS *Jane Adams* and then signed on as Deck Cadet aboard the SS *John G. Brady* on October 12, 1943, for the ship's maiden voyage to the South Pacific. He signed off in June 1944 to return to Kings Point and the completion of his training.

The SS *Logan Victory* sailed from San Francisco without escort to bases at Eniwetok and Ulithi delivering Army ammunition. From Ulithi, the *Logan Victory* sailed in a convoy to Kerama Retto, the logistics base for the invasion of Okinawa. At 0100, on April 6, 1945, shortly after arriving at Kerama Retto, the *Logan Victory* was ordered to shift to an explosives anchorage, which had been established between Hokaji Shima and Koba Shima. At 0700, the SS *Logan Victory* anchored between the SS *Hobbs Victory* and the SS *Pierre Victory* in a triangular formation, with the *Logan Victory* at the northern apex. The *Logan Victory*'s crew and Armed Guard detachment had been at "battle stations" off and on since 0330.

According to eyewitness accounts and after action reports, an attack by approximately eight kamikaze aircraft began at 1640 with an attack by a single engine plane on the SS *Pierre Victory*. According to

Cadet-Midshipman Hawken's report on the loss of the ship, the Master, Chief Mate, and Second Mate were all on the bridge when the attacks began. It is unknown where Third Mate Keith Treseder was. Gun crews from the three ships in the explosives anchorage and other ships in the vicinity began firing at the attacking planes. The Commanding Officer of the *Logan Victory*'s Armed Guard unit claimed that the aircraft was destroyed by the *Logan Victory*'s five-inch gun. Immediately afterward (1645), a second kamikaze was sighted coming in from north end of Koba Shima. Although the kamikaze was seen to be hit numerous times by the *Logan Victory*'s machine guns, they failed to disable the airplane. The kamikaze struck the ship on the port side, just aft of the deckhouse, at 1647.

Gasoline and incendiaries aboard the kamikaze caused the *Logan Victory* to burst into fire. Spread by exploding ammunition, the fire was soon out of control. As a result, the ship was abandoned at 1657 in the one surviving lifeboat and several rafts. The ship sank at 1902, about two and a half hours after being hit. The survivors were picked up by the USS *Strategy (AM 308)*, YMS *86,* and other small naval craft.
Cadet-Midshipman William A. Lau, Engine Cadet, recounted the attack in his report on the loss of the SS *Logan Victory:*

> The writer's watch was from four to eight in the engine room. About 1615, the Chief Engineer came down and told those in the engine room that a Japanese suicide plane had crashed into an LST. The guns of subject vessel were firing continuously. About 1645, a loud explosion aft of the deckhouse was heard. The writer was standing by the throttle. Flames and large pieces of white hot metal came tumbling down on top of the turbines. The lights went out immediately. The only light came from the flames.

> The Fireman was first up the ladder, then the Second Assistant Engineer shut off the throttle and the writer followed him up the ladder and came out on the main deck passageway on the port side. The entire after part of the deckhouse was a mass of flames so the writer ran through the passageway to the forward part of the house and up the ladder to the boat deck. On the ladder were all types of wood and debris that had been blown through the passageway. The writer was trying to get to his room but as the flames were coming down the passageway it was apparent that he could not, so he ran to the port side of the boat deck. Both lifeboats were on fire. The Second Mate was seen to jump over the side and many more were doing the

same. The writer followed and was soon swimming faster than he ever had before. His first thoughts were that the ship would blow up any minute and to get away as far as possible.

Keith Treseder was one of twelve members of the *Logan Victory*'s fifty-six-man crew killed in the attack along with three members of the Naval Armed Guard and an Army officer.

For his merchant marine service, Keith W. Treseder was posthumously awarded the Mariner's Medal, the Combat Bar with star, the Pacific War Zone Bar, the Victory Medal, and the Presidential Testimonial Letter.

According to Treseder's niece Julie Treseder Cadogan, Keith W. Treseder was the fourth of William Q. Treseder and Julia Worthen Treseder's six sons. Quillian, Earnest, and Rex were Keith's older brothers. His younger brothers were Glen and Gordon. Julie is Glen's daughter. Keith's father was a Deputy U.S. Marshall. Keith entered the San Mateo Basic School on January 18, 1943, and graduated from Kings Point in 1944.

Donald Joseph Tynan

Born:	August 16, 1922
Hometown:	Yonkers, NY
Class:	1943
Service:	Merchant Marine
Position / Rank:	Third Assistant Engineer
Date / Place of death:	April 16, 1944 / 40-05 N, 69-24 W
Date / Place of burial:	April 16, 1944 / Lost at Sea—40-05 N, 69-24 W
Age:	21

Donald J. Tynan was appointed a Midshipman, USNR, on September 18, 1942, and graduated in January 1944 with Section A-144. He signed on as Third Assistant Engineer aboard the SS *John Sergeant* at the Port of New York on January 19, 1944. In late March 1944, the SS *Pan Pennsylvania* returned to New York from a voyage to the United Kingdom. Donald J. Tynan signed on as Third Assistant Engineer for the next voyage.

On April 15, 1944, the six-month-old SS *Pan Pennsylvania*, at that time the largest tanker in the U.S. Merchant Marine, sailed from New York in Convoy CU-21 loaded with 140,000 barrels of gasoline bound for Barry, Wales. The following morning, the ship was about two hundred miles east of the mouth of the New York Harbor while the convoy finished forming for the voyage to England. At approximately 0805, the *Pan Pennsylvania* was torpedoed by *U-550*. The torpedo struck on the port side at number 8 tank. Survivors later noted a "gusher of red" pouring from the side of the ship.

Some crew members who had been having breakfast at the time of the attack jumped overboard; others tried to launch one of the lifeboats. The engines were reversed and secured while the ship settled at the stern. At 0845, the Captain, noting that the engine room was on fire while fumes from the cargo were getting "heavy and sickening," ordered the remaining crew to abandon ship. The survivors of the *Pan Pennsylvania* were picked up by three of the convoy escorts, USS *Peterson (DE 152)*, USS *Gandy (DE 764)*, and USS *Joyce (DE 317)*. Later that morning, these ships sank *U-550*. The hulk of the SS *Pan Pennsylvania* capsized but remained afloat until it was sunk by aircraft on April 18, 1944.

SS *Pan Pennsylvania* burning while its assailant, *U-550*, sinks

Of the *Pan Pennsylvania*'s fifty merchant crew and the thirty-one-man Armed Guard detachment, fifteen crew members, including Donald J. Tynan and ten Navy sailors died in the attack.

For his merchant marine service, Donald J. Tynan was posthumously awarded the Mariner's Medal, the Combat Bar with Star, the Atlantic War Zone Bar, the Victory Medal, and the Presidential Testimonial Letter.

Donald J. Tynan was the third of Captain Thomas J. Tynan and Veronica Kelly Tynan's four children. The oldest child was Donald's sister, also named Veronica. His brothers were Brandon (one year older) and Robert (five years younger). When Donald was a boy, his father was already sailing as Master. However, since the 1940 U.S. Census identifies Veronica Tynan as a widow, Thomas J. Tynan died during the 1930s. The 1940 U.S. Census also indicates that Veronica Tynan was employed as a "cafeteria operator" in a public high school, while Brandon was employed as a clerk in a public school. Donald's younger brother, Robert, graduated from Kings Point in 1950.

Richard I. Victorino

Born:	October 11, 1921
Hometown:	Morgan Hill, CA
Class:	1944
Service:	Merchant Marine
Position / Rank:	Second Mate
Date / Place of death:	November 7, 1945 / Near Los Banos, CA
Date / Place of burial:	November 1945 / Santa Clara Mission Cemetery, Santa Clara, CA
Age:	24

Richard Victorino, a 1944 graduate of the U.S. Merchant Marine Academy, was accidentally shot in the stomach at the "Duck Club," seven miles northwest of Los Banos, California, on November 7, 1945. He was declared dead at 1225 that day.

After his appointment as midshipman, USNR, on October 12, 1942, Richard sailed as Deck Cadet aboard the SS *Benjamin Curtis* in 1942 and 1943. Crew lists indicate that he signed on aboard the SS *B. F. Irvine* as Second Mate on February 11, 1945, for a voyage to the South Pacific, returning to Seattle on August 9, 1945. He had previously served as Third Mate and Junior Third Mate aboard the SS *Robin Wentley* in 1944 on voyages to the South Pacific, including Saipan, Eniwetok Atoll, and Pearl Harbor, Hawaii.

Memorial at Santa Clara Mission Cemetery

Based on his merchant marine service, at the time of his death, Richard I. Victorino had earned the Pacific War Zone Bar, the Victory Medal, and the Presidential Testimonial Letter.

Richard Victorino was married to Dorothy Victorino at the time of his death. He was the older of

John I. Victorino and Mary Bettencourt Victorino's two sons; his younger brother was named John.

According to the 1930 and 1940 U.S. Census, Richard's father was a dairyman at a dairy farm outside of Gilroy, California.

Kenneth Alva Waters

Born:	January 13, 1920
Hometown:	Hartford City, IN
Class:	1943
Service:	Merchant Marine
Position / Rank:	Third Mate
Date / Place of death:	September 21, 1943 / Khorramshahr, Iran
Date / Place of burial:	September 21, 1943 / Christian Cemetery, Khorramshahr, Iran
Age:	22

Kenneth A. Waters reported to the U.S. Maritime Commission Cadet School at Algiers, Louisiana, on the evening of September 22, 1941. After completing his initial training, he was detached on December 4, 1941, to join the SS *Zoella Lyke*s as Deck Cadet. He signed on aboard the SS *Zoella Lykes* on December 23, 1941, and remained aboard until he signed off on September 30, 1942. He then reported to Kings Point, where he was assigned to Section A-105 before completing his training at Kings Point in April 1943. After graduation, he served as Third Mate aboard the SS *Francis Lewis* from May to July 1943.

On July 15, 1943, at Philadelphia, Pennsylvania, Kenneth A. Waters signed on aboard the SS *Exhibitor* as Third Mate. The ship sailed without escort on the evening of July 22, 1943, for Freemantle, Australia, via the Panama Canal. Upon arrival at Freemantle, the *Exhibitor* was assigned to a convoy for the voyage to the Persian Gulf. The *Exhibitor* arrived in the Persian Gulf on September 12, 1943. By September 19, the *Exhibitor* was anchored off the Iranian port of Khorramshahr and began discharging its cargo.

At 1505, on September 19, 1943, while he was supervising cargo operations, Kenneth Waters was pinned between the body of a truck that was being unloaded and the ship's number 2 resistor house. Two hours later, he was taken ashore by boat to the U.S. Army Twenty-First Station Hospital for treatment. There he was diagnosed with traumatic rupture of the duodenum and shock resulting from the accident. Despite the efforts of the doctors and staff at the station hospital, Kenneth Waters succumbed to his injuries at 0602, September 21, 1943. He was buried the same day.

Based on his merchant marine service, Kenneth A. Waters was posthumously awarded the Atlantic War Zone Bar, the Mediterranean-Middle East War Zone Bar, the Pacific War Zone Bar, the Victory Medal, and the Presidential Testimonial Letter. Kenneth A. Waters is among the more than 1,800 names listed on the World War II memorial on the grounds of the Blackford County, Indiana Courthouse.

Kenneth A. Waters was the second of Walter W. Waters and Frances Templeton Waters's three children and their oldest son. Kenneth's sister, Hope, was three years older, while his brother, Calvin, was five years younger.

According to the 1930 U.S. Census, Walter Waters was employed as a machinist in a gear factory. By the 1940 U.S. Census, Walter was still working as a machinist, while Frances was working as a sales woman in a department store. At the same time, Kenneth is listed has having completed one year of college, while little brother Calvin was working on a newspaper delivery route.

The April 1943 edition of *Polaris* described Kenneth Waters upon his graduation:

> Kenneth A. Waters, referred to as Fluid, really doesn't know whether he's coming or going. Regarded by the prelims as a great sage. Is the mathematical genius of his class and happily proves it for the edification of all.

Robie Knowles Wentworth

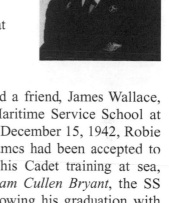

Born:	June 19, 1921
Hometown:	Kennebunk Beach, ME
Class:	1944
Service:	Merchant Marine
Position / Rank:	Third Assistant Engineer
Date / Place of death:	August 30, 1944 / 55-30 N, 7-30 W
Date / Place of burial:	August 30, 1944 / Lost at Sea—55-30 N, 7-30 W
Age:	23

On October 29, 1942, Robie K. Wentworth and a friend, James Wallace, left Kennebunk Beach, Maine, for the U.S. Maritime Service School at Sheepshead Bay, New York. Six weeks later, on December 15, 1942, Robie Wentworth wrote to his parents that he and James had been accepted to the U.S. Merchant Marine Academy. During his Cadet training at sea, Robie sailed as Engine Cadet on the SS *William Cullen Bryant*, the SS *John P. Holland,* and the SS *Abner Nash*. Following his graduation with Section B-318, Robie Wentworth signed on aboard the SS *Jacksonville*, a T2-SE-A1 tanker, as Third Assistant Engineer on August 19, 1944. Also signing on aboard the *Jacksonville* was Cadet-Midshipman Leroy P. Lawrence, the Deck Cadet.

SS *Jacksonville*

On August 30, about fifty miles north of Londonderry, Northern Ireland, the *Jacksonville* was maneuvering with four other ships to split off from Convoy CU-36 to sail for Loch Ewe, Scotland. The ship had just completed an eighty-six-degree turn to take its place at the end of a single column on the port side of the convoy when it was struck by a torpedo from *U-482*. The *Jacksonville*'s gasoline cargo ignited immediately. Within seconds of the torpedo's explosion, the entire ship was on fire, with flames shooting hundreds of feet into the air. Witnesses on other ships said that they could hear the ammunition in the ready service boxes exploding. Less than five minutes after the first torpedo, *U-482* fired another torpedo, breaking the ship in two. With no time to launch either lifeboats or rafts, all but two members of the ship's crew and Armed Guard perished. The only survivors were two men who jumped overboard before the flames caught them.

Based on his merchant marine service, Robie K. Wentworth was posthumously awarded the Mariner's Medal, the Combat Bar with star, the Atlantic War Zone Bar, the Victory Medal, and the Presidential Testimonial Letter.

Robie K. Wentworth was the eldest of Warren K. Wentworth and Mabel V. Wentworth's thirteen children. He graduated from Kennebunk High School in 1940, where he played football, basketball, and baseball. Robie's family owned and operated the Wentworth Hotel. The family lived in the hotel during the winter months and in a nearby cottage during the summer "tourist" months. Robie's college plans were dashed by a combination of his father's high medical bills for rheumatic fever and a severe drop in the tourist trade in 1939 and 1940. In September 1941, Robie and his brother Bailey began working at the South Portland Shipyard building Liberty ships. Robie's longtime girlfriend Irmena was known as the "pinup" of Section B-318. The two were engaged to be married when the *Jacksonville* returned from this voyage.

In 1988, eleven of his section mates placed a plaque in the Memorial Arbors at Kings Point in Robie's honor. Sometime later, his family wrote a detailed biography of Robie. The following poem was found in the memorabilia that Robie's mother's kept of him:

To My Soldier Son

Today I watched you go away, You
left on that long, long ride.
You were so straight, my tall dark son My
heart just swelled with pride.
When you are so far away, my dear I'll
miss you so, I know,
But I feel that whatever may come, I'll be
proud of where're you go.
You've been such a pal to your mother, dear, I'll
treasure each precious hour,
And pray that God will keep you safe, 'Till
you're come home with me once more.

To the day she died, Robie's mother believed that he would somehow
return to her.

Frederick Cowper Whitehead Jr.

Born:	December 16, 1918
Hometown:	Roanoke, VA
Class:	1943
Service:	USNR
Position / Rank:	Asst. Engineering Officer / Ensign
Date / Place of death:	April 20, 1944 / Mediterranean
Date / Place of burial:	April 20, 1944 / Lost at Sea Mediterranean; Tablets of the Missing at North Africa American Cemetery, Carthage, Tunisia
Age:	25

Frederick C. Whitehead was sworn in as a Midshipman, USNR, at the U.S. Merchant Marine Academy on September 18, 1942. Just a few weeks later, on October 6, 1942, he signed on as Engine Cadet aboard the passenger ship SS *Santa Paula*, which was serving as a U.S. Army troop transport. He completed his at-sea training aboard the *Santa Paula* on April 5, 1943, and returned to Kings Point to complete his education.

On December 24, 1943, Frederick C. Cowper, along with his classmates in Section A-240, graduated from Kings Point. After a few weeks of leave, he was sworn in as an Ensign, U.S. Naval Reserve, on January 15, 1944. He reported to the U.S. Navy Supervisor of Shipbuilding, New York, New York, on January 20, 1944, for further assignment. One week later, he was assigned to the destroyer USS *Lansdale (DD 426)*, a USS *Benson (DD 421)* class destroyer, then on duty in the Mediterranean. U.S. Navy records indicate that Ensign Whitehead reported aboard the *Lansdale* on March 26, 1944, at Oran.

Between April 10 and April 20, 1943, the USS *Lansdale* was assigned to escort convoys along the north coast of Africa from Oran, Algeria to Bizerte, Tunisia, in the face of determined air and submarine attacks, including attacks by German radio-controlled bombs, the first so-called smart bombs. On April 18, 1944, the *Lansdale* sailed from Oran to join

Convoy UGS-38, bound for Bizerte. Because the *Lansdale* was equipped with equipment to "jam" the radio frequencies the Germans used to control their smart bombs, the *Lansdale* was assigned to the convoy's port (seaward) forward corner.

USS *Lansdale* (DD 426)

On April 20, the convoy was making way past Cape Benegut off the Algerian coast. As twilight came, about two dozen German Ju 88s and He 111 bombers armed with torpedoes attacked the convoy in three successive waves. The first wave destroyed the SS *Paul Hamilton*, killing Kings Point Cadet-Midshipman Edward Zapletal and everyone else aboard.

Destruction of SS *Paul Hamilton*

The *Lansdale*, silhouetted by the explosion of the SS *Paul Hamilton*, was targeted by several aircraft from the second and third waves of German planes. In the ensuing action, the *Lansdale*'s gunners shot down two attacking planes while the Commanding Officer, Lieutenant Commander D. M. Swift, maneuvered to dodge torpedoes launched by others. However, the *Lansdale* could not dodge all of the torpedoes. At 2106, the *Lansdale* was hit on the starboard side at the forward fire room, where Ensign Whitehead, the assistant Engineering Officer, was on duty.

All of the crew in the forward fire room, including Ensign Whitehead died instantly. The ship took an immediate list to port and began circling clockwise due to jammed steering gear.

Despite the best efforts of the crew, the *Lansdale*'s port list increased to eighty degrees, at which point the Commanding Officer ordered the crew to abandon ship. When the survivors were mustered, forty-seven men, including Ensign Whitehead, were missing and presumed dead.

Ensign Frederick C. Whitehead, USNR, was posthumously awarded the Purple Heart and the European-African-Middle East Area Campaign Medal. Based on his merchant marine service as a Cadet-Midshipman, he was also awarded the Atlantic War Zone Bar, the Mediterranean-Middle East War Zone Bar, the Victory Medal, and the Presidential Testimonial Letter.

Frederick "Fred" Cowper Whitehead was the oldest of Frederick Cowper Whitehead and Myrtle Lee Whitehead's three sons. Fred's brothers were John and Richard. According to the 1940 U.S. Census and city directories, Frederick Sr. was employed as an engineer for the Chesapeake and Potomac Telephone Company. The 1941 yearbook of High Point College (now High Point University) lists Fred Cowper Whitehead as a member of the school's sophomore class.

Fulton Edison Yewell Jr.

Born:	September 28, 1921
Hometown:	Baltimore, MD
Class:	1943
Service:	Merchant Marine
Position / Rank:	Second Mate
Date / Place of death:	December 2, 1943 / Bari, Italy
Date / Place of burial:	December 2, 1943 / Lost at Sea Bari, Italy
Age:	22

Fulton E. Yewell entered the U.S. Merchant Marine Cadet Corps on July 11, 1941, when he reported to the Cadet school at Fort Schuyler, New York. However, he did not receive a Naval Reserve appointment due to his ". . . inability to meet naval physical requirements." Despite this setback, his performance at the Cadet school as of August 30, 1941, was noted as being "superior." During his at-sea training, Fulton served aboard the SS *Cranford* until it was torpedoed by *U-155* on July 30, 1942. He returned to Kings Point as a member of the Tin Fish Club wearing the Combat Bar with Star and Atlantic War Zone Bar.

After graduation from Kings Point with Section A-105, Fulton Yewell signed on as Third Mate aboard the SS *John L. Motley* at Baltimore, Maryland, on June 4, 1943, shortly after it was delivered from its builders, Bethlehem-Fairfield Shipbuilding, to the War Shipping Administration. Also joining the ship on the same day were Cadet-Midshipmen Edward Howard (Deck Cadet) and Jay Litton (Engine Cadet). The *John L. Motley* made one voyage to the Mediterranean and returned to New York from Oran, Algeria in mid-September 1943. Coast Guard records show that Fulton Yewell was promoted to Second Mate and signed on it that capacity on October 16, 1943. After loading a cargo of ammunition, the *John L. Motley* sailed on its second voyage to the Mediterranean, reaching the crowded harbor of Bari, Italy, on November 28, 1943.

On December 2, 1943, the *John L. Motley* was moored alongside the jetty at Bari, discharging its cargo, when a massive German air attack on the port took defenders by surprise. The attack and ensuing explosions sank seventeen ships and put the harbor out of use for three weeks. This attack became known as "Little Pearl Harbor."

Explosion of either *John L. Motley* or SS *John Harvey* at Bari, Italy

A Naval Armed Guard member on the SS *John Bascom*, moored next to the *John L. Motley*, reported that the *Motley* sustained three bomb hits, one in number 5 hold, one in number 3 hold, and one down the vessel's stack. The crew was able to control the fires caused by the first strike, but after the second hit, the fires on board raged out of control, burning through the vessel's mooring lines and setting her adrift. The subsequent explosion of the *Motley*'s cargo killed everyone on board, including Fulton E. Yewell Jr. and Cadet-Midshipmen Edward D. Howard and Jay F. Litton.

The damage caused by German bombs to the *John L. Motley* did not end there. The explosion on the *John Motley* set off a chain reaction on the nearby SS *John Harvey*, which was carrying a secret cargo of mustard gas munitions. The *John Harvey*, which had already been hit and was on fire, disintegrated when the *Motley* exploded, releasing deadly mustard gas into the air and water around the vessel. The death toll in Bari was more than one thousand civilians and Allied seamen. Six Kings Point Cadets were lost on three different vessels.

Thousands more seamen and civilians sustained serious injuries caused by the exposure to mustard gas. The effect of these injuries was exacerbated by the fact that doctors in the area didn't realize they were treating mustard gas victims.

Upon his death, Fulton E. Yewell had earned, or was posthumously awarded, the Mariner's Medal, the Combat Bar with two stars, the Atlantic War Zone Bar, the Mediterranean-Middle East War Zone Bar, the Victory Medal, and the Presidential Testimonial Letter.

Fulton E. Yewell was the only son of Fulton E. Yewell Sr. and Rose Delano Yewell. Baltimore City Directories from the 1920s indicate that Fulton Sr.

was a builder. However, the couple was divorced sometime in the 1920s. The 1930 U.S. Census shows that Fulton and his mother were living with Fulton's uncle, John S. Delano, a Chesapeake Bay Pilot. By 1940, according to that year's U.S. Census, Fulton's mother was married to William M. Burich, and Fulton is listed as Mr. Burich's stepson. Mr. Burich worked as a salesman for a local dairy.

The April 1943 edition of *Polaris* described Fulton Yewell upon his graduation:

> "Steamboat" is famous for the speed with which he completes his examinations. Famed for his double-jointedness, being able to bend in any direction. Can turn around and look himself over. Is opposed to everything traditional and loudly makes it known.

U.S. Maritime Commission Cadet Officers Who Died during World War II

The men listed in this section were enrolled in the U.S. Maritime Commission Cadet Corps (USMCCC) between 1937 and 1941. Nineteen of the twenty-five men were classified as Cadet Officers after they received their USCG officer's license following graduation from a state Maritime Academy: six from Pennsylvania Nautical School, five from Massachusetts Nautical School, four from New York Merchant Marine Academy, and three from California Maritime Academy. One man came up through the hawsepipe, studied for his license, became a company Cadet and later a Cadet Officer. Some of the other USMMCCC men did not obtain a Coast Guard license. Among the other USMMCCC members, one went on to become a Chief Mate and two became Second Mates. See Index C for a list of the Cadet Officers and the reference to pages where they are named.

Six of the men died serving as U.S. Navy Officers: a Lieutenant died on his submarine when it was attacked by Japanese forces; an Ensign died when his aircraft crashed in Iceland; another Lieutenant died when his submarine was sunk by Japanese forces off the Japanese coast; an Ensign died while in charge of a landing craft that was shelled and demolished by a German 88 during the amphibious assault on Salerno, Italy (he was awarded the Silver Star for his actions that day); a Lieutenant died when a Japanese shore battery shelled his ship; and another officer died of an illness near Pearl Harbor.

A Cadet Officer serving as an Army Air Corps Second Lieutenant died when his aircraft crashed in England following bombing raids on Germany. Another former Cadet Officer serving as a civilian crew member on a U.S. Army mine planter died when a storm sunk his ship. While delivering an aircraft to China for the government in 1944, another former Cadet Officer, serving as a civilian navigator, died following the crash of his aircraft in Cuba. One man, after signing off his ship as a First Assistant Engineer in

1943, died of unknown causes; and another died in an automobile accident in Baltimore in 1941.

The remaining men died serving on merchant ships; two in aircraft attacks and five when their ships were torpedoed. Another died as a POW, when the Japanese ship carrying POWs was torpedoed. A Chief Mate died in a storm; another Chief Mate died in a shipboard accident and a Second Mate died in a storm when his ship broke up. Two of the men died just before the United States entered the WW II; one in an automobile accident, and the other was apparently a suicide.

All but two of the twenty-five men are listed on the 1946 Kings Point War Memorial and the Alumni Association's *Kings Point Log* as graduates of the U.S. Merchant Marine Academy. One man not on the War Memorial is R. N. Simmons, who entered the U.S. Navy as a Midshipman on November 22, 1940, and died as a Navy Officer. He is included since there is evidence that for a period of time in 1939, he was in the USMCCC. The other man was not known of until recently.

Robert Walker Allen

Born:	April 18, 1919
Hometown:	Edgewood, PA
Class:	1940—USMMCC Cadet Officer
	1939—Pennsylvania Nautical School
Service:	USNR
Position / Rank:	Submarine Officer / Lieutenant
Date / Place of death:	January 10, 1943 / 5-40 S, 152-2 E
Date / Place of burial:	January 10, 1943 / Lost at Sea—5-40 S, 152-2 E; Tablets of the Missing at Manila American Cemetery Manila, Philippines
Age:	23

Robert W. Allen was appointed a Cadet, Merchant Marine Reserve, on March 25, 1939, while he was attending the Pennsylvania Nautical School. Following his graduation from Pennsylvania Nautical School later that year, he began sailing as a Cadet Officer (engine) when he signed on aboard the SS *Asura* on December 20, 1939. According to crew lists on file in New York, he signed on as Third Assistant Engineer aboard the SS *Exilona* in March 1940 and remained aboard in that capacity until August 1940. During his time aboard the SS *Exilona,* he apparently applied for an appointment as Ensign, USNR. Upon his acceptance of the appointment on September 16, 1940, he was placed on active duty and was initially assigned to the USS *Arkansas* (BB 33).

After completing this assignment, Robert Allen was transferred to the Submarine School at New London, Connecticut. Upon graduation, he was assigned to the USS *Argonaut* (SM 1). The *Argonaut*, one of the largest submarines in the U.S. Navy, was designed to lay mines. In January 1942, the *Argonaut* began conversion to a troop carrying submarine at the Mare Island Naval Shipyard. After the conversion, the *Argonaut* carried Marines of the Second Raider Battalion to Makin Island for a diversionary raid. The *Argonaut* retrieved them upon completion of the raid two days later.

After returning from the raid, the *Argonaut* was assigned to operate out of Brisbane, Australia. In December 1943, the *Argonaut* sailed from Brisbane for a patrol area in the Solomon Islands between New Britain and Bougainville. On January 10, 1943, the *Argonaut* sighted a convoy of five freighters, escorted by Japanese destroyers, and attacked. A U.S. Army plane was flying over the scene and witnessed the *Argonaut*'s attack on the convoy.

USS *Argonaut*

Although the *Argonaut* successfully torpedoed at least one destroyer, the other escorts counterattacked with depth charges. The Army plane circling above noticed the *Argonaut* surfacing at an odd angle, its bow protruding upward from the waves, indicating that the counterattack had damaged the *Argonaut*. The destroyers surrounded the submarine and pumped shells into her bow, sinking her. All 105 men aboard the *Argonaut* including Lt. Allen were lost.

Lt. Robert W. Allen, USNR, was posthumously awarded the Purple Heart Medal, the American Defense Service Medal, the Asiatic-Pacific Area Campaign Medal, and the World War II Victory Medal. For his merchant marine service, he also earned the Merchant Marine Defense Bar.

At the time of his death, Robert Allen was married to Dorothy Danton Allen. Robert W. Allen was the second of Kenneth Pratt Allen and Isabel Louise Bortree Allen's four children. Robert's older brother was Kenneth. His younger siblings were Donald and Mary. According to the 1930 U.S. Census, Kenneth Allen was employed by the local power company.

George Walter Alther Jr.

Born:	April 14, 1918
Hometown:	Melrose, MA
Class:	1940-USMMCC
	Cadet Officer
	1939-Massachusetts
	Nautical School
Service:	Merchant Marine
Position:	Second Mate
Date / Place of death:	July 14, 1943 Avola, Sicily
Date / Place of burial:	July 14, 1943 / Lost at Sea Avola, Sicily
Age:	25

According to Maritime Commission records, George W. Alther was assigned to the SS *President Monroe* as a Cadet Officer in September 1939. Prior to being assigned to the *President Monroe,* he was employed aboard ship as a Quartermaster for the Eastern Steamship Company. In 1940, George Alther was promoted to Third Mate aboard the *President Monroe*. He subsequently served in the same capacity aboard the *President Buchanan* until 1942. Sometime in April 1942, George Alther signed on aboard the MS *Chant*, the former MS *Hulda Maersk*, which was owned by the War Shipping Administration and operated by American President Lines.

The *Chant* sailed for Scotland, where it was loaded with aviation gasoline in drums plus a deck cargo of coal and two motor launches for the embattled island of Malta. The *Chant* sailed in Convoy WS-19Z to Gibraltar with three other ships. Upon their departure from Gibraltar to Malta, the ships and their escort became part of one of the great convoy battles of World War II, Operation Harpoon. The convoy was escorted by a powerful task force of twelve Royal Navy ships, known as "Force X," which included the antiaircraft carrier cruiser HMS *Cairo*. The escort proved to be not quite powerful enough. On the run through the Mediterranean, the convoy and its escorts fought off attacks by Italian cruisers, destroyers, high-altitude bombers, dive bombers, and torpedo bombers. On June 15, 1942, after days of fighting off attacks, a bomber got through the escort's antiaircraft fire, hitting the *Chant* with one of its bombs. The bomb struck the *Chant* at number 4 hold, igniting the gasoline and setting off explosions in the rest of the gasoline and the ammunition for the ship's guns. George Alther and nearly all of the crew were able to abandon ship and were rescued by the British minesweeper HMS *Rye* (J-76). He arrived back in New York aboard the SS *Queen Mary* on September 19, 1942.

George Alther signed on as Second Mate aboard the SS *Timothy Pickering* at the Port of New York on December 11, 1942. Also signing on were four Cadet-Midshipmen: Christopher Brennan (deck), William Lyman (deck), Warren Marks (engine), and Lawrence McLaughlin (engine). On the morning of July 13, 1943, just three days after the Invasion of Sicily began; the *Timothy Pickering* arrived off the British Army's invasion beach at Avola, Sicily, with 130 British soldiers aboard. In addition, the ship was carrying an almost-identical cargo to that of the ill-fated MS *Chant:* munitions, TNT, high-octane gasoline, artillery pieces, and trucks. On the morning of July 13, the vessel was anchored in the harbor, about half a mile from shore, with the bow in and the starboard side closest to the shore. The crew had begun unloading the vessel's cargo.

At 1040 (GCT), the Allied shipping off Avola was attacked by German dive bombers. One of them dropped a single five-hundred-pound bomb on the *Timothy Pickering* at its number 4 hold. The bomb detonated in the ship's engine room, causing a massive explosion of the ship's cargo with resulting fire. The explosion left a gaping hole in the starboard side of the ship, causing it to quickly begin sinking. With no time to either launch lifeboats or be given an order to abandon ship, the crew began to leave the ship immediately, leaping over the side into the oily waters or sliding down ropes and the anchor chain. In May 1944, the Academy's newspaper, *Polaris*, printed a report on the loss of the *Timothy Pickering,* which expanded on the report of the sinking by Cadet-Midshipman Brennan, one of only twenty-nine survivors.

> The ticklish cargo of explosives and high-test octane was being gently worked over the side to waiting supply barges when one such raider appeared and began to attack. The plane's bomb landed squarely into the open number four hatch of Brennan's ship. The explosion was instantaneous. Sheets of yellow flame and billowing clouds of smoke rose hundreds of feet in the air. Two adjacent ships were set afire; others were bombarded with huge chunks of metal. Cadet-Midshipmen on other vessels heard the explosion some 50 miles out at sea. To stunned observers nearby, the doomed ship seemed to dissolve into thin air.

However, Brennan was the only survivor of four Cadet-Midshipmen who signed on aboard the *Timothy Pickering*. The other three perished in the explosion and ensuing fire. In addition to the three Cadet-Midshipmen, nineteen other crew members, eight Naval Armed Guard sailors, and one hundred British soldiers perished.

 Second Mate George W. Alther Jr., the *Timothy Pickering*'s twenty-five-year-old Second Mate and 1940 Cadet Officer, was killed while helping the ship's wounded Armed Guard officer abandon ship. For this action, he was posthumously awarded the merchant marine's highest honor, the Distinguished Service Medal. For his merchant marine service, George W. Alther was also awarded the Mariner's Medal, the Combat Bar (with two stars), the Merchant Marine Defense Bar, the Atlantic War Zone Bar, the Mediterranean-Middle East War Zone Bar, the Pacific War Zone Bar, the Victory Medal, and the Presidential Testimonial Letter. The Liberty ship *George W. Alther* was also named in his honor.

George W. Alther was the oldest of George W. Alther Sr. and Hilda Alther's four sons. George's younger brothers were Edward, Frederick, and Richard. Hilda Alther died in 1940. The 1940 and 1930 U.S. Census indicates that George Alther Sr. was a railroad Fireman working on steam locomotives.

Frederick William Baumann Jr.

Born:	July 2, 1922
Hometown:	Cresco, PA
Class:	1942—USMMCC
	1941—Pennsylvania Nautical School
Service:	Merchant Marine
Position:	Junior Third Assistant Engineer
Date / Place of death:	January 9, 1943 / 56-15 N, 22-00 W
Date / Place of burial:	January 9, 1943 / Lost at Sea—56-15 N, 22-00 W
Age:	20

Frederick W. Baumann was a Cadet MMR on August 29, 1940, while he was attending the Pennsylvania Nautical School. On April 11, 1942, he received his seaman's papers from the U.S. Coast Guard in New York, New York, which permitted him to sail as a Cadet. He signed on aboard the SS *Louise Lykes* as Engine Cadet on May 9, 1942, and signed off on September 18, 1942, apparently to sit for his Third Assistant Engineer's license. Exactly one month later, he signed on aboard the SS *Louise Lykes* as Junior Third Assistant Engineer.

SS *Louise Lykes*

The SS *Louise Lykes* sailed without escort from New York on January 2, 1943, carrying a cargo of ammunition and other war supplies bound for Belfast, Northern Ireland. The ship was hit by four torpedoes fired from the surfaced *U-384* at 2025 on the evening of January 9, 1943. According to German Navy records, the *Louise Lykes* cargo exploded with what was described as "a terrible blast," forcing *U-384* to dive to avoid being struck by pieces of the wreckage. There were no survivors among the fifty merchant crew, thirty-four Naval Armed Guard sailors, and ten U.S. Army personnel aboard.

Another former U.S. Maritime Commission Cadet Officer, Harry A. Wolfe Jr., and five Cadet-Midshipmen from the U.S. Merchant Marine Academy, Michael M. Chrobak, Charles C. Gassner, Allen G. Miller, Robert C. Vancure, and Eugene W. Walters, were all killed, making the sinking of the SS *Louise Lykes* the single deadliest sinking in the Academy's history in terms of Cadet losses.

Based on his merchant marine service, Frederick W. Baumann was posthumously awarded the Mariner's Medal, the Combat Bar, the Atlantic War Zone Bar, the Mediterranean-Middle East Bar, the Victory Medal, and the Presidential Testimonial Letter.

Frederick W. Baumann was the eldest of Frederick W. Baumann Sr. and Pearl B. Fancher Baumann's three children. Frederick's brother Robert was three years younger, while his sister, Evelyn was four years younger. According to U.S. Census information, the Baumann family lived on a farm in Pennsylvania.

Thorndike Joseph Berwick

Born:	August 29, 1915
Hometown:	Methuen, MA
Class:	1939—USMMCC Cadet Officer
	1938—Massachusetts Nautical School
Service:	Merchant Marine
Position:	Second Assistant Engineer
Date / Place of death:	October 23, 1941 / Baltimore, MD
Date / Place of burial:	October 27, 1941 / Elmwood Cemetery, Methuen, MA
Age:	26

Thorndike (spelled Thorndyke in some records) J. Berwick graduated from Massachusetts Nautical School in April 1938 with a U.S. Coast Guard license, issued on April 8, 1938, as Third Assistant Engineer, steam and motor. He began sailing with the American Pioneer Line as a Cadet Officer aboard the SS *West Cusetta* on April 15, 1938. On November 4, 1938, he was transferred to the SS *City of Elwood*. On March 29, 1939, he was promoted to Junior Third Assistant Engineer. He continued sailing aboard the SS *City of Elwood* as Junior Third Assistant Engineer and Third Assistant Engineer until 1941. According to his U.S. Coast Guard records, Thorndike Berwick served as Junior Third Assistant Engineer aboard the SS *Capulin* from March 5, 1941, to April 24, 1941. One month later, on May 22, 1941, he signed on as Second Assistant Engineer aboard the MS *Jeff Davis* and signed off at the end of a coastwise run on June 9, 1941.

According to his obituary, Thorndike J. Berwick was killed in an automobile accident on October 23, 1941, in Baltimore, Maryland. The funeral was held on October 27 at the home of his grandparents, Mr. and Mrs. Joseph Camire in Methuen, Massachusetts, followed by a Catholic Requiem High Mass at St. Mary's Church in Methuen.

Based on his merchant marine service, Thorndike J. Berwick was eligible to receive the Merchant Marine Defense Bar, the Victory Medal, and the Presidential Testimonial Letter.

Thorndike Berwick was the oldest of Louis P. Berwick and Yvonne G. Camire Berwick's four children and one of their two sons. His siblings were Louise, Marceline, and Louis P. Jr. In the 1930 U.S. Census, Louis Sr.'s occupation is listed as electrician.

Carl Bialek Jr.

Born:	April 30, 1915
Hometown:	New Hackensack, NY
Class:	1939—USMMCC Cadet Officer 1938—New York MMA
Service:	U.S. Navy
Position / Rank:	Co-pilot or Navigator / Ensign
Date / Place of death:	November 2, 1941 / near Krisuvik, Iceland
Date / Place of burial:	November 2, 1941 / near Krisuvik, Iceland
Age:	26

After graduating from New York Merchant Marine Academy, Carl Bialek sailed as a Cadet Officer (engineer) aboard the SS *American Traveler* until early 1939. Crew lists on file in New York, New York, indicate that he signed on aboard the passenger ship SS *Manhattan* as a licensed Junior Engineer on April 28, 1939, at New York, New York. The last crew list entry for him on the SS *Manhattan* was upon the ship's arrival in New York on November 15, 1939. He subsequently applied for and received his commission as Ensign, U.S. Naval Reserve, and was ordered to active duty. He completed naval aviation training on April 25, 1941, and was assigned to fly seaplanes.

PBM-1 "Mariner"

Ensign Carl Bialek was a crew member (either copilot or navigator) of a Navy Martin PBM-1 "Mariner" (Serial number 1248) seaplane that crashed into a mountainside while returning to its base in Keflavik, Iceland, on November 2, 1941. The aircraft was assigned to Patrol Squadron 74 (VP-74), an element of the pre-World War II "Neutrality Patrol" in the North Atlantic.

During the two weeks preceding the crash, the USS *Kearny* (DD432) had been torpedoed, and the USS *Reuben James* (DD 245) was sunk by U-boats while on neutrality patrol.

According to the crash report,

> The plane crashed as a result of insufficient and unreliable aids to navigation under instrument flying conditions. The pilot maintained his course on the assumption that it was a safe course based on the radio-direction finder bearing on Reykjanes Point, which bearing was incorrect.

Ensign Carl Bialek, USNR, Ensign Carl M. Thornquist, USNR, 2nd Lt. William P. Robinson, USA, and all nine enlisted crewmen on board were killed in the crash.

Carl Bialek, the son of Carl Bialek and Bertha Bialek, grew up on the family poultry farm near Wappinger's Falls in Duchess County, New York. The couple had a daughter Martha, Carl's older sister, who worked as a bookkeeper.

Charles Emil Blair

Born:	May 8, 1918
Hometown:	Port Arthur, TX
Class:	1940—USMM Cadet Corps
Service:	Merchant Marine
Position:	Able Bodied Seaman
Date / Place of death:	May 16, 1942 / Gulf of Mexico 28-52 N, 90-20 W
Date / Place of burial:	May 16, 1942 / Gulf of Mexico 28-52 N, 90-20 W / Lost at Sea
Age:	24

Charles Emil Blair was a member of the Merchant Marine Cadet Corps and completed training as a Deck Cadet on November 26, 1940. However, there is no notation in his U.S. Coast Guard record that he received a license as Third Mate. Coast Guard records show that he sailed as Deck Cadet aboard the SS *American Press* (1939-1940), the SS *Liberator* (1939), the SS *Effingham* (1939), the SS *Almeria Lykes* (1938, 1939), the SS *Ruth Lykes* (1938), and the SS *Ethan Allen* (1937-1938). Following completion of his Cadet Corps training, he sailed as an able bodied seaman aboard several ships on coastwise voyages. Coast Guard records show that he was a survivor of the torpedoing of the SS *Papoose* on March 19, 1942.

In May 1942, Charles E. Blair signed on aboard the tanker MV *William C. McTarnahan* as an able bodied seaman. The ship was in ballast en route to Port Isabel, Texas, from New York with a crew of thirty-eight merchant mariners and seven Armed Guard sailors. The ship was sailing without an escort and was not zigzagging, since U-boats were not believed to be operating in the Gulf of Mexico. However, the German Navy had just sent the U-boats of its Tenth U-boat Flotilla to the Gulf of Mexico to disrupt the flow of oil and other war supplies to the East Coast and foreign destinations. In May 1942 alone, U-boats operating in the Gulf of Mexico sank fifty-six ships.

At about 10:00 a.m., on May 16, 1942, when the *William C. McTarnahan* was thirty-five miles east of Ship Shoal Light, Louisiana, *U-506* sighted it and another ship, the tanker SS *Sun*. The submarine attacked the *Sun* first, hitting it on the port bow, damaging it, but not sinking it. The *U-506* then attacked the nearby *William C. McTarnahan*. Two torpedoes hit the *McTarnahan* on the starboard side at the number 2 tank and engine room. The resulting fire killed all crew members in the aft section of the ship. However, the ship remained afloat, and the submarine surfaced to try to sink it with gunfire. Over the next thirty minutes, *U-506* fired approximately fifteen shells at the *McTarnahan*, hitting the ship several times, while the surviving crew abandoned ship in two lifeboats and two life rafts. Believing that the ship was sinking, *U-506* submerged and left the scene. Four hours later, fishing vessels directed by a U.S. Coast Guard patrol plane arrived in the area to rescue the survivors and take them to Houma, Louisiana.

Seventeen of the *McTarnahan*'s crew members, including Charles E. Blair, were lost in the attack. Ironically, despite *U-506*'s best efforts, the *McTarnahan* did not sink. The ship was repaired and returned to service.

Based on his wartime service, Charles E. Blair should have received the Mariner's Medal, the Combat Bar with Star, the Atlantic War Zone Bar, and the Presidential Testimonial Letter.

Charles Emil Blair is identified in U.S. Coast Guard documents as the son of Mrs. J. E. Blair of Port Arthur, Texas. However, even though letters were written by Mrs. Blair from a Port Arthur, Texas, address, seeking information about her son's death, four years later, mail sent to his mother at that address was returned with no forwarding address.

SS *William C. McTarnahan*

James J. Coffey

Born:	1923	
Hometown:	Jamesburg, NJ	
Class:	1942—USMCC Cadet Officer	
Service:	Merchant Marine	No Photograph Available
Position / Rank:	Second Mate	
Date / Place of death:	March 2, 1943 / 62-10 N, 28-25 W	
Date / Place of burial:	March 2, 1943 / Lost at Sea—62-10 N, 28-25 W	
Age:	20	

Little is known about James J. Coffey before he signed on aboard the *SS Meriwether Lewis* as Second Mate on January 25, 1943. In early 1942 the crew list for the U.S. Army Transport *Maui* shows him as Junior Third Officer. The crew list indicates as of that time he had 2 ½ years of experience at sea.

When James Coffey signed on aboard the *SS Meriwether Lewis*, the ship had four Cadet-Midshipmen from the U.S. Merchant Marine Academy; Randall P. Bourell (Deck) Alan Clark (Deck), Daniel J. Maher (Engine), and Francis McCann (Engine). On February 18, 1943 the *Meriwether Lewis* with its four Kings Point cadets sailed from New York as part of convoy HX-227 bound for the United Kingdom and then to Murmansk, Russia. The ship was loaded with a cargo of vehicle tires, ammunition, and according to some references, a deck cargo of PT Boats.

According to German Navy records, the *Meriwether Lewis* was identified as a straggler from a convoy, and unsuccessfully attacked by *U-759* in the early morning of March 2. The submarine was unable to re-attack the *Meriwether Lewis* due to problems with its engines, but it was able to contact *U-634* and lead it to the straggler. The *U-634* fired four torpedoes at the *Meriwether Lewis*, hitting it with one of them. The damage was apparently sufficient to stop the ship, but did not sink it. The submarine hit the *Meriwether Lewis* with two more torpedoes, the last of which detonated the ship's ammunition cargo. Although there was plenty of time to abandon ship, the USCGC *Ingham* (WPG 35) found only a 30-mile line of floating tires during its two day long search for the *SS Meriwether Lewis* and crew. Thus, the ship's entire crew of forty-four, including

Second Mate James J. Coffey, the four Kings Point Cadet-Midshipmen, and 28 members of the Naval Armed Guard perished in the sinking.

Based on this voyage and his previous voyages James J. Coffey was posthumously awarded the Mariner's Medal, Combat Bar with star, Atlantic War Zone Bar, Pacific War Zone Bar the Victory Medal, and the Presidential Testimonial Letter.

Charles Henry Doell

Born:	May 5, 1920
Hometown:	West Roxbury, MA
Class:	1941 USMMCC Cadet Officer
	1940 Massachusetts Nautical School
Service:	Merchant Marine
Position:	Third Mate
Date / Place of death:	November 23, 1942 / 42-25 N, 48-27 W
Date / Place of burial:	November 23, 1942 / Lost at Sea 42-25 N, 48-27 W
Age:	22

Charles H. Doell signed on aboard the tanker SS *Caddo* as Third Mate on July 17, 1942, at New York, New York. The *Caddo*'s crew list indicates that the five-foot-eleven-inch, 150-pound Doell had been going to sea for four years at that time. U.S. Coast Guard records show that Charles H. Doell had received his license as Third Mate on October 14, 1940, shortly after his graduation from the Massachusetts Nautical School (now Massachusetts Maritime Academy). U.S. Merchant Marine Cadet Corps records identify Charles H. Doell as a Cadet Officer in 1940. He received his license as Second Mate on May 14, 1942.

SS *Caddo*

On November 11, 1942, the *Caddo* sailed from Baytown, Texas, for Reykjavik, Iceland, with a cargo of over one hundred thousand barrels of diesel oil and fuel oil and three hundred drums of gasoline for the U.S. Navy. The ship steered evasive courses after leaving Baytown and maintained five lookouts at all times. However, on the morning of November 23, 1942, the ship was sighted and attacked by *U-518*. The crew of the *Caddo* saw the torpedo track and turned to port toward the torpedo, but the evasive action was too little, too late. At about 0640 (GCT), the *Caddo* was hit by a torpedo on the port side at the pump room, just forward of the after accommodation house. The explosion ripped up the deck above the pump room, flooded the pump room, demolished the port side lifeboat/raft, and disabled the radio transmitter.

The tough tanker took about ninety minutes to sink, affording the entire crew time to abandon ship in the three surviving lifeboats. Ten minutes after the *Caddo* slipped beneath the waves, *U-518* surfaced and took the Master, Paul B. Muller, and Chief Mate, Bendik Lande, prisoner. Captain Muller later died in a German prison camp. Bendik Lande survived his imprisonment and was repatriated following the war. The remaining survivors were divided between three boats.

Only six of the seventeen men in first boat were alive to be rescued by the MS *Motomar* on December 8, 1942, 650 miles south of where the *Caddo* was sunk. When the six survivors were landed at Marcus Hook, Pennsylvania on Christmas Eve, 1942, they noted the kind treatment they received from the Spanish crew of the Motomar. The forty-one crewmen and Armed Guard sailors in the second and third lifeboats, including Third Mate Charles H. Doell, were never seen again.

U.S. Coast Guard identification photo of Charles H. Doell

Based on the above, Charles H. Doell would have been posthumously awarded the Mariner's Medal, the Combat Bar with star, the Atlantic War Zone Bar, the Victory Medal, and the Presidential Testimonial Letter.

Charles H. Doell was the oldest child and only son of Henry Doell and Mildred L. Smith Doell. Esther, who was four years younger, was Charles's sister. In 1940, Henry Doell was employed as an insurance broker at James Simpson & Company.

David Lincoln Edwards

Born:	February 12, 1918	
Hometown:	Brighton, MA	
Class:	1940—USMMCC Cadet Officer 1938—Massachusetts Nautical School	
Service:	Merchant Marine	
Position:	Chief Mate	
Date / Place of death:	February 23, 1943 / 46-15 N, 38-11 W	
Date / Place of burial:	February 23, 1943 / Lost at Sea—46-15 N, 38-11 W	
Age:	25	

David Edwards served aboard the USS *Nantucket* as a Cadet from March 28, 1936, to April 5, 1938. He started his officer career on August 1, 1938, as a Cadet Officer assigned to the Coast and Geodetic Survey ship SS *Hydrographer*. He subsequently sailed as Cadet Officer aboard the SS *Delnorte* and as Third Mate aboard the SS *Delplata, Delorleans,* and *Delmundo*. On August 13, 1942, the latter ship was torpedoed and sunk. However, David Edwards survived the sinking and returned to sea. He signed on aboard the SS *Jonathan Sturges* on or before January 12, 1943. Among the ship's crew on that date were Cadet-Midshipmen Harry Burlison, Grover Leitz, Ralph Kohlmeyer, and William Wilson.

After safely delivering its cargo to England, the *Jonathan Sturges* was returning to New York with Convoy ON-166 from Liverpool to New York City when it fell behind the convoy on the night of February 23/24, 1943. The ship, with a crew of forty-four merchant mariners and a Naval Armed Guard of thirty-one, was carrying 1,500 tons of sand ballast. In bad weather and poor visibility, the *Sturges* was making 6 knots, about half its full speed. At about 1:00 a.m., the vessel was struck in the forward part of the ship by two torpedoes fired by *U-707*. The engines were secured, but the ship, which had apparently been broken in two, began to sink bow first. Survivors recalled that the explosions gave off a sweet odor and left a sweet taste in their mouths for hours after the incident.

Although the Radio Officer was able to send a distress signal, there was no time to await a reply, as the crew abandoned ship. Two lifeboats and four life rafts were successfully launched. According to the post-sinking report of the survivors, nineteen men were able to get into one lifeboat, while the Master, Chief Mate David Edwards, and fifteen others were in the other boat. The other twenty-four survivors were able to reach the four life rafts. However, the boats and rafts were soon separated.

On February 27, three days after the sinking, the boat with nineteen men aboard met up with a lifeboat carrying three survivors from the Dutch ship SS *Madoera* who had been in the same convoy. Eight of the *Sturges* survivors climbed into the *Madoera*'s boat. Although one of the *Jonathan Sturges* crew eventually died of exposure, the other eighteen (along with the three *Madoera*'s survivors) were rescued by the USS *Belknap* (DD 251) on March 12, 1943. However, the other lifeboat with its seventeen survivors was never seen again. Of the twenty-four men on the life rafts, only six survived. These men were rescued on April 5 by *U-336* and spent the rest of the war as prisoners of war.

Based on his merchant marine service, David L. Edwards was posthumously awarded the Mariner's Medal, the Combat Bar with two stars, the Atlantic War Zone Bar, the Victory Medal, and the Presidential Testimonial Letter.

David L. Edwards was the son of Harry Phillip Edwards Sr. of Brighton, Massachusetts. He had at least one sibling, brother Harry Jr. At the time of his death, he was married to Marie Edwards, who was living in New Orleans, Louisiana.

When David Edwards served aboard the USS *Nantucket* as a Cadet, the ship was a training ship assigned in 1901 to the Massachusetts Nautical School, now Massachusetts Maritime Academy. With the exception of its reactivation and service in the U.S. Navy during World War I, the *Nantucket* served as the Massachusetts Nautical School's training ship until 1940. In that year, the former USS *Nantucket* was transferred to the U.S. Merchant Marine Academy to serve as its training ship. Two years later, the *Nantucket* was renamed the *Emery Rice*. After eighteen years of service to Kings Point, the *Emery Rice* was scrapped in 1958. However, the "heart" of this early piece of Kings Point history, the ship's engine, remains at Kings Point as a national historic engineering landmark.

William Maxwell Farr

Born:	September 29, 1915	
Hometown:	Allentown, PA	
Class:	1939—USMMCC Cadet Officer 1938— Pennsylvania Nautical School	
Service:	Merchant Marine	No Photograph
Position:	Deck Cadet Officer	Available
Date / Place of death:	November 16, 1941 / Allentown, PA	
Date / Place of burial:	Unknown / Union-West End Cemetery, Allentown, PA	
Age:	26	

William M. Farr was accepted into the U.S. Merchant Marine Cadet Corps Cadet Officer program as Deck Cadet Officer on June 8, 1938. According to the U.S. Coast Guard, he was issued a license as Third Mate at Philadelphia, Pennsylvania, on May 25, 1938. On June 9, 1938, he was assigned to the SS *Capulin,* which was loading cargo at Baltimore, Maryland. However, on June 15, he was reassigned to the SS *Sarcoxie,* which was also loading cargo in Baltimore. He signed on aboard the SS *Sarcoxie* on June 21, 1938, and sailed aboard that ship until he left the ship on February 23, 1939. On June 7, 1939, William Farr signed on as able bodied seaman aboard the SS *Exermont.* He signed off on August 10 after completing a voyage to the Mediterranean. There are no records that William M. Farr served at sea again, although the 1940 U.S. Census lists his occupation as "seaman," and the 1940/1941 Allentown city directories list his occupation as "Cadet Officer."

William M. Farr was the youngest of Jacob L. Farr and Mabel L. Farr's five children. William, known as "Bill" to the family, had two brothers, L. Donald and Harvey. His two sisters were Elizabeth and Louise. The Farr family owned a shoe factory and several shoe stores in Pennsylvania, which did business as Farr Brothers. He is listed in the yearbook of Lehigh University as studying arts at the university in the class of 1938. However, at some point, he began his nautical education. His residence in 1941 indicates that he is living with his father, the president of Farr Brothers

Company, and his mother. According to surviving family members, the cause of William M. Farr's death was suicide.

William M. Farr Headstone

Although the Farr Building, the company headquarters for Farr Brothers Co., still stands at the corner of Eighth and Hamilton Streets in Allentown, Pennsylvania, the Farr family sold the business in 1980.

Paul Greene

Born: October 31, 1919
Hometown: Dorchester, MA
Class: 1939 Massachusetts
                   Maritime Academy
                   1939 USMMCC Cadet
                   Officer
Service: Merchant Marine
Position: First Assistant Engineer
Date / Place of death: December 5, 1943 /
                   Unknown
Date / Place of burial: Unknown
Age: 24

Paul Greene was appointed a merchant marine Cadet, Merchant Marine Reserve, U.S. Naval Reserve, on April 25, 1939. His address is shown as USS *Nantucket*, which was the training ship for the Massachusetts Maritime Academy. He graduated from the Academy on September 26, 1939. On October 16, 1939, Paul Greene signed on aboard the SS *President Van Buren* (later renamed SS *President Fillmore*) as Cadet Officer (engine). He served aboard the ship continuously until January 23, 1942, when he signed off as Second Assistant Engineer. Crew lists on file in various ports show that he subsequently sailed as second assistant on the SS *President Buchanan* (March-September 1942). He then signed on as Second Assistant Engineer aboard the SS *James Fenimore Cooper* on October 30, 1942, and signed off on June 15, 1943, as First Assistant Engineer.

On March 7, 1942, Paul Greene applied for a commission as an Ensign, USNR. He was appointed Ensign, USNR (E-M), on December 17, 1942, effective November 20, 1942. However, as he was at sea aboard the SS *James Fenimore Cooper* at the time, his acceptance was delayed until he returned to port. However, the appointment was cancelled on August 28, 1943, as he had not accepted the appointment by that date.

Nothing is known about Paul Greene's whereabouts or fate after he signed off the SS *James Fenimore Cooper* at New York, New York, on June 15, 1943. He is not listed among the war dead by the U.S. Coast Guard, which was responsible for keeping track of all merchant mariners. Research to determine the circumstances of his death is ongoing.

Based on his merchant marine service, at the time of his death, Paul Greene had earned the Combat Bar, the American Defense Bar, the Atlantic War Zone Bar, the Mediterranean-Middle East War Zone Bar, the Pacific War Zone Bar, the Victory Medal, and the Presidential Testimonial Letter.

Paul Greene was the only son and youngest child of George G. Green and Lillian Hird Greene. Paul's older sister was Margaretta. Their father was killed in WW I, leaving their mother to raise them. The 1930 and 1940 U.S. Census indicates that the Greene family was living with Lillian's parents in Boston (Dorchester), MA. The same records show that Lillian was working as stenographer and private secretary in a law office. U.S. Navy records show that Paul Greene attended Boston English High School from 1933 through his graduation in 1937.

The Naval Officer who interviewed Paul Greene for his commission as Ensign noted the following about him:

> Quiet, shy but seems to have good judgment and to be dependable, more mature than he looks.

Theodore Albert Heidt

Born:	March 5, 1920
Hometown:	Glendale, NY
Class:	USMC Cadet Corps 1939
Service:	Merchant Marine
Position:	Chief Officer
Date / Place of death:	November 4, 1945, Kahului, Maui
Date / Place of burial:	Unknown
Age:	26

Theodore A. Heidt joined the U.S. Merchant Marine Cadet Corps in March 1939 and served as Deck Cadet aboard the *Scanstates, Mormacsun, Deer Lodge,* and *Mormacyork* on voyages to Europe and South America. He subsequently sailed as Third Mate aboard the SS *Argentina* and as Second Mate aboard the SS *George Weems*. He signed on as Chief Mate aboard the C1-M-AV1 cargo ship SS *Link Splice* on August 28, 1945, at Savannah, Georgia. The *Link Splice* sailed later for Hawaii via the Panama Canal.

By November 4, 1945, the *Link Splice* had reached Kahului, the port for the Hawaiian island of Maui. As the Chief Mate, Theodore Heidt was standing the evening 4 to 8 watch on deck supervising cargo handling and the ship's lines. At approximately 1900, the ship's Captain, Joseph N. Gonyeau, noticed that the ship's gangway was out of position. He went to inform the Chief Mate of the fact but could not find him. While talking with the ship's purser, the Captain reported that he heard screaming and yelling on deck. The Captain and purser immediately went on deck and found that Theodore Heidt had been pulled into a winch by the gangway line. From the lack of other crew members around, it was apparent that he had attempted to handle the gangway himself rather than calling the deck crew on watch to help him with it. Apparently, he had become fouled in the gangway line while the winch was operating and was unable to disengage himself from the line. The line pulled him into and around the winch several times, wrapping him in the line and crushing him as the line was tightened by the winch.

The Captain, purser, and other members of the crew were able to extricate Theodore Heidt from the winch and called for medical assistance. One U.S. Public Health Service doctor and two U.S. Navy doctors arrived on the scene but could not save him. Theodore Heidt was declared dead at about 1940 November 4, 1945. After preparation for burial by a local mortician, Heidt's body was repatriated to the United States on board the *Link Splice* the ship on which he served. According to crew records on file in New York, the ship returned to New York from Hawaii on December 4, 1945.

Based on his merchant marine service, Theodore A. Heidt was entitled to the Atlantic War Zone Bar, the Mediterranean-Middle East War Zone Bar, the Pacific War Zone Bar, and the Victory Medal.

At the time of his death, Theodore A. Heidt was the husband of Irene A. Heidt of Kew Gardens, Long Island, New York. He was the only son of Alfred A. Heidt and Frieda Heidt. Alfred Heidt managed a bar and grill.

James Morley Hendy

Born: September 9, 1918
Hometown: Santa Barbara, CA
Class: 1941—USMCC Cadet Officer
1941—California Maritime Academy
Service: Merchant Marine
Position: Chief Officer
Date / Place of death: November 19, 1944, at sea Aboard USS *Rixey* (APH 3)
Date / Place of burial: November 20, 1944 / at Sea, 07-07 N 131-57E
Age: 26

James M. Hendy was appointed a Cadet Officer, U.S. Merchant Marine Cadet Corps, in December 1941 and assigned to the SS *Cape Alava*. According to crew lists on file in New York, by April 1942, he had been promoted to Third Mate aboard the *Cape Alava* and completed a voyage to Bombay, India, in that capacity. Other records indicate that he left the *Cape Alava* in England in early 1943 and signed on aboard the SS *Erin* at Bristol, United Kingdom, on February 18. The *Erin* arrived at New York on March 15, 1943. He signed on as Chief Mate aboard SS *Gilbert Stuart* at New York, New York, on March 1, 1944. After a voyage to England, he signed articles again at New Orleans, Louisiana, on July 14, 1944, before the ship sailed for the South Pacific.

By October 1944, the *Gilbert Stuart* had arrived in Hollandia, New Guinea. On October 29, 1944, the ship sailed for San Pedro Bay, Leyte, Philippine Islands, with five hundred Army troops and their equipment plus about six thousand drums of motor gasoline in the lower holds. The ship arrived at San Pedro Bay on November 4. In the following days, the ship anchored off Dulag and then shifted to an anchorage off of Red Beach south of Tacloban. During its stay in San Pedro Bay, enemy air attacks were frequent, with up to four "red alerts" each day.

On the morning of November 18, the first red alert came at 0515 (local), bringing the crew, Armed Guard, and Army longshoremen to their general quarters stations. Roughly two hours later, at 0715, another red alert was received. The gun crews began firing as enemy aircraft attacked the ship, shooting down two of them. However, a third aircraft attacked from dead ahead. Several of the ship's 20 mm machine guns began firing at the plane, shooting its tail off. The damaged bomber crashed into the starboard side of the bridge. The aircraft's bombs fell into the midships section of the ship, while the burning wreckage of the aircraft spread across the after portion of the ship. The aircraft's engine actually fell into the number 4 lower hold, which contained two thousand drums of motor gasoline, but did not start a fire.

At the time of the attack, most of the Deck Department was on deck working with the Army longshoremen unloading cargo. Fire broke out along the entire length of the deck following the attack. The aft gun crews flooded the aft magazine, released a life raft, and then swam from the stern to the bow to assist in the firefighting. The rest of the crew immediately manned fire hoses; within a few minutes, firefighting and rescue craft had joined the ship. The fire was brought under control by the ship's crew and men from several Navy ships in the area without igniting the remaining cargo of gasoline.

USS *Rixey* (APH 3)

Of the thirty-eight merchant crew and twenty-nine Naval Armed Guard on board, five crew members and one Navy gunner were killed in the attack. In addition, five Army longshoremen working aboard the *Gilbert Stuart* were also killed. Many more men, including Chief Mate James M. Hendy, were wounded in the attack or burned by the fires. Several of the *Gilbert Stuart* badly injured men, including James Hendy, were transferred to the evacuation transport USS *Rixey* (APH 3) for transport to hospital facilities in Manus, New Guinea. However, the extent of James Hendy's wounds and third-degree burns resulted in his coming aboard the *Rixey* in severe shock. Despite continuous administration of plasma, two transfusions of whole blood, and the best efforts of the *Rixey* medical staff, James M. Hendy succumbed to his wounds at 1655 on November 19, 1944. He was buried at sea in a service conducted by Chaplain Lieutenant L. E. Cook, USNR, at 1000 on November 20, 1944.

The ship sailed from San Pedro Bay under its own power on November 22 with the help of the surviving members of the ship's Armed Guard, since many of the Deck Department sailors were killed or injured. The ship arrived safely in Hollandia a few days later and returned to San Francisco, California, on January 27, 1945, from Milne Bay, New Guinea.

Based on his merchant marine service, he would have received the Mariner's Medal, the Combat Bar, the Atlantic War Zone Bar, the Pacific War Zone Bar, and the Victory Medal.

James was the only son of Joseph H. Hendy and Grace Miriam Maxfield Hendy, and husband of Dorothy P. Hendy. James and Dorothy were married in 1943 and lived at 1336 Garden Street, Santa Barbara, California. James' father was born in England and was a homebuilder. The 1940 census shows that James was living at home working as a Carpenter's helper. James was born in Fruitland, Idaho, along with his older sister, Miriam Sara Hendy.

Oliver Meeker Jones

Born: February 6, 1917
Hometown: Hartford, CT
Class: 1939—USMMCC
Service: Merchant Marine
Position: Second Mate
Date / Place of death: March 7, 1942 / off
Sable Island, Halifax, NS
Date / Place of burial: March 7, 1942 / Lost at
Sea / Off Sable Island,
Halifax, NS
Age: 24

According to his U.S. Coast Guard file, Oliver M. Jones began going to sea as an apprentice seaman on December 7, 1935, aboard the SS *Scanpenn*. After sailing as Cadet aboard the SS *Scanyork* and SS *City of Fairbury,* he received his certificate of service as Deck Cadet from the U.S. Coast Guard at New York, New York, on April 29, 1937. Sometime thereafter, Oliver M. Jones became one of the first members of the U.S. Merchant Marine Cadet Corps. After sailing as Deck Cadet for two more years aboard other Moore-McCormack Lines ships, including the SS *Scanstates*, Oliver M. Jones received his U.S. Coast Guard license as Third Mate, oceans, on June 20, 1939.

SS *Independence Hall*

Oliver Jones continued working for Moore-McCormack, sailing as fourth officer aboard the SS *Mormachawk*, and Junior Third Mate aboard the SS *Brazil* and *Mormacswan*. On November 1, 1941, he signed on aboard the SS *Independence Hall*, a World War I "Hog Islander," at Norfolk, Virginia. Four months later, the SS *Independence Hall*, loaded with general cargo, was in Halifax, Nova Scotia, waiting to sail in Convoy SC-73. The convoy, bound for Liverpool, sailed on March 6, 1942, but thick fog and heavy seas caused the *Independence Hall* to lose the convoy almost immediately upon departure from Halifax. The rising seas battered the twenty-two-year-old ship, washing the number 4 life raft, the ship's deck cargo, and one of the ship's able seamen overboard.

The Captain, Eugene Currot, turned the ship into the wind and spent two hours in a fruitless search for the missing seaman. By the time he abandoned the search, the ship was amid increasingly heavy seas. Soon after, the ship's crew heard the cry, "All men put on life jackets." At that point, according to the ship's Naval Armed Guard Commander,

> We all rushed out into the alleyway and saw through the door that the forward part of the ship had been carried away. It was about 100 yards distant. After the ship broke in two the engineers on watch stayed at their posts for hours working the ship back at slow speed, I believe, into the wind and seas. They stuck to their posts until "abandon ship" had been ordered, and certainly did a wonderful job."

Unfortunately, nearly all of the ship's deck officers, including Second Mate Oliver M. Jones, were in the forward portion of the ship, which had broken off. None of the officers and men in this part of the ship survived.

The senior surviving deck officer, Third Mate Walter J. Lee, took command of what was left of the *Independence Hall* and prepared the remaining life rafts and lifeboats for lowering. When he finally ordered the crew to abandon ship, it ran aground. With the heavy seas and surf, the only option for the survivors was to remain aboard the stranded hulk until a rescue could be attempted. By late morning of the next day, the wreck had been spotted by a PBY "Catalina" patrol plane, which directed several warships to the wreck. After several unsuccessful rescue attempts, men and boats from the HMS *Witch (D 89)* were able to rescue the survivors of the *Independence Hall*. For his heroism and leadership as Third Mate of the SS *Independence Hall*, Walter J. Lee was awarded the Merchant Marine Distinguished Service Medal.

Based on his merchant marine service, Oliver Meeker Jones was posthumously awarded the Merchant Marine Defense Bar, the Atlantic War Zone Bar, the Victory Medal, and the Presidential Testimonial Letter.

Oliver M. Jones was the younger of Richard Pratt Jones and Ruth Meeker Weld Jones's two sons.

According to U.S. Census information, Richard P. Jones was a farmer living in South Windsor, Connecticut. Oliver's mother and father died in March 1932. He lived with his older brother, Richard, in Jersey City, New Jersey, when he was not at sea. Oliver was a member of the Children of the American Revolution and Sons of the American Revolution as descendant of Richard Abbey, a Connecticut soldier in the American Revolution. A marker for Oliver M. Jones is in the Center Cemetery, South Windsor, Connecticut.

**Oliver Meeker Jones,
South Windsor, CT**

Walter Hay Lee

Born:	August 23, 1913
Hometown:	Los Angeles, CA
Class:	USMCC Cadet Officer—1940
Service:	Merchant Marine
Position:	Second Mate
Date / Place of death:	September 18, 1944 / 02-52 S, 101-12 E
Date / Place of burial:	September 18, 1944 / Lost at Sea 02-52 S, 101-12 E
Age:	31

Walter H. Lee is believed by his relatives to be the first Chinese American licensed officer in the U.S. Merchant Marine. Walter started out in the merchant marine in 1933 as an Ordinary Seaman aboard the SS *Golden Peak* of the Oceanic and Oriental Navigation Company sailing to the Far East. On September 14, 1934, he received his U.S. Coast Guard certificate as able bodied seaman. He continued sailing aboard the SS *Golden Peak* in this capacity for the next two years. By March 3, 1936, he had been promoted to Deck Cadet aboard the SS *Golden Star*. After just one year of study and training aboard the Golden Star, Walter earned his license as Third Mate from the U.S. Coast Guard on April 6, 1937.

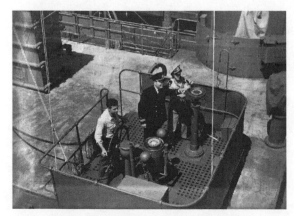

Walter Lee (in blues) George Duffy (khakis) and Stan Gorski on flying bridge of *American Leader*

It is unknown in what capacity Walter sailed during the two years after he received his Third Mate's license. However, he began sailing as a Cadet Officer (deck) aboard the SS *Sawokla* on May 20, 1939. After a year sailing as Cadet Officer, he signed on as Junior Third Mate aboard the SS *Sea Witch* on June 30, 1940. He signed off as Third Mate on May

5, 1941. Six weeks later, on June 17, 1941, he signed on as Third Mate aboard the MS *American Leader*. With the exception of the month he took off in the fall of 1941 to sit for his Second Mate's license examination, Walter H. Lee served continuously aboard the *American Leader* thereafter.

On April 13, 1942, at the Port of New York, two Kings Point Cadet-Midshipmen joined the ship, Joseph DiCicco (engine) and Gordon Tyne (deck). According to the account of Captain George Duffy, then the ship's Third Mate, the ship was carrying a general cargo of war supplies, including boots, barbed wire, and vehicles, along with a deck cargo of nine twin-engine bombers, bound for Russia via Persian Gulf ports. The ship was also loaded with several thousand tons of steel ingots for India. The *American Leader* was armed with a handful of antiquated weapons manned by nine Navy sailors.

MV *American Leader*

After discharging its cargo, the *American Leader* loaded a cargo of rugs, chemicals, and other raw materials in India before sailing for Colombo, Ceylon (Sri Lanka), to load baled rubber and liquid latex. Upon completion of loading, the ship sailed for Cape Town, South Africa, arriving there on September 7, 1942. From Cape Town, the ship was ordered to continue westward, without escort, toward the Straits of Magellan.

At about 1930, on September 10, while Walter Lee was standing his bridge watch as Second Mate, the *American Leader* ran afoul of the German Navy commerce raider *Michel*. During the brief, one-sided engagement, ten crew members, including Cadet-Midshipmen Gordon Tyne and Joseph DiCicco, were killed, two lifeboats were destroyed, and Walter Lee was wounded in the leg. The forty-eight survivors (thirty-nine crew and nine Armed Guard sailors) became prisoners of war, joining a growing group from the *Michel*'s earlier victims. Despite receiving medical care aboard the *Michel*, Walter Lee's wounded leg never healed properly.

Two months later, the *Michel*'s Commanding Officer turned his prisoners of war over to Japanese authorities in Batavia, Java (present-day Djakarta, Indonesia). According to accounts of the survivors, most of the *American Leader*'s survivors were put to work by the Japanese building a railroad in the jungle. Because of his leg injury, Walter Lee was not considered fit enough for the work parties and remained in camp. According to documents in his U.S. Coast Guard record, a short wave radio message from Walter Hay Lee was received by U.S. authorities in early 1943. By June, his prisoner of war status had been officially confirmed.

In September 1944, Walter Lee and several other *American Leader* survivors were killed in the sinking of the prisoner of war transport *Junyo Maru* when it was torpedoed by HMS *Tradewind*. Other *American Leader* survivors were killed in the sinking of the *Tomahaku Maru*. Of the fifty-eight men aboard the *American Leader* when it sailed from Cape Town, only twenty-eight made it home after the end of the war.

In 2006, a moving memoir of Walter H. Lee was written by his nephew, Christopher Lee, the son of Walter's younger sister Edna.[1] In his memoir, Christopher Lee recounts visits to the Lee family by some of Walter's shipmates in which they told them about Walter's days as a prisoner of war. Christopher Lee notes that the survivors of the *Junyo Maru* told the family that

> as the prisoners were swimming toward shore, Walter was trying to help someone else. The sailors said that Walter was always helping someone. He was just that type of person. They waited for him, but Walter said, "I'm fine, you go on ahead." When they looked back he was gone.

On Sunday, June 4, 2000, a Dutch Navy squadron visiting Indonesia conducted a memorial service to the prisoners of war who perished in the sinking of the *Junyo Maru*. A memorial wreath with the names of deceased inscribed on it, including those of Walter Hay Lee and his shipmates from the MS *American Leader*, was dropped on the ocean at the location of the sinking.

---

[1] "An Officer and a Chinaman: A War Hero I Never Met," *Topography of War: Asian American Essays*, Asian American Writer's Workshop, 2006.

Walter Hay Lee was posthumously awarded the Mariner's Medal, the Combat Bar with star, the Atlantic War Zone Bar, the American Defense Bar, the Victory Medal, and the Presidential Testimonial Letter.

Walter was the youngest of Thing "Leo" (known as "Goongsie" to the family) Lee and Chan She Lee's two sons and the third of their four children. Mr. Lee was a successful businessman who owned a clothing store, Leland's Men's Furnishing, as well as a cigar store. Thing Lee's ownership of these stores was very important to the family, as under the laws of the time, only Chinese men who owned business could bring wives over from China. Although his brother and sisters went to local high schools, Walter attended Polytechnic High, where he majored in engineering. However, he began sailing as an Ordinary Seaman before he graduated.

Christopher Lee wrote the following about what Walter was like:

> Edna recalls that when Walter came home on leave, he would use a car for a date and to go out with his friends. He and George shared a car, but George was always more "relaxed" about upkeep. Edna remembers Walter muttering and fuming: "That George! All he does is *drive* the car. He never washes or cleans it. He just doesn't take *care* of things!" And he'd get a bucket of water, go out and wash the car with spit, polish and vigor. Whether it was life at sea of just the difference in the brother's personalities is hard to say. Probably both.

Robert W. Lorenz

Born:	June 23, 1917
Hometown:	New York, NY
Class:	USMCC Cadet Officer—1941 New York Maritime—1940
Service:	U.S. Naval Reserve
Position / Rank:	Submarine Officer / Lieutenant
Date / Place of death:	On or about September 17, 1943 / near Shira Saki, Honshu, Japan
Date / Place of burial:	On or about September 17, 1943 / Lost at Sea near Shira Saki, Honshu, Japan— Tablets of the Missing at Honolulu Memorial Honolulu, Hawaii
Age:	25

U.S. Navy records indicate that Robert Lorenz entered the U.S. Naval Reserve on June 25, 1939, while he was a student at the New York State Merchant Marine Academy. He graduated on September 27, 1940. After graduation, he applied for and was accepted into the Cadet Officer Program of the U.S. Merchant Marine Cadet Corps. He was assigned for training to the U.S. Coast and Geodetic Survey Ship *Explorer*. He served aboard the *Explorer* from October 16, 1940, until January 25, 1941. The Captain of the *Explorer* said in his report dated May 3, 1941,

Cadet Officer (D) Robert Lorenz

Mr. Lorenz displayed an unusual amount of ability and energy. He was considered the most capable of all the Cadets assigned this vessel. He is highly recommended for receiving a Certificate of Ability and for any other award that can be issued.

While he was assigned to the *Explorer*, he applied for appointment as an Ensign, U.S. Naval Reserve, and assignment to active duty. While he was waiting for his commission, he was assigned to the U.S. Maritime Commission Cadet School at Fort Schuyler, New York. He was commissioned with a date of rank of February 14, 1941, but did not receive active duty orders. In the meantime, he signed on as Cadet Officer aboard the passenger ship SS *Uruguay* as Cadet Officer (deck) on April 11, 1941. He was promoted to Junior third officer for the ship's next voyage, signing on in this capacity on May 20, 1941. In July 1941, he asked the Navy when he would be ordered to active duty. This letter appears to have broken a bureaucratic log jam, as he was ordered to active duty on August 20, 1941. He signed off of the SS *Uruguay* on September 22, 1941, in order to accept his commission and report for active duty on September 24.

After initial processing, Ensign Lorenz left New York on September 29 and reported aboard the USS *McCawley* (AP 10) on October 4, 1941. Ensign Lorenz was assigned to duty as a Junior watch and division officer and assistant boat group officer until he was detached on September 27, 1942. In February 1942, the *McCawley* made a trip to Iceland with troops for defense of that key island. Upon its return to New York, the *McCawley* was transferred to the Pacific Fleet. Upon its arrival in Wellington, New Zealand, the *McCawley* became the flagship of Rear Admiral Richmond K. Turner, USN, Commander of Amphibious Forces for the Navy/Marine Corps amphibious landings at Guadalcanal. On June 15, 1942, he was promoted to Lieutenant (jg). Upon his detachment from the *McCawley* on September 27, 1942, to attend submarine school, which he had requested on April 1, 1942, his Commanding Officer stated the following in his report on fitness of officers:

> Very good personal and military character. In action at Guadalcanal
> Aug. 7-9 & Sept 18, 1942, with creditable performance of duty.

On October 19, 1942, Lieutenant (jg) Lorenz reported for submarine school at New London, Connecticut, for training to become a submarine officer. Two days later, he was assigned to USS *O-6 (*SS *67)*, a World War I—era submarine used by that time for training submarine sailors. After two months aboard the *O-6,* he was detached on December 18, 1942, to report to the submarine school to complete his training in submarines. Shortly before being detached from USS *0-6,* he applied for transfer to the regular U.S. Navy. His request was denied because New York Merchant Marine Academy was not recognized as a Naval Reserve Officers Training Corps unit. Following three months of additional training at New London, on March 27, 1943, Lieutenant Lorenz, along with several other officers, was transferred to Commander, Submarine Force Pacific, for duty. Upon his arrival in Pearl Harbor, Lieutenant Lorenz was assigned to Submarine Division 43 for temporary duty aboard one of its submarines and ultimate assignment to USS *Pompano* (SS 181).

USS *Pompano* **(SS 181)**

According to his service record, Robert Lorenz was promoted to full Lieutenant on May 1, 1943. He reported aboard the *Pompano* on May 12, 1943, the day after it began its refit period following its fifth war patrol. Lieutenant Lorenz was aboard for the *Pompano*'s sixth war patrol, although he was not fully qualified in submarines until the very last days of the patrol. After a thirty-day long refit at Midway, the *Pompano* departed on its seventh war patrol on August 20, 1943. The *Pompano* orders were to patrol the east coast of Honshu, Japan, from August 29 to September 27, and then to return to Pearl Harbor. The *Pompano* attacked and sank two Japanese ships and damaged a third in early September.

A recent reanalysis of Japanese Navy records indicates that unbeknownst to the *Pompano* crew, one of its fuel tanks had been damaged and was leaking oil. On September 17, Japanese antisubmarine forces spotted a moving oil slick off the northern coast of Honshu, about a mile off of the Shira Saki Lighthouse. The oil slick was attacked by both aircraft and antisubmarine patrol craft, resulting in large quantities of oil floating to the surface in a fixed location. On July 23, 2012, a U.S. Navy minesweeper operating off Shira Saki detected what is described as a "possible submarine" lying on the bottom.

USS *Pompano* (SS-181) memorial
Juniper Hill Park, Frankfort, Kentucky

The USS *Pompano* was stricken from the U.S. Naval Vessel Register on January 12, 1944. Lt. Robert Lorenz and the rest of the crew of the USS *Pompano* were declared dead on January 4, 1946.

Lt. Robert Lorenz, USNR, was posthumously awarded the Purple Heart, the American Defense Service Medal, the American Campaign Medal, the Asiatic-Pacific Campaign Medal, the World War II Victory Medal, and the Submarine Combat Patrol Insignia with one star. He was also awarded the Merchant Marine Defense Bar. His name is inscribed on the Tables of the Missing at the Honolulu Memorial, Honolulu, Hawaii.

Robert W. Lorenz was the younger of Julius Lorenz and Eugenia Rieger Lorenz's two sons. Following graduation from Straubenmuller Textile High School in June 1936, Robert attended New York University and Columbian Preparatory School (Washington DC) before entering New York Merchant Marine Academy in 1938. Robert and his older brother, Theodore, grew up in a hotel in Westchester, New York, where their father was either the owner or manager.

Henry Duke McNabb

Born:	November 19, 1917
Hometown:	Stockton, CA
Class:	1939—USMMCC Cadet Officer 1939— California Maritime Academy
Service:	U. S. Naval Reserve
Position / Rank:	Salvage Boat Officer / Ensign
Date / Place of death:	September 9, 1943 / Salerno, Italy
Date / Place of Burial:	Unknown / Casa Bonita Mausoleum, Stockton, CA
Age:	25

Ensign Henry Duke McNabb graduated from California Maritime Academy in 1939. Shortly after graduation, he was appointed a Cadet Officer in the U.S. Merchant Marine Cadet Corps and served aboard the Coast and Geodetic Survey Ship *Pioneer* from June to October 1939. By January 24, 1940, Henry McNabb had secured employment with Standard Oil Company of California (Chevron) as an able bodied seaman aboard the tanker SS *J. C. Fitzsimmons*. Crew lists on file in Seattle, Washington, indicate that he was still employed in that capacity in August 1940.

Henry D. McNabb was commissioned into the Navy on September 15, 1942, at San Francisco, California. He reported to the Navy's amphibious training base, Little Creek, Virginia, on October 29, 1942. On December 2, he was transferred to the attack cargo ship USS *Arcturus* (AKA 1) (formerly the SS *Mormachawk*), and reported aboard the following day. After a voyage to the South Pacific, the *Arcturus* returned to the U.S. East Coast for repairs and preparation for the Invasion of Sicily. On July 8, 1943, the USS *Arcturus* was one of the many amphibious ships supporting the landings on Sicily.

USS *Arcturus* (AKA 1)

After the completion of operations at Sicily, the USS *Arcturus* was assigned Operation Avalanche, the Invasion of Salerno, Italy. This was the first Allied assault on the continent of Europe. Assigned to Task Force 81, the Southern Attack Force, the USS *Arcturus* sailed from Oran and arrived off the beaches of Salerno on September 8, 1943. The landings began at 0335 on September 9.

Ensign McNabb was assigned to duty as the *Arcturus* Salvage Boat Officer, in charge of *LCM 15* (landing craft, mechanized), with its four-man crew and five enlisted men of the boat salvage and repair party. On September 9, between 0900 and 1000, while Ensign McNabb and his men were assisting a British Landing Craft at Blue Beach, *LCM 15* came under fire from a German 88 mm shore battery. The gunfire killed Ensign McNabb and five of his men, wounded three of the other four men, and sank *LCM 15*.

Ensign Henry D. McNabb, USNR, was posthumously awarded the Silver Star, the Navy's third-highest award for valor, and the Purple Heart for his actions during the landings at Salerno. In addition, he also earned the European-African-Middle Eastern Campaign Medal. For his merchant marine service, Henry D. McNabb also earned the Merchant Marine Defense Bar and the Pacific War Zone Bar.

Henry Duke McNabb was the only son of A. Jack McNabb, a Stockton, California, Police Officer, and Wilmoth McNabb. The 1920 U.S. Census shows the family living in Dallas, Texas, where Jack's occupation was listed as Carpenter. However, the 1930 census shows Jack and Duke McNabb living in Stockton, California, but there is no mention of Wilmoth in the household. City Directories for Stockton, California, from 1940 to 42 indicate that Jack McNabb had remarried a woman named Eva.

Sometime after August 1940, Henry Duke McNabb was employed as a firefighter with the Stockton, California, Fire Department. A memorial page on the Stockton Fire Department's web site indicates he was the only one of twenty-five Stockton firefighters that did not return safely home at the end of the war. The street in front of Stockton Fire Station number 14 was renamed McNabb Street in his honor on September 9, 1994, the forty-first anniversary of his death.

Theodore Scharpf

Born:	May 27, 1920
Hometown:	Brooklyn, NY
Class:	1941—USMMCC Cadet Officer
	1940—New York MMA
Service:	Merchant Marine
Position:	First Assistant Engineer
Date / Place of death:	January 27, 1943 / 36-37 N, 30-55 W
Date / Place of burial:	January 27, 1943 / Lost at Sea—36-37 N, 30-55 W
Age:	22

Theodore Scharpf entered New York Merchant Marine Academy in 1938 and was aboard its Training Ship, SS *Empire State,* for its 1939 cruise to Europe and the Far East. Following his graduation in 1940, he sailed as Cadet Officer aboard the SS *Deltargentino* and SS *Veragua.* On September 13, 1941, he signed on aboard the SS *Lancaster* as Third Assistant Engineer and remained there through several voyages, including a voyage to Murmansk and back in Convoy PQ-15 and QP-13.

According to U.S. Coast Guard records, Theodore Scharpf signed on aboard the SS *Charles C. Pinckney* on January 1, 1943. The ship sailed with Convoy UGS-4 from Hampton Roads, Virginia, on January 13, 1943, loaded with ammunition, a general cargo of war supplies, and mechanized equipment bound for Casablanca. The *Charles C. Pinckney* was one of three ships, including the SS *City of Flint* and the SS *Julia Ward Howe,* which fell behind the convoy on January 21, 1943. All three ships, no longer protected by the convoy escort of six U.S. Navy destroyers, were sunk by U-boats within a week.

On January 27, the *Charles C. Pinckney* was about two hundred miles south-southwest of Fayal Island, Azores. During the morning, the watch sighted a submarine far off on the horizon, traveling parallel to the *Charles C. Pinckney,* apparently at great speed. The gun crew fired a few shots at the submarine, but even at maximum elevation, these did not come close to their target. The *Charles C. Pinckney* then increased to its maximum speed of 11 knots.

Late in the afternoon, the *Charles C. Pinckney* changed course to proceed directly away from the submarine, but the crew was unable to tell whether or not the submarine followed. At about 2145, local time, the Chief Mate observed a torpedo, fired by *U-514* heading directly for the ship, and ordered a hard-right rudder, but the order came too late. The torpedo struck just behind the ship's bow. The explosion detonated part of her cargo, which blew off the bow and killed two men in the forward gun crew. On the Captain's order, the crew abandoned ship immediately, with all but one of the boats lowered successfully. The gun crew remained on the ship at great peril to their own lives, given the cargo of munitions on board. When the German submarine surfaced near the port beam, the gun crew engaged, forcing the sub into an emergency dive, and leading the gun crew to believe they'd sunk the sub.

SS Charles S. Pinckney

Since the ship did not immediately sink, the crew reboarded the ship to see if it could be repaired. After inspecting the ship's engines, the Chief Engineer reported that it would not be possible to raise steam and continue sailing the ship. However, the crew was able to collect additional supplies and send a distress signal. Around midnight, *U-514* fired two more torpedoes; the second torpedo hit the *Charles C. Pinckney*, causing the crew to abandon ship again. Soon thereafter, *U-514* approached the boats and questioned the survivors.

The four lifeboats began making way for the Azores but were unable to stay together in heavy seas during the second night. One lifeboat, carrying six crew members, including the second officer, and eight Naval Armed Guard sailors, was picked up on February 8 by the Swiss ship *Caritas I*, and later landed at Horta, Fayal Island. The other three lifeboats were never seen again. Of the seventy-three persons aboard the SS *Charles C. Pinckney* (forty-two crew, twenty-nine Naval Armed Guard sailors, and two U.S. Army security officers), only these fourteen were rescued.

Theodore Scharpf, along with Cadet-Midshipmen Vincent Corrigan and Robert L. Lamac, was among those lost.

Based on his service aboard, the SS *Charles S. Pinckney*, and his previous merchant marine service, Theodore Scharpf was posthumously awarded the Mariner's Medal, the Combat Bar with star, the Atlantic War Zone Bar, the Victory Medal, and the Presidential Testimonial Letter. He would also have been eligible for the Soviet Commemorative Medal awarded in 1995 by the then Soviet Union to U.S. Merchant Mariners who sailed in the Murmansk convoys.

Theodore Scharpf was the younger of Margaret Scharpf's two sons. Theodore's father died sometime in the 1920s. Emat, Theodore's older brother, was fifteen years older and employed as a bank examiner in 1930. The 1940 census does not identify an occupation for either Theodore or his mother, although it appears that they had taken in a boarder.

Robert Campbell Simmons

Born:	July 9, 1920
Hometown:	Newburyport, Massachusetts
Class:	1939—USMC Cadet Corps
Service:	U.S. Army Air Corps
Position / Rank:	Bombardier / Second Lieutenant
Date / Place of death:	September 27, 1944 / Elmside Farm, near Nailstone, England
Date / Place of burial:	Cambridge American Cemetery, Plot E, Row 6, Grave 1
Age:	24

U.S. Maritime Commission records indicate that Robert C. Simmons was a member of the U.S. Merchant Marine Cadet Corps from June 27 to November 18, 1939.

Robert C. Simmons subsequently enlisted in the U.S. Army Air Corps on July 23, 1942, as an aviation Cadet and was promoted to Second Lieutenant on October 7, 1943. Subsequently, he completed Bombardier School and was assigned to fly B-17G bombers with the 849th Bombardment Squadron (Heavy), 490th Bomb Group, and Eighth Air Force operating out of Eye Air Base, Suffolk, England.

On the night of September 27, 1944, Simmons was participating in a low-level training mission aboard the *Heavenly Body* (tail number 43-37776), a B-17G. At 2045, local time, the aircraft's nose dropped, and its port wing struck the ground. The resulting crash killed all of those aboard.

At the time Second Lieutenant Simmons was killed, his unit was flying strategic bombing missions over Germany. U.S. Air Force records indicate that Robert C. Simmons was awarded the Air Medal with three Oak Leaf Clusters. This indicates that Second Lieutenant Simmons had participated in as many as thirty-five combat missions over Europe at the time of his death. The memorial plaque is near the site of the crash of the "Heavenly Body."

Robert C. Simmons was the son of Herbert W. Simmons and Grace C. Simmons. In 1930, Hubert Simmons was employed as a bridge tender while the family lived with his grandfather, a fisherman. By 1940, Robert had a much younger brother, Herbert Jr.

Memorial Plaque placed near the Crash Site of "Heavenly Body"

Robert Navarre Simmons

Born:	April 6, 1917
Hometown:	Seattle, WA
Class:	1939—USMMCC Cadet Corps
Service:	USNR
Position / Rank:	Executive Officer / Lieutenant
Date / Place of death:	May 18, 1945, Okinawa / 26-11.5 N, 127-37 E
Date / Place of burial:	Honolulu Memorial, Plot M, Row 0, Grave 916
Age:	28

Robert N. Simmons became a member of the U.S. Merchant Marine Cadet Corps in August 1939. Crew lists on file in Seattle, Washington, show that he signed on as Deck Cadet aboard the SS *West Ivis* of the Pacific Argentine Brazil Line on February 16, 1940, at Seattle, Washington, for a voyage to the Caribbean and East Coast of South America. It is unknown when he signed off the SS *West Ivis*, but he neither continued serving with the Merchant Marine Cadet Corps nor received a license from the U.S. Coast Guard.

U.S. Navy records indicate that Robert N. Simmons entered the U.S. Navy as a Midshipman on November 22, 1940, after previously enlisting on August 9, 1940. He was promoted to Ensign, USNR, on February 28, 1941, and reported aboard the USS *Drayton* (DD 336) on April 8, 1941, at Pearl Harbor. The USS *Drayton* was at sea escorting the USS Lexington (CV 2) when the Japanese attacked Pearl Harbor on December 7, 1941. After operating out of Pearl Harbor and the U.S. West Coast for most of 1942, the *Drayton* spent the next ten months in combat in and around Guadalcanal and the Solomon Islands. By the time Robert Simmons was transferred from the *Drayton* on August 19, 1943, he had been promoted to Lieutenant.

Lieutenant Simmons was assigned to the USS *Longshaw* (DD 559) as its executive officer when the ship was commissioned on December 4, 1943. After its shakedown cruise and crew training, the *Longshaw* sailed for duty with the Pacific Fleet. By May 1945, the *Longshaw* was involved in combat duty in the Central Pacific, Philippines, Taiwan Strait, Southeast

Asia, and Okinawa without returning to the United States. The *Longshaw* reported for duty off Okinawa on March 24, 1945, and spent the next two months providing shore bombardment supporting troops fighting ashore and antiaircraft protection for ships supporting the landings. As a result, the crew was operating in combat conditions twenty-four hours per day.

USS *Longshaw* under way in the Pacific

According to the USS *Longshaw*'s after action report, by May 18, 1945, the ship's crew was exhausted. At 0719, on May 18, 1945, while maneuvering, the ship ran hard aground on a reef. For two hours, strenuous efforts were made to free the *Longshaw*. During that time, the Japanese relocated a shore battery, which took the ship under fire at 1101.

The ship received several hits in quick succession, causing extensive damage and an explosion that blew the bow off. The Captain ordered the crew to abandon ship but was wounded and apparently died shortly thereafter. Lieutenant Simmons was apparently killed during the Japanese shelling.

The hulk of the USS *Longshaw* was destroyed by gunfire and torpedoes later that day.

During his naval service, Lt. Robert N. Simmons, USNR, was awarded the Bronze Star, the Purple Heart, the American Defense Service Medal, and the Asiatic-Pacific Campaign Medal with at least three stars. In addition, for his service in the merchant marine, he was eligible for the Merchant Marine Defense Bar.

Robert N. Simmons was the youngest son of Clyde Barrett Simmons and Beatrice Eva Navarre Simmons. Interestingly, the middle name of both of his siblings was also Navarre. On March 27, 1941, Robert N. Simmons wed Winifred Sandoe. Of their four years of marriage, they were with each other just eight months. However, from their marriage, two children were born, including author Craig Vetter, who wrote a memoir about the father he never knew based on his letters to Winifred, *All My Love, Samples Later: My Mother, My Father, and Our Family That Almost Was. A Story of Life and War.*

Thaddeus Theophilus Trzebuchowski

Born: January 29, 1919
Hometown: Brooklyn, NY
Class: 1941—USMC Cadet
                          Officer 1939—New York
                          MMA
Service: Merchant Marine
Position: Chief Mate
Date / Place of death: December 11, 1943 /
                          U.S. East Coast 40-43 N,
                          71-58 W
Date / Place of burial: December 11, 1943 /
                          U.S. East Coast 40-43 N,
                          71-58 W—Lost at Sea
Age: 24

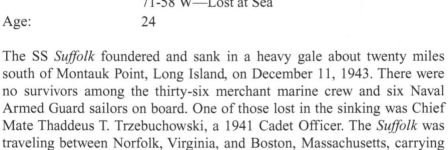

The SS *Suffolk* foundered and sank in a heavy gale about twenty miles south of Montauk Point, Long Island, on December 11, 1943. There were no survivors among the thirty-six merchant marine crew and six Naval Armed Guard sailors on board. One of those lost in the sinking was Chief Mate Thaddeus T. Trzebuchowski, a 1941 Cadet Officer. The *Suffolk* was traveling between Norfolk, Virginia, and Boston, Massachusetts, carrying a cargo of coal.

The vessel transmitted her final message at midday, December 11, stating she was foundering in heavy weather. The Navy sent out several vessels to try to aid the crew of the *Suffolk*, but these were unable to reach the vessel. The search was abandoned several days later when neither wreckage nor survivors had been sighted. However, at least one raft was launched successfully from the sinking ship. On December 31, the USS *Reeves* (DE 156) came upon a raft from the *Suffolk*. However, the only two occupants of the raft, a Navy gunner and a member of the crew, had died days earlier from exposure.

Thaddeus T. Trzebuchowski had previously served as second class Deck Cadet aboard the TV *Empire State* (1939), Deck Cadet (Cadet Officer) aboard the MS *Exton* (1940), and Third Mate aboard the SS *Gatun* (1941), the SS *Atlantida* (1941), and the MS *Idaho* (1942). Crew lists for these ships describe him as being five feet seven inches tall and weighing 135 pounds with his next of kin identified as his father, M. Trzebuchowski. He left at least one sibling, his brother Francis A. Trzebuchowski, who sought additional information about his brother's death in 1944.

Robert Stanley Walter Jr.

Born:	November 19, 1917
Hometown:	Washington, DC
Class:	1937-39—USMCC Cadet Officer 1937—Pennsylvania Nautical School
Service:	Army Coast Artillery
Position:	Mate (Civilian)
Date / Place of death:	January 8, 1942 / U.S. East Coast
Date / Place of burial:	January 8, 1942 / U.S. East Coast—Lost at Sea
Age:	25

U.S. Coast Guard records show that Robert S. Walter received his license as Third Mate, oceans, unlimited, on May 26, 1937, the day after he graduated from Pennsylvania Nautical School. He signed on as Cadet Officer aboard the SS *President Roosevelt* shortly after receiving his license. Crew lists on file in New York, New York, indicate that he remained aboard the SS *President Roosevelt* until 1939. He then served as Junior Third Mate aboard the SS *American Trader* until later that year. On February 23, 1940, he signed on aboard the SS *Manhattan* as Junior Third Officer. In November 1940, he signed on aboard the SS *Artigas* as Junior Third Mate. He remained aboard the *Artigas* until July 1941. Based on his subsequent employment, he must have become employed by the U.S. Army shortly after leaving the *Artigas*.

On January 7, 1942, the U.S. Army mine planter *General Richard Arnold* was called out to rescue a sister mine planter, *L-88*, off of the Isles of Shoals, near Portsmouth Harbor, New Hampshire. The *Arnold*, a ninety-eight-foot ship built in 1909, gallantly made its way through stormy weather to aid the disabled *L-88*, which had been drifting in the storm for more than six hours. The *Arnold* reached the *L-88* at 2030 and made itself fast to the *L-88*. The two ships, powered only by the *Arnold*, could not make any progress back to port and hove to using the *Arnold* engines until a larger mine planter, the *General Absalom Baird*, could tow the *L-88* back into port.

The *Baird* arrived at the scene at around midnight and began towing both ships back to harbor. However, ice had been building up on the *Arnold* since it left port, and both ships were heavy with ice. At 0050, on January 8, the *Arnold* reported that it was taking on water by the stern. The crew manned the pumps but was unable to keep the water from rising. By 0130, the water had risen over the pumps and put out the fires in the boiler, leaving the *Arnold* helpless. Fifteen minutes later, the *General Richard Arnold* suddenly plunged under the waves. The *L-88* would have been dragged down by the sinking *Arnold* if the *L-88*'s crew had not rushed on deck to cut the lines binding them fast to the doomed ship. The Master of the *General Richard Arnold*, William H. Chasteen, was able to jump from the bridge into the icy waters as the ship sank. He was the only survivor; the rest of the crew, including Mate Robert S. Walter Jr., were lost.

U.S. Army mine planter *General William H. Arnold*

Based on his merchant marine service, Robert S. Walter was posthumously awarded the Merchant Marine Defense Bar, the Atlantic War Zone Bar, the Victory Medal, and the Presidential Testimonial Letter.

Robert S. Walter was the oldest son of Robert Sr. and Anne R. Walter. Robert had an older sister, Jane, and a younger brother, George. According to the 1920 U.S. Census, Robert Sr. was vice president of Army and Navy Preparatory School in Washington DC. However, by the 1930 census, Robert Sr. is identified as being a life insurance agent.

Richard Bryce Wilkie

Born:	November 24, 1916
Hometown:	Los Angeles, CA
Class:	1940—USMMCC Cadet Officer 1939—California Maritime Academy
Service:	U.S. Naval Reserve
Position / Rank:	Repair Ship Officer / Ensign
Date / Place of death:	June 21, 1941 / San Diego, CA
Date / Place of burial:	June 26, 1941 / Fort Rosecrans National Cemetery, San Diego, CA Officer Section A, Site 214
Age:	24

Headstone at Fort Rosecrans National Cemetery

Ensign Richard B. Wilkie was appointed as a merchant marine Cadet, USNR, on April 23, 1940, after his graduation from California Maritime Academy in 1939. On May 21, 1940, he signed on aboard the SS *President Pierce* as Cadet Officer for a voyage to the Far East, including Yokohama, Japan. Upon the ship's return to California, Richard Wilkie applied for a Naval Reserve commission. After a second trip to the Far East, Richard B. Wilkie accepted his appointment as Ensign, USNR on September 3, 1940.

Ensign Wilkie was immediately assigned to the repair ship USS *Medusa (AR 1)*, based at Pearl Harbor. He was transported to Hawaii aboard the USS *Tippecanoe (AO 21)* and reported aboard the USS *Medusa* on October 4, 1940. On October 23, less than three weeks after reporting aboard the *Medusa*, Ensign Wilkie was transferred to Pearl

Harbor's Naval Hospital, suffering from what would later be determined to be tuberculosis of the spine.

After initial treatment, Ensign Wilkie was transferred to the West Coast for further treatment. He was transported aboard the USS *Neches (AO 5)* and reported to the U.S. Naval Hospital, Balboa, California, on December 11, 1940. However, the treatments available in San Diego did not cure Wilkie's condition. As result, in June 1941, he requested medical retirement from the U.S. Navy. However, he died at the U.S. Naval Hospital on June 21, 1941, before this request could be processed. The cause of death was listed as tuberculosis of the spine.

Although he did not receive any U.S. Navy awards during his brief service, he earned the Merchant Marine Defense Bar for his merchant marine service.

Richard B. Wilkie was the son of William S. Wilkie and Rose Talange Wilkie. According to the 1920 U.S. Census, he had a sister, Marjorie.

Harry Arthur Wolfe Jr.

Born:	October 26, 1920
Hometown:	Kingston, PA
Class:	1942—USMMCC Cadet Officer 1941— Pennsylvania Nautical School
Service:	Merchant Marine
Position:	Third Mate
Date / Place of death:	January 9, 1943 / 56-15 N, 22-00 W
Date / Place of burial:	January 9, 1943 / Lost at Sea—56-15 N, 22-00 W
Age:	22

Harry A. Wolfe signed on aboard the SS *Louise Lykes* on November 7, 1941, as a "Cadet Officer" in the ship's Deck Department. The ship completed a voyage to South Africa and returned to New York on March 31, 1942. Six weeks later, on May 9, 1942, Harry Wolfe was promoted to Junior Third Mate for a voyage to South Africa and the Red Sea. He continued as the *Louise Lykes* Junior Third Mate for a voyage to North Africa, from which the ship returned to New York on December 12, 1942.

SS *Louise Lykes*

The SS *Louise Lykes* sailed without escort from New York on January 2, 1943, carrying a cargo of ammunition and other war supplies bound for Belfast, Northern Ireland. The ship was hit by four torpedoes fired from the surfaced *U-384* at 2025 on the evening of January 9, 1943. According to German Navy records, the *Louise Lykes* cargo exploded with what was described as "a terrible blast," forcing *U-384* to dive to avoid being struck by pieces of the wreckage. There were no survivors among the fifty merchant crew, thirty-four Naval Armed Guard sailors, and ten U.S. Army personnel aboard.

Another former U.S. Maritime Commission Cadet Officer, Frederick Baumann, and five Cadet-Midshipmen from the U.S. Merchant Marine Academy, Michael M. Chrobak, Charles C. Gassner, Allen G. Miller, Robert C. Vancure, and Eugene W. Walters, were all killed, making the sinking of the SS *Louise Lykes* the single deadliest sinking in the Academy's history in terms of Cadet losses.

Based on his merchant marine service, Harry A. Wolfe was posthumously awarded the Mariner's Medal, the Combat Bar with star, the Atlantic War Zone Bar, the Mediterranean—Middle East Bar, the Victory Medal, and the Presidential Testimonial Letter.

Harry Wolfe was the only son of Harry A. Wolfe Sr. and Emily Wolfe; they also had an older daughter, Margaret. According to the 1940 U.S. Census, Margaret and her husband, Robert Bell, were living with the Wolfes. At that time, Harry Sr. was employed as an electrician at a local iron works.

Walter William Zech

Born:	April 16, 1916
Hometown:	Philadelphia, PA
Class:	1939—USMMCC Cadet Officer 1937— Pennsylvania Nautical School
Service:	China National Aviation Corp.
Position:	Aircraft Navigator
Date / Place of death:	March 8, 1944 / Camaguey, Cuba
Date / Place of burial:	Unknown / Philadelphia, PA
Age:	27

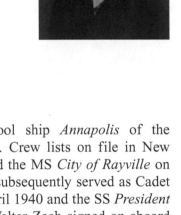

Walter W. Zech graduated from the school ship *Annapolis* of the Pennsylvania State Nautical School in 1937. Crew lists on file in New York show that Walter Zech signed on aboard the MS *City of Rayville* on March 3, 1939, as Cadet Officer (deck). He subsequently served as Cadet Officer (deck) aboard the SS *Lightning* in April 1940 and the SS *President Roosevelt* in July 1940. On July 24, 1940, Walter Zech signed on aboard the passenger ship SS *Washington* as a Junior Deck Officer on voyages that returned to New York from the West Coast via the Panama Canal. His physical description shows that he was five feet eleven inches tall and weighed 170 pounds.

According to the *Philadelphia Evening Bulletin*, on March 11, 1944, Walter Zech had raised his license to First Mate. However, by July 1943, Walter Zech had completed a special course in aircraft navigation at the University of Miami. After completing this course, he was employed by Pan American Airlines before switching to China National Aviation Corporation as a navigator ferrying aircraft from the United States to China via India.

On Tuesday, March 7, 1944, he was serving as navigator on a China National Aviation aircraft ferry mission of two aircraft, which took off from Morrison Field (now known as Palm Beach International Airport). The two aircraft were bound eventually for Calcutta, India, via Caribbean Island bases, Natal, Brazil, and across the South Atlantic to Accra, Africa.

On this trip, the lead pilot decided to stop for refueling at Camaguey Army Air Corps Base, Cuba, rather than Nassau or Kingston, Jamaica.

Newspaper accounts indicate that Zech's aircraft had trouble immediately after takeoff from Camaguey on Wednesday, March 8. Witnesses said that the plane attempted to return to base but crashed on its approach for an emergency landing. All four of the plane's occupants, including Walter Zech, were killed. Walter Zech was originally assigned to the other aircraft, but for some reason, he changed aircraft.

Walter Zech was the husband of Stella Zech and had a son, Walter Ray, who was living in Miami at the time of his death. He was one of Ruth Zech Willis's three sons. Walter's brothers were Stanley and Harry. Walter also had a sister named Erica.

According to the 1930 U.S. Census, Walter's father died in the 1920s, leaving his mother a widow. The census indicates that Walter's mother was a schoolteacher. According to the report of his death in the *Philadelphia Evening Bulletin*, from March 11, 1944, Walter graduated from Philadelphia Central High School in 1934.

**Walter Zech with his wife, Stella
and son, Walter Ray, in Miami, 1943**

Gone, but Never Forgotten

James Hoffman, a 1944 graduate of Kings Point, plays a very special role in this book. He grew up in Cambridge, Illinois, applied for admission to the Cadet Corps in May 1942 while still in high school was accepted and was called to training at Pass Christian in September. He arrived several weeks before the recently acquired campus was ready for students; he spent those first few weeks aboard the training vessel SS *North Star*. In early October, Hoffman and his two dozen classmates moved all their possessions, along with all the training equipment, aboard the *North Star*, into the former Inn by the Sea resort.

After eight weeks of preliminary training, on November 13, Cadet-Midshipman Hoffman was shipped out on the SS *Wade Hampton*, a Delta Line freighter on its maiden voyage that carried a load of sugar from Santiago, Cuba, to the Domino Sugar plant in Baltimore. The *Wade Hampton* then went to New York, where she picked up a general cargo of war materiel, including two PT boats stowed on deck. In mid-February 1943, she joined convoy HX-227 headed for Russia on the notorious Murmansk run.

The *Wade Hampton* never made it. She fell behind her convoy due to bad weather and was torpedoed on February 28. Hoffman wound up in a lifeboat for three hours, at the end of which, a British corvette rescued him and his fellow survivors. He recalled that his sea project went to the bottom with his ship. In a sense, the crew of the *Wade Hampton* was lucky; of the fifty-nine people onboard, including the naval Armed Guard, only nine died.

Hoffman and his fellow survivors soon found themselves aboard the SS *Santa Catalina*, en route to Liverpool. They were put up in a so-called survivors' pool, a hotel taken over for the war effort. As Hoffman recalled, "They had a dining room where you could get a meal. A good thing for us because we had no money . . . We'd lost everything except the clothes on our backs . . ." Like other American Mariners at the survivors' pool, Hoffman watched the bulletin boards for a ship returning to the United States. He found a berth on a British liner that was speedy enough to traverse the North Atlantic unescorted. He arrived in New York, reported to the Maritime Commission's training office, and received a replacement uniform and a week's leave.

At the end of the week, he received his new papers from the Coast Guard and assigned to the SS *Borinquen*, a converted passenger liner that ferried troops and other passengers back and forth between New York and the Mediterranean, with stops at Casablanca, Algiers, Palermo, and other ports. For a teenage Mariner, even an experienced one, it was a whole new world, full of dangers and novelty.

In late September 1943, Hoffman arrived at Kings Point for his advanced training, in time for the formal dedication of the campus on September 20. He completed his advanced training as an Engineering Cadet and graduated in June 1944. He was commissioned as Ensign in the U.S. Navy and served the remainder of World War II as an Engineering Officer aboard the USS *Regulus* and USS *Rescue* in the South Pacific. He was aboard the *Rescue*, a hospital ship, in Tokyo Bay on September 2, 1945. From the ship's deck, he watched the nearby USS *Missouri* as the Armistice signing took place. The *Rescue* had the important role of rescuing American POWs released by the Japanese that day.

He was recalled to active duty in the Navy in 1951, promoted to Lieutenant, and served aboard the USS *Leo* and USS *Thomas Jefferson* during the Korean War. He saw duty in a variety of ways, including service in-country in Korea and at Eniwetok for the hydrogen bomb trials.

Following the Korean War, he remained on inactive duty and after several years retired from the U.S. Navy.

Like many WWII survivors, Hoffman pursued a civilian career, got married, and made his way through his adult life and work. But his dramatic wartime experiences never fully left his mind—nor did the fact that the merchant mariners of World War II had never been accorded veteran's status. It was a promise made by President Franklin Roosevelt, but ignored for decades by subsequent administrations. As Hoffman and many others saw it, this was a blatant injustice—one which was not remedied until 1988, when judicial pressure forced the Air Force (the agency with congressional authority to determine veteran's status) to extend formal veteran's recognition and a limited GI Bill of Rights to the merchant mariners of WWII.

This retroactive recognition was extended to the Cadet-Midshipmen who died on their training voyages, whose stories were told in the preceding pages of this book. Thinking about the implications of this chain of events, Hoffman realized that there was almost no chance that, nearly a half-century after the fact, the families of the Cadets would ever receive the long-overdue veteran-recognition documents. So working with Captain George McCarthy, Hoffman lobbied the Coast Guard to issue an individual certificate for each Cadet killed in action and to send those documents to Kings Point.

After a certain amount of arm-twisting, the Coast Guard acquiesced. But it soon became clear that the Academy, although supportive of Hoffman's and McCarthy's efforts, didn't have the resources to track down families across the country to hand over the documents. So Hoffman volunteered for that task himself: "I said, 'Okay, fine. I'll start looking for the families. And soon as I find one, I'll notify you, and you can get the document for that Cadet sent out to the family.' And that's what I started doing, back in late 1988 or early 1989." Starting with a list of next of kin that the Academy had, Hoffman began digging. To put it mildly, it was a tough slog. More than four decades had passed. Families had moved, died out, or simply disappeared. Hoffman haunted libraries, scoured old newspapers, contacted veterans' groups, and otherwise dug deep, looking for relatives, in most cases, siblings or nephews and nieces of the deceased Cadets.

Near the close of 2004, Thomas G. Schroeder, a 1957 graduate of the Academy, joined the search for the families of the 142. Like Hoffman, Schroeder had put in hundreds of hours in the ongoing effort, and

Hoffman noted that Schroeder had been particularly helpful in winning the cooperation of many individuals during the long and difficult search.

Hoffman and Schroeder turned up all the families eligible to receive the veteran's document; it was a labor of love. "I want to give them the document that honors their loved one," Hoffman said. "So I keep at it." When Hoffman died, Tom Schroeder kept at it and he reached the last family in 2013.

Many of the photographs, letters, and other personal comments that appear in this volume are there thanks to Hoffman's and Schroeder's tireless efforts. The memories of the Cadet-Midshipmen and the USMMA alumni profiled in this book are much richer through their efforts. They may be long gone, but thanks to their fellow Mariners, they will never be forgotten.

Jim was honored by the Kings Point Alumni and the Academy in 2003 with the Peter Rackett Lifetime Achievement Award; and on May 17, 2005, the Academy dedicated the James Hoffman Advanced Learning Center.

James Hoffman died on May 5, 2011, and was buried with full military honors with gun salutes.

Kings Point Graduate Books and Reminiscences

Amborski, Leonard E. *The Last Voyage: Maritime Heroes of World War II.* New York: Ambor Press, 2001.

Billy, George J. and Billy Christine M, *Merchant Mariners at War, an Oral History of World War II,* University Press of Florida, 2008

Clark, Captain John W. *SSS.* Kings Point: American Merchant Marine Museum, 2000.

Cruikshank, Jeffrey L., and Chloe G. Kline. *In Peace and War: A History of the U.S. Merchant Marine Academy at Kings Point.* New York: Wiley Books, 2007.

DeGhetto, Kenneth. "Sea Log." Unpublished account of the author's sea year.

Elliott, Lt. Earnest W. Memoir of a Merchant Mariner in World War II, 2000, personal experiences as a Cadet and officer in WW II; prepared for family and friends. Copy is in USMMA Library archives.

Mitchell, C. Bradford. *We'll Deliver.* Kings Point: USMMA Alumni Association, 1977.

Moore, Captain Arthur R. *A Careless Word . . . A Needless Sinking: A History of the Staggering Losses Suffered by the U.S. Merchant Marine, Both in Ships and Personnel, during World War II.* Kings Point: American Merchant Marine Museum, 1985.

Moses, Sam. *At All Costs: How a Crippled Ship and Two American Merchant Mariners Turned the Tide of World War II.* Random House Trade Paperbacks, 2007.

Nicholes, Captain Walter S. *The Seagoing Years: Memoirs of a Boy at War.* Privately published in 2011.

Reminick, Gerald. *Death's Railway: A Merchant Mariner on the River Kwai.* Palo Alto: The Glencannon Press, 2002.

Risk, James L. *The Forgotten Convoy of North Russia...Recollections of.*

Risk, James L. *Recounting of a Convoy Stuck at Molotovsk, Russia, from March-December 1943.*

Quarterly Newsletter. Lake Norman YMCA, December 2006, pages 15-20; and story enlarged in a compact disc of same name.

Roland, Alex, W., Jeffrey Bolster, and Alexander Keyssar. *The Way of the Ship: America's Maritime History Reenvisioned, 1600-2000.* New York: Wiley Books, 2007.

Rosen, Herman E. *Gallant Ship, Brave Men.* The S. S. John Drayton, Liberty Ship, American Merchant Marine Museum, Kings Point, NY 2004.

Runyan, Timothy J., and Jan M. Copes. *To Die Gallantly: The Battle of the Atlantic.* Boulder: Westview Press, 1994.

Slezak, Michael A. "My World War II Experiences in the Maritime Service." Unpublished manuscript, last modified July 1, 1992.

Snider, Andrew J., and others. *Annals of the U.S. Merchant Marine Academy: Class of 1942 History Project.* CD-ROM.

Varga, Frank. "Popop's War, 2004." Unpublished account of the author's sea year and after, prepared for family. Copy is in USMMA Library archives.

Acknowledgment of Sources Contained in the Book

Part 1 is generally drawn from a draft manuscript dated March 20, 2008, by Jeffrey L. Cruikshank and Chloe G. Kline, *The Cruikshank Company,* provided under contract to the American Maritime History Project. This work has been significantly modified with many additions and deletions. Sources utilized in this work included interviews with graduates, quotations from *Polaris*, the USMMA Cadet-Midshipman magazine, and several government publications. References also include material drawn from the following:

Heinicke, Captain Richard, Jr. "Perilous Seafaring, 1942-1945." Unpublished manuscript

Tarrant, V. E. *The U-Boat Offensive, 1914-1945*. Annapolis: Naval Institute Press, 1989.

White, David Fairbank. *Bitter Ocean: The Battle of the Atlantic, 1939-1945*. New York: Simon & Schuster, 2006.

Williamson, Gordon. *Wolf Pack: The Story of the U-Boat in World War II*. Oxford: Osprey Publishing, 2003.

Part 2 contains extensive detailed research by Thomas McCaffery, class of 1976. It was drawn from USMMA archives and many other Federal Archives; photographs came from USMMA and family members. Some early research information was drawn from a draft manuscript dated March 20, 2008, by The Cruikshank Company provided under contract to the American Maritime History Project.

Cover Design
Marek X. Mutch, Bay Village, Ohio

Photographs
The majority of the photographs were received from the U.S. Merchant Marine Academy and the U.S. Maritime Commission. Photographs of the men honored in this book that include their family members were received from family members who provided them for use in this testimonial book. We thank them for their vital contribution.

The cover photo of the painting *The Last Five Shells* by Tom Lowell was provided by the American Merchant Marine Museum, Kings Point, New York. The Monument photo was provided by the Bland Memorial Library, Kings Point.

Index A Cadet-Midshipmen

for each Cadet-Midshipman

Index B Graduates

for each Graduate

Index C Cadet Officers

for each Cadet Officer

General Index

Appendix A

Chronological List of Deceased Cadets and Graduates

Date	Name	Date	Name
June 21, 1941	Richard Bryce Wilkie	November 2, 1941	Carl Bialek
November 16, 1941	William M. Farr	January 8, 1942	Robert S. Walter Jr.
February 20, 1942	Richard Lewis	February 20, 1942	Robert See
March 7, 1942	Oliver Meeker Jones	March 19, 1942	Howard Payne Conway Jr.
April 6, 1942	Richard H. Holbrook	May 4, 1942	Carl Brandler
May 9, 1942	Glenn R. Bruaw	May 9, 1942	Irwin S. Ebel
May 16, 1942	Charles Emil Blair	May 26, 1942	John P. Brewster
May 28, 1942	Peter N. Chunosoff	June 8, 1942	Kenneth McAuliffe
July 5, 1942	Calvert Sumner Foote	July 30, 1942	Vincent Gordon Cathey
September 10, 1942	Robert Joseph C. DiCicco	September 10, 1942	Gordon A. Tyne
September 13, 1942	Norbert Amborski	September 19, 1942	Ceslau A. Maciorowski
September 24, 1942	Robert Valentine Palmer	September 24, 1942	Burton G. Bergeson
September 24, 1942	Jonathan F. Sturges	September 27, 1942	Edwin Joseph O'Hara
September 27, 1942	Arthur R. Chamberlin Jr.	September 29, 1942	Robert J. Bole III
September 29, 1942	Chester E. Klein	October 7, 1942	Robert S. Nauman
October 7, 1942	Louis Joseph Rovella	October 9, 1942	Samuel Schuster
October 17, 1942	Joseph P. Alexander	October 17, 1942	Joseph William Krusko
		November 2, 1942	Walter P. Seperski
November 2, 1942	Bernard Washington Spilman	November 4, 1942	Robert Everhart
November 4, 1942	Herman Garritsen	November 4, 1942	Peter Smith
November 7, 1942	David Hogan Frohn	November 7, 1942	Richard P. Farrell
November 7, 1942	William R. Weis Jr.	November 7, 1942	George Edgar Guilford
November 7, 1942	James Dale Herndon	November 7, 1942	Fred Pennington
November 14, 1942	William B. Ginnelly	November 18, 1942	Otto E. Kern Jr.
November 23, 1942	Charles Henry Doell	November 19, 1942	Meyer Egenthal
November 19, 1942	William Vaughan O'Hara	December 2, 1942	Joseph Giovinco
December 2, 1942	Henry Levett	December 7, 1942	Drew Allen
December 7, 1942	Philip G. Branigan	December 7, 1942	Leonard L. Erhlich
December 7, 1942	Henry E. Harris Jr.	December 7, 1942	Walter C. Hetrick Jr.
December 7, 1942	John J. McKelvey	December 12, 1942	George John Viridakis

December 31, 1942	Edward J. Ackerlind	December 31, 1942	Warren Benjamin Carriere
January 1, 1943	Denniston Charlton Jr.	January 1, 1943	Benjamin P. Gafford
January 5, 1943	Albert Milton Limehouse	January 9, 1943	Frederick William Baumann
January 9, 1943	Michael M. Chrobak	January 9, 1943	Charles C. Gassner
January 9, 1943	Allen G. Miller	January 9, 1943	Robert C. Vancure
January 9, 1943	Eugene Weaver Walters	January 9, 1943	Harry Arthur Wolfe
January 10, 1943	Robert Walker Allen	January 27, 1943	Vincent Corrigan
January 27, 1943	Robert Louis Lamac	January 27, 1943	Theodore Scharpf
February 2, 1943	William Rutherford Linde	February 2, 1943	Edward J. Gavin
February 2, 1943	Samuel T. Tyler	February 2, 1943	Jay A. Hammershoy
February 2, 1943	Richard E. Holland	February 2, 1943	George R. Race
February 5, 1943	David H. Pitzely	February 5, 1943	James H. Province
February 13, 1943	Harry Quayle Jr.	February 21, 1943	Maxwell Hollander
February 23, 1943	Harry M. Burlison	February 23, 1943	Ralph J. Kohlmeyer
February 23, 1943	Grover P. Lietz	February 23, 1943	William C. Wilson
February 24, 1943	John R. Gordon	February 28, 1943	George C. Miller Jr.
March 2, 1943	Randall P. Bourell	March 2, 1943	Alan R. Clarke
March 2, 1943	Daniel J. Maher	March 2, 1943	Francis T. McCann
March 2, 1943	James J. Coffey		
March 10, 1943	Michael Buck Jr.	March 10, 1943	Howard T. McGrath
March 10, 1943	James R. Rowley	March 10, 1943	John P. Tucek
March 10, 1943	Arthur J. Gradus	March 10, 1943	Charles W. Tamplin
March 11, 1943	James Sinclair Cordua	March 11, 1943	Edwin Hanzik
March 11, 1943	James Oscar Moon	March 11, 1943	Rafael Ramirez Rivera
March 11, 1943	Edwin P. Wiggin	March 16, 1943	John R. Lambert
March 16, 1943	Richard Record	March 17, 1943	Lee T. Byrd
March 17, 1943	LeRoy W. Kernan	March 17, 1943	Walter J. Meyer
March 17, 1943	Robert F. Miller	March 17, 1943	William H. Parker
April 11, 1943	James A. Hope	April 11, 1943	James J. Magee
April 11, 1943	Jack Stadstad	April 23, 1943	Aubrey G. Connors
April 23, 1943	Stephen N. Siviglia	May 19, 1943	Thomas Kellegrew
June 1, 1943	John O. Talbot	June 1, 1943	Benjamin H. Wilkinson
June 6, 1943	Henry J. Bogardus Jr.	June 10, 1943	John M. Carter
June 10, 1943	Alphonse I. Miller	June 10, 1943	Joseph J. Landron Jr.
June 30, 1943	Donald A. Kennedy	July 8, 1943	John H. Watson, III
July 9, 1943	William H. Green Jr.	July 9, 1943	John N. Stewart Jr.
July 13, 1943	George D. McCall	July 14, 1943	George W. Alther Jr.
July 14, 1943	William L. Lyman	July 14, 1943	Warren P. Marks
July 14, 1943	Lawrence McLaughlin	August 4, 1943	William E. McCann
August 19, 1943	Robert J. Derick	August 19, 1943	Roscoe J. Prickett Jr.
August 29, 1943	Robert W. Lorenz	September 9, 1943	Henry D. McNabb
September 14, 1943	George E. Pancratz	September 14, 1943	William S. Sempell
September 20, 1943	Alan A. Atchison Jr.	September 21, 1943	Donald S. Wright
September 21, 1943	Kenneth A. Waters	September 26, 1943	Roland E. Netcott
November 1, 1943	Peter J. Biemel	December 2, 1943	Edwin D. Howard

December 2, 1943	Jay F. Litton	December 2, 1943	Fulton E. Yewell Jr.
December 2, 1943	Marvin W. Brodie	December 2, 1943	Richard B. Glauche
December 2, 1943	Alvin H. Justis	December 2, 1943	Francis B. Tone
December 5, 1943	Paul Greene	December 11, 1943	Thaddeus T. Trzebuchowski
January 6, 1944	Joseph Leonard Driscoll	January 10, 1944	Ronald E. Nolan
March 7, 1944	Walter W. Zech	April 16, 1944	Donald J. Tynan
April 19, 1944	William J. Secunda	April 20, 1944	Frederick C. Whitehead
April 20, 1944	Edward S. Zapletal	June 1, 1944	Michael F. Kostal Jr.
June 12, 1944	Floyd K. Callesen	July 2, 1944	Floyd W. Roach
July 2, 1944	George M. Rutan	July 17, 1944	Walter F. Kannberg
July 18, 1944	Bernard Shultz	August 28, 1944	Gordon W. Lyons
August 20, 1944	Robie K. Wentworth	August 20, 1944	Leroy P. Lawrence
September 18, 1944	Walter H. Lee	October 4, 1944	Charles F. Gerstacker
October 10, 1944	Edward Lemerise	October 31, 1944	Harry Grant
November 1, 1944	William J. O'Neill Jr.	November 2, 1944	Thomas B. Carey Jr.
November 10, 1944	Lloyd S. Strom	November 20, 1944	James M. Hendy
December 10, 1944	Charles W. Hogue	December 12, 1944	Joseph R. Lawrence Jr.
December 18, 1944	Alfredo I. Anido	December 28, 1944	Donald J. Kannitzer
January 2, 1945	Edwin R. Stauffacher Jr.	January 4, 1945	Peter C. Y. Chue
January 15, 1945	Arthur C. Forsyth	January 15, 1945	Edward S. Sherman
January 20, 1945	Roy J. DuChene Jr.	February 1, 1945	Antonio V. Graziano
February 5, 1945	Clarence B. Dengler Jr.	February 23, 1945	Niles K. Stevens
March 20, 1945	Isidore Schaffer	April 2, 1945	Gordon A. Herstam
April 6, 1945	Alexander Harris	April 6, 1945	Keith W. Treseder
April 6, 1945	Richard P. Anderson	April 9, 1945	Jay R. Rosenbloom
April 10, 1945	John W. Artist	April 10, 1945	Dante L. Polcari
April 11, 1945	George P. Grieshaber	April 18, 1945	Herbert E. Anderson
May 5, 1945	Alfredo J. Dell'Aquila	May 11, 1945	Howard S. Bartlett
May 18, 1945	Robert N. Simmons	May 24, 1945	Thomas G. Jones
November 4, 1945	Theodore A. Heidt	November 7, 1945	Richard I. Victorino

Appendix B

U.S. Merchant Marine Academy Cadet-Midshipmen Who Died During World War II
Hometown, Year Born, Ship, Action That Took Their Life

Name	Hometown	State	Month Year Born	Deck or Engine	Ship	Sunk or Event Month Year	Action T Torpedo
Ackerlind, Edward J.	Minneapolis	MN	5/20	Engine	SS *Maiden Creek I*	12/42	Storm Damage. Life boat lost.
Alexander, Joseph Peter	Attica	GA	4/21	Deck	SS *Angelina*	10/42	T
Amborski, Norbert	Buffalo	NY	9/20	Engine	SS *Stone Street*	9/42	T
Artist, John Walter	Brooklyn	NY	4/27	Engine	SS *Saint Mihiel*	4/45	Collision at sea explosion
Atchison, Alan Arlington, Jr.	St. Louis	MO	11/22	Deck	SS *Theodore Dwight Weld*	9/43	T
Bergeson, Burton Gale	Lake Park	MN	6/22	Deck	SS *John Winthrop*	9/42	T
Biemel, Peter John	Cleveland	OH	9/24	Engine	SS *Salmon P. Chase*	11/43	Air Attack Italy
Bogardus, Henry J., Jr.	Montclair	NJ	3/23	Engine	SS *William King*	6/43	T
Bole, Robert J., III	Drexel Hill	PA	7/20	Deck	MS *Wichita*	9/42	T
Bourell, Randall Price	Olney	IL	1/21	Deck	SS *Meriwether Lewis*	3/43	T
Brandler, Carl A.	Maybank	TX	1918	Engine	SS *Munger T. Ball*	5/42	T
Branigan, Philip George	Teaneck	NJ	7/22	Deck	SS *James McKay*	12/42	T
Brewster, John P.	Teaneck	NJ	3/19	Engine	SS *Syros*	5/42	T
Brodie, Marvin W.	Columbus	OH	2/22	Engine	SS *John Harvey*	12/43	Air Attack Italy
Bruaw, Glenn R.	York Haven	PA	11/21	Deck	SS *Heredia*	5/42	T
Buck, Michael, Jr.	Mount Kisco	NY	2/20	Engine	SS *James Sprunt*	3/43	T

Burlison, Harry Moulton	Minneapolis	MN	12/21	Deck	SS *Jonathan Sturges*	2/43	T
Byrd, Lee Thomas	Benson	NC	4/22	Deck	SS *Harry Luckenbach*	3/43	T
Carey, Thomas Bernard, Jr.	Hartford	CT	10/24	Engine	Lost in training	11/44	Scarlet Fever
Carriere, Warren B.	New Orleans	LA	8/19	Deck	SS *Maiden Creek I*	12/42	Storm Damage. Life boat lost.
Carter, John McCormick	Rockville	MD	6/21	Engine	SS *Esso Gettysburg*	6/43	T
Cathey, Vincent G.	Andrews	NC	1/23	Engine	SS *Robert E. Lee*	7/42	T
Chamberlain, Arthur R., Jr.	Piedmont	CA	11/21	Deck	SS *Stephen Hopkins*	9/42	Raider
Charlton, Denniston, Jr.	Great Neck	NY	12/23	Deck	SS *Arthur Middleton*	1/43	T
Chrobak, Michael M.	Linden	NJ	9/21	Engine	SS *Louise Lykes*	1/43	T
Chunosoff, Peter N.	Brooklyn	NY	11/22	Deck	SS *Alcoa Pilgrim*	5/42	T
Clarke, Alan R.	Ridgewood	NJ	2/22	Deck	SS *Meriwether Lewis*	3/43	T
Connors, Aubrey George	Lincolnville	ME	11/22	Deck	SS *Robert Gray*	4/43	T
Conway, Howard P., Jr.	Charlotte	NC	1/19	Engine	SS *Liberator*	3/42	T
Cordua, James Sinclair	Lost Creek	WV	1/22	Deck	SS *William C. Gorgas*	3/43	T
Corrigan, Vincent J.	Glendale	NY	7/22	Engine	SS *Charles C. Pinckney*	1/43	T
Derick, Robert John	East Hartford	CT	4/23	Engine	SS *J. Pinckney Henderson*	8/43	Collision Fire
DiCicco, Joseph C.	Brooklyn	NY	9/22	Engine	MS *American Leader*	9/42	T
Driscoll, Joseph Leonard	Brooklyn	NY	8/23	Deck	SS *Robert Erskine*	1/44	Storm Ship Grounded Drown Italy
DuChene, Roy Joseph, Jr.	Detroit	MI	2/26	Deck	Lost in training	1/45	Pneumonia
Ebel, Irwin S.	Brooklyn	NY	3/23	Engine	SS *Heredia*	5/42	T
Egenthal, Meyer	Brooklyn	NY	3/22	Engine	SS *Sawokla*	11/42	Raider and T
Erhlich, Leonard L.	Brooklyn	NY	6/23	Engine	SS *James McKay*	12/42	T
Everhart, Robert R.	Bala Cynwyd	PA	3/22	Deck	SS *William Clark*	11/42	T
Farrell, Richard P.	Los Angeles	CA	7/20	Deck	SS *Nathaniel Hawthorne*	11/42	T
Foote, Calvin S.	Scranton	PA	4/22	Deck	SS *Pan Atlantic*	7/42	Bombed
Frohn, David H.	Los Angeles	CA	7/21	Deck	SS *Francis Drake*	11/42	Drown in port
Gafford, Benjamin P.	Sherman	TX	3/22	Engine	SS *Arthur Middleton*	1/43	T
Garritsen, Herman G.	Ridgewood	NJ	2/22	Engine	SS *William Clark*	11/42	T
Gassner, Charles C.	Pittsburgh	PA	9/21	Deck	SS *Louise Lykes*	1/43	T
Gavin, Edward J.	West Orange	NJ	4/23	Engine	SS *Dorchester*	2/43	T

Gerstacker, Charles F.	Cleveland	OH	7/20	Engine	Lost in training, San Mateo	10/44	Drown
Ginnelly, William Bernard	Philadelphia	PA	10/22	Engine	SS *Scapa Flow*	11/42	T
Giovinco, Joseph	Brooklyn	NY	4/24	Deck	SS *Coamo*	12/42	T
Glauche, Richard B.	Chicago	IL	4/24	Deck	SS *John Harvey*	12/43	Air Attack Italy
Gordon, John R., Jr.	Brooklyn	NY	1/20	Engine	SS *Nathaniel Greene*	2/43	Air Attack and T
Gradus, Arthur J.	Long Island City	NY	6/23	Deck	SS *Richard Bland*	3/43	T
Green, William Henry, Jr.	Louisiana	MO	11/22	Engine	SS *Samuel Heintzelman*	7/43	T
Guilford, George E.	Centralia	KS	7/21	Engine	SS *La Salle*	11/42	T
Hammershoy, Jay Arthur	Glenbrook	CT	3/22	Engine	SS *Henry R. Mallory*	2/43	T
Hanzik, Edwin	Huntington Station	NY	2/22	Deck	SS *William C. Gorgus*	3/43	T
Harris, Alexander W.	Greenville	SC	11/25	Deck	SS *Hobbs Victory*	4/45	Kamikaze off Okinawa
Hetrick, Walter Charles, Jr.	Lawrence	NY	8/20	Deck	SS *James McKay*	12/42	T
Holbrook, Richard H.	Wayland	NY	1/22	Engine	SS *Bienville*	4/42	Bombs and Cruiser
Holland, Richard E.	Scranton	PA	5/22	Deck	SS *Henry R. Mallory*	2/43	T
Hollander, Maxwell	Atlantic Beach	NY	9/18	Deck	SS *Rosario*	2/43	T
Hope, James Arthur	Avalon	PA	4/21	Deck	SS *Edward B. Dudley*	4/43	T
Howard, Edward David	Sylvania	OH	5/24	Deck	SS *John L. Motley*	12/43	Air Attack Italy
Justis, Alvin H., Jr.	Lynchburg	VA	8/24	Engine	SS *John Harvey*	12/43	Air Attack Italy
Kannitzer, Donald J.	Seattle	WA	10/25	Deck	SS *John Burke*	12/44	Kamikaze Mindoro P.I.
Kellegrew, Thomas	Brooklyn	NY	10/21	Engine	SS *John Drayton*	5/43	T
Kennedy, Donald A.	Brooklyn	NY	5/24	Engine	SS *Lee S. Overman*	6/43	Shipboard Accident
Kern, Otto E., Jr.	Detroit	MI	2/21	Deck	SS *Richard Henry Lee*	11/42	Auto Accident
Klein, Chester E.	Elmhurst	NY	6/20	Engine	MS *Wichita*	9/42	T
Kohlmeyer, Ralph Jacob	Rego Park	NY	10/19	Engine	SS *Jonathan Sturges*	2/43	T
Krusko, Joseph W.	Yonkers	NY	3/20	Deck	SS *Angelina*	10/42	T
Lamac, Robert Louis	Bronx	NY	9/21	Deck	SS *Charles S. Pinckney*	1/43	T
Lambert, John R.	Del Rio	TX	5/24	Deck	SS *James Oglethorpe*	3/43	T
Landron, Joseph J., Jr.	Brooklyn	NY	10/22	Engine	SS *Esso Gettysburg*	6/43	T
Lawrence, Leroy Pinneo	Hartford	CT	7/21	Deck	SS *Jacksonville*	8/44	T

Levett, Henry Alexander	Summit	NJ	1/23	Deck	SS *Coamo*	12/42	T
Lewis, Richard E.	Oswego	NY	4/23	Deck	SS *Azalea City*	2/42	T
Lietz, Grover Paul	Okawville	IL	3/21	Engine	SS *Jonathan Sturges*	2/43	T
Limehouse, Albert Milton	Birmingham	AL	11/21	Unknown	Lost in training	1/43	Illness Nephrosis
Linde, William Rutherford	Hartford	CT	10/21	Engine	SS *Jeremiah Van Rennselaer*	2/43	T
Litton, Jay Francis	Detroit	MI	8/24	Engine	SS *John L. Motley*	12/43	Air Attack Italy
Lyman, William L., Jr.	Upper Montclair	NJ	3/23	Deck	SS *Timothy Pickering*	7/43	Air Attack Italy
Magee, James Joseph	Philadelphia	PA	9/23	Deck	SS *Edward B. Dudley*	4/43	T
Maher, Daniel Joseph	East Boston	MA	7/23	Engine	SS *Meriwether Lewis*	3/43	T
Marks, Warren P.	Nutley	NJ	9/23	Engine	SS *Timothy Pickering*	7/43	Air Attack Italy
McAuliffe, Kenneth,	Metairie	LA	1924	Unknown	SS *Tela*	6/42	T
McCall, George Duncan	Hartselle	AL	3/22	Deck	SS *Robert Bacon*	7/43	T
McCann, Francis T.	Johnson City	NY	8/24	Engine	SS *Meriwether Lewis*	3/43	T
McCann, William Edward	Detroit	MI	9/20	Engine	SS *Thomas Paine*	8/43	Malaria India
McGrath, Howard T.	New York	NY	6/23	Engine	SS *James Sprunt*	3/43	T
McKelvey, John J.	Patterson	NJ	10/20	Deck	SS *James McKay*	12/42	T
McLaughlin, Lawrence Daniel	Woodbridge	NJ	8/23	Engine	SS *Timothy Pickering*	7/43	Air Attack Italy
Meyer, Walter John	New York	NY	2/22	Engine	SS *Harry Luckenbach*	3/43	T
Miller, Allen George, Jr.	Philadelphia	PA	9/23	Deck	SS *Louise Lykes*	1/43	T
Miller, Alphonse Ignatius	Toledo	OH	7/23	Deck	SS *Esso Gettysburg*	6/43	T
Miller, Francis Robert	Chestertown	MD	11/24	Engine	SS *Harry Luckenbach*	3/43	T
Miller, George Carter, Jr.	Jacksonville	FL	4/23	Deck	SS *Wade Hampton*	2/43	T
Moon, James O.	Stone Mountain	GA	6/23	Engine	SS *William C. Gorgas*	3/43	T
Nauman, Robert S.	Chicago	IL	9/21	Engine	SS *Firethorn*	10/42	T
Netcott, Roland Edward	Independence	IA	UNK	Engine	Lost in training 9/26/43	9/43	Unknown
Nolan, Ronald Earl	Algiers	LA	11/24	Deck	SS *Wildwood*	1/44	Pneumonia
O'Hara, Edwin Joseph	Lindsay	CA	11/23	Engine	SS *Stephen Hopkins*	9/42	Raider
O'Hara, William Vaughan	Cambridge	MA	8/21	Deck	SS *Sawokla*	11/42	Raider and T
Palmer, Robert V.	Richmond Hill	VA	10/22	Engine	SS *West Chetac*	9/42	T

Pancratz, George Edward	Little Falls	MN	4/23	Deck	SS *Bushrod Washington*	9/43	Air Attack Italy
Parker, William Henry	Newport News	VA	5/23	Deck	SS *Harry Luckenbach*	3/43	T
Pennington, Fred	Newville	AL	10/21	Deck	SS *La Salle*	11/42	T
Pitzely, David Harold	Bronx	NY	7/24	Deck	SS *West Portal*	2/43	T
Polcari, Dante L.	Medford	MA	4/21	Deck	SS *Saint Mihiel*	4/45	Collision, explosion
Prickett, Roscoe J., Jr.	Little Rock	AR	12/24	Deck	SS *J. Pinckney Henderson*	8/43	Collision Fire
Province, James Henry	Detroit	MI	10/20	Engine	SS *West Portal*	2/43	T
Quayle, Harry, Jr.	Garfield	UT	5/22	Deck	SS *Daniel H. Lownsdale*	2/43	Explosive device in Libya
Race, George R.	Schenectady	NY	4/19	Engine	SS *Henry R. Mallory*	2/43	T
Record, Richard	Oklahoma City	OK	6/24	Engine	SS *James Oglethorpe*	3/43	T
Rosenbloom, Jay R.	Kansas City	MO	6/26	Deck	SS *Charles Henderson*	4/45	Ship Exploded Bari Italy
Rowley, James R.	Little Neck	NY	3/22	Deck	SS *James Sprunt*	3/43	T
Rovella, Louis J.	Philadelphia	PA	6/23	Engine	SS *Firethorn*	10/42	T
Schuster, Samuel	Philadelphia	PA	2/23	Deck	SS *Examelia*	10/42	T
See, Robert J.	Brooklyn	NY	2/19	Engine	SS *Azalea City*	2/42	T
Sempell, William Stewart	Brooklyn	NY	1/24	Engine	SS *Bushrod Washington*	9/43	Air Attack Italy
Shultz, Bernard	Brooklyn	NY	10/22	Deck	SS *Cape Ugat*	7/44	Illness at sea buried New Guinea
Siviglia, Stephen Neuman	Brooklyn	NY	5/24	Engine	SS *Robert Gray*	4/43	T
Smith, Peter J.	Norwood	MA	7/21	Engine	SS *William Clark*	11/42	T
Spilman, Bernard Washington	Arlington	VA	12/20	Engine	MV *Zaandam*	11/42	T
Stadstad, Jack N.	Garden City	NY	11/21	Engine	SS *John Drayton*	4/43	T
Stewart, John Norton, Jr.	Pass Christian	MS	2/24	Deck	SS *Samuel Heintzelman*	7/43	T
Sturges, Jonathan Ford,	Fairfield	CT	6/19	Engine	SS *John Winthrop*	9/42	T
Talbott, John Odell	Bellefonte	PA	10/23	Deck	SS *John Morgan*	6/43	Collision Explosion
Tamplin, Charles W.	Troy	OH	8/23	Deck	SS *Richard Bland*	3/43	T
Tone, Francis Bernard	Easton	PA	7/23	Engine	SS *Samuel J. Tilden*	12/43	Air Attack Italy
Tucek, John P.	Rutherford	NJ	8/22	Deck	SS *James Sprunt*	3/43	T
Tyler, Samuel T., Jr.	Wilmington	NC	2/24	Deck	SS *Dorchester*	2/43	T
Tyne, Gordon A.	Gloucester	MA	10/22	Deck	MS *American Leader*	9/42	T

Vancure, Robert Charles	Youngstown	OH	10/19	Engine	SS *Louise Lykes*	1/43	T
Viridakis, George John	New Haven	CT	5/24	Unknown	Lost in training	12/42	Illness TB
Walters, Eugene Weaver	Brownsville	PA	7/20	Deck	SS *Louise Lykes*	1/43	T
Watson, John H., III	Madison	NJ	8/21	Deck	SS *Peter Minuit*	7/43	Shipboard accident died in Bermuda
Weis, William R., Jr.	Oakland	CA	3/21	Deck	SS *Nathaniel Hawthorne*	11/42	T
Wiggin, Edwin P.	Quicksand	KY	7/24	Deck	SS *William C. Gorgas*	3/43	T
Wilkinson, Benjamin Harris	Wilkinsburg	PA	7/18	Deck	SS *John Morgan*	6/43	Collision Explosion
Wilson, William Crocker	Loudonville	NY	1/24	Deck	SS *Jonathan Sturges*	2/43	T
Wright, Donald Samuels	Moline	IL	3/24	Deck	SS *Cornelia P. Spencer*	9/43	T
Zapletal, Edwin Steve	Milwaukee	WI	1/23	Deck	SS *Paul Hamilton*	4/44	Torpedo Air Attack Med

Appendix C

U.S. Merchant Marine Academy Cadet Corps Cadet-Midshipmen Survivors of Vessels Lost through Enemy Action as of October 15, 1943

These men were members of the "Tin Fish Club"

ALANO, Raffaele
ALLEN, William Stanford
AMSBERRY, Boyd Carleton
ANDELSON, Lester Malcom
ANDERSEN, Martin Gregor
(2) ANDERSON, Carl, Jr.
ANDERSON, Erick Wallace
ANDERSON, Leland B., Jr.
ANSEL, Charles Hamlin
ARMOUR, Mark Robert
AVARY, William Warner
AYERS, Bruce Meeker
BABCOCK, Milton Thorpe
BARLOW, George D.
BARROWCLOUGH, Howard J.
BARTON, Keith Ferdie
BARTON, Robert Winfield
BARWICK, William Ellsworth
BATES, Warren Harding
BECKER, Philip Derway
BELL, George Roderic, Jr.
BELLAH, Maurice
BENNETT, Harold H.
BENSON, Robert Elmer
BERRIMAN, Joseph Cave
BEST, Joseph Frank, Jr.
BETTS, Dennis Rozzel
*(2) BIRD, Ralph William
BLACKA, Thurman H.
BLAIR, George T.
BLANTON, Will Virgil
BLUM, Irving Meyer
BOERNER, Robert Rudolph
BOLAND, Francis Joseph
BOOTH, Joseph Wilson

BOUTON, Clyde Sanford, Jr.
BOUTYETTE, Jean
BRADFORD, Francis C.
BRADY, Thomas Patrick
BRENNAN, Christopher James
BRODSKY, Jerome
BROOKS, Jacob, Jr.
BROUGHTON, James Charles
BROWN, Arthur Z.
BROWN, Hoyt William, Jr.
BURRES, Jack Gordon
BUXBAUM, Leopold Charles
CAHILL, Edward Patrick
CAIN, Frank Haywood
CALDWELL, William Pitts
CALLAHAN, John William, Jr.
CAMPBELL, James
CANAVAN, Patrick Francis
CARAS, James Charles
CARBOTTI, Michael James
CARMINES, Charles Dixon
*CARNEY, Edward Joseph
CHAPMAN, William King
CHARLTON, Marshall Jay
CHRISTENSEN, Harry Edmund
CHRISTOPHER, Joseph Francis
CHURCHMAN, Leslie
CLARK, Robert G.
COFFEY, William Mathew
COMSTOCK, Bartholomew James
CONNELL, Robert Hildreth, Jr.
CONNOLLY, Patrick James
COOK, Dale Owen
COONEN, James Willard
COOPER, Herbert Bertram

CORL, Eldon Alexander
*(2) CORLISS, Robert Milton
CORRIGAN, John
COTTER, Christopher
CROSS, William Reid, II
CROTTY, Leo J.
CUMMINGS, John Barrett
CURTIS, Calvin Charles
CUTRONA, Enrico
**DALES, Francis A.
DAMON, Robert Earl
D'AURIA, Giovanni
DAVIES, James Clarence
DAVIES, William Goldie, Jr.
*(2) DAVIS, Edward S., Jr.
DAY, Wesley Fletcher
DeBAUN, Robert Fallon
DEGNEN, Joseph Francis
*DEITZ, Morton
*DeMARCHES, Devo
DENGLER, Clarence Bert, Jr.
DENNISON, William James
DeREMER, William J.
DESPOSITO, John Joseph
DICOSIMO, Frederick
DORE, William F. H.
DOWLING, James
DOYLE, Robert McElroy
DRAPER, John Samuel
DREW, Burton Charles
DRINKWATER, George Henry
DRUMHELLER, Maurice A.
(2) DUDLEY, Robert H.
DUHRELS, Fred
DUNCAN, Ulric Dahlgren

639

DUNHAM, Byron
DUNN, John Gordon
DUNNE, Francis
DURR, William S., Jr.
ECKMANN, Harold Adam
EDERA, Eugenia
EDGAR, Lauren Freemont
ELLARD, Trant Horace
ELLIOTT, James Martindale
ELLIOTT, William James
ERB, Arthur Eugene
ETEROVICH, Ivan
EWING, Paul Crangle
FAHRNER, Willard Floyd
FAJANS, Wayne Douglas
FALLONE, Pasquale Carlo
FARLEY, Neil George
FARLEY, Rex Jay
(2) FARRELL, George, Jr.
FARRELL, Joseph Patrick, Jr.
FAWCETT, Richard Edward
FEDOR, Louis Paul
FELDER, Ira Dee
FENNESSEY, Donald F.
FITZGERALD, Edward M.
FITZPATRICK, James John
FLEISCHER, William A.
FORD, William Hoyt
FRANKS, William Joseph
FREIHOFER, Warren Curtis
FRIEDEMANN, Joseph W.
FUQUA, James Gill
GAGLIANO, Joseph Anthony
GALLAGHER, John Thomas
GARIBALDI, George Dominic
GETCHELL, Patrick Francis
GIBSON, Walter F.
GILBERT, Mitchell L.
GOYNE, Robert Evan
GRANT, John
GRAY, Walter A., Jr.
GREEN, George
GROSS, Carl Clarence
GRUSH, Bernard Vincent
GURLEY, Franklin C., Jr.
GUY, Raymond Stewart
HAGER, Louis Cornelius
HALEY, Edmund C., II
HALVORSON, John Evan
HAMMILL, Thomas Anthony
HANSON, Howard A.
HARDER, Orrin Howard
HARDY, Peter John Spencer
HARLEY, John Auguton
HARRIMAN, Clinton H., Jr.
HARTER, Donald Ralph
HATCHER, Orville Paul
HEALEY, William J., Jr.
HEALY, Edward
HEDENBERG, Robert James
HELLING, Robert Ellsworth

HEMSLEY, George R.
HENDERSON, Albert E., Jr.
HENYAN, Richard Rice
HERBERT, John Tyson
HEWITT, James Joseph
HOFF, William Robert
HOFFMAN, James
HOGAN, Raymond
HOKE, Dayrel Gibson
HOLBY, William Graham
HOLCOMB, Kenneth Grant
HOLMES, Gordon
(3) HOLUBOWICZ, Romauld Paul
HORN, Marion F.
HOWLAND, Charles Taggart
HUTCHISON, Joseph Howard
JAKOBSON, Eric Eugene
JAYSON, Herman Louis
JEFFREY, William Leroy
(2) JENNIS, Joseph Hyman
JOHNSON, Robert Louis
JOHNSON, Warren R.
JOHNSON, Wilbur
JOHNSTON, Bertrand Francis
JONES, Glenn Daniel
JOOS, Francis Thomas
JOYCE, Albert Thomas
KAPLAN, Nathan Julius
KARSTEN, John William
KAUTZ, William George
KAVANAGH, Edward
KAYLOR, Charles Burril
KEATING, Leo Chester, Jr.
*KELLY, Charles F.
KELLY, Patrick Raleigh
KENNEDY, James Joseph, Jr.
KESSOCK, James Miller
KETCHAM, Arthur, Jr.
KILBRIDE, John Jay, Jr.
KILMER, Frederick Dennis
KISLING, Jacob Harvey
KLEIN, Carlton David
KLEIN, David Francis
KNIEP, Robert
KRAMER, Cletus Edward
KRIEGER, Alfred H.
(2) KROGMANN, John Clement
KUDER, Reid Gottlieb
LAWRENCE, Joseph Richard
LENK, Joseph Richard
(2) LEONARD, Thomas Patrick
LEONARD, William John
LESSING, Frederick James
LINDEN, Bernard J.
LINDROTH, Ernest R.
LISSNER, James, Jr.
LIVELLI, Paul Samuel
LIVINGSTON, Patrick Howard
LOESER, Aloysius N.
LOPEZ, Warren Joseph
*LOWE, Ansel Hardy

LUEDDECKE, John Henry
LUZINSKI, Robert John
LYSK, Stephen C.
McCABE, Edward Joseph
McCARRON, James Joseph
McCARTHY, Gerald Thomas
McCLURE, John Lincoln
McCORMICK, Nicholas
McMANUS, Benjamin Patton
MacDOUGALL, Bruce A.
MacKENZIE, William Murray
MacLEAN, Donald
MACE, William Ross, Jr.
MACY, John Entwistle
MAGEE, John Merton
MANEGOLD, Milton George
MARKS, William
MARTIN, William Francis
MARTINEZ, Benedict
MARTZ, Carl Edwin
MASSET, Harold August
MERRILL, James M.
MIESNER, Vincent J.
MILLIGAN, Paul L., Jr.
MILLS, James Franklin
MILOS, John Joseph
MITCHELL, Vincent
MITCHELL, William Thomas
MOCK, Ralph L.
MOORE, Albert Reed, Jr.
MOPPER, Kahart Kenny
MORRIS, Gilbert W., Jr.
MOYES, Anthony James
MUENZEN, Thomas Bryant
MUHLENBRUCK, Howard Dick
MUKHALIAN, Henry T.
MURPHY, Paul Francis
NASCZNIEC, Frank P.
NELSON, Charles Adrian
NEMITZ, Ralph Henry
NEWMAN, Leonard
*NEWSOME, Frank Noel
NIEVES, Benjamin
NIXON, Thomas Forbes
NOLAN, Chester Conrad
NORSTRAND, Robert Howell
(2) OBERHOLSER, Leland Spoon
O'CONNELL, Edward
O'CONNELL, John Francis
OLIVER, William Francis
ORNDORFF, Henry Russell
OSBORNE, Stanley
OTTO, Richard George
PABARCUS, John Peter, Jr.
PAGANELLI, Joseph
PANCRATZ, George Edward
PARKER, Hunter Andrew
PASSELL, Laurence
PATERSON, Fredrick William
PAUL, John Francis
PAYNE, James Harrison

(2) PERKINS, Paul E.
PERKS, Oran Frederick
PERRON, Gerard
PERSON, Raymond Norval
PETERSEN, Chester L.
PETERSON, Alfred Ray
PETERSON, Charles J.
PETTINATO, Nicholas R.
PHILLIPS, William L.
PIERCE, Bernard Francis
POLIFRONI, Nicholas
PRAY, Robert Edgar
PRICE, Maurice Warren
QUERN, Albert Frederick
QUIDORT, Eugene Clinton
QUIN, James Norval, Jr.
QUINN, John Joseph
RAMSEY, William John
RAPKIN, Abraham
REED, Joseph Christopher
REESE, Donald J.
RHEIN, Robert James
RICH, William
RITTENHOUSE, Edward S.
RITTER, Henry J.
ROBERTS, Frank C., Jr.
ROCHE, Richard R.
ROGOW, Melvin Bernard
ROSEN, Herman
ROSENTHAL, Homer Stanley
ROSENTHALER, Milton
ROSS, Frank Fuller
SAFFER, Howard
SALLING, James M.
SAUER, Charles Adam
SAWYER, Sherman Goethals
SCHERMERHORN, James Britt

* (2) SCHNEIDER, Leon Henry
SCHOFIELD, Benjamin
SCHULER, Charles Joseph
SCOFIELD, Richard Cary
***SCRUGGS, John Howard
SEARCY, Roy Dennis
SEMBRICH, Alfred Stefhano
SEMMLER, Arthur 0.
SHANNON, James
SHAPPEE, James Burton
SHIFFLER, John Edward
SHOTWELL, Roger Ward, Jr.
SHURSKIS, Sigmund William
SITTMANN, Walter G.
SMAHA, Jack Harold
SMALL, George Charles
SMITH, Richard Hugh
SMITH, Robert Seward
SMITH, Walter Bryce
SMOLEN, Barnet
SNIDER, Paul G.
SONSKY, Allen
SPECKHARD, Robert R.
SPEIGELMAN, David L.
STACKHOUSE, Wilson
STEFFENSEN, James Peter
STEIN, Arthur
STEINGRESS, Frederick M.
STEINMAN, Frank Henry, III
STEUART, John Thomas
STEWART, James M.
STILWELL, Edward Peter
SULLIVAN, John Gerald
SUMMERHAYES, Donald Wren
SUNESON, Austin Roger
TAYLOR, Franklin S.
TETZLAFF, Oscar

THOMAS, Samuel B., Jr.
**THOMAS, William Morris
TOSCANO, Joseph A.
TRAVIS, James B.
TROWER, Luther Lee
*TUTONE, John C.
TYSON, Victor Eyre
URSIN, George, Jr.
VALENTINE, Russell
VERBURG, Robert Junior
VETTER, Jack
VETTER, Robert Lane
VISCONTI, Albert
WAGENSEIL, Warren C.
WALL, Jacques Francis
WALSH, Charles Francis
WARLAND, Knute
WATERS, John M.
(2) WATSON, Warren Colwell
WAXMAN, Robert Charles
WEBB, Allen Gilbert
WEIDNER, George Joseph
WELCH, Edward
WENDT, Charles C., Jr.
(2) WERTHMAN, Robert Henry
WILLIAMS, Charles B.
WILLIAMS, Paul Ray
WILLIAMSON, Winston W.
WILSON, Cameron
WITCRAFT, William David
WOODWARD, William H., Jr.
WORTMAN, David
YEWELL, Fulton E., Jr.
YORK, Daniel A.
YUSKA, Elmer
ZASLOFF, Elias
**ZITO, Frederick, Raymond

Total Survivors as of October 15, 1943   399
Total lost or missing as of October 15, 1943   113
TOTAL   512

Symbols:
*   Wounded in action & Awarded   (2) Survived two vessels lost in
      Mariners Medal   Enemy action
**   Awarded Distinguished Service   (3) Survived three vessels lost in
      Medal   Enemy action
***   Awarded Order of the Purple Heart

Source: The National Archives and Records Administration (War Shipping Administration U.S. Merchant Marine Cadet Corps Training Organization)

Appendix D

Distinguished Service Medal Citations

Edwin J. O'Hara

The President of the United States takes pleasure in presenting the Merchant Marine Distinguished Service Medal to

Edwin Joseph O'Hara

Engine Cadet on SS *Stephen Hopkins*, September 27, 1942

For extraordinary heroism under unusual hazards.

Two enemy surface raiders suddenly appeared out of the morning mist to attack the small merchantman upon which he was serving. Heavy guns of one raider pounded his ship, and machine guns from the other sprayed her decks for one-half hour at close quarters. The heroic gun crew of O'Hara's ship exchanged shot for shot with the enemy, placing thirty-five shells into the waterline of one of the raiders until its crew was forced to abandon their sinking ship. The gun Commander was mortally wounded early in the action, and all of the gun crew were killed or wounded when an enemy shell exploded the magazine of their gun.

At the explosion, O'Hara ran aft and single-handedly served and fired the damaged gun with five live shells remaining in the ready box, scoring direct hits near the waterline of the second raider. O'Hara was mortally wounded in this action. With boilers blown up, engines destroyed, masts shot away, and ablaze from stem to stern, the gallant merchantman finally went under, carrying O'Hara and several of his fighting shipmates with her.

The magnificent courage of this young Cadet constitutes a degree of heroism which will be an enduring inspiration to seamen of the United States Merchant Marine everywhere.

For the President

Admiral Emory Scott Land

George W. Alther Jr.

The President of the United States takes pleasure in presenting the Merchant Marine Distinguished Service Medal to

George W. Alther Jr.

Second Mate on SS *Timothy Pickering*, October 14, 1943

For heroism above and beyond the call of duty.

The vessel in which he was serving in 1941 was bombed by enemy planes, and again a ship in which he served in 1942 was bombed and sunk. During an enemy air attack on a Sicilian port, his third wartime vessel, loaded with ammunition, TNT, aviation gasoline, and British troops, was hit by a 500-pound bomb. The ship was split in two—ammunition exploded in the holds—and the water around the ship was a surface of burning gasoline. The gunnery officer was wounded on the lower deck amidship which was enveloped by flames; but with utter disregard for his own safety, Second Officer Alther went to his assistance, and in so doing gave his life.

In unhesitatingly risking, and subsequently giving, his life in a heroic attempt to rescue a wounded fellow officer, he maintained and enhanced the finest traditions of the United States Merchant Marine.

For the President

Admiral Emory Scott Land

Francis A. Dales

The President of the United States takes pleasure in presenting the Merchant Marine Distinguished Service Medal to

Francis A. Dales

Deck Cadet-Midshipman on SS *Santa Elisa*/SS *Ohio*, August 8-15, 1942

For heroism above and beyond the call of duty.

His ship was a freighter carrying drums of high-octane gasoline, one of two American ships, in a small British convoy to Malta. Orders were to "get through at all costs." Heavily escorted, the convoy moved into the Mediterranean, and before noon of that day, the enemy's attack began. From then on, the entire convoy was under constant attack from Axis planes and submarines. Assigned the command of an antiaircraft gun mounted on the bridge, Dales contributed to the successful defense of his ship for three days.

At 4:00 on the morning of the fourth day, torpedo boats succeeded in breaking through, and two attacked from opposite sides. Sneaking in close under cover of darkness, one opened point-blank fire on Dales's position with four .50-caliber machine guns, sweeping the bridge and killing three of his gun crew in the first bursts. The other sent its deadly torpedo into the opposite side of the freighter. Neither the heavy fire from the first torpedo boat nor the torpedo from the second drove Dales and his crew from their gun. With only flashes to fire at in the darkness, he found the target, and the first boat burst into flames and sank. But the torpedo launched by the other had done its deadly work. The high-test gasoline cargo ignited, and the American ship was engulfed in flames. Reluctantly, orders were given to abandon her.

Two hours later, the survivors were picked up by a British destroyer, which then proceeded to take in tow a tanker that had been bombed and could not maneuver. After five hours of constant dive-bombing, the tanker was hit again—her crew abandoned her—and the destroyer was forced to cut her loose. But the cargo she carried was most important to the defense of Malta, and it had to get through. The rescue destroyer and another destroyer steamed in—lashed themselves to either side of the stricken tanker—and dragged her along in a determined attempt to get to port.

Dales and four others volunteered to go aboard the tanker and man her guns in order to bring more firepower to their defense. The shackled ships, inching along and making a perfect target, were assailed by concentrated enemy airpower. All that day, wave after wave of German and Italian bombers dived at them and were beaten off by a heavy barrage. Bombs straddled them, scoring near misses, but no direct hits were made until noon the next day, when the tanker finally received a bomb down her stack which blew out the bottom of her engine room. Though she continued to settle until her decks were awash, they fought her through, until dusk that day brought them under the protection of the hard-fighting air force out of Malta.

The magnificent courage of this young Cadet constitutes a degree of heroism which will be an enduring inspiration to seamen of the United States Merchant Marine everywhere.

For the President

Admiral Emory Scott Land

Elmer C. Donnelly

The President of the United States takes pleasure in presenting the Merchant Marine Distinguished Service Medal to

Elmer C. Donnelly

Deck Cadet-Midshipman on SS *Daniel Huger*, May 9, 1943

For heroism beyond the call of duty.

His ship was subjected to a two-hour high level bombing attack by seventeen enemy planes. As a result of a near miss, bomb fragments pierced the hull and the cargo of high octane gasoline exploded. Despite heroic efforts to combat the flames, two to three hundred feet high, the fire was soon out of control and the ship was abandoned. Upon the arrival of the shore fire brigade, it was decided to try to save the ship with foamite.

It was necessary to have a few men return to the ship, enter the adjacent hold, and play a hose on the heated bulkhead to prevent the raging fire from spreading. Cadet-Midshipman Donnelly was one of the five who volunteered to risk his life in an attempt to save part of the cargo, which was so necessary to the continuance of war operations. That the fire was eventually brought under control and most of the cargo saved was due in no small measure to his outstanding bravery.

His willingness to risk his life to save his ship, and his heroic conduct during the fire, are in keeping with the finest traditions of the sea.

For the President

Admiral Emory Scott Land

Carl M. Medved

It is my privilege to present the Merchant Marine Distinguished Service Medal, authorized by the secretary of transportation, posthumously to

Carl M. Medved

Cadet-Midshipman (Engine) on SS *Daniel Huger*, May 9, 1943

For heroism beyond the call of duty.

His ship was subjected to a two-hour high level bombing attack by seventeen enemy planes. As a result of a near miss, bomb fragments pierced the hull and the cargo of high octane gasoline exploded. Despite heroic efforts to combat the flames, two to three hundred feet high, the fire was soon out of control and the ship was abandoned. Upon arrival of the shore fire brigade, it was decided to try to save the ship with foamite. It was necessary to have a few men return to the ship, enter the adjacent hold, and play a hose on the heated bulkhead to prevent the raging fire from spreading.

Cadet-Midshipman Medved volunteered to risk his life in an attempt to save part of the cargo, which was so necessary to the continuance of war operations. That the fire was eventually brought under control and most of the cargo saved was due in no small measure to his outstanding bravery.

His willingness to risk his life to save his ship, and his heroic conduct during the fire, are in keeping with the finest traditions of the sea.

Captain William G. Schubert
Maritime Administrator [1]

---

[1] Medved's award was presented posthumously to surviving members of Medved's family on August 29, 2003, by Maritime Administrator Captain William G. Schubert. Medved was one of three Cadets on the *Daniel Huger* who qualified for the Distinguished Service Medal; because of a delay in his return to the U.S. after the war, his authorization for the medal, which had been set in motion by Superintendent Giles Stedman, was never processed. Almost sixty years later, his authorization papers were discovered in the Academy archives by Eliot Lumbard, who enlisted the help of Superintendent Stewart and Maritime Administrator Schubert to process the long delayed award. Medved was overjoyed to learn that his heroic actions would at last be recognized; sadly, however, he died only weeks before the presentation of the medal in August 2003.

Walter G. Sittman

The President of the United States takes pleasure in presenting the Merchant Marine Distinguished Service Medal to

Walter G. Sittman

Engine Cadet-Midshipman on SS *William T. Coleman*, July 20, 1943

For exceptionally meritorious conduct and intrepidity in action.

During the evening and throughout the night of March 19, 1943, while Cadet-Midshipman Walter G. Sittman's vessel was moored in company with several other vessels in port on the north coast of Africa, a concentrated air attack was made on the assembled vessels by strong formations of enemy aircraft. As the bombing, torpedoing, and strafing action commenced, two ships moored to the same buoy, and one of which was fast aft to Cadet-Midshipman Sittman's vessel, was loaded with ammunition, bombs, and high octane gasoline.

The stricken vessel, which was hit by several bombs forward and aft, was ablaze within a matter of seconds; her cargo of ammunition and bombs exploding and flying in all directions. Immediately preparations were underway to slip moorings in order to stand clear of the burning vessel. Engineers were ready below and up forward preparations were made to unmoor. Cadet-Midshipman Sittman and the Radio Operator volunteered to cut the moorings aft. The stern of the vessel was but six feet from the stern of the blazing ship, and the extreme heat plus bursting shells and bombs made this mission extremely hazardous. Within a few minutes, the volunteers had accomplished their mission, and their ship was able to proceed a safe distance from the burning vessels, which soon disintegrated with a terrific explosion.

The magnificent courage and complete disregard for his own personal safety shown by Cadet-Midshipman Sittman in his effort to save his ship, cargo, and the lives of his shipmates constitutes a degree of heroism which will be an enduring inspiration to seamen of the United States Merchant Marine everywhere.

For the President

Admiral Emory Scott Land

William M. Thomas

The President of the United States takes pleasure in presenting the Merchant Marine Distinguished Service Medal to:

William M. Thomas Jr.

Engine Cadet-Midshipman on SS *Edgar Allan Poe*, November 8, 1942

For extraordinary heroism above and beyond the line of duty.

The ship upon which he was serving was loaded in all holds with highly explosive war material when attacked by torpedo and shell fire from enemy submarine. The torpedo struck amidship, demolishing the engine and rupturing all steam and fuel pipes. The engineer and Fireman on watch met immediate death. An Oiler, blown to the top of the cylinder heads, lay helpless as a result of multiple wounds. Hearing his cries, Thomas descended into the darkness of the steam-filled wreckage and carried the injured man to the deck. By this time, all undamaged lifeboats were away. Launching a small balsa life raft, he succeeded in getting the wounded man over the side and lashed him securely to the raft. Thomas then swam alongside the raft for about twenty hours until they were picked up by a rescue ship.

His magnificent courage and disregard of his own safety in saving the life of a shipmate constitute a degree of heroism which will be an enduring inspiration to seamen of the United States Merchant Marine everywhere.

For the President

Admiral Emory Scott Land

Phil C. Vannais

The President of the United States takes pleasure in presenting the Merchant Marine Distinguished Service Medal to

Phil Cox Vannais

Engine Cadet-Midshipman on SS *Daniel Huger*, May 9, 1943

For heroism beyond the call of duty.

His ship was subjected to a two-hour high level bombing attack by seventeen enemy planes. As a result of a near miss, bomb fragments pierced the hull and the cargo of high octane gasoline exploded. Despite heroic efforts to combat the flames, two to three hundred feet high, the fire was soon out of control and the ship was abandoned. Upon the arrival of the shore fire brigade, it was decided to try to save the ship with foamite. It was necessary to have a few men returned to the ship, enter the adjacent hold, and play a hose on the heated bulkhead to prevent the raging fire from spreading.

Cadet-Midshipman Vannais was one of four who volunteered to risk his life in an attempt to save part of the cargo, which was so necessary to the continuance of war operations. That the fire was eventually brought under control and most of the cargo saved was due in no small measure to his outstanding bravery.

His willingness to risk his life to save his ship, and his heroic conduct during the fire, are in keeping with the finest traditions of the sea.

For the President

Admiral Emory Scott Land

Frederick R. Zito

The President of the United States takes pleasure in presenting the Merchant Marine Distinguished Service Medal to

Frederic R. Zito

Engine Cadet-Midshipman on SS *Fitz John Porter*, March 1, 1943

For heroism beyond the line of duty.

The ship in which he served was torpedoed at night. The crew abandoned the fast-sinking ship in an orderly fashion except for one man. This man, a Fireman weighing 250 pounds, lost his hold in descending the Jacobs ladder. In his struggles to catch himself, he became so fouled in the boat falls that he was hanging head down and helpless. Zito left his position in the lifeboat, climbed hand over hand up the falls, and attempted to extricate the now thoroughly panic-stricken man. Thwarted in his efforts to free the Fireman, the young Cadet cut the falls above them with his clasp knife, and both men fell into the sea. Zito worked desperately to remove the ropes from the still struggling Fireman. Failing in this, he, now at the point of exhaustion, took the entangled man in tow until both were picked up by a lifeboat.

Zito's heroism in thus saving the life of one of his shipmates at great risk to his own is in keeping with the finest traditions of the United States Merchant Marine.

For the President

Admiral Emory Scott Land

Appendix E

U.S. Merchant Marine Medals and Awards

Distinguished Service Medal

The Merchant Marine Distinguished Service Medal is the highest award which can be bestowed upon members of the U.S. Merchant Marine. The medal is the service's equivalent of the Medal of Honor because merchant mariners, even those on inactive duty in the naval reserve, are not on active duty and therefore not eligible for the Medal of Honor. It is awarded to any seaman in the U.S. Merchant Marine who, on or after September 3, 1939, distinguished themselves by outstanding conduct or service in the line of duty. Regulations state that not more than one medal shall be issued to any one person, but for each succeeding instance sufficient to justify the award of a medal, they will be awarded a suitable insignia to be worn with the medal.

Meritorious Service Medal

The Merchant Marine Meritorious Service Medal was awarded to any seaman of any ship operated by or for the War Shipping Administration, who was commended by the administrator for conduct or service of a meritorious nature, but not sufficient to warrant the Merchant Marine Distinguished Service Medal.

Mariner's Medal

The Mariner's Medal is the U.S. Merchant Marine's equivalent of the Military Purple Heart. The medal is awarded to any seaman who, while serving in a ship during a war period, is wounded, suffers physical injury, or suffers through dangerous exposure as a result of an act of enemy of the United States.

Gallant Ship Unit Citation

The Merchant Marine Gallant Ship Citation Ribbon is awarded to officers and seamen who served on a United States vessel or to a foreign-flagged vessel, which at the time of service, participated in outstanding or gallant action in marine disasters or other emergencies for the purpose of saving life or property at sea. At the center of the ribbon is a silver seahorse device.

Nine ships, and their crews, were awarded the Gallant Ship Unit Citation during World War II:

SS *Adoniram Judson*   SS *Stanvac Calcutta*
SS *Cedar Mills*   SS *Stephen Hopkins*
SS *Marcus Daly*   SS *Virginia Dare*
SS *Nathaniel Greene*   SS *William Moultie*
SS *Samuel Parker*

Combat Bar or Ribbon

The Combat Bar was awarded to members of the merchant marine who served on a ship when it was attacked or damaged by an enemy or an instrument of war, such as a mine during the Second World War. This award is a ribbon bar only, without a medal. Further prescribed is the issuance of a silver star, to be attached to such bar, to seamen who were forced to abandon ship when it was attacked or damaged. For each additional abandonment of ship, an additional star is attached.

Other Merchant Marine Bar or Ribbon Awards

Defense

This bar or ribbon was awarded to members of the merchant marine who served aboard United States merchant ships between September 8, 1939, and December 7, 1941.

Atlantic War Zone

This bar or ribbon was awarded to officers and men of ships operated by the War Shipping Administration for service in the Atlantic war zone between December 7, 1941, and November 8, 1945. This theatre of operations comprised the North Atlantic Ocean, South Atlantic Ocean, Gulf of Mexico, Caribbean Sea, Barents Sea, and Greenland Sea.

Mediterranean-Middle East War Zone

This bar or ribbon was awarded to officers and men of ships operated by the War Shipping Administration for service in the Mediterranean-Middle East war zone between December 7, 1941, and November 8, 1945. This theater of operations comprised the Mediterranean Sea, Red Sea, Arabian Sea, and Indian Ocean, west of eighty degrees, east longitude.

Pacific War Zone

This bar or ribbon was awarded to officers and men of ships operated by the War Shipping Administration for service in the Pacific war zone between December 7, 1941, and March 2, 1946. This theatre of operations comprised the North Pacific, South Pacific, and the Indian Ocean, east of eighty degrees, east longitude.

World War II Victory Medal

This was awarded to members of the crews of ships who served thirty days or more during the period between December 7, 1941, and September 3, 1945.

Awards or Medals Issued by U.S. or Foreign Militaries to Merchant Mariners Prisoner of War

May be awarded to any person who was a prisoner of war after April 5, 1917 (the date of the United States entry into World War I). The person's conduct, while in captivity, must have been honorable. This medal may be awarded posthumously to the surviving next of kin of the recipient.

Philippine Defense

Presented to any service member of either the Philippine military or an Allied armed force who participated in the defense of the Philippine Islands between December 8, 1941, and June 15, 1942.

Philippine Liberation

Presented to any service member of both Philippine and Allied militaries who participated in the liberation of the Philippine Islands between the dates of October 17, 1944, and September 2, 1945.

Soviet Commemorative Medal

Awarded by the Russian government upon the "Fiftieth Anniversary in the Victory of the Great Patriotic War" to U.S. merchant mariners who participated in the Arctic convoys to the city of Murmansk.

Service and Other Emblems
Honorable Service Button

Awarded to members of the crews of ships who served for thirty days during the period between December 7, 1941, to September 3, 1945.

Merchant Marine Service

Prescribed as an identifying insignia to be issued to all seamen.

Service Flag and Lapel Button
A merchant marine service flag and a service lapel button are prescribed for display by members of the immediate families of seamen serving in the American Merchant Marine during the war period. If the seaman symbolized is killed, or dies while serving, the white star will have been superimposed thereon by a gold star of smaller size so that the white forms a border. The service lapel button is of enameled metal, and its design is of a miniature of the service flag.

A family member might wear a "son in service" pin that family members would wear to show support for a son, brother, or husband serving in the merchant marine during WWII.

Appendix F

USMMA Graduates Killed in Service Since January 1, 1947

Enemy Action-Military

William N. Donnelly IV   On November 25, 2010, while leading his Marines of Second Platoon, Kilo Company, Third Battalion, Fifth Marine Infantry Regiment, on a dismounted infantry operation in Helmand Province, Afghanistan, First Lieutenant William Donnelly, USMC, a graduate of the class of 2008 was killed in action.

Francis L. Toner IV   On March 27, 2009, Lieutenant (Junior grade) Francis Toner, USN, a civil engineering corps officer and 2006 graduate, was assigned as the garrison engineer, Combined Security Transition Team. While he was running at Camp Shaheen, Afghanistan, with a group of other naval officers, the group was taken under fire by an Afghan dissident. Lieutenant Toner distracted the shooter by offering himself as a target, thereby saving all but one female officer in the group at the cost of his own life.

Aaron N. Seesan   On March 21, 2005, First Lieutenant Seesan, a 2003 graduate, was leading his platoon of the Seventy-Third Combat Engineer Company on a search for roadside explosive devices in Iraq. One of the devices exploded, mortally wounding him. Although he survived the explosion, he died of his wounds at Landstuhl, Germany.

John Lavish	On August 1, 1967, Captain John "Larry" Lavish, USAF, a graduate of the class of 1963, was assigned as air liaison officer to the Third Battalion, Republic of Korea Marine Corps. While he and his men were coordinating air support to the Korean Marines, he was killed when his armored personnel carrier struck a mine. Lavish had survived 151 missions in F-4 Phantoms over Vietnam and had been selected for promotion to major.

Enemy Action-Merchant Marine

John A. Bishop	On August 23, 1968, John Bishop, a graduate of the class of 1946, was serving as First Assistant Engineer aboard the SS *Baton Rouge Victory*. While the ship was in the Saigon River, a Viet Cong swimmer placed a limpet mine on the hull at the engine room. When the mine exploded, he lost his life when the engineers on duty were killed.

USMMA Graduates
Killed Other than by Enemy Action While in War Zone
Since January 1, 1947
Military

John A. Beving	During Desert Storm in Iraq, on August 8, 1992, while flying with HMLA "Scarface" Squadron 367 in an AH1W helicopter for HMLA "Scarface," Captain Beving, USMC, class of 1986, was wearing night vision goggles over the dunes of Kuwait during a training mission in support of Operation Desert Stay. He and his copilot were killed when their aircraft crashed. His remains lie in the Rosecrans National Cemetery in San Diego, California.
Mark D. Jackson	During Desert Storm in Iraq, on 3/24/1991, Lieutenant Jackson, USNR, class of 1985, died of injuries sustained in an automobile accident in Dhahran, Saudi Arabia. His was the first death

of a naval reservist recalled to active duty in Operation Desert Storm; reportedly it was in a collision of military vehicles.

Merchant Marine

Raymond W. Reiche

During the Vietnam War, while serving aboard the States Marine C-2, SS *Badger State*, Second Mate Reiche, class of 1968, on 12/26/1969, lost his life while attempting to save the vessel from aerial bombs that were loose in the ship's holds, in extremely rough seas while en route to Vietnam. The vessel ultimately sank from exploding bombs. Only fourteen crew members survived.

USMMA Graduates
Killed on Active Duty While Training
Since January 1, 1947

Allen R. Schuchman

Second Lieutenant Schuchman, USAFR, class of 1950, while pilot of an F-94B all-weather fighter interceptor during training on 12/17/52, hit terrain while attempting a landing at Elmendorf AFB, Anchorage, Alaska.

Thomas E. Fitzpatrick

Lieutenant (Junior grade) Fitzpatrick, USN, class of 1951, on 2/28/1955, was a "checkout" pilot in an F9F-8 Cougar, leading a flight between two aircrafts and crashed into hills near Modesto, California, due to engine or electrical failure. He was killed when the ejection seat failed and he was forced to bailout at high speed.

Thomas J. Campbell

Lieutenant Campbell, USN, class of 1952, on 3/14/1962, during recovery operations in the Western Pacific aboard the USS *Hancock* (CVA-19), Pilot Campbell crashed his F3H Demon fighter jet on the carrier deck and went over the side.

James A. Reneau	Lieutenant (Junior grade) Reneau, USN, class of 1960, while in training on 2/12/1964, off NAS Miramar for a deployment to the Western Pacific in a Navy F-4 Phantom II, the pilot Reneau was killed in a low altitude rollover combat maneuver during a failed ejection sequence.
Dennis P. Hritz	Lieutenant (Junior grade) Hritz, USN, class of 1977, on 2/28/1978, during a routine training flight in a TH-1L Bell Iroquois helicopter trainer from NAS Whiting Field, Milton, Florida, exploded over Bay Minette, Alabama, killing all onboard including Hritz. His Commanding Officer awarded his wings posthumously.
Thomas D. Waterbury	Lieutenant Waterbury, USN, class of 1985, on 4/15/1992, in Training Squadron 4 in the Gulf of Mexico, while practicing takeoffs from the USS *Forrestal* (CV-59), the T-2C Buckeye trainer, in which Waterbury was an instructor pilot in the rear seat, crashed immediately after takeoff. Waterbury ejected, but was not found. The other instructor pilot was rescued.
Kenneth M. Graff	Second Lieutenant Graff, USMC, class of 2001, on 9/23/2002, was killed when his four-seat Piper Cherokee crashed between a tree and a house in E. Milton, Florida, while soloing in a prospective aviator program of FAA certified instruction, while waiting for formal instruction at the Naval Aviation Schools Command in Pensacola, Florida.
Jerry R. Smith	Lieutenant (Junior grade) Smith, USN, class of 2003, Carrier Airborne Early Warning Squadron 120, on 8/28/2007, perished with two other crew members of an E-2C Hawkeye command and control aircraft after launching off the USS *Harry S. Truman*, while Smith was completing carrier qualification exercises off the Virginia Capes in the Atlantic Ocean. Neither the plane nor the crew members were recovered. Smith had earned his wings on May 2006, qualifying in the T-45A Goshawk jet.

USMMA Graduates
Killed While Serving Their Nation
Under Special Circumstances
Since January 1, 1947

Elliot M. See Jr.

See, class of 1949, and Astronaut Charles Bassett were killed on 02/28/1966 when their T-38 jet trainer crashed into the McDonnell Aircraft Building 101, known as the McDonnell Space Center, adjacent to the Lambert Field Airport in St. Louis, Missouri, where they were going to train in a Gemini spacecraft simulator. See was a member of the 1962 NASA Group 2 and acted as backup pilot for Gemini 5. He was in line to fly as prime crew pilot for Gemini 8 but was promoted to be command pilot of Gemini 9. Investigative panel concluded that pilot error (flying too low to the ground) was caused by poor visibility due to bad weather.

Robert D. Colin

Colin, class of 1974, was killed on 09/11/2001 when terrorists flew a commercial jet liner into the South Tower of the World Trade Center, New York City. He worked for Aon Corporation (Insurance) on the ninety-ninth floor.

Gilbert F. Granados

Granados, class of 1975, was killed on 09/11/2001 when terrorists flew a commercial jet liner into the South Tower of the World Trade Center, New York City. He worked for Aon Corporation (Insurance) on the ninety-eighth floor. A Lieutenant Commander in the U.S. Coast Guard Reserve, the U.S. Coast Guard Station at USMMA, Kings Point, New York, was named for Granados in 2003.

Source U.S. Merchant Marine Academy Alumni Foundation, *(Revised 01/24/2011)*